"Any man or woman who decides to run for President of the United States would be wise to read *Intellectuals and the American Presidency*. In his seminal work Tevi Troy identifies and explains the key to a successful presidency—and does so clearly and persuasively. As a Republican I hope Democrats do not read it—but if they do it will be good for our country." —**Martin Anderson**, Hoover Institution

"Ideas have consequences, and intellectuals have, or are supposed to have, ideas. Since the early 1960s, the administrations of each president have brought intellectuals into their folds, with a view toward using their ideas to come up with good public policy. The extent to which they have succeeded—or failed—at this is the subject ot Tevi Troy's *Intellectuals and the American Presidency,* a book that bids fair to become the definitive work on the subject—and which will deliver to its readers some interesting surprises about the role of intellectuals in politics and public policy."—**Michael Barone**, editor, *U.S. News & World Report*

"As presidential politics grows more superficial, the general assumption is that intellectuals—people who deal in ideas—grow less relevant. Tevi Troy shows how wrong and lazy that assumption is. With striking clarity and in rich historical detail, he reveals that, for better and for worse, intellectuals are crucial to the success and survival of a modern president."—**Peter Beinart**, editor, *The New Republic*

"In this witty and wise study, Tevi Troy tells how modern presidents have increasingly been surrounded, and at times hounded, by academics, writers, and other intellectuals. From Franklin Delano Roosevelt's 'brain trust' through John F. Kennedy's 'best and brightest' right down to the present, the White House has become a haven both for political operatives who specialize in winning votes *and* for intellectual personalities who specialize in spinning ideas. Troy superbly profiles how presidents from Roosevelt to George W. Bush and their top political advisers have coped, co-opted, or crossed swords with intellectuals. For anyone with a serious interest in how we got where we are in American politics and the presidency, this book is must reading." —**John J. DiIulio Jr.**, former director, White House Office of Faith-Based and Community Initiatives

"Tevi Troy has done the impossible! He's written an interesting and engaging analysis on the role of White House eggheads without resorting to excessive nudity or violence."—**Jonah Goldberg**, syndicated columnist and editor of *National Review Online*

"Tevi Troy tells the delicious tale of how presidents exploit the ambition and insecurity of intellectuals—or ignore them at their peril. Highly recommended for thinkers who thirst to be on cable t.v." —**Stephen Hess**, Brookings Institution

"Tevi Troy has given us a fascinating slice of history, in a well-written, balanced and meticulously researched package. *Intellectuals and the American Presidency* provides illumination about both the modern presidency and the role of ideas (and idea people) in American politics and policy."—**Norm Ornstein**, American Enterprise Institute, and columnist, *Roll Call*

"Love them or hate them, intellectuals are players in American politics. Good politicians realize this, and act accordingly. Tevi Troy smartly chronicles the surprising successes and occasional humorous failures of presidents who courted America's elusive yet vocal intellectual establishment. This lively and readable study is must-reading for lovers of history and politics alike." —**Jack Valenti**, chairman, Motion Picture Association of America, and former aide to Lyndon Johnson

"Tevi Troy's *Intellectuals and the American Presidency* is original and readable—required reading for intellectuals, presidents, and the rest of us." —**Ben Wattenberg**, American Enterprise Institute, and host of *Think Tank*

"The tale of presidents and intellectuals, sometimes awkward, sometimes cozy, invariably important, is too often ignored. Not so in Tevi Troy's illuminating and enlightening new study. A fitting read for the talking head era." —**Jay Winik**, author of *April 1865: The Month That Saved America*

INTELLECTUALS AND THE AMERICAN PRESIDENCY

INTELLECTUALS AND THE AMERICAN PRESIDENCY

PHILOSOPHERS, JESTERS, OR TECHNICIANS?

TEVI TROY

ROWMAN & LITTLEFIELD PUBLISHERS, INC.
Lanham • Boulder • New York • London

ROWMAN & LITTLEFIELD PUBLISHERS, INC.

Published in the United States of America
by Rowman & Littlefield Publishers, Inc.
4720 Boston Way, Lanham, Maryland 20706
www.rowmanlittlefield.com

12 Hid's Copse Road
Cumnor Hill, Oxford OX2 9JJ, England

Distributed by National Book Network

British Library Cataloguing in Publication Information Available

Library of Congress Cataloging-in-Publication Data

Troy, Tevi, 1967-
    Intellectuals and the American presidency : philosophers, jesters, or technicians? / Tevi Troy.
      p. cm. — (American intellectual culture)
    Includes bibliographical references and index.
    ISBN 0-7425-0825-0 (alk. paper)
    1. Presidents—United States. 2. Presidents—United States—Staff. 3.
Intellectuals—United States—Political activity. I. Title. II. Series.

JK521 .T76 2002
973.92—dc21

                                    2001048521

To Kami Troy

"She opens her mouth with wisdom,
and the teaching of kindness is on her tongue."
Proverbs 31:26

CONTENTS

ACKNOWLEDGMENTS

It is impossible for me to thank everybody who helped me in the long process of writing this book but that is not going to stop me from trying. This project began while I was a graduate student at the University of Texas, and I would like to thank my graduate advisers, Professors Elspeth Rostow and the late and lamented Bob Crunden. The University of Texas was generous in supporting my research, as were the Institute for Humane Studies, the Heritage Foundation's Salvatori Fellowship, and the Hudson Institute, which housed me for a year while I wrote.

As no researcher can survive without libraries, I must thank the staffs at the Kennedy Library in Massachusetts, the Johnson Library in Texas, the Ford Library in Ann Arbor, the Nixon Archives at the University of Maryland, the Carter Center in Georgia, and the Hudson Institute Library in Indianapolis. The Library of Congress is a national treasure, and I am indebted to the staffs at the Manuscript Reading Room, the Photo Archives, and most especially Mary Yarnell in the Loan Division.

Rowman & Littlefield has done a great job with this book, including former editor Steve Wrinn, new editor Mary Carpenter, and production editor Lynn Gemmell. In addition, Eldon Eisenach may not remember this, but he introduced me to Bill McClay, who brought me to Rowman & Littlefield and has supported this project and me in innumerable ways.

My parents, Dov and Elaine Troy, have been incredibly helpful and supportive to me in this endeavor, as they have been to me in all things. I also owe an unpayable debt to my brothers, Dan and Gil Troy, who have provided me with the impossible challenge of living up to both their accomplishments and expectations.

My sisters-in-law, Cheryl and Linda, have been with me throughout this process, and their respective children—Aaron, Leora, and Ariel, and Lia, Jonah, and Aviv—have joined at various steps along the way. My friends, and they know who they are, are truly too numerous to mention. Three in particular, John McConnell, Vin Cannato, and Ira Carnahan, took the time to read and comment on longer versions of this book than the one you hold before you.

Finally, I would like to thank my new family, my in-laws, Vita and Ray Pliskow, and my wife, Kami. She has been patient beyond all expectations with the late nights and sudden deadlines that came with writing this book. I cannot yet thank but I must acknowledge our new son, Ezra. While he may spend the next few years reading Dr. Seuss and the like, I look forward with pride to the prospect that he may read this book someday.

1

INTELLECTUALS AND THE MODERN PRESIDENCY

In April 1998, Texas Governor George W. Bush visited Stanford University's Hoover Institution. At the time, Bush was far from assured that he would receive the 2000 Republican presidential nomination. Although he led a crowded field of Republican presidential hopefuls, his lead was by no means insurmountable. In addition, some pollsters wondered whether the poll respondents even knew they were voting for the Texas governor and not his father, the former president. During his visit, Bush attended a meeting at the home of former Secretary of State George Shultz, a Hoover Fellow. At that meeting, Bush sufficiently impressed Shultz and his Hoover colleagues, and they agreed to form an ad hoc advisory committee to assist Bush in his quest for the presidency.

By seeking—and winning—the support of intellectuals, Bush gave himself a major head start in the so-called invisible primary preceding the presidential election year. With the backing of most top GOP intellectuals, especially those in conservative think tanks like Hoover and the American Enterprise Institute, Bush helped stave off a number of primary challenges from the right. In addition, having a team of intellectuals to augment his policy shop also gave Bush and his campaign more heft in the eyes of the media. While intellectuals did not win the campaign for him, they certainly gave him an important early boost and a coherent message in the form of "compassionate conservatism."

In contrast, Bush's opponent Al Gore had relatively few public interactions with intellectuals. Unfortunately for Gore, his most famous "intellectual," feminist writer Naomi Wolf, had to downgrade her public role after reports of her hefty $15,000 monthly salary and New Age advice on Gore's wardrobe became public. As a result, Wolf became more of an obstacle for Gore than anything else. Without a core group of prominent intellectual backers, Gore's campaign suffered through a number of periods of drift, frequently reinventing itself in the search for a catchy and coherent message.

The tale of the 2000 primaries and election does not mean that Republicans own the intellectuals. Far from it. If anything, Republicans generally start campaigns at a disadvantage with most American intellectuals. Not coincidentally, Democratic presidents have historically been more successful in using intellectuals to help shape their message. In 1992, for example, Bill Clinton brilliantly used the moderate intellectuals situated in and around the Democratic Leadership Council and the Progressive Policy Institute to demonstrate that he was a different kind of Democrat from the liberals who had lost three consecutive presidential elections. At the same time, President George H. W. Bush, Clinton's seemingly unbeatable rival, paid relatively little attention to conservative intellectuals or staffers trying to bring new ideas into the White House. Partially as a result of their different approaches to intellectuals, Clinton emerged as the candidate of new ideas, while Bush seemed to lack vision and soon found himself voted out of office.

Both George W. Bush in 2000 and Clinton in 1992 understood that fighting for intellectual support matters. They were by no means the first presidential candidates to understand the importance of intellectuals. Franklin D. Roosevelt, for example, used the brain trust of professors in his 1932 campaign. In 1960 John F. Kennedy used historian Arthur Schlesinger and economist John Kenneth Galbraith to reassure voters previously predisposed to liberal icons Adlai Stevenson and Hubert Humphrey.

Presidents who have sought intellectual support have not done so because of the small number of votes intellectuals cast, or even because intellectual staffers are indispensable in campaigns. Rather, every president since 1960 has had to address the question of intellectual support because their relations with intellectuals help shape the candidate's public image. Intellectuals cannot elect a president, but they can help make a candidate electable. They do this by making presidents appear to be men of vision and conviction. In turn, this image helps presidents in the eyes of the media, party activists, and ultimately voters.

INTELLECTUAL AMBASSADORS

Successful presidents of the past forty years have used intellectuals to help shape their image. The two most successful strategies, discussed in this work, include maintaining positive relations with the intellectual community or some segment of it and hiring an assistant from academic or quasi-academic circles specifically to assist the president in dealing with the intellectual community. Unlike most White House aides, these ambassadors have no specific administrative or policy responsibilities but are supposed to smooth relations between the president and America's increasingly important intellectual community. As the stories of the past eight administrations show, the interrelation of intellectuals and presidents has developed into a crucial factor in determining presidential success.

Intellectuals did not just suddenly arrive at the White House door and start dispensing advice. The circumstances behind the hiring of the first intellectuals in the White House developed slowly and culminated in the 1960s, as intellectuals attained stature and presidents felt that they needed a liaison to the increasingly important intellectual community. In the same decade that intellectuals reached this position of power, though, they also attained their greatest notoriety.

The 1960s were tumultuous years in which the Vietnam War and racial tensions threatened to tear the country apart. Lyndon Johnson encountered race riots during every summer of his presidency except 1966. Vietnam led to student protests and family divisions as the nation endured a rising body count on the nightly news. All of these events helped shatter confidence in American institutions and contributed to the sense of disorder plaguing the land. While the intellectuals were typically nonviolent protesters, they were not exactly passive either. In its cover story on the Newark riots of summer 1967, the *New York Review of Books*, a left-wing intellectual journal, printed a diagram showing how to build a Molotov cocktail for urban warfare. Many intellectuals influenced the tone and tenor of the demonstrations, as leaders of the student protests cited radical antiwar intellectuals to justify their actions. As a result of these tensions, the same decade that saw the opening of new opportunities in the White House for intellectuals also witnessed intellectuals creating more difficulties for presidents. Presidents Lyndon B. Johnson and Richard M. Nixon both found that simply hiring a representative intellectual could not overcome the roiling tensions of America in the 1960s. Partially as a result of this inability to quell intellectual criticism, both Johnson and Nixon left office without exhausting their eligibility for the office.[1]

INTELLECTUALS IN AMERICAN LIFE

The growing prominence of intellectuals in the White House came about as a result of two converging trends: the entrance of intellectuals into mainstream American society and the development of the modern presidency. The first part of this two-step process, the movement of intellectuals into mainstream American society in the twentieth century, resulted from America's remarkable economic expansion. While there had been intellectuals in America dating back to Puritan times, before 1890, as Columbia University historian Richard Hofstadter has argued, "practically every man of letters had to have a primary source of income." This need for outside income limited intellectuals to the clerical or leisure classes. As intellectuals came mainly from these classes, their patrons tended to come from these classes too.[2]

As America became an industrial power toward the end of the nineteenth century, however, the status of intellectuals changed. Industrialization brought affluence, which facilitated intellectual development in a number of ways. Industrialists like John D. Rockefeller and Andrew Carnegie, who had accumulated vast new fortunes, used part of their wealth to endow universities, foundations, magazines, and, later, think tanks, all of which helped create financial support mechanisms for intellectuals. Rockefeller, for example, helped endow a university—Chicago—as well as his eponymous foundation. Similarly, Stanford University, Carnegie-Mellon University, the Brookings Institution, and the *New Republic* magazine owe their existence to the largesse of wealthy individuals.[3]

Most important, perhaps, affluence helped create what the historian Robert Wiebe called a new middle class. The members of this class could afford to send their children to school for longer periods of time. In addition, this class, which largely consisted of urban professional men and women, believed in the concept of leveled democracy, that "almost anyone with incentive, it seemed, could acquire the skills of a profession." Along with this belief in professions came professionalization, the establishment of standards to govern fields such as law, medicine, and education. All of these fields required education. As historian Burton Bledstein has noted, "For the middle class in America, degree-granting education was an instrument of ambition and a vehicle to status in the occupational world."[4]

Although the professions required increasing levels of education, the members of the new middle class were not themselves intellectuals. They did, however, help establish the Progressive Era belief in the expert, the sense that more educated individuals understand problems better than less educated individuals and therefore can solve problems better than amateurs. This notion of expertise and perfectibility continued long after the Progressive Era waned; the eventual development of intellectuals as White House advisers was a lagging manifestation of this belief.[5]

The progressive notion of the professional attorney or physician helped pave the way for the professional intellectual. Doctors and lawyers, however, have an independent support mechanism—the individuals who pay for their services. Intellectuals, in contrast, usually lack such a mercantile relationship with people. Intellectuals' remuneration comes from more indirect sources, from students who pay to attend their classes or readers who buy the books or magazines that print their articles. The growing new middle class provided an audience that could support professional intellectuals. In addition, the new middle class, which emphasized education for its children, also provided a pool of future intellectuals, who no longer needed to come from the upper class. In the years following the Progressive Era, as America became more democratic and more affluent, intellectuals became increasingly numerous and more important.

The professional intellectual was more than what the dictionary classifies as one "possessing a high degree of understanding [and] given to pursuits that exercise the intellect." The professional intellectual was what the late Christopher Lasch called a "person for whom thinking fulfills at once the function of work and play." While Lasch captured much of the essence of an intellectual by uniting work and play, he missed another important element of an intellectual—the need for appreciation of one's work. Professional intellectuals are, as the sociologist Talcott Parsons has argued, "scholarship" intellectuals, absorbed by the university system, as opposed to "creative" intellectuals, who exist outside the university system. Even though scholarship intellectuals are not necessarily artists, they nevertheless have a burning need for recognition. In order to satisfy this need, scholarship intellectuals look to a number of media, including the written word, the classroom, or, increasingly throughout the twentieth century, the government.[6]

THE MODERN PRESIDENCY

More than any other event, the development of the modern presidency brought intellectuals into American politics. Given their supposed inability to interact with average citizens, intellectuals rarely ran for political office and limited themselves to writing books on political subjects or informally advising politicians. Although progressive presidents Woodrow Wilson and Theodore Roosevelt both had intellectual tendencies and had written books before reaching the White House, neither had intellectuals on his White House staff. Roosevelt, for example, consulted with intellectuals such as Columbia's Nicholas Murray Butler, yet he lacked an administrative apparatus for hiring assistants full-time. Woodrow Wilson was the only Ph.D. to serve as president, but he too had a very limited circle of advisers. Wilson did use intellectuals in the Inquiry, a group of scholars enlisted to help plan for peace after World War I. The Inquiry, however, was a temporary committee. For the most part, presidents lacked staffs, and intellectuals had no official role to play.[7]

Presidents began hiring assistants after Congress appropriated funds to hire clerks during the Buchanan administration in 1857. Lincoln ran the Civil War with only two secretaries, John Nicolay and John Hay, the latter of whom became secretary of state under William McKinley. McKinley also hired the first White House aide, George Courtelyou. A holdover from the Grover Cleveland administration, Cortelyou helped McKinley cope with the growing administrative duties of the presidency. He later became postmaster general and secretary of the Treasury under Theodore Roosevelt.

In the nineteenth century, presidents usually looked to Congress for a legislative agenda. In the first two decades of the twentieth century, however, the role of the regulatory state expanded into areas such as food and drugs, agriculture, and banking. As a result, the president found his purview expanding but not his power. In order to meet the needs of the new century, presidents would need to expand their administrative power.[8]

This expansion took place under Franklin Delano Roosevelt. In his three-plus terms in office, from 1933 to 1945, Roosevelt presided over the birth of the modern presidency. In response to the needs of the Great Depression, Roosevelt expanded the president's influence, visibility, and administrative power. These changes contributed to an opening and an increased role for intellectuals in politics.

Roosevelt began to change presidential traditions before he was elected. Since George Washington, presidents had stood for, rather than run for, office, offering few policy prescriptions along the way. Roosevelt, however, ran a much more active campaign, giving both the traditional stump speeches and radio addresses. Historian Gil Troy notes that before Roosevelt, campaign analysts would ask whether a candidate would stump; after Roosevelt, they asked when candidates would start stumping. In order to write these speeches, Roosevelt relied in part on a group of professors known, thanks to the coinage of Roosevelt's aide Louis Howe, as the brains trust. Columbia professors Rexford Tugwell, Raymond Moley, and Adolph Berle made up the core of this group, more familiarly known as the brain trust.[9]

The group was founded in response to candidate Roosevelt's request that Moley assemble expert advice on key issues. The academics would come to Hyde Park by train from New York and depart the same evening. This practice unnerved many old-time politicians, who saw little need for academics to get involved in politics. John Nance Garner, FDR's vice presidential nominee, sent a message to Roosevelt during the campaign: "Tell the governor that he is the boss and we will follow him to hell if we have to, but if he goes too far with some of these wild-eyed ideas we are going to have the shit kicked out of us."[10]

Part of the reason for this discomfort was Moley. He embarked on the assignment to assemble academic experts a little too eagerly, leading some wags to joke that the only way to get an appointment with Moley was by going through FDR. But a larger part of this discomfort stemmed from the novelty of intellectuals in politics. As historian David Kennedy observed, "The Brain Trusters, especially the ever-present Moley, attracted much public notice in late 1932 and early 1933. They were a novelty in American political culture."[11]

Although they caused discomfort in some quarters, the brain trusters helped Roosevelt maintain relations with the liberal intellectual community, a project that future presidents would pursue as well. During the campaign, for example, Berle convinced Roosevelt to advocate an economic council, in part because "the liberal wing of the party, particularly the intellectuals, are very firm in favor of an economic council." While Roosevelt's (or any candidate's) campaign statements had little bearing on his policies in office, Berle's comment demonstrates that Roosevelt and the brain trusters felt the need to seek intellectual support and that there was a perceived link between intellectuals and liberals. While the need to appease intellectuals became more important in future administrations, Roosevelt evidently saw this necessity as well.[12]

After the campaign, each of the professors received an appointment in the Roosevelt administration. Roosevelt's including intellectuals excited some people, particularly liberals. Harry Elmer Barnes, author of The Liberal Viewpoint, a column in the New York World-Telegram, called the president-elect's "apparent determination to secure expert advice . . . the most novel and promising item in Franklin D. Roosevelt's approach to the Presidency." The next day Barnes asserted that Moley would "be most powerful and useful as a liaison man between the 'brain trust' and the politicians and plutocrats with whom Mr. Roosevelt will have to deal." Barnes cooed that "for this task Professor Moley has no superior in the whole American academic profession." Barnes concluded with a prediction: if Roosevelt listened to his brain trust, he would have the "most intelligently planned administration in our national history." If he did not listen to them, however, "both the country and Mr. Roosevelt will be the losers."[13]

Although contemporary analysts like Barnes romanticized the brain trust, the group exerted little influence in the administration itself. In addition, none of them had White House appointments; Moley served as assistant secretary of state, and Tugwell had the same position in the Department of Agriculture. Berle refused a full-time appointment, acting instead as special adviser to the Reconstruction Finance Corporation. The absence of White House appointments was partially a function of the lack of White House jobs at the time. In addition, as Arthur Schlesinger Jr. later discovered, the brain trusters never regained the level of influence they had held during the campaign, particularly in the period leading up to the 1932 Democratic National Convention in Chicago. Finally, Roosevelt reserved places at his side for those personally close to him, such as Louis Howe (at first) and his press secretary, Stephen Early. While Roosevelt used intellectuals to his advantage, they were far from his most trusted aides.[14]

In retrospect, even the brain trusters did not consider themselves to have been a vital part of the administration. While preparing a book on the brain trust in 1964, Tugwell wrote a letter to Moley suggesting that their most important contribution had been as "the upholders of several important attitudes," including "sound money, modified by the need for unemployment relief and debt easing; strictly national policies; realistic agricultural policy that FDR rather wanted to fudge on when it came to unpopular crop restriction." Tugwell added that their service as a brain trust ended after Roosevelt's "inauguration on the theory that we then became officials and not a brains trust."[15]

Moley, for the most part, agreed. He remembered that Berle had made only three major contributions, all of them on the campaign trail. Moley added that his "relationship with Berle was never very good after the election," speculating that their distance may have resulted from the fact that Berle "felt that he deserved something better in the Administration." With respect to the main conclusion, Moley agreed with Tugwell, noting that he had "taken the position that the Brain Trust officially did not operate after the election, although you and I were close in the months that followed." The popular perception remains that the brain trusters served as the idea men of the Roosevelt administration, the participants evidently did not share that view.[16]

Although the role of brain trusters was more limited than the one future public intellectuals would play, they did establish the precedent for full-time intellectual involvement at the presidential level, in both campaigns and administrations. But Tugwell, Berle, and Moley were not the only intellectuals to join the Roosevelt White House. While Roosevelt pressed an ambitious legislative agenda that included both the first and second New Deals, he often lacked the administrative staff to meet the needs of his expanding presidency. In 1936, near the start of his second term, Roosevelt established the President's Committee on Administrative Management, headed by Louis Brownlow. In 1937 the Brownlow committee reported to Congress that "the President needs help." To provide this help, the committee suggested that Congress give the president the right to hire six administrative assistants, each at a salary of $10,000. Employing words that later became famous, the committee recommended that these assistants "should be possessed of high competence, great physical vigor, and a passion for anonymity." Brownlow intended to "give the President a few administrative assistants to take much work off his shoulders and serve him in a strictly confidential capacity." Following the committee's suggestions, Roosevelt issued Executive Order 8248, which increased the size of both the White House staff and the administrative agencies.[17]

Congress, however, proved less eager than Brownlow to increase Roosevelt's power. Many congressmen bitterly opposed the Reorganization Act, proposed in 1938, which would have institutionalized the Brownlow committee's suggestions. New York Republican Bertrand H. Snell feared that the six assistants would be "nonpublicized brain children lacking any practical experience in public affairs." Missouri Republican Dewey J. Short went further, arguing against having "theoretical, intellectual, professorial nincompoops who could not be elected dog-catcher" assist the president. While these characterizations may have been descriptive of some White House aides, Republican Congressman Hamilton Fish of New York, who represented Roosevelt's home district, made an even more outrageous charge. The fiery Fish warned that the reorganization represented "a step to concentrate power in the hands of the president and set up a species of fascism or Nazism or an American form of dictatorship." While Fish's fears may have been exaggerated, his concerns centered on the very rise of the expert, which had made intellectuals relevant in the first place.[18]

Based partially on these accusations, Congress rejected the Government Reorganization Act. A blander bill, which gave the president his assistants but no new departments, passed in March 1939. Roosevelt signed the bill on April 3, creating the Executive Office of the President.[19]

The expanded federal government, especially the Executive Office of the President, created new opportunities for the legions of young and not so young idealists who had been moving to Washington since Roosevelt's inauguration. These new arrivals either started full-time careers in Washington or went through the "revolving door," alternating between jobs inside and outside the city. In his memoirs, for example, John Kenneth Galbraith recalled that his colleagues at the Department of Agriculture under Roosevelt included Abraham Fortas, Alger Hiss, Adlai Stevenson, and George Ball, all of whom would become influential in the following decades. Washington had opened its doors to the intellectually minded, and they did not hesitate to walk through them.[20]

THE POLITICS OF THE NEW CLASS

These two converging streams—the increasing importance of American intellectuals and the modernization and growth of the American presidency—came even closer in the 1950s. The 1952 contest between Dwight D. Eisenhower and Adlai E. Stevenson brought intellectuals into the forefront of a presidential campaign for the first time since Roosevelt's run in 1932. In 1952, however, intellectuals had a much larger audience, namely, the emerging New Class. Educated, affluent, interested, this New Class developed out of the affluent society America had become in the late 1940s.

The term "New Class" came from a 1957 book by Milovan Djilas of the same title. Djilas, a Yugoslav sociologist, used the term to refer to Yugoslavia's communist

elites. The phrase gained currency among American intellectuals as a convenient way to refer to newly educated Americans who traded in information
rather than capital. Characteristics of the New Class included more education,
higher income, and a higher likelihood of living on the East or West Coast than
the average American had. According to Daniel Bell, a sociologist and one of the
chief chroniclers of the New Class, the Serviceman's Readjustment Act of
1944—better known as the GI Bill—was instrumental in creating this New
Class. The GI Bill sent thousands of Americans—most of whose parents had not
attended college—to America's vast collection of universities. In 1956, the final
year of the GI Bill, American institutions of higher learning granted almost
240,000 more degrees and employed almost 150,000 more faculty members
than in the bill's first year. This influx of students and faculty not only provided
more jobs for the intellectually minded but also created a better educated and
larger market for highbrow writing. These college-educated children became
the audience for America's intellectuals, who overwhelmingly supported
Stevenson's presidential campaign.[21]

According to Richard Hofstadter, Stevenson's "appeal to intellectuals overshadowed anything in recent history." Columnist Stewart Alsop even coined the
word "egghead" specifically with regard to the liberal intellectuals of that 1952
campaign. CBS reporter Eric Sevareid noted that Stevenson "captured the
imagination of intellectuals, of all those who are really informed; he has excited
the passions of the *mind*."[22]

In addition to their swooning over Stevenson, a number of prominent intellectuals also worked on his campaign. According to biographer Porter
McKeever, Stevenson's speechwriting team represented "the most remarkable
assemblage of writing talent ever brought together for a political campaign." In
this group, known as the Elks Club because they worked out of the third floor of
the Springfield Elks Club, "at least four Pulitzer Prize winners were at work virtually all the time amid the ebb and flow of ideas, rhetoric, and people." This
group included John Kenneth Galbraith and Arthur M. Schlesinger Jr.—fellow
Harvard professors, popular authors, and cofounders of Americans for Democratic Action.[23]

Galbraith felt that liberals should wear the egghead badge with pride: "As the
party of the eggheads, we should similarly and proudly make use of our brains
and experience." Stevenson recognized that the support of these intellectuals
added to the perception of his being an egghead, joking, "Eggheads of the world
unite! You have nothing to lose but your yolks!" Despite Stevenson's rather flip-
pant approach, this perception proved as much a liability as an asset, as he lost
to Eisenhower in 1952 and 1956.[24]

Partially as a result of perceptions created by the Stevenson campaign, calling
someone an intellectual in the 1950s and 1960s effectively meant calling that

person a liberal. While not all liberals were intellectuals, most intellectuals were indeed liberals. The absence of conservatism among intellectuals was so complete in this period that literary critic Lionel Trilling, a member of the famous "New York intellectuals," described conservative thought as "irritable mental gestures which seem to resemble ideas." This dismissal demonstrates that liberal intellectuals found little reason to believe that there could be such a thing as a conservative intellectual. Yet in a country as diverse as the United States, at some point conservatives, no matter how irritable, would have to develop thoughts that did more than "resemble" ideas. Conservatives, however, would have to wait for a while. Despite individual conservative intellectuals such as William F. Buckley Jr. and Wilmoore Kendall, intellectualism and liberalism seemed inextricably linked through the mid-1960s, a situation that thrilled liberals and infuriated conservatives.[25]

POSTWAR INTELLECTUAL GROWTH

Even though Stevenson lost to Eisenhower twice, his appeal among intellectuals showed that intellectuals brought advantages to presidential campaigns as well as liabilities. Massachusetts senator and presidential aspirant John F. Kennedy took in this lesson, calculating that the advantages of intellectuals could actually outweigh the liabilities. Kennedy proved instrumental in making more room for intellectuals in presidential politics, first in his campaign and later in the White House. According to Kennedy's analysis, prominent intellectual involvement could appeal to and win votes among the growing New Class.

Intellectuals also gained stature in this period because of the Cold War. The Korean War had already demonstrated that military confrontation between West and East could be bloody and inconclusive. As a result, American brainpower began emerging as the key to gaining the upper hand in the post–World War II geopolitical struggle against the Soviet Union. In 1958, after the Soviet Union had beaten the United States into space with Sputnik, the first artificial earth satellite, Americans looked to experts to reassure them of their global—and moral—superiority. According to Hofstadter, after Sputnik "the national distaste for intellect appeared to be not just a disgrace but a hazard to survival." Washington issued a call for experts and intellectuals answered. The initial reliance on scientific experts helped encourage reliance on other experts, including policy experts. By the 1960s, Hofstadter found Washington "hospitable to Harvard professors and ex-Rhodes Scholars."[26]

Also in the 1950s, a number of intellectuals found increased stature in the emerging popular culture. A series of fairly specialized books that made general points about the nation boosted the reputations (as well as the bank accounts) of a number of previously obscure intellectuals. Books like David Riesman's *The Lonely Crowd*, John Kenneth Galbraith's *The Affluent Society*, and C. Wright Mills's *The Power Elite* became popular beyond the authors' (and certainly their publishers') expectations. All of these works recognized the wealth and comfort of America in the 1950s yet criticized various flaws in the American character. In *The Affluent Society*, for example, Galbraith created a long-lasting conception of a wealthy America that needed to spend money on public works instead of individual pleasures. Riesman feared that advanced, "other-directed" individuals lacked interior motivation and a sense of morality. Mills, who was even more critical of American society, warned that a small, unelected elite dominated the country's decision-making process. All three books became best-sellers and their ideas became part of the national zeitgeist.[27]

As intellectuals gained increasing respect (and respectability), they stepped up their participation in presidential campaigns. Although Stevenson's electoral defeats prevented these intellectuals from entering White House positions until the 1960s, every presidential contest after 1952 would include intellectuals on one or both sides. Intellectuals were now ready for more serious involvement in politics.[28]

PUBLIC INTELLECTUALS

Eric Goldman defined the liberal intellectuals of the 1950s and 1960s as "a large, amorphous group of academics, writers, editors, staff people at foundations, certain types of lawyers, and a scattering of others who made their living primarily from talking, writing, research or some combination of these." Goldman, like Talcott Parsons, recognized that artists could be intellectuals, although he limited his definition to individuals with a policy orientation. Different writers have developed names for these newly involved intellectuals, variations on Russell Jacoby's phrase "public intellectuals." The names attempted to capture the new level of intellectual involvement in American public affairs, both in and outside of government.[29]

These public intellectuals were often relatively well-known generalists who were willing to speak or write about most subjects, but always injecting their own worldview into their various endeavors. Public intellectuals usually supported themselves without institutional employment. The most famous group of public intellectuals, the New York intellectuals, often worked as freelance writers, edited small magazines, and taught part-time at universities, unlike tenure-track professors. Given this unaffiliated status, their livelihood often depended on their productivity, encouraging prolific writing. As a result, their frequent writings made the New York intellectuals—and public intellectuals in general—influential beyond their numbers. This disproportionate level of influence made politicians, and presidential candidates in particular, pay more attention to vocal intellectuals than to similarly sized but less prolific groups. In Kennedy's case, for example, paying attention meant specifically seeking out liaisons to the intellectual community, not from the New York intellectuals but from the developing group of Washington, or political, intellectuals. The increased prominence of political intellectuals and their influence among the growing New Class enhanced the role of intellectuals in the White House, as politicians attempted to coopt the voices of the intellectual elites and, hence, the votes of the New Class.[30]

INTELLECTUALS IN THE WHITE HOUSE

The increasing importance of intellectuals in shaping public discourse led to a new development in American politics, the hiring of public intellectuals to advise on a broad range of issues of interest to the New Class elites. Most presidential aides are smart, literate, and well educated, but they are not necessarily intellectuals. Public intellectuals usually have an academic or a quasi-academic background and a preexisting reputation, usually stemming from authorship of a well-received book.

Some extremely smart White House aides stopped short of serving as intellectuals in their respective administrations. Theodore Sorensen, Ben Wattenberg, and William Safire were all smart, educated, literate advisers and speechwriters who nevertheless lacked the credentials and preexisting independent reputations to qualify as public intellectuals. Sorensen, for example, had spent almost all of his adult life as a Kennedy assistant, neglecting his own projects, not to mention his own reputation. Wattenberg received his position as a result of writing *The Real Majority* but made a name for himself as a public intellectual after leaving the Johnson White House. Safire, who did not complete his undergraduate work at Syracuse University, had worked in public relations and political campaigns (for Richard M. Nixon in 1960 and 1968 and Jacob K. Javits for Senate in 1962) before joining the Nixon White House. His real fame as a public intellectual came after his White House status, as a popular columnist for the *New York Times*.[31]

The new public intellectuals were also different from other aides in that they served the president *as intellectuals*, assisting the president in the formulation of ideas and in relations with the intellectual community. For this reason, intellectual advisers with one specific policy portfolio, such as foreign or economic policy, do not qualify. Henry A. Kissinger, for example, might have qualified as a public intellectual while at Harvard, but Nixon chose him exclusively as his foreign policy adviser, not as a broad-based intellectual adviser.

In recent years, presidents have developed the Office of Public Liaison, with individual aides reaching out to specific communities. These liaisons have of necessity tended to be members of the target group. White House liaisons to the black and Jewish communities, for example, are almost always black or Jewish. Sensitive minority groups who need a specific advocate in the White House appreciate representatives from their own group. Similarly, public intellectuals chosen to serve as ambassadors to the intellectual community require good standing in the intellectual community. They also needed experience with members of the New Class, who were usually familiar with developments among the intellectuals.

As ambassadors to the intellectual community, and indirectly the New Class, intellectual advisers performed many of the same tasks as the diplomatic corps, explaining to the president what those in the intellectual world were thinking in general, and what they thought of the president in particular. Outside the White House, the ambassadorial function required defending the president from varying degrees of intellectual attack. This job proved relatively simple for Schlesinger, for example, as President Kennedy enjoyed fairly solid support among the intellectuals. Under Johnson, however, this task became much more difficult, since many intellectuals turned against Johnson over the Vietnam War.

Serving as the president's ambassador to intellectuals necessitated representing the president among more than just the relatively small group of well-known public intellectuals and a marginally larger cohort of academics. Presidents have used intellectuals to represent the White House among groups that were not necessarily intellectual but could serve as bellwethers of intellectual opinion: liberal organizations, college students, and members of the press. Intellectuals founded liberal organizations such as Americans for Democratic Action and remained active in their operation. Thus, obtaining an ADA endorsement would serve as a fairly reliable indication of intellectual support. College students represented the group perhaps most influenced by intellectuals, not only among their own professors but with respect to reading popular works by public intellectuals. Tom Hayden, author of the Port Huron Statement, the 1962 manifesto of the radical Students for a Democratic Society, derived many of his ideas from C. Wright Mills's *Power Elite*. Finally, journalists often read intellectual works, and they were best able to impart those ideas to the reading public. As a result, presidents have relied on intellectual advisers to keep them abreast of developments in these related spheres.

In addition to serving as the president's ambassador to intellectuals and intellectually minded groups, intellectuals in the White House often performed a more cerebral task, serving as individuals who could bring new thoughts and a coherent perspective to the administration. Without specific portfolios, intellectual advisers have had more time and a greater inclination for reading than the presidents they served, and they could suggest ideas that would not otherwise have come to the president's attention. This practice not only kept presidents aware of contemporary intellectual developments but also served as a conduit for new policy ideas.

DIFFERENT APPROACHES TO INTELLECTUAL ASSISTANCE

The 1960s were a particularly volatile decade, as the Vietnam War, race riots, student protests, and assassinations rocked the country. Partially as a result of this unrest, what Allen Matusow called "the fever of discontent rising in intellectual circles," the bulk of intellectual opinion shifted from general support of the Kennedy administration to general opposition to the administrations of Johnson and Nixon. This shift made relations with intellectuals more contentious but increasingly important. In addition, the very existence of the position showed that whatever the leanings of the American intellectual community, those who walked the corridors of power now heard the intellectuals' voices.[32]

This proximity to power led to an existential problem for the intellectuals themselves. Intellectuals had historically counted on outsider status in their critiques of American society. As Irving Howe observed, "Whenever intellectuals become absorbed into the accredited institutions of society they not only lose their traditional rebelliousness but to one extent or another *they cease to function as intellectuals*" (emphasis original). Because identifying with those in power dampened their ability to criticize, intellectuals needed to prove that they remained outsiders. The intellectuals in the White House, as direct advisers to the president, had a particularly difficult time making that claim. This tension has challenged the use of intellectual advisers almost from its inception.[33]

Since 1960, intellectuals have become increasingly important, shaping the millions of words written about presidents that determine presidential support and reputations. Consequently, every president has had to deal with the intellectual community. Reaching out to public intellectuals has been one way for presidents to capture the advantages of support from intellectuals. A president, however, does not need a single ambassador to the intellectuals as much as he needs to show an interest in what intellectuals have to say. In recent years, no president has hired a single public intellectual to serve as full-time ambassador, largely because of the inability of any one liaison to appeal to the fragmented intellectual community. Still, presidents like Ronald Reagan and Clinton, who could not appeal to all intellectuals, managed to appeal to the intellectuals they needed. Reagan, for example, had the undying loyalty of conservative intellectuals, which helped stave off the bitter attacks of the liberal intellectuals who despised him. Clinton, even more cleverly, used both moderate New Democrat intellectuals as well as northeastern establishment intellectuals whenever either group suited his purposes. Presidents who hired one public intellectual for this role found that one ambassador does not necessarily bring about good relations with the intellectuals.

In short, hiring a single public intellectual is only one strategy for garnering intellectual support. The crucial development over the past forty years has been the growth of the intellectual community and the favors they can bestow on both presidents and potential presidents, in arenas ranging from elite opinion to the electoral college. The fact is that modern presidents need to appeal to at least some segment of the intellectual community. Recent presidents have tried to accomplish this difficult task in a variety of ways. However they have tried to do this, every recent president—and most candidates—have had to address the issue of appealing to the intellectuals who will ultimately pass judgment on their actions.

2

ARTHUR SCHLESINGER: COURT INTELLECTUAL

In 1960, American intellectuals stood at the height of their influence. They tended to live in New York or Boston, shared similar political views, largely associated with the Democratic Party, and for the most part supported America in its Cold War struggle with the Soviet Union. These "Cold War liberals" criticized the conformity of the American masses while championing the American system.

GETTING THE NOMINATION

John F. Kennedy, Harvard '39, sported a coterie of intellectual advisers as well as his own intellectual bona fides. He cultivated his reputation as both the intellectual president and the intellectuals' president. The only president ever to win a Pulitzer Prize, Kennedy published his honors thesis as a book, hired conspicuously brainy assistants, and maintained regular contacts with the academics of his home state at Harvard and MIT. In his memoirs, Ted Sorensen—one of the smartest Kennedy assistants—calls Kennedy not only an intellectual but an intellectual giant. Kennedy accepted this categorization. According to Sorensen, Kennedy even referred to himself as "something of an ivory tower president."[1]

Yet, as with most observations about Kennedy, the appearance did not necessarily correspond to the reality. Kennedy's apparent rapport with intellectuals developed as a result of a serious effort to woo them. Although he recruited academics for his campaign, Kennedy's reputation as the intellectuals' president did not fully harden until after his death in 1963.[2]

During the early stages of the 1960 campaign, Kennedy knew that he was not the intellectuals' favorite, and he resented it. At one dinner party with Nancy and Theodore H. White, he complained about Stevenson's most-favored-politician status among intellectuals: "Kennedy asked the other seven diners why it was that Adlai Stevenson was considered an 'egghead' and he, Kennedy, wasn't." Reporters also knew where Kennedy stood with the intellectuals. As reporter Thomas Winship wrote at the time, "Many professors frankly say they like Humphrey more than Kennedy and admire Stevenson more." This situation began to change, however, after Arthur Schlesinger Jr., perhaps the country's best-known intellectual, joined Kennedy. Of course, Schlesinger only made this move after making a pragmatic decision that his true favorite, Adlai Stevenson, would not be entering the race.[3]

Liberal intellectuals had a number of reasons not to like Kennedy. Sorensen claimed that "the intellectual journals of opinion had doubts about his credentials as a liberal, about his religion and, above all, about his father." Kennedy's father was, understandably, the biggest obstacle to intellectual support. Joseph P. Kennedy had a reputation as an anti-Semite, bootlegger, racketeer, speculator, and womanizer. In addition, he had little regard for intellectuals. These alleged crimes, however, constituted venial sins compared to his chief failing: resisting Franklin D. Roosevelt's anti-Nazi stance before World War II. Kennedy had been Roosevelt's ambassador to England when the war began and had opposed Roosevelt's attempts to aid the British until the January 1941 institution of lend-lease, the program that "loaned" American war matériel to the struggling British.[4]

Joseph Kennedy, however, was not his son's fault. And Kennedy understood the burden his father's reputation placed on him. In 1960, upon hearing that Martin Luther King Sr. took Kennedy's Catholicism as a reason to diverge from Martin Jr.'s support for Kennedy, the Massachusetts senator famously remarked, "Well, we all have fathers, don't we?"[5]

Intellectuals, however, hesitated before backing Kennedy for reasons beyond his lineage. According to Sorensen, Kennedy was "considered with some disdain to be an intellectual by most Massachusetts politicians and considered with equal disdain to be a politician by most Massachusetts intellectuals." As a result, even the idea of Kennedy's running hurt him in the liberal intellectual community. In late 1959, Kennedy stood a distant third in the pantheon of liberal candidates, behind the twice-defeated Stevenson and the outspoken liberal senator from Minnesota, Hubert H. Humphrey.[6]

Kennedy's middle-ground position—being neither a complete pol nor a complete egghead—probably helped in the general election of 1960. But in order to reach the general election, Kennedy needed to obtain the Democratic Party's nomination. Without the support of intellectuals, the fight for the nomination would have been that much more difficult. Fortunately for Kennedy, he had started making inroads into the Cambridge intellectual community before he was a presidential candidate, and the run for the presidency strengthened his interest in gaining the support of intellectuals. When Kennedy sought such support earlier—as a candidate for the Senate and later as a senator—liberal intellectuals had not yet seen him as a threat to their favorite, Stevenson.[7]

Kennedy hired Sorensen, a young lawyer from Nebraska, who became, according to Theodore White, "J.F.K.'s intellectual chief-of-staff." In addition to Sorensen, Kennedy looked outside for supplemental assistance in order to "keep pace with his demand for new ideas and material." As Sorensen put it, "While the Senator was a brainy man, his intelligence included the ability to know his own limitations of time and knowledge and to draw on the brains of others."[8]

Schlesinger, a staunch Stevensonian in 1956, had long-standing ties to the Kennedy team. At the time, Kennedy was considering a run for the 1956 vice presidential nomination under Stevenson, a post eventually captured by Tennessee Senator Estes Kefauver. When the Kennedy team sought political intelligence regarding Stevenson's preferences, they looked to Schlesinger, who, Sorensen recounts, "quietly kept us informed of thinking within the Stevenson camp."[9]

Kennedy's failure to capture the vice presidential nomination only whetted his appetite to seek the presidential nomination. This next step required more than informal links to writers affiliated with Joseph Kennedy, like former Securities and Exchange Commission head James Landis and *New York Times* reporter Arthur Krock. Asking professors for advice, as John Kennedy had done in the Senate, established relationships with intellectuals but did not require any real work or commitments from either Kennedy or the professors. To win intellectual support for his presidential run, however, Kennedy needed to do more.

According to Sorensen, the desire to win over intellectuals, and in turn capture the White House, led Kennedy in 1959 to "make all files and facts available without condition or limitation to [Williams College] Professor James MacGregor Burns for the only serious pre-Presidential biography published." Despite his reluctance to turn over his private papers, Kennedy chose Burns, a prominent liberal political science professor, Sorensen recalled, "not because he assumed that Burns would write a panegyric (which Burns didn't) but because he believed that Burns's ability, and his standing in the liberal intellectual community, would give the book stature among the audience we hoped it would reach."[10]

In addition to opening up his files to Burns's prying eyes, Kennedy needed to establish a formal intellectual organization, ostensibly to provide ideas and advice but, more important, to put intellectuals on a masthead as official Kennedy supporters for the 1960 race. The organization that accomplished this task was the Academic Advising Committee. As Theodore White described the group in gushing prose: "From New England come ideas coined by the finest minds of academe; at Harvard and MIT a campus elite of brilliant professional talent forms an advisory committee surveying the far horizon of American moods and problems." In setting up this group, Sorensen enlisted the assistance of Amherst professor Earl Latham and a young graduate student, Deirdre Henderson.[11]

The Academic Advising Committee met for the first time in December 1958 at the Commander Hotel in Cambridge. After this initial organizational meeting with Sorensen, Henderson maintained contact with the individual professors. According to *Washington Post* reporter Thomas Winship, writing in the days before political correctness, "pretty Deirdre Henderson" would call "on the various professors who have done various chores." And, Winship told his readers, Henderson was more than just a pretty face: "Henderson—a bright person—can take notes and pick up already-prepared memoranda, articles, or recent speeches. This saves the professor the time-consuming job of pounding out a new finished paper." As a result of this system, Winship concluded, Kennedy stood "on the verge of 'owning' a remarkable segment of New England's university and industrial brain power—lock, stock, and speechwriting pad."[12]

Latham soon lost his top position at the AAC to Harvard law professor Archibald Cox. In January 1960, Kennedy wrote to Cox that although Latham had been doing a satisfactory job, Kennedy "need[ed] a faculty member on the scene who can lead and stimulate the group to make sure we are getting the maximum use of it—I do not feel we have been up to now." In addition to Cox, Harvard economist John Kenneth Galbraith and Schlesinger constituted the key triumvirate of the AAC.[13]

The committee had two main tasks. The first and most straightforward was to enlist professorial assistance in specific policy areas. Operating under Sorensen's supervision, Henderson did most of this work. For $3.00 per hour, she collected the various position papers that the professors proffered, forwarding them to Sorensen in the Washington office.[14]

In addition to Henderson, Richard Goodwin, a young lawyer hired as part of the Kennedy staff's precampaign cerebral upgrade, also had paper-requesting authority. In a 1960 letter to Cox, Goodwin listed areas in which Kennedy needed advice. "The Senator has requested position papers on the following subjects," the letter began. The subjects included minerals, reclamation, grazing land, water, projects certain states will be interested in, industrialization of the West, mining, and tariffs." And, lest Cox or his friends forget that Kennedy operated on a political, not academic, timetable, Goodwin added that "he [Kennedy] did want them as soon as possible."[15]

From a policy standpoint, the memos collected from the AAC had very little impact on the Kennedy campaign. According to Sorensen, "Not all their material was usable and even less was actually used." The committee did prove worthwhile, Sorensen found, in that it "provided a fresh and reassuring reservoir of expert intellect at a time when the Senator's speech schedule was exhausting both our intellectual and physical resources." Committeeman Abram Chayes was also skeptical of the project's usefulness, saying, "[I] just remember a terrible sense of inadequacy in the response of this collection of brains; nobody really was able to come up with anything terribly important."[16]

The committee, however, had another purpose. As Sorensen explained, "No announcement was made at the time about the committee's formation, but its very existence, when known, helped recruit Kennedy supporters in the liberal intellectual 'community' who had leaned to Stevenson or Humphrey." Kennedy and Sorensen recognized intellectuals' importance as a constituency. Furthermore, Sorensen admits that this consideration constituted the committee's purpose, since "the liberal intellectuals, with few delegates but many prestigious and articulate voices, could be a formidable foe, as Barkley and Kefauver had learned." With the committee, though, they felt covered, as "Kennedy's 'academic advisers' formed an important beachhead on this front."[17]

Bringing intellectuals on board the Kennedy train required more than just commissioning position papers. Kennedy, as already noted, had a few obstacles to overcome. In 1959, he still needed to face down the ghost of Senator Joseph R. McCarthy. When McCarthy had bullied the Senate and the nation with his invisible list of communist infiltrators, Senator Kennedy had remained strangely quiet. Worse, Robert F. Kennedy, Jack's younger brother, had worked for McCarthy, along with McCarthy's hatchet man and liberal bête noire, Roy Cohn. Kennedy allies later excused these two problems by noting that Bobby quit McCarthy's staff and that the senator had been bedridden when the Senate voted to censure McCarthy. In their memoirs, written after Kennedy's death, both Schlesinger and Sorensen stoutly defend Kennedy from the charge that he ducked the McCarthy issue. Schlesinger made the curious claim that Kennedy's stance differed little from the rest of his party. Furthermore, according to Schlesinger, the only reason Kennedy attracted the charges of cowardice on McCarthy stemmed from the title of Kennedy's book *Profiles in Courage*. Sorensen, in his defense of Kennedy, blamed himself for not voting in Kennedy's place during the senator's illness. While the veracity of Kennedy's defense is not important here, the intensity of the defense is.[18]

Schlesinger also wrote Kennedy a familiar "Dear Jack" letter advising the senator on this issue. Schlesinger explained that the McCarthy issue had staying power: "As you know better than I," Schlesinger wrote, "the McCarthy thing is the great talking-point against you, the one thing which has caused most doubt about you (and which, indeed, is hard to defend)." Lest Kennedy think Schlesinger was just restating the obvious, Schlesinger let Kennedy know that the professor was wearing his adviser hat: "How does one handle all this?" Hoping that the issue would quiet down, Schlesinger told the candidate to avoid the issue, informing him that "my instinct on the matter is that the best answer lies, not in explanations of the past, but in what you do now." Fortunately for Kennedy, McCarthy had died in 1957, three years after his political death and two years before the Kennedy family began its pursuit of the presidency.[19]

Kennedy responded warmly to Schlesinger's missive: "I agree with you that my best course now is a positive one." Recalling the utility of their past attempts to improve his reputation on the McCarthy issue, Kennedy continued: "We have had some success—where people were willing to listen—in pointing out that the past record is not what most people believe." In his concluding lines, Kennedy stroked his pet intellectual: "I do not know if I mentioned to you before how impressed both Ted and I were with your memorandum on the future role of the Democratic Party. We are the wiser for reading it, and intend to use it further."[20]

Kennedy probably felt the need to stroke Schlesinger because, at the same time, Humphrey was also seeking Schlesinger's loyalties. Schlesinger had worked with Humphrey and Max Kampelman, Humphrey's legislative counsel, since 1947. As late as December 1959, Schlesinger was still writing speeches for Humphrey. After one such effort, Humphrey lavished praise on Schlesinger: "I am eternally grateful to you for the superb draft you prepared for my speech at the Eleanor Roosevelt Testimonial dinner. It was just right—and I felt good giving it."[21]

By early 1960, although Schlesinger had not officially declared himself, he was taking Kennedy's side in disputes between the two competing senators. In a February letter to ADA chairman and Humphrey supporter Joseph L. Rauh Jr., Schlesinger warned that Humphrey's attacks on Kennedy imperiled the liberal cause. "It would seem to me that Hubert is making a great mistake in indulging in personal attacks on Jack (if he is actually doing so)," Schlesinger wrote. "Such attacks," he argued, "constitute a disservice to the Democratic Party and to liberalism." Unsolicited, he advised Rauh to "tell Hubert to be himself and campaign on the basis of what he stands for. If he wants to mention Kennedy at all, it would be far smarter to praise Jack than to damn him." Given the fact that Humphrey was competing directly against Kennedy, actively praising his opponent seemed curious advice, indeed.[22]

Even with this apparent declaration of Schlesinger's loyalties, in March 1960 enough people were still unsure of Schlesinger's leanings that the Humphrey campaign prepared a draft letter in which Schlesinger and other prominent liberals—including Reinhold Niebuhr, Francis Biddle, and Rauh—would endorse

Humphrey. The letter, dated March 17, 1960, and addressed "Dear Friend," read, in part, "The five of us signing this letter to you deeply believe that Senator Hubert Humphrey is best qualified to be the next President of the United States."[23]

That same week, though, Schlesinger was writing a detailed letter to Kennedy on how to pick up liberal votes: "If you win by a decisive margin in Wisconsin, I believe that the liberals in the party ought rapidly to unite behind your candidacy." Schlesinger addressed the issue of the politicians to whom he had been previously loyal, explaining, "This means that two men especially should be persuaded to come out for you—Stevenson and Humphrey. I should be prepared to use what influence I have with both to try and get them to do this after Wisconsin."[24]

By April 1960, Humphrey was fighting not just Kennedy but Schlesinger as well. In a bitter April 18 letter to Schlesinger, three weeks before the crucial West Virginia primaries, the beleaguered candidate complained about the Kennedy campaign's sensitivity to criticism. Humphrey denied making "any personal attacks on Jack." Instead, Humphrey said, "What I have done is to point out some of the differences in our public records." This tactic was perfectly legitimate, he explained, as "I have never believed it was wrong in any political contest to 'take a look at the record.'" Finally, Humphrey exploded: "Enough of this. I am a friend of Jack Kennedy, but I refuse to believe he is a God and I refuse to worship at his political shrine." Although Humphrey may have found the outburst cathartic, it is unlikely that Humphrey's comments helped him very much with Schlesinger.[25]

Schlesinger did not respond to Humphrey in the way one would expect a chastised professor would answer a sitting U.S. senator and presidential candidate. He attacked Humphrey right back. After an initial declaration of semineutrality, "I do not want to pose as a spokesman for anyone except myself," he put himself in the position of defender of liberalism: "I do think that there is a considerable body of opinion in the Democratic party committed to the objective of a liberal candidate and a liberal platform but not committed to a specific candidate." Schlesinger warned Humphrey that "it is absolutely stupid and futile now to observe the spectacle of the two liberal candidates swinging angrily on each other and trying to knock each other out of the ring while the conservatives sit in the audience and egg them on." Finally, so that Humphrey should not think that this had been a private communication, Schlesinger added that he was "sending a copy of this letter to Jack."[26]

As the letter shows, Schlesinger and Humphrey clearly had enjoyed a close relationship, however strained the campaign may have left it. Although Schlesinger had committed to Kennedy, Schlesinger apparently could have worked for Humphrey without any qualms, although he probably would have preferred Stevenson to either of them. Thus his choice of Kennedy appears to have been more practical than ideological. Schlesinger felt the need to justify his position in the name of liberalism, not Kennedy partisanship. This higher-cause rhetoric allowed him to rationalize the break from his friend Humphrey. Politics, goes the old saw, is about choices. Schlesinger evidently learned this lesson early on.

Right after Schlesinger sent his letter to Humphrey, he sent a very different one to Kennedy. "Just a note to send warmest congratulations on your remarkable victory yesterday," Schlesinger wrote, referring to the decisive West Virginia primary. In addition to warm wishes, Schlesinger added his spin on the victory's impact on the liberal votes. "I would hope that in the next few weeks the key northern liberals will come out for you," Schlesinger wrote, "and I will do what I can to help bring this about." As Schlesinger was writing to Humphrey to quiet any anti-Kennedy rhetoric, he was also writing to Kennedy hoping to bring Humphrey's supporters to the Kennedy camp.[27]

In June, a month after the West Virginia primary had knocked Humphrey out of the race, sixteen prominent liberals endorsed Kennedy in an open letter to Americans for Democratic Action, *The Nation*, and the *Progressive*, three liberal institutions. Addressed to "Fellow Liberal[s]," the letter explained the political situation as follows: "Until recently liberals have divided their support for the Presidency among Hubert Humphrey, John Kennedy and Adlai Stevenson. All three men have demonstrated the kind of effective leadership which would make them great presidents." The situation had changed after West Virginia, the letter explained: "The purpose of this letter is to urge, now that Senator Humphrey has withdrawn from the race and Mr. Stevenson continues to stand aside, that the liberals of America turn to Senator Kennedy for President." The *New York Times* reported the endorsement, informing readers that "sixteen former backers of Adlai E. Stevenson issued an 'open letter' to 'fellow liberals' tonight urging them to unite behind Senator John F. Kennedy of Massachusetts as the Democratic Presidential nominee." The signers included, among others, the historians James MacGregor Burns, Henry Steele Commager, and Allan Nevins, Galbraith, Schlesinger, and *New Republic* editor Gilbert Harrison. With Humphrey out of the race, Stevenson wavering, and Kennedy having momentum, intellectuals likely felt that Kennedy was the best they were going to get.[28]

Whatever their motivations, all of this posturing did have an effect. Walter Lippmann, the dean of American political columnists and a prominent member of the eastern intellectual elite, reported that the Academic Advisory Committee helped dispel his doubts about Kennedy. As Lippmann recalled, the "Cambridge braintrust, whom I had known very well . . . had done a great deal in convincing me that Kennedy was a good man to have. I mean, their support was very impressive to me." Winning Lippmann's support constituted a coup for the Kennedy campaign. Previously, the influential columnist had supported Adlai Stevenson. Lippmann and other intellectuals did not just automatically support Kennedy because of the senator's natural attraction to the intellectual community. The Kennedy team had to work for it. Obviously, the belief that Kennedy had this natural link to intellectuals was a myth. Like the so-called natural swing of baseball great Ted Williams, Kennedy's "natural" links to intellectuals stemmed from persistence, focus, and hard work.[29]

By the time the nominating season ended, the media had established Kennedy's reputation as one who had a facility with intellectuals, if not a natural link. A number of articles appeared describing Kennedy's team of academic supporters. In one such article, a *Business Week* writer described Kennedy as "the master cultivator of the intellectual." And for liberal intellectuals, the 1960 election gave them little choice. Although liberal intellectuals did not like Kennedy running mate Lyndon Johnson, and some retained doubts about Kennedy, liberal intellectuals loathed Richard Nixon. While the actual campaign for the presidency seesawed through one of the closest contests in modern times, the battle for the liberal intellectuals effectively ended after the Democratic convention in Los Angeles.[30]

TRANSITION TO THE PRESIDENCY

Intellectuals played a lesser role in the fall campaign than they had in the struggle for the Democratic nomination. In August 1960, Schlesinger attended the annual convention of Americans for Democratic Action, the group that he had cofounded in 1947. Schlesinger wrote in a letter to Kennedy that the ADA endorsed Kennedy reluctantly, and only because of the intensity of their hatred for Nixon. Schlesinger went on to explain the hostility that liberals and intellectuals felt toward Kennedy (terms that Schlesinger used interchangeably) and suggested how Kennedy could mollify them. Schlesinger recognized the Democratic domination of college faculties, reporting that "Scholars-for-Nixon now claims support from 4000 faculty members. You could get support from three times as many in a short time if someone would get to work right away on it."[31]

In a contest decided by two-tenths of a percentage point, almost anything could have constituted the determining factor. Clearly, Harvard professors supported him by a wide margin. According to the *Harvard Crimson*, the faculty backed Kennedy by 284 votes. Not surprisingly, his biggest edge came among professors in the social sciences, a staggering 83 percent of whom backed the hometown candidate. While neither college graduates nor Harvard professors constitute a sample of American intellectuals, the latter figure probably measured Kennedy's support better than the former.[32]

Once elected, Kennedy also took an academic approach to the transition. Before the election, he assigned Columbia political science professor Richard Neustadt to prepare a plan for the transition. Neustadt had just written *Presidential Power*, a popular and critically acclaimed study of presidential effectiveness. In late 1960 and early 1961, Neustadt sent JFK a series of detailed memos on how to organize and staff the presidency, giving him goals, timetables, and priorities.[33]

Also on the transition, Deirdre Henderson continued helping in academic matters, researching various scholars as prospective nominees for selected offices. On November 22 she recommended that the president-elect use professorial assistance in the transition. Henderson thought that, "given their semi-detachment from the political world . . . many of the professors could be most helpful in giving their evaluation of appointments." Henderson assured Kennedy that she was not naive about this semidetachment, though: "This is not to say that they do not have their particular biases, but on the whole I find, having worked closely with approximately seventy of your advisers over the past year and a half, that they are anxious to offer advice with no view to reward or self-advancement." Of course, they did not advise without thought of any compensation, but, she found, "their satisfaction seems to be in knowing that they can channel their ideas through someone who can appreciate their views."[34]

Academics received a variety of appointments in the new administration: Jerome Wiesner from MIT became the White House science adviser; John Kenneth Galbraith went to India as ambassador; MIT professor Walt Rostow became deputy assistant for National Security Affairs under former Harvard dean McGeorge Bundy. All of these men had specialties and their positions reflected their expertise and interests. This left Schlesinger, Kennedy's best-known intellectual, a historian with no policy expertise or experience, adrift without a position, despite his invaluable work in helping Kennedy win the nomination. Although Kennedy did not name it at the time, in choosing a position best suited for the talents and temperament of Arthur Schlesinger, Kennedy established the model for future intellectuals in the White House.[35]

ARTHUR SCHLESINGER:
INTELLECTUAL IN THE WHITE HOUSE

Given Schlesinger's unusual résumé in the political realm, Kennedy's hesitation deciding what to do with Schlesinger makes sense. Schlesinger was born in

Columbus, Ohio, in 1917, the son of Progressive Era historian Arthur Schlesinger Sr. Schlesinger Jr. graduated summa cum laude from Harvard in 1938, spent a year as a Henry Fellow at Cambridge, and then entered Harvard's prestigious Society of Fellows for three years. Although Schlesinger did the research for *The Age of Jackson* as a fellow, the society was not a degree-granting program. Schlesinger, one of the twentieth century's best-known historians, never earned a Ph.D. During World War II, Schlesinger did intelligence work, mainly for the Office of Strategic Services. After the war, Schlesinger taught at Harvard, where he wrote his first eight books, books that, according to an only slightly hyperbolic Mitchell Ross, "had been read by half of literate America."[36]

While Kennedy pondered Schlesinger's fate, Schlesinger appears to have had his own troubles coping with Kennedy's indecision. In his own book, *A Thousand Days*, which probably placed the author in the best possible light, Schlesinger asked the president-elect if his prospective position "was firm enough in his mind for me to request leave from Harvard." In his private correspondence he expressed even more anxiety. To his friend, columnist Joseph Alsop, Schlesinger wrote, "I continue happy about the New Frontier and only hope that the summons comes to join it before too long."[37]

Although Kennedy did not rush into hiring Schlesinger, he and Schlesinger had thought about where the historian would best fit. Schlesinger had also discussed the matter with Robert Kennedy during the transition. In addition, he sent the president-elect a long memo in early January, explaining that he had "been giving some thought to the question of where or how I could be useful in the White House." First, he reviewed the new White House organization, in which "Ted Sorensen will be generally in charge of the domestic front, plus speech-drafting, etc.; and Mac Bundy will be generally in charge of the foreign front." These people would handle quotidian concerns, "considerably immersed in each day's crises." Schlesinger, in contrast, wanted to translate his generalist's skill into a more wide-ranging position, although he made the request in a roundabout manner: "should there not be someone in the White House concerned with long-term projects, definition and presentation of programs and policy, independent program review, and the like." In addition, Schlesinger provided an added incentive for hiring him, a continuation of his campaign role: "I should add that it might also be of use to have someone in the White House in whom labor and liberals would find what you once called 'visual reassurance' and whom they could trust as a channel for communications." This channel of communication became the essential element of Schlesinger's position.[38]

In this letter, Schlesinger demonstrated his understanding that Kennedy would appreciate the political advantages of a White House liaison to the intellectual left. In addition, in requesting to be made aide without portfolio,

Schlesinger removed himself from making important decisions and left himself open to future sniping that he was out of the loop by working in the East Wing.

Schlesinger sent a copy of this memo to his father, who wrote that the position would be "an indispensable service, especially if JFK will give you your hand." The question of Schlesinger's hand stemmed from two issues. First, there was the matter of Kennedy and what kind of manager he would be. Schlesinger Jr. had known Kennedy for almost two decades by this point, so this could not have been too great a concern. In addition, the position Schlesinger proposed—thinker without portfolio—was a new one on the White House staff. At this point, the concept of an official, salaried, task-specific White House staff dated back only twenty years. While Schlesinger could propose to do this "indispensable service," neither he nor Kennedy could know how it would turn out.

The amorphous nature of the position confused other staffers who tried to describe it. Since so many Kennedy aides wrote memoirs, there are a number of different descriptions of Schlesinger's duties. Sorensen described Schlesinger's position as a contact person with "liberals and intellectuals both in this country and abroad, as an adviser on Latin-American, United Nations and cultural affairs, as a source of innovation, ideas and occasional speeches on all topics, and incidentally as a lightning rod to attract Republican attacks away from the rest of us." Although the description sounds benign, a close reading reveals Sorensen's attempt to diminish Schlesinger's role. First, the phrase "occasional speeches" serves as a reminder that Sorensen, not Schlesinger, was the principal wordsmith. Sorensen exhibited some sensitivity on this point. As Goodwin, who had his own clashes with Sorensen, recalled, "Occasionally when a Sorensen speech draft was unsatisfactory, Kennedy would give it to Arthur Schlesinger with the injunction: 'Rework this a little, but don't tell Ted I asked you.'" Goodwin's comment reveals that all of them, including Kennedy, recognized Sorensen's sensitivity.[39]

Sorensen's other subtle dig came in the observation that Schlesinger played the role of lightning rod, implying that Schlesinger was a kind of beard, separate and apart from the real policymakers. Even with respect to Schlesinger's role as adviser on UN affairs, his true function was to serve as liaison to the UN ambassador and to the favorite of intellectuals—Adlai Stevenson. Schlesinger's responsibility, to keep the ambassador happy, was really an extension of Schlesinger's service in helping bring intellectual support to Kennedy.[40]

Other aides also downplayed Schlesinger's role. According to political operatives Kenneth P. O'Donnell and David F. Powers, Schlesinger was "special assistant without a special portfolio, to be a liaison man in charge of keeping Adlai Stevenson happy, to receive complaints from the liberals, and to act as a sort of household devil's advocate who would complain about anything in the administration that bothered him." O'Donnell and Powers's description has the same substance as Sorensen's and a touch more insolence.[41]

The most irreverent description of Schlesinger's role came from Robert Kennedy, who remembered that his older brother "liked Arthur Schlesinger, but he thought he was a little bit of a nut sometimes. He thought he was sort of a gadfly and that he was having a helluva good time in Washington. He didn't do a helluva lot, but he was good to have around." In addition, Kennedy remembered, "he wasn't brought in on any major policy matters, but he'd work on drafts of speeches." O'Donnell, Sorensen, and Bobby Kennedy may have been the three men closest to the president and, according to their recollections, Schlesinger did not serve a vital function in the White House.[42]

Even Goodwin, who allied himself with Schlesinger on a number of issues, felt it necessary to identify Schlesinger's exact location in the White House. Goodwin noted that Schlesinger was "on the other side of the mansion, in the East Wing," where the First Lady's staff worked, as opposed to the more policy- and president-oriented West Wing. Schlesinger, Goodwin added, occupied a "more luxurious, but more remote domain." Still, Schlesinger worked in the White House for three years and kept himself busy, whether in the East Wing or elsewhere. And, of course, outsiders assume that anyone who works in the White House, even as an intellectual, has the presidential imprimatur.[43]

THE HISTORIAN

In the White House, Schlesinger worked on the arts, gave general political advice, helped create the White House library, provided a liaison with the mainstream intellectual community, and, most unofficially, served as a liberal lightning rod, giving cover to the rest of the staff. Although he specifically requested a position with such diffuse responsibilities, the intangible nature of his posting left him unsatisfied, at least at the beginning. As his good friend (and fellow exile from the policy realm) John Kenneth Galbraith recalled, Schlesinger at first felt "unhappy and uncertain concerning his White House assignment. He [had] a good address but no clear function."[44]

Despite this initial unhappiness, Schlesinger soon settled in to his new post. His first and primary role was as intellectual and historical adviser in the White House. This assignment included keeping the president informed of intellectual developments and making sure the White House operated in a manner that would be conducive to both historical research and positive historical review.

Schlesinger stressed the importance of this latter notion to the president very early in the administration. In a February 1961 memo, written less than one month after Kennedy's inauguration, Schlesinger outlined Kennedy's weighty responsibility in terms of the historical record. Evidently responding to a Kennedy query, Schlesinger wrote, "You raised the question the other day as to what papers you could properly take away from the White House at the expiration of your term. The answer is that you are expected to take away *all* your papers." In addition, the staff members bore the responsibility of the historical record as well. As a result, according to Sorensen, Kennedy "agreed that procedures should be established to record the firsthand recollections of participants in crucial events while our memories were still fresh."[45]

At the time, Schlesinger claimed that he did not intend to write a history or memoir of Kennedy's administration and that he planned to leave during a second term. In the same memo, he told Kennedy that he did not see himself "as being here on an historical mission; that I have no work of contemporary history under contemplation, except to finish *The Age of Roosevelt*; and that, unless you wish me to do so, I plan to do nothing personally in collecting material on the Age of Kennedy." Even so, Kennedy and the rest of his staff assumed that Schlesinger would write a history of the administration. In April, less than one hundred days after Kennedy had entered the White House, U.S.-trained Cuban rebels failed in an attempted invasion of the Bay of Pigs. Schlesinger, although not privy to all of the planning, had been one of the few advisers who opposed the endeavor. After the fiasco, Kennedy tellingly remarked, "Arthur wrote me a memorandum that will look pretty good when he gets around to writing his book on my administration." Then he added, sarcastically (according to Schlesinger), "Only he better not publish that memorandum while I'm still alive."[46]

Schlesinger was not writing his book clandestinely. Although he had been taking "fragmentary" notes at the outset, the president's reaction to the Bay of Pigs incident changed his mind. "I hope you kept a full account of that," Kennedy remarked to him. Schlesinger responded that he had thought that, in the interests of open conversation, Kennedy "did not want us to keep full accounts of anything." Kennedy, chastened by the postinvasion blame ducking, responded, "No, go ahead. You can be damn sure that the CIA has its record and the Joint Chiefs theirs. We'd better make sure we have a record over here. So you go ahead." Thus instructed, Schlesinger proceeded to keep more comprehensive notes.[47]

Schlesinger reminded Kennedy of the need to keep an accurate record after the Cuban missile crisis. In October 1962, the CIA told Kennedy that the Soviet Union had placed nuclear missiles capable of reaching the United States in Cuba, just ninety miles from Florida. Kennedy responded by imposing a naval blockade of Cuba until the Soviets backed down and removed the missiles. After the fear of a nuclear showdown subsided, Schlesinger, who did not sit in on the meeting of the ExComm crisis management team, sent a memo to the president about the historical record. "Now that the worst is over, may I plead the interests of history and hope that you might be able to set down your impressions of the week while they are still vivid in your mind," Schlesinger wrote, showing himself to be a bit of a historical nudge. Schlesinger apparently intended for Kennedy's reflections to serve future historians. Still, the note keeps open the possibility that Schlesinger himself might be one of those served in the "interests of history," as he ultimately was.[48]

In 1963, three years into the administration, Schlesinger sent the president a series of memoranda discussing the various approaches to an official history of the Kennedy administration. In the third memo, in late February 1963, he reviewed the advantages and disadvantages of a single "house historian" versus specialists for specific areas. Schlesinger reminded Kennedy that "you decided that you did not want either a continuing White House historian or ad hoc specialists brought in from outside to write up specific episodes. You also decided that you did not wish to encourage Dick Neustadt's idea of using Cuba and Skybolt as 'cases' in a book on Presidential decision-making." Given that, he warned, Kennedy still needed to choose an approach.[49]

In March, Schlesinger decided to increase the pressure. In a memo entitled "Your Obligation to Future Historians," Schlesinger took the position of "a representative of the historical interests of the Administration" in order to "beg" Kennedy to do two things: first, "to dictate the circumstances of the decision to resume atmospheric testing while they are still fresh in your mind"; second, to "set aside five or ten minutes every afternoon to note the major events of the day." Were it not for Kennedy's tragic assassination later that year, Schlesinger doubtless would have continued to nag Kennedy on this subject.[50]

Although Schlesinger failed in his attempts to encourage presidential reflection, he had more success in carrying another aspect of his professional life into the White House. As one of the country's most visible intellectuals, Schlesinger was well suited to keep the president up-to-date on intellectual developments. The fact that his friends were responsible for most of the major intellectual developments simplified Schlesinger's task. Whenever one of his friends wrote something that the president would find of interest, Schlesinger could offer to introduce that person to the president. In this way Schlesinger could report on the intellectual community and act as liaison at the same time.

For example, when Alfred Kazin, one of the New York intellectuals, planned an article for the *American Scholar* on intellectuals and the Kennedy administration, Schlesinger told the president about the upcoming article, adding that Kazin would like to meet him. Schlesinger plugged Kazin as "a lively and interesting man" and told the president that he felt Kennedy "would enjoy talking to him."[51]

Kennedy apparently agreed and let Schlesinger invite Kazin down for lunch. The three men had a pleasant meal, the highlight of which was Kennedy's question as to the relevance of the encounter: "But what has all of this to do with the papers waiting for me on my desk?" Nevertheless, Kazin wrote an article that Schlesinger and Kennedy took as negative. In the article, "The President and Other Intellectuals," Kazin averred that Kennedy was the most intellectually minded president since Woodrow Wilson or, perhaps, Theodore Roosevelt, which was not saying very much. Whereas some columnists had chastised Kennedy for *not* writing the book *Profiles in Courage*, speculating that Sorensen was the author, Kazin attacked the president for having written it: "It is the kind of book that reads like a series of excerpts even when you read it through; and indeed it seems composed of excerpts—excerpts of reading, excerpts of anecdotes." Although this comment was accurate, it was also a little harsh toward the sitting president of the United States.[52]

Kazin's main point was that an affinity toward reading did not make one an intellectual. Therefore, according to Kazin, Kennedy had snookered intellectuals who saw him as one of them. Kazin attacked the academics in the administration for their inability to prevent the Bay of Pigs, asking, "Where, then, is the meaningful relation of intellectuals to power? Is it only to write memoranda, to 'educate' the decisions that others make?" Finally, Kazin saw Kennedy's intellectual standing as a pose, the preening of "a would-be intellectual who happens to be President of the United States." Intellectualism was a phase of American superficiality, he concluded, as "to be an 'intellectual' is the latest style in American success, the mark of our manipulatable society."[53]

If the fact that Kazin was so critical despite having met with Kennedy embarrassed Schlesinger, he did not show it in his memoir. "Kazin manfully resisted seduction," Schlesinger observed, as if intellectual circles saw it as macho to hit one's host with the loaf of broad he served. Even Kennedy laughed off the article, mock complaining to Schlesinger that "we wined him and dined him and talked about Hemingway and Dreiser with him, and I later told Jackie what a good time she missed, and then he went away and wrote that piece!"[54]

The Kazin experience did not deter Schlesinger from plugging other friends of his. In early 1962, Schlesinger recommended that Kennedy grant an audience to Richard Rovere for a *New Yorker* profile. "Since Rovere is both a brilliant and friendly writer, I hope you will decide to let him go ahead with this project." If Schlesinger's personal word were not enough, he added his historian's analysis to bolster his position. "I don't know how much impact a *New Yorker* profile would have on the current political atmosphere, but I am sure that a Rovere profile at this point would be a source of great importance for future historians." Unlike Kazin, Rovere did not disappoint, praising Kennedy's "extraordinary political intelligence," which formed the "essence of his political attractiveness."[55]

Schlesinger also sent jokes about the administration itself into the Oval Office. In March 1963, Schlesinger sent Kennedy a Jules Feiffer cartoon with the following note, "You may—or may not—enjoy Feiffer's impression of a typical White House meeting." The six-panel cartoon had Chester "Chet" Bowles, one of the administration's liberals, bumbling into a staff meeting late, with the excuse, "Sorry I'm late, Chief. I was finishing up a book review." Kennedy, trying to cover his annoyance, responded, "Try to be prompt, Chester. The rest of us manage to get our book reviews done on our own time." Schlesinger apparently felt comfortable that the president had a sense of humor about such matters.[56]

Schlesinger directed a steady stream of these types of memos onto the president's desk, as many as ten a month. Since Kennedy did not have a chief of staff or hierarchical staff organization, he probably saw most if not all of this barrage of articles, books, speeches by Schlesinger, and letters from friends. In this way, Schlesinger kept Kennedy in touch with the intellectual–cultural world. Although this task was not an official part of his job description, Schlesinger quickly made it his most regular assignment, making these updates a major element of his position.

THE ART CONNOISSEUR

The job of keeping intellectuals happy also benefited from demonstrating presidential appreciation of the arts. As a result, early in the administration, Schlesinger pushed Kennedy in an artistic direction. In February, less than a month after Kennedy's inauguration, Schlesinger sent the president a long memo, ostensibly about Latin America, but emphasizing the importance of positive relations with intellectuals: "Intellectuals, of course, have become a dynamic political force through much of the world, especially in the new nations. In many cases these newly-liberated intellectuals see the United States as materialistic, vulgar, obsessed with comic books and television, hostile to higher cultural and spiritual values." According to Schlesinger, intellectuals, in America and abroad, took a condescending attitude toward the United States. He felt that Kennedy had an opportunity to change this perception and let him know it. "You are a writer and historian. Your wife is a patron of the arts. You have appointed intellectuals to positions in your administration. You summoned the leading artists and writers in America to your inauguration." By virtue of these assets, Kennedy gave "the intellectual community of the United States a sense of being important to the country once again."[57]

While this was an improvement over the perceived anti-intellectualism of the Eisenhower years, for Schlesinger it was not enough. It represented a good start, though, "a splendid foundation from which to launch a new image of America as a land which deeply values artistic and cultural achievement." And here Schlesinger reached the point, his policy recommendation, a concerted administration effort to maintain this newfound goodwill. Schlesinger offered a number of suggestions for accomplishing this, "for example, receiving leading artists and scholars at the White House; the appointment of a serious commission on government and the arts; stories about the books you and the First Lady have been reading; appearances on notable cultural occasions, etc." This memo provides a blueprint for Schlesinger's activities as Kennedy's informal adviser on the arts. More important, it predicts many of Kennedy's activities, as, in this area at least, he tended to follow Schlesinger's advice.[58]

In November 1961, cellist Pablo Casals performed at the White House, the first in a well-publicized dinner series for artists. Other guests at these dinners included composer Igor Stravinsky, literary critic André Malraux, and some of the West's Nobel Prize winners. Kennedy famously called this group "the most extraordinary collection of talent, of human knowledge, that has ever been gathered together at the White House, with the possible exception of when Thomas Jefferson dined alone."[59]

Afterward, Schlesinger told Kennedy, who had little interest in music, that the Casals dinner "had an extraordinary effect in the artistic world." After the dinner, he reported, "when the advisory council for the National Cultural Center met, a number of people said to me in the most heartfelt way how much the Administration's evident desire to recognize artistic and intellectual distinction meant to the whole intellectual community." Schlesinger also informed Kennedy of a column by the *New York Herald Tribune*'s John Crosby calling Kennedy "the best friend culture . . . has had in the White House since Jefferson." The repeated Jefferson references were not accidental. Jefferson's reputation for erudition and taste appealed to Kennedy and the New Frontiersmen. Kennedy had reportedly read Jefferson's first inaugural address on his own inauguration day and judged it "better than mine."[60]

In addition to good press and favorable comparisons with Thomas Jefferson, Schlesinger argued that the artist coddling had a tangible and positive effect. "All this is of obvious importance, not only in attaching a potent opinion-making group to the Administration, but in transforming the world's impression of the United States as a nation of money-grubbing materialists." Even better, he noted, "all this has taken place without any criticism, so far as I am aware." Both Kennedy and Schlesinger treated the intellectuals as a constituency to be courted. As a member of that constituency, Schlesinger would have favored them more than Kennedy, who needed to satisfy a variety of constituencies. Still, both men took this constituent-service approach to intellectual activity.[61]

Schlesinger not only advised the president on general artistic developments and possible invitees to White House events, but he also managed the inchoate

President's Council on the Arts from inside the White House. He and his good friend August Heckscher, the special consultant for the arts, met and kibitzed over potential arts policies. Then one of the men, usually Schlesinger, would pass the recommendations to the president.

Although Kennedy had appointed Heckscher in early 1962, the two men apparently waited a few months before proceeding in earnest. In August of that year, Heckscher met with the president and offered some preliminary suggestions, sending the notes of the conversation to Schlesinger. In the meeting, Heckscher proposed a number of arts-related policies, of which Kennedy approved three: a council on the arts, a conference on the arts, and tax breaks for supporting artistic endeavors. The president, however, drew the line at government funding to the arts. "He doubted," Heckscher remembered, "whether we should go into direct subsidies. How would one decide which institutions to support?" Despite the president's disapproval, Congress funded the controversial National Endowment for the Arts just five years later, on Johnson's watch.[62]

When Kennedy did something that pleased artists, Schlesinger made sure to let his boss know. After all, Schlesinger's job included pleasing the artistic community, and if artists expressed approval, it meant that Schlesinger was doing something right. In late October 1963, Schlesinger sent Kennedy a memo on this subject: "You will be interested in the *New York Post*'s response to [Kennedy's speech at] Amherst." The editorial was so glowing that Schlesinger needed to add a postscript, "*I did not* inspire this editorial, nor did [*Post* editor James] Wechsler write it" (emphasis in original). In the speech, Kennedy had praised poetry's place in society, claiming that "when power corrupts, poetry cleanses." Consequently, poetry was vital to democracy, as "the highest duty of the writer, the composer, the artist is to remain true to himself and to let the chips fall where they may." The *Post* editorialists loved this message, seeing in it a mission for America: "If the precepts of this noble speech become the guidelines of American society, we are indeed entering not the decline, as some pessimists proclaim, but the golden age of American civilization."[63]

POLITICAL LIGHTNING ROD

As the 1962 midterm elections approached, Schlesinger began taking a larger role in electoral politics, writing a nine-page analysis of the upcoming elections entitled "The Presidency and Mid-Term Elections." This paper, which looked at the approaches of previous presidents to midterm elections and the results, came up with three conclusions. First, "Presidential intervention in mid-term elections has increased steadily over this period." Second, "there is no evidence that presidential intervention has at any point played a decisive role in determining the outcome of these elections." Schlesinger put his recommendation in his third conclusion: "History suggests that it would be a mistake for the President to turn the 1962 mid-term election into a test of personal confidence by actively intervening in the form of personal endorsement or advocacy of (or opposition to) individual candidates." On the one hand, this seems to be the appropriate role for a public intellectual in the White House, using his expertise in a certain field to give the president practical advice on a subject. On the other hand, a Pulitzer Prize–winning professor of history could probably have been put to better use than writing political memos that could have been written by a savvy twenty-three-year-old history major. Kennedy did not necessarily need someone of Schlesinger's stature to tell him that "sixty years ago, mid-term elections were primarily *local* elections" and cull quotes such as Theodore Roosevelt saying, "By George, I sometimes wish I was not in the White House and could be on the stump and speak frankly." Even if a junior staffer wrote the memo and had Schlesinger look it over for inaccuracies, it would seem a more appropriate allocation of resources.[64]

Kennedy did not always follow Schlesinger's political advice. According to Sorensen, Schlesinger had written "a thoughtful memorandum" arguing against presidential participation in the midterms because history showed that presidents received the blame for the inevitable losses. Schlesinger gave as examples Wilson in 1918 and Roosevelt in 1938, two incumbents weakened by participating in midterm elections in which their parties made weak showings. Kennedy ignored this advice, and the Democrats made a strong showing, losing only two seats in the House of Representatives and gaining a surprising four seats in the Senate. Of course, Kennedy's resolve in the Cuban missile crisis, which occurred in October, just prior to the election, contributed to the triumph.[65]

Schlesinger often acted as liberal point man in the administration, intervening on behalf of both prominent liberals and liberal issues. Sometimes these interventions concerned issues close to Schlesinger's heart. Regarding the hardline anticommunist John Birch Society, Schlesinger wrote Kennedy a memo describing the history of both the Birchers and their opponents. Schlesinger wanted Kennedy to support the anti-Birchers, telling him that "those who are fighting the Birch movement in Wichita, Pasadena, etc., would be enormously heartened by some expressions from you condemning the movement and saluting those who are supporting traditional American views of freedom of expression and conscience." Later that year, Kennedy spoke out against "those on the fringes of our society who have sought to escape their own responsibility by finding a simple solution, an appealing slogan or convenient scapegoat." From the language, tone, and historical perspective of this comment, it appears that Schlesinger had some success in pushing the president toward this position.[66]

Although Schlesinger had far less power than many conservatives feared, allegations concerning his influence caused Kennedy numerous headaches. Even before the 1962 congressional elections brought Schlesinger into the role of political adviser, Schlesinger played the additional political role of liberal magnet for conservative criticism. This role required deft handling. Kennedy needed to keep Schlesinger visible and happy to satisfy liberals and provide a target for conservatives. At the same time, though, Kennedy did not wish for Schlesinger to assume a high profile or become involved in actual policy making. According to Washington journalist and Kennedy confidant Ben Bradlee, "Kennedy had only one true professional historian working in the White House. This was Schlesinger, whom he admired as a historian, liked enormously as a person, but whose liberal politics he felt were impractical."[67]

Even if Schlesinger's politics had been more "practical," Kennedy would have needed to keep him at arm's length because of the political attacks conservatives directed at the historian. The columnist Walter Winchell criticized Schlesinger for being patronizing in comments he had made in a 1960 *Encounter* article on heroic leadership. Winchell quoted Schlesinger: "Heroic leadership should seem the most effective means of charging semi-illiterate people with a sense of national and social purpose." According to Winchell, Schlesinger's condescension did not end there: "'If the crisis can be met in no other way,' wrote JFK's No. 1 advisor, 'it must be met that way.'" Winchell, who carried on a long-standing and bitter feud with Schlesinger's friend Jimmy Wechsler of the *New York Post*, appears to have made two mistakes. First, Schlesinger was in no way Kennedy's top adviser, although he may have been Kennedy's best-known White House aide. Second, Winchell appears to have made Schlesinger's speculative comments much worse than the innocuous musings they actually were. Political appointees in America continue to be held captive by the printed word, and they should be responsible for what they have written. Still, the incident showed some political wisdom on Kennedy's part. By bringing Schlesinger into the White House but not giving him much power, Kennedy allowed conservative ire to fall on Schlesinger, letting other aides work productively in their relative obscurity.[68]

In addition to knocking Schlesinger individually, conservatives also hit Schlesinger on the issue of ADA, which Schlesinger had cofounded. In July 1962, for example, the conservative newspaper *Human Events* published an eleven-article supplement detailing ADA participation in the administration. The *Los Angeles Times* also devoted a special series to ADA. Robert Hartmann, Washington bureau chief for the *Times*, wrote seven articles on the organization, which the *Times* then reprinted together. Hartmann argued that the ADA merited examination because it was unusual that a "14-year-old organization . . . with a budget of less than $200,000 a year, regarded as an albatross by many Democrats and as anathema by most Republicans . . . can staff a new administration with three White House aides, three cabinet officers and 31 key appointments."[69]

The critics had good reason to question Schlesinger's link to ADA. Although Hartmann was correct to deny a sinister conspiracy, ADA did influence government affairs, through both its members in the administration and the frequent contacts ADA leadership had with ADA members employed by Kennedy. Schlesinger, for example, was in constant contact with ADA offices in Washington. Some of the interaction was completely innocuous, such as Schlesinger's observation to ADA national director Violet Gunther, "Whatever happened to [Ronald] Reagan? Wasn't he once a great Hollywood liberal?" Years later, Schlesinger and Gunther would not be the only two liberals wrestling with this question.[70]

Schlesinger also liked to let ADA know when it had influence on government policy. In a letter to Paul Seabury, chairman of the group's executive committee, Schlesinger dropped a very unsubtle hint that the committee's words had influenced presidential policy: "I am grateful for your letter of November second on behalf of the ADA Executive Committee. I attach herewith a copy of the statement on the subject issued the same day by the President. I am happy to note a certain parallelism between the two documents!" Schlesinger pointed out this "certain parallelism" for a number of reasons. First, it made him, as an ADA member and sympathizer, feel pleased about the presidential statement. Second, this word migration made ADA members happy, both about Schlesinger's position and about Kennedy in the White House. Third, and most important, this was part of Schlesinger's job, to make sure that ADA and other representatives of the intellectual left approved of the man in the Oval Office. Despite his closeness to the ADA, Schlesinger recognized the need to limit the association while he worked in the White House.[71]

Another aspect of Schlesinger's responsibilities as lightning rod required a moderately high profile—of his left side. In early 1962, Schlesinger let Kennedy know that Larry Spivak of NBC's *Meet the Press*, "an old friend of mine," wanted Schlesinger to appear on the show. Spivak, Schlesinger explained, felt that "the opposition was building me up as a sort of socialist monster, and that an appearance on *Meet the Press* would show the nation that my ideas are reasonable and my personality innocuous." Schlesinger's first reaction was negative; he "demurred and said that presidential assistants were charged with a passion for anonymity." Then he had second thoughts, telling the president that "if the Republicans continue to portray me as a major national threat, there might be some point in considering Spivak's suggestion." Kennedy did not agree, scrawling "NO" on the original memo and sending it back to Schlesinger. While Kennedy wanted Schlesinger to have a high profile among liberal intellectuals, he wanted Schlesinger to keep a relatively low profile nationally.[72]

WHITE HOUSE LIBRARIAN

Schlesinger passed only one project on to his successors—the White House Library. The unfinished nature of this project did not stem from a lack of effort on Schlesinger's part but the late date on which he began the endeavor. This project brought him in close contact with the First Lady, as part of her White House redecoration project, contributing to the perception of Schlesinger as an East Wing aide.

Mrs. Kennedy approved of the library idea but did not quite want to get involved. Letitia Baldridge, Jackie's social secretary, wrote to Schlesinger that "Mrs. Kennedy wants you to handle this whole thing without even consoling [sic] her. If you could just report to me or send me a carbon copy occasionally, we will be in clover."[73]

Once Schlesinger received the First Lady's approval (and pledge of noninterference), he wrote letters to various librarians and historians regarding the project, including his father, who sent the letter back with his recommendations scrawled on the original. Knowing historians as well as he did, Schlesinger Sr. made at least one unsolicited recommendation: "To get the full co-operation of your consultants I think it would be well to send them stamped envelopes for the return of the document."[74]

Schlesinger then sent "a basic White House library list" of 2,741 vital books to twenty-five prominent historians, asking them for "recommendations as to which books should be omitted and further books which should be included." After collecting his responses, Schlesinger spent a few months collating the information and creating a draft list of books. Then Mrs. Kennedy reappeared, seeking a progress report, telling Schlesinger that "I'm ashamed to say I really don't know what is happening on our Library Committee, except that absolutely no progress is being made." Evidently her desire to be left out of the loop had been a temporary one. While she had Schlesinger's attention, she added her instructions as to what the library should look like, revealing in her inimitable way what she thought of public libraries: "I don't think it should be used as a working library or that anyone in the White House should be able to borrow from it. As you know, that way, books will gradually disappear and we will have to have hideous numbers on the backs."[75]

Schlesinger, unruffled, wrote back to Jackie: "Do not despair about the library. . . . As you will see from this letter, the basic list of books has been completed."

Given that part of his reason for working on the library project stemmed from his desire to have books available for the White House staff, he probably disagreed with Mrs. Kennedy's desire to keep the library semiprivate. Instead, he tactfully wrote, "I agree with you that it ought not to be a library from which the White House staff could borrow books; but I do think that it ought to be a library to which the staff can turn if necessary." In conclusion, he reassured her once again that the project would proceed apace: "In short, I think the Library is making progress." If nothing else, the letter demonstrates an admirable ability to placate the First Lady.[76]

In his last official communiqué on the library, Schlesinger updated James Babb, who originally suggested the idea of the library, on the status of the project. "So far as I understand it, President Johnson wishes very definitely for the library to continue." Schlesinger concluded with a jab at the new president: "I do hope we can avoid twelve volumes covering the social, economic and natural history of Texas!"[77]

SCHLESINGER'S LEGACY

In a letter to Schlesinger's father, Kennedy wrote that he found Schlesinger "of inestimable assistance and I do believe that his work here in the White House will make his later writings on Roosevelt and American history generally more perceptive." Part of this statement is obviously intended to make the senior Schlesinger proud. On the other hand, Kennedy avoids mentioning any White House accomplishments, preferring instead to focus on the job's beneficial impact on Schlesinger Jr. One reason for this omission could be that Kennedy viewed Schlesinger's historical perspective as his chief asset. In that case, Schlesinger's subsequent work, the invaluable if hagiographic *A Thousand Days*, vindicates Schlesinger's selection.[78]

If the measure of an intellectual assistant's success is the public's perception of the president's relationship with intellectuals, then Schlesinger belongs in the intellectual assistants' hall of fame. Not all of Kennedy's success on this front, though, stems from Schlesinger's doing. Kennedy did a very capable job of reaching out to intellectuals with the Academic Advisory Committee. In addition, having Sorensen—who Richard Neustadt said had "the most extraordinary intellect in Kennedy's entourage"—with him for over a decade, helped. Kennedy's résumé, which lists him as having studied at Harvard, Princeton, Stanford, Yale, and the London School of Economics (although only Harvard granted him a graduating degree), also added to the reputation.[79]

Stories in the press about Kennedy's affinity for the *New Republic* further bolstered Kennedy's image among liberals and intellectuals. Early in the administration, Newsweek reported that the president entered a National Security meeting "engrossed" in a magazine that was "perhaps unknown to all but one-half of one percent of the population. It was *The New Republic*." Under Kennedy, the article continued, the magazine's "circulation has spurted from 34,120 to 40,278. *The New Republic* has become almost 'must' reading on the New Frontier." But Kennedy was not the only *New Republic* addict in the administration; "its readers include U.N. Ambassador Adlai Stevenson, Presidential Assistants Theodore Sorensen and Arthur Schlesinger Jr., Interior Secretary Stewart Udall, and Agriculture Secretary Orville Freeman." Articles like this helped Kennedy's stature among intellectuals, Schlesinger or no Schlesinger.[80]

In Norman Podhoretz's book *Making It*, he described the feelings of the New York intellectuals under Kennedy as akin to bliss: "from having carried a faint aura of disreputability, the title 'intellectual' all at once became an honorific, and much began to be made in Washington as elsewhere of leading representatives of this particularistic class." The Family, as Podhoretz called the New York intellectuals, did not expect such deference from the nation's political class. The new attention exhilarated Podhoretz, who recalled that Family members "knew and were even friendly with members of the White House staff; they read our magazines and the pieces and books we ourselves wrote, and they cared—it was even said the President himself cared—about what we thought. Would Roosevelt have cared? Would Truman? Would Eisenhower?" To get such a strong reaction, Kennedy and Schlesinger had to have done something right.[81]

Despite the perception of Kennedy's closeness with liberal intellectuals, Kennedy's troubles with ADA demonstrate that such was not always the case. It was Lyndon Johnson's boorishness and disdain for the "Harvards" that made Kennedy's relations with intellectuals idyllic, and in retrospect only. Even with Schlesinger, the Academic Advisory Committee, and art dinners, the intellectuals were hard to satisfy and did not really trust Kennedy. Compared with Lyndon Johnson, however, Kennedy was the intellectuals' best friend. In this sense, then, Johnson was Kennedy's biggest asset in his reputation with the intellectual constituency.

Nevertheless, Schlesinger, who held operational responsibility for Kennedy's relations with the intellectuals, proved generally successful in his task. Although intellectuals like Kazin and the ADA conventioneers occasionally griped about the president's commitment, intellectuals by their nature constitute a vocal and complaining lot. Compared with the domestic upheaval of the Johnson era, the Kennedy period represented a veritable honeymoon period between the White House and intellectuals.

Although Schlesinger helped keep intellectuals happy, his work in the policy realm was not nearly as successful. There were good reasons for this. As his résumé demonstrates, Schlesinger's experience made him hard to classify in a policy sense.

As a historian, not an economist or even a political scientist, Schlesinger did not have a natural post in the White House. He was obviously very bright, but not necessarily an expert or even interested in the inner workings of domestic policy. So Kennedy put him to work in the only appropriate role he could find—that of a generalist intellectual, responsible for cultural exchange, relations with other academics, and spotting intellectual trends.

In his three years at the White House, Schlesinger wrote articles and film reviews, corresponded with the nation's intellectual and cultural elites, advised John F. Kennedy on literary and some political matters, worked with Americans for Democratic Action in promoting liberalism in America, and accumulated the research for his next book, *A Thousand Days*. In short, his job at the White House paid him $20,000 to be . . . Arthur Schlesinger. For Kennedy, this was a bargain. Schlesinger, with his high standing among the relatively unified intellectual community, helped Kennedy become president, gain good reviews as president, and become even more popular in the years following the tragic assassination in Dallas.

3

LYNDON JOHNSON
VERSUS
THE "HARVARDS"

The apparent consensus among American intellectuals fragmented during Lyndon Johnson's presidency. Although Johnson did not cause the breakup on his own, he bore some of the blame and much of the suffering. Many disenchanted intellectuals directed their ire over Vietnam at the White House, where Johnson's boorishness contrasted poorly with his predecessor's refinement. Johnson served during both the escalation of the Vietnam War and the postlegislative civil rights movement, issues that bitterly divided intellectuals and the country. Anti-Johnson intellectuals also found a wider audience as the baby boomers matured and college teaching needs grew. This need for teachers led to the professionalization of the intellectuals. In accepting secure positions with possibilities of tenure and pensions, intellectuals also accepted geographical dispersion, increasing their stability but at the same time decreasing their concentration compared with the previous generation's intellectuals.

JOHNSON AND SCHLESINGER

A look at Lyndon B. Johnson's relations with American intellectuals must begin where an examination of Kennedy's relations left off—with Arthur Schlesinger. Johnson's southern conservative image and demeanor poisoned his relations with northern intellectuals, most notably Schlesinger. Schlesinger's experience with the crude but smart Texan demonstrates how Johnson's often troubled relations with intellectuals developed into open warfare during his presidency.

Schlesinger's relationship with Johnson dated back to 1953, when Johnson criticized an article by Schlesinger. They began corresponding in 1957, starting their relationship on the wrong foot, even for people who did not like each other. Johnson's February 1957 letter to Schlesinger began with an accusation: "I understand you have some ideas on what the Democrats should do in terms of making issues looking towards the election in 1958. From what I have heard, I am inclined to think that you are not too convinced that I am going about it in the right way." Johnson put Schlesinger in his place by reminding the professor of Johnson's position: "As Majority Leader of the Senate, I have some problems which I do not think you are too aware of." Johnson completed his missive with an invitation wrapped around a threat. "I hear that you come to Washington quite often. . . . Let me know the next time you are coming so that we can arrange an appointment to talk over some of these problems. I suspect that you will find I will go a long way toward convincing you that it is not as easy as you think." Johnson's letter made his disdain for unelected intellectual kibitzers quite clear.[1]

The letter must have unnerved Schlesinger. Not only was one of the nation's most powerful officials aware of Schlesinger's private conversations, but he also had a good idea about Schlesinger's peregrinations ("I hear that you come to Washington quite often"). Worst of all, Johnson cared enough about Schlesinger's comments to let Schlesinger know that he was in Johnson's zone of awareness. Schlesinger waited, appropriately, until Valentine's Day before attempting reconciliation in a self-deprecating manner: "May I say that I am, of course, grateful for your interest in my views. These views are of no importance, however, except as they reflect misgivings prevalent among Northern Democrats." In addition to belittling his own views, Schlesinger expressed his sympathy for Johnson's position vis-à-vis his own: "I can well imagine that the responsibility of leadership on the firing line presents problems of which outsiders are not aware. I would welcome indeed a chance for a discussion on this and other points and I will let you know in advance before my next visit to Washington." Regardless of whether Schlesinger was sincere, he certainly took the right tone to assuage the angry Johnson.[2]

Schlesinger's deference must have helped matters, for Johnson's next letter to Schlesinger displayed a friendlier tone: "I am in complete agreement with your observation that the Democratic Party will never win a national election as the party of 'retrenchment, economy, and inadequate public service.'" Johnson also tried to make Schlesinger feel needed, writing that "my assistant George Reedy, whom you met, tells me that he is familiar with some of [Walt] Rostow's ideas and that they are worth exploring. If he should be in the vicinity, I would like to meet him. It would also be helpful to talk to Galbraith and [Seymour] Harris." Finally, Johnson lauded Schlesinger: "Your suggestions were definitely helpful in clarifying my own thinking. Keep them coming! Our party needs the best brains and ideas that we can get together." In this letter, Johnson now agreed with Schlesinger and praised him excessively, two signs that Johnson did not despise someone. To someone he truly liked, though, he probably would not have been as hyperbolic.[3]

By the next March, the two men were on a first-name basis, and Schlesinger felt comfortable enough to send Johnson a long letter suggesting a major increase in public spending. Schlesinger, demonstrating a historian's version of Keynesianism, warned that a budget surplus would lead to a tax cut: "the extra money pumped into the economy will be dissipated in consumer spending; it means longer cars, bigger fins and larger television sets." Schlesinger obviously disapproved of tax cuts going back to taxpayers. Schlesinger told Johnson that during a time "when we are losing ground in our competition with the Communists, the arguments are overwhelming for using the money acquired through budgetary deficits to meet urgent national needs rather than dispersing it generally and ineffectually for gadgets and gimmicks."[4]

Johnson immediately wrote back that "every once in a while when the skies are overcast, and it is difficult to determine an exact course, a mariner comes across a break in the clouds that reveals a very useful star which is ideal for navigators. Your letter was in that category." Regardless of one's opinion of Johnson's metaphor, Johnson apparently approved of Schlesinger's views, which express Keynes's ideas about increasing public-sector spending pumped though John Kenneth Galbraith's popularizing microphone.[5]

Schlesinger later remembered that the two men had an amiable, if not intimate, relationship: "We had a perfectly affable acquaintance, though I am sure that Johnson regarded me with a certain detachment, as some kind of Eastern intellectual associated with Adlai Stevenson, for whom he did not have a high regard." Schlesinger and his friends, for their part, viewed Johnson as a southern conservative associated with segregationist Georgia Senator Richard B. Russell.[6]

Just as Schlesinger's friends knew about the professor's imbroglio with Johnson, they knew about the rapprochement as well. In a letter thanking Schlesinger for a civil rights award nomination, Joe Rauh teased Schlesinger about his new-found friend. "Nor is my appreciation any less just because you have become chief brain truster for Lyndon Johnson, who has just accomplished the demise of the Republican Party single-handedly. As for me, I shall stick with Eugene Debs and Averell." The leadership of Americans for Democratic Action apparently considered advising Johnson to be a cardinal offense.[7]

For the next two years, Schlesinger and Johnson stood at cross-purposes; Johnson was maneuvering for the Democratic nomination while Schlesinger was a key player in the "Stop Johnson" movement, backing Kennedy as the best way to accomplish this goal. Nevertheless, Schlesinger and Johnson corresponded frequently during this period, never mentioning the Massachusetts senator looming between them.

Later, of course, Kennedy did win the nomination Johnson coveted. Kennedy's selection of Johnson as his running mate represented a step backward in the carefully planned campaign to obtain the support of intellectuals. By that time, however, the intellectuals had no choice but to back Kennedy, as they found Richard Nixon was anathema. Although the precise tale behind Kennedy's selection of Johnson remains murky and contested, Kennedy clearly had to consider factors other than the reactions of East Coast intellectuals.

For his part, Johnson had little regard for the East Coast intellectuals. He could not understand why well-educated liberals embraced Kennedy and not Johnson. As he told Doris Kearns years later, "It was the goddamndest thing, here was a young whippersnapper, malaria-ridden and yallah, sickly, sickly. He never said a word of importance in the Senate and never did a thing." Johnson, meanwhile, was the nation's most effective legislator. Nevertheless, Johnson continued, "somehow, with his books and his Pulitzer Prizes, he managed to create the image of himself as a shining intellectual, a youthful leader who could change the face of the country," a development Johnson resented at least as much as Kennedy himself resented Stevenson's ties to intellectuals. Despite Johnson's disgust with Kennedy's reputation, the rest of the political world seemed to play it up, further frustrating Johnson.[8]

Kennedy had to work hard for his reputation among intellectuals in 1959 and 1960; by the time of his death, however, writers had cemented Kennedy's standing among the intellectuals. Lewis Mumford wrote that Kennedy had been "the first American President to give art, literature, and music a place of dignity and honor in our national life." Although Mumford's statement gave short shrift to Thomas Jefferson and Theodore Roosevelt, Mumford did not exaggerate as much when he observed that those interested in the arts had lost "a staunch friend."[9]

As expected, Johnson disliked both the worshipful praise of Kennedy and the comparisons, in which Johnson inevitably came up short. According to Princeton historian Eric Goldman, who would soon replace Schlesinger as house intellectual, Kennedy's good press goaded Johnson: "The more Lyndon Johnson heard the cultivated Kennedy from Harvard compared with his boorish Texas self, the more he held himself back on occasion, at other times deliberately exaggerated Lyndon Johnson from Johnson City, drawl, boisterousness, banality and all." As a result of this constant comparison, Goldman remembered, "[LBJ] could readily do without a number of the JFK entourage, most especially those 'overbred smart alecks who live in Georgetown and think in Harvard.'"[10]

Despite Johnson's dislike for many members of Kennedy's staff, he kept several of them when he became president. Even though most of the Kennedy people, with the notable exception of Kennedy himself, had treated Johnson poorly during the administration, Johnson felt the need to send a healing message to the wounded nation. In the most recent example of vice presidential succession at the time, Harry Truman had felt the need to hire as many of his own people as possible in order to distinguish himself from Roosevelt. Johnson brought in some of his own men, Texans like Jack Valenti and Marvin Watson, but on the whole the Kennedy people stayed on at first.[11]

Schlesinger wanted to resign immediately after Kennedy's death, but Johnson insisted that he remain. According to Schlesinger, "I resigned the day after Dallas. He called me in and made an eloquent plea to the effect that he needed me more than Kennedy had and so on, which I found rather impressive at the time. I later discovered that he said the same thing to everybody else." Original or not, Johnson's plea worked, as Schlesinger "agree[d] to stay on for the transition."[12]

Even though he stayed on, everyone knew that Schlesinger did not belong in the new administration. As Kennedy aide Lee White remembered, "Well, Schlesinger, of course, didn't stay [under LBJ]. He left right away, and he should have. It was not his dish of tea. Arthur did not have a sort of an operating responsibility. He was at the ball park, but he wasn't in the ball game."[13]

On January 25, 1964, Schlesinger wrote his letter of resignation to Johnson, claiming that he did so "with great regret; but, as I told you when you so generously urged me to stay on after President Kennedy's death, I had long since resolved that in any case the time had come for me to return to scholarly work." He added some praise for Johnson, writing that "I cannot depart without assuring you of my admiration for your wise and strong leadership in these shadowed weeks since November 22."[14]

Johnson wrote an equally disingenuous note back to Schlesinger: "With much regret, I accept your resignation as Special Assistant to the President." Of course, Johnson being Johnson, he had to add some exaggerated praise: "I know the academic world will be richer for your return. But the White House will not be quite the same without you. We shall miss the fresh insights of your scholarship and the liberality of your spirit." Johnson may have missed Schlesinger's "insights" and "spirit," but he probably did not miss him personally. Schlesinger left the White House on March 1, 1964.[15]

With Schlesinger gone, Johnson sought his own link to the academic and intellectual worlds. Johnson took two approaches to setting up this link. He filled the position that Schlesinger had left with an academic he did not fully trust. This would turn out badly. Johnson's second approach was to hire smart people with political savvy who could speak to academics but also to Johnson. While this second approach proved more successful, in the end, perhaps no strategy could have patched the unmendable tear in Johnson's relationship with American intellectuals.

ERIC GOLDMAN: "WRETCHED, RASH, INTRUDING FOOL"

Lyndon Johnson clearly had ambivalent feelings about American intellectuals. Educated at Southwest Texas Teacher's College, he often felt inferior to those educated at America's elite universities. On the other hand, he had overcome a poor upbringing and a less prestigious diploma to become president. As a result, he often felt superior to those who started with more but attained less.

In addition to this ambivalence, Johnson did not trust intellectuals who wrote and read but did not risk. According to Alan Reinert, in his introduction to Billy Lee Brammer's *The Gay Place*, "Billy Lee was the first and last intellectual that Lyndon Johnson ever really trusted. He welcomed his careful perspective and reflective temper, the inward bent of his mind, and he trusted him because he could dominate him, or so it seemed." Brammer, as a Texan, had worked as a speechwriter for Johnson and was able to speak Johnson's language. His 1961 roman à clef starred Arthur Fenstemaker, a Johnson-like governor of Texas: larger-than-life, profane, and relentlessly pragmatic. In the novel, Hoot, the governor's brother, asks Jay McGown, a Brammer-like aide, "You have any ideas? Jay. Don't any of you people have any ideas?" Jay, accustomed to the governor's ways, replies: "I haven't had an idea in two years. The Governor usually has all the ideas." This typical exchange captures Johnson, who liked having smart people around him but also liked having all the ideas.[16]

In addition, Johnson disapproved of twentieth-century America's definition of intellectuals. Johnson had no use for "objective" RAND Institute number crunchers. According to Jack Valenti, Johnson's closest aide for the first few years, Johnson did not "like cold intellectuals around him. He wants people who will cry when an old lady falls down in the street." Valenti, a Harvard MBA, was very smart but not generally considered an intellectual. This perception irked Johnson, who observed that "Jack is really an intellectual. People would admit it if he didn't come from the wrong side of the Mason-Dixon line."[17]

Still, despite his reservations, Johnson was not opposed to intellectuals. According to Goldman, "[Johnson] was not even really anti-intellectual. He was much too curious, and all the while he blasted intellectuals, he continued to look up to men of the books and kept trying to find ones who did not annoy him too much." Goldman's analysis demonstrates the recurring ambivalence that led to Johnson's struggles with intellectuals. His problem was not one of comprehension. As Goldman concluded, "Lyndon Johnson simply had no equipment which would permit him to understand intellectuals." Johnson admired intellectuals yet felt superior to them; he wanted their ideas but did not understand their approach.[18]

In addition to his own confusion, Johnson needed to do something to address the power of intellectuals in the 1960s, particularly with his party and with the press. He adopted a two-pronged solution, developing an informal "quiet brain trust" of outside advisers and hiring a new public intellectual, Eric Goldman, to manage their ideas inside the White House.

Unlike Schlesinger with Kennedy, Goldman neither worked on a campaign for Johnson nor had a long-standing relationship with him. Goldman's link to the White House came through an ex-student. Early in the administration, some of Johnson's top advisers—Abe Fortas, Horace Busby, Bill Moyers, and George Reedy—formed a small group designed to secure intellectual support. The group also included Dick Nelson, a younger White House aide, who suggested that the group consult Goldman, one of Nelson's professors at Princeton.

In response to a White House request, Goldman sent in his "suggested list of men for the 'quiet brain trust'" in December 1963, just two weeks after Kennedy's death. Goldman chose eight men who were "at the top of their fields" and expressed sympathy with "the purposes of the Administration." He tried to vary them by age, geography, and field. The aides, knowing Johnson's tastes, specifically told Johnson to extend his search beyond the northeast. According to Goldman, "[Walter] Jenkins, joined by Moyers, stressed that they should represent the West and South as well as the North and East."[19]

Five days after Goldman submitted his list of suggested brain trusters, he met with the aides working on the project in the White House. The group decided to establish a special group of academicians, specialists, and writers that the president could consult for advice and ideas. They also determined that this group was to remain informal and that "Professor Goldman should be given status as a member of the President's staff on whatever basis is appropriate." According to Goldman, the president recruited Goldman by insisting, "I badly need help—I badly need it. And I especially need the help of the best minds in the country." Johnson favored both the phrase and the concept of the "best minds in the country," even if he did not always like the people who owned those minds.[20]

Goldman's new job included the following roles: "To compile lists of able imaginative persons around the United States in various fields to be able to generate ideas, opinions, drafts, and advice." In addition, Goldman was to "receive requests from the President or his staff to obtain and furnish ideas and suggestions" and "to see to it that drafts of high literary quality which might be helpful to the White House staff are produced." Finally, the top White House aides expected Goldman "to prepare concise memoranda on given subject representing the boiling down of the results of Dr. Goldman's consultations, research, etc." In all, it was a challenging role, intellectually conceived, but more policy oriented than Schlesinger's fluffier position; considering Johnson's anti-intellectualism, it may have been doomed from the start. Making the position even more challenging was the fact that Goldman was supposed to do the job on a part-time basis.[21]

Goldman did not necessarily want it that way. Once brought into the loop, he wanted to make it both official and full-time. Moyers reported to Johnson that he and Valenti had discussed Goldman's status with the professor: "Jack Valenti and I have talked to Eric Goldman and he wants to come aboard full time as a Special Assistant to the President. He, of course, would like to get the salary that other top assistants receive." This latter request was a sticking point, as Johnson, although a rather profligate spender of congressional funds, turned into a tightwad with executive office disbursements. Moyers knew of Johnson's reluctance to spend and tried to assure the president that Goldman, if hired, would give them their money's worth. "In our discussions with him," Moyers wrote, "we made it clear that someone is needed to do the rose garden statements as well as to prepare ideas and projects. He says he would like to continue to serve as an idea man as well as to take on the rose garden job." Moyers informed Johnson that Goldman would be willing to take on all tasks, including those that seemed beneath a distinguished Princeton historian. Although this argument did not convince Johnson to hire Goldman as a special assistant, it did adumbrate Goldman's responsibilities in the White House.[22]

In addition to his parsimony, Johnson had another reason for his reluctance to make Goldman a special assistant, namely, the shadow of Arthur Schlesinger. The White House wanted to make it clear that Schlesinger and his position belonged to an earlier administration. Goldman remembers that the normally serene Johnson aide Walter Jenkins insisted that Goldman was not replacing Schlesinger: "Jenkins' mild voice rose as he told me, 'You are not the Johnson Arthur Schlesinger. Nobody is going to be the Johnson Schlesinger. Nobody is going to be the Johnson anything of Kennedy. *This is a different Administration*'" (emphasis original). Jenkins's vehemence probably gave an indication of the depth of Johnson's feelings as well.[23]

At the February 3 press conference announcing Goldman's appointment as "coordinator for the reception of the work of the Nation's scholars and specialists," White House press secretary Pierre Salinger went out of his way to distinguish Goldman from Schlesinger. Salinger explained that Goldman would "serve without pay as a consultant and adviser to the President." Upon being asked, "Does he become the new Dr. Schlesinger?" Salinger replied in strong terms for a normally diplomatic press liaison. "Dr. Schlesinger played a special role for President Kennedy," Salinger, himself a Kennedy holdover, explained. "I could not compare the two roles." Salinger elaborated: "Mr. Schlesinger was the liaison between the White House and the UN, among other things, and it is not anticipated that Dr. Goldman will perform such functions." Goldman's real role, Salinger told the press, would be "to serve in assisting the President in the collection of ideas." Even Schlesinger himself, the man against whom the Johnsonites were defining Goldman, felt the need to make this point. In an oral history, Schlesinger insisted that "Eric Goldman was not my successor in any sense." Still, Schlesinger did not take the idea too far. When he needed to pass on the job of ministering to the nascent White House Library, he went right to Goldman. The Johnsonite aides, so eager to emphasize distinctions between the two regimes, would never have sanctioned such a direct transfer of responsibility.[24]

The Johnson aides distinguished Goldman from Schlesinger to protect their boss and his administration. Their comments, though, also had an unintended impact on Goldman's White House tenure. By emphasizing Goldman's part-time status and the lack of a special, Schlesingerian link to the president, these aides made clear that Goldman was not a presidential intimate, had an undefined non-policy oriented role, and would receive no salary. The new guy was off to an inauspicious start.

Goldman himself did not help matters. He was temperamentally unsuited for the Johnson White House, which was inhabited by many young unknowns who went on to become more famous. Goldman was already in his late forties and, although he had written several well-known and respected books, accomplished very little after his White House tenure. Like Schlesinger, Goldman lacked the "passion for anonymity" that the Brownlow committee recommended for White House aides. Unlike Schlesinger, Goldman was not famous to begin with. He had some exposure as the moderator of NBC's *Open Mind*, a public affairs television program. He had written for *Time* during World War II, and his books had been well received among historians. Still, all of these flirtations with Lady Fame did not even approach the level of Schlesinger's flamboyant affair.[25]

In Goldman's acceptance letter, he flattered Johnson: "Judging by the type of leadership you have been giving the nation—and speaking now not as a member of your staff but as a historian—I am convinced that you will prove one of the few genuinely great Presidents in the history of the United States." Strong words, perhaps, but Goldman assured Johnson that he was there to help in this regard, telling the president, "I am happy and proud to contribute whatever I can toward that end." This letter shows that Goldman was quite conscious of his standing in the White House hierarchy but also quite aware of his position as house historian, who could always place Johnson and surrounding events in historical perspective.[26]

Providing this historian's perspective developed into Goldman's primary responsibility in the White House, as he constantly informed Johnson and his aides of anniversaries, history lessons, and parallels between current and past events. Although Goldman demonstrated an understanding of this element of his job, his conception of the position did not always match the understanding of Johnson, his other aides, or the press, especially regarding the Schlesinger connection. While the Johnsonites tried to deny the genesis of Goldman's position, Goldman saw himself as Schlesinger's direct occupational descendant. Referring to his new position, Goldman remembered, "The post was certainly new. My fellow historian, Arthur Schlesinger, Jr., working under President Kennedy and also engaged in a variety of duties had been the first to be thought of in this way; I was the second." In this instance, Goldman was correct, as Goldman's responsibilities and Schlesinger's proved to be quite similar.[27]

Both men carried the responsibility of being the president's "idea man." Goldman did not like this characterization: "As far as much of the press was concerned, I was now the 'idea man,' a silly title and one obviously damaging to what I was trying to do." The notion of the idea man attracted a great deal of attention. Goldman received a letter from the King of the Cats himself, Harlem Congressman Adam Clayton Powell, saying, "Your appointment to the unique position as 'ideas' man for our President is an excellent choice." As usual, a complimentary note sent to the White House either included or preceded a request. In this case, Powell included the request, telling Goldman that "after you have settled into the job, I would like for us to get together, because I also have 'ideas.'" Goldman responded to Powell with a noncommittal note, saying, "Now that I will be in Washington a good bit of the time, I hope that our paths will cross so that we can talk over matters of mutual interest." In Washington terms, Goldman's response was as affirmative as a "maybe" from a Japanese trade negotiator.[28]

Despite what people like Powell thought, the job of idea man did not necessarily amount to operational responsibility. In terms of specific tasks, Goldman often did the same things that Schlesinger had. According to Goldman, some of his responsibilities "were similar to those carried out by aides whom no one would have thought of calling an 'intellectual,' and others of which could have been executed with at least equal competence by a man unaccoutered by a Ph.D., a professorship, or any other mark of intellectualism." This mirrors Schlesinger, who had his finger in many areas but primary responsibility over none. Goldman also performed many jobs that did not need a distinguished historian. Both men, however, gave others the perception that they were more than just political assistants. Goldman remembered being "considered—inside the White House and particularly outside it—different to a degree because in some sense I was supposed to 'represent' the intellectual community." Schlesinger also benefited and suffered from this perception.[29]

GOLDMAN AND THE FIRST LADY

A mixed blessing enjoyed by intellectuals in the White House was a presumed link to the First Lady. Goldman observed that "the 'resident intellectual' is inevitably drawn into the work of the First Lady, for she and he represent 'culture'; and the manifold activities in which she must, or does, participate." Although working for the First Lady often involves aides in more prominent projects and ingratiates them with the president, it also gives off the aura of working in unserious, non–policy related areas, not unlike wearing a clown suit at a convention of IBM salesmen. To their chagrin, both Goldman and Schlesinger donned the costume during their White House tenure.[30]

Goldman's work for the First Lady included a great deal of speechwriting. In one week in 1965, Goldman wrote Mrs. Johnson's remarks for speeches at the commencement exercises at the College of the Virgin Islands (June 3), the American Booksellers Convention (June 6), and Radcliffe College (June 9). He also ghostwrote some of her published works, including, for example, her foreword for the book *With Heritage So Rich* (1966). Despite what Goldman may have felt, Mrs. Johnson took advantage of Goldman's speechwriting talents as often as possible.[31]

Whatever his feelings about writing for the First Lady, Goldman probably liked writing for the president's daughters even less. Goldman wrote speech drafts for both Johnson daughters. In addition, he stage-managed an interaction between Lynda Johnson and Goldman's friend, the distinguished historian David Herbert Donald. "In a recent conversation," Goldman wrote to Lynda, "I mentioned to [Donald] your special interest in [Reconstruction] and he has sent you—through me—an inscribed copy of his Sumner biography, for which he won the Pulitzer Prize." In case young Lynda did not know how to respond to the gift, Goldman wrote that "the Book and a draft of a suggested reply are enclosed." Goldman's suggested reply warmly complimented his historian friend: "I certainly know of the brilliance of your scholarly work in those fields. I very much appreciate your sending me the book, especially with its gracious inscription, and I look forward to reading it whenever I can find a long enough interlude in my college work."[32]

As a professor only two years earlier, Goldman had graded the papers of college students. Now he was ghostwriting for two girls in their teens. From Goldman's point of view, writing for Mrs. Johnson and her daughters left him in the less serious novelty position of intellectual in residence rather than the policy position in the West Wing. Goldman's role in the White House with respect to the various Johnson family members resembles that of a freelance magazine writer. The president represented the prestigious magazine Goldman wanted to write for. Mrs. Johnson and her daughters constituted secondary jobs that Goldman took in order to survive.[33]

WHITE HOUSE HISTORIAN

Most of Goldman's responsibilities—both assigned and self-designated—in the White House related in some way to his historical training. His most frequent self-designated assignment was to link historical anniversaries to current events. He had a particular affinity for anniversaries, telling the president when he could mention a particular anniversary in a speech. Goldman also created a file of "notations of some upcoming anniversaries with suggested remarks which might be used in conversation (in a way that would get into the press), in ad libs, or otherwise." Johnson approved of this idea in a general way. The suggestion, though, also says something about Goldman, as only someone with duties as general as Goldman's could have had the time to think of such an idea in the overworked Johnson White House.[34]

Filling the speech and anecdote files did not exhaust the possibilities anniversaries had to offer. Goldman liked anniversaries so much that he urged Johnson to establish a rotating monthly exhibit honoring famous Americans born in each thirty-odd-day period. In addition to his love of anniversaries, Goldman generally advised Johnson on intellectual matters, from mundane matters of magazine articles and interviews to managing Johnson's links with the intellectual community. This task became more important as the Vietnam War progressed and Johnson's relations with intellectuals worsened. Ultimately, Goldman was unable to extinguish these sparks and was badly singed by the ensuing flame.

For the first two years, Goldman took on rather innocuous tasks. When Johnson assistant Eliska Hasek asked Goldman to ghostwrite a presidential article for the *Centennial Review of Arts and Sciences*, Goldman interceded to protect the president's intellectual credibility. "I don't think that President Johnson should do this," he wrote to Hasek. "To begin with, the Centennial Review of Arts & Science is a magazine of extremely limited circulation and no great repute." Goldman added another, more compelling, reason. "[CRAS editor] Weisinger asked me to do this article a long time ago and I declined. I don't think the President should be asked after a staff member." Although this incident shows Goldman to be a bit of a magazine snob, he was probably right in suggesting that Johnson not degrade himself with contributing to a small magazine or accepting a secondary assignment.[35]

In the same month, Goldman found a project worthy of the president's byline. Goldman wrote to Valenti that the American Heritage Publishing Corporation was preparing "a sixteen volume guide to the states of the United States, incorporating historical as well as current information about each of the 50 states." Goldman felt that "it would be a good idea if President Johnson did contribute the Foreword and I enclose a draft." In these two incidents, Goldman earned his consultant's paycheck. The average White House aide may not have known the relative merits of the two aforementioned publications. As a professional historian, Goldman needed to know these things.[36]

In a similar vein, Goldman sifted through requests and offers from intellectually minded individuals. During the 1964 campaign against Arizona Senator Goldwater, Williams College professor James MacGregor Burns asked Goldman for an interview with Johnson in preparation for a *Life* article. Johnson approved the request. Goldman then wrote a memo preparing Johnson for the meeting that told the story of Burns's falling out with the Kennedys. Burns had written a favorable biography of John F. Kennedy that contained only one unfavorable comment, which questioned Kennedy's level of commitment. According to Goldman, that suggestion "angered the Kennedy group and it particularly stuck in the craw of Ted Sorensen, who was still protesting it publicly years later." As a result, Goldman explained, "Burns' relationship to the Kennedys was consequently somewhat one-sided—he being very anxious to be in but being held off." Goldman told Johnson the story of Burns's troubles with the Kennedy clan to endear Burns to Johnson and to show that Burns did not reside in the Kennedy camp, unlike so many of his intellectual brethren.[37]

Goldman liked to use his historical talents to compare current events to past ones and determine what worked and what had not. In August 1964, Goldman undertook a review of previous Democratic presidential campaigns in the twentieth century, looking at past Democratic platforms, acceptance speeches, and congressional legislation records. Goldman informed Johnson that "the kind of acceptance speech which I understand you have in mind—broad-gauged, high-level, relatively non-partisan . . . fits in with the better precedents." As a result of his research, Goldman suggested that "in the case of incumbents, the past tendency has been to disconnect the acceptance speech from the highly partisan convention and to emphasize that the man who was the candidate was the President of the United States." According to Goldman, this method had two advantages, as it was "sound both politically and in terms of the national interest." Johnson heartily approved of Goldman's work, which, after all, vindicated his own inclinations, writing an effusive note to Goldman saying, "This was excellent. I am proud of you."[38]

Goldman also tried to place the 1964 campaign in historical perspective, linking it with the elections of 1800, 1860, and 1932, as "occasions when the American people had to make a basic choice." According to Goldman, 1964 belonged with these three other elections. "It might be noted that each time the American people voted not to go back to some allegedly better past but to move forward along the general lines of humane, progressive thinking." Here Goldman fell victim to a genuine loss of perspective, which led him to submit a simplistic and tendentious analysis. Presumably, Americans see every election as providing a basic choice about the country's direction. Only with time do historians gain the perspective necessary to determine which elections truly provided such stark contrasts. Furthermore, the three elections that Goldman mentioned—1800, 1860, and 1932—represented three of the key "realigning elections" in American history. To place the 1964 election in that pantheon was not only incorrect but also hubristic.[39]

Finally, when the Johnson camp knew they had won the election, Goldman sent Moyers a memo describing "election eve broadcasts by incumbent Presidents." Goldman's study led him to make a number of suggestions regarding this broadcast, the first being that "the President deliver the address in his home of Texas." Second, Goldman "suggest[ed] that he be introduced by [vice presidential candidate] Senator Humphrey speaking from his home in Minnesota." Moyers, who annotated the memo, wrote, "We're going to do this" in the margin next to this proposal. If not, Goldman wanted former President Harry S. Truman to introduce Johnson, an idea Moyers had already examined, writing, "He's too ill, we're told." As for the content, Goldman recommended "that the speech revolve around the major theme of the president's campaign—consensus, what it has meant to us and what it can mean to us." This notion elicited a terse "good" from Moyers's margin marker. At the top of the memo, Moyers wrote: "To: Eric Goldman. Thanks. This very helpful." Of course, Goldman had not suggested anything earthshaking or even new, but it is reassuring to have a historian tell you what has worked before.[40]

After the election, Goldman remained focused on ceremonies and events for a time, although Johnson did not always approve the suggested events and Goldman did not always hide his disappointment at these rejections. In late December 1964, Goldman had a conversation with Justice Arthur Goldberg, a good friend of the president, about expanding the Presidential Medal of Freedom program. Goldman reported the results of the talk to Johnson, emphasizing the fact that the suggestion came partially from Goldberg. According to Goldman, Goldberg, as secretary of labor, "was the man who worked out the program under President Kennedy," although Goldberg's "plan was more sweeping than the one adopted." Now Goldberg wanted to return to his original plan and Goldman "heartily concur[red]."[41]

Goldman carbon copied the memo to Goldberg, who replied, "Your memo to the President is just right. I hope that the response is favorable." Johnson, however, disapproved the project, perhaps because he felt that expanding a Kennedy program would not benefit his administration. Goldman wrote to Goldberg, "I have received back word from the President the memo concerning the Presidential Medal of Freedom. I am afraid he disapproved it and he disapproved it without giving any reason." Goldman then put the ball back in Goldberg's court, saying, "Perhaps there is some way that you can take this up with him again informally on an appropriate occasion. I hope so." Even when he lost,

Goldman did not give up hope. Goldman would need this stubborn attitude over the next year and a half of his White House tenure, as he found himself mediating between two increasingly bitter and unyielding forces, President Johnson and the bulk of the American intellectual community.[42]

EGGHEAD IN THE MIDDLE

If Goldman spent his first two years mainly as White House historian in residence, he spent his second two years embroiled in Johnson's prickly relations with intellectuals. Since the president and the liberal intellectual community started out distrusting each other, Goldman had an exceedingly difficult task. As the Vietnam War escalated, these relations worsened, and Goldman's job grew harder, requiring increasing sensitivity and tact in dealing with two groups that considered him their colleague—the White House and the intellectuals. Goldman did not prove up to the job, trying to maintain loyalties in two camps and failing in both. Although an intellectual in the White House needs good relations with the academic community in order to do his job effectively, good relations with the president and his staff are essential to keeping the job.

From the very beginning, Goldman knew of his responsibilities in this regard. Responding to a congratulatory note from William Shirer for taking over the "Think Factory," Goldman replied that "the job is essentially one of organizing and operating brain trusts in domestic and foreign affairs and carrying on a continuing liaison with intellectuals and experts outside those brain trusts." As Goldman's tenure in the White House continued, of necessity, he worked with the brain trusts less and tried to manage the position of liaison more.[43]

Goldman originally started, as already noted, with the brain trusts. Before the White House even announced Goldman's appointment, Goldman contacted twelve scholars concerning the State of the Union address. Goldman reported back to the president that his anti-intellectual reputation preceded him, as "some of the men expressed surprise. They said they had not expected the President to be so interested in the suggestions of 'intellectuals.'" At this point, though, ignorance rather than hostility characterized the president's relations with intellectuals. Goldman sensed an opportunity to bring the parties together, since some of the intellectuals "were especially glad that men from a number of institutions and parts of the country were being consulted. They felt that the previous Administration had tended to limit itself too much to one group." Johnson must have enjoyed reading of this one "edge" he had over Kennedy.[44]

In terms of advice rendered, though, the contacts failed to meet Goldman's expectations, as he found "their suggestions for definite new programs . . . unclear or obviously inappropriate." Goldman told Johnson that he "was disappointed by . . . the extremely small number of fresh ideas." He maintained his optimism about future contacts by suggesting that "perhaps they had too little time and probably I contacted too few brilliant younger men with flexible minds and too many people who, in the course of acquiring their considerable reputations, lost a good deal of their inventiveness." As the Kennedy campaign had discovered five years earlier, Goldman learned that asking intellectuals for advice would not necessarily solve the country's problems, not to mention Lyndon Johnson's.[45]

After the White House made Goldman's appointment official, Goldman tried to make his contacts with intellectuals more official as well. Goldman sent out an extensive mailing to recruit scholars to this process. Contemporaneously with the initial letter seeking ideas, Goldman set up a White House meeting with twenty-seven of America's best-known intellectuals. The meeting took place on March 19, 1964, two days after *New York Times* columnist James Reston reported that the Johnson administration lacked intellectual support. Goldman reacted very defensively to the column, sending a memo to Walter Jenkins arguing that the forthcoming meeting belied Reston's observation. "At least five of the people," Goldman wrote to Jenkins, "[John Kenneth] Galbraith, [Richard] Hofstadter, [Clinton] Rossiter, Margaret Mead, and [David] Riesman—are quite well known to the general public interested in serious books and their works have sold into the hundreds of thousands."[46]

Two of Goldman's five "popular" intellectuals, Galbraith and Hofstadter, did not show up at the meeting. Galbraith sent Goldman a note regretting his inability to attend and hoping for "a successful session." Galbraith added a note of caution to his good wishes: "Perhaps you should warn your volunteer Houses and Hopkins of Harry Truman's observation on Baruch. 'One should not boast of giving a President advice. He always has more than he can use.'"[47]

Despite Galbraith's skepticism, the meeting, with twenty-two invitees in attendance, came off well. Goldman invited a far more geographically diverse group of intellectuals than Kennedy consulted in either his campaign or the White House. Johnson's antieastern bias and his position as president of the country (as opposed to Kennedy's as senator from Massachusetts) required Goldman to look beyond the northeastern corridor. Johnson apparently approved of the invitees and the meeting. The president wrote Goldman a note thanking him for "what I understand was a masterful job of keeping on one track a wide assortment of intellectual wizards!"[48]

Despite the group's wizardry, Goldman left the meeting unconvinced. In an April Fool's Day letter to Sargent Shriver, Goldman expressed his "hope" that "the group of experts on domestic affairs will fulfill its possibilities." An empirical experiment, Goldman revealed, did little to justify his hopes. He had asked the group for "suggestions concerning the type of education which might be offered in the camps set up under the poverty program." They had sent in their suggestions to Goldman and, he told Shriver, "I enclose some of the results. None of these seem to me exactly epoch-making but I send them along just in case they might be of some help." This absence of epoch-making results was apparently a recurrent finding following big meetings of intellectuals.[49]

Although many of the responses failed to meet Goldman's expectations, Cornell professor Clinton Rossiter did not disappoint. Goldman wrote to Johnson that Rossiter, who "is generally recognized as the country's leading academic authority on the office of the Presidency," shared some ideas worth examining. In the meeting, Rossiter, author of the classic *The American Presidency*, had emphasized the "unique qualities of the American Presidency." Rossiter listed five specific qualities—that the presidency "provides a steady focus of leadership"; "strikes a felicitous balance between power and limitations"; "is a priceless symbol of our continuity and destiny as a people"; "has been tested sternly in the crucible of time"; and "is, above all, an office of freedom." Goldman indicated that Johnson should keep these points in mind as he exercised the highest powers in the land. Although it lacked specific policy prescriptions, this constituted the kind of memo that Johnson, or any president, could appreciate. Rossiter's authorship provided intellectual gravitas, Goldman's distillation vindicated the notion of having an idea collector, and it reminded Johnson of the awesome powers, history, and responsibility of the presidency. This last function was probably the most important, as presidents often lack people who have the authority to lecture them on the responsibilities they bear.[50]

In September, Goldman wrote but did not send an angry letter to James Reston concerning four *Times* articles on the White House and intellectuals. The *Times* had incorrectly reported that the Johnson White House lacked intellectuals. Goldman, somewhat understandably, took this assertion personally. After having a conversation with Reston, Goldman wrote that "all four of these articles were written without speaking to me." In general, Goldman objected, "I get the impression that I don't exist as far as the Times is concerned."[51]

At the time, though, Johnson's approval was more important for Goldman than press attention. On October 3, Goldman scored the double coup of having the White House act on two ideas he pushed—a dinner for student leaders and the establishment of the White House Fellows program. The ideas for the two programs came from University of North Carolina president William Friday and Carnegie Endowment president John Gardner, respectively. Goldman's successes attracted the attention of U.S. commissioner of education Francis Keppel, who wrote to Goldman, "The Balanchine of the intellectual ballet has struck again. Your Saturday affair was a splendid performance. Bravo!" Keppel's praise, though hyperbolic, contained more than a kernel of truth. That day, October 3, 1964, was probably the best one of Goldman's tenure. After this high point, though, a smart broker would have profited by selling Goldman stock short.[52]

THE WHITE HOUSE FESTIVAL OF THE ARTS

In addition to his usual duties of reminding Johnson of various anniversaries and giving history lessons on demand, Goldman headed a new, high-profile project in 1965, the White House Festival of the Arts. Goldman generated the idea for the festival, following a small spur from White House social secretary Bess Abell. Abell had visited Goldman's office in February 1965 and suggested, with spring approaching, "How about doing something 'cultural' that would go well with the season?" Abell mentioned Kennedy's success with the Pablo Casals event as an example and then added, "Of course we didn't want to imitate the Kennedys, but could I think of something along that line?" Abell's approach typified the Johnson staff's attitude toward Kennedy. They wished to imitate his successes but on their own terms, and without anyone outside the administration comparing the Johnson team with the Kennedys.[53]

Abell's suggestion in itself did not inspire Goldman. In fact, Goldman recalled, "Bess Abell had a way of talking about culture that made me wince." But Abell's suggestion fit into Goldman's other plans. Goldman's assistant, Dr. Barbaralee Diamonstein, "had been urging me to give greater attention to ways by which the White House could encourage the cultural renaissance occurring in many American communities." At the same time, Goldman thought, "there was the matter of the newly established National Council on the Arts, which could use a little projecting into public awareness." Goldman responded to these three contemporaneous stimuli by conceptualizing "a 'White House Festival of the Arts,' an outgoing, warm, colorful White House salute to the Americans who were building up the museums and symphonies in the local communities, organizing reading and discussion groups, staging their own arts festivals." Goldman returned to Abell with this idea of an "appropriately Johnsonian . . . across-the-board representation of many of the arts" festival. Abell hesitated, as she was reluctant to bring intellectuals into the White House: "Writers and artists," she commented. "These people can be troublesome." Although Goldman could barely contain his contempt for Abell, the social secretary was right to worry about Goldman's "troublesome" colleagues.[54]

Ignoring Abell's concerns, on February 25 Goldman submitted to Johnson "a suggestion that in the early Spring you and Mrs. Johnson sponsor a White House Festival on the Arts." Goldman assured the president that the festival would not burden the president, as "this would be a day-long event . . . but the participation of you and Mrs. Johnson would be quite limited." Overall, Goldman declared, "the point of the Festival would be to express White House interest in the arts now being performed in the United States."[55]

In retrospect, Goldman felt obligated to defend the proposal memo from two unspoken accusations—one from the intellectual community and one from the White House. Goldman sensed that some intellectuals believed the festival was intended to coopt opponents of the Vietnam War. Goldman denied that the festival had anything to do with intellectual alienation concerning Vietnam, since "the memorandum was sent to the president on February 25, 1965, before he ordered systematic bombing of North Vietnam and before the Dominican intervention, and hence before there was any great outcry against the foreign policy." This statement is true, as far as it goes. On the other hand, the festival did follow the escalation linked to the 1964 Gulf of Tonkin Resolution. In addition, Johnson had experienced trouble with intellectuals even before his foreign policy controversies deepened. From the White House side, Goldman sensed a feeling that the festival made him some kind of supplicant to the artistic and intellectual communities. He objected to this notion, insisting that "nothing in the memo suggested that Lyndon Johnson was supposed to emerge faunlike as a devotee of the arts."[56]

Despite these tensions, both Johnsons, Lyndon and Lady Bird, responded positively to Goldman's suggestion, with only minimal hesitation. The president wrote on Goldman's memo, "I like this, ask Bill M. and Jack V. to see me about it before I take final action." The First Lady also approved, with reservations, scribbling, "I think it is an excellent idea *if* brilliantly executed by someone who works and shoves and *works* and *shoves*." Mrs. Johnson's comment helped get the event approved but also pressured the executors to come through with the requisite excellence.[57]

Goldman heard nothing from Johnson between the president's tentatively positive comments on the February 25 memo and the final approval, issued on May 22, only twenty-two days before the scheduled June 14 event. For the next three weeks, Goldman and Diamonstein organized the conference in every detail, from selecting the participating artists and guests to borrowing paintings for the White House walls. Goldman marveled at Diamonstein's ability to cajole museum directors into sending precious art work to the White House (and paying for the shipping themselves). As word of the festival spread, Goldman found himself besieged with requests for tickets to the event. Although Goldman had received requests for tickets to all previous events, he had "never experienced anything like the assault for an invitation to this event." As the event neared, Goldman stood in an enviable position, as the aide in charge of a popular, newsworthy, and fun event.[58]

Two weeks before the festival, the artistic community hit Goldman with a sucker punch, instantly moving him from most-envied to least-envied aide. On May 30, Robert Lowell, a poet selected to read at the festival, sent Goldman a letter withdrawing his acceptance. Lowell wrote that he had "accepted somewhat rapidly and greedily." Upon reflection, however, Lowell, who had been a conscientious objector during World War II, decided that he was now "conscience-bound to refuse your courteous invitation. I do so now in a public letter because my acceptance has been announced in the newspapers, and because of the strangeness of the Administration's recent actions." By "recent actions" Lowell meant Johnson's foreign policy, specifically the escalation of the Vietnam War. Lowell felt that the United States was "in danger of imperceptibly becoming an explosive and suddenly chauvinistic nation, and may even be drifting on our way to the last nuclear ruin." Lowell's analysis demonstrated that his true strength lay in poetry rather than strategic thinking. Lowell also "enclos[ed] a public letter to President Johnson, which I intend to release to the press."[59]

The letter disturbed Goldman, who knew that this development would damage the president's already frayed relations with intellectuals. While wearing his White House hat, his "first reaction to the letter was fury." Then he switched to his Princeton professor hat and "decided that my initial reaction was off base and that the letter had been written by a sincere and troubled man. He was wrong, it seemed to me, but for reasons I had to respect." Despite his newfound respect for the poet, Goldman still felt obligated to try to change Lowell's mind. Goldman warned Lowell that "the letter would infuriate [LBJ] and that he would deem it an insult to him personally and the office of the President." Not only was Lowell unmoved, but he had sent the letter to the *New York Times* before sending it to the White House. This action understandably angered Goldman. After all, sending a private letter to a newspaper before the intended recipient sees it violates proper etiquette, not to mention decency.[60]

The next day, the *New York Times* printed the story of Lowell's withdrawal on page one. In addition to printing the entire letter, *Times* reporter Richard Shepard placed the letter in the context of a broader struggle between the president and American intellectuals. According to Shepard, "Mr. Lowell's rejection was the latest manifestation of sharp discontent with American policies in Vietnam and the Dominican Republic in some intellectual circles." Shepard added that "John Hersey and Saul Bellow, two other writers, said they would attend but expressed strong disagreement with the Administration's foreign policy." Overall, Shepard noted, "Condemnation of [President Johnson's] foreign policy has been more frequent recently among writers as well as college teachers and students."[61]

The *Times* article embarrassed the Johnson administration by highlighting two of the most serious public relations weaknesses, namely, the Vietnam War and intellectual discontent. Goldman, however, no longer directed his anger toward Lowell. In his continuing movement between perspectives, Goldman sympathized with the *New York Times* for printing the story, writing that "in view of its inherent news interest, I was scarcely surprised that the *Times* played it prominently." In contrast, Goldman "was interested to learn that President Johnson took the placement as another example of the hostility of the *Times* toward him." Once Johnson saw the *Times* article, he backed away from the forthcoming festival.[62]

Although he possessed a volcanic temper, Johnson might not have reacted so angrily to Lowell in a different context. Alas, the arts festival did not take place in a vacuum. As Shepard observed in discussing the Lowell letter, during the four months between Goldman's memo suggesting the event and the actual festival in June, intellectual (not popular) opinion had begun to turn against the Vietnam War. Goldman explained that, in this period, anti-Johnson and anti-Vietnam "criticism had flared in intellectual and artistic circles." The first teach-in, an all-night university protest against the war, took place at the University of Michigan on March 24, 1965, indicating rising student dissatisfaction with the war.[63]

Goldman had noticed this inchoate discontent; it was his job to keep abreast of these developments. He erred, however, in not considering such roilings very significant: "What was happening in 1965 was that a particular group among the intellectuals and artists, probably a minority," had started to oppose the Vietnam War. Goldman observed that all intellectuals did not oppose Johnson, but "primarily ... academics and writers." And only certain kinds of academics and writers, especially professors in certain fields, "the social sciences and the humanities." To these groups, Johnson now had three strikes against him. He had received the first strike long ago, by dint of being a sometime conservative Texan from a little-known college. The second strike whizzed by him in November 1963, when Kennedy's death permanently placed Johnson in the shadow of a martyred president. The third strike came in 1965, when Johnson swung and missed an unhittable pitch in the form of Vietnam. After this, Goldman wrote, "The doctrine, regardless of accuracy, was fixed: Lyndon Johnson does not love intellectuals and artists (which was mostly true), and President Kennedy did (which was true to a certain extent and in some ways)." Over the next few years, Johnson faced an unrelenting assault from this segment of intellectuals that Goldman described, prompting British journalist Henry Fairlie to note, "I have found nothing more strange or unattractive than the way in which American intellectuals take pleasure in reviling President Johnson."[64]

In 1965, according to Goldman, "one center of the intellectual attack on the president's foreign policy was the *New York Review of Books*, a journal which in a way was an accident of American trade unionism." After Lowell sent his withdrawal letter to Johnson, Lowell's wife, Elizabeth Hardwick, told Robert Silvers, editor of the *NYRB*, about the withdrawal. Silvers then drafted a telegram to Johnson supporting Lowell's decision. The telegram told Johnson: "We hope that in this and other countries [people] will not conclude that a White House arts program testifies to approval of Administration policy by the members of the artistic community." The *Times* picked up this story as well, writing that "twenty writers and artists, including six Pulitzer Prize–winning poets, voiced support for Robert Lowell, the poet, for rejecting an invitation to a White House arts festival because he objected to United States foreign policy." The *Times* added—incorrectly—that "none of the twenty had been invited to participate in the festival June 14."[65]

Embarrassingly enough, Goldman had placed three of the twenty signers—Dwight Macdonald, Larry Rivers, and Mark Rothko—on the invitation list for the festival. After seeing the telegram, Goldman erased Rothko and Rivers from the list, but the White House had already sent out Macdonald's invitation, making it too late to prevent Macdonald's attendance. Despite Goldman's attempts at damage control, the telegram worsened Johnson's already sour mood, prompting the president to threaten that he would not attend the festival.[66]

After the splash his telegram created, Robert Silvers continued his assault on the festival, commissioning Macdonald to cover the festival for the *NYRB*. Macdonald then sent in another telegram, this one accepting Goldman's invitation and describing his intention of writing about it. Goldman and Johnson knew not to expect a positive portrayal. In actuality, only five invitees (including Lowell) declined to attend because of the war. But, Goldman reported, fourteen others declined without cause, perhaps for the same reason. In addition, he remembered, "among those who replied affirmatively, to my knowledge at least fifteen attended with serious doubts in their minds." Furthermore, John Hersey, who was scheduled to read at the festival, decided not to read from one of his novels, instead choosing *Hiroshima* as his text, a work decrying "the destructive potential of war." These varied responses inspired Johnson's complaint that "some of them insult me by staying away and some of them insult me by coming."[67]

With the atmosphere changing unfavorably for the president, as the festival neared, Bess Abell became Goldman's watchdog, making sure that none of the artists embarrassed the president any further. Goldman bristled under this supervision, particularly when Abell told him that, since Arthur Miller was a communist, they could not "have him and his play in the White House." When Goldman objected to this declaration, Abell exploded, telling him that "these people of yours—and this festival—have done nothing but cause trouble for the President. But if you insist, I'm tired of trying to make the festival sensible. Remember, Miller is your responsibility." Abell's watchdogging taught Goldman that he stood in an impossible position, stuck between bitter and intractable op-ponents: "The festival of the arts had once seemed so minor and so pleasant a task. Instead it kept raising the nastiest kind of problems and ones which only too plainly could escalate." On the one hand, "friends from the intellectual and artistic community, who had no way of knowing what was actually going on in the White House called me to say sadly or bitterly, Why have you made yourself a tool of this sham propaganda festival?" Abell's comments showed that Gold-man lacked sympathizers in the White House as well. Still, the opposition strengthened Goldman's resolve: "come hell or high water, come my friends, en-emies, the West Wing, Bess Abell or Lyndon Johnson himself, I was determined to do everything humanly possible" to ensure that the festival had an "inflexible commitment to quality and to intellectual and artistic freedom."[68]

Despite Goldman's resolution, White House opposition continued to mount. Two of the Johnson administration's most influential figures, Lady Bird and aide Marvin Watson, joined the antifestival bandwagon. For her part, Mrs. Johnson invited Goldman to lunch, trying to get him to prevent John Hersey from reading the *Hiroshima* passage. Mrs. Johnson told Goldman that "the President is being criticized as a bloody warmonger. He can't have writers com-ing here and denouncing him, in his own house, as a man who wants to use nu-clear bombs." She then said, three times, that "the President and I do not want this man to come here and read this." After the incident Goldman felt that, in the eyes of the Johnsons, "I was now a copiously certified, card-carrying 'these peo-ple.'"[69]

Watson also gave Goldman his opinions about the festival, and in language far stronger than the First Lady's. When an unnamed old Texas friend of Watson's, whom Goldman asked for help, told Watson to think about "the influence of the intellectual community," Watson lost his patience, exclaiming, "F—— the intel-lectual community." Following the First Lady's and Watson's sentiments, the White House tried to undercut the festival. First, "an order came from the Pres-ident: the festival was to be blacked out. No reporters, photographers or televi-sion people except those already invited as guests were to be present." In addi-tion, Goldman noted that "for one of the few times in the Johnson years, a White House project was publicly identified with someone other than the President or First Lady. The identification was no compliment to me."[70]

In the end, the festival itself came off fairly successfully, with the expected readings, films, and performances. Even Dwight Macdonald, the festival's blus-tering bad boy, acknowledged that "logistically, the Festival was a great success." There were some glitches, however, and the media remembered them more than the successes. A large part of the problem came from the fact that, with Lowell absent, "for many, perhaps a majority of the intellectuals, artists and critics, the salient personality of the festival was the man who was not there." In addition, Macdonald continued to cause trouble, distributing a pro-Lowell petition during the festival. This constituted a minor problem, as only seven people signed the petition. Charlton Heston humbled Macdonald by telling him that "having convictions doesn't mean that you have to lack elementary manners. Are you really accustomed to signing petitions against your host in his home?" In addition to these invitee-driven problems, Johnson himself compounded matters by giving a somewhat impolitic speech in which he told the guests that they had "been asked to come not because you are the greatest artists of the land, although in the judgment of those who made up the guest list you may be." Comments like those did not help Johnson's already strained relations with the intellectual and artistic communities.[71]

In his appraisal of the festival, Howard Taubman of the *Times* agreed that President Johnson withheld his full charm potential. According to "seasoned White House observers," most probably Goldman, evidence of presidential reserve included the facts "that press photographers and television cameras did not have freedom to make a complete record of the proceedings," "that the President himself did not receive all the guests personally at the late afternoon reception," and, finally, "that apart from shaking hands with a few visitors he did not stay after delivering his talk." Overall, according to Taubman, "the festival, it was felt, underlined the difficulties and advantages of bringing about direct communication between the President and the intellectual and artistic community." Even with the controversies surrounding it, Taubman concluded that "the 'Festival of the Arts' not only paid tribute to the arts but demonstrated to the nation and the world that democracy in action began in the White House." Goldman particularly liked the fact that the *Times* made this point. Strangely enough, in this, perhaps the festival's most positive appraisal, Taubman did not mention Goldman's name once.[72]

Finally, except for the *Times*, most postfestival print analysis cemented the perception of failure surrounding the event. The last word published at the time (before Goldman's memoir five years later) belonged to Macdonald. After rebuffing the festival, accepting an invitation, and then trying to undermine the event, Macdonald found himself scorned by Goldman and berated by Heston. Macdonald finally got to tell his tale in the *New York Review of Books*. After spending one page justifying his acceptance and another mocking the guest list, particularly the patrons of the arts, and then noting that the White House misspelled his name, Macdonald launched his revenge in earnest. He reserved most of his scorn for Goldman, who "looked most unfestive throughout his festival— the only really happy-looking people, in fact, were Duke Ellington and his bandsmen." Macdonald portrayed Goldman as a man without a country type:

"Poor Dr. Goldman, caught like Polonius ('wretched, rash, intruding fool') between the fell and incensed points of mighty antagonists."[73]

Even before Macdonald's piece appeared, Mrs. Johnson felt that the media portrayal misrepresented the festival. In her diary entry for the day after the event, she called the day "Black Tuesday." Mrs. Johnson remembered that the festival had not caused the administration's problems, as the "disasters of the Arts Festival were a 'pebble in the shoe,' but the real rocks are the constant black background of Vietnam and Santo Domingo." After waking up, the First Lady "called in Liz [Carpenter] and Bess [Abell] to have a post-mortem on the Festival of the Arts, and we discussed the one-by-one hammer blows of the front-page stories—*New York Times*, *New York Herald Tribune*, even the *Washington Post*." Mrs. Johnson and her aides felt that all the stories had a similar cast, as "all of them seemed to delight in faulting their country and their President." Instead of looking at the festival's bright spots, the media "accented only Robert Lowell's not coming, John Hersey's coming and lecturing, Dwight Macdonald's passing around a petition for his fellow guests to sign, disapproving of the President's foreign policy." In contrast, Mrs. Johnson fondly remembered "thrill[ing] to Helen Hayes, Marian Anderson, Roberta Peters, the whole cast of the Glass Menagerie, Catherine Drinker Bowen, and poet Phyllis McGinley—all 'playing' on the White House stage on one day." The First Lady recognized that not everyone saw the festival her way. Employing a curious phrase, she called the protests surrounding the event "the fly on top of the feast." Mrs. Johnson clearly wanted to emphasize the "feast" part of the image, but it is hard to erase the thought of a fly sitting on top of all that food.[74]

Contrary to Goldman's perceptions, Mrs. Johnson felt sympathy for, not anger at, Goldman, remarking, "Poor Dr. Goldman. He has worked so hard. And yet the total result must have been a towering headache, if not heartbreak." Mrs. Johnson's private sympathy did not assuage Goldman, who felt rather bitter about the whole event. He knew that he had failed in his overarching responsibility of promoting presidential relations with the intellectual community. In fact, he had done the opposite. In terms of relations with the general, *New York Review of Books*-reading intellectual community, Goldman recognized that "the White House Festival of the Arts had been an unmitigated disaster. Almost everything that happened after Lowell's letter and President Johnson's reaction to it had added bricks to a wall between the President and these groups." Goldman could find solace only in the fact that "mercifully, much of the story was unknown."[75]

For this failure, Goldman saw enough blame to go around. In his awkward, in-between position, he "had seen a President reacting with arrogant know-nothingness, and influential figures in the cultural world reacting with an equally arrogant know-it-allness." This statement highlights Goldman's inadequacies in his position. Goldman, assigned by Johnson to the position of liaison between the president and the intellectuals, ended up hating both parties, largely because the two forces hated each other. In the previous administration, in contrast, Schlesinger served as liaison between a president and intellectuals who generally liked each other. When forced to choose between the two, Schlesinger, unlike Goldman, sided with the president. Unlike Schlesinger, Goldman tried to serve two masters, and when he tried to satisfy both, he only incurred double wrath.[76]

GOLDMAN POSTFESTIVAL

After the White House Festival of the Arts debacle, Goldman never returned to Johnson's good graces. The two men had never been close, but the festival pushed them even farther apart. Johnson initially felt that Goldman could help him interact with the intellectual community. Now that the whole country knew that Goldman's presence lessened intellectual antipathy not one bit, Johnson had no more use for the Princeton professor. From the close of the festival on, the White House consulted Goldman more infrequently and seldom listened to his advice; the White House had initiated the countdown for Goldman's exit.

For his part, Goldman felt that he had worked very hard on the festival and that his work went unrewarded. He never received a full-time White House position or salary but did receive assignments that required a full-time commitment. As a result, when Goldman received a new assignment after the event, he refused. Valenti had sent Goldman a memo requesting information on the National Geographic Society. Goldman sent it back, saying, "I regret that I must return this." Goldman explained that "during the last four months I have been working six to seven days a week on White House matters that could not be set aside, under an absolute limitation of pay for two days a week. . . ." As a result, Goldman wrote, "I'm afraid I am now forced to concern myself with making a living as well as working for the White House." Given the deferential tone usually found in White House memos, Goldman's statement sounds absolutely icy. The timing of this rebuff, three days after the festival, could not have been a coincidence.[77]

By late 1965, Johnson was not even expressing approval of Goldman's historical suggestions. In December 1965, Goldman suggested to Johnson "that early in 1966 you establish a new national institution—the Presidential Professorships in American History. The establishment of these Professorships would be part of your observance of the coming Bicentennial of the American Revolution." Goldman found the idea exciting, writing to the Carnegie, Ford, and Rockefeller Foundations for support. All of them rejected the idea. In early January, Moyers put a damper on the idea, telling him that he was "not enthusiastic about the Presidential Professorships. The Dick Hofstadters and David Donalds are going to publish great books with or without grants." Moyers was right about prolific historians like Donald and Hofstadter, who did not need presidential grants to write their books. Joe Califano ended the idea a few months later, writing to Goldman that "the President has disapproved the proposal for Presidential professorships." Clearly, Goldman's tenure was approaching the end.[78]

Goldman's last close interaction with the president came in May 1966, when Johnson gave a speech at the dedication of Woodrow Wilson Hall at Princeton's Wilson School of Public and International Affairs aimed at recapturing intellectual support. Goldman wrote the original draft of the president's speech, which he sent to Moyers along with a memo suggesting that his draft would "strike an overwhelming number of intellectuals as sympathetic and understanding but firm." The speech would show intellectuals that Johnson "fully grasps their high value and wants to work with them but at the same time he remains President of all the people and can countenance no pettiness or irresponsibility from any group." Overall, Goldman felt that the speech could "do a lot to dispel the rancorous feeling in some intellectual circles that [Johnson] neither understands nor cares about them."[79]

Three thousand spectators greeted Johnson at Princeton with an honorary doctorate and a standing ovation. Two to three hundred antiwar protesters also attended the speech. Johnson spoke for twenty-eight minutes, during which, according to Goldman, "the audience listened closely and thoughtfully." After the president finished, Goldman recalled, the audience "stood again after prolonged applause." The *New York Times* reported the speech as a reply to Senator William Fulbright's accusation that the administration suffered from an "arrogance of power." In the speech, Johnson accused the intellectual community of a corresponding "affluence of power," which they earned only after enduring the "pain" of having "once walked on the barren fringes of authority."[80]

After the speech, Johnson flew back to Washington with aides Doug Cater, Donald Hornig, and Goldman. On the plane, Goldman recalled, "the President had a Dr. Pepper and potato chips. He spoke mostly of Senator Fulbright and opposition to his Vietnam policy in academic and intellectual circles." Apparently, the president felt undisturbed by Fulbright and the Princeton protesters that day. Goldman wrote that "the President's remark as he entered the plane for the flight back summarized the trip. 'Well,' he said, 'it's been a nice day.'" After returning to the White House, Goldman wrote a thank-you note to the president: "Thank you for taking me with you to Princeton. It was fascinating—and deeply instructive— to listen to you on the plane." Perhaps Goldman felt that by telling Johnson how "instructive" Goldman found his comments on intellectuals, Goldman could show that he did not belong among Mrs. Johnson's "those people."[81]

GOLDMAN'S DEPARTURE

His influence long gone, Goldman knew he needed to leave the White House. He had felt the urge to depart right after the arts festival, partially because he "had been developing sizable doubts about the whole conception of the position of White House 'intellectual-in-residence.'" The president's ambivalence about intellectuals forced him to hire an intellectual to appeal to intellectuals while rebuffing the intellectual in order to appeal to the public at large. As a result, Goldman complained, this ambivalence left observers "wondering just how much the President considered [the intellectual] a genuinely needed staff member."[82]

Goldman did not share either of these reasons for leaving in his (handwritten) resignation letter. Goldman blamed his departure on a desire to return to teaching, telling Johnson that "inevitably my White House work over the last thirty-four months has curtailed the time that I can give to my regular occupation and I now think it best that I return to that work." As a result, Goldman wrote, "I would like this letter to serve as my resignation as Special Consultant to the President."[83]

Mrs. Johnson's farewell message to Goldman came first, and she praised Goldman warmly, telling him that "we are going to miss you!" She wanted him "to know how much I appreciate the suggestions and talents which you so graciously extended to my various projects and speeches." Finally, she added that in those speeches, "the words were always a little more golden because of your knowledge and gifted hand."[84]

The next day, Goldman received a farewell letter from the president. Johnson did not even try to stop Goldman, his usual practice, even with someone he disliked (like Schlesinger), writing simply: "I regret deeply your letter of resignation. Yet, ironically, I find myself a captive of my own policy and admonitions. As you well know, one of the keystones of my administration is better and broader education." Johnson also provided tepid praise for Goldman's work, telling the historian, "Your service here has been valuable. You leave your special mark—the historic perspective—on many of the programs which have come into being." Johnson's coolness emerges from this letter in two ways. He did not offer the usual effusive praise, and he failed to refer specifically to anything Goldman had done.[85]

Regardless of whether she had forgiven Goldman for the arts festival, Mrs. Johnson accepted his resignation with warmth and grace. As for the president, he proved unable to hide the mutual antipathy between the two men. As Goldman recalled, "President Johnson had made plain his dim view of me, and he certainly would not have been my choice for a fishing trip."[86]

Goldman deserves much of the blame for this enmity. In addition to the festival fiasco, he also deserved partial blame for his inability to mend the rift between the president and intellectuals, which, after all, represented his primary responsibility. In addition, other White House aides recognized that Goldman was just not up to the job. His fellow historian Arthur Schlesinger revealed that two of Goldman's colleagues, Kennedy holdovers "Moyers and Goodwin . . . both found him very unsatisfactory." Schlesinger himself felt that Goldman "didn't fit into the way government operated," which may represent a compliment in some senses, although Schlesinger clearly did not mean it as such. Finally, Schlesinger summarized Goldman's service as follows: "he certainly wasn't brought in on policy questions, and later became disenchanted."[87]

Part of Goldman's disenchantment also derived from certain embarrassing incidents during his tenure. Goldman endured one more of these imbroglios before he left the White House, this one concerning his resignation itself. Once again, Goldman shared a good deal of the blame for the occurrence. Johnson typically liked his aides to resign quietly, without a statement from the White House or the departing staffer. Goldman violated the policy by giving a "backgrounder" to reporters announcing his departure, angering Johnson yet again. At the September 6 briefing session, Goldman not only told the reporters of his departure but also, "in the course of the conversation," made another point, one that he "had wanted to state." Goldman noted that "it seemed to me that President Johnson's relations with the intellectual community, and educated Americans generally, had deteriorated woefully, and that some of the fault was attributable both ways." He also answered that he planned to write a book about the Johnson administration.[88]

The press conference infuriated Johnson. Not only had Goldman violated Johnson's policy, but he also criticized the administration while doing so and indicated that he was writing a book that presumably would criticize the administration even further. Johnson then decided to have Bill Moyers announce Goldman's departure in a press conference meant to undercut Goldman and the forthcoming book. According to Goldman, "Johnson had instructed [Moyers], 'Don't attack him personally, but take care of the book.'" Following the president's instructions, Moyers did his telegenic best to marginalize Goldman's role in the Johnson White House, going far out of his way to make the point. After Moyers announced that Brandeis American studies professor John P. Roche would be joining the White House staff, one reporter asked the perfectly reasonable question, "Is this a direct replacement?" Moyers replied adamantly, "No, it is not, Hugh." He added, in case any of the reporters did not know, "Mr. Roche will be full-time and he will be moving here. Mr. Goldman has been a part-time consultant since April of 1964." Then, without being asked, he volunteered that Goldman had only "worked, for example, 148 days in 1964, 117 days in 1965, and 66 days in 1966, on a part-time basis." In contrast, Moyers said, "Mr. Roche will be full-time. There is no relationship between their duties." Moyers did not misrepresent the situation. In fact, everything Moyers said was correct. The point is that, not having been asked, Moyers did not need to provide the hours that Goldman had worked.[89]

Moyers continued the anti-Goldman barrage by dismissing the notion that the president even employed a single liaison between the White House and the intellectual community, saying that "the President has never felt that one man could carry that responsibility, Pat." Moyers stated that the White House had "tried to involve the academic community, experts, scholars, and others on a working level" and that "the 1964 and 1965 task forces" each "had a healthy share of academic experts." Clearly Moyers meant to say that the president did not need any one intellectual, particularly Eric Goldman. The president's independence also stemmed from "the fact that the President expects men like Mr. Califano, Mr. McPherson, Mr. Semer, Mr. Cater, Mr. Rostow, myself—all of whom work on a variety of matters—to develop our own relationship with members of the academic community." Moyers told the reporters that "you cannot consider the academic community a union. You have to deal with it on an individualistic basis with people on functional assignments." As a result, Moyers emphasized, "no one man can be or can be expected to be the liaison." Although Moyers made some good points, the ideas he expressed must have been news to Goldman, who heard the White House press secretary say that Goldman's job had not existed.[90]

When a reporter asked Moyers a question about Goldman's comments that "the President distrusts Ivy League intellectuals or people from Eastern colleges," Moyers categorically denied the accusation, insisting, "That is not true. I, who have spent several hours of each day with the President, know it is not true." Then he took a razor directly to Goldman's jugular, saying, "It is a fact that Mr. Goldman has spent most of his time working directly with Mrs. Johnson and Mrs. Carpenter in the East Wing." As a result of these duties, Moyers added, Goldman's "meetings with the President have not been more than a dozen in the course of two and a half years." Instead of issuing a stock answer, Moyers attacked Goldman's White House responsibilities. The East Wing slight echoed Goodwin's crack about Schlesinger's status in the Kennedy administration. Moyers's defensiveness in regard to Goldman's responsibilities resembled the administration's defensiveness in originally engaging Goldman. Then, as in this situation, the administration's spokesman did not wish to admit that the new intellectual in the White House would be replacing the previous one.[91]

Despite Goldman's underhanded behavior, the Johnson team could have handled Goldman's departure in a more professional and dignified manner. The vendetta against Goldman backfired in the press, further weakening Johnson's ties to intellectuals. Peter Lisagor wrote in the *Philadelphia Inquirer* that Goldman departed "convinced that the best that can be hoped for in the relations between President Johnson and the Nation's intellectuals is a precarious co-existence." Lisagor called the arts festival a "fiasco" and furthered the perception of the "mutual antagonism that exists between the President and the literati, especially those from Eastern universities." This antagonism, of course, stemmed from "the President's Southwestern Populist disdain for the products of the Ivy League schools and his tendency to favor courses diametrically opposed to those advocated by Eastern intellectuals." By trying to diminish the damage of Goldman's departure, Moyers's hostile press conference only served to cement preexisting perceptions of Johnson's unease with thinking men.[92]

The editorial pages picked up on Goldman's departure as well. A *Washington Star* editorial entitled "So Long, Eric," wrote sarcastically that Goldman's departure "was accompanied by the graciousness we have grown accustomed to in these circumstances." The editorial was referring to the fact that "Press Secretary Moyers went out of his way to note that Professor Goldman saw the president not more than a dozen times and worked mostly with Mrs. Johnson and her press secretary." The editorialist ruefully came to the conclusion that Goldman's "kind of idea man is neither needed nor possible in our present system of government." In the American system, "an idea man as such will almost inevitably fall into Mr. Moyers' purgatory of the women's quarters, halfway between beautification and cultural tea." This reference to the intellectual in the White House as occupying a somewhat effeminate position, in contrast to the male, policy positions, plagued Schlesinger as well.[93]

Of course, the situation was not all Johnson's fault, for Goldman had initiated the chain of events by contravening Johnson's wishes and briefing the press. Furthermore, Goldman's indecision and selfishness had helped put Johnson in the difficult position to begin with. Still, Johnson was the leader of the free world, while, according to Moyers, Goldman was a marginal former aide to the First Lady. The press knew enough to train their guns on the big target.

While the press pilloried Johnson's handling of the affair, Goldman received letters of support from friends and acquaintances such as David Donald and Herbert Mitgang. Campaign chronicler Theodore White wrote a miserably typed letter to Goldman asking to discuss the fact that the "academics, professors, intellectuals who now envelope [*sic*] politics in the U.S.A. has increased to the critical point." White asked Goldman a machine-gun burst of questions: "How has all this come about? . . . Why the dominance of East Coast Ivy League academics? Why the sterility of Mid-Western campuses? Are the intellectuals of court there as philosophers, or jesters, or technicians? Etcetera." In truth, White probably knew the answer to this question at least as well as Goldman. In his quadrennial examinations of presidential elections, White saw this growth of intellectuals in politics as a component of the maturation of American politics. As society grew more complex, the increased need for specialization contributed to the new need for intellectuals, especially in politics. White later wrote a *Life* magazine series on "Action-Intellectuals," "the large and growing body of men who choose to leave their quiet and secure niches on the university campus and involve themselves instead in the perplexing problems that face the nation." Though White knew this, he also knew that he could get the point across more strongly if he could get Goldman to make it.[94]

As a result of Johnson's attack on him, Goldman left the White House a hero, returning to the good graces of his fellow intellectuals. For his part, Johnson remained in the White House for two more years before leaving without running for reelection. In that period, he had a number of extremely smart, intellectually minded aides, including Doug Cater, John Roche, and Ben Wattenberg. All three of them helped keep Johnson abreast of trends among students and academics. Cater, in particular, spent a great deal of time cultivating professors. But after the Goldman fiasco, all of Johnson's aides served as policy aides as well. Johnson never again made the mistake of having just one intellectual serve him just as an intellectual.

Today, decades after his death, Johnson continues to be known as an anti-intellectual president. The truth is that Johnson had help in gaining his reputation, both inside and outside the White House. Johnson entered the presidency bringing problems with the intellectuals that Eric Goldman could not solve. Unfortunately for both Johnson and Goldman, Goldman never managed to attenuate Johnson's rifts with intellectuals, and in many respects he widened the gap.

4

MAN THE BARRICADES: NIXON AND MOYNIHAN

By 1968, analysts had much more difficulty classifying intellectuals as a politically unified group: "liberal intellectual" stopped being a redundancy. While most intellectuals remained liberals, theirs was no longer the consensus position. By the end of the decade they endured derision from both their left and their right. On the left, radical intellectuals vehemently condemned the Vietnam War and supported the student protest movements feared by their colleagues. Other dissenters within the intellectual class believed that the linear extension of "Cold War liberalism" was opposition to the youthful extremism of Chicago and the siege of the Pentagon, as well as the continuing demands of the civil rights movement. Although not all of them accepted the appellation, by the end of Nixon's presidency many of these intellectual dissenters had a new name: neoconservatives.

Richard Nixon became president in 1969 after a long career in politics. Throughout the course of his controversial career, he had acquired many enemies, most of them on the left. The left's historic antipathy toward Nixon stemmed largely from his relentless anticommunism. In his 1946 congressional campaign against incumbent Democrat Jerry Voorhis, Nixon accused his opponent of accepting support from a communist-dominated political action committee. As a congressman, Nixon led the charge against accused communist spy Alger Hiss. In his 1950 campaign for the Senate, Nixon called his opponent, Congresswoman Helen Gahagan Douglas, "pink" and compared her voting record with that of communist-sympathizing New York Congressman Vito Marcantonio. Liberals never forgave Nixon for these actions. Worst of all, from the perspective of anti-anticommunist intellectuals, Nixon won all of these battles.

Unsurprisingly, in 1960, Kennedy dominated Nixon in the quest for intellectual support, best symbolized by his incredible 83 percent showing among Harvard professors. In the process, Kennedy stuck Nixon with the adhesive reputation that the Whittier, California, native had "no class." Kennedy's charm and intellect notwithstanding, Arthur Schlesinger found that many of his friends in Americans for Democratic Action backed Kennedy only because they hated Nixon so much. Two years later, after losing the 1962 California gubernatorial election to Edmund G. "Pat" Brown, Nixon could have been referring to intellectuals as easily as reporters when he uttered his famous statement, "You won't have Nixon to kick around anymore."[1]

Despite the mutual antipathy between intellectuals and Nixon, biographer Stephen E. Ambrose reports that Nixon sought "the respect and admiration of the intellectuals and the establishment." Although he hated their politics, Ambrose continued, Nixon nevertheless "respected and admired [intellectuals], and spoke of himself as one of them," even telling reporter Jules Witcover that "some people have said I'm sort of an egghead in the Republican party." As a result, during his "wilderness years" between 1962 and 1968, Nixon tried to keep himself up-to-date on contemporary thought by reading heavily, particularly Book of the Month Club selections and *New York Times* nonfiction best-sellers.

Under Nixon's outward disdain for American intellectuals, biographer Jonathan Aitken felt that "somewhere inside him Nixon had a hunger for intellectual study." This hunger remained inside Nixon because many of his political associates harbored even deeper anti-intellectual attitudes. As a result, Nixon "took pains to conceal [his reading] from his less intellectual cronies in the law and politics, but his private notes and memoranda of the period clearly illustrate the deeper nature of his literary tastes."[2]

Because of this ambivalence, when Nixon became president, he sought out his very own intellectual aide. Nixon needed someone having an intellect and erudition he could respect but not necessarily accepting the conventional wisdom of the northeastern intellectual establishment. Nixon wanted someone with an unimpeachable scholarly record, a willingness to work for the unpopular (among intellectuals, anyway) Nixon, and a healthy disdain for American intellectuals. To fill this apparently contradictory role, Nixon selected Daniel Patrick Moynihan.

DANIEL PATRICK MOYNIHAN

Moynihan was born in Tulsa, Oklahoma, on March 16, 1927. He had a difficult childhood, growing up in a single-parent family in New York's Hell's Kitchen.

Lyndon Johnson aide and Moynihan friend Harry McPherson learned that "Pat shined shoes every day from the time he was 13 until he was 16, and then worked as a stevedore for two years until by chance and grit he was picked up by somebody in a position to help him get through high school." Afterward, Moynihan studied at Tufts and the London School of Economics under anti-Marxist political scientist Michael Oakeshott, who introduced Moynihan, "earlier than most, to the fact that the socialist idea had spent itself as an economic doctrine." Hence Moynihan's lifelong anticommunism.[3]

Moynihan's first political job came as an assistant to Democratic New York Governor W. Averell Harriman in 1955. During the Kennedy administration, Moynihan moved to Washington to serve as assistant secretary of labor. While working in the Department of Labor, Moynihan did two things that helped make him famous. First, he cowrote a book entitled *Beyond the Melting Pot: The Negroes, Puerto Ricans, Jews, Italians, and Irish of New York City* with Nathan Glazer in 1963.[4]

Beyond the Melting Pot was a best-selling look at New York's various ethnicities. In the book, Glazer and Moynihan tried to refute the idea of the melting pot, arguing that "the melting pot . . . did not happen." The book had separate chapters describing the tendencies and prospects for each group in the title, written with a frankness that would probably not pass muster in today's more sensitized environment. In the chapter on blacks, for example, Glazer painted a discouraging statistical portrait of the black community in New York City. He observed that "the rate of illegitimacy among Negroes is about fourteen or fifteen times that among whites." He cited this as a factor in black problems, finding that "prejudice, low income, poor education explain only so much."[5]

Even at the time, Moynihan and Glazer recognized the incendiary potential of their subject. They warned readers that "some of the judgments—we will not call them facts—which follow will appear to be harsh. We ask the understanding of those who will be offended." At the time, though, neither author had any idea of just how sensitive their subject would become, although they—especially Moynihan—would eventually learn.[6]

Despite, or perhaps because of, the book's controversial arguments, *Beyond the Melting Pot* became one of those occasional books that enters the national lexicon. The book's success, however, had the disadvantage of extending the controversy. A few years later, Harry McPherson told President Johnson that Moynihan was losing his bid for the New York City Council in part because "he wrote a book 'Beyond the Melting Pot,' a very hard-nosed look at New York's ethnic politics." Despite this legacy, *Beyond the Melting Pot* was by no means Moynihan's most controversial work during this period. That honor went to his Labor Department–sponsored report, *The Negro Family: The Case for National Action*, better known as the Report on the Black Family or the Moynihan Report.[7]

The Moynihan Report provided the basis for Johnson's June 4, 1965, speech at Howard University, a speech that established the intellectual underpinnings for affirmative action and promulgated the link between illegitimacy and poverty in the black community. Johnson's staff knew that the speech held potential for controversy. Before Johnson gave the speech, his aides obtained the approval of civil rights leaders Martin Luther King Jr., Roy Wilkins, and Whitney Young.[8]

After the speech, someone in the administration leaked that the ideas on illegitimacy came from an unsigned Department of Labor report. Investigative columnists Rowland Evans and Robert Novak first reported that Moynihan wrote the "much-suppressed, much-leaked Labor Department document." The Moynihan Report found that "at the heart of the deterioration of the fabric of the Negro society is the deterioration of the Negro family." This deterioration, the report argued, stemmed from characteristics developed during slavery, when slave owners would remove black fathers from their families. Although the author acknowledged that "both white and Negro illegitimacy rates have been increasing," the higher base of black illegitimacy made single motherhood a greater problem in the black than in the white community. This "breakdown of the Negro family . . . led to a startling increase in welfare dependency." Many of these ideas grew out of *Beyond the Melting Pot*. Although Glazer, not Moynihan, wrote the segment on blacks, as coauthor, Moynihan had certainly read and approved of the chapter.[9]

This analysis spurred quite a controversy. The first rumblings, according to Moynihan, came from within the government itself. In an article in *Commentary*, he described, using the passive voice to avoid naming names, how the assault spread: "Word began to flow forth from the recesses of the Department of Health, Education, and Welfare that I was a 'subtle racist,' that the Negro people had been insulted and further that the facts were wrong."[10]

As a follow-up to the Howard speech, Johnson had called for a White House conference entitled To Fulfill These Rights. At the conference, held in November 1965, journalist Mary McGrory noted that participants treated Moynihan as a "nonperson." Before the conference even began, a group of one hundred civil rights leaders held a preconference conference, in which they issued a statement insisting "that the question of 'family stability' be stricken entirely from that agenda." At that point, Moynihan realized that "the issue of the Negro family was dead."[11]

In addition to the ostracism, a spate of articles, most of them from what Moynihan called the "liberal left," attacked Moynihan and his thesis. In the *Amsterdam News*, a black newspaper, columnist James Farmer accused Moynihan of providing "a massive academic cop-out for the white conscience." Writing in *The Nation*, William Ryan came to similar conclusions, finding Moynihan guilty, albeit unintentionally, of "a new form of subtle racism." *Crisis*, the magazine of the NAACP, reprinted Ryan's article with the title "The New Genteel Racism." In one of the more measured analyses, Frank Riesman wrote in *Dissent* that "the basic defect in the Moynihan thesis is a one-sided presentation of the consequences of segregation and discrimination."[12]

To Moynihan, the liberal firing squad aiming at him was firing at one of their own: "I had spent much of my adult life working for racial equality . . . had set the theme and written the first draft of President Johnson's address . . . which he was to describe as the finest civil rights speech he ever gave, only to find myself a symbol of reaction." Furthermore, he knew that he had been playing with fire and had attempted to avoid exactly the kind of controversy that ensued: "I *had* been prudent that time. Exceedingly prudent. Prudent to the point of almost misrepresenting evidence in order to avoid any implication of blame." He compared the reaction of his newfound enemies to Hannah Arendt's depiction of totalitarianism. The critics, he argued, like the totalitarians, promoted a smothering system not permitting internal dissent.[13]

The shower of print criticism, as well as some death threats, depressed Moynihan. He recounts—melodramatically—that without a supportive phone call from liberal theologian Reinhold Niebuhr he might not have survived. Hyperbole aside, the episode provided a valuable lesson for Moynihan—that he needed to be extremely careful in matters of race.[14]

After leaving the administration and losing a race for city council in New York, Moynihan opted for the relative safety of academia. He moved to the Harvard–MIT Joint Center, where he wrote *Maximum Feasible Misunderstanding: Community Action in the War on Poverty*, a devastating critique of the failure of the War on Poverty. Typically, Moynihan blamed the failures on out-of-touch bureaucrats and intellectuals. According to Moynihan, "the War on Poverty was not declared at the behest of the poor: it was declared in their interest by persons confident in their judgment in such matters."[15]

In addition to his problems with the War on Poverty, Moynihan carried a lingering resentment about his own treatment. In a letter to Harry McPherson concerning the difficulty of discussing urban unrest, Moynihan wrote: "I will forbear to expand on what the view within the bureaucracy is as to what happened to me and to the persons with me, but if my head were sticking on a pike at the South West Gate of the White House grounds the impression would hardly be greater." After his experience, Moynihan had little confidence that those who remained after him would speak boldly or even honestly about race. Moynihan remained bitter about his treatment and very suspicious of bureaucrats, reporters, and the intellectual left. These attitudes made him the perfect adviser for Richard Nixon.[16]

MOYNIHAN AND NIXON

How Nixon came to hire Moynihan as his assistant for urban affairs remains unclear. Since Moynihan had attained a measure of notoriety by the late 1960s, Nixon had encountered Moynihan's name before the 1968 campaign. According to Ambrose, during the wilderness years, conservative Columbia economics professor Martin Anderson "introduced Nixon and his aides to the works of Daniel Patrick Moynihan of Harvard, and of other liberal sociologists, that attacked the current welfare system." James Reichley writes that Congressman Melvin Laird identified Moynihan as someone who had the potential to present a conservative alternative to laissez- faire. Moynihan believed that Nixon associate Leonard Garment had brought Moynihan's name to Nixon's attention. Whoever first spotted Moynihan, the campaign knew of his work, as Nixon praised Moynihan in a speech as a "thoughtful liberal."[17]

Once Nixon won the election, Moynihan's name kept popping up. Speechwriter Ray Price cited Moynihan as a "new liberal." Laird, slated to be secretary of defense, suggested appointing Moynihan as secretary of health, education, and welfare. This fell through largely because, according to Reichley, "Nixon seems at that time to have viewed academic intellectuals as normally better suited to staff than to line positions." Theodore White reported that Nixon had originally wanted Moynihan as secretary of labor, only to have labor leaders veto the choice. In the end, Nixon nominally gave Moynihan the urban affairs portfolio, based on Moynihan's *Public Interest* article on the same subject. In reality, though, Nixon hired Moynihan as his adviser on the turbulence of the 1960s, much of which emanated from the newly fragmented intellectual community.[18]

By hiring a lifelong Democrat like Moynihan, Nixon purposely broke with a number of conventions. Contrary to previous presidents' motivations in hiring prominent professors like Goldman and Schlesinger, Nixon did not hire Moynihan to assuage the academic–intellectual community. Political scientists Everett Ladd and Seymour Martin Lipset had "found that Nixon was supported by only 19 percent of social scientists in 1968." With this record, Nixon knew far too well that he had no chance of appealing to America's intellectuals. According to Donald H. Rumsfeld, Nixon's director of the Office of Economic Opportunity, Nixon felt that his "role was *not* to make an agreement with the leaders of [elite] institutions, but to reach *underneath* them regardless of any discord with the elites at the top." Consequently, Nixon wanted someone familiar with the academic community who had legitimate standing as a respected intellectual and yet could make the populist anti-intellectual arguments, criticizing the increasingly antiestablishment and congenitally anti-Nixon intellectual community. As *Business Week* described it, Moynihan brought in "ties, friendly and otherwise, with a broad assortment of writers and random intellectuals."[19]

In addition, Nixon shocked many conservatives and flummoxed certain liberals by bringing a Kennedy–Johnson Democrat into a policy-making position. While presidents usually appoint token members of the opposition party, they ordinarily do so in administrative positions like the cabinet or areas of occasional bipartisan consensus like foreign affairs. Kennedy, for example, hired Republican C. Douglas Dillon as secretary of the Treasury, a position in which Dillon could reassure Wall Street and run a large department but not create new policy initiatives. Moynihan, in contrast, joined the administration in order to bring in new, presumably liberal, ideas.

The liberal in Moynihan struggled—briefly—with Nixon's offer. He felt skeptical, admitting that he "knew from the start that it could not work." Engaging in his best Hamlet imitation, Moynihan later asked, "How could I, a lifelong Democrat, direct domestic policy in a Republican administration? I was not flesh of their flesh—not blood of their blood." On the other hand, he relished the challenge, asking, "How could I refuse to try?" Moynihan took the job for both the challenge and the access. He told the *New York Times* that Nixon "was pretty much asking me to come down and tell him what I thought." Given that, Moynihan felt that he had no choice but to provide the president with a (somewhat) liberal voice.[20]

Nixon's ploy to win over liberals by hiring Moynihan worked, to a degree. According to the liberal columnist Mary McGrory, Moynihan's appointment represented a sign of conciliation from Nixon. Soon after Nixon's inauguration, McGrory found that "the Democrats are bemused by the new Nixon style. Some who made a career of despising him are now wishing him well." Of course, they did not become Nixon fans overnight; many remained skeptical, agreeing that "Moynihan was a dazzling choice, but say[ing], 'Of course, he won't last six months.'" McGrory noted that many blacks disagreed with their white liberal allies, as the black community held "profound reservations about the author of the Moynihan report." Overall, though, McGrory felt that "Moynihan's presence is still the most powerful signal that Nixon means business in the cities."[21]

Moynihan sent the column to Nixon, thereby ensuring that Nixon would see that the appointment of Moynihan had brought both good press and approval from prominent liberals. Moynihan informed the president that McGrory engaged in "one of the favorite guessing games around Washington, namely how long [fellow former Democratic appointee] Henry Kissinger and I will be here." McGrory also suggested that if Moynihan left, he "might 'document' [his] 'disenchantment.'" Moynihan had two responses to the suggestion. He assured the president that he had "no intention of leaving until my two years are up." He offered a caveat to this guarantee: "Mind, the black extremists could eventually raise such a ruckus that I would be of no value to you and would have to leave, but that would be your decision." This caveat proved prescient, as Moynihan did finally anger many black activists, although they did not force his eventual resignation.[22]

Moynihan also assured the president that "regardless of what happens I wish to offer my solemn commitment that I will not write anything political about my experiences in the White House" and sent carbon copies to H. R. Haldeman, Nixon's chief of staff, and John D. Ehrlichman, Nixon's counsel. This commitment seems a bit disingenuous, not to mention unwise. Public intellectuals write books: it is part of what they do. In addition to the low believability quotient, Moynihan did write a book about his experiences in the White House, *The Politics of a Guaranteed Income*. In it, Moynihan circumvented his commitment from the post-McGrory letter by writing only about the story of the Family Assistance Plan, not the totality of his experiences in the White House. Still, Nixon, who understood how the game was played, probably knew all along that Moynihan would write some kind of book about the Nixon years. With respect to White House speechwriter William Safire, for example, Nixon had said, "This is Safire, absolutely trustworthy, worked with us in '60. But watch what you say, he's a writer." Safire took this comment as an invitation to take notes; Moynihan most likely had a similar attitude.[23]

Despite the twin looming threats—a damaging resignation and/or memoir—associated with Moynihan, Nixon truly liked his urban affairs adviser. Beyond the external differences between an eastern liberal intellectual and a conservative western politician, the two had a lot in common. Both had escaped youthful poverty with their smarts, and they both resented those in the eastern establishment who had not had to work for their positions yet condescended toward scrappers like Moynihan and Nixon, who did. As a result, Moynihan enjoyed a good rapport with a president who did not like or trust many people. Haldeman recalled that this rapport helped Moynihan obtain "a lot of access to the president. Nixon liked him. He just sparkled with ideas and you knew he constantly got things brewing." At the same time, Haldeman recognized and wanted to take advantage of Moynihan's gift for self-promotion, observing that, in addition to Moynihan's ability to "get ideas in front of the President, he could also get them in front of the camera."[24]

Moynihan had a self-deprecating way of letting people know the frequency of his visits with Nixon, telling *Business Week* that "the poor fellow [Nixon] is seldom more than three hours away from another meeting with me." This closeness to Nixon added to Moynihan's policy-making influence. Another important factor boosting Moynihan's profile came from the primacy of urban issues in 1969. Urban unrest helped extend his influence from the seemingly circumscribed field of urban affairs to cover all domestic policy. This urgency had carried over from the Johnson years. Moynihan recalled that "urban rioting had consumed the domestic energies of the Johnson administration in its last phase." The problem had reached such proportions, he continued, that "when the Nixon staff took over in the White House it was presented with pads of forms to be used in calling out the National Guard. Blank spaces were provided for date, time, and place." Given this context, having control over all urban policy constituted a wide agenda.[25]

Although Nixon liked Moynihan, others had a different opinion of him and his appointment to the administration. According to White House aide Martin Anderson, "Haldeman and Ehrlichman regarded Moynihan's appointment as a master stroke, a way of bringing in a Democrat and giving the impression that this would indeed be an open administration, with a very broad base. They thought they could use him as a figurehead, with no real authority." This plan backfired, Anderson recalled, because "Moynihan was practically the only person in the White House, with the exception of Bryce Harlow, with previous experience in Washington. Not surprisingly, he turned out to be extraordinarily effective." Anderson, as a member of the conservative wing of Nixon aides, often found himself frustrated by this effectiveness.[26]

In addition to specific policy memos, Moynihan wrote to Nixon on a wide array of subjects. When Nixon told Moynihan that he liked biographies, Moynihan provided the president with a list of ten recommended biographies. Nixon shocked Moynihan by reading all ten of them, including Robert Blake's *Disraeli*, an eight-hundred-page effort that even Moynihan had not read.[27]

Moynihan also gave Nixon an implicit recommendation of his own book. When Robert H. Bartley reviewed *Maximum Feasible Misunderstanding* in the *Wall Street Journal*, Moynihan forwarded the review to Nixon, along with a memo explaining that the (quite positive) review would "give [Nixon] a good idea of what is in that book." Moynihan probably felt that the review would appeal to Nixon because Bartley, the *Journal*'s future editor, concentrated on Moynihan's description of the defective social science—and hence, social scientists—behind the War on Poverty. Nixon apparently liked what he saw, scrawling in the margins "very interesting" and "I think I'll have to read the book."[28]

MOYNIHAN, NIXON, AND
THE INTELLECTUALS

Moynihan's frequent and flowing memoranda, with reviews of books, suggested reading lists, and stories of his press successes, appealed to Nixon, which itself was one of Moynihan's responsibilities. In addition to these generalized duties, though, Moynihan also had specific policy areas, with perhaps the most important one being to keep Nixon informed of where he stood with the always troublesome intellectuals. Nixon did not expect Moynihan to repair his relations with the intellectual community. Consequently, Moynihan's role was to report to Nixon on the intellectual mood of the country and advise the president on his relations. According to historian John Robert Greene, "Moynihan and Nixon shared a common enemy—the intellectual Left." Nixon expected Moynihan to let him know what was taking place on the other side of the gap.[29]

One point that Moynihan emphasized was the developing intolerance on the left, with which Nixon agreed. Two years before joining the Nixon administration, Moynihan, presumably a member of the left but chastened by his experience with the Report on the Negro Family, called the left "as rigid and destructive as any force in American life." Statements like this made Moynihan a rare breed, a "Nixon liberal." Conversing with Nixon and working in the Nixon White House did little to change Moynihan's dislike for leftist intellectuals.[30]

As Moynihan saw it, the left of the 1960s had "adopted almost wholesale the arguments of the right," the very right that had driven Moynihan to be a liberal in the first place. Moynihan described the process as "a symmetrical, almost elegant, process of transfer. The extreme left adopted stances of the extreme right; the traditional left, those of the traditional right; the moderate liberals, those of moderate conservatives." This complex switch not only explained Moynihan's antipathy to the left but also helped rationalize his association with a Republican administration. After all, if the left held the positions of the hated right, then the right represented a legitimate opposition to the New Left.[31]

As Nixon's liberal, Moynihan embarked on an agenda that he knew Nixon would approve—analyzing the activities of America's intellectuals. For example, one of Moynihan's first memos to the president warned that those most susceptible to intellectual influence had harmed Nixon's predecessor. According to Moynihan, Lyndon Johnson "was the first American president toppled by a mob. No matter that it was a mob of college professors, millionaires, flower children, and Radcliffe girls." Moynihan further warned that America's "leading cultural figures are going—or have gone—into opposition" and that, in opposition, "it is their pleasure to cause trouble, to be against." This memo was distinctive only in that it was the first of many similar missives on the subject of America's antiestablishment figures, especially the intellectuals.[32]

Although Moynihan's anti-intellectual analyses frequently took the form of memoranda to the president, he also spoke his mind in more public media, passing on the remarks and their reception to the Oval Office. In June 1969, Moynihan gave a commencement address at Notre Dame criticizing intellectuals and radicals on campuses. Moynihan theorized that America was facing a religious, not political, crisis. According to Moynihan, the politicization of the search for spirituality lay at the heart of most radical protests. In sum, Moynihan felt that radical protests represented "the quest for divinity [in] a secular form."[33]

After the speech, Moynihan sent the president a memo about the Notre Dame remarks and some reactions to them. Moynihan's critique of America's youth inspired "almost uniformly favorable" reactions, he told the president. Moynihan enclosed one of those reactions, a favorable editorial in the *Wall Street Journal* arguing that "Mr. Moynihan's insights help to show that the attitudes of the rebellious students merely reflect the intellectual currents of our times," currents that Moynihan, Nixon, and the *Journal* all disdained. In conclusion, the editorialist wrote that, unlike the student protesters, "Modern Man must recognize that there are answers he must seek, if not in his soul, at least in his innermost self."[34]

In addition to the *Journal*, Moynihan noted, *Life* and the *American Scholar* had also approved of his theory. Moynihan told the president that the periodicals he mentioned represented "an impressive variety of political leanings and professional interests," all of whom "seem to share a general agreement on this subject." Nixon, a more prolific memo annotator than either Kennedy or Johnson before him, liked what Moynihan had to say, writing "good job!" in the margin and adding that "it is reassuring to have a true intellectual in residence!" Nixon saw Moynihan as a real or "true" intellectual, respected by the intellectual establishment but also open-minded and unhindered by ideological baggage.[35]

Moynihan did more than criticize the existing intellectual establishment. He also tried to identify and recruit other intellectuals, like him, who disapproved of the prevailing academic winds. To the extent that this often entailed bringing more liberal Democrats into the White House, Moynihan faced opposition from Republican loyalists on the White House staff. According to *Los Angeles Times* reporter Stuart Loory, Moynihan organized an unofficial and covert "friends of Pat" series of visitors to brief Nixon on "how they see the state of the union." The "unlikely gurus" included professors Aaron Wildavsky, David Riesman, and James Q. Wilson. Loory reported that Moynihan "was emerging as the link between RN and the academic community—a group with whom presidential relations have been tenuous at best." When asked about these secretive meetings, Moynihan replied "that he'd prefer questions about his sex life."[36]

Notwithstanding Moynihan's reluctance to discuss these meetings, he was bringing these people to the White House for consultation, even trying to hire one of them—Aaron Wildavsky of Berkeley—as his assistant. In order to sell Nixon on Wildavsky, Moynihan wrote, "If I were to suggest the leading political scientists in the nation under age fifty (he is 39) Wildavsky would certainly be in the first twenty, probably the first ten." Moynihan added that "it would be widely agreed that he is just about the only prominent social scientist on the Berkeley campus who has never stopped resisting the SDS and the crazies generally."[37]

It seems clear that Moynihan needed to do a lot of convincing to get another Democrat considered for a position in the Nixon White House. In this case,

Moynihan's overwhelming endorsement and his assurance that Wildavsky was Nixon's kind of Democrat proved insufficient to overcome White House suspicions. Nixon had his staff check out Wildavsky independently.

Ten days later, Egil "Bud" Krogh wrote a memo to Ehrlichman presenting him with three conclusions, one negative and two positive, about Wildavsky. According to Krogh, Wildavsky "has been, and is, a Democrat and cannot, as [Ehrlichman assistant] Edward Morgan notes be considered 'our guy.'" On the plus side, Wildavsky "has been very much a hard-liner against student violence in any form," a valued quality in the Nixon administration. Based on these findings, Krogh recommended that Ehrlichman "interpose no objection to hiring Wildavsky." He acknowledged that Wildavsky was not the optimal choice, as "it would be easy, and preferable, I should think, to find a tough Republican for the job." On the other hand, Krogh decided, "I don't think Moynihan is comfortable with tough Republicans." Despite this endorsement, Wildavsky never received the urban affairs job.[38]

Failing to have his appointees approved, in his second year, Moynihan changed his strategy for bolstering Nixon's support among the academically inclined. By this point, Moynihan may have realized the futility of trying to attract the backing of traditional intellectuals for a Republican administration, even if, as Moynihan believed, Nixon came a lot closer to Moynihan's ideals than the increasingly "fascistic" left. Moynihan's new strategy involved exhorting the White House staff to find intellectual supporters within the Republican Party, or at least among non-Democrats. Unable to bring the Republicans intellectual gravitas from outside the party, Moynihan now sought success from within. Many of Moynihan's prospects in this endeavor later emerged as important neoconservatives.

As part of this process, Moynihan tried to convince the administration of the need for real conservative intellectuals. To accomplish this goal, Moynihan realized that he needed more than Nixon's ear, so he took his case to Haldeman and Ehrlichman. Moynihan sent Nixon's top aides a nineteen-page memo, a length unheard of in most administrations. Moynihan, however, not only broke the convention of shorter memoranda but managed to make it compelling reading.

The July 24 paper followed earlier "brief discussions of the difficulty the administration seems to have in linking up with competent, respected conservative thinkers." Moynihan acknowledged that the lengthy memo was a burden to those already laboring under a staggering amount of paper. But he "had not the time, as they say, to write a brief memorandum, and so I send you this, as I felt both of you were interested in the subject." Just in case Moynihan had not captured their attention, he added, "You should be [interested]: the Presidency is at stake."[39]

Moynihan's "impression of Republicans, after living among them as an interested and sympathetic observer for almost two years," was devastating. Republicans, "as a group . . . have almost no confidence that any serious thinker could be with you on any issue of consequence. Economists, perhaps, but few others." Even worse, he wrote that "to a Republican a serious thinker is a liberal Democrat or a left wing anti-democrat." Moynihan being Moynihan, he compared the Republican situation to that of demoralized "English Catholics in the mid-nineteenth century," who felt intellectually inferior to the Anglican establishment yet stood on the cusp of an intellectual and spiritual revival. Moynihan saw Republicans in the same light, since the "inadequacies" and "vulgarity" of liberalism were driving "increasing numbers of men and women of no especial political persuasion to realize that something is wrong somewhere." Moynihan saw these independents as "the president's natural allies." Unfortunately, Moynihan observed, he was not seeing "them brought into our counsels . . . because of a sense of inadequacy hereabouts." Moynihan summarized the defeatist Republican attitude as: "Better stick with Kate Smith and the Silent Majority. They aren't very smart, but then neither are we."[40]

Moynihan's rather candid words indicate that he felt very comfortable speaking frankly with Ehrlichman and Haldeman, that he knew he was right and did not care what they said, or that he felt confident that he could intimidate a lawyer and an advertising executive, like Ehrlichman and Haldeman, on the subject of intellectuals. In any case, they were unlikely to challenge his tale of the English Catholic revival, which reads somewhat like a parable about the then nascent rise of neoconservatism.[41]

On page 12, Moynihan assured his readers that "*there is a point [to] this endless essay*," that "the failure within the administration to grasp the intellectual coherence of the administration's program has led to a great deal of the most serious kind of trouble." According to Moynihan, the administration fell into a trap: "Attacked, we attacked back. We began to raise our voices. Mistakes began to engender mistakes. All along there was one repeated phenomenon: we acted in such ways as to increase the moral authority of our opponents and to diminish our own." Moynihan feared that the administration lacked moral authority partly because of the lack of potent Republican voices in the administration and in the culture at large.[42]

As a result of this dearth, Moynihan wrote, when someone attacked the administration, "nobody defends us." Unlike liberals, Moynihan suggested, "No one in the Congress, certainly no 'liberal' Republican helps us. No one writes articles for us, much less books, or plays, or folk songs." Although Republicans had to overcome the obstacle of liberal cultural dominance, Moynihan did not absolve the administration of blame for this situation, as they did a poor job of defending themselves. Of administration spokesmen, only the vice president "has sought to take up some of the intellectual issues of the time and to argue the conservative case." This did not succeed, however, as his crusade "has been a disaster for the president," even though "many things the Vice President says are true, at least I would think so." Vice President Spiro Agnew suffered from the fact that "opinion is so concentrated on the liberal left that Agnew's mildly conservative positions are easily portrayed as the voice of the Radical Right." As a result of this unbalance, Agnew's "attacks enabled the opposition to ignore anything of substance he said, and to depict even his most reasoned statements as the frenzied precursors of Fascist Repression," despite the fact that "anyone so fortunate as to be attacked by the Vice President becomes an instant culture hero." In sum, Moynihan found that "in the contest for moral authority, they win."[43]

Moynihan saw himself as a one-man army trying to rectify the bleak situation, indicating that he had "spent eighteen months in this building pouring gin into various newspapermen, and I can attest that it is possible to get them to consider the possibility that what I say might be true." Although he had made great strides in this effort, he told Ehrlichman and Haldeman that he couldn't "do it anymore. It needs to be done by real Republicans." Consequently, Moynihan urged that Nixon "begin associating with academics and intellectuals who are capable of understanding what he is up to, and able also to expand his own understanding on the basis of their special competencies." Moynihan insisted that "there are such persons. There are hundreds of them." Unfortunately, Moynihan said, reminding his readers of his introduction, "it seems impossible for a Republican activist really to believe this."[44]

Moynihan felt that a group of intellectual Republicans and Republican sympathizers could help ease the president's burden. Given his narrow time window, Moynihan hoped "that if anything is to be done there would still be time for me to be of some possible help." Moynihan's memo inspired some movement in this direction, although he never found the group of Republican defenders that Moynihan and, presumably, Nixon sought. In terms of intellectuals in the administration, Moynihan's paper showed that in ten years intellectuals had moved beyond the role of adviser/updater on academic affairs to a point where Moynihan could—with only partial hyperbole—classify his work as representing the "'intellectual raison d'être' of the administration." As for Haldeman and Ehrlichman, their only written response to the memo appeared to be an attached note by Haldeman, with only two words on it: "ask E"; perhaps Haldeman asked Ehrlichman if he had read the whole thing.[45]

Given the extent of the threat Nixon faced (Moynihan had already told Nixon that Johnson was "toppled by a mob"), Moynihan urged the president "to protect the fundamental institutions of the nation, and of these, the universities are presently the ones most threatened." Protecting these institutions, Moynihan insisted, was "an intellectual task," one that could "not succeed without effective argument and marshaling of facts." Moynihan suggested Sidney Hook as one soldier in this war. Hook, a former Marxist who became a staunch anticommunist, had awakened many of the neoconservatives to the dangers of communism. He also spoke out against student radicalism. Moynihan assured the president that "there are more Sidney Hooks. We should encourage them. Certainly if you are to continue seeing university types, you ought to see a few who agree with *you*."[46]

Moynihan suggested that one reason for Nixon's having few intellectuals on his side was that "the administration is very weak at identifying non-Republicans who share your tough mindedness on these areas." Nixon expressed skepticism at this statement, underlining it and writing to Haldeman, "H just what we need to add to our 23%," presumably referring to Republicans' weak support on campuses. As if he had anticipated Nixon's defeatism, Moynihan then summarized the Republican attitude as follows: "Anyone who is not a hard hat Republican is presumed to be a soft liberal. Since hard hats don't talk so good, we end up needlessly deprecating our own positions." Of course, there was something strange about Moynihan's insistence that Nixon find conservative intellectuals; if such creatures had been readily available, Nixon probably would not have hired Moynihan.[47]

In November, Moynihan wrote the president a thirteen-page memo warning of "a struggle going on in this country of the kind the Germans used to call a *Kulturkampf*." Nixon's opponents—the opponents of order—had on their side "the adversary culture which dominates almost all channels of information transfer and opinion formation," which, he observed, "has never been stronger, and as best I can tell it has come near to silencing the representatives of traditional America." One place where Moynihan saw evidence of this Kulturkampf was at the *New York Times*, where editor Abe Rosenthal oversaw "a news room still predominantly made up of old time liberal Democrats who can be counted on to report a story in a straight-forward manner." Unfortunately, Moynihan reported, "every time one of [the veterans] goes and is replaced by a new recruit from the Harvard Crimson or whatever, the Maoist faction on West 43d Street gets one more vote. No one else applies."[48]

Moynihan did not paint this bleak portrait just to depress the president. He saw a cadre of people who could help the administration obtain "some class in its supporters." Contrary to his previous comments about finding intellectuals on the right, Moynihan explained that *the most effective allies of the administration with respect to issues of civic order and the legitimacy of the established institutions are likely now to be found among writers on the left rather than those on the right.*" These writers of the left, mainly friends of Moynihan, were leftist only in the sense that Moynihan was: they were nominal Democrats. Moynihan called these people, including Irving Kristol, Norman Podhoretz, and Nathan Glazer, "a potentially enormously influential source of support for a positive and reasonably optimistic view of American society—before, during, and after the Nixon administration." As a result, Moynihan continued, "this source should be encouraged, given access to the Administration, and just as importantly listened to." Moynihan called this group "the true conservatives . . . defending what America has been able to achieve." Defending America was not the role of the left at the time; in reality, Moynihan was pointing out to Nixon the emerging neoconservatives.[49]

Moynihan added an appendix listing potential allies among intellectuals and providing a biographical blurb and Moynihan's assessments of each man, all of them either sympathetic to the administration or at least enemies of the New Left. As he expected the president to use his candidates, Moynihan intended the appendix to receive wider circulation within the White House. He wrote the bios in the staccato style befitting introductions of the Dirty Dozen. For example, he described Lionel Trilling as follows: "Columbia. English literature. The leading academic literary scholar of the nation. A man of transcendent rationality, and fierce opposition to authoritarian trends everywhere." Similarly, he described Irving Kristol, somewhat inaccurately, in the following manner: "NYU. Political Scientist. Publisher with Dan Bell of the *Public Interest*. Well known to the President, who had him to a small stag dinner last spring." In order to underscore the president's unpopularity among the faculty at elite universities, Moynihan wrote that Nathan Glazer "recently said to me that he would suppose he was the leading defender of the Nixon Administration on the Harvard campus."[50]

Although the length of the memo and its appendix would have caused Lyndon Johnson to send it back to the author, Nixon not only read the memo but acted on it. He passed it on to Haldeman, who sent the appendix back to Moynihan, telling him, "Now get a reading from [White House speechwriter Patrick J.] Buchanan + VP as to these & additions—as people we should be cultivating." Haldeman recalled in his diaries that Nixon was "impressed by a long Moynihan memo, gist of which is the lack of real intellectuals in the Administration." Haldeman added that Nixon agreed "and wants E, et al, to recruit in this direction." Distilling Moynihan's ideas, Haldeman wrote that "as of now have no real ferment of new ideas and no real tough intellectual challenge of present ideas or programs. Main problem is most intellectuals are not on our side. Also Moynihan makes point we've failed to get our story across about what we have done." As a former advertising man, Haldeman closed the entry by summing up the situation in words familiar to him: "The old PR complaint."[51]

In addition to soliciting Buchanan's opinion about Moynihan's list, Haldeman had also told Moynihan to seek Vice President Agnew's advice on the subject. On December 22, Haldeman assistant Bruce Kehrli told Higby that "Art Sohmer of the VP's office called with the VP's comments on the Moynihan list of intellectuals." Agnew, who had been the administration's most public critic of intellectual excesses, "did not have any additions or deletions but recommended Hook, Kristol, Nisbet, and Lipset, all of whom he knew, be cultivated." Of Agnew's favorites, only Nisbet was a Republican, demonstrating that despite his partisan reputation, Agnew kept an open mind concerning party affiliation.[52]

Perhaps because he was a conservative, University of California professor Robert Nisbet attracted the most attention in the cross-pollination of memoranda in the West Wing. At the end of December, Moynihan's last week in the White House, Haldeman told the president that "Buchanan, with some input from Dr. Moynihan, has put together the attached list of intellectuals and academics that he feels we should be cultivating." After reading Haldeman's list, Nixon added two, writing in the margin, "Have Buchanan ch[eck] out Nisbet + Tonsor." Steven Tonsor, a history professor at Michigan, attracted Nixon's interest because he was a "McC. frd." or friend of Council of Economic Advisers chairman Paul McCracken. Knowing that Moynihan was about to leave, Haldeman explained that "the President understands [Nisbet] might be someone we would want to consider bringing in as the House intellectual to replace Moynihan's contribution in that particular area. He feels we need someone on hand fulltime to talk to and work up ideas for the staff." Despite the interest, though, Nisbet never got the job, nor did anyone else.[53]

IN THIS CORNER: MOYNIHAN
VERSUS BURNS

The administration never hired a replacement full-time intellectual, but not for a lack of trying by Pat Moynihan. Nixon, however, had given Moynihan a broader mandate than just advising on intellectual issues. As adviser on urban affairs, Moynihan held a key position on most domestic issues, especially race, cities in general, and welfare policy. Moynihan did not, however, have unlimited influence on these issues. In fact, for the first six months of the job, Moynihan had a shadow following every move he made. The shadow was named Arthur Burns.

Moynihan and Burns had nothing in common other than high IQs. Moynihan was an intensely political American-born Irish Catholic Democrat sociologist; Burns was an aristocratic, academically inclined German Jewish Republican economist. The men did not even agree on vices, as Moynihan was an infamous drinker while Burns favored a pipe. Somehow Nixon appointed these two opposites as his top two advisers on domestic policy.

Both men at first resisted joining the Nixon White House. Moynihan, despite his partisan reservations, could not pass up the opportunity to have the president's ear. As an old friend of Nixon's, Burns already had the president's ear but, having worked in the Eisenhower White House as chairman of the Council of Economic Advisers, did not wish to serve on the White House staff again. Nixon, though, had promised Burns the chairmanship of the Federal Reserve Board when it came available and asked him to serve as special adviser to the president until that point. Burns reluctantly agreed.

Nixon declared that he viewed Burns and Moynihan as equals on the White House flowchart. Consequently, actual power derived from each man's ability to influence the president and make things happen. Although Burns had the advantage of a much longer relationship with the president, Moynihan proved willing to work harder at getting his points across. According to Stephen Hess, Moynihan's deputy, "Moynihan was expert at dealing with the president. This was, after all, the third president he had worked for. He kept a steady stream of memos flowing into Nixon, and these began to have an effect." Hess explained that Moynihan suggested policies in rapid-fire succession "and Burns found that he was spending most of his time reacting to proposals developed by Moynihan's staff." Hess recalled that "Burns did a very good job at this. He was a very intelligent critic. But he did not have the time or the staff, once the administration was under way, to develop many initiatives on his own." Moynihan's tenacity kept Burns constantly playing defense.[54]

Moynihan and Burns had the reputation of lining up on opposite sides of any issue that came before them. In retrospect, Moynihan said that their "debate was never nasty and that, in my view, Burns was far more often correct in his forecasts than I was. An economist of formidable power, he is even more an intellectual in that singularly brilliant Middle-European Jewish tradition." At the time, however, Ehrlichman, who served as a buffer between the two men, recalled that they were like "oil and water." Early in the administration, their feud "got to be a game of who talked to the President last. . . . As quickly as Burns walked out, Moynihan would come in and undo everything that Burns had done."[55]

To counter Moynihan's initiatives, Burns needed to keep track of his doings. Only a few weeks after the inauguration, Burns requested that his assistant Martin Anderson, a young economics professor from Columbia, attend Moynihan's Council of Urban Affairs (CUA) meetings. Cabinet secretary John Whittaker, in forwarding this request to Haldeman, explained that "Marty already attends the Urban Affairs Sub-Committee meetings as Burns' representative and Burns wants Marty at the full Urban Affairs Council meetings for continuity." Although

Whittaker's explanation sounds perfectly innocuous, given the context of the Moynihan–Burns feud, the request for Anderson's attendance may have been an early indication of tension in the White House.[56]

Although Burns used Anderson to try and keep up with Moynihan, Burns most often would reply to Moynihan's memoranda and comments directly. In March, for example, Burns sent the president a rebuttal of Moynihan's urban program, "Toward a National Urban Policy." Burns called his proposal "A Program for the Cities" and stressed two broad themes, "tax incentives and voluntary action." Burns told the president that he had "some reservations about the message proposed by Dr. Moynihan. It advocates a substantially larger role for government in our society. Moreover, the cost of its recommended program is likely to prove very troublesome." Although he had some good points, Burns apparently pushed his ideas rather strongly for Haldeman and Ehrlichman. On the same day that Burns sent this memo, Haldeman wrote in his diary that "Arthur Burns is now driving E[hrlichman] nuts, as he did me (and still does)."[57]

Another type of confrontation between the two men took place over Nixon's request for a reading of Pete Hamill's article in *New York*, "The Revolt of the White Lower Middle Classes." Hamill's article described how white working-class citizens felt neglected by a government of elites that catered to the intractable poor. Nixon requested responses to the article from both Moynihan and Burns.[58]

Typically, Moynihan weighed in first, and with a longer response than Burns would provide. Moynihan told the president that he was "entirely right to have been disturbed by Pete Hamill's article." He added that "Hamill and I correspond, and he tends to view me as a good guy, albeit a professor. He is not at all anti-intellectual, but he is hardly much taken with what passes for intellectualism in New York at the moment." This sentiment put Hamill, Moynihan, and Nixon all in agreement on the subject of the current state of intellectuals.[59]

Moynihan felt that the article presented the administration with two major tasks: "to enable that working class to see what it *is* getting out of government . . . [and] to reconcile the group to the astonishing onset of role reversal of other groups . . . which has shocked and disoriented almost everyone, but most especially this *group* which places unusual emphasis on the importance of people behaving 'like they should.'" Moynihan gave as an example the story of Marion Barry, head of a black organization called Pride, Inc., who "tore up a parking ticket threw it at the cop and called him a motherf***er." Moynihan complained that "the United States Government has set [Barry] up in the resentment business," which the white lower middle class in turn resented. Moynihan called for the "dissol[ution of] the black urban lower class, turning it into a 'black lower middle class' in its own right, and simultaneously seek[ing] the ethical and political

formulations that will restore legitimacy in the eyes of its elite youth," a tall order. To accomplish this, Moynihan backed a broad income strategy that could
include tax reform, a hunger plan, Family Security, revenue sharing, and man-
power training.[60]

Burns took a somewhat different tack. He saw Hamill's article as "a clear, and
perhaps not too early, warning to government that new spending programs,
higher taxes, and romantic promises of urban reconstruction are not welcomed
as words of wisdom by many millions of the white working class." Burns's solutions included a strong law-and-order stance, an anti-inflation campaign, and an
insistence that "people on welfare must be subject (wherever applicable) to a
strict work requirement." Overall, Nixon took ideas from both memos, stressing
the fight against crime and inflation, as well as backing elements of Moynihan's
income strategy.[61]

In addition to demonstrating specific policy differences, these memoranda
highlight other important differences between the two men. Unlike Moynihan,
Burns summarized Hamill by quoting his article, not talking about his relationship with Hamill. More important, Burns was a specialist with specific ideas on
economic policy. Moynihan, as a public intellectual, had opinions on everything.
This is not to suggest that Moynihan was a dilettante. Rather, he was acting as
what Daniel Bell would call a postideological thinker. When faced with a problem, Burns suggested answers; Moynihan suggested looking at the causes behind the problems. Burns, the economist, was very direct and provided specific
policy responses. Moynihan, in contrast, was the generalist, more verbose and
fearful of answers. While not optimal for policy positions, Moynihan's postideological, wide-ranging background was typical of the public intellectuals, who
sought methods rather than policy prescriptions. While Moynihan's approach
was more accepted on campus, it was not always appreciated in the White
House.[62]

The press found out about the Burns–Moynihan feud, much to Nixon's con-
sternation. In a September 1969 memo on the public perception of Nixon's
western White House in San Clemente, Pat Buchanan warned the president
about the disputes in the administration. Buchanan indicated that the disputes
"between Burns and Moynihan . . . are being waged in the public press; there is
a growing call among editorialists that the President put his foot down."[63]

The feud began to take its toll on both the president and the administration.
Bryce Harlow reported that "Nixon was getting bored with Burns. He became
tired of having Burns lecture him. Burns did not realize it, but he was beginning
to get on the president's nerves." Ehrlichman, who increasingly had to serve as
intermediary between the two groups, complained that "confusion began to
spread through the departments. Nobody was sure whether the Burns group or

the Moynihan group really spoke for the administration." Although Moynihan appeared to accept the matter good-naturedly, Burns fumed at having Ehrlichman stand between him and the president.[64]

In a normal business, management would alleviate the feud by firing one—or both—of the principals. Although Moynihan may have been more effective, he probably would have been the one to go because of Burns's long-standing relationship with Nixon. Washington being neither logical nor profit oriented, both men received promotions. Nixon appointed Moynihan, as well as Bryce Harlow, counselor to the president with cabinet rank, while Burns got his desired appointment to the Federal Reserve Board. Haldeman and Ehrlichman announced at the cabinet meeting in the first week of December 1969 that "the President's Domestic Affairs staff has been realigned in order to take into account the elevation of Dr. Moynihan and Bryce Harlow and Dr. Burns' departure for the Federal Reserve." What this meant was that, although both men received better titles, Burns lost all of his staff and Moynihan lost most of his, except for deputy Stephen Hess and staff assistants Chester Finn and Christopher DeMuth.[65]

Despite the superior rank, Moynihan knew what the change signified. Buchanan reported in one of his news summaries that "Moynihan had given several interesting interviews recently. In at least three of them there is some speculation as to how long he will last here." Buchanan suggested that "the increasing commentary that Moynihan is being 'kicked upstairs' may be injurious to our urban expert's sense of pride." Buchanan added that Moynihan "seem[ed] to be laying the groundwork and rationale for a potential departure—if that is the course of action decided upon." Nixon underlined the passage regarding Moynihan's pride and passed Buchanan's information on to Ehrlichman, instructing Ehrlichman to "watch this." With the twin promotions, both Moynihan and Burns lost some influence with the president. The shouting around the president quieted down, though, which is what Nixon wanted after all.[66]

PAT'S POLICIES

With a real policy advisory role, Moynihan was a more complete White House adviser than either Schlesinger or Goldman had been. Although Moynihan's advice on intellectuals made Nixon happy, opportunities for lasting impact came in the policy realm. Moynihan's policy suggestions came mainly in three overlapping areas: urban, racial, and welfare policy.[67]

When Nixon entered office, urban riots had erupted every summer since the Watts riots of 1964, culminating in the disasters following the 1968 assassination of Martin Luther King Jr., which helped elect Nixon. Despite the problems

he faced in the cities, Johnson had put a low priority on urban affairs, often refusing to meet with mayors. In September 1966, for example, Johnson rebuffed
a suggestion by Doug Cater that he meet with selected mayors. Johnson wrote
to Cater that "[Chicago Mayor Richard J.] Daley can see me anytime but the VP
usually deals with the Mayors."[68]

Moynihan's view of urban affairs differed from that of Johnson and his advisers. The problem of urban riots tortured Moynihan, and he was determined to
help prevent their recurrence. In 1970 he published *Toward a National Urban
Policy*, an anthology of solutions for America's urban ills. Although the book
came out a year after he started working at the White House, Moynihan wrote in
the preface that he had been working on and thinking about the project since
1964. In the eponymous opening essay, Moynihan observed that "the United
States does not now have an urban policy. The idea that there might be such a
policy is new." Moynihan advocated changing this situation, backing an urban
policy that included attacking poverty, improving black status, and promoting
decentralization in the interests of "social peace." Moynihan also wrote that "in
the Spring of 1969, President Nixon met in the Cabinet room with the mayors
of ten American cities," distinguishing Nixon from Johnson at the very beginning of the administration.[69]

In addition to meeting publicly with the mayors, Nixon differed from Johnson in having an urban affairs adviser. In this role, Moynihan started pressing
Nixon on urban policy even before he took office. On January 9, 1969, Moynihan addressed a memo on the urban crisis to the president-elect suggesting an
"optimistic posture," as he promised to "assume that our problems are manage-
able if only we will manage them." Moynihan added that "this is the only position
possible for government." In the memo, Moynihan ranged from the eighteenth-
and nineteenth-century origins of democracy to the contemporary threat to
democratic breakdown and concluded that "what is now termed 'the crisis of
the cities' is more a moral and cultural crisis than a material one. Indeed it is frequently the former that produces the latter." Although the memo lacked specific
suggestions, Moynihan hoped to help Nixon solve the moral and cultural crisis.
The memo represented a typical Moynihan offering: erudite yet commonsensi-
cal, predicting disaster along with suggesting a nonspecific way out.[70]

Although the memo may have been typical Moynihan, it was not typical Washington, where memoranda tend to focus on specific policy solutions rather than
long-term analyses of solutions. Despite this, or perhaps because of it, Nixon
liked the memo, passing it on to special assistant Len Garment, a former law part-
ner of Nixon's. In forwarding the memo to Garment, Haldeman wrote that Nixon
"wanted to emphasize that this is not a final policy paper but rather the kind of
incisive and stimulating analysis which he thinks should be constantly brought to

the attention of policymakers." While Haldeman's comments demonstrated that Nixon liked the memo, they also implied that Nixon and Haldeman did not view more cerebral aides like Garment and Moynihan as real policymakers.[71]

In his time in the White House, Moynihan would challenge this nonpolicy perception of his role. Moynihan made sure he and his staffers on the Urban Affairs Council had offices near Nixon's in the West Wing. Moynihan knew from previous experience that "proximity is everything." This tactic helped Moynihan get his ideas in front of Nixon.[72]

The Urban Affairs meetings themselves represented another element of Moynihan's effectiveness strategy. The UAC had weekly scheduled meetings with preprinted agendas and follow-up minutes distributed. The first UAC meeting, on January 9, 1969, had a discussion of the administration's "national growth policy proposal" first on the agenda. For the second item, "Dr. Moynihan would then describe the outlines of a national growth policy, including both urban and rural development." These sorts of meetings suited Moynihan's style, as he preferred broad programs and general directional suggestions over legislative nitty gritty.[73]

Two weeks after this first meeting, Nixon issued Executive Order 11452, officially creating the Urban Affairs Council. As urban affairs "czar," Moynihan had a particular dislike for anyone circumventing his authority. In a memo to Ehrlichman, Moynihan complained that the administration had made certain departmental appointments without consulting him. Moynihan obviously had some pull in the White House, as Peter Flanigan wrote a memo to political operatives Darrell Trent and Harry Flemming, ordering that "all candidates for positions in the Urban Affairs area be discussed with Dr. Moynihan." Flanigan proposed a rule of thumb in these matters: "When in doubt as to the propriety of informing Dr. Moynihan, settling the doubt in favor of our bringing too many names, rather than too few, to his office." This broad mandate helps demonstrate the extent of Moynihan's influence in the first year of the administration. It also shows that Moynihan could be rather insistent on getting his way. While Moynihan certainly had other talents, incidents like this one indicate that working with him proved trying at times.[74]

Despite Moynihan's occasional petulance, his UAC meetings often proved genial, if not amusing. In the first meeting, for example, with Nixon in attendance, Burns and Agnew asked Moynihan to provide an overview for an urban program. Moynihan responded that he "would be glad to undertake such a task, on the condition that—and I realize that one does not ordinarily impose conditions on the President of the United States—on the condition that no one take it seriously." According to the meeting notes, "everyone roared, including the President, who first blinked, and then joined in the laughter."[75]

Although the UAC produced relatively few policies, Moynihan's work on it led to his "Toward a National Urban Policy," the anchor essay in his book. The essay, which examined the problems of American cities more than the solutions, appeared in *Public Interest* before coming out in book form. Moynihan sent a copy of the published essay to the president, informing Nixon that the magazine was "edited by Irving Kristol, of whom the Vice President is a bit of a fan!" Moynihan explained that the essay "emerged from the effort begun in the Urban Affairs Council last January to 'assist the President in the development of a national urban policy.'" As a result, Moynihan continued, the "quasi-official" document "represent[ed] one of the more specifically intellectual products of your administration."[76]

The month after sending the *Public Interest* article to the president, Moynihan received his "promotion" to counselor. After this move, which widened his scope, Moynihan decreased his emphasis on urban affairs, along with the volume of paper he produced on urban issues. The UAC meetings continued, but they accomplished less. In February 1970, the UAC went on the road for publicity purposes, meeting with Mayor Richard G. Lugar in Indianapolis. This move was the equivalent of propping up a television show's sagging ratings by including a well-known guest star: the ratings may receive a temporary bump, but the product does not change very much. At the meeting, Moynihan outlined his ten-point urban policy, which did not appear to have changed from the earlier meetings, adding an eleventh point: to be of good cheer. Moynihan felt that "while the American city had been in its winter, and still was in its February, 'the spring of the American city is not far away,' and that there was an increasing awareness of its plight."[77]

When asked by Nixon biographer Jonathan Aitken what the UAC had accomplished, Moynihan did not cite any specific program. He did, however, credit the administration with "chang[ing] the atmosphere." Moynihan claimed that "there weren't any race riots under Nixon, partly because local communities could see that his administration was moving on jobs, schools, decentralization of power and welfare reform." Two years earlier, though, without the benefit of hindsight, Moynihan had not given Nixon quite as much credit for ending urban riots. In November 1970, Moynihan informed the president that "major civil disorders in the Negro residential areas of large cities have—almost abruptly—ceased" but that "it is not possible to call this an achievement of the administration." Moynihan did tell the president to take credit for the development, explaining that "as you are blamed when it rains . . . you might as well take credit when the sun shines." This analysis said more for Moynihan as a public relations specialist than as an urban expert. On the other hand, the Nixon administration did deserve some credit for ending urban strife. By creating the UAC and giving Moynihan a prominent bully pulpit, Nixon showed that he was taking urban problems seriously. This gesture—which received steady publicity in the weekly meetings—did not end urban rioting, but it did help, as Moynihan put it, "change the atmosphere."[78]

Although, by Moynihan's own admission, most accomplishments of the UAC were non–policy specific, the best-known domestic policy recommendation of the Nixon administration did grow out of it. Moynihan felt that the Family Assistance Plan, the administration's proposal to overhaul the welfare system, would help solve many of the nation's urban ills. The FAP called for direct transfer payments to families earning below a certain income threshold in order to bring them up to that level. It was part of Moynihan's "income strategy," which encouraged people to solve their own problems by providing them with enough money to make their own choices.

In *The Politics of a Guaranteed Income*, his account of the Family Assistance Plan's rise and fall, Moynihan claimed that "the Family Assistance Plan was a product of the Urban Affairs Council, in ways a consequence of it." While this is true, Moynihan recognized that the idea for the plan did not originate with the UAC. He found earlier manifestations of the plan in European social theory, Canada's welfare plan during World War II, and Milton Friedman's suggestion of a negative income tax (of which FAP was a variant), from the 1940s.[79]

In addition, versions of a Family Assistance–type plan had existed in the federal bureaucracy since at least 1963, when the Labor Department's policy planning staff, which Moynihan headed, wrote a policy paper on the subject. Afterward, planners at the Department of Health, Education, and Welfare had presented the plan to Secretary John Gardner and Secretary Wilbur Cohen. Robert Finch inherited the idea under Nixon. For better or worse, Moynihan felt that the negative income tax had a certain momentum: "Had [Finch] rejected it, it would have been prepared for his successor, Secretary Elliot L. Richardson. Bureaucracy was at work."[80]

Moynihan's perception of bureaucratic inevitability argues against the importance of intellectuals, or at least policy experts, in the development of domestic programs. In the case of the FAP, though, Moynihan had pushed the idea as a private citizen for a number of years before joining the Nixon administration. In 1966, for example, Moynihan wrote to Harry McPherson backing a family allowance, which "would benefit 80 percent of the American people in one stroke." Moynihan warned that in the past welfare reform had led to a "savage reaction of the Federal bureaucracy in H.E.W. and Labor, and to some extent O.E.O., and the even wilder resentment on the part of what might be called the Civil Rights left." While this fear of the bureaucracy stemmed in part from Moynihan's experience with the Moynihan Report, he was correct to see the possible obstacles to welfare reform.[81]

A few years later, as UAC chairman, Moynihan continued pushing family allowances. He created the Nixon administration's variant on the negative income tax, pushing it against resistance in the federal bureaucracy, the White House, and later the Congress. Moynihan received this mandate from the president because of Nixon's genuine interest in improving the welfare system. In January 1969 the president expressed his thoughts on the subject to his assistants with input on welfare policy. Nixon wrote that the "New York welfare mess is probably typical of a problem which exists all over the country." To prove that he was serious about the matter, Nixon warned his assistants that he did "not want this swept under the rug or put aside on the ground that we want to have an 'era of good feeling' with the bureaucrats as we begin." This take-charge attitude on welfare coincided with Moynihan's interest in the subject.[82]

Moynihan believed that Nixon emphasized welfare because of his strict Quaker upbringing, which created Nixon's "Puritan ethic" views on welfare. To someone with Nixon's working-poor background, Moynihan felt that "welfare was at very least a mark of failure, and in certain circumstances a badge of shame." As a result, Nixon turned to Moynihan, who also grew out of the working poor, to answer his queries about welfare, such as "why the AFDC welfare rate suddenly (in the mid-1960s) lost its earlier dependence on the unemployment rate." As Alexander Butterfield put it in the memo making this request, the president "is interested in the causes." This interest distinguished Nixon from Johnson, who preferred action memoranda to analysis. It also explains why Moynihan enjoyed access to the president, who liked Moynihan's analytical approach.[83]

Moynihan felt that domestic policy demanded an analytical approach. In *The Politics of a Guaranteed Income*, he complained that "strategic abstractions— containment, massive retaliation, graduated deterrence—are common enough in foreign affairs, but relatively rare in social policy, where political leaders have preferred to assert goals rather than modes of achieving them." The UAC established a subcommittee on welfare reform, headed by HEW Secretary Finch, that tried to accommodate Moynihan's observation that "welfare was a problem that had created itself. The rolls rise because they are there." Another, related problem that Moynihan found, in response to a direct query from Nixon, was that <u>"THERE SEEMS TO HAVE BEEN SOME CHANGE IN ATTITUDE. WELFARE WOULD SEEM TO BE LESS STIGMATIZING NOW THAN IN THE PAST."</u>[84]

Moynihan felt that the FAP would solve these problems. It would eliminate poverty by providing lump-sum payments to families earning under $1,600 a year. FAP exempted earnings up to $13.85 a week in order to encourage participants to work. It would also eliminate the question of stigma by sending checks directly to families, diminishing the need for social workers. This component of the plan especially pleased both Moynihan and Nixon. According to historian Stephen Ambrose, when presented with the plan, Nixon asked Moynihan, "Will FSS get rid of social workers?" Moynihan responded, rather gleefully, "It will wipe them out!" In addition to the plan's merits, both men saw the elimination of generally liberal social workers as an added bonus.[85]

With all the work going into preparing something as complex as FAP, Moynihan warned the president in April that "the press seems to be getting hold of the general outline of the Family Security System and that we have to expect that the story will break fairly soon." Moynihan explained that, given the number of people involved in planning the program, "a gradual seepage" was inevitable. As a result, Moynihan recommended to Nixon that "if you decide to adopt the plan you should announce it soon after Congress returns." Moynihan told the president that the plan would "be the centerpiece in your domestic program—truly an historic proposal."[86]

Nixon forwarded Moynihan's note to Ehrlichman, explaining that he had already "decided to go ahead on this program." Ironically, given Moynihan's concern about leaks, Nixon admonished Ehrlichman, "Don't tell Finch or M[oynihan] et al; but get a plan ready for implementation by 1st of next week." Although Moynihan had participated in every step of the process until that point, Nixon first informed Ehrlichman of his decision, purposely shutting out Moynihan and Finch, who had also played an important role.

Although Nixon had made his decision in April, he did not announce the plan until August 8, 1969. When Nixon asked if people liked the plan, Moynihan replied, "Like it! Why, there are more telegrams coming in than at any time since Johnson announced he was quitting!" Then he added, "Enjoy it while you can, Mr. President. The criticism will soon start."[87]

Moynihan was right about the criticism. He expected conservative Republicans, starting with Burns inside the White House, to oppose the plan, which they did. Opposition from the left proved more surprising, although not completely unexpected. Moynihan described FAP as "a complex social science proposal, which was to be judged by a profession that by and large loathed him." Liberal organizations such as the National Welfare Rights Organization opposed the plan, claiming that FAP stood for F*** America's Poor. Black organizations, such as the Urban League, opposed the plan too, incurring Moynihan's anger against the group's leader, Whitney Young.[88]

Liberal opposition to FAP had an impact. Twenty years later, in a letter to Anthony Lewis, ultraliberal point man for the *New York Times*, Moynihan was still complaining about the left's opposition to FAP. Moynihan wrote that "liberals commenced to denounce the proposals as reactionary, racist, Lord knows what." These denunciations had a stronger effect inside the White House than outside. According to Moynihan, "From the outside this might not have seemed much harassment or rejection. From the inside it seemed a continuous, relentless barrage." This barrage discouraged White House staffers working on FAP and also played into Nixon and Moynihan's view of public discourse as dominated by liberals. Moynihan recalled that he "watched the high spirits of the reformers gradually subside. It was no use. [The Nixon people] would never be accepted as reformers. And so? And so, why bother?" Getting their cues from Nixon and Moynihan, White House staffers felt that intellectuals, liberals, and the media all opposed them.[89]

Moynihan also had trouble selling FAP to skeptical liberals and conservatives. Moynihan blamed the failure, as he did so many things, on the lack of Republican intellectuals in the administration or supporting it: "Here, as in much else, the Republican party suffered from its lack of intellectuals and publicists who could speak with authority to the concerns of this constituency." Moynihan felt that liberals could line up opponents to denounce the FAP, while Republicans lacked advocates to sing its virtues.[90]

The House Ways and Means Committee approved the FAP on March 5, 1970, and the entire House passed the plan on April 16. In May, Moynihan published a pro-FAP article in a *Saturday Review* issue devoted to the program. Moynihan sent Nixon a copy of the article with a cover note assuring the president that Moynihan would "see that this is circulated to the Senate." "More importantly," Moynihan added, "the *Saturday Review* has an enormous influential circulation and it should do quite a bit of good on its own." Nixon liked what Moynihan had done and wrote back, "*Good* get it broadly circulated."[91]

Despite Moynihan's best efforts, the FAP failed to pass in the Senate. The opposing forces, including the coalition of social welfare forces, proved too strong for the administration to overcome. FAP demonstrated that an intellectual in the White House could initiate a bold new idea, but getting bold legislation passed proved to be a different matter.

MOYNIHAN AND RACE

While FAP proved to be Moynihan's best-known policy suggestion, it was not his best-known move in the White House. As with his experience in the Johnson administration, Moynihan again found the subject of race relations both messy and controversial. Regardless of the subject's explosiveness, Moynihan saw himself as an expert on race. He had coauthored a book on the subject, strongly supported civil rights, and had spent a great deal of time on the issue of race relations during the Johnson administration. Consequently, Moynihan often advised Nixon on racial matters.

In Moynihan's first memorandum to the president, he talked of the need to dissolve the black lower class, now known as the underclass. This class, he warned, was "unstable and essentially violent." In addition, he argued that this underclass fomented black radicalism and anti-Semitism. He informed the president that "among Jews . . . there is a rising concern, in some quarters approaching alarm, over black anti-Semitism. They foresee Negro political power driving them from civil service jobs, as in the New York City School system. They see anti-Semitism becoming an accepted political posture." In response to these developments, he recommended, as a political matter, a deescalation "of the rhetoric of crisis about the internal state of the society in general, and in particular about those problems—e.g., crime, de facto segregation, low educational achievement—which government has relatively little power to influence."[92]

Moynihan frequently suggested this strategy of rhetorical deescalation, which corresponded to the views of many of Moynihan's former liberal colleagues. These nascent neocons viewed blacks as another immigrant group climbing the status ladder. Given this view, the best strategy was to provide legal protection from discrimination and then sit back and let them climb. To members of the civil rights community, however, this approach represented a very real danger. From their perspective, they had worked to put civil rights on the agenda. Now that they had succeeded, the government wanted to move on to other issues, without ensuring complete equality for blacks. Moynihan, of course, saw things very differently. To him, civil rights supporters had succeeded in pushing their agenda but did not want to lose their influence, so they were seeking out new problems to solve. One thing was true, however: a deescalation of racial rhetoric did not serve the desires of the civil rights community's leaders.[93]

Even though his approach differed from that of the civil rights community, Moynihan, as an urban Democrat in a very white Nixon administration, had more contacts in the black community than most of his White House colleagues. While Moynihan was not the administration's official black liaison—Robert Brown had that position—according to Ehrlichman, Nixon did not feel comfortable speaking with Brown. As a result, Moynihan often briefed Nixon on developments in the black community.[94]

Moynihan adopted this role early in the administration. In February 1969, he warned the president that the administration's attempts to reach out to the black community had not been successful. One indication of this lack of success that Moynihan reported was that Urban League president "Whitney Young continues to 'bad mouth' you, as the saying goes." Nixon did not like this news. He felt that "Young *may* have decided to go all the way to get King's mantle—and in addition to satisfy the militants. Why don't you have a meeting with him and lay it

on the line? If he has drawn the sword we should know it—and act accordingly."
By asking Moynihan to set up this meeting, Nixon demonstrated that he respected
Moynihan's expertise with regard to the black community. Relying on Moynihan
for peaceful relations with the black community mirrored using him for similar
reasons with intellectuals. Although Moynihan was closer than most Nixon
staffers to both of these groups, he had also angered both with his frankness.[95]

Both Nixon and Moynihan believed that blacks would and should make
steady progress and that "radical" civil rights organizations did not perform a
service for the communities they claimed to represent. As a result, Moynihan's
memoranda and comments on the black community encountered general agreement from the president and the rest of his staff. Many in the civil rights community, however, disagreed with these views. This disagreement came to a head
when Moynihan invited Ralph Abernathy, president of the Southern Christian
Leadership Conference, to a UAC meeting.

Abernathy arrived at the May 13 meeting with an entourage that included
Marian Wright Edelman, Jesse Jackson, and Andrew Young. This group joined
Abernathy in the Cabinet Room encounter with Nixon. Five separate accounts
of the ensuing meeting dispute some of the most basic details. The Nixon aides
agree that Abernathy read off a long list of demands, although accounts of
Nixon's reaction to Abernathy's monologue differ. Abernathy does not recount
making any demands, only that he was subjected to a session of "economic double-
talk." Ray Price, writing the White House notes of the meeting, simply indicated
that Abernathy and Nixon "exchanged messages." After that, Nixon "said he
had to go because of an urgent message from [Kissinger] in Saigon. Abernathy
insisted that [Nixon] hear his reply." Before Nixon could leave, though, "Dr.
Abernathy detained him, asking for a moment to reply." Nixon listened and then
left, and Agnew replaced Nixon as chair of the meeting.[96]

According to Ehrlichman, however, after Abernathy issued his demands and
Nixon replied, the president, "furious . . . got up and left the room [as] Moynihan did his best to salvage something." Although this account could correspond
to Price's tale, Haldeman appears to have been at a different meeting entirely. As
he wrote in his staccato diary style, "UAC had Ralph Abernathy. Pretty ridiculous. He brought six, or eight, of his cohorts and read a long list of demands.
Tried to trap P into meeting with the rest of his group, or ordering the rest of his
group to do so. No luck. P handled beautifully." In Nixon's account, "the long
session was a shambles because [Abernathy] was either unprepared or unwilling, or both, to have a serious discussion. Instead he postured and made
speeches." Nixon remembered that, despite the posturing, Abernathy "seemed
pleased that we had made this effort and at the end thanked me profusely for taking the time to meet with them."[97]

According to Price's notes, after both Nixon and Agnew had left the meeting, "Dr. Moynihan interrupted the meeting with an urgent report from the Indian Treaty Room." It seemed that a group of "Poor People who had been assembled there at 10:00 had been led to believe that Dr. Abernathy would be returning in about an hour." When Abernathy did not return, as a result of his long harangue, the group was "restive and impatient (by now it was about 1:00), and they were threatening a demonstration." This threatened demonstration irked Abernathy, who "insisted that they hadn't come with any intention of staging a demonstration; and he hoped that some of the Cabinet would accompany him, to give evidence to the Poor of their concern." The meeting finally broke up, "a little after 1:00, after a bit less than three hours." Abernathy proceeded to the Indian Treaty Room along with HUD secretary George Romney and transportation secretary John Volpe.[98]

Everyone agrees on what Abernathy did next. Recalling that the meeting had made him "angrier than [he] had been in a long time," Abernathy denounced Nixon and the administration, calling the meeting "the most disappointing and the most fruitless of all the meetings we have had up to this time." This reaction infuriated everyone in the administration. Typically, Haldeman described Abernathy's action in clipped tones: "Abernathy went out and stabbed us on TV. Proved again there's no dealing with these people. They obviously want confrontation, not solutions." This incident particularly disturbed Moynihan, who paced in front of the president "embarrassed and outraged," telling Nixon that Abernathy's betrayal "was unconscionable and I promise you it will never happen again."[99]

Moynihan's prediction came true, although not for the reason Moynihan suggested. Haldeman recorded that the staff meeting the next "morning was mainly about reaction to Abernathy yesterday. We were had, and now they all realize it. Hope a lesson is learned." According to Ehrlichman, the lesson was that "for the next four years anyone who suggested that the president meet with a group of blacks could expect to hear about Moynihan's meeting with Ralph Abernathy and the leaders." Although Abernathy cowed the staff, the incident disturbed Nixon less. He told Moynihan that "the problem as I see it, is that they don't think that I care. We must demonstrate to them that we do care by our actions and not just by our words." Ironically, with respect to relations with black America, the president would consistently find his actions—including initiating affirmative action programs such as the Philadelphia Plan—ignored while the administration's words got them into trouble.[100]

While Moynihan probably thought that 1969 was a year full of racial controversy for the administration, 1970 made the preceding year look tame. Moynihan began the year by writing his most famous memorandum—one of the most famous memoranda in White House history—the "benign neglect memo." The memo began by informing Nixon of gains in black income: "In quantifiable terms, which are reliable, the American Negro is making extraordinary progress." Moynihan backed up this claim statistically, showing black gains in income and education but ruefully noting that the "illegitimacy rate rose once again."[101]

In the memo, Moynihan made four major recommendations: a White House conference to discuss black concerns; a deescalation of racial rhetoric to allow for black progress; more research on the prevention of crime; and recognition of nonradical black leaders instead of the headline-grabbing, militant Black Panthers. The Panthers, Moynihan explained, had just had a star-filled fund-raising party at Leonard Bernstein's Manhattan apartment, which Tom Wolfe later immortalized in his essay "Radical Chic." Nixon, apparently appalled by the tale, scrawled in the margin that the Panther party demonstrated "the complete decadence of the American 'upper' class intellectual elite."[102]

In addition to his recommendations and the Panther tale, Moynihan told Nixon that "there is a silent black majority as well as a white one," one that had "generally been ignored by the government and the media." Nixon agreed with the point, although he felt that the "silent" supporters among blacks numbered only 30 percent. This idea of the silent majority especially appealed to Nixon because he had coined the phrase himself, referring to his base of support in the heartland. This group also had the added benefit, in Nixon's and Moynihan's eyes, of resisting the influence of elite opinions, particularly in the news media. By invoking the support of this black silent minority, Moynihan was trying to show that many blacks really supported the Nixon administration.[103]

Since Moynihan did not really recommend any serious administration action, the memo should have, like most White House papers, slipped from view as soon as the president placed it in his out box. Unfortunately for Moynihan, though, six weeks after he wrote it, someone in the administration leaked the memo to the press. Out of the 1,650 words in the memo, press reports focused on only two. In recommending a period of deescalation, which, in itself, was not a new idea, Moynihan used the infelicitous phrase "benign neglect," a phrase that came from the Earl of Durham's 1839 report concerning Canadian self-government. The day the memo leaked, Sunday, March 1, the *New York Times* ran a headline reading "'Benign Neglect' on Race is Proposed by Moynihan."[104]

Needless to say, the leak angered Nixon. According to Haldeman, Nixon was "cranked up about two major leaks in the *New York Times* today, especially one of Moynihan memo about blacks." In retaliation, Nixon requested "a complete freeze on *Times*, etc." Haldeman felt that the press had "immediately taken [the phrase] out of context." Regardless of the "freeze" on the Times, the White House never discovered the identity of the leaker.[105]

In any event, the damage was done. The day after the *Times* printed the memo, *Times* columnist Anthony Lewis laced into Moynihan. He predicted that "blacks would think that any period of neglect would be not benign, but hostile. And they would be right." By Tuesday, press calls had swamped Ron Ziegler, the president's spokesman. Moynihan had to call a special press conference to defend the memo and specifically the phrase "benign neglect." The same day, the *Times* solemnly editorialized on the "sad" document, calling it an "astonishingly optimistic memorandum" whose recommendations "can only encourage the most retrogressive elements" in government.[106]

By Saturday, the civil rights community had issued its official response. The title of the front page article in the *Times* told the entire story: "21 Rights Leaders Rebut Moynihan: Assert Benign Neglect Idea Is 'Symptomatic of Effort to Wipe Out Gains.'" In addition to black civil rights leaders, the twenty-one signers also included prominent Jews, such as Dore Schary of the B'nai B'rith Anti-Defamation League and Rabbi Arthur Lelyveld of the American Jewish Congress. The group called the memo a "flagrant and shameful document." Rebutting the claim of black gains, they claimed that "these gains have been significant, but they have not been monumental." This constitutes, at best, a semantic difference. Nevertheless, the stance demonstrated that the civil rights establishment had no patience for any government official discussing black gains, just as, five years earlier, after the Moynihan Report, black leaders had no patience for a discussion of black problems.[107]

The Nation, which had run some of the harshest anti-Moynihan pieces following the Moynihan Report five years earlier, fired a new round of grapeshot. An unsigned editorial told Moynihan that he had "repeated the offense," calling his memo "mischievous, cruel and ridiculous." *Time* ran a cartoon showing a battered Native American telling an African American about the experience of "benign neglect." Nixon recalled that Moynihan tendered his resignation in the wake of the controversy, but the president refused it.[108]

Even though he kept his job after the benign neglect memo, Moynihan endured an extremely difficult month. At the end of March, Haldeman recorded that he had "Moynihan in to see me, disturbed about staff leaks designed to screw him, especially via [White House aide Clark] Molenhoff. Made point he's ruined in Democratic Party because of the 'benign neglect' memo. He's really distressed, mainly because he has nowhere left to go." His position inside the administration suffered too, as both his access and his memo output diminished sharply.[109]

Although the tide of anti-Moynihan sentiment eventually subsided, friends and enemies alike remembered "benign neglect." In all likelihood, Moynihan and Nixon both saw themselves as problack constituents but antiblack leaders. While this approach may have helped them soothe the cities and preside over a period of material and integrational gains for blacks, it did not leave either man with a good reputation in the black community. As recently as 1994, when black activist Al Sharpton unsuccessfully ran against Moynihan for the New York Democratic Senate nomination, Sharpton referred to his opponent as "Daniel Patrick 'Benign Neglect' Moynihan."

EXEUNT MOYNIHAN

Although the benign neglect episode did not drive Moynihan from the White House, he knew that he would not remain much longer. He had never intended to stay more than two years and, if he had considered changing his mind, his promotion above control over domestic affairs dissuaded him from staying on. He had promised Nixon that he would return to Harvard after Congress passed FAP. In late 1970, as the administration saw that FAP would die in the Senate, Moynihan began preparing to leave.[110]

In mid-November, Moynihan met with Nixon to discuss moving to the position of U.S. ambassador to the United Nations. Moynihan tentatively accepted. On November 20, the *Boston Globe* reported that Moynihan would take the UN job; on that same day, the Senate Finance Committee voted down FAP. Then Moynihan changed his mind, deciding to return to Harvard. He wrote to the president explaining his change of heart and then met with Haldeman to discuss his decision. Haldeman remembered that Moynihan explained his choice with a "whole range of reasons." Haldeman told Moynihan that Nixon "understood, but would want critiques and suggestions from him as he has done all along."[111]

Moynihan did not leave silently. He gave a powerful valedictory address to the year-end briefing and reception for cabinet and subcabinet officials. In what he called his "Christmas Charge," Moynihan reminded the officials that they had entered office during the "worst of times." The country "was coming apart" and "the agony was elemental, irresolvable, and nigh to universal." Given that situation, Moynihan called the administration's accomplishments "considerable, even remarkable." Recognizing he may have sounded Pollyannish, Moynihan laid out the reasons for optimism, which included greater prospects for peace in Vietnam, the disappearance of urban unrest, the cooling of racial rhetoric, and increasing integration in the schools. Moynihan called this "all in all, a record of some good fortune and much achievement." Unfortunately, Moynihan complained, the administration had received little credit for its accomplishments.[112]

Given the situation as he saw it, Moynihan offered "three exhortations, and the rest will be silence." First, he insisted that they "be of good cheer and good conscience. Depressing, even frightening things are being said about the administration. They are not true." Moynihan had been making this suggestion, in various manifestations, since the beginning of the administration. He had also made

his second suggestion—"to resist the temptation to respond in kind to the un-
truths and half truths that begin to fill the air"—many times before. In his per-
oration, Moynihan suggested that, in order to accomplish the first two exhortations, "it is necessary for members of the administration, the men in this room,
to be far more attentive to what it is the President has said, and proposed."
Moynihan complained that "time and again, the President has said things of
startling insight, taken positions of great political courage and intellectual dar-
ing, only to be greeted with silence or incomprehension." As a result of administration inaction, "the people in the nation who take these matters seriously
have never been required to take us seriously." Moynihan concluded that "a large
vision of America has been put forth. It can only be furthered by men who share
it." Moynihan's remarks were the equivalent of vitamin pills for the lawyers and
advertising executives in the embattled Nixon White House.[113]

Moynihan's speech was leaked to the press, although this particular leak led
to a positive press clipping. William Randolph Hearst quoted heavily from the
speech in a front-page editorial in the *Seattle Post-Intelligencer*. Hearst especially
liked Moynihan's optimism about the alleviation of America's problems. Hearst
explained that Moynihan's words had added credibility because Moynihan was
"a pillar of the Ivy League Eastern Intellectual Establishment." Despite Moynihan's "establishment" background, Hearst concluded that Moynihan's acco-
lades for Nixon and the administration "could only have come from an honest
man who had observed first hand."[114]

Ironically, although Hearst's words may have represented the last words written about Moynihan as a member of the Nixon administration, they provided
the kind of payback Nixon had sought in hiring Moynihan. Nixon wanted people, specifically leftists, intellectuals, and activists, to look at Moynihan and determine that the president was serious about branching out in new directions.
With respect to intellectuals, for example, Nixon hoped that Moynihan, as an intellectual himself, would provide cover for Nixon's views on intellectuals. But
Nixon also hired Moynihan because they shared similar views on the elitism and
monotonous leftism among American intellectuals. As a result, precisely because
Moynihan was Nixon's type of intellectual, he could not help the anti-intellectual
Nixon with the prickly intellectual community and could only suggest that the
president seek out other intellectuals like himself.

SEARCH FOR A REPLACEMENT
INTELLECTUAL: KAHN AND KRISTOL

Moynihan was right to point out that Nixon lacked intellectuals on his team. After Moynihan left, Nixon sought, unsuccessfully, a replacement. Although Nixon

spent most of his second term on foreign policy and Watergate, where he did not need a single intellectual ambassador, having a link to the intellectuals, someone to explain his side of the story, might have helped during Watergate.

In addition to lacking a link to the intellectuals when he needed one, Nixon really wanted an idea man in the White House to replace Moynihan. In January 1971, just days after Moynihan's Christmas charge farewell, Haldeman reported that Nixon "got into a discussion of the need for a staff intellectual." According to Haldeman, Nixon had "in mind Robert Nisbitt [sic] in California." Nixon felt that he needed "one highly regarded academic," like Nisbet, "to stimulate thinking, give the P someone to talk to from time to time, and to work with the rest of the staff generating ideas."[115]

The Nixon White House sought other intellectuals in addition to Nisbet, including former Trotskyite James Burnham, although Buchanan warned Haldeman to "be a little leery of approaching Burnham on our Domestic Policy." Haldeman agreed to add Burnham "to our list of intellectuals." Another candidate was Arthur Burns's White House assistant, Martin Anderson. In suggesting Anderson to Ehrlichman, Haldeman wrote that Nixon wanted to place "a Conservative, who is known as such, into a top level fulltime position in the Domestic Council." In this vein, Nixon thought, rehiring Anderson could serve "as a signal to the Conservatives."[116]

Neither Burnham nor Anderson joined the Nixon White House as an intellectual adviser, but the search continued through the post-Moynihan years. More important, perhaps as a result of Moynihan's nagging, Nixon tried to find his kind of intellectual. In this vein, the administration courted two men—Irving Kristol and Herman Kahn.

Kristol, a former Trotskyite who had served as an editor for *Commentary*, *Encounter*, and the *Reporter*, was working at Basic Books as well as copublishing— with Daniel Bell—*Public Interest*. Moynihan, who was a good friend of Kristol's, had suggested Kristol's name as a promising intellectual for Nixon to cultivate. Kristol had attended a 1970 stag dinner with the president and failed to impress Haldeman, who complained that "Kristol didn't add much." Despite Haldeman's disinterest, Kristol still had his supporters in the White House, including the president, even after Moynihan left.[117]

In March 1971, Nixon's aides noticed Kristol's piece in the *New York Times Magazine* entitled "Pornography, Obscenity, and Censorship," in which Kristol issued a call for "liberal censorship." White House aide George Bell recommended that Nixon call Kristol to "encourage . . . his views toward a responsible approach to censorship of pornography." In case Nixon did not remember Kristol from Moynihan's recommendations and the stag dinner, Bell added that "Kristol is a leading intellectual—one we can use as a supporter. His son, Bill, worked as an intern for Pat Moynihan." Buchanan and Colson seconded the rec-ommendation.[118]

According to Philip Nobile, Nixon considered appointing Kristol as a wide-ranging domestic policy adviser in his second term. This followed Kristol's pub-lic endorsement of Nixon in 1972, a move that angered many of Kristol's fellow intellectuals, including Lionel Trilling, one of Kristol's mentors. Despite the en-dorsement, though, Nixon never made the appointment, although the refusal may have come from Kristol, who, after serving in the army, vowed that he "would never, never again work as a functionary in any large organization, and especially not for the U.S. government."[119]

Nixon's other favorite post-Moynihan intellectual, Herman Kahn, had made his name as a global strategist but felt comfortable discoursing on any topic. Kahn withdrew from graduate programs in physics and mathematics at Cal Tech before receiving his Ph.D., partially because he "felt that narrow training created intel-lectual blinders that could prevent a specialist from seeing the 'big picture.'" As a result, he did not limit the advice he gave the president to any narrow subjects.[120]

Kahn met with Nixon and his Domestic Council in early 1973. Before the meet-ing, Kahn sent Nixon a briefing book outlining some of his thoughts. In the brief-ing book, which was in capital letters, Kahn explained his theory of the Counter-reformation, which he saw as a movement rising in opposition to the "counterculture" of student radicals. The Counterreformation resembled Nixon's idea of the "Silent Majority" that resented the excesses of the New Left. Kahn's views on most American intellectuals meshed with Nixon's. Kahn defined an intel-lectual as "ONE WHO FORMS HIS JUDGMENTS CHIEFLY ON THE BASIS OF INDIRECT EXPERIENCE AND WHO WORKS WITH WORDS AND IDEAS RATHER THAN ACTIONS AND THINGS." He traced the growth of influence of American intellectuals to the loss of confidence following Sputnik, when Americans sought expert opinions to surpass the Soviets and to reassure themselves of their global—and moral—superiority.[121]

In the end, no one replaced Moynihan as the Nixon administration's ambas-sador to the intellectuals. While this stemmed in part from Nixon's antipathy to in-tellectuals, it also came about because of the roller coaster ride that Nixon took over the next few years. Heading into the 1972 election, Nixon was riding high, as he crushed liberal North Dakota Senator George McGovern in one of the greatest landslides in American history. McGovern, who was the favorite of the radical anti-war intellectuals, was considered outside the mainstream of the American people. For this reason, Nixon had no need for an emissary among the intellectuals. In fact, he was better off allowing McGovern to maintain the support of the intellectuals while Nixon pointed to that support as a reason for nonintellectuals—the bulk of the country—to stick with Nixon.

In the years following his reelection, Nixon did not focus on reaching out to the intellectuals, largely because he was consumed with Watergate. While doing so might have helped dampen the animosity the intellectual community held toward Nixon in this period, it is unlikely that any amount of effort in wooing academics, or any other constituency, could have saved him from the scandal that ended his presidency.

With Nixon starting in such a deficit with America's intellectuals, there was little Moynihan or anyone else could do to help improve his standing in that community. When Nixon faced the Watergate crisis, intellectuals clamored just as loudly as (if not more loudly than) anyone else for Nixon's head. Yet Moynihan did serve an important purpose. As a liberal antiradical hired by Richard Nixon, he helped shatter some categories and preconceptions regarding intellectuals in America. Furthermore, in the White House, Moynihan helped encourage new types of thinking among Nixon's aides and Moynihan's friends in the academy and the intellectual world. The Nixon–Moynihan alliance helped move disaffected liberal intellectuals to the right and served as an important factor in the creation of a new conservative alternative.

5

BOB GOLDWIN AND THE FORD INTERLUDE

No matter what he accomplished in office, Gerald R. Ford will be remembered as an accidental president. Before replacing Spiro T. Agnew as vice president, Ford had shown little interest in running for national office, let alone the presidency. In fact, Ford was the only person ever to become president without having won anything higher than a local election. Given his general lack of preparedness, it is unsurprising that Ford came into office without a ready slate of intellectuals.

GERALD FORD AND THE ACCIDENTAL PRESIDENCY

Unlike Kennedy, Johnson, and Nixon before him, Gerald Ford lacked a prepackaged reputation regarding his views on intellectuals. A genial, unassuming man, Ford had neither Nixon's and Johnson's ambivalent disdain toward intellectuals nor Kennedy's haughty superiority. Accordingly, he chose an intellectual adviser free of the controversial reputation of a Schlesinger or a Moynihan—former University of Chicago professor Robert Goldwin. At the end of Goldwin's tenure, however, through no fault of Ford's or Goldwin's, the short-lived tradition of relying on one intellectual to reach out to the larger community would be no more.

Goldwin was born in New York on April 16, 1922. World War II delayed his entrance into college, as he served in the U.S. Cavalry from 1942 to 1946. After the war, he earned his B.A. at St. John's College in Annapolis and his master's and doctorate in political science from the University of Chicago in 1963. While at Chicago, Goldwin served as director of research for Charles Percy's failed campaign for governor and also worked on Percy's successful Senate campaign.[1]

From 1960 to 1966, Goldwin was director of the Public Affairs Conference Center in Chicago, where he organized quasi-academic conferences involving academics, politicians, and businessmen. It was at one of these conferences that he met Congressmen Gerald Ford from Michigan and Donald Rumsfeld from Illinois. Goldwin taught at Kenyon College from 1966 to 1969 before moving to St. John's again, where he served as dean from 1969 to 1973. In the same period, Rumsfeld, with whom Goldwin had remained friends, became Nixon's ambassador to NATO in 1973 and hired Goldwin as an assistant. After Nixon resigned, President Ford hired Rumsfeld to replace Alexander Haig as White House chief of staff or, as Ford preferred calling it, staff coordinator.

The Ford administration took a while to get its bearings. The Ford people found that just getting rid of Nixon aides like Haig and speechwriter John McLaughlin was exhausting. With the White House in turmoil, it took the new administration a while to get everything sorted out, and selecting an ambassador to the intellectuals was a relatively low priority. By November 1974, four months after the administration began, the Ford White House was as settled as it was going to get. Rumsfeld persuaded Goldwin to forgo a new position at the University of Pennsylvania and become a special consultant to President Ford.[2]

Although his official title was special consultant, Goldwin had numerous unofficial titles, both in the media and in the White House. Media appellations included "the president's professor" (*Time*), intellectual-in-residence (William Safire), "tutor to the president (*National Journal*), and Gerald Ford's idea broker (*National Observer*). Within the White House, his title varied according to whether the individual in question liked Goldwin. Ford, who liked Goldwin, called Goldwin his "resident intellectual"; speechwriter Robert Hartmann, who did not like him, called Goldwin "Rumsfeld/Cheney's resident 'intellectual.'" Press secretary Ron Nessen rather neutrally called Goldwin "the White House liaison with the academic community." Goldwin, for his part, stuck to the official title, just calling himself special consultant.[3]

According to the announcement of Goldwin's appointment on December 9, he would "work with the Domestic Council and others in the White House to help assure the flow of information, ideas, and suggestions to the President, especially from individuals outside the government." Goldwin was on the lookout for ideas. He had little confidence in getting the ideas he needed from the mainstream academic community. Goldwin openly disassociated himself from the word "intellectual," which he considered "fishy." At the start of his tenure, he told an interviewer, "I think of 'intellectuals' as people who have a real distaste, sometimes even contempt, for the commonsense approach, which is fundamentally the political approach." As a result, he felt that "'intellectuals' don't have much that is helpful to say to people who have to run the government."

According to Goldwin, intellectuals did not "even have much to say to the ordinary citizen, except that 'You have no standards of taste, you don't understand things as they really are, and the only way to have a better society is to reorder it according to our principles rather than yours.'" Goldwin's bitterness toward the American intellectual community stemmed from his feeling that intellectuals looked down on ordinary Americans. Clearly, attitudes had changed since Kennedy had sensed electoral benefits in capturing the intellectuals' imagination in 1960.[4]

Goldwin's first assignment for Ford was, appropriately enough, organizing a private, one-man seminar with neoconservative writer and editor Irving Kristol. Kristol was a frequent intellectual resource for the Ford White House, especially during Goldwin's first months on board. For this first meeting, which was not announced to the press, Goldwin wrote Ford a brief memo detailing Kristol's background and giving Ford some straightforward talking points explaining what they wanted from Kristol. Ford's second point is instructive regarding Goldwin's role: "I've asked Bob Goldwin to invite people like you, who are knowledgeable about matters of importance to the White House, for informal conversation with me and others in the White House." What they were looking for, Goldwin suggested Ford say, were "fresh ideas, new ways of looking at political and social problems."[5]

In their hour-long conversation, Kristol suggested that Ford meet with more than one intellectual at a time. Ford liked the idea, and Goldwin began assembling seminars with multiple scholars. Goldwin's next seminar discussed the national mood. Guests at the seminar included Daniel Boorstin, Martin Diamond, and James Q. Wilson, precisely the kind of conservative academics Moynihan had been urging Nixon to cultivate. The Boorstin–Diamond–Wilson seminar, held on December 9, took place the same day the White House announced Goldwin's appointment to the press. The topics included the upcoming State of the Union address, a request for low-cost ideas, the bicentennial, and the violent crime problem. Goldwin wrote to Rumsfeld that he intended to explain the difference "between the people we hope to bring in to the White House for these conversations and 'intellectuals,' who are not helpful and who will not be invited to participate in these discussions." This distinction demonstrated very early on that Goldwin did not see himself as a liaison to the mainstream intellectual community. He viewed intellectuals with skepticism, if not disdain, for an unwillingness to take what he saw as a commonsense approach to the nation's problems.[6]

At the press briefing announcing both Goldwin's appointment and the Boorstin–Diamond–Wilson dinner, Ford press secretary Ron Nessen explained that Goldwin would "be working with the Domestic Council, and his primary job will be to bring in new ideas and new people into contact with the senior staff

members here and with the President." Nessen joked that Goldwin, in his new capacity, "set up a working dinner tonight for the President with three distinguished
American scholars, or four if you count me." More seriously, but in a way equally
amusing, Nessen responded to a question regarding Ford's curiosity about ideas as
follows: "Ever since he came to office, and even before he came to office, Sarah, the
President always felt a great need to be exposed to ideas."[7]

The next day, Nessen briefed the press on the dinner, explaining that "as
soon as we sat down at the table, the discussion turned to the philosophy of information distribution in America and especially on newspapers as educators of
people. That sort of flowed into a discussion of the mood of the country and a
certain amount of pessimism that seems to be in the country." Nessen said that
Boorstin had "talked about his theory of self-destructing ideals; that is, Americans have always had high ideals and always achieved their ideals. After you have
achieved your ideals, you sort of feel let down and you don't know what to go on
to next." The discussion then moved to the 1950s. Since that time, "there has
been a feeling that the quality of life has not improved for people in America as
much as they had anticipated it would." The participants offered the belief that
the bicentennial would offer an opportunity to "remind Americans that things
have improved a great deal in this country."[8]

Although Nessen was relatively short on specifics, the press briefing and the
media attention disturbed Wilson, who asked Goldwin if he found the subsequent "stories in *Time* and *Newsweek* as troublesome as do I?" Wilson felt that
"if the President is to benefit to the greatest degree from such meetings, those
participating in them should feel that they can speak with utmost candor." Goldwin took care of the problem by forwarding the Wilson note to Nessen, who kept
future summits quieter.[9]

In the first three months of his new job, Goldwin attracted a great deal of media attention, receiving profiles in, among others, the *Chicago Tribune*, *National
Journal*, the *New York Times*, *Newsweek*, *Time*, and the *Washington Star-News*.
In an interview with *Science* magazine soon after his appointment, Goldwin expanded on his new role, explaining that he was supposed to bring interesting
ideas to the attention of Ford and the White House staff. While seminars would
be a part of this process, Goldwin would also send the president and Rumsfeld
memos and articles filled with ideas and policy suggestions. According to Goldwin, he was seeking individuals who were "not the kind of people who think of
calling up the White House when they have an idea; their natural tendency is to
sit down and write an article." Although some of these ideas might have filtered
their way to the president anyway, Goldwin's job was to speed up the process,
as well as make sure that some of the better ideas did not fall through the
cracks.[10]

Fred Barnes noted in the *Washington Star-News* that Goldwin was not looking for "specialists in a single field, but those with broad learning." As Goldwin put it, he was looking for "people who have a very broad view of things, what you might call the presidential viewpoint." This recurring theme of broadness over specialization demonstrated an emerging view among conservatives that American intellectuals were becoming too specialized, at the expense of accessibility.[11]

Goldwin's first few months saw a flurry of activity in the form of seminars, memos to the president, and correspondence with outside intellectuals. As previously noted, a disproportionately large amount of Goldwin's early correspondence came from Kristol. Ford evidently liked Kristol, and Goldwin frequently went to Kristol for advice and personnel recommendations. In late 1974, in the months following Kristol's meeting with Ford, Kristol suggested appointees for Librarian of Congress, three members of the Council of the National Endowment of the Humanities, assistant secretary of state for educational and cultural affairs, and director of the National Institute for Education.[12]

In recommending a Librarian of Congress, Kristol suggested to Goldwin that "it would be nice, if at some moment, you could explain in a few sentences to Don Rumsfeld why it is so important that this job not be turned over to the librarians." Kristol obviously knew that Goldwin had Rumsfeld's ear. Kristol evidently considered cultural positions extremely important reflections of the nation's cultural state and wanted appointees a cut above the average political functionaries.[13]

Clearly, Goldwin liked Kristol, but Kristol also had a following among some of the other senior staffers. In January 1975, Rumsfeld's deputy Richard Cheney wrote to Goldwin: "I greatly appreciate receiving the stuff you've been sending me. . . . Anything that comes in from Kristol or others, I'd love to see." Cheney also suggested bringing in Kristol for specific tasks, telling Goldwin that "it might be a good idea if you sent the Conference Board speech to Irving Kristol and marked for him those portions that relate to his letter on the need to defend the middle class." With this kind of support, it is not surprising that Goldwin felt comfortable asking Kristol for advice on so many subjects.[14]

In early 1975, Kristol, who saw nonliberal intellectuals moving away from universities and toward reliance on foundation largesse, suggested some sort of recognition for what Kristol called "the men who head small and sometimes obscure foundations which support useful research and activities of a kind that the Ford and Rockefeller Foundations take a dim view of." According to Kristol, the foundation heads were "unbeknownst to it, being helpful to this Administration, to the Republican party, and to conservative and moderate enterprise in general." As examples, Kristol went on to list the Smith-Richardson, Merrill, Scaife, Earhart, and Lilly foundations, all of which became crucial in the development of a network of conservative think tanks that the Reagan administration would use so effectively in the 1980s.[15]

Word of Kristol's cooperation spread beyond the White House, leading other intellectuals, such as the Hudson Institute's Herman Kahn, to try to join the action. Kahn wrote to Goldwin rather starkly, saying that he heard "from Irving Kristol that you are in charge of moving intellectual ideas into the White House. I have lots of them. Should we get together?" Goldwin gave Kahn the only possible correct response: "Of course we should get together." This response, while flattering, did not commit Goldwin or Ford to anything. Irrespective of the number of ideas Kahn had, his rather forward missive did not raise him up into the Kristol category.[16]

Another intellectual who wanted to emulate Kristol was Claremont-McKenna professor Harry Jaffa, who, like Goldwin, was a follower of Leo Strauss. However, Jaffa was a West Coast rather than an East Coast Straussian. In addition, while Jaffa was a brilliant scholar and author of the invaluable *Crisis of the House Divided*, he also had a reputation for criticizing his friends far more than his enemies. After Jaffa had written Goldwin a particularly hectoring letter, Goldwin wrote back with a sarcastic reply: "Your letter of December 19 had a slightly complaining tone to it for not getting sufficiently prompt responses or action when you write me. You wrote to me in July 1973 that President Nixon should resign—and he did. What better results can you expect from a single letter?"[17]

Although his letter had a somewhat nasty edge to it, Goldwin's new position protected him from any vitriol in return. Jaffa's reply—which came in five days rather than the month Goldwin took—displayed an uncharacteristically soft touch. First, Jaffa quoted their shared mentor Strauss, who had once joked that "while England slept, and Churchill talked, [New School professor] Ernst Kris silently saved Europe." Jaffa added, almost apologetically, "Had I known that you, armed with my letter, were busy persuading President Nixon to resign, I would not have allowed that complaining tone to creep into my letter!" Jaffa had served as an all-purpose intellectual for Barry Goldwater and had written the famous line "Extremism in the defense of liberty is no vice, and moderation in the pursuit of liberty is no virtue." Now, with Goldwin inside the White House and Jaffa and others anxious to get in, Goldwin was not having any trouble getting letters returned.[18]

While other intellectuals wanted to, and often did, help out Goldwin, Kristol still had the best access. In one memo, Goldwin wrote that "Kristol is the most articulate spokesman today of ideas and themes that are wholly in accord with the spirit and style of the Ford Administration." The piece that prompted this high praise was Kristol's analysis of the American Revolution, which found that America had "much more to be proud of than we seem to realize. The American Revolution was unique because it was so successful." This perspective, like the one prevalent at the Boorstin-Diamond-Wilson dinner, served as an effective counter to the regnant pessimism of the period.[19]

Enamored of Kristol's perspective, Ford's team considered hiring him. Goldwin first raised the possibility in a memo to Rumsfeld and Ford, saying that "this judgment leads me to recommend that an effort be made to find a high-level position in the White House or Administration for Kristol, so that we have the benefits of his intelligence and expressive abilities on a full-time basis." Goldwin also argued that Kristol himself had shown how he could be recruited. According to Goldwin, Kristol had recommended that the administration hire a professor. In doing so, Kristol "assumed that the man would be initially unwilling but then went on to say, 'I see no reason why he should be permitted to languish comfortably up there. It's time he performed some service for this country and I am sure he would do this task extremely well.'" Goldwin then recommended to Rumsfeld "that we say the same thing to Kristol."[20]

As in the Nixon adminstration, this idea never came to anything, probably because of Kristol's same long-standing post–military service promise never again to work for a large organization. Another compelling reason for Kristol's not coming aboard may have been that Goldwin already had the job that might have suited Kristol best. In any event, Kristol continued to serve as what Goldwin called him on another occasion, "the Universal Resource," weighing in favor on issues as diverse as common situs picketing, the earnings limit for senior citizens, and Ford's energy plan.[21]

In addition, Kristol's recommendations on intellectuals were extremely influential. On March 10, 1975, for example, Kristol wrote to Goldwin that he "was chatting on the phone with [University of Toronto professor] Allan Bloom last night and . . . got the distinct impression that he sort of feels left out of things." Kristol explained that he understood the reasons for not having Bloom at one of the seminars, since "no one else would get a chance to put a word in edgewise." Nevertheless, he felt that Bloom deserved something, "given the numbers of splendid young scholars he is turning out, he certainly deserves it." Goldwin wasted no time following through on Kristol's suggestion, sending Bloom a letter requesting that Bloom "write to me from time to time as thoughts occur to you, on any topic of importance that I might adapt and convey to others here in the White House?" While Kristol may not have had an official job in the Ford White House, Goldwin and his colleagues took Kristol's suggestions seriously. With the rise of think tanks and employment opportunities for nonuniversity scholars, access without responsibility became ideal in many ways.[22]

THOUGHTS ON RACE

One issue that preoccupied many nonuniversity scholars, particularly the neoconservatives, during the Ford administration was affirmative action. Affirmative action represented the real divide between liberals, who saw equality of results as the next step in the civil rights battlefield, and the neocons, who strongly supported equal rights but drew the line at government-mandated equal results. The reason the neoconservatives stood at the front line of the debate was that old-line conservatives had lost the battle on civil rights and in general lacked credibility on civil rights issues. As a result, conservatives had trouble making the anti–affirmative action case in the 1970s, and the neoconservatives stepped into the breach.

The seeds of this development had been growing for over a decade. In 1963 Nathan Glazer and Pat Moynihan's *Beyond the Melting Pot* warned of high illegitimacy rates in the black community, a concern repeated by Moynihan in the Johnson administration. In 1970, Moynihan got in trouble again with his infamous "benign neglect" memo. Nixon, in part to allay criticism from the civil rights community, promulgated the Philadelphia Plan, which set affirmative action in motion among the executive agencies. By 1974, without much fanfare or even a vote, affirmative action was well on its way to becoming official U.S. policy, and it seemed that a small but feisty group of neoconservatives stood alone in opposition.[23]

Goldwin was particularly frustrated by the federal government's widespread adoption of affirmative action goals and timetables in hiring, especially since these programs had been put in place without any instruction from Congress. As Goldwin later described it, affirmative action was an example of the all too common phenomenon of "bureaucratic projects acquir[ing] a life of their own, vast programs that have no traceable legislative basis." According to Goldwin, "the affirmative action program has no legislative basis." It started with an executive order that had no details in it other than the phrase "affirmative action." It went on to be adopted by the Department of Labor and then Health, Education, and Welfare. Then it spread to higher education, where its presence most disturbed Goldwin. According to Goldwin, "Everybody knows now what a massive impact that has had on higher education throughout the country, and no one can undo it." A program that began with one executive order developed "a life of its own without ever having been through any kind of congressional hearings, deliberations, debates, votes or anything else that is usually the basis for a large program."[24]

Goldwin made these points to Ford after Ford told Jewish leaders of his "aversion to quotas" and his belief that "the law should be changed." As Goldwin explained, "the source of the 'quota' problem is not to be found in legislation." Rather, the problem came from "the phrase 'goals and timetables,' which occurs in regulations of the Department of Labor and the Department of Health, Education, and Welfare." This phrase came from the agencies' interpretation of President Johnson's Executive Order 11246, even though, Goldwin noted, the "Executive Order does not use the phrase 'goals and timetables,' or anything like it."[25]

Goldwin recommended that Ford could "end the 'quota' problem [by] . . . eliminat[ing] goals from the regulations of Labor and HEW." As Goldwin put it, "Whomever they favor, quotas are quotas and discrimination is discrimination. They should have no place in our laws or regulations."[26]

Unsurprisingly, Kristol often served as Goldwin's guide in this matter as well. Kristol recommended that Goldwin contact UCLA economist Thomas Sowell. Goldwin found Sowell perhaps "the most interesting of Kristol's recommendations" for the position of Librarian of Congress. Goldwin described Sowell as "black, . . . a Ph.D. from the Economics Dept. of the University of Chicago and like that school in his thinking." Goldwin also noted Kristol's view that "Sowell's autobiography, called *Black Education: Myths and Tragedies*, is a wonderful book and recommends it highly." A few months after this conversation, Sowell joined a Ford seminar, along with Gertrude Himmelfarb (Kristol's wife), Ed Banfield, and Herbert Storing.[27]

Sowell criticized affirmative action as unfair to whites and harmful to blacks. He sent Goldwin a research paper he had written on affirmative action, writing in an accompanying letter that "the hard statistics present an even more unfavorable picture than I had expected [of affirmative action], for it is *ineffective* as well as burdensome." Sowell's anti–affirmative action stance harmed him with the liberal black community, which monolithically backed affirmative action and saw opposition, particularly black opposition, as a betrayal. When Ford nominated Sowell for a slot on the Federal Trade Commission, the Congressional black caucus came out in force against him. As Goldwin wrote to Cheney, the members of the black caucus "accuse[d] him of being an Uncle Tom." Goldwin felt that this pressure should not deter the nomination, telling Cheney that it "will redound to the President's credit if we stand *firm* on the nomination." Despite Goldwin's backing, Sowell withdrew his name from consideration, telling Goldwin that he "declined to continue as a nominee for the FTC because I could no longer continue in this costly limbo after losing credence in the reports of the personnel people in the White House."[28]

Goldwin also sought out Nathan Glazer, who was perhaps the leading opponent of affirmative action in the 1970s, as well as one of the most prominent neoconservatives. He had written *Beyond the Melting Pot* with Moynihan and would later coedit *Public Interest* with Kristol. Glazer's book *Affirmative Discrimination* was one of the first full-blown attacks on racial quotas and had a tremendous impact among neoconservatives. Goldwin told Glazer that the book was "a welcome and rational addition to a field which has suffered too long from an excess in irrationality."[29]

Despite Goldwin's abiding interest in the subject, he proved unable to change the direction of U.S. policy or even engage Ford on the issue. Of course, it is perfectly understandable that an administration that never really enjoyed popular support would act warily around this explosive issue. Affirmative action took hold in the bureaucracy quickly, and more popular, more conservative regimes, specifically the Reagan administration but also the Republican Congresses of the 1990s, failed to roll back affirmative action. Furthermore, Ford never really had his heart in it. More than two decades after leaving office, Ford wrote an op-ed piece in the *New York Times* defending the University of Michigan's race-conscious admissions policies, warning that two lawsuits opposing race-conscious admissions "pose a threat to . . . diversity." Ford is not the only one now reconciled to a policy he once opposed. Glazer, once affirmative action's chief enemy, later came out in favor of race-based admissions, arguing that such policies were the only way to ensure that blacks would attend the top schools. Unlike Ford and Glazer, however, Goldwin remained an opponent of affirmative action, but his lone voice failed to do much to stop its practice during the Ford administration.[30]

SPEECHWRITING: THE LONG
NATIONAL NIGHTMARE

Another frustration Goldwin encountered in the Ford White House was the nasty internecine warfare that surrounded the speechwriting process. While Goldwin thrived in the job of setting up seminars for the president and maintaining contact with the leading conservative intellectuals, White House speeches were a minefield of conflicting egos and countervailing interests. Goldwin's frustration was not unique in the Ford White House and was symptomatic of a far greater problem.

Early in the administration, Goldwin complained to Cheney and Rumsfeld that "at 7:30 PM I was asked by Jim Cannon to attempt a complete rewrite of the draft of a Message to Congress, with a deadline of mid-morning the next day." Goldwin dutifully undertook the task and met the deadline, and then "was told it was excellent and would be used, but, as I suspected, another revision was done later the same day and in the end not a word of my effort remained in the text." This kind of immediate demand for a product that is never used is not unusual in politics, but it is frustrating. The reason for telling Cheney and Rumsfeld was "that this assignment forced me to put to one side the other high priority projects both of you had asked me to work on." Goldwin then somewhat naively recommended that "from now on that whenever anyone else asks me to undertake a task I refer them to one you for consideration and approval."[31]

Although Cheney wrote "ok" on the memo, he could not have thought this would solve the problem. The Ford White House had perhaps the most dysfunctional speechwriting operation since Judson Welliver started the White House speechwriting shop in the Harding administration. The primary (although not the sole) reason for this was Robert T. Hartmann.

Hartmann wrote—and fought for—the line "our long national nightmare is over" in Ford's inaugural address. Although he had served as Ford's vice presidential chief of staff, Hartmann did not serve as chief of staff once Ford became president. As Nessen later described Hartmann, "He lost out in the White House power struggle. He took it badly." Hartmann, as counselor to the president and director of the White House speechwriting staff, was supposed to approve every official word that came out of the Ford White House, an enormous and nearly impossible task.[32]

Hartmann was intensely loyal to Ford and correctly saw his closeness to Ford as the source of whatever power he had in the White House. Even after the administration ended, Harmann still felt he needed to prove the closeness of his relationship with Ford. In his memoir, he included an appendix listing the Ford presidential and vice presidential staffs. As if the juxtaposition of the lists did not make the point, he placed black stars next to individuals who had been with Ford before the presidency and underlined the names of those who had served under Nixon, whom Hartmann saw as enemies.[33]

As with all power struggles, the fault was not one-sided. According to Nessen, Rumsfeld "brought order out of anarchy in the Oval Office. But his manner and ambitions sparked rivalries." Memoirs of the Ford administration almost universally note the staff struggles over speechwriting. Cheney later claimed that "one of the problems we always had, frankly, was trying to integrate the speechwriting process with the policy process. And with the political process." National security adviser Brent Scowcroft agreed, saying, "It's one of the things we did the least well." These sentiments led to anti-Hartmann campaigns, as well as retaliatory actions by Hartmann. As Nessen wrote, "Hartmann was a frequent target—and source—of staff sniping, dating from the anti-Haig campaign during Ford's first days in the White House."[34]

Hartmann's manner and speeches irritated Goldwin. As a Rumsfeld hire, Goldwin was loyal to Rumsfeld, which made Goldwin automatically suspicious in Hartmann's eyes. For his part, Goldwin thought of Hartmann as a hack speechwriter, telling one interviewer that "Hartmann saw no need for continuity in a speech. He felt that each sentence had to carry its own weight, and that no overall theme need be developed." Interviewer James Reichley wrote that Goldwin "worked with Hartmann in the White House (or in Hartmann's view, against him)." Goldwin also reflected later on some of the deficiencies of the

White House staff: "Personality clashes were an aspect of the institutional procedures, and if you omit those things you omit a very important part of the description of the Ford White House. I have in mind Robert Hartmann especially, but also other very senior people."[35]

Goldwin felt that Ford's speeches needed more heft and less fluff. After seeing one draft of a Pearl Harbor anniversary speech sent to him by Ford aide Michael Raoul-Duval, Goldwin responded: "This is embarrassing—it's a bit too melodramatic. Since he's speaking in Hawaii, maybe some will want to be grappled with Hula Hoops." On another occasion, Goldwin sent Nessen a column called "Confessions of an Optimist in Time of Crisis" by neoconservative writer Ben Wattenberg. He included a note: "In case you missed it, I send you this excellent article by Wattenberg. It is excellent on three counts: the useful information, the unusual argument, and the upbeat tone. It should be useful for speeches." Nessen—who shared Goldwin's view of Hartmann—praised the article, adding, "I hope the President and his speechwriters are seeing this and other thought provoking articles."[36]

Despite his frustrations with Hartmann, Goldwin did not have operational responsibility for speeches and could do little about the situation. Goldwin seems to have been called in only for the big nationally broadcast speeches, which often tended to be collaborative, and somewhat slapdash, efforts. Nessen reported that Hartmann's draft of a 1975 fireside chat that would lay out Ford's program to the nation was "awful—ten minutes too long, full of clichés, flowery, with the major points blurred." When he reported this to Rumsfeld, Rumsfeld suggested, "Why don't you write the speech?" Nessen did just that, which he saw as "the first challenge to Hartmann's status as Ford's speechwriter." Nessen's draft, however, was not the only challenge, as he found out later that "Rumsfeld had ordered still another draft from Alan Greenspan and Robert Goldwin, the White House liaison with the academic community." The final version, Nessen reported, included "parts of my draft, the Greenspan–Goldwin text and Rumsfeld's ideas," pointedly lacking Hartmann's input. According to Nessen, this kind of haphazard conduct became standard procedure, as "the writing operation was so unreliable that other staff members were quietly recruited to produce presidential speeches and statements."[37]

A similar speech-by-committee approach marked the president's series of bicentennial addresses in July 1976. Goldwin prepared a memo for most of the White House senior staff (not including Hartmann) of bicentennial themes that the White House could use in celebrating the upcoming anniversary. Goldwin's four-point memo stressed the importance of integrating optimism about the future with the founding principles. While the founders had cherished the idea of individual freedom, the two intervening centuries had seen the rise of powerful and at times constructive forces which nevertheless could potentially threaten that freedom. Goldwin wrote that "our task for the third century is to make sure that indi-

vidual freedom is enhanced and not overwhelmed by big government, big industry, mass media, mass education, or any other form of the tyranny of bigness."[38]

At the same time, Hartmann was moving ahead with his own plans for the bicentennial speeches. Hartmann, who claimed he "was hired neither as speech
writer nor press secretary but primarily as an idea man," reached out to the intellectual community for ideas on bicentennial speeches. Hartmann called, "at
Ford's suggestion, Dr. Daniel Boorstin (Librarian of Congress) and Dr. [sic] Irving Kristol and asked them to propose thematic outlines. Then I wrote my own."
Hartmann then "removed the names of the authors, marked with a Roman nu-
meral and on June 8 delivered them to the President." As usual, Hartmann's
paranoia harmed him more than it helped him. As he notes in his memoirs, "In
fooling Ford, I also fooled myself and history. I have lost my code key and cannot match all the names with the numerals."[39]

Hartmann also sought input from "Ford's Yale law professor and LBJ's Under
Secretary of State, Eugene Rostow; President Theodore M. Hesbergh of Notre
Dame; Dr. Martin Diamond of Northern Illinois University; and Dr. Herert Storing
of the University of Chicago." Finally, he "got so bighearted and broad-minded that
I also invited Baroody, Gergen, Goldwin and Marsh to contribute Bicentennial
drafts. Nobody should be able to complain their talents were overlooked."[40]

Goldwin responded to Hartmann's "big-hearted" gesture with a seven-page
memo outlining six speech ideas, including some elaborations on Kristol's memo
to Hartmann. Kristol emphasized that the American Revolution succeeded because of its realism and its universal appeal, an appeal that continued for two centuries via immigration and kinship based on universal political values, not narrow
concerns such as language or religion. Goldwin's memo also added some of his
own ideas, many of them from the larger memo he had distributed earlier, which
served as a draft for a Ford article in *U.S. News and World Report*.[41]

Despite the desultory nature of the process, the product—as Hartmann
called them, "eight good to excellent speeches in five days"—was a success. He
remarked that the "President's Bicentennial speeches, which he conscientiously
rehearsed, did Ford much credit." The president was pleased as well, remembering that "not a single incident marred our festival. The nation's wound had
healed." Although the president's speeches had helped unite the country, they
unfortunately tended to have the opposite effect on his staff.[42]

CONCLUSION: THE THINK TANK BECKONS

The bicentennial project was Goldwin's last major endeavor in the Ford White
House. On September 16, 1976, he submitted his resignation to the president, effective October 30: "After the most rewarding two-year period of my life—thanks

to you, Mr. President—I think the time has come for me to return to more familiar duties outside the government." Goldwin added that he would "always be
grateful for the opportunity that came my way to share in a momentous achievement in American history; I mean your success in lifting American self-respect
from the depths of August 8, 1974, to the heights of July 4, 1976." Goldwin was
not going far; he would be accepting an "appointment to the American Enterprise Institute for Public Policy Research, here in Washington, as Resident
Scholar and Director of Seminar Programs." Goldwin promised to remain
"ready to serve you and your Administration whenever called upon."[43]

Ford accepted the resignation with some flattery of his own, telling Goldwin
that he had "every reason to be proud of your role in facilitating a close and mutually beneficial relationship between the White House and our fellow citizens
engaged in education and the arts." Ford wrote that he was particularly grateful
"for the valuable series of Presidential seminars which you arranged. The opportunity for such candid and stimulating exchanges with many of the leading
thinkers in our country has meant a great deal to me personally and has added
an important dimension to this Administration."[44]

It is fitting that Goldwin, unlike previous academics leaving the White House,
left the administration for a position at a think tank, not a university appointment. This move demonstrated that the world of the intellectuals, particularly
conservative intellectuals, had reoriented itself away from the universities. Student uprisings at Yale, Columbia, and Cornell, among other places, frightened
and repelled many conservative professors. These professors, including Goldwin, Cornell's Walter Berns and Thomas Sowell, and Yale's Robert Bork, rejected the death threats and indifference to academic freedom they saw on campuses and moved to the freer and more politically involved world of the think
tank. The conservative intellectuals who began affiliating with think tanks like
AEI were not political activists, most having shunned politics earlier in their academic careers. The threat posed by the student revolts of the 1960s, however,
changed their minds. Involvement in politics now seemed necessary in order to
protect the universities—and themselves—from threats to the established order.
At the same time, they also had to face the harsh reality that the universities did
not necessarily want them, either. Think tanks, being free from protesting students and hostile colleagues, served as a safe haven for conservative scholars.

Interestingly enough, Gerald Ford, when he left office, also affiliated with a
think tank, also AEI—the first president to do so. Ford's affiliation, although
mainly a nominal one, was another sign of the rise of think tanks. Although
Goldwin may have felt there was nowhere else to go, Ford's move indicated that
think tanks like AEI had attained new stature.

Despite Goldwin's impressive credentials, he served in a more limited role than
his predecessors. Ford used Goldwin as a seminar holder more than a policy ad-

viser, making him more of an idea generator than a policy implementer. In addition to this difference in duties, Goldwin, as a conservative Straussian philosopher, could make no pretense of serving as liaison with his more liberal academic colleagues. The invitees at the Goldwin seminars were mainly conservatives and neoconservatives, many of whom were not on campuses or would be leaving campuses soon. While the number of conservative intellectuals had grown since before the 1960s, they still lacked a discernible presence on most campuses.[45]

In some ways, Goldwin was not the liaison with the traditional academic community, but with what Sidney Blumenthal dubbed the "counterestablishment." While Moynihan had suggested that Nixon seek out new intellectual blood, Goldwin actually went out and brought in Republican intellectuals to consult with the president. This counterestablishment group of intellectuals viewed the mainstream academic and intellectual institutions—the Ford Foundation, Harvard, the *New York Times*—with a mix of envy and disdain, knowing that they and their views were not welcome in these places. The sarcasm regarding these institutions reveals a knowing cynicism far different from Pat Moynihan's frustration with these organizations or Eric Goldman's reverential feelings toward them.

An example of this knowing cynicism can be seen in Goldwin's recollection of a conversation he had with James Q. Wilson. Wilson, co-originator of the "broken windows" theory arguing for a vigilant police response to all crimes, had just assisted Goldwin in preparing a speech for Ford on crime. Responding to the speech, the *New York Times* editorialized that "while the President talked about mandatory jail terms, he neglected to talk about half-way houses, work release programs, or other re-entry programs which might serve to rehabilitate." Wilson, Goldwin, and the other neoconservatives could not stand what they saw as an overly utopian and naïve emphasis on rehabilitation rather than incarceration for criminals, and the editorial incensed Goldwin. He wrote a memo to the file indicating that he "called James Wilson to tell him about the *New York Times* editorial, knowing that Wilson makes it a practice not to read the *New York Times* editorials ('for the sake of his health')." Goldwin's sarcastic aside demonstrates the frustration that neoconservatives felt with the prevailing liberal attitudes of the time, attitudes that they considered soft-headed and divorced from reality as well as from solid social scientific evidence.[46]

Goldwin's disdain for the *New York Times* editorial board was a telling indication of the loss of shared touchstones within the American intellectual community. Cultural and intellectual organs were becoming more polarized—not to mention easier to start and support—and conservatives and liberals began flocking to the outlets that reflected their respective views. A large part of this development stemmed from the fact that conservatives felt shut out of the establishment organs, a slight that people like Irving Kristol tried to rectify by helping fund the growing network of neoconservative scholars, magazines, and think tanks. Conservatives no longer felt at home with the establishment and consequently tried to create their own counterestablishment.

The neoconservatives' disdain for the northeastern intellectual establishment demonstrated their recognition that they would never be part of that establishment, coupled with the confidence that they alone remained devoted to the free exchange of ideas. This attitude was also a precursor to the Reaganite model of conservative intellectuals from conservative institutions as policy experts.

In addition to the impossibility of a conservative serving as an ambassador to the intellectual community-at-large, the Ford administration's tenuous electoral status also diminished Goldwin's role. Largely as a result of the circumstances of Ford's ascendancy, the Ford administration was more reactive than its immediate predecessors, more interested in crisis management than in new initiatives. According to the historian John Greene, "For the most part, Ford's domestic agenda was less an articulated agenda and more an exercise in crisis management—dealing with brush fires in areas such as civil rights, urban issues, and labor problems." This approach often led to unclear staff assignments and confusion regarding responsibilities. Greene added that "depending on the situation, Ford turned to a staff member or a cabinet member to deal with the flare-ups. Depending on the person responsible for the situation, the outcome was different each time." This ad hoc methodology made it difficult for someone like Goldwin to establish a routine relationship with the president.[47]

In addition, Ford, who became president without running for the office, never articulated a vision of what he wanted for the country. When Goldwin tried to get Ford to lay out his vision, he met with indifference if not disinterest. In one incident, Goldwin and Cheney tried to get Ford to provide some guidance for possible themes the administration could follow. In an effort to get Ford to overcome his reticence in discussing ideas, Cheney and Goldwin asked, "What do you wish to be identified with?" Ford's answer, "I like people," failed to provide the guidance they sought.[48]

Ford's affability, while genuine, did not help him establish a serious thematic or intellectual throughline for his administration. During the Ford administration's brief twenty-eight-month tenure, Goldwin tried mightily to plug this hole, as well as help defeat the pervasive national cynicism that followed Nixon's resignation. In this regard, Goldwin kept close tabs on the intellectual community, including the growing body of conservative thinkers. He did not, however, have a strong hand in policy creation. When Goldwin eschewed a return to academia, he marked a crucial turning point in the history of intellectuals and the modern presidency. By opting for a position in the burgeoning Washington think tank community, Goldwin ushered in the beginning of a new era for both liberal and conservative intellectuals in the White House.

6

JIMMY CARTER: DANCING TO HIS OWN TUNE

With Jimmy Carter's ascension to power in the 1976 election, Washington welcomed a true outsider for the first time since intellectuals had entered politics in full force after World War II. Indeed, Carter was the first president since Woodrow Wilson never to have worked in Washington before being elected. Even Wilson, having grown up in Virginia and served as a professor and university president, had a far better understanding of American intellectuals than Carter did.

Furthermore, Carter did not share a political philosophy with any segment of the nation's intellectual or political establishment. Having been elected without their help, he did not feel indebted to either group. Not only was Carter's philosophy sui generis, he felt no real obligation to hire people who might change or represent his philosophy. For this reason, Carter never hired a single intellectual as adviser or ambassador.

JIMMY CARTER'S UNIQUE PHILOSOPHY

For good and for ill, and more than any other modern president, Carter was his own man. He lacked political and intellectual debts, but he also lacked the experiences and unifying insights such debts would have purchased. As Gaddis Smith observed, "There is a very personal quality to his rhetoric, a constant reference back to his own life and his own experience. . . . He was not a widely read or traveled man, and his illustrations, his references, and his comparisons were drawn very largely from his own life."[1]

There is no doubt that Carter was extremely smart. According to Kenneth Morris's insightful *Jimmy Carter: American Moralist*, Carter "was noticeably intelligent and had enormous capacity for information." At the same time, however, "little in his mostly technical education or his practical background as a naval officer and agri-businessman equipped him to grasp the synthesis of abstract ideas that is the hallmark of social and cultural interpretation." Similarly, Burton Kaufman, an extremely sympathetic biographer, found Carter "highly intelligent, intro-spective, and thoughtful, but . . . not ideological, philosophical, or conceptual."[2]

People who worked with Carter agreed. Hamilton Jordan, Carter's chief cam-paign strategist, recalled his first impression of Carter was of "a man of considerable intelligence who had a commonsense approach to Georgia's problems." James Fal-lows, a Carter speechwriter who was hired out of Washington rather than Georgia, described Carter as "a smart man but not an intellectual in the sense of liking the play of ideas, of pushing concepts to their limits to examine their implications." Carter had a high intellect, but he was more of a concrete than an abstract thinker.[3]

To his credit, Carter was an original thinker, one who promulgated his own set of beliefs instead of fitting into an established pattern. This approach offered many advantages while he was running for office—a process Carter called "a graduate course in America." For one thing, someone who eschewed existing ideologies could portray himself as a fresh voice on the campaign trail. Further-more, it made a candidate harder to pin down, and subsequently made it harder to pin a party's unpopular beliefs on such a candidate. Fallows, for example, joined Carter's campaign precisely because the Georgia governor was so hard to type. Fallows recalled that Carter, "alone among candidates, might look past the tired formulas of left and right and offer something new."[4]

Carter intentionally pursued this nonideological approach in the campaign at the request of his advisers, a tight-knit circle of native Georgians known as the Georgia mafia. Atlanta attorney Charlie Kirbo, one of Carter's closest confi-dants, urged him "not to run his campaign on an intellectual approach to issues, but on a restoration of confidence in government." Carter took this advice and, according to Morris, "campaigned on neither issues nor vision." Instead, Carter campaigned by "offering the nation his morality and competence."[5]

While Carter took Kirbo's advice and made the most of it, it is unclear that he could have worked any other way. He was extremely uncomfortable with ideol-ogy and, according to Morris, lacked "a solid intellectual foundation for his po-litical views." To the extent that Carter did have an ideology, it was not detectable along any standard philosophical continuum. Carter's ideology was a combina-tion of southern populism, evangelical Protestantism, progressivism, the civil rights movement, and popular-culture moral sentiments absorbed through mu-sicians like Bob Dylan. As Morris described it, "the result was a synthesis that was at once evangelical, southern, universalistic, contemporary—and quintes-sentially American." Despite its "quintessentially American" nature, this mix was not an intellectual one, and few intellectuals shared his unique viewpoint.[6]

Even if Carter's views had resided in a standard ideological framework, Carter was not that interested. He truly believed that he had something fresh to offer, a unique ideology unavailable in Washington. As Clifton and Pierce Mc-Cleskey explained, "It cannot be too strongly stressed that Carter's 'outsider' approach to the nomination was much more than a campaign ploy or a reflection of his political experience in Georgia."[7]

Carter and his advisers also felt that he could not have been an insider even if he had wanted to be. Fallows recalled that "during the campaign, [Carter] had enjoyed receiving the busloads of eastern experts, wrinkled and cranky after the three-hour ride from Atlanta to Plains—knowing that they'd tell their friends at Brookings and Harvard about the brilliance of the simple country boy, knowing also that they'd call him a dumb southern redneck when he made his first mistake." This tale illustrates many levels of distrust, not only between Carter and the elite intellectuals but also within the minds of Carter and the Georgian mafia of advisers. Carter knew that the northeastern intellectuals would not accept him, so he mocked them for their elitism. This approach is reminiscent of Lyndon Johnson, another southern Democrat who desperately sought intellectuals' approval while he disdained them personally. Even Johnson, however, made more of an effort to get intellectuals to like him than Carter did.[8]

Despite his discomfort with intellectuals, Carter managed to complete the campaign with the general support of the party elites. This was largely due to the efforts of Stuart Eizenstat, the only member of the Georgia mafia with Washington experience. Eizenstat, a Harvard-trained lawyer, had served on Johnson's speechwriting staff before returning to his native Georgia. With Carter, he became issues director for the campaign and later transition coordinator for policy and domestic policy adviser in the White House.

As issues director for the campaign, Eizenstat was responsible for establishing links with intellectuals, which was no mean feat. Carter lacked his own ties with intellectuals, and his long-shot campaign failed to draw in many supporters at first. In their first briefing at the Brookings Institution, arranged by Brookings scholar Henry Owen in 1975, "one of the participants asked what this person was, you know, running for." As Eizenstat recalled, "He couldn't believe that [Carter] was running for President. Not because he wasn't intelligent and didn't seem on the ball but just because nobody had ever heard of him."[9]

Despite these early difficulties, Eizenstat was increasingly successful at recruiting as Carter won more primaries. He "began to cultivate people from around the country who were substantive experts in their field; get ideas from them, get papers from them." As the historian Robert Wood described it, Eizenstat "fulfilled for Carter Sorenson's earlier role with Kennedy." Eizenstat set up campaign task forces for domestic, foreign, and economic policy. The Brookings Institution, the University of Wisconsin, and University of Pennsylvania were important centers for Carter, and his supporters there included Arthur Okun, Charles Schultz, and Donna Shalala.[10]

Carter's reliance on Brookings represented a new phenomenon for a campaign, and the development of the new intellectual model of the think tank technocrat. While Robert Goldwin had started to bring think tank scholars into the White House and had even left the White House for a think tank, Carter's use of Brookings brought technocrats into the process at a far earlier stage. As the number and influence of think tanks grew, the use of think tanks rather than individuals for policy mining made good sense. First, the potential of an organization was available to be harnessed, thereby attenuating the problems of knowledge gaps or personality flaws in an individual. In addition, think tank technocrats are often better suited to policy work than more theoretically minded academics. Finally, think tanks have ideological reputations, and heavy reliance on one organization could help identify a candidate's ideological moorings. In Carter's case Brookings, while on the left, is more of a pragmatic than an ideological institution. In Brookings, Carter, who was trying to run as a pragmatist, not an ideologue, found a good match.

Although Brookings was helpful, Eizenstat was in charge. According to Larry Klein, a University of Pennsylvania economist who worked with the campaign, Eizenstat "ran the intellectuals in the campaign." Klein also noted that "as the campaign progressed, it became more establishment oriented, less radical in ideas, and the influence by academics declined dramatically." Despite Klein's evident disappointment, this shift made sense. As the campaign ended, Carter needed to move beyond campaign mode and adopt a set of governing principles. Carter won the election because of a brilliant campaign staff and a nation that had tired of Watergate. Now the question was whether they could govern.[11]

With the campaign over, Eizenstat settled in as director of domestic policy with a staff of forty-three, mostly lawyers, below him. Eizenstat freely admitted that he "did not often think of advisers with the category of academics in mind." As a result, according to Wood, "although Eizenstat would deny any break with academics or outside experts in general, no major academic figure served as an architect of public policy in the Carter administration." With no major academics, the administration began with Eizenstat as the central policy player, and one of the few staffers with daily access to the president. He brought with him to the White House a one-hundred-page draft plan of the Carter domestic policy agenda. As he would soon find out, though, very little in the Carter administration followed any sort of plan.[12]

GOVERNING OVER CAMPAIGNING

The central irony of the Carter administration was that everything that had been so successful on the campaign trail made life difficult in office. Carter's crack

Theodore White asked Arthur Schlesinger Jr. if his role in the Kennedy White House was as "Philosopher, jester, or technician?"

Princeton professor Eric Goldman found himself in the unfortunate position of suspect to both the Johnson White House and his erstwhile academic colleagues.

Richard Nixon chose Pat Moynihan as his intellectual precisely because Moynihan wrote things that angered the regnant intellectual establishment.

Although Moynihan and civil rights leader Ralph Abernathy managed to smile for the cameras, Moynihan's frankness on issues regarding race often got him into trouble.

Bob Goldwin came to the Ford White House through Don Rumsfeld, pictured on the wall of Goldwin's office at the American Enterprise Institute. (Photograph courtesy of American Enterprise Institute)

Pat Caddell's polling helped put Jimmy Carter in the White House, but his reading of Christopher Lasch's best-selling *Culture of Narcissism* led to the disastrous "malaise" speech. (Photograph courtesy of the Carter Library)

Martin Anderson, shown here in front of the Nixon White House, played an important role for Republican presidential candidates from Nixon to George W. Bush.

Anderson was closest to Ronald Reagan, serving as Reagan's "one-man idea factory."

Jim Pinkerton tried to bring in ideas like the New Paradigm to the first Bush White House, but found himself stymied by OMB Director Richard Darman, who mocked Pinkerton's approach, joking "Brother, can you paradigm?" (Photograph courtesy of Creation Waits Photography)

Bill Galston, shown here with the American Enterprise Institute's Michael Novak, helped pave the path for Bill Clinton's New Democrat campaign in 1992. Galston, like many of his fellow Democratic Leadership Council's allies, took a back seat to traditional party activists in the Clinton White House. (Photograph courtesy of American Enterprise Institute)

Despite having taught Al Gore at Harvard and promoted Gore's career for decades, *New Republic* owner Marty Peretz played a relatively minor role in Gore's 2000 campaign. (Photograph courtesy of Anne Peretz, photographer)

campaign staffers, who had brilliantly executed a plan that took Carter from unknown to president, found themselves far better suited to campaigning than governing. With few exceptions (most notably Jody Powell), the Georgia mafia evac-
uated Washington immediately after the administration ended. Even Carter's
relative anonymity worked against him. With Carter in office, what seemed like
freshness on the campaign trail felt like the morning after a one-night stand. Similarly, Carter's intellectual vagueness, which allowed him to avoid being typed on
the campaign trail, made it hard for him to connect with the ideological allies who
communicate a positive message about a politician to voters and the grass roots.

Carter's staff shared the president's disdain for satisfying ideological allies. As
Carter's secretary of health, education, and welfare Joseph Califano recalled,
"Carter's staff seemed naïve to a fault and appeared to believe the anti-
Washington rhetoric that had carried Carter to the White House." Califano was
right about the staff, but he forgot to add that the president shared their viewpoint.[13]

While Carter's staff had problems with Washington, not all of the difficulties
were their fault. Carter oversaw a national Democratic Party that was in disarray,
with its northern liberal and southern conservative components in regular disagreement. Within a generation, most of the southern conservatives would become Republicans while the Democrats made progress recruiting liberal Republicans in the North and East. In 1976, however, this process was still working
itself out. As Jordan complained, "We . . . had no unifying Democratic consensus,
no program, no set of principles on which a majority of Democrats agreed."[14]

Still, Carter's lack of a discernible ideology did not make things any easier. His
muddled approach frustrated many a party regular. Eric Goldman, who knew
something about idea gathering from his days with Johnson, lamented the lack of
a unifying principle by placing Carter in a historical context. According to Goldman, "Carterism may be totally lacking in the scourging of a Theodore Roosevelt, the cathedral summoning of a Woodrow Wilson, the rollicking iconoclasm
of an FDR. Carterism does not march and it does not sing; it is cautious, muted,
grayish, at times even crabbed."[15]

The harshest assessment of Carter's fuzziness came from a member of his
own staff. In May 1979, James Fallows, after resigning from the administration,
wrote "The Passionless President" for the *Atlantic Monthly*. Califano described
the article as "a tale of incompetence, mediocrity, and sniping on the White
House staff," but it was really much worse than that. Fallows's article challenged
Carter's basic ability and desire to be president in the first place.[16]

Fallows described Carter as selfish and lacking in sophistication, unwilling to
make any effort to learn how to do the job of president effectively. According to
Fallows, Carter lacked "the ability to explain his goals and thereby to offer an object for loyalty larger than himself." As a result, he continued, in perhaps the article's harshest sentence, that "the central idea of the Carter Administration is

Jimmy Carter himself, his own mixture of traits, since the only thing that finally gives coherence to the items of his creed is that he happens to believe them all." Even though Carter might have positions on individual matters, "no one could carry out the Carter program, because Carter has resisted providing the overall guidelines that might explain what his program is." In sum, Fallows found, he "came to think that Carter believes fifty things, but no one thing."[17]

Fallows also spotted a similar weakness among Carter's staff members, whom he found almost completely uninterested in policy. As Fallows described it, "in other administrations, there have been assistants whose interest in policy was faint—Dave Powers for Kennedy, Pa Watson for Roosevelt, Marvin Watson for LBJ—but this time there is almost no one at the upper level (apart from Eizenstat and Brzezinski, the designated hitters for policy) with a serious interest in how the public's business is performed." In addition, he noted that "in two years in the government, I had not one serious or impassioned discussion with a member of the senior staff about what all those government programs meant, which of them, if any, really worked, how the government might be changed." Carter not only lacked a philosophy for himself but seemed unwilling to look for one among his staff. In addition to lacking a prominent intellectual on his staff, Carter presided over an administration with an almost complete absence of policy-interested aides.[18]

Fallows's description of Carter is a devastating one. To Fallows, Carter could not do the one thing that any president must do in order to maintain his hold in a democracy—be able to explain himself to the American people. To be fair to Fallows, he did not just wait until he left the administration to make these complaints. He tried, in vain, to express his concerns while on the staff. In one memo, written to press secretary Jody Powell during the first year of the administration, Fallows asserted that "we have to sell policy, not personality." According to Fallows, the sui generis, noncategorical president needed to get specific on issues and make thoughtful speeches rather than off-the-cuff remarks. Fallows further argued that "we should make these speeches sound as good as possible, they should really be designed to be read rather than heard." Fallows was not just saying this because he was one of the speechwriters; Fallows understood that for an administration to convey its message, it needed to sell that message to "a few tens of thousands of talkative people in journalism, in the universities, in the associations and unions, and in the government itself—for it is these professional opinion brokers who set the tone for how we are perceived by the millions who watch television and read the newspaper and magazines." It is precisely these people, those children of the GI Bill, the new millions who had graduated from college in the 1950s and 1960s, to whom prominent intellectuals as political aides were meant to appeal. Fallows saw that the administration was failing to reach those people in particular, and that these educated elites therefore could not—and would not—preach the gospel of Carter to an increasingly cynical and concerned nation at large.[19]

Fallows knew that he and his fellow speechwriters could not sell the message if they did not themselves understand what it was. As he urged in the memo, "The President should make his reasons clear to those who are helping him explain them." Fallows elaborated, explaining that "no speechwriter can do a decent job if he or she doesn't know what his employer thinks. The earlier the President can let us know his wishes, and the more we're allowed at least to observe the first stages of policy making, the better job we can do in explaining the policy that's finally decided." This memo is remarkable for the starkness with which it made this one central point: Not even his own speechwriters knew where Jimmy Carter stood on the issues.[20]

Unfortunately for the administration, nothing came of this memo, and Fallows took his complaint directly to the "talkative" class that he felt the administration was failing to reach. As Fallows lamented in a subsequent interview, Carter suffered from a form of ideological inertia, strongly resisting almost any kind of change. As Fallows put it, "If there is a single grievous flaw I find in Carter, it is his complacency about the people he has around him and the ideas that come to him. There's no passion in him to find better people, to find better ideas. He is satisfied with those he has." This was an exceptionally dangerous predisposition for a president, especially one who was presiding over a severe and often frightening period of change.[21]

THE MALAISE MORASS

In July 1979, two months after the appearance of Fallows's embarrassing and damaging piece in the *Atlantic*, the Carter administration was reeling. In addition to the growing notion—fostered by the Fallows piece—that the administration did not quite have it together, the nation was also in the midst of a recession and an oil crisis. The administration needed to turn things around, and Carter was, for once, receptive to suggestions.

Carter ended up taking the advice of his pollster, Pat Caddell. Caddell was a twenty-nine-year-old wunderkind who had started his own polling business, Cambridge Survey Research, while a senior in Harvard in 1971. In 1972 he served as McGovern's chief pollster. In that same year, Carter met Hamilton Jordan and Caddell media adviser Gerald Rafshoon at the Democratic National Convention. Four years later he served as Carter's chief campaign pollster and was a member of what *Business Week* called "Carter's brain trust for the campaign." After the 1976 election, Caddell and Rafshoon established offices at 1775

Pennsylvania Avenue, a few blocks from the White House, but continued to advise Carter and participated in the White House's Wednesday strategy meetings.[22]

Caddell's strength was his ability to paint a picture of the national mood based on what Carter called his "remarkably accurate" polls. According to Morris, Caddell, the only non-Georgian in Carter's inner circle, had a talent for a "kind of abstract intellectual meandering that attracted the more practical-minded executive to him." As such, Morris continued, "Caddell remained virtually alone as the administration's point man for ideas, and Carter welcomed his contribution."[23]

Caddell attracted a great deal of media attention during the Carter administration. In addition to his office near the White House, he shared a house with Rafshoon, and then Jordan and Tim Kraft. Caddell's youth and unique appearance also caught reporters' attention. The *National Journal* described Caddell as a Dickensian character with an Eton schoolboy haircut, a "pear-shaped figure draped in Harvard Square three-piece suits." While consulting at the White House, Caddell's other high-profile clients included the Saudi government, which had paid him a controversial $80,000 retainer during the campaign. When asked about the potential for a conflict of interest, press secretary Jody Powell explained simply, "If Caddell and Rafshoon were involved in making policy decisions, there would be a conflict of interest. They are not."[24]

Although Caddell did not have a line position in the White House, there was no gainsaying Caddell's influence. According to the *National Journal*, Caddell "helped persuade Carter to emphasize symbols of security rather than policy moves in the early months of the Administration—what has become known as Caddell's 'style-over-substance' pitch." In addition, Eizenstat, who certainly had policy influence, freely admitted that he and Caddell "talk[ed] all the time," adding that he found Caddell "extremely useful as a substance man."[25]

Most of all, though, the media focused on Caddell's closeness to the president. As political analyst Alan Baron said in *Newsweek*, "No American President, and probably no foreign leader, has relied on a pollster to the degree that Carter does Caddell." Caddell took advantage of this closeness in the spring of 1979 to convince the president that they needed to take drastic action to turn his polls around. On April 23, he wrote a worried memo to the president warning that Carter was heading on a path to lose the 1980 election. A month later, on May 30, Caddell helped arrange a White House dinner with guests such as *Washington Monthly* editor Charles Peters, Jesse Jackson, sociologist Daniel Bell, former Johnson press secretary Bill Moyers, and University of Rochester historian Christopher Lasch. Caddell was most taken with Lasch, the son-in-law of historian Henry Steele Commager and author of the best-selling *The Culture of Narcissism*.[26]

Lasch's book was a depressing look at America in the late 1970s. On the very first page, he warned that America was in a period of "malaise" and suffering from a "crisis of confidence," unlike Henry Luce's evocative description of an American century. In Lasch's analysis, America lacked confidence, the schools were collapsing, and the middle class was beginning to act like the poor by living only for the present. This may have been true for America at the time, but it was certainly not the message the American people wanted to hear from their leaders.[27]

This view, however, appealed to Caddell, a notorious pessimist. Yet Caddell did not just give Carter Lasch's book to present to the nation. Led by Caddell, Carter embarked on a long period of self-reflection and soul-searching in the summer of 1979. The most intense part of this period came in the first two weeks in July, beginning on July 3, when Carter was scheduled to give a speech to the nation on the oil crisis. Caddell convinced Carter to postpone the address and rethink it.

Caddell's idea to cancel the speech met with considerable opposition within the White House, most notably from Eizenstat and Vice President Walter Mondale. While both men felt that postponing the July 3 address added to the atmosphere of crisis in the White House, they also felt that Caddell was taking Carter down the wrong path. According to the journalist Sidney Blumenthal, "Caddell and Vice President Walter Mondale argued heatedly. Caddell demanded a transcendental 'breakthrough' that would recapture the 1976 Carter. Mondale regarded Caddell's semi-mystical talk of a national crisis of the spirit as literally insane." Eizenstat was perhaps even more opposed. He had been working on a standard energy speech and "thought it was a mistake to cancel it and was just as surprised as the next person when I found out that it had been." And he was even more opposed to what happened over the next two weeks.[28]

Carter had gone up to Camp David before the scheduled address armed with a series of polls and a memo from Caddell describing the national mood. According to Carter, Caddell "seemed certain that the problem transcended the simple issue of energy, and applied to the basic relationship between the people and their government and other major institutions; Americans were rapidly losing faith in themselves and in their country." Caddell's advice was "to focus not only on energy, but to think seriously about addressing this more general subject." As for the objections, Carter saw Mondale's position as recalcitrance, recalling that Mondale "was distraught, and could not become reconciled to my abruptly canceling the speech and then methodically bringing in groups of advisers to help me make further plans while the nation was in a quandary about my intentions." Eizenstat, despite his influence, was just a staffer who lost an interstaff struggle.[29]

Based on Caddell's suggestion, Carter "decided to invite to Camp David small groups of key advisers—governors, local officials, members of Congress, executives from business and labor, economists and energy experts, religious leaders, a small group of experienced political advisers, and some of the most senior and respected news reporters"—approximately 130 in all. While Carter found the overall experience to be among the most thought-provoking of his presidency, some of the sessions worked out better than others. As Carter recalled, the session "with the economists was a waste of time; they all expounded their own conflicting theories, and seemed to be unwilling or unable to consider the views of others or to deal in a practical way with the economic problems I was having to face every day."[30]

The goal of the process was to shop a new message to the nation, and a team of Carter speechwriters began working on various drafts. In one memo, Rafshoon described the range of advice to Carter as being "from the extreme optimism of the Vice-President to Stu's desire to have a very substantive speech to Pat's apocalyptic first draft." Rafshoon also put himself in the anti-Caddell camp, warning that "if we give the speech that Caddell has proposed, it will be very counterproductive to what we are trying to do. It could even be a disaster." Rafshoon felt that "people don't want to hear you *talk* about their problems and they certainly don't want to hear you *whine* about them. . . . Leadership begins with a sense of knowing where you're going. The Caddell speech sends all the opposite signals." While he felt that Caddell's speech was "an interesting academic treatise," he cautioned that "people want you to do something, to be a President, to be a leader—not to philosophize about it." Rafshoon, of course, had his own model for the speech—a short, three-part speech, detailing the problem, Carter's program, and America's ability to solve any crisis. In the problem section, Rafshoon did allow that the mood of the country was not good and suggested that "the first one-third should recognize the seriousness of the energy problem and the broader concept of the malaise of the country," demonstrating that the m-word—malaise—was being bandied about the White House.[31]

Rafshoon also recalled that even after the whole team of speechwriters, including Hendrik Hertzberg, Gordon Stewart, Wayne Granquist, and Caddell, finished a draft, Carter "basically rewrote the whole speech." After that, they went back and forth two more times, and the speechwriters "won about 50 percent of our arguments which means that he won 50 percent of his." Then, finally, Carter "made the finishing touches."[32]

The final product, echoing Lasch, was called "Energy and the Crisis of Confidence," was one of the most famous presidential speeches of the century. Carter gave the speech on July 15, watched by 65 million Americans, double the number who had watched previous speeches. Sidney Blumenthal described the speech as Carter coming "down the mountain and deliver[ing] a speech replete with morally uplifting themes." As Eizenstat recalled, the speech married the idea of "this inertia or malaise in America" with the idea that "the way to eliminate it was to find a common mission, a common goal that might be in a common enterprise," namely, "energy security independence."[33]

The nation responded positively to the speech, at first. As Eizenstat recalled, the speech "was initially quite well received," and Carter's poll numbers rose in the immediate aftermath. But not everyone agreed. Califano thought it "was a banal address," written "for Pat Caddell's polls and to manipulate the emotions of the people exposed in them." Immediately after the speech, when Carter asked Califano his opinion, the best Califano could come up with was "it's the best-delivered speech I've seen you give." According to Morris, Robert Bellah, who had been at the White House dinner in May as well as a Camp David session, "hated the malaise speech, and thought it was 'pathetic' attempt at 'morale boosting.'" Teddy Kennedy, who was in the process of challenging Carter for the Democratic nomination in 1980, probably was the one who dubbed the speech "the malaise speech"—even though the word "malaise" did not appear in the text—and the name stuck. In a 1992 episode of *The Simpsons*, a statue of Carter appears with the words "Malaise Forever" sculpted into the pedestal.[34]

After the speech, Carter fired four of his cabinet officers, including Califano, which fostered a sense of crisis and a sense that the White House was not in control of matters. As Eizenstat put it, "Whatever positives came out of that were more than overcome by the negatives which resulted from the way in which the cabinet shake-up was accomplished." By September Carter's approval ratings had sunk to a dismal 19 percent.[35]

With the beginning of the drop in the polls, Carter and Caddell endured relentless attacks in the press. One particularly unfair editorial in *Business Week* complained that "no one in the Administration is making economic policy. Even worse, those who have the President's ear—such as Jordan, the new chief of staff, and pollster Patrick Caddell—know nothing about economic policy." Today, Carter is often remembered mainly for the malaise speech, and this is unfair. The speech was not as bad as is commonly believed, and it was initially successful in raising Carter's approval ratings. And in fairness, Carter certainly faced a number of other crises and problems that contributed to his defeat for reelection the next year. But Carter was not blameless, either. In failing to articulate a clearly defined ideology, Carter allowed himself to be defined by that one speech, something a politician should never do, no matter how good the speech may be.[36]

Caddell was not fully at fault, either. He described to Blumenthal how he tried to work with the White House policy makers "to develop themes for the 1980 race." When he asked the question, What is our vision of the future? Caddell found that "in the White House there was silence, shrugged shoulders up and down the line." This silence is reminiscent of President Ford's weak response that he wanted to be remembered for liking people. The voters sensed this and voted out both administrations. According to Blumenthal, the "principal lesson

Caddell learned from Carter's loss to Reagan was that we have to campaign on principles and ideas. Reagan is a man of convictions and belief. You can only best him when you put forward ideas that you fervently believe." As two writers from *Newsweek* put it, "Caddell's findings become Carter's philosophy." Unfortunately for Carter, Caddell's findings revealed that the American people lacked confidence in their leader, which was a poor philosophy on which to run a reelection campaign. Carter and Caddell, who offered Carter's own quirky belief system and Caddell's reliance on polls, could not respond to Reagan's campaign of principles and ideas, even though Caddell believed them to be unpopular ideas.[37]

In analyzing the Caddell method, Blumenthal felt that "the weakness of Caddell's intellectual method is that one cannot adduce an ideology from studying the short-term anxieties of the electorate, however useful that study may be for designing particular campaigns." Similarly, the weakness of the Carter method was that the American people were never able to adduce an ideology from Carter until the malaise speech, when they did not like what they heard.[38]

In fact, this problem continued to haunt Carter throughout his 1980 reelection campaign. In July 1980, a year after the malaise speech, speechwriter Bernard Aronson fretted over Carter's inability to express his ideology in his speeches. Aronson wrote a memo in response to Jack Watson, Jordan's replacement as chief of staff, who had, according to Aronson, asked staffers "to submit ideas about how to solve what he called the 'presentation' problem—the fact that Carter's public image is so much poorer than his performance or record deserves." Although he gamely tried to address the problem, Aronson recognized that "after trying as a presidential speechwriter to put these thoughts into practice and failing, I have no illusions about the dimensions of the challenge." The real problem was that "fundamentally, these—or any other ideas for themes—can only be successful if the President adopts them as a point of view; it is not something a speechwriter can accomplish." Aronson understood that speeches cannot provide much unless the writers receive clear direction from the top. The Carter administration continually failed to provide that direction, and the speechwriters, talented though they were, could not create a presidential rhetoric that articulated Jimmy Carter's worldview.[39]

Jimmy Carter was the first president since Kennedy who did not have a full-time ambassador to intellectuals on staff and he suffered as a result: Carter felt the absence of a one-man lightning rod for ideas. While previous administrations learned that having an intellectual on board was no panacea, Carter was the first president to learn that not having such a staffer to help shape and define the administration's mission could be damaging. In a postaffluent, increasingly educated society, an administration could not long survive if no one knew what it

7

REAGAN AND THE RISE OF THE CONSERVATIVE INTELLECTUAL

Jimmy Carter did not need an intellectual on staff: his belief system was so idiosyncratic that nobody other than he could possibly understand or articulate what he wanted. Unfortunately for Carter, after four years of his administration, the American people did not understand him, either. Oddly enough, Ronald Reagan also had no use for a specific emissary to the intellectuals—for precisely the opposite reason.

RONALD REAGAN WAS HIS OWN BAROMETER

Ronald Reagan wore his vision on his sleeve. Many disagreed with him, but everybody knew what he believed. Reagan was an unabashed conservative and was not shy about it. Furthermore, Reagan the candidate and Reagan the president both believed what Reagan the governor and even Reagan the spokesman for General Electric believed. As Dinesh D'Souza put it, "Reagan's public philosophy, elaborated over two decades, was so well known that any competent person could say with a high degree of accuracy how the president would respond to a particular initiative."[1]

Reagan supporters and opponents alike agreed that Reagan's philosophy was public and had been so for a long time. David Stockman, who served as Reagan's director of the Office of Management and Budget, called him "ancient ideologically," a comment that seemed to refer both to his positions and how long Reagan had held them. As Bernard Aronson, a Carter speechwriter, described it, Reagan was "a man whose basic speech has not changed in two decades."

Aronson saw this as a terrible weakness, but, he added during the 1980 campaign, "Incredibly, Ronald Reagan . . . has positioned himself as the more dynamic candidate." Aronson recognized that Reagan was doing something right and recommended to his boss that "what we need first is a presidential rhetoric that describes and defines the world as Jimmy Carter sees it." Of course, if voters did not understand the world as Carter saw it by 1980, they were never going to do so.[2]

It was Carter's very fuzziness that paved the way for Reagan. As Reagan speechwriter Peggy Noonan explained it, "There was no Reagan without Carter. Only four years of steady decline and lack of clarity could have lurched the country over to this—this actor." Despite the controversial nature of Reagan's conservatism and the fact that Reagan's advisers tried to soft-pedal his ideology, Reagan's clarity of vision composed part of his appeal to the electorate in 1980. Reagan's strength was in his ability to articulate and make palatable a philosophy that the nation's political elites had long denigrated.[3]

Reagan's victory, however, was far more than just a reaction against Carter's lack of vision. Reagan benefited from a cresting wave of conservatism that was sweeping away tired liberal ideas that had gone unchallenged for too long. As Noonan described it, "People were thinking. That doesn't quite express it. People were driving intellectual bulldozers and knocking down rotting old ideas." Martin Anderson, one of Reagan's chief policy advisers, also used a shifting-ground metaphor, describing Reagan's election as "something in scope and power equivalent to an intellectual earthquake that would shake the political establishment of the United States—and the world—for some time to come."[4]

Reagan's election was certainly part of a larger movement. American conservatism, famously dismissed by Lionel Trilling in 1950 as a series "of irritable mental gestures which seem to resemble ideas," had overtaken liberalism from behind. As Gregg Easterbrook wrote in the *Atlantic* during the Reagan administration, "In vigor, freshness, and appeal, market-oriented theories have surpassed government-oriented theories at every turn. This feat has been accomplished in the main by circumventing the expected source of intellectual developments—the universities." Furthermore, conservatism's triumph benefited from the help of some of Trilling's former students and disciples, like the neoconservatives Irving Kristol and Norman Podhoretz.[5]

Martin Anderson described conservative ascendancy as the "logical outgrowth of policy ideas and political forces set in motion during the 1950s and 1960s, ideas and forces that gathered strength and speed during the 1970s, then achieved political power during the 1980s, and promise to dominate national policy in the United States for the remainder of the twentieth century." This movement gained strength from its diverse elements, all of which were reacting against traditional, tired liberalism. These elements, Anderson continued, included:

> the traditional Republicans and the old conservatives who formed its core; the libertarians who gave it consistency and sharply defined goals . . . the neoconservatives whose desertion from the Left seemed to confirm the validity of the movement and who infused that movement with new intellectual vigor; the New Right with their political enthusiasm and persistence; and the Moral Majority with their large numbers and moral certitude.[6]

The various elements of this movement saw Reagan's election as a victory for the movement as a whole, in a way that the left never saw a victory in Carter's election four years earlier. Carter had run selling himself as his chief asset. Reagan, in contrast, ran as a spokesman for a movement and, ironically, was more successful personally than Carter had been at the same time.

In the same way that the right saw Reagan's election as a win for its ideas, the left recognized the 1980 election as a loss. Professor and Democratic activist Robert Reich told Richard Reeves that "what the Republicans accomplished during the last fifteen years was a triumph of ideas, an intellectual victory." The main fruit of that victory, Reich explained, was that conservatives had "shifted the burden of proof onto government." Bill Galston, another professor-cum-Democratic activist, rejected the notion that Reagan lacked ideas, explaining that "there were ideas in the Reagan campaign last time. That's how he won, on the strength of ideas." Galston, trying to motivate his party to turn things around for the 1984 election, warned, "It's almost impossible to overrate the importance of ideas in politics."[7]

Other Democrats expressed similar frustrations. Pat Moynihan, elected senator from New York in 1976, complained that "the Republican party simply left us behind. They became the party of ideas and we were left, in Lord Macauley's phrase, 'The Stupid Party.'" Walter Mondale, after leaving the vice presidency in 1981, declared his intention to go off and think for a year. After chronicling all of these depressed liberals, Reeves observed that the Democrats "had set the agenda for fifty years; now they didn't know where they were going anymore." The left's vocalization of its sense of loss only added to the right's feelings of triumph.[8]

While Reagan won the presidency as the representative of a newly vibrant conservative movement, knowing what he thought and running an idea-based campaign by no means made Reagan an intellectual. On this score, no one had any illusions. As Reagan biographer Lou Cannon described it, "Even some of Reagan's friends and supporters on the right had their doubts about his intellectual candlepower." According to journalists Rowland Evans and Robert

Novak, neoconservative thinker Norman Podhoretz "liked Reagan when he met him in 1980 but had to attest that he certainly was no intellectual." Dinesh D'Souza, who could not have been a more sympathetic biographer, wrote that "even though [Reagan] was the most ideological man to occupy the White House in half a century, he was the furthest thing from an intellectual." Reagan, for his part, understood that not being an intellectual had its advantages.[9]

Reagan, of course, had his defenders as well. Although he was not an intellectual, he had ideas and he knew how to communicate them. As the Georgetown University professor and Reagan's UN ambassador Jeane Kirkpatrick put it, "He was not an intellectual, not a professor, [and] not a journalist—but he was a person who communicated." Reagan and his staff, both in the campaign and in the administration, were at least as concerned about communicating ideas as they were about the ideas themselves. As Don Regan, Reagan's Treasury secretary and later his chief of staff, recalled, "No government in history can have been more sensitive to the media, or more driven by the printed word and the television image, than the Reagan Administration." While the comment's tone was in line with the rest of Regan's bitter memoir, it demonstrates the understanding the administration—and especially the president—had for the importance of communicating ideas as well as just having them.[10]

Reagan's White House aides consistently stressed the importance of having Reagan communicate his message. As White House political director Lyn Nofziger wrote in a memo to chief of staff James Baker and deputy chief of staff Michael Deaver, "The great communicator needs to communicate." Given this premise, Nofziger continued, "it is necessary for the President to go around the media directly to the people." This recommendation was precisely the opposite of James Fallows's suggestion to Carter about communicating his message. Fallows had thought that Carter needed to spread his message to "a few tens of thousands of talkative people in journalism, in the universities, in the associations and unions, and in the government itself. . . . [the] professional opinion brokers who set the tone for how we are perceived by the millions who watch television and read the newspaper and magazines." Nofziger, in contrast, recommended the opposite approach. Fallows's elites knew what Reagan thought and generally disapproved. Nofziger argued that Reagan needed to circumvent these elites and go straight to the people with his message.[11]

Reagan's aides recognized that they had a tremendous asset in Reagan, and they sought to take full advantage of that asset. White House communications aide David Gergen summarized Reagan's abilities, saying, "He has spoken to the American people through prime time television more often and more effectively than any other President." Reagan was much better in this sense than any of his immediate predecessors. As Gergen concluded, "Ronald Reagan is making more use of 'the bully pulpit' of the Presidency than almost any of his predecessors—and again, with greater effect." It is hard to imagine such a memo in the Carter or Ford White Houses, both of which had weak communications strategies and principals who lacked clear vision.[12]

Traditionally, the task of a public intellectual in the White House was twofold: first, to help signal where the president stood on an ideological scale and, second, to shore up support among the intellectual community, an increasingly important interest group, if not for their numbers then for the volume of their voices. Of course, these two tasks were linked. Signaling that the president stood with intellectuals shored up relations with them, and it had the added advantage of encouraging coopted intellectuals to write more favorably about the administration.

Neither of these models fit Reagan's needs. With Reagan's strong sense of vision, and his skill in communicating his vision, he did not need an intellectual to explain where he stood. In addition, since mainstream academics and intellectuals had little regard for Reagan, he did not try to use intellectuals to appeal to American academics. As Jay Winik described Reagan's elite opponents, "countless magazine articles portrayed him as lazy and out of touch, academics scoffed at his reluctance to read every position paper and master the fine print of every policy detail, and a dismissive press quoted legions of think tank experts and activists denouncing his work habits and policies." Reaching out to these unstinting adversaries would not have changed intellectual opposition to him, and it might have backfired among the smaller but loyal group of conservative intellectuals who did like Reagan.[13]

Intellectual antipathy toward a Republican president was not unique to Reagan. As Theodore White explained, "the thinking and scholarly classes had in 1913 begun to abandon the Republicans, a party founded by thinking men, for Democratic Professor Woodrow Wilson." But opposition to Reagan surpassed the standard intellectual disdain for Republicans.[14]

Despite not needing an intellectual for any of the traditional reasons, Reagan nevertheless made use of what White called a developing "corps of intellectual outriders, absent in Republican politics since Theodore Roosevelt had given up the White House seventy-two years earlier." Reagan developed relations with a host of conservative intellectuals, but because he knew so strongly what he believed, he did not really need any one of them. As a result, Reagan did not have any one intellectual aide. What he often did need, however, were detail experts. In his campaign and later in his administration, Reagan used conservative intellectuals in line positions, where they could handle the fine points. He did not need them for the message or to tell him what he believed. He needed them to help show him how to carry out what he believed.[15]

REAGAN'S ONE-MAN THINK TANK

The most prominent among Reagan's intellectuals was economist Martin Anderson, who took a leave from Stanford's Hoover Institution to join the campaign. An aide to Arthur Burns in the Nixon White House, Anderson served as both issues director and coordinator of outside intellectual talent for the Reagan campaign. He was no stranger to campaigns, either, having directed policy research in the 1968 Nixon campaign.

Anderson learned the importance of ideas in politics early in his career. During the Nixon campaign, he "learned that policy advisers from the intellectual world could be a tremendous asset to a campaign." In subsequent years, Anderson became more convinced of this fact, observing that "ideas are the key to creating policy, but people are the key to implementing that policy." Anderson believed that ideas represented the first element in a process by which policy came about. Anderson saw this process as one in which "ideas come out of the intellectual world, are transformed by the world of presidential campaigns into items on the national policy agenda, and then how those ideas become law in Washington, D.C., and govern us and affect our daily lives."[16]

Anderson first joined Reagan's camp in 1975 and engaged in what he called "a systematic effort to introduce the nation's best economists to Reagan." This effort was in turn "part of a more general effort to recruit an army of intellectuals to advise and counsel Reagan on the entire range of policy issues." As part of this effort, Anderson brought together "461 of America's top intellectuals," to that point "the largest and most distinguished group of intellectuals ever assembled for an American political campaign." In many ways, this effort reaped the harvest that Moynihan and Goldman sowed in trying to develop neoconservative and conservative alternatives to the regnant liberalism on American campuses.[17]

Anderson collected his policy experts painstakingly; as he described it, "To get people to serve, I telephoned most of them personally." Seventeen scholars from Hoover alone signed up with the Reagan task forces. Anderson then organized them into issue areas, where they created both a formidable policy operation and a shadow government that was able to slide into the administration after Reagan's victory.[18]

Anderson also helped focus Reagan intellectually. Anderson's first memo to Reagan, Policy Memorandum No. 1, laid out the key themes of the Reagan campaign, which became the key themes of the Reagan administration. These themes included conquering inflation, lowering tax rates, indexing tax brackets, cutting spending, and jump-starting economic growth. While Reagan believed in all of these things generally, Anderson focused all of these ideas into a coherent economic program, one the subsequent administration would try to follow.[19]

Although Anderson felt close to Reagan, he had no illusions of indispensability. When campaign manager John Sears, a relative newcomer to the Reagan entourage, set up an alternative Washington policy shop to Anderson's California operation, Anderson quit the campaign in protest, and Reagan batted nary an eye. According to Evans and Novak, Sears was glad to see Anderson go, as he had complained that Anderson had "closed his mind to new ideas and was not fulfilling his mission of discovering exciting new positions for the candidate." When Sears later overreached by trying to fire Reagan confidant Ed Meese and was in turn fired by Reagan, Anderson returned and continued collecting ideas and intellectuals as before.[20]

THINK TANKS DEFINE THE AGENDA

Even before the 1980 campaign began in earnest, Anderson worked on creating a policy agenda for Reagan. While he was still at Hoover, Anderson suggested (and later served as the chief compiler for) a draft agenda for a Republican president, "an 868-page anthology entitled *The United States in the 1980s*." Anderson later counted "seventeen of the people who contributed to or advised on the book [and] held important positions in the Reagan administration." The book so closely mirrored Reagan's thinking that, according to journalist Sidney Blumenthal, years later, when Reagan was president and Mikhail Gorbachev leader of the Soviet Union, "Gorbachev seemed to regard the anthology by the conservative think tank as the product of an American equivalent of the Soviet Politburo, a document with the force of an official directive."[21]

Another think tank book that had an important impact on the Reagan administration was *Mandate for Leadership*, the Heritage Foundation's agenda anthology. Heritage was a different kind of think tank, founded in 1973 exclusively to influence Capitol Hill, to fill what Blumenthal called "the desperate daily need for intellectual meat to feed the hearings, the speeches, the unrelenting policy grinder." According to Heritage founder Edwin J. Feulner, its mission was to be "an activist version of Brookings."[22]

Mandate for Leadership filled the new administration's need for meat as well. According to Feulner, "Seven days after the election, we met with Martin Anderson, Dick Allen, Ed Meese and others in the basement of the Hay-Adams and we delivered them the first draft copies of 'Mandate for Leadership.'" Seen as the "bible of the Reagan transition," *Mandate for Leadership* became a prized possession in Washington, even making the *Washington Post* best-seller list. The new president gave a copy of the book to each of his cabinet members as a starting point for what they should accomplish.[23]

The book grew out of the Heritage attempt to answer the question, What is the conservative agenda, particularly for the "first one hundred days" of a Republican administration? Heritage assembled a few hundred experts to answer the question. As Feulner saw it, the Reagan administration would be a struggle "between those who have done their homework and are ready with imaginative ideas, and those who try to hide their intellectual poverty behind a facade of once-fashionable liberal clichés." In Washington during the early days of the Reagan administration, reading *Mandate* counted as doing homework.[24]

The growth of institutions like Hoover and Heritage, along with the American Enterprise Institute, represented an important shift in American intellectual life. As social scientist Everett Carll Ladd documented, humanities and social science professors at research universities were—and probably still are—much more liberal than professors in the hard sciences and the population at large. With liberals dominating the academy, conservatives felt excluded. As a result, think tanks became alternate homes for conservative scholars, places where they could develop policies, compare ideas, and wait for opportunities to go into government so they could implement those policies.[25]

These think tanks became a crucial element of the Reagan revolution. Reeves described the difference between Republicans and Democrats as follows: "While the Democratic Party depended intellectually on the ideas of the New Deal and the hit-or-miss work of liberal authors and academics, Republicans institutionalized the business of political thinking and the marketing of policy ideas." In the period leading up to Reagan's election, Reeves explained, "dozens of conservative institutions staffed with aggressive scholars, researchers and pamphleteers . . . pulled together and honed a coherent set of ideas, a view of America and the world that was persuasively articulated by Reagan." As the leftist journalist John B. Judis put it, "conservatives . . . developed a political and governing elite capable of sustaining the movement."[26]

Both Reeves and Judis displayed more than a touch of jealousy at what the right accomplished. While Reeves and his allies maintained their stronghold in what he called the "hit-or-miss" world of the academy, liberals envied the efficiency with which conservatives went about their business. Conservatism's rise followed the model laid out by the theory of late industrialization, in which latecomers develop an industrial base without the inefficiencies of the early developers. While liberals became academics and then learned that they could influence policy, conservatives lagged and then developed a successful operation designed specifically for influencing policy.

With books like *Mandate for Leadership* and *The United States in the 1980s*, the Reagan administration did not need anyone to find ideas for it. All the ideas had been laid out already. The administration needed the people populating the think tanks to implement those ideas; for their part, Feulner and his allies were eager to help in order to ensure that Reagan stuck to the plan in the face of establishment opposition. As Feulner warned, *Mandate for Leadership*'s "proposals were not well received by that segment of the political establishment whose main preoccupation since the election of Ronald Reagan has been to reinterpret the election results as a victory for 'pragmatism' over 'ideology.'" Feulner claimed that these people, "the self-appointed guardians of political fashion, whom Irving Kristol has called 'the new class,' advise the new President to 'avoid ideology,' which roughly translates into an admonition to reject any substantive changes in the direction of government."[27]

Feulner did his best to ensure that this New Class mentality did not creep into the new administration. Heritage set up an operation to help staff the administration, hoping to guarantee that only conservatives received important positions. As Judis noted, Heritage's "computerized personnel office, manned by Louis Cordia, former deputy director of the Environmental Protection Agency, funneled conservative professionals into government jobs." Heritage recommended many candidates, and none came more highly recommended than those who arrived with either a letter or phone call from Feulner vouching for them. While intellectuals composed only a tiny percentage of those hired through this process, the process itself had its roots in the conservative intellectual movement.[28]

INSIDE THE WHITE HOUSE

While Heritage worked from the outside to maintain the administration's ideological purity, Anderson worked from within to ensure that the administration remained committed to Reagan's conservative principles. Anderson was more of a scholar than an implementer. Once inside the White House, as assistant to the president for policy development, his role changed; while he could have been considered the campaign's intellectual, he did become the White House's intellectual. Part of this stemmed from Anderson's own success. Not only were Reagan's positions staked out on most issues, but Anderson had already had his say on the staffing of the administration, both affirmatively and negatively. For example, at the chairmanship of the Council of Economic Advisers, Anderson pushed hard for Murray Weidenbaum, head of the Center for the Study of American Business at Washington University in St. Louis. Anderson said he supported Weidenbaum because Weidenbaum had a pragmatic streak, and "the last thing we needed was a brilliant academic theorist who had no appreciation for the reality of Washington and the stakes involved." In addition, Anderson had been walking a fine line between supply-side and non-supply-side theorists, or so-called traditionalists, and Weidenbaum did not fall neatly into either camp.[29]

Anderson could also veto individuals, as he did in the case of Chester "Checker" Finn as assistant secretary of education. According to Evans and Novak, Anderson, who had seen his mentor Burns lose battle after battle in the Nixon White House to Pat Moynihan, was determined not to let another Moynihan gain a foothold in the Reagan White House. To prevent that, "he quietly exercised a veto on anybody who had been closely associated with Moynihan," such as Finn, a former Moynihan aide.[30]

As the preceding incidents demonstrate, Anderson held a great deal of power in staffing the administration, and staffing it in a conservative way. This made Anderson a powerful influence over the administration's day-to-day decisions. According to Morton Blackwell, a movement conservative who worked in the White House, "the most important achievement of this Administration is the literally hundreds and hundreds of appointees who share the President's philosophy who have been credentialed in Government. For conservatives, this is the great watershed." But on issues besides personnel, Anderson brought a nonconfrontational approach with him into the White House. His general attitude was, "We know where Reagan has been, what he's said, what the history is." Given this explicit and public expression of the administration's position on most issues, "As long as the departments and agencies are moving in that direction, excellent. We do not want to fight with them. It is very easy for the White House staff to get into a position where you begin to compete with the departments and agencies and you look at them as adversaries. That is the dumbest thing in the world." In this way, according to Robert Pear of the *New York Times*, Anderson kept "an eye on emerging policies to ensure that they conform with Mr. Reagan's views." This approach made Anderson the "White House's intellectual gatekeeper," who "provide[d] intellectual underpinnings for Mr. Reagan's positions."[31]

Within the White House, Anderson played the role of what Ed Meese called the "conscience of the administration." Anderson "served as a member of each of the councils dealing with Domestic and economic policy. He served, in a sense, as the President's 'quality assurance' representative, raising questions when policy proposals seemed to diverge from Reagan's objectives." According to Pear, Anderson, "the White House's intellectual-in-residence," deserved credit for the fact that "President Reagan has adhered more closely to his campaign promises than other chief executives."[32]

Despite Anderson's influence over the administration's philosophical bent, he never emerged as a central power broker. Part of the reason for this was structural. The most important power centers in the administration were David Stockman's

Office of Management and Budget and the Legislative Strategy Group, a new organization chaired by chief of staff James Baker. As David Stockman, a member of the LSG, somewhat arrogantly put it, "The LSG was, in fact, the very top of the heap in the whole of Washington." With LSG and OMB regnant, Anderson's Office of Policy Development was relegated to a supporting role.[33]

But another reason for the development of Anderson's role was Anderson himself. Anderson, subject to one of the administration's rampant leaks, was accused of being "more a scholar than a manager." When confronted with this revelation by a reporter, Anderson did not disagree. In fact, he actively disliked being a manager, explaining that "the idea of having a lot of people working for me and controlling them is not my idea of fun."[34]

In addition to not taking a serious managerial role, Anderson also refrained from bringing in new ideas for the administration. According to Lou Cannon, Anderson "did not see his role as that of an innovator of a host of new policy proposals." Instead, Anderson saw OPD as "'an implementer' of basic Reagan economic policies." As Anderson later recalled, "We weren't developing policy; we were trying to figure out how to implement policy. That was the key." This position made a great deal of sense, as Reagan already knew what he wanted, and the biggest obstacle to accomplishing Reagan's agenda was a lack of time. Anderson wisely recognized this and did not seek new initiatives, instead focusing on accomplishing Reagan's long-standing goals.[35]

For his part, Anderson did not mind the perception that he was out of the loop, explaining that "as long as OMB and the [LSG] are doing something I don't have to do, that's fine with me—more power to them." This did not mean that Anderson was passive. As he noted, "when they're doing something I don't agree with, that's when I get involved." For example, when attorney general William French Smith broached the idea of a national identity card at a cabinet meeting, the libertarian-leaning Anderson quickly stepped in and quashed the idea.[36]

Unsurprisingly, Anderson did not last long in the Reagan White House, quitting after just one year in order to return to Hoover and work on his book, *Revolution*. (He had already declined the position of vice chair at the Federal Reserve, a position taken by Alan Greenspan.) Some of Washington's conventional wisdom watchers saw Anderson's departure as a victory for the pragmatists over the conservatives, or the traditional economists over the supply-siders. Ann Crittenden of the *New York Times* opined that, with Anderson's departure, "economic policy has been returned to traditional conservatives—officials who are managers and pragmatists rather than theorists."[37]

Anderson, however, felt comfortable that he had fulfilled his role as "keeper of the sacred scrolls." As he told Crittenden when he left, "Ronald Reagan is still surrounded by people who are philosophically at one with him. The policies that were set in the first year of the Administration—federalism, a stronger defense, less government spending—will be followed. It's just the tactics that have changed." Anderson had helped Reagan attain the White House, had placed conservatives who agreed with the Reagan philosophy in key administration posts, and had, in his one year in the White House, helped set the ideological tone for the administration. With all that accomplished, and especially with the administration focusing more on policy implementation than development, Anderson did not really need to stay any longer in the administration.[38]

Anderson's analysis was generally correct. While Baker and his allies ran the White House, they ran it in a conservative way. Being pragmatists meant that they made necessary compromises with a Democratic House of Representatives, compromises that purists like Anderson found distasteful. But the policies they pursued were generally conservative ones, as Reagan's conservatism laid out a clearly marked path for others to follow.

In the years following Anderson's departure, the administration continued along the same path Reagan had established from the start. This happened, in large part, because the administration had hired literally dozens of scholars from the newly emergent conservative think tanks. As Stockman described it, Reagan "conveyed the impression that since we all knew what needed to be done, we should simply get on with the job." Mike Deaver had a similar understanding, explaining that it was "Reagan's force and style that moved the governorship and the presidency. . . . He was at the center of what made things work, what moved things." With Reagan serving as the touchstone for an administration filled with alumni of conservative think tanks, the Heritage Foundation estimated that "60% of the policy recommendations in Mandate [For Leadership] I were adopted."[39]

Reagan speechwriter Peggy Noonan, in her savvy memoir of her time in the Reagan White House, cites her conversation with "a smart and sophisticated man" who also worked in the White House to explain how Reagan administered. According to Noonan's friend, Reagan did not rule as much as "the idea of Reagan ruled." In this model, "everybody around [Reagan] had a good idea of who he was and what he would do. He'd been in public life for twenty years, they knew what he stood for." Of course, some people adhered to the model better than others. As Noonan explained, "There were those who read the book, and those who'd seen the picture. Stockman, Darman, Marty Anderson—they'd read the book; they had an elaborate and detached sense of who the president was and what was going on." Evans and Novak had a similar theory: "Because Reagan came to office with a driving ideology that informed his every action, and which demanded compliance by his colleagues in government, his administration was uniquely different. Ronald Reagan was the administration."[40]

CONSERVATISM IN THE OUT YEARS

While Reagan succeeded in unifying conservatism and making it triumphant, conservatism's very successes caused problems of their own. Just as liberalism had expanded to the point where no one intellectual could speak for liberalism, conservatism, even though the intellectual community at large saw it as just emerging, had already grown too big to stand without internal divisions. Anderson adumbrated this problem in his description of all the different strands of conservatism that Reagan had brought together. In acknowledging that Reagan's skill united all of these elements, Anderson made the implicit point that without such skills, these movements would return to standing alone.

One early indication of possible rifts in the new conservative family came in 1981, in the debate over the head of the National Endowment for the Humanities. Melville Bradford, a well-known conservative historian from the University of Dallas, seemed poised to get the job. Instead, an unknown philosophy professor named William Bennett landed the position. At the time, Bennett was serving as director of the National Center of the Humanities in North Carolina, a position he inherited when the previous director died unexpectedly. Bennett owed both his jobs at the NEH and the National Center to patronage from the neoconservative, or ex-Democratic, wing of the Republican party. Gertrude Himmelfarb, the wife of Irving Kristol and a prominent historian, had recommended Bennett for the job as the assistant director at NCH. And numerous neoconservatives, including Kristol, pushed successfully for Bennett's appointment to NEH. While Bennett won the battle, many old-line conservatives—who viewed the neoconservatives as well-funded Johnny-come-latelies—harbored grudges about the incident for a long time to come.[41]

The truth was that all of the elements that helped put Reagan in the White House could not stay united forever. Even Anderson's unwillingness to bring in Finn because of Finn's Moynihan connections highlighted early cracks in the dam. Conservative intellectuals were certainly fortunate that they had Reagan as a unifying figure. Reaganism *was* conservatism in the Reagan years, in a way that Carterism, Clintonism, or Johnsonism were never liberalism.

This development served Reagan well; he did not need any one intellectual to demonstrate where he stood. It did not, however, hold together conservatism in his aftermath. After Reagan—and, to be fair, after the Cold War—conservatism had a much harder time explaining its core principles.

Reagan was also well served by Anderson, who was a unifying figure in that he was not a neoconservative, but rather a longtime Republican who had served in the Nixon administration. Working at Hoover, however, a think tank at least sympathetic to neoconservatives, allowed Anderson to avoid that dichotomy. He was also able to blur the differences between supply-siders and non-supply-siders, although he complains that he was unfairly labeled as an antisupply-sider. Even so, Anderson did not last long in the administration, helping staff the administration and then returning to academic life, where he felt more comfortable. Reagan, for all his unifying skill, also inhabited a fortunate moment of unity before conservatism felt fully comfortable on its own.

In the years after Reagan, conservative intellectuals broke up into frequently fighting camps, making it hard for conservatives to agree on a candidate and hard for candidates themselves to agree on any one intellectual. While Reagan was president, however, conservative intellectuals generally agreed to back Reagan, just as liberals united in disdain for him. The strong and for the most part unwavering feelings Reagan brought to the surface among intellectuals of left and right alike explained why Reagan did not need a goodwill ambassador among America's intellectual elites. Both sides had already made up their minds on the subject.

8

GEORGE BUSH:
SEARCHING FOR THE
"VISION THING"

George Bush had a problem. He was less ideological than Ronald Reagan, and he wanted a less ideological administration than Reagan's had been. Unfortunately, by toning down Reagan's conservative message, Bush opened himself up to a media barrage of accusations that he had no agenda, no philosophy. But when he picked an issue on which to take a stand, the same pundits called him overly conservative and accused him of exploiting an issue for political purposes. Bush spent much of his administration between the rock of being a weather vane and the hard place of not having any ideas. Once trapped in this media-created paradigm, Bush found it extremely difficult to escape.

Bush's aides exacerbated the problem. Those who lacked ideas and initiative dominated the administration, while those who had ideas found themselves ignored or, worse, stifled. Although the Bush administration appointed some intellectuals to White House positions, it did not select a public intellectual for a high-profile position. William Kristol, perhaps the best-known intellectual in the administration, served as chief of staff for Vice President Dan Quayle but did not advise the president and frequently clashed with Bush's advisers. Another intellectually minded aide, Jim Pinkerton, proposed a series of ideas known as the New Paradigm but found his plans blocked by Richard Darman, Bush's budget director, who mocked Pinkerton's plan by quipping, "Brother, can you paradigm?" And domestic policy adviser Roger Porter, a professor at Harvard's John F. Kennedy School of Government, developed a reputation among his aides for chasing ideas away from rather than into the Oval Office.[1]

Given a poor contrast with Reagan and given a White House staff where those with power lacked vision and those with vision lacked power, Bush also had a hard time expressing his own beliefs. It is unsurprising that the media and the public perceived Bush as devoid of vision. Yet this perception is unfair to Bush, whose vision was more evident in his Gulf War victory than any of his legislative initiatives. The war with Iraq helped usher in a decade of low oil prices, world stability with the United States as the international peace guarantor, and the economic boom of the 1990s, effectively making it a successful domestic vision. Bush's real problem was his inability—or his refusal—to articulate this vision, a task that could have been made immeasurably easier by employing some kind of intellectual surrogate.

THE CONTRAST WITH REAGAN

Bush's contrast with Reagan stemmed from both inherent and studied factors. Nothing could hide the fact that Bush was very different from Reagan. Bush lacked both the fervor of Reagan's beliefs and the clarity of his expression. Bush aide Charlie Kolb compared the difference between Bush and Reagan to Isaiah Berlin's distinction between the fox—who knows many things—and the hedgehog—who doggedly pursues one true thing. Reagan, Kolb felt, was "unmistakably a hedgehog—someone who lived by a "single, central vision, one system more or less coherent or articulate, in terms of which they understand, think and feel." Bush, in contrast, was all fox, a man who would "pursue many ends, often unrelated and even contradictory, connected, if at all, only in some de facto way." The way this played out in their respective administrations was that Reagan "had a clearly defined roadmap of where he wanted to go and what he wanted to accomplish," while Bush "replaced substance with form."[2]

Reagan's Treasury secretary and later chief of staff Don Regan discerned the difference between Reagan and Bush in their choice of reading material, noting that Reagan generally recited passages from the conservative *Washington Times*, while Bush usually quoted the *New York Times*, adding "this is a big difference." Another reading-related distinction lay in reading itself. While Martin Anderson called Reagan a "closet bookworm," Bush joked with journalists about his lack of interest in reading. *Time* reporters Michael Duffy and Dan Goodgame quoted Bush's own description of his 1991 vacation plans as "a good deal of golf . . . a good deal of tennis, a good deal of horseshoes, a good deal of fishing, a good deal of running—and some reading. I have to throw that in for the intellectuals out there." As David Brooks observed in reviewing Bush's collection of letters written during his career in public life, Bush, "while bright . . . doesn't have an intellectual bone in his body." The Bush White House reflected its principal. While Reagan liked intellectuals and liked having them around him, Kolb found the Bush White House "borderline anti-intellectual."[3]

Bush did not derive his worldview from books but from his understanding of Washington, from the people he knew, from the process of governing. In all of these areas, he far surpassed Reagan. Reagan saw Washington from an outsider's perspective, while Bush knew the town like an insider. This fact is hardly surprising, given that Reagan, like Carter before him, had never lived in Washington before being inaugurated as president. Bush, however, lived in Washington almost exclusively from 1966 through his election as president, leaving only to serve as head of the U.S. consulate in Communist China and as the U.S. delegate to the United Nations in New York. Outside of two terms as a congressman from Houston, all of Bush's political positions had been appointive, not elective.

The contrast between Reagan the outsider and Bush the insider was perhaps the biggest difference between the two politicians. As Duffy and Goodgame observed, "It was Reagan's ideology and his outsider status that lay behind his confrontational style and his demands for fundamental change." Bush, in contrast, "had no interest in changing the world." While Reagan famously told Americans in his inaugural address that government was the problem, not the solution, to their problems, Bush began his 1988 campaign by saying, "I do not hate government."[4]

Bill Kristol, who served under both Reagan and Bush, explained that "Bush really was a creature of Washington and didn't like the idea of populist pressure on Congress or on the executive branch. Reagan was the opposite. He always understood himself to be, whatever the self-deception and whatever the limitations, basically a populist spokesman for the people against the establishment." Whatever else he was, George Bush could not plausibly claim to be antiestablishment.[5]

In sum, even Bush's many friends admitted that he lacked a discernible ideology. Duffy and Goodgame quote an anonymous friend of the president as saying, "Loyalty is his ideology, his vision." The British observers Colin Campbell and Bert A. Rockman explained Bush to their countrymen by calling him "a Tory," not "a neoconservative or a Reaganite." As such, Bush "is not turned on by ideas, but he is equally not turned off by them either." Comparing him with Carter, they observed that "Bush is more comfortable with facts than with theories, a virtue perhaps for decision making and a liability for cultivating party passions." As a result of these inherent differences, Campbell and Rockman found, "We all knew what Ronald Reagan wanted: less, except for the military. But we do not really know what George Bush wants."[6]

Recognizing the inherent differences between him and his predecessor, Bush intentionally ran an operation that was very different from Reagan's. With respect to speechwriting, Mark Rozell found that "Bush was acutely aware that he lacked Reagan's skills and he refused advice to be more dramatic—more "Reaganesque"—in his presentations." Bush knew he "lacked a Reaganesque flair for speech and did not inspire people the way in which his predecessor did." Bush's lack of flair led to an oft noted disdain for his speechwriters, in contrast to the near reverence shown them in the Reagan administration. Under Reagan, Kolb recalled, speechwriting "had been a center of ideological ferment inside the White House, a focal point for the debate over presidential policy." Bush preferred anonymous wordsmiths, toiling out of sight, removed from whatever meager discussion of issues might be occurring, while crafting passionless prose to convey the message handed to them. As a result, Kolb felt, "Bush saw little need for speeches to explain much of anything. His public remarks lacked content, depth, inspiration, and, frequently, even elementary grammar."[7]

While Kolb's comments stem from a certain bitterness as a staffer frustrated with his superiors, many other commentators have observed that Bush wanted a less influential speechwriting department than Reagan had. Rozell notes that Bush would "delete rhetorical flourishes from speech drafts and explain that he did not want to sound too much like Reagan." John Podhoretz, one of the Reaganites in the Bush White House, complained that Bush "kicked the speechwriting department out of its nice digs . . . decreed that speechwriters would no longer be allowed to eat in the White House Mess, and limited the top salary for speechwriters to $40,000."[8]

Even Bush loyalist Boyden Gray, who rarely had an unkind word to say about the president, acknowledged that the speechwriting staff lacked the status of Reagan's writers. According to Gray, "the speech writers, with all due respect, were not of the same caliber as their predecessors in Bush's office when he was vice president, and their absence did affect his ability to communicate." Whatever the reasons for the difference between the Bush and Reagan speechwriting operations, the two administrations clearly treated speechwriting differently. Kenneth Thompson unearthed the following statistic: "Reagan gave about 180 speeches a year and had nine speechwriters, while Bush gave up to 400 speeches a year but had only five speechwriters."[9]

According to Reagan biographer Lou Cannon, "what George Bush dismissed as 'the vision thing' was for Reagan the central purpose of the presidency." Despite Cannon's critique, Bush's move away from Reagan was part of a conscious effort. According to Duffy and Goodgame, Robert Teeter, Bush's pollster, "realized that the nation was alienated by the excesses of the Reagan era but recognized that it was also unwilling to embrace the Democratic alternative. He felt that the public wanted only a minor course correction." Teeter's polling also revealed that while the public worried about debt, education, and the environment, Americans also "feared . . . any sweeping attempt by Washington to address these and other issues might only make things worse." This realization led to a deliberate attempt to create a nonideological, relatively unambitious presidency.[10]

The public diffidence stemmed partly from the fact that the situation had changed vastly between 1980 and 1988. While Bush was running for president, the Cold War was winding down. The Berlin Wall fell early in his presidency, ending the Cold War that had dominated American foreign policy for four decades.

On the domestic front, America seemed to be in far better shape than it had been eight years earlier. The American economy had recovered from the disasters of the late 1970s and early 1980s, tempered by a sobering stock market dip in October 1987. In addition, the Iran–Contra affair had dampened the public desire for an overly ambitious agenda. As the 1980s drew to a close, the American people seemed wholly uninterested in activist government. As Bush said in his inaugural address, "The old solution, the old way, was to think that public money alone could end these problems. But we have learned that that is not so."[11]

In addition to a diffident public, Bush faced a divided Republican Party, unsure of its agenda in the post-Reagan era. In many ways the Republicans were victims of their own successes. While Reagan was president, the Republican Party stood for whatever Reagan said it did. After Reagan, however, the picture became far less clear. The post-Reagan conservative movement was deeply split, comprising evangelical Christians, libertarians, paleoconservatives, and neoconservatives. All of them had agreed with Reagan on the prosecution of the Cold War, but otherwise they had very different views of what Reagan stood for. Bush could not have kept all of these disparate elements satisfied even if he had wanted to.

Overall, the fractured nature of conservatism probably helped Bush more than it hurt him. With the split movement having trouble articulating where it wanted to go, Bush encountered less of a need to pursue an overarching goal or policy. This served Bush's nature well. As Bush stated at the start of his 1988 campaign: "I am a practical man. I like what's real. I'm not much for the airy and the abstract. I like what works. I am not a mystic, and I do not yearn to lead a crusade."[12]

THE VISION THING

Despite, or perhaps because of, his efforts to distance himself from Reagan, Bush could never avoid the obvious comparisons with Reagan. Given this context, Bush faced a lose-lose scenario. If he had followed Reagan's views, he would have been criticized for being a wimp or a Reagan lackey. But breaking from Reagan carried its own set of dangers. As Chase Untermeyer, a long-time Bush ally, explained, "If he had articulated a different vision for his administration, perhaps people would have had grounds to say he was trying to betray Reagan."[13]

Largely because of this contrast, Bush found himself tagged early and forever with the reputation as having "no vision." Bush's own rhetoric, or lack thereof, played a key role in establishing this reputation. At the beginning of 1987, *Time*'s Robert Ajemian reported that a friend of Bush advised the vice president to spend some time at Camp David figuring out "where he wanted to take the country." Bush's response: "Oh, the vision thing." Once Bush made the mistake of referring to his relative incoherence as "the vision thing," journalists pounced on the infelicitous phrase as a shorthand description of Bush's views and later of his presidency.[14]

Of course, Bush was not the only 1988 candidate who had trouble articulating his views. As Bill Schneider wrote, "Dole calls it 'the V word,' while Bush awkwardly refers to 'the vision thing.'" Bush, however, won, and this one ill-conceived phrase rapidly colored everything Bush did. The consistency with which the press hewed to this message was remarkable. No politician, not Reagan, not Clinton, not even Roosevelt, could ever have stuck to any one message as well as the press stuck to the message that Bush lacked "the vision thing."[15]

The problem of the campaign continued throughout the Bush presidency. Immediately after Bush's victory, journalists began describing "Bush as a man with no agenda, no 'vision' for the nation's future." This label came at Bush from every side, liberals and conservatives, print media and television, administration allies and opponents on the hill.[16]

Once the Beltway hardened on the view of Bush as visionless, he could never shake it. As Barbara Hinckley described matters in her book, *The Symbolic Presidency*, "During the first months of George Bush's presidency, the press criticized the lack of 'vision' in his speeches, the absence of a clear sense of direction in his leadership, and his low public profile." Even before the election took place, Ken Walsh of *U.S. News and World Report* concluded that Bush's "content-free campaign" would limit Bush to what he called "the passive mandate." Other journalists did not take much more time to come to the same conclusion. By March 1989, Ann Devroy and David Hoffman of the *Washington Post* called the Bush administration "a ship without a rudder." As his vice president, Dan Quayle, learned, once the media begin to pile on, wriggling free from reporters' universal conclusion is nearly impossible.[17]

Among the talking head set, nearly all of them, whatever their politics, believed that George Bush had no vision to offer the American people. By March, one day's *Hotline*, an influential Beltway compilation of daily news stories and television talk show highlights, listed no less than five different pundits expressing different versions of the same theme: George Bush had no agenda. George Will referred to "a Bush presidency hollow at its moral center." Pat Buchanan opined that a tombstone reading "'Here lies our education president,' doesn't quite cut it." David Broder wrote that Bush faced "questions about the scope, direction and pace of his presidency that neither he nor anyone else can definitively set to rest at this point." Kevin Phillips wrote that neither Congress nor the president had any "larger vision or philosophy." And Cal Thomas explained that looking beyond the "transition fog" of the Bush administration, "one sees only more fog."[18]

Of course, Bush could not blame the media entirely for his reputation. Even his own administration appointees had trouble explaining what Bush represented. One Bush official said, "If you asked sophisticated voters, if you held a gun to their heads and said, 'Tell me four things George Bush is for, or you die,' they couldn't tell you." Similarly, Bush aide Jim Pinkerton, when told that Bush approved of the administration's progress on cutting down leaks, complained that "the reason there are no leaks is easy to understand: There's nothing to leak."[19]

Bush compounded this problem when he was unable to explain his goals. As Fred Barnes wrote in the *New Republic*, Bush suffered from "moderate Republican's disease: he has nothing to say." At one point, Bush could not tell a reporter a single goal he wanted to accomplish, instead responding with a rambling 150-word muddle mentioning the economy, drug-free schools, Head Start, and big government, concluding, "So when I talk about education, I'm talking about all those things." In his autobiography, Bush covered the question about his vision by asserting, "It was all there in everything I'd said as a candidate and done in nearly twenty years of public life." While Bush may have felt that this covered all the bases, it clearly did not satisfy his critics. As Kerry Mullins and Aaron Wildavsky asked, "What is one to think of a president who, after some thirty-odd years in politics, has few apparent policy preferences?" While Bush thought his career in politics had answered the question, most observers felt that his career had raised more questions than answers.[20]

THE BUSH TEAM

In staffing his administration, Bush primarily chose aides like himself: smart, competent, and dedicated to public service, but not overly ideological. The Bush transition collected sixteen thousand résumés, and, according to George Hackett of *Newsweek*, primarily chose "pragmatic problem solvers" over "ideological cowboys." Ann Devroy quoted one transition official as saying, "Our people don't have agendas. They have mortgages. They want jobs."[21]

Even if Bush's mortgage holders had been more proactive, the administration provided little room for ideological innovation. In addition to Bush's discomfort with the vision question, chief of staff John Sununu and Office of Management and Budget director Richard Darman—both pragmatists—maintained tight control over all aspects of domestic policy with bullying and intimidation tactics. As press secretary Marlin Fitzwater explained, "Sununu's staff meetings were a farce in which no one said anything for fear of being publicly humiliated by Sununu or Dick Darman."[22]

Analysts and participants alike agreed that Sununu and Darman dominated policy making in the Bush White House. Republican Congressman Vin Weber noted that "when you ask how to influence decision-making in the Bush White House, it's always the same answer: Sununu." Political scientist Dilys Hill concluded that "the President's image in domestic affairs was as the captor of his top aides—particularly Sununu and Darman—who dominated decisions. John Podhoretz put it more simply: with respect to domestic policy, "Sununu and Darman and their trusted aides were the loop." The two men possessed most of the power in the Bush White House and felt no need to share it with anyone else.[23]

One result of the Sununu–Darman axis is that Bush used the White House staff as an idea-generating body less than other presidents did. As David Mervin points out, Bush began his administration with only thirteen assistants to the president, compared with twenty-two for Reagan before him and twenty for Clinton after. In Mervin's interpretation, "As an unambitious, conservative, guardian president with a limited agenda, an aversion to image-making and a distaste for florid speech-making, Bush had less need of an extensive staff." The Bush staff lacked the Reaganites' zeal, and the few Reaganites on staff felt uncomfortable. According to Rozell, when Bush did bring in some Reaganites such as Podhoretz, Andrew Ferguson, and Tony Snow in 1991 and 1992, "they came in feeling a little bit out of place in the Bush White House because they were Reaganites and they felt that Bush had not lived up to their belief that George Bush was elected to a third Reagan term."[24]

Overall, Podhoretz felt, the Bush "White House staff, almost every member of which had been hired by Sununu himself, was astoundingly mediocre—politically shortsighted, ideologically deprived, inclined to elevate the importance of the trivial and discount the significant." Podhoretz's analysis may be unfair. As a Reaganite, Podhoretz was predisposed to dislike Bush and his staff. Furthermore, his memoir demonstrates his feeling that vocal conservatives received a raw deal from the Bush White House. Nevertheless, Podhoretz was certainly correct that the Bush White House was reactive rather than proactive and that most of the initiative was stifled by Darman and Sununu. As Joel Aberbach described it, "Bush and his key appointees . . . have much in common with stereotypical bureaucrats, pragmatism, lack of an overall vision (the vision thing) and an affection for governing."[25]

Although Darman and Sununu ran herd over a generally submissive White House staff, there were a few aides who had the potential to serve as idea men or as ambassador to the intellectual community. Given Bush's discomfort with articulating a larger vision, he could have used the help in formulating his goals for his presidency. Unsurprisingly, no one ever emerged in the role.

The most likely candidate for an agenda setter in the Bush White House was Roger Porter, assistant to the president for economic and domestic policy, the first person ever to possess both portfolios. Porter, a professor at Harvard's Kennedy School, had served in both the Ford and Reagan administrations and had written a book about his experiences under Ford, *Economic Policy Making in the White House*. Although not quite prominent enough to be considered a public intellectual, Porter did have an independent academic reputation before coming to the White House.

Porter worked extremely hard, practically living in the White House during his tenure. He was also willing to cover up for weaknesses elsewhere in the administration. The administration held a two-day governors' summit on education in September 1989. Logically, education secretary Lauro Cavazos should have been the point man for such an event. Unfortunately, Cavazos was an ineffective holdover from the Reagan administration, and Bush did not trust him to get the job done. Consequently, Porter organized the summit behind the scenes, and the summit received relatively good press. ABC's Bill Blakemore reported that after the summit, "Even the skeptics among the governors are now saying that it appears they are getting an education president." The next year, when Bush finally fired Cavazos, Porter's name appeared on the short list for replacements, although the position ultimately went to Lamar Alexander.[26]

Aside from filling in for semiabsent cabinet secretaries, Porter had the difficult job of assembling ideas for the administration's domestic initiatives. For most of the administration, this was the quietest front, but in 1992, with the memories of the Gulf War receding and the recession dominating media attention, Porter brought forth a number of policy packages to demonstrate the Bush agenda. Susan Page of *Newsday* commented that the various packages Porter presented demonstrated "the disarray that has enveloped the White House." Ann Devroy reported the joke that reporters were calling Bush the environmental president "because he loves recycling so much."[27]

While Porter encountered most of his problems from his bosses and those outside the White House, he also faced some serious trouble from subordinates. Porter received universally bad reviews from other staffers in the White House. Charles Kolb devoted most of his book to criticizing what he saw as Porter's ineffectiveness, complaining that Porter was "a most important player in the Bush White House, not so much for what he did as for what he chose not to do." Podhoretz referred to Porter as "a man of almost infinite limits." Fitzwater, more of a peer than a junior, who was far less of a Reaganite than either Kolb or Podhoretz, wrote that "Porter was an academic, a student of the game, a staffer who had worked for three presidents but never really understood the combination of special interests, public opinion, and party politics that dictate so many decisions in Washington."[28]

Unlike Kolb or Podhoretz, Fitzwater did not seem to hold a grudge against Porter. Nevertheless, Fitzwater provided perhaps the harshest depiction of Porter, recounting how Porter's Office of Policy Development was responsible for writing all White House fact sheets, despite the fact that "Roger couldn't write his name in less than three pages." As a result, Fitzwater and other senior staffers had to "teach political fact sheet writing to a tenured professor of government at Harvard University who had already written two books on the presidency."[29]

According to Andrew Card, who served as deputy chief of staff under Sununu, Porter's operation served more as a research center or think tank than a policy implementation office. While Porter joined with Sununu and White House Counsel Boyden Gray in the late night discussions that formed the basis for the Clean Air Act, as Card notes, "Porter was more the clerk in that process, with the policy direction coming significantly from Sununu and Gray." Porter also had similar troubles with Darman, as he "was frequently cut out of the process in a Machiavellian way by Darman." All in all, Gray concluded, Porter languished on the sidelines of policy making, as "Darman and Sununu often conveniently kept Porter out of the game."[30]

As Card notes, while OPD's secondary role may have stemmed partly from Porter's cautious nature, Porter's real problem was the same one faced by the rest of the White House staff. According to almost every account, Darman and Sununu dominated the policy debate in the White House, and they browbeat anyone who tried to break their dominance or even provide a different perspective. While Porter's ineffectiveness clearly frustrated activist staffers like Kolb, the Darman–Sununu stranglehold over policy placed additional limits on Porter's ability to get things done.

Whatever the reason for Porter's passivity, the fact remains that he never established OPD as an important power center in the Bush White House. Just as Martin Anderson found that the LSG, with Baker and Stockman, became the crucial power center in the Reagan White House, the Sununu–Darman axis dominated discussion under Bush. And later in the administration, when Bush felt unhappy with the drift of his domestic policy, he brought in agriculture secretary Clayton Yeutter to serve as domestic policy czar over Porter, leaving him even further out of the decision-making process. In the ultimate indignity, Yeutter even relieved Porter of his office.

Another OPD staffer who chafed under Porter's passivity and Sununu and Darman's aggressiveness was Jim Pinkerton. Pinkerton was a Stanford graduate who had played an invaluable role as an opposition researcher during the presidential campaign—having discovered Willie Horton, the dangerous prisoner Governor Dukakis furloughed.

In the White House, Pinkerton often overshadowed Porter, which made Pinkerton, the deputy assistant to the president for policy planning, a threat to Porter and an annoyance to Darman. David Mervin called Pinkerton "the closest in the Bush White House to an intellectual in residence." Similarly, Duffy and Goodgame referred to him as the "White House idea man." Clearly very smart and interested in ideas, Pinkerton lacked an independent intellectual reputation predating his time in the White House and therefore could not serve as an ambassador to the intellectual community. Since Porter did not act as a public idea broker, and with no other intellectuals on the Bush staff, the role of idea man fell to Pinkerton by default.[31]

Responding to the perceived domestic policy vacuum, Pinkerton advocated an empowerment agenda that he deemed the New Paradigm. The New Paradigm comprised programs designed to promote individual choice and decentralized government—school vouchers, empowerment zones for inner cities, and welfare reform. While Pinkerton and a few others—Kolb, HUD secretary Jack Kemp, vice presidential chief of staff Bill Kristol—saw the New Paradigm as a possible organizing principle for Bush domestic policy, Darman rejected the idea out of hand. In a speech before the Council for Excellence in Government, Darman derided the New Paradigm, calling it neo-neo-ism and questioning the premise that it was either new or a paradigm. The very phrase made him think, "Brother, can you paradigm?" While the New Paradigm never went far during the Bush administration, many of the New Paradigm ideas reappeared a few years later in Newt Gingrich's "Contract with America."

PARADIGMLESS DRIFT

With Darman's rejection of the New Paradigm ideas, the Bush administration was left once again with the perception of not having an agenda. Darman's and Sununu's proudest achievement was their 1990 negotiation of a budget deal with Democratic congressional leaders. The deal, designed to reduce the budget deficit, contained spending caps to limit outlays as well as revenue raisers in the form of a tax increase. This deal violated the central promise of Bush's campaign, the famous "Read my lips: No new taxes" pledge. Darman and Sununu felt that the deal's spending restrictions made violating the tax promise worthwhile. The media, not to mention the American people, focused solely on the broken promise, adding to the perception of a directionless administration.

In addition to suffering in the media, the shift on taxes really hurt Bush among conservatives. Conservatives had long suspected Bush, although Bush's pledge had helped alleviate their concerns during the 1988 election. When it became clear during the budget negotiations that Bush would back a tax hike, Congressman Newt Gingrich deserted the administration negotiators and helped lead the fight against the administration's deal in Congress. Later, after the deal passed, National Republican Congressional Committee head Ed Rollins angered Bush by advising conservative members to run against the administration in the 1990 elections. Rollins lost his job over the incident, and conservatives continued to feel betrayed by Bush.

Breaking the tax pledge, losing the conservatives, and rejecting the New Paradigm agenda did not hurt Bush initially. Buoyed by the Gulf War victory against Iraq, Bush's approval ratings reached a high of 91 percent in mid-1991. Unfortunately for Bush, the postwar high plummeted as the nation sank into a recession in 1991–1992. During this recession, many reporters and pundits began citing Kevin Philips's influential 1990 book, *The Politics of Rich and Poor: Wealth and the American Electorate in the Reagan Aftermath*. Philips, a former campaign strategist for Nixon, argued that under Reagan, America saw "the sums of wealth quietly intensify, [and] the sums involved took a mega-leap." This new concentration of wealth created resentment among the have-nots and set the stage for a major upheaval in American politics in the 1990s.[32]

In addition to the external developments, by 1992, the pundits, conservatives, and White House staff had all been beating the conventional wisdom drum that Bush lacked an agenda for three years, making it extremely difficult for Bush to change the perception about him. Matters grew worse in the spring of 1992, when Los Angeles erupted in violence after the acquittal of four police officers caught on videotape beating Rodney King. With L.A. burning, the administration became truly desperate for a domestic agenda. The White House announced that Porter had "been charged with surveying federal agencies for new ideas."[33]

Despite the newfound interest in domestic initiatives, though, the same problem remained: the president refused to articulate a cohesive agenda. On May 1, with the riots still raging, Bush spoke to the nation from the Oval Office. In his speech, he tried to give a message of hope and reconciliation: "We must keep on working to create a climate of understanding and tolerance, a climate that refuses to accept racism, bigotry, anti-Semitism, and hate of any kind, anytime, anywhere." Bush concluded by assuring the nation that "the violence will end. Justice will be served. Hope will return." Bush's speech, while conciliatory, lacked the indignation or the solutions that many Americans sought.[34]

Vice President Dan Quayle, in contrast, responded to the riots with the most famous speech of his life. Quayle, who complained in his memoir that the administration lacked "a driving creed," gave Americans both indignation and solutions. Quayle's speech complained that "our inner cities are filled with children having children, with people who have not been able to take advantage of economic opportunities, with people who are dependent on drugs or the narcotic of welfare." The speech struck a chord, largely because of Quayle's observation that "it doesn't help matters when prime time TV has Murphy Brown—a character who supposedly epitomizes today's intelligent, highly paid, professional woman—mocking the importance of fathers, by bearing a child alone, and calling it just another 'lifestyle choice.'" While the media derided Quayle for the Murphy Brown reference, the hard-hitting speech showed far more leadership than Bush's stolid call for unity. When chief of staff Sam Skinner refused to back Quayle, the president seemed to fear Quayle's ideas and lack ideas of his own. The contrast between Bush, seemingly devoid of ideas, and Democratic nominee Bill Clinton, a one-man idea factory, put Bush on the defensive throughout the 1992 campaign.[35]

IN DEFENSE OF BUSH

Bush clearly suffered from the perception that he lacked an agenda or a vision for America. And he certainly would have benefited from having a public intellectual on staff, someone who could have demonstrated that the president was interested in and was looking for ideas. But the lack of a famous intellectual on staff does not mean that the conventional wisdom of a visionless Bush accurately depicted his presidency. Bush's vision for the presidency was not necessarily activist on the domestic front, but that is not to say that it was not a vision.

Bush suffered in part from unrealistic journalistic expectations. As Rozell put it, "When Bush did not conform to a model of presidential leadership that demanded bold, early initiatives, journalists defined his leadership as lacking." Journalists wanted to see a bold first-one-hundred-day agenda, and when Bush failed to produce one, reporters determined "that he did not adequately use his honeymoon period to set the nation's agenda."[36]

Part of this, observed Fitzwater, stemmed from the press's own inherent biases, complaining that "you liberal writers are just like the Democrats in Congress. You think government isn't doing anything unless it's taxing and spending and creating new bureaucracies." Fitzwater had a point. After eight years of the Reagan agenda, Bush had a right to adopt a governance strategy, one that would implement the Reagan reforms without creating whole new policies. Of course, this strategy worked when the nation faced good times but fell apart in the face of a recession or other kind of crisis.[37]

The journalists and pundits had settled on their view of Bush as ineffectual long before the people soured on him. As Rozell observed, "Bush's leadership approach did not initially bother the public as much as it bothered leading journalists. The president maintained very good public approval ratings throughout much of 1989." Furthermore, the journalists' rejection of Bush may have not been innocent either. According to one study, 89 percent of journalists voted for Clinton over Bush in 1992, more than double the percentage in the population at large.[38]

Although most journalists indeed seemed to dislike Bush—if not him personally, then his leadership style—their complaints about Bush seemed accurate, especially in contrast to Reagan. While Reagan ran an activist presidency, one eager to establish bold new policies and push the nation in a new direction, Bush was content with a guardian presidency, aimed at consolidating recent gains and adjusting to the new status quo. Reagan ascended to the presidency during a time of crisis; Bush inherited peace and prosperity. Reagan united disparate elements into a Republican Party willing to agree on certain core principles; Bush inherited a fractious Republican Party that could not agree on who or what represented the Reagan legacy. Reagan rode into office on a wave that swept working congressional majorities into office with him; Bush faced a Democratic Congress determined to humiliate him.

Given these different personalities and different circumstances, Reagan and Bush had to take different approaches to the presidency. Reagan's Legislative Strategy Group helped set the agenda for both Congress and the presidency. Bush, in contrast, relied on the veto strategy to shape legislation under a Democratic Congress. The veto strategy, which David Mervin credits to Roger Porter, proved successful in that Congress overrode only one of Bush's forty-four vetoes. Although this was not an exciting strategy, and it allowed the Democrats to paint Bush as an obstructionist president devoid of ideas, it was the best Bush could have done under the circumstances.[39]

While the Democrat-controlled Congress limited Bush's legislative options, he did have a more global vision for America. Unfortunately, the Bush strategy was not the kind journalists usually embrace. As Rozell notes, "The press coverage of presidents emphasiz[ing] the notion that the President must be someone with a vision . . . reflects something of a bias." Presidents who cannot secure a bold agenda through Congress by definition lack vision. Rozell is correct to observe that "this assessment is unfair to presidents like Ford and Bush who governed with Democratic Party majorities in the legislature."[40]

Consequently, the Gulf War victory represented the crowning achievement of the Bush administration, both internationally and domestically. With the legislative door closed by a hostile Congress, Bush needed to express his vision through executive action. As Duffy and Goodgame note, "Bush's approach to domestic affairs was in many cases a mere extension of his approach to foreign policy. Bush often said, 'Building a better America doesn't stop at the water's edge.' In many ways for Bush, it began there." With the defeat of Iraq, Bush demonstrated his belief in stability, prosperity, and a world led by America, both economically and politically. While Bush served as president for less than a third of the 1990s, much of the decade —dominated by an economic boom and a strong, unchallenged America—bore Bush's stamp.[41]

Bush did articulate this vision on occasion. In a speech to the American Enterprise Institute in late 1991, Bush explained, Coolidge-like, that "America's fundamentals are sound." To Bush, the most important one of these fundamentals was "of course, the cornerstone of our American idea, the bedrock belief in freedom that led us from Valley Forge to Desert Storm to the new world now unfolding around us." Bush felt that Desert Storm encapsulated his vision, and he believed the American people saw things the same way.[42]

Ironically, when Bush did try to make this vision a campaign theme, it was the New Paradigmers who best characterized his views. As Fred Barnes reported in the *New Republic*, Bush believed that the line "If we can change the world, we can change America" encapsulated his approach to both America and the world. Gingrich aide Jeff Eisenach wrote the line and passed it on to Pinkerton. Bush incorporated it into speeches and campaign commercials in 1992, trying to convey his idea that international stability would create American prosperity.[43]

Unfortunately for Bush, he could change the world, but he could not change the conventional wisdom. Despite these late attempts to articulate a vision, Bush failed to capture the imagination of a recession-weary American people. One senior White House official commented, "It's not that he doesn't believe anything, it's that he doesn't see much connection between expressing beliefs and acting on them in a serious way." In this, Bush suffered from the lack of a prominent staff intellectual who could have represented the vision and clarified Bush's commitment to it. But Bush had little interest in the symbolic elements of the presidency, and his administration suffered because of it. This, again, stemmed from Bush's personality. As Fitzwater observed, "George Bush is a very complex and multidimensional person. Yet because he compartmentalizes so many aspects of his life, including his friends, few people see the full range of his talents." Bush's compartmentalizing nature made it hard for him to express—or to have anyone express for him—a single, unifying vision, and this mistake probably cost him his job in 1992.[44]

9

BILL CLINTON: AT HOME WITH THE INTELLECTUALS

Bill Clinton used intellectuals more successfully than any president since Kennedy. From the beginning of his campaign, when he carefully cultivated the centrist intellectuals in the Democratic Leadership Council, through the depths of his impeachment trial, when much of the intellectual establishment rose as if as one to defend the president, Bill Clinton consistently harnessed his good relations with intellectuals to his advantage. Surprisingly, Clinton also discovered that this critical aid came quite cheaply.

In scoring this coup over the intellectuals, Clinton benefited immensely from his educational background. As a Rhodes scholar and a graduate of Georgetown University and Yale Law School, Clinton already had a leg up over most of his predecessors in the postwar era. Furthermore, Clinton's modest upbringing proved that he secured his slots without benefiting from any old boy network. Although Gerald Ford had also attended Yale Law, Ford did so before Yale Law School had acquired its current reputation as the most elite of elite graduate programs. On top of his domestic schooling, Clinton's Rhodes scholarship served as the final sign of approbation, not only granting him the ultimate imprimatur but also introducing him to many of the superstars of his generation, individuals with whom he would remain close throughout his political career.

Clinton had a genuine love of ideas and academic discourse. Clinton read an impressive number of books for anyone, let alone the nation's chief executive. Early in his presidency, Clinton let slip the fact that he tried "to read at least thirty minutes a day," not counting weekends or airline trips, when he would "read for a couple of hours at a time." Most of the books he read were current, and he often allowed word of his latest read to trickle out, thereby flattering the author and even boosting book sales. Furthermore, his regular diet of op-ed pages and opinion journals included the *New York Times*, the *Washington Post*, *Harper's*, the *New Yorker*, the *New Republic*, and the *Atlantic*, the very list favored by America's intellectual establishment.[1]

In addition to reading what intellectuals write, he also liked hearing what they have to say. Inviting prominent intellectuals to come the White House before the State of the Union address was an annual ritual. Guests at these dinners included, among others, Alan Brinkley, Theda Skocpol, Paul Starr, Garrison Keillor, David Herbert Donald, Henry Louis Gates Jr., Alan Ehrenhalt, Robert Putnam, Benjamin Barber, Amitai Etzioni, Amy Guttmann, Randall Kennedy, and Jane Mansbridge. Clinton did not contact such people just once a year but regularly solicited them for advice. Yale professor Stephen Carter, for example, was a regular source of book suggestions.[2]

As a result of this campaigning, Clinton was quite popular among the professoriate. He did not require the services of a public intellectual in the Arthur Schlesinger mode to keep him abreast of developments in academe; he followed these developments and maintained these contacts for the most part by himself. Granted, Clinton is rather unique and cannot be easily imitated by another president wishing to ingratiate himself with the intellectual elites. But his success in dealing with American intellectuals, despite the fact that he often disappointed them politically, demonstrates that cultivating the intellectual community can reap rich rewards.

BILL CLINTON AND THE DLC

Clinton's most important action in his quest for the nation's highest office may have been serving as chairman of the Democratic Leadership Council. Al From, a former congressional and White House aide, founded the DLC in 1985, after Reagan's forty-nine-state victory over Walter Mondale. From, a 1965 Northwestern University graduate, believed that the Democrats suffered electorally from domination by liberal interest groups like NOW, the AFL-CIO, and the NAACP. As New Democrat chronicler Kenneth Baer wrote, the Democrats "for the past thirty years had been seen as profligate 'tax-and-spenders,' reflexive defenders of federal government programs, pacifist isolationists, and advocates of an active social liberalism." From created the DLC to rescue the Democratic Party from some of these liberal excesses.[3]

From succeeded spectacularly. He found ready funding from corporations happy to help wrest the Democrats from the grip of liberal interest groups. The group's $2.5 million annual budget supported Capitol Hill offices, a staff of twenty, a five-person think tank, the Progressive Policy Institute, and a $225,000 annual salary for From. Thanks to some judicious salesmanship, From also obtained the ear of the future president. In 1989, From visited Clinton in Arkansas, enticing the Arkansas governor with the prospect of the presidency. From told Clinton, "If you take the DLC chairmanship, we will give you a national platform, and I think you will be president of the United States." From also promised Clinton staff and campaign funds to help advance the agenda, two essential elements for victory in the so-called invisible primary of electoral expectations. Clinton listened to both From's promise and his agenda, serving as DLC chairman in 1990.[4]

The agenda came from two PPI fellows, William Galston and Elaine Kamarck, who wrote an influential paper, "The Politics of Evasion," which argued that the Democrats needed to reach beyond their base of interest groups to win back the White House. Galston and Kamarck observed that as long as the public viewed the Democrats as the party of "tax and spending policies that contradict the interests of average families . . . [and] welfare policies that foster dependence rather than self-reliance" they had no chance of winning national elections. A Democrat who changed this perception, who criticized dependency and argued for responsibility, would reclaim the keys to the White House. As Galston later described it, "I argued that the Democratic party could not hope—and did not deserve—to regain a presidential majority until it shifted its orientation in a number of respects," including defense, social policy, and economics.[5]

When Clinton ran for the presidency, the DLC agenda proved remarkably effective on the campaign trail. In the fall of 1991 Clinton gave three New Democrat-style speeches at Georgetown University, on the New Democrat philosophy, on an economic policy that did not stress class warfare, and on a more robust foreign policy. These well-attended events helped shape and solidify perceptions of Clinton as a New Democrat among the influential Washington media. Former DLC policy director Bruce Reed wrote the successful addresses, which were heavily influenced by Galston. The Georgetown addresses were the most important speeches Clinton gave in the primary season, and possibly the most important speeches of the entire campaign.

Clinton certainly benefited from good luck. Bush's strength following the Gulf War scared off some of the best-known Democrats, and the 1991 recession sapped Bush's strength. Yet Clinton, with the help of From and the DLC, also made his own luck, criticizing the race-baiting rapper Sister Souljah in front of a black audience, arguing for responsibilities in addition to rights, and calling for the end of welfare as we know it. Clinton's willingness, indeed eagerness, to take on entrenched left-wing interests demonstrated to the American people that he was a different sort of Democrat. He was able to make this case because of the ideas and agenda provided by the DLC.

By running as a New Democrat, Clinton ended the long-standing perception of the Democrats as the new politics party. Even the party platform, which had previously been a laundry list of special interest sacred cows, had a DLC tone to it. According to the *New York Times*, the 1992 platform, with discussions of individual responsibility and demands for welfare reform, contained "whole sections that would have been hooted down not too many years ago." With the DLC rhetoric on the campaign trail and the recast platform, Clinton successfully convinced Americans that he was a different sort of Democrat.[6]

As a result of the DLC makeover, Clinton won the 1992 election, and the DLC and Al From attained new heights of fame and stature. One liberal transition official referred to From—the domestic policy coordinator of the transition—as "the intellectual godfather of Clinton's candidacy," who, as a result, "is going to get some of the spoils." From evidently thought so too, telling one reporter that he expected the DLC to "be for the Clinton administration what the Heritage Foundation was for the Reagan administration. . . . An idea factory to help Bill come up with new approaches." Like the Heritage Foundation's *Mandate for Leadership* in 1980, the DLC book, *Mandate for Change*, suddenly became quite popular, with 137,000 copies in print by December 1992.[7]

Despite its triumph, the DLC had some powerful enemies in the Democratic Party, those who represented the very interests that the so-called New Democrats repudiated. Jesse Jackson, a leader of the Democratic far left, jested that DLC stood for the "Democratic leisure class" and referred to the organization as "the Southern White Boys Club." Left-wing Senator Howard Metzenbaum growled that From "doesn't know **** from Shinola." With such powerful antagonists in its own party, the DLC found the transition something of a viper pit, with many recommended appointees ending up mortally wounded.[8]

Clinton's appointments looked far more old Democrat than New. David Gergen of *U.S. News and World Report* expressed surprise that there were not more intellectuals among the appointees. Paul Gigot characterized the new staff as "not diverse enough in the thinkers associated with the ideas that made Mr. Clinton 'a different kind of Democrat.'" Instead of fishing in the New Democrat pool, Clinton placed most of his emphasis on hiring women and minorities to top positions.[9]

When the transition ended, Clinton had not appointed any DLC staff members to top administration positions—cabinet posts or commissioned slots in the White House. Of the fifteen authors in the PPI anthology, *Mandate for Change*, only one—Galston—had secured an administration post at the end of the transition. Galston and DLC issues director Bruce Reed both garnered positions as assistants to domestic policy adviser Carol Rascoe. Kamarck had a particularly difficult time, reportedly getting blackballed for a position as assistant secretary for welfare and family policy at the Department of Health and Human Services before ending up as an aide to Vice President Al Gore. As Dan Balz and Ronald Brownstein observed, the DLCers in the administration gained "White House jobs sufficiently senior to affect a broad range of specific policies but not powerful enough to influence the administration's overall direction." Paul Gigot warned, rather presciently, that the few New Democrats who were appointed ran "the risk of being 'Pinkertoned'—left free to think on their own, humored sometimes, but ultimately ignored the way Jim Pinkerton was in the Bush White House."[10]

DLC members did not hide their frustration. Morton Kondracke of *Roll Call* wrote that the DLC and PPI were "bewildered and disappointed" by the dearth of jobs. One DLC operative told the *New Republic* that "if he had known how Clinton would turn out, he might have cast a protest vote for Perot last November." The new administration was so laden with old-line liberal Democrats that a DLC staffer who made the cut into the administration joked, "I always knew that signing on early to the campaign would help you get a job, they would say. I just didn't know it was the Dukakis campaign."[11]

There were a number of reasons for this purge of nonliberal potential appointees. First, the DLCers, while they had helped Clinton secure the presidency, had also made bitter enemies within the party, liberals like Reverend Jackson and Senator Metzenbaum who had a vested interest in keeping the party as it was. In addition, one of the oldest traditions in American politics is that all of the party's elements must gain a portion of the spoils. In the Democratic Party of 1992, the spoils system left room for blacks, feminists, Jews, and union officials. Moderate southern white males, while crucial to winning a general election, did not constitute a powerful interest group within the already victorious Democratic Party. Finally, Hillary Rodham Clinton, who was more liberal than her husband, was a crucial factor, pushing for many liberals whom she knew from her own lifetime of political activism.

This was not the first time a moderate southern governor won the presidency only to disappoint his more conservative backers. In 1976, Jimmy Carter secured the support of moderate Democrats, including the Cold Warriors of the Coalition for a Democratic Majority. When it came time for staffing the Carter administration, the CDM members found themselves left out, with the exception of Peter Rosenblatt, who received a low-ranking posting to distant Micronesia. As Elliot Abrams, a member of the group, lamented, "They froze us out completely. We got one unbelievably minor job. It was a special negotiator position. Not for Polynesia. Not even for Macronesia. But for Micronesia." Many of the frustrated job seekers, like Abrams, went on to become neoconservative Reagan backers in the 1980 election.[12]

The DLCers fared slightly better than the CDMers had, but not by much. Those staffers who found employment faced the challenge of working within an administration that had rejected most of their ideological allies. Bill Galston, one of the few New Democrats to secure any kind of position in the young administration, was appointed a deputy assistant to the president and worked on national service, children, and families, issues that he had emphasized while at PPI. Galston, a graduate of Cornell and the University of Chicago, had previously served as issues director for the 1984 Mondale campaign.

While Galston served in the White House, he argued for the DLC position on hot-button issues within his purview. According to senior Clinton adviser George Stephanopoulos, Galston was one of the minority urging an end of racial quotas, arguing that "affirmative action was a good idea that had gone bad over time." He also took a strong stand on letting states experiment with welfare reform, boasting to Michael Barone of *U.S. News and World Report* that "the administration has not turned down a single request from a state to waive federal welfare rules." Other Galston initiatives included the education program Goals 2000, the National and Community Service Act, and the Earned Income Tax Credit. His positions often put him at odds with both the left and the right. With Goals 2000, for example, Galston recalled that the left felt that the new standards would harm poor and minority children, while the right feared new impositions from Washington.[13]

Not shy about expressing his positions, Galston found himself out of step with an administration that eschewed New Democratic ideals and personnel. As Galston told *Time* after he left the White House, "in '92 our ideas captured the country but not the party," leaving Galston less popular in a Democratic White House than in the nation at large.[14]

Galston's ideas helped shape the Clinton approach to welfare, but by the time the administration agreed to welfare reform, Galston had already departed, leaving in early 1995. When Galston left, he claimed that he wanted to spend more time with his family. Most commentators dismissed his explanation, claiming that Galston "was frustrated" in an administration "dominated by liberals" such as deputy chief of staff Harold Ickes. Clinton consultant Dick Morris put matters even more strongly, claiming that Galston and White House counselor David Gergen "had quit in disgust at the [White House's] leftward drift."[15]

Whatever the truth was behind Galston's departure, both Galston and his former organization clearly enjoyed more influence with Clinton before the 1992 election than after. Galston admitted that a major source of tension in the administration "involved accommodating the liberal tendencies that still dominate the party and the centrist views the president ran on." According to FEC commissioner and former Heritage Foundation official David Mason, the DLC and PPI "were situated to be the think tank of the Clinton Administration. And it hasn't worked out that way." Although Clinton clearly had campaigned as a New Democrat in 1992, once in the White House, he did not govern that way.[16]

Largely as a result of the New Democrats' inability to secure top-level White House positions, the first two years of the Clinton administration demonstrated a strong left-wing bias. Clinton's first budget, passed without any Republican votes, contained the largest tax increase in American history. In fact, according to Democratic Senator Daniel Patrick Moynihan, the tax hike represented the "largest tax increase in the history of public finance in the United States or anywhere else in the world."[17]

More memorably, the administration spent much of the first two years working on the massive health care restructuring plan. The health care plan task force, led by Hillary Rodham Clinton and management consultant Ira Magaziner, collected six hundred people in thirty-eight subgroups and working groups, nearly all of them liberals, and spent $13.4 million in creating a byzantine 1,342-page new system that purported to guarantee some minimal level of health care to all Americans. John Judis of the *New Republic* called the plan a "proposal of stunning—but, given the nature of the industry necessary—complexity." The plan died in the Democratic Congress without a vote in September 1994. In the November elections, Clinton's party lost control of both houses of Congress for the first time in forty years.[18]

QUEST FOR THE THIRD WAY

While the New Democrats found themselves frustrated by the leftward drift of the first two years of the Clinton White House, liberals in the administration felt that the White House was not liberal enough. Clinton political guru—and unabashed liberal—James Carville famously complained that he wished to be reincarnated as the bond market. In Carville's view, the bond market (i.e., Wall Street), not liberal ideals, set the administration's policies.

Carville's complaint was echoed by Robert Reich of the Kennedy School. Reich, a friend of Clinton since their Rhodes scholar and Yale Law School days, served as Clinton's first secretary of labor. In 1968 Reich had told a *Time* reporter that he hoped "to be a kind of cross between a philosopher and a political hack," and he had gotten his wish in the intervening years. Although Reich taught at the Kennedy School, he lacked a Ph.D. Therefore his peers did not always consider him a fellow scholar, and he was often dismissed as "a popularizer and self-promoter." At the same time, he was deeply involved in politics, where the party faithful saw him more as an egghead than as a team player.

Reich's no-man's-land status revealed the perils of a career as a professional public intellectual. While he may have found the vocation he had told *Time* he always wanted, getting what one thinks one wants as a twenty-year-old does not always constitute a gift.[19]

Reich's tenure at the Labor Department was often frustrating. There's no doubt that he came to the job with high hopes. In the beginning of his memoir he writes that "for many years before, I had researched and written about investing in our nation's most precious resource—its human capital—and about reversing the long-term slide toward widening inequality of income, wealth, and opportunity. Now I had a chance to implement my ideas under a president who shared them." It did not take Reich long to learn, as the DLCers had, that running for office on an issue and governing on that issue were very different things. For the first two years of the Clinton administration, Reich found that Treasury Secretary Lloyd Bentsen's warnings about the deficit trumped Reich's desire for expensive new government "investments."[20]

After the 1994 election, things just became worse for Reich. With the administration reeling from devastating losses in the Congress, Clinton stopped tacking left and began a famous quest for the Third Way. The master behind this effort was Dick Morris, an abrasive New York political consultant who had known Clinton for twenty years. Morris, who consulted for Democrats and Republicans alike, advised the adoption of a triangulation strategy, seeking answers beyond traditional notions of right and left. While the strategy proved effective for Clinton, it did not make Morris popular among the administration liberals like Reich, who felt Morris was advocating capitulation to Republican ideas. Reich's belief, expressed to *The Nation* after he had left the cabinet, was that it was "important for progressive Democrats not to be co-opted by a watered-down version of Republicanism."[21]

Even worse for Reich, Morris's obnoxious manner exacerbated his ideological heresy. According to Reich, in his first encounter with Morris, the consultant burst into Reich's office and told him, "You have a lot of good ideas. . . . The president likes your ideas. I want them so I can test them." Reluctantly, Reich passed on some thoughts. A short while later, a less complimentary Morris informed Reich: "I tested your ideas. One worked. Two didn't." Needless to say, Reich found this policy-by-poll approach dismissive of his work, not to mention extremely distasteful. As Reich described it, "There used to be a policy-making process in the White House. It wasn't perfect by any means, but at least options were weighed. B [Clinton] received our various arguments about what was good for the nation. Now we have Morris and his polls." While Reich had not liked losing to Bentsen in the early days, at least he was losing the battles on policy grounds. With Morris in the picture, everything took a backseat to his polls.[22]

To Reich's dismay, there was little doubt that Morris, or at least his ideas, were in control during this period. As Morris's rival George Stephanopoulos unhappily described matters, "From December 1994 through August 1996, Leon Panetta managed the official White House staff, the Joint Chiefs commanded the military, the cabinet administered the government, but no single person more influenced the President of the United States than Dick Morris." In this period, during which the president declared the era of big government over and signed the welfare reform bill and the Defense of Marriage Act, it seemed that the New Democrats were finally getting some of what they wanted.[23]

Yet these concessions to the New Democrat mantra must have rankled the DLC almost as much as liberals like Reich. Morris may have popularized the notion of triangulation, but he did not invent the Third Way. The Third Way was what the DLC had always thought. In 1993, before Clinton summoned Morris to Washington for emergency surgery, Al From was explaining that the DLC "agenda isn't liberal or conservative. It is both, and it is different." With Clinton's 1995 reinvention and 1996 reelection, Morris received much of the credit, while the DLC had few representatives in the White House. Although the quest for the Third Way had begun with DLC intellectuals, when it came they had little to do with it.[24]

SECOND TERM: SCANDAL AND BLUMENTHAL

Morris and his triangulation strategy helped usher Clinton into a second term. With no more elections ahead of him, Clinton theoretically should have been able to reveal his true self (whatever that was) and govern according to his heart. Unfortunately for Clinton, his second term quickly bogged down in scandal. Even Morris left in scandal before the election, caught in a tryst with a prostitute whom he allowed to eavesdrop on White House phone calls. The Morris scandal, however, would pale before the one involving the president.

During Clinton's first term, the strategy toward the various scandals surrounding the president and First Lady was to delay all investigations until after the 1996 election. Clinton succeeded, but the effort had the unfortunate effect of lumping the various scandals together, leaving none of the parties particularly happy. For their part, the Clintons felt like perpetual targets. From their opponents' view, mixing together multiple scandals precluded the clarity necessary to stoke the flames of outrage among the American people. Either way, in late 1997, almost a year into Clinton's second term, the Whitewater and Filegate scandals, which were being investigated by independent counsel Ken Starr, became hopelessly entangled in the Paula Jones sexual harassment case when Jones's lawyers began pursuing allegations of Clinton's affair with a White House intern named Monica Lewinsky. When some—still anonymous—source leaked this information to Starr's team, the independent counsel began to investigate allegations of perjury and obstruction of justice, leading eventually to Clinton's impeachment in the House and acquittal in the Senate.

The events that dominated the news in 1998 and 1999 had two effects on the Clinton administration's relations with intellectuals. First, the impeachment episode, by becoming the major political story for more than a year, crippled any chance Clinton had for generating any new policy initiatives or even a strategic vision for his second term. Second, Clinton's early solicitousness toward intellectuals and the academy bore fruit during the scandal, as many of the scholars who joined the president at White House dinners led the fight against his impeachment.

Clinton began 1998 as he had all of his previous years in office, with a meeting of intellectuals to help him prepare for the State of the Union address. According to John Maggs of the *National Journal*, Clinton wondered if he should "seize the opportunity to assume the mantle of reformer Theodore Roosevelt, or leave that for the next president." When Clinton gave the address, after news of the Lewinsky scandal had grabbed headlines around the world, he gave the most subdued SOTU of his presidency, passing on the opportunity to speak of Roosevelt and the reform agenda. As Bruce Solomon of the *National Journal* observed, in the second Clinton term "big ideas are notable these days for their absence."[25]

Although Clinton's second term was short on big new ideas, big thinkers had not absented themselves. The administration had carefully cultivated liberal intellectuals for years—with dinner invitations, idea requests, and, most of all, attention after twelve years of administrations they could not abide. Now the embattled president needed to cash in his chits and secure the support of the liberal intellectual establishment. By and large, the intellectuals responded to the president's request, and the man who helped make it happen was Sidney Blumenthal.

Blumenthal joined the White House payroll as an assistant to the president in August 1997. An extremely talented journalist, Blumenthal had worked for the *Washington Post*, the *New Republic*, and the *New Yorker* over twenty-five years, writing articles and books, and generally skewering conservatives with a razor-sharp stylus. He also wrote a number of well-received books, including *The Rise of the Counterestablishment*, which described the development of institutions on the right and provided a blueprint for what would be called the vast right-wing conspiracy.[26]

Blumenthal had unusually close access to the Clintons, maintaining a link that Clinton had severed with most other reporters. However, Blumenthal's relations with the Clintons damaged his credibility as a journalist in many quarters. Howard Kurtz of the *Washington Post* observed that rival reporters branded

Blumenthal the "capital's chief suck-up, a craven sellout who defended Bill and Hillary Clinton against the world even as he carefully cultivated them in private conversations." The *New York Observer* called him a "longtime cheerleader for Clinton" and joked when he joined the White House that he "will now be paid by the White House for his boosterism."[27]

Blumenthal's sin was not writing positively about the Clintons; if that were the case, many journalists would have been guilty. Blumenthal, it was alleged, crossed the line from journalism into advocacy by advising the Clintons, getting information from Republicans as a journalist, and then sharing it with his Democratic allies, writing speeches or providing speech ideas for Hillary, and refusing to write anything negative about the Clintons that he learned in the course of their many conversations. The *New Yorker* replaced Blumenthal as its Washington editor because of his refusal to write about Clinton's scandals, such as the budding Whitewater investigation. Michael Kelly, Blumenthal's replacement, ordered Blumenthal away from the *New Yorker*'s Washington office because, Kelly said, "I did not trust him." Kelly even suspected that Blumenthal was seeking a White House job. Because of such suspicions, Blumenthal lost his credibility as a journalist. When he started at the White House, the *New Republic*—his former employer—puckishly suggested that he was due White House back pay.[28]

Of course, some reporters admired and even envied Blumenthal's access. Michael Lewis wrote in the *New York Times Magazine* that Blumenthal was just doing his job: "documenting the world as it appeared to Bill Clinton." According to Lewis "Blumenthal's access and ability meant that the *New Yorker*, for a brief, shining moment, gave you some brief sense of just how weirdly uncomfortable were our new first couple." Even Lewis, however, admitted the damage caused by Blumenthal's lack of objectivity, acknowledging that "before long, the name Sidney Blumenthal was an inside-the-Beltway joke."[29]

Lewis recognized an essential irony, that Blumenthal's very access to the best possible news source eviscerated his effectiveness. With his journalistic career stalled while the Clintons remained in office, Blumenthal joined the White House, taking a position with impressive and wide-ranging job responsibilities. According to his affidavit filed during the Starr investigation, Blumenthal worked on numerous hot-button issues—including trade, environment, Social Security, education, crime, welfare, and tobacco—wrote speeches, and served as the administration's liaison with Great Britain. With respect to the administration's scandal problems, he advised the president on "the effect of the [Starr] investigation on his official duties, including how best to frame his public statements, his legislative agenda, and his dealings with foreign countries in light of that investigation."[30]

According to Dana Milbank of the *New Republic*, Blumenthal also "served as the White House point man in the development of a new way of packaging

Clinton's brand of centrist government." This was a curiously new role for Blumenthal, who had long been critical of New Democrat or Third Way thinking as a betrayal of Democratic Party traditions. By this point, however, the Third Way had a new appeal, as potentially allowing Clinton to claim a larger legacy than just the second president ever impeached by Congress. As Baer speculated, "This imperative could also explain the intense interest that Hillary Clinton, a prominent liberal, and Sidney Blumenthal, a White House aide who as a journalist had been critical of the DLC, took in the Third Way."[31]

The Third Way gained even more cachet with the election of Tony Blair as prime minister of Great Britain, ending almost two decades of Conservative rule. Blumenthal, as the White House expert on the Third Way, went to England with Hillary Clinton in 1998 to discuss the Third Way with Blair and his advisers. Of course, Blumenthal's primary focus was on framing the Third Way domestically. He even set up a "bury the hatchet" meeting, again with Hillary, with New and Old Democrats in search of common goals.

Blumenthal also worked on the continuing series of White House dinners for intellectuals, trading on his lifetime of good relationships with much of the liberal intellectual establishment, which resulted from his years as a journalist and an author. Blumenthal's skills, as well as Clinton's facility and comfort with the intellectual community, were very useful during the Lewinsky scandal. With his journalistic background and take-no-prisoners approach, Blumenthal worked on shaping the story. This task landed Blumenthal in some legal trouble when the independent counsel investigated him for spreading the tale that Lewinsky stalked the president, implying that the president was blameless and the former intern less than stable. Blumenthal was also widely reputed to have been the source for the *Salon* story that House Judiciary Committee chairman Henry Hyde had an affair thirty years earlier.

Blumenthal also served as point man for the White House counterattack against Starr and any journalists who presented Starr's point of view. Jeffrey Toobin, who also sided with the White House on the Lewinsky scandal, wrote that Blumenthal served as one of "Clinton's most zealous defenders." As Toobin explained, Blumenthal's "contribution to the defense effort was to take on Starr's staff." Even when he did not interact with reporters directly, he was the brains behind the pro-Clinton spin, sending anti-Starr "material to the Democratic National Committee, where the fruits of his media research were distilled into talking points, and directed reporters to the resulting product."[32]

Newsweek reporter Michael Isikoff, who did most of the heavy lifting in uncovering the Lewinsky scandal, saw Blumenthal's role as more sinister. According to Isikoff, Blumenthal provided misleading information to *New York Times* columnist Anthony Lewis regarding the questions Starr's grand jury posed to

Blumenthal, making the questions seem more sinister than they really were. After his testimony, Blumenthal also gave a misleading statement to the press outside the courthouse, implying that the independent counsel had tried to stifle Blumenthal's freedom of speech by interrogating him regarding his press contacts with specific organizations. As Isikoff explained, "It was Blumenthal in his answer who mentioned specific news organizations, not any of Starr's prosecutors in their questions."[33]

Blumenthal's role as point man in the White House war against Starr made Blumenthal the chief enemy of conservatives in Washington. Jonah Goldberg of the *National Review* described Blumenthal as "Clinton's Rasputin and the first lady's Beria" and "the man who has done more to make smearing the president's concubines a cabinet level job than anyone." The *New York Post* called Blumenthal "Bill's dirt devil" and the "top White House smear-meister." Blumenthal also ended his long-standing friendship with left-wing Clinton hater Christopher Hitchens over the affair, when Hitchens testified that Blumenthal had smeared Lewinsky when the two men met with their wives for lunch. Hitchens's affidavit contradicted Blumenthal's sworn testimony and put Blumenthal in jeopardy of perjury.[34]

Overall, Blumenthal's record in defending the president during the scandal is mixed. While he succeeded in getting negative information about Starr and his team into the press, in doing so he also garnered a fair degree of notoriety and bad press for himself. On the other hand, in drawing attention to himself, he served as a lightning rod for the president, drawing some attention away from Clinton and helping the president survive the scandal.

In addition to shaping the media spin, the White House also worked closely with academic intellectuals to defend the president. When the House Judiciary Committee called on the White House to provide witnesses to defend Clinton in the impeachment hearings, the White House eschewed factual witnesses, relying almost exclusively on academics to assail the process. After hearing from the fourteen White House witnesses, Hyde joked that the committee had "heard from so many college professors that I think I'm going to ask if we can get college credit for attending the seminars."[35]

BLUMENTHAL AND WILENTZ

The most vocal of the witnesses was Blumenthal's friend and Princeton University professor Sean Wilentz, who harangued the Judiciary Committee members for creating "a nauseating spectacle" and warned them that their "reputations will be darkened for as long as there are Americans who can tell the difference between the rule of law and the rule of politics." Wilentz received almost universally bad reviews for his histrionic performance. The *New York Times* called Wilentz's testimony "a gratuitously patronizing presentation," while Goldberg described Wilenz as "the biggest academic buffoon of the impeachment hearings."[36]

But Wilentz was not testifying solely as a scholar. He had organized a petition of 412 historians who opposed impeachment and placed a full-page ad in the *New York Times* on October 30, 1998, only slightly less critical of the Republicans than Wilentz's actual testimony had been. The ad asserted, without proof, that "the current charges against [President Clinton] depart from what the Framers saw as grounds for impeachment." Many of the signers, including Samuel H. Beer, Albert Camarillo, David Herbert Donald, Henry Louis Gates, and Orlando Patterson, had participated in the White House dinners at which Clinton had so carefully cultivated the intellectual community.[37]

Like Wilentz's testimony, the letter emerged as a partisan endeavor. According to a report in the *American Enterprise* magazine, the address given in the ad was the Washington office of a left-wing organization, People for the American Way. Its tax-exempt foundation, founded by Hollywood producer Norman Lear, paid for the ad, not the four hundred signatories, as the ad implied. Another revelation about the ad came the same month from *George* magazine. Blumenthal, "who fancies himself the White House's resident intellectual," not only served as "the historians' 'connection at the White House,'" but he also "helped the historians create the ad." As one editorialist noted, when asked about the controversy, Wilentz "denie[d] Blumenthal wrote the ad (but not the group's connection to him)."[38]

The ad was therefore misleading, as Goldberg put it, because "the tone and tenor of their open letter was that they were nonpartisan experts on what the Constitution has to say and what history has to tell us. After all, these were 'historians speaking as historians.'" These stories revealed, however, that the ads were not the unsolicited product of outrage by the nation's historians, but part of a larger defense strategy coming from the White House and facilitated by People for the American Way and Wilentz's buddy Blumenthal.[39]

In November 1999, months after the conclusion of the impeachment trial, Wilentz arranged for Blumenthal to give the Willard and Margaret Thorp Lecture in American Studies at Princeton. Blumenthal, who spoke on "Presidents and Democracy: An American History," argued in favor of Clinton's Third Way, describing it as "a movement neither reiterating the old left and its programs formulated in the crucible of unreformed industrialism and economic scarcity nor weakly mimicking the right and its reflexive doctrine of market infallibility and government fault." Creating this synthesis, Blumenthal claimed, made Clinton the true Madisonian, in contrast to conservatives, who were "busily fabricating a past to fit their political doctrines." Clinton's success at redefining "the Madisonian synthesis" incurred the wrath of conservatives, who impeached the president in "an attempt to overturn two presidential elections. But the President, of course, was acquitted."[40]

Wilentz also continued to defend the president long after the end of the impeachment drama. In February 2000, he wrote a much talked about piece in the *New Republic* debunking the existence of Clinton fatigue—the notion that the nation had tired of Clinton and that Gore would suffer as a result. Wilentz left no room for doubt, arguing that "by every meaningful standard, statistical and historical, Clinton fatigue is an utter hoax." He blamed this hoax on "the dogma-cursed state of American political commentary." In the column's sequel, Wilentz attacked "anti-Clinton denial" on the left and the right, claiming that "the likeliest story of this political year" would be the election of "the purveyor of continued peace and prosperity: Clinton's vice president, Al Gore." As he had during the impeachment battles, Wilentz aimed his ire at Clinton's opponents, but he also extended his argument to include a ringing and unqualified defense of Clinton's entire presidency. According to Wilentz, all of Clinton's critics must be wrong, just as Clinton himself could do no wrong.[41]

Wilentz, interviewed in the *Daily Princetonian* after Blumenthal spoke at Princeton, claimed that "Blumenthal is the closest thing to an intellectual that has been in the White House since the 1960s." Wilentz was right that there had not been a full-time public intellectual in the White House in decades, since Bob Goldwin in the 1970s under Ford. Blumenthal came closer to the Schlesinger model than anyone had in the previous three administrations. But the two men, although they may have fit the same model in the White House, were very different. Schlesinger had been a serious, Pulitzer Prize–winning scholar before coming to the White House. Although a partisan Democrat, Schlesinger was not the kind of hit man that Blumenthal was, either as a sharp-penned journalist or a rabid Clinton defender.[42]

Although Blumenthal played the role of liaison to the academic community and had a preexisting intellectual reputation, it is not clear that he qualifies as an intellectual, public or otherwise. He came from journalism, not academia, and he took an exceptionally partisan approach to the role. While Wilentz was right that Blumenthal transcended "the stereotypical poll-driven aide," it is unclear from his journalistic and White House work that he was a "political thinker." Nevertheless, Clinton needed a loyalist like Blumenthal, especially during the dark days of the Lewinsky scandal. Thanks to the unstinting allegiance of people like Blumenthal inside the White House and Wilentz on the outside, Clinton not only survived the scandal but probably had the best relations with the academic community of any president since Kennedy.[43]

CONCLUSION

In his generally scathing book criticizing all the actors in the Lewinsky scandal, *An Affair of State*, Richard Posner reserves special ire for the intellectuals who defended Clinton in the affair, particularly those who signed the historians' ad in the *New York Times*. According to Posner, throughout the affair "representative figures of the academic Left have been notable for the partisanship, precipitance, and moral insensitivity of their commentary on l'affaire Clinton." According to Posner, the intellectual elites' response to the crisis demonstrated "the incapacity of the academic community, including some of its brightest lights in law, history, moral philosophy, and political theory, to contribute helpfully to a governmental crisis." While Posner may have had a point about bias in the academy, the fact is that the intellectual community, encouraged by Blumenthal, served Clinton well during his presidency. This does not make them any more responsible, but it does mean that Clinton and Blumenthal understood the power of the intellectual establishment and how to harness that power effectively.[44]

Overall, Clinton was successful with intellectuals and had good relations with them. Unfortunately, due to the scandal, he did not make the best use of this resource, relying on intellectuals to defend him in a mud-slinging war rather than trying to provide a coherent vision for the country. The lesson of the Clinton administration, however, was that good relations with intellectuals paid dividends. The New Democrat intellectuals of the DLC and the PPI helped Clinton capture the presidency in 1992, and the unyielding support of the liberal intellectual establishment during the Lewinsky crisis helped him keep his presidency. The irony of Clinton's good rapport among intellectuals was that Clinton seemed unable to present a coherent vision throughout his presidency. He tacked right when it suited him around elections and moved left when he wanted or needed the support of his party.

Clinton's waverings did not go unnoticed. The New Democrats complained rather loudly when they felt left out in the early part of the administration. On the other side, Arthur Schlesinger, while a vocal Clinton defender, also noted the irony of the left's defense of Clinton, even as many New Democrats abandoned him during the crisis. Despite occasional cavils, Clinton managed to keep both sides relatively happy throughout his presidency. The lesson of the Clinton administration with regard to intellectuals is that maintaining a reservoir of goodwill among the intellectuals pays dividends.

10

BUSH, GORE,
AND BEYOND

The 2000 presidential campaigns of Texas Governor George W. Bush and
Vice President Al Gore defied expectations. In a traditional election, Gore,
the Democrat, would have been surrounded with academics and intellectuals,
while Bush, the Republican, would have maintained a swarm of political consultants, pollsters, and elected officials, while downplaying ties to the intellectual
world. As it turned out, the opposite happened. Bush quickly secured the support of conservative think tank experts and advertised his links to that community, while Gore maintained a relatively small policy staff and downplayed his
more natural ties to the academic community.

The candidates' own weaknesses helped account for these developments.
Bush, dogged by a perception that he lacked the policy depth to be president,
assembled a large team of well-known policy experts to counter that perception.
Bush thereby aimed to reassure voters that even if he did not know all the issues,
he at least had a team around him that could guide him through the process. As
University of Texas political scientist Bruce Buchanan put it, "Bush is not a policy wonk, so he has to rely on people who are." Gore, in contrast, constantly
tried to demonstrate that he was a regular guy, not the stiff policy wonk relentlessly caricatured in the mainstream press. Part of this effort included downplaying his actual ties with well-known intellectuals.[1]

GEORGE BUSH'S POLICY ARMY

Bush played his hand better. Despite Bush's degrees from Yale University and Harvard Business School, he managed to benefit from maintaining low expectations.

Early in his campaign, Bush earned the support of top scholars at the American Enterprise Institute and the Hoover Institution, probably the two most prestigious conservative think tanks. The Hoover connection attracted more press attention. The Stanford University–based think tank, named the world's best by the *Economist*, housed some of the biggest stars in the conservative universe, including Nobel Prize–winning economist Milton Friedman, former Secretary of State George Shultz, and Reagan policy guru Martin Anderson. In April 1998 Bush visited Hoover, where Michael Boskin, George H.W. Bush's chair of the Council of Economic Advisers, set up a meeting at Shultz's house for Bush and some of Hoover's top scholars. During the meeting, Anderson recalled, "We all kind of looked at each other and said, 'Hey, this guy's really good.'" Anderson did not miss the fact that in addition to being "really smart and sharp and quick," Bush was governor of the nation's second-largest state, a natural launching pad for a presidential run.[2]

A few months after the meeting, in July 1998, Bush, who had not yet announced for the presidency, called for Boskin, Anderson, Shultz, and Stanford provost Condoleeza Rice to visit him in Austin. After that meeting, Anderson said, "So, on an as-if basis, we agreed to set up a policy shop." The well-organized policy shop resembled an army, with more than one hundred experts broken up into separate teams under three major divisions. Former Indianapolis Mayor Steven Goldsmith headed the domestic division, AEI economist Larry Lindsey captained the economic division, and Rice ran the foreign policy apparatus. In addition to Rice, Hoover scholars filled three domestic policy slots and five on economics. As the *Stanford Review* noted breathlessly, if not accurately, "No one has seen anything of this scope before at this stage of a candidacy."[3]

In addition to the formal policy groupings, Bush had a number of advisers who helped shape his "compassionate conservative" message, such as University of Texas professor Marvin Olasky, Princeton University professor John DiIulio, and Manhattan Institute scholar Myron Magnet. Other architects of the compassionate conservative message included UCLA professor James Q. Wilson, who had helped in seminars with President Ford; National Center for Neighborhood Enterprise president Robert Woodson; and Goldsmith, who assembled a meeting of compassionate conservatives with Bush to hone the message. Olasky and Magnet, however, had the closest association with the new ideology. As Bush biographer Bill Minutaglio described it, Olasky and Magnet were "instrumental in shaping the bedrock of Mr. Bush's public policies—something the leading GOP presidential contender describes with the catch phrase 'compassionate conservatism.'" According to Minutaglio, Bush told Magnet in 1997 that Magnet's 1992 book, *The Dream and the Nightmare*, changed the governor's life. Magnet's book, recommended to Bush by chief strategist Karl Rove, argued that cultural forces unleashed by society's elites trickled down and caused tremendous damage among the underclass, whose members lacked the resources to recover from bad choices. As Magnet himself described it, "The book kind of contains the formula for compassionate conservatism."[4]

Even though Olasky lived in the same city as Bush, he only met Bush through an elaborate series of circumstances, in a textbook case of how ideas filter through the culture and end up with politicians. In Olasky's book *The Tragedy of American Compassion*, he agreed with Magnet that government welfare programs encouraged dangerous behavior and contributed to the underclass. Olasky also argued that what the public sector had caused, the private sector— churches, volunteer organizations, and civic-minded corporations—could fix. Former secretary of education William Bennett gave the book as a Christmas gift to Congressman Newt Gingrich. Gingrich, a former college professor who had just managed the Republican takeover of Congress, put the book on his much-publicized reading list for all members of the new Republican majority. Rove saw the book on the reading list and recommended it to Bush.[5]

Bush's intellectual arsenal served him in good stead throughout the 2000 campaign, as journalists constantly derided his grasp of policy but quickly added that Bush had assembled an array of conservatism's top thinkers to advise him. As conservative columnist George Will put it, while Bush was no intellectual, he was "comfortable around people of high intellectual quality, and has a cadre of them devising theoretical justification for his instinctive proclivity—call it 'strong executive conservatism.'" While most other pundits were less friendly, they could not overlook the fact that Bush recognized his perceived limitations and surrounded himself with top policy experts.[6]

The movement of intellectuals in and out of Austin throughout 1998 and 1999, reminiscent of Franklin Roosevelt's summoning of the brain trust to Hyde Park for miniseminars in his 1932 campaign, attracted some negative press as well. *Washington Post* columnist Michael Kelly, for example, mocked the "historic flocking" to Austin of "planes filled with think-tankers and policy-paperers." Kelly joked that "there were flights from Washington to Austin so filled with egos that flight attendants agonized in the galleys over which to stroke first." Despite the mocking, the essential point could not fail to get out— that Bush surrounded himself with top policy experts. As James Carney wrote in *Time*, "The fear that continues to fester about Bush—as we read about his periodic foreign policy gaffes and then hear him blithely assert that what he doesn't know he can learn from his advisers—is that at 53 he has the same cavalier attitude toward knowledge that he had at 21: he could learn what he needs to know, but he doesn't seem to think it's worth his time." The harshness of this comment was blunted by the necessary reference to the group of experts that

Bush had assembled. In this sense, the teams of scholars protected Bush from the worst of the media derision.[7]

The Bush scholars served another purpose as well, signaling to conservative activists and readers of right-leaning publications that Bush planned to run a conservative administration. As AEI scholar Norman Ornstein put it, the conservative intellectuals around Bush made "a statement that his presidency will be a little bit more like Ronald Reagan's than George Bush's." While Bush was not the most conservative candidate in the primaries, his policy team demonstrated to party conservatives, who make up a large percentage of Republican primary voters, that Bush, while electable, was still sufficiently conservative to satisfy them. This reassurance came in handy when Bush faced both a furious primary challenge from Arizona Senator John McCain and the third-party candidacy of right-wing columnist Pat Buchanan.[8]

AL GORE'S APPROACH

While Bush gained extra sheen from the academic bright lights around him, Gore often found himself trying to cover up his intellectual advisers. Gore had the reputation of a "wonk," Ivy League–speak for a nerdy know-it-all, derived from spelling the word "know" backward. Gore was the kind of candidate who enjoyed reading the five-hundred-page policy tomes that Bush eschewed. Even though Gore's Harvard grades had not been much better than Bush's Yale scores—both men earned their share of Cs—Gore developed the persona of a thinking man's politician, rather than Bush's "common man" approach. *Earth in the Balance*, Gore's best-selling policy tome, which quoted more existential philosophers than most American high school teachers can name, was instrumental in developing that persona.[9]

Gore also had long-standing friendships among the liberal intellectual establishment. Martin Peretz, editor of the *New Republic*, had been a Gore friend and adviser since Peretz taught Gore at Harvard thirty years earlier. Yet Gore and Peretz rarely appeared in public together, and Peretz was careful to stay away from the campaign, even spending much of the year 2000 in Israel, far away from his old friend.

While Peretz's backing did not hurt Gore, an all-out pro-Gore attitude did occasionally harm Peretz and his magazine's reputation. In September 1997, Peretz fired *New Republic* editor Michael Kelly, allegedly because Kelly refused to run an unsigned editorial, penned by Peretz, defending Gore from allegations of campaign finance abuses. Kelly had insisted that the piece be signed, while Peretz presumably knew that a Peretz piece defending Gore would have had limited impact. Furthermore, according to Kelly, he had warned Peretz that the magazine would be examining Gore with a more critical eye, leading to the firing. Peretz disagreed with Kelly's version, arguing that the Gore connection had nothing to do with the decision to fire Kelly. According to Peretz, since his backing of Gore was 100 percent upfront, there was nothing wrong with it: "It's no secret that I am a friend and admirer of his." As a result, he claimed, "Whatever I write is so clearly personal in nature that no one will say I'm trying to come off as an Olympian and neutral judge of these matters." Although Peretz remained close to Gore, having a public relationship with the vice president involved enough danger for Peretz that he never took the kind of public profile affiliation with the campaign that people like Olasky or Magnet had with the Bush campaign.[10]

Gore also faced problems with another author and adviser, feminist writer Naomi Wolf. Wolf caused the campaign severe embarrassment when *Time* revealed that the Gore campaign had paid her $15,000 a month for advice on how to attract support among women and young voters. Wolf received her money through consulting firms in an apparent effort to mask her salary in required Federal Election Commission reporting. After the relationship became public, the campaign kept her on board but reduced her salary by two-thirds.

A bigger problem for Gore than the excessive salary and ensuing cover-up was the advice itself. Most of Wolf's advice seemed to fit into the role of helping the campaign reach out to young women. But Wolf also provided two pieces of advice that led to relentless caricaturing in the media. First, Wolf told Gore to be an "alpha male" rather than the "beta male" that a vice president was necessarily supposed to be. Furthermore, Wolf advised Gore to wear earth tones rather than the standard blues and reds that he—along with most politicians—had worn in the past.

Although the alpha male and earth tone suggestions constituted only a small part of Wolf's advice, her role was problematic on a number of levels. Most obviously, the method of payment contributed to the perception that there was something to hide. In addition, while Wolf dressed Gore, Bush had a team of experts providing real policy advice on a wide variety of subjects, creating an unfavorable contrast. Wolf's alpha male suggestion, in addition to sounding overly New Age, fostered the impression that Gore was not his own man and would change his style to suit political purposes. Presumably, a real alpha male does not need to be told to act like an alpha male. Finally, the Gore campaign reluctantly but inevitably had to defend Wolf's controversial body of work, usually explaining that Gore had not read all of Wolf's books. This problem worsened when Wolf appeared on ABC's *This Week* to defend herself, against the wishes of the top brass at the Gore campaign, who had probably leaked the anti-Wolf stories to begin with. As Myron Magnet wrote in the *Wall Street Journal*—after Wolf had attacked Magnet's work—some of the "loopy ideas" that Wolf had to defend on *This Week* included "that women should release their 'shadow slut'; that parents should teach their children to masturbate their friends, so as to avoid the dangers of intercourse; that sure, abortion is killing someone, but that's okay, as long as we have 'acts of redemption,' little ceremonies saying how sorry we are to have done it."[11]

As a result of all of these problems, Gore suffered from a severe anti-Wolf backlash. Brookings scholar Stephen Hess said, "The idea that they paid her this kind of money for stuff she would have been thrilled to provide for nothing is evidence of how far the Gore operation has gone amok." *New York Times* columnist Maureen Dowd called Wolf "the moral equivalent of an Armani T-shirt, because Mr. Gore has obscenely overpaid for something basic," namely, to be told to be his own person. Even the staid and Gore-friendly *New York Times* editorial page made a joke about Wolf: "Her advice to Mr. Gore seems pretty reasonable, except for the earth tones." After the incident, Wolf lay low, only to resurface six months later when the tumult had diminished. According to the *New York Post*'s Deborah Orin, Wolf returned to the campaign in July 2000, "happily bragging" to friends that she was "back in the loop as Gore trie[d] to reinvent his campaign once again."[12]

In addition to having somewhat controversial advisers like Wolf and Peretz, Gore also relied heavily on top experts within the Clinton administration, including economic adviser Gene Sperling and Treasury secretary Lawrence Summers. Although these people had know-how and access to the latest information, this path created problems for Gore as well. First, using Clinton appointees made it harder for Gore to emerge from the Clinton shadow. In addition, using full-time administration appointees raised inevitable questions about use of federal resources for political activities. These potential problems limited his ability to use the Clinton policy aides to their fullest effect.[13]

Finally, although Gore had his own policy staff, it was a much smaller operation than the Bush machine. As Ceci Connolly and Glenn Kessler of the *Washington Post* reported, Gore maintained "a strikingly small paid policy staff." Bush had a full-time staff of ten—not counting all of the outside policy experts—led by the well-regarded former Senate aide and Bush administration official Joshua Bolten. As the *Washington Post* put it, Bush "built one of the best policy shops any presidential candidate has assembled and relies on a network of advisers that includes some of the brightest conservative thinkers in the country." In contrast, Gore's staff consisted of ex-Progressive Policy Institute scholar and Gore vice presidential aide Elaine Kamarck, Kamarck's assistant, and former White House aide Sarah Bianchi.[14]

Part of the reason for the small staff may have been that Gore did not seem to need his policy shop very much. Clinton administration staffers provided much of the heavy lifting, and there were indications that Gore did not listen to the policy shop's recommendations. Kamarck was a New Democrat, best known for coauthoring the pro–Third Way "Politics of Evasion" essay with Bill Galston. But as Jonathan Cohn pointed out in the *New Republic*, Gore was quite publicly running an Old Democrat campaign, trying to appeal to the Democratic Party's four pillars: labor, feminists, blacks, and other minorities. While this kind of campaign appealed to Gore's liberal campaign manager, Donna Brazile, it was exactly the kind of politics that Kamarck and her allies in the Democratic Leadership Council had been fighting for over a decade. Cohn found it strange that Kamarck would condone the Brazile approach, wondering if Kamarck felt that "after 8 years of moving the Democratic Party to the right, she thinks it's time to nudge it back to the left." The other strange thing about the Old Democrat campaign is that Gore had been closely affiliated with the whole New Democrat movement, even helping write some of the earliest DLC press releases.[15]

From the other side of the spectrum, John Miller and Ramesh Ponnuru of the *National Review* agreed that Gore had apparently abandoned the New Democrats. Not only did Gore disagree with the DLC position on issues like federalism, Medicare, and Social Security, but in all of those cases, the DLC was far closer to Bush's position than to Gore's. As Kamarck put it, "The only reason [the DLC] ideas got as far as they did is because people thought we had to do something. We don't have to do something anymore." As Miller and Ponnuru explained it, Kamarck believed that "economic prosperity . . . made it possible for the vice president to avoid a DLC-driven agenda of entitlement reform."[16]

While Gore and Bush took different approaches to bringing in expert policy assistance, their main opponents for the nomination, Bill Bradley and John McCain, respectively, ran as their own senior policy advisers and suffered for it. Having outside intellectuals advise a candidate on positions is not the only reason to bring in the experts, although it helps. Bringing in well-known intellectuals can reassure party activists—those further down what David Brooks called the "intellectual continuum"—that a particular candidate is ideologically acceptable. Both McCain and Bradley suffered on this front. Since McCain ran largely to Bush's left, it was relatively easy for Bush to paint McCain as insufficiently conservative for the Republican party faithful. But McCain's relative lack of outside assistance made the Bush campaign's job even easier. According to Fred Barnes of the McCain-friendly *Weekly Standard*, McCain did not have "his act together on domestic policy," refusing to put in the effort to craft a unified domestic policy vision. As Barnes put it, McCain needed "policy advisers with . . . talent and seriousness, and he needs to spend as much quality time with them as he does with reporters." The fact that Bush had the bulk of conservative intellectuals and think tanks on his team highlighted McCain's deficiencies on this front.[17]

Bradley, in contrast, tried to run to Gore's left and therefore should have had additional appeal to the activists and ideologues who make up a disproportionate share of both parties' primary electorates. Despite the Bradley campaign's leftward tilt, Gore still managed to attack Bradley from the left, accusing Bradley of opposing Medicaid and having supported Reagan's budgets. Bradley aided Gore by stubbornly serving as his own senior policy adviser. As Melinda Henneberger explained in the *New York Times*, Bradley was "in charge of tone, direction, vision. . . . Both in a political sense and on policy, Bill Bradley is his campaign." As a result of this approach, Bradley had only a few members of the Democratic intelligentsia on his team to defend him from Gore's relentless attacks. As the McCain and Bradley experiences demonstrated, failure to bring in outside policy experts could unnecessarily expose candidates to new vulnerabilities.[18]

THE "ANTI-SMARTY" CAMPAIGN

Despite the role intellectuals played in the 2000 campaign, it remains clear that the days of the full-time White House ambassador to the intellectual community writ large are in the past. Bush managed relations with intellectuals better than Gore did, but he also benefited from the mood of the electorate. Having intellectuals in the White House might have seemed appealing in 1960, but by 2000 Americans seemed to prefer likability to book smarts. As Jonathan Chait of the *New Republic* explained, the conventional wisdom that "the only thing standing between George W. Bush and the presidency is a persistent reservation about his intellect" was all wrong. In contrast, he argued, "Bush hasn't done a bad job masking his boredom with the details of governance; he's done an excellent job of flaunting it." According to Chait, Bush was "a brilliant candidate not despite of his anti-intellectualism but because of it."[19]

Richard Berke, writing in the *New York Times*, agreed. Bush's perceived lack of intellectual curiosity was more of an advantage than a disadvantage. According to Berke, "just as a recurrent theme in this presidential race has been whether Gov. George W. Bush has the intellect to be a successful president, so some Gore advisers worry that their candidate may come off, as President Harry Truman would put it, as too much of a 'smarty.'" While Bush just had to prove that he was smart enough to be president, Gore had "the arguably tougher job of proving that he is not a condescending smarty-pants."[20]

Both writers agreed that Bush's admitted lack of interest in "reading a 500-page book on public policy or something" helped Bush in the 2000 campaign. Lack of interest in policy by itself, however, did not make a candidate appealing. As Marty Anderson put it, Bush had "a secret weapon. It's the same one Eisenhower had. Clinton's got it. Even when they disagreed with his policies, they still like him." Bush, along with Clinton before him, had the most important trait in American presidential politics: likability.[21]

Chait also saw another, more negative, aspect of Clintonism as an important factor in Bush's appeal in 2000. Chait blamed Clinton for "the anti-intellectual turn of the political zeitgeist," which was "rooted in boredom, not anger, and it [arose] not from a hatred of Clintonism but from an approval of it." Clinton talked to everyone, to intellectuals, to his own aides, to opponents, to the American people. Despite Clinton's own appeal to intellectuals and close relations with them, his constant talking contributed to a mood in which the public enjoyed having a president who could talk to them, not lecture at them.[22]

EARLY BUSH

It is difficult to assess an administration's long-term relationship with intellectuals without looking back at the administration as a whole. Still, the launch of the Bush presidency was instructive in that it provided a sense of the direction Bush wanted to take. In the early days of the Bush presidency, think tanks played a prominent role in staffing the new administration. His transition team consulted heavily with scholars from AEI, Hoover, the Hudson Institute, and the Heritage Foundation, which produced many of its famous lists. The production of the Heritage lists caused a bit of a stir when the *New York Times* reported that Virginia Thomas, the wife of Supreme Court Justice Clarence Thomas, helped gather names of candidates for the Bush transition. The *Times* reported the story, and other papers followed, because the disputed election ended up in the Supreme Court, where Justice Thomas voted in favor of Bush. Mrs. Thomas's actions, the *Times* claimed, raised "possible conflict of interest claims." Whatever the merit of the charges, the story demonstrated that the Heritage Foundation was playing a role in the formation of the Bush administration. Working at the Heritage Foundation does not make one an intellectual, and those recommended by Heritage were by no means all—or even most—intellectuals, but Heritage's role did demonstrate that Bush took conservative ideas seriously.[23]

Following the brief transition, the early days of the Bush administration revealed that George W. Bush appeared to be following the Reagan model of using intellectuals to help staff his administration without relying on any one intellectual as his ambassador to the academic world. Bush was not likely to serve as his own ambassador to the intellectuals, as Clinton did, but he was not likely to ignore them, either. As Peggy Noonan put it in the *Wall Street Journal*, "Mr. Bush fils, like Mr. Reagan, has respect for the power of ideas and has surrounded himself with people with ideas."[24]

As such, refugees from AEI, Heritage, and the Hudson Institute took important administration posts, both in the White House and throughout the government. Although the think tanks did well, Bush did not hire any single White House ambassador to the intellectual community. Again, this followed the Reagan model of hiring conservatives who love ideas but not focusing on any one intellectual adviser.

The most prominent intellectual in the administration was the political scientist John DiIulio, whom Bush tapped to head the Office of Faith-Based and Community Initiatives, the cornerstone of Bush's compassionate conservative agenda. DiIulio, a former student of James Q. Wilson at Harvard, described himself as "the noncosmopolitan intellectual." Wilson, perhaps the most brilliant American academic in the period examined in this volume, called DiIulio "one of the three or four best graduate students I ever had." *Newsweek* described him as "an exuberant iconoclast," who was "impossible to tie to single political ideology." Reverend Eugene Rivers called him "Joe Pesci with a Ph.D."[25]

As the various descriptions indicated, DiIulio was a scholar in the Moynihan mold, an ethnic Democrat from modest means with little patience for elitism on the right or the left. Like Moynihan, DiIulio also had more enemies on the left than on the right. But also like Moynihan, he took the issue of urban poverty seriously and was willing to try a wholly new approach to the problem. Unfortunately, the events of September 2001 profoundly changed the Bush administration's approach. Yet even before the terrorist attacks of September 11 refocused the administration on the war on terrorism, DiIulio announced his departure and return to academia. DiIulio left the White House on September 15, 2001.

Unlike his predecessor, Bush was never a headline grabber. While conservative think tankers swirled through the transition and DiIulio made pugnacious comments in the press, Bush remained in the background. Even when establishment intellectuals came to visit the White House, they met with White House staffers as a group. According to the *Washington Post*, "Bush adviser Karl Rove invited [Fred Greenstein] and other scholars, such as Yale political scientist Stephen Skowronek, to the White House for a guest lecture on the modern presidency to Bush aides."[26]

On the whole, however, Bush showed little interest in reaching out to the so-called mainstream intellectual community. According to columnist Michael Kelly, Bush ignored the liberal intellectual establishment, thereby "making the liberal establishment unhappy to a point approaching hysteria." According to Jane Mayer of the *New Yorker*, Bush passed up a chance to attend Yale's three-hundredth anniversary party, an opportunity his predecessor would never have skipped. Bush, when given the chance, would not even acknowledge that he was born in Connecticut, making Texas a key part of his rejection of the whole elitist package symbolized by Ivy League schools in northeastern states. As Mayer

put it, Bush's "storied antipathy to Yale, which some have interpreted as an expression of populism, has become an integral part of his political packaging."
This political packaging called for concerted efforts among conservative
thinkers but studied indifference to the hostile intellectual establishment.[27]

REPUBLICAN VERSUS DEMOCRATIC STRATEGIES

Although Bush brought in presidential scholars to talk to his staff, for the most part
Bush and his staff focused on garnering the support of openly conservative think
tankers. Clinton, in contrast, focused mainly on winning over select establishment
intellectuals at America's top universities one-on-one and not focusing on the
Washington-based think tanks. Despite the fact that they took very different tacks,
both men were fairly successful in their efforts with intellectuals, mainly because
they recognized the strengths and weaknesses of the intellectuals on their own side.

The contrast between the successful Clinton and Bush approaches demonstrates the degree to which the American intellectual community had become
fragmented over four decades. While the establishment intellectual community
remained reliably liberal, conservatives built their own counterestablishment
with right-of-center thinkers and talking heads. The two communities rarely in-
tersected, and each had independent relations with the politicians of its party.
Yet they served an important purpose for their respective parties, and Democratic and Republican presidents developed completely different strategies for
dealing with intellectuals in ways that served them best.

DEMOCRATS AND DIFFUSE ESTABLISHMENTARIANS

As each side needed a different approach to relations with the intellectuals, each
side had its own advantages and disadvantages. Democrats had a natural edge
among the so-called establishment intellectuals at the elite universities and intellectual magazines. The thinkers at these organizations inclined themselves to
support Democratic candidates and presidents and were therefore susceptible
to wooing from those quarters. These intellectuals had credibility in the mainstream press and therefore could be helpful in shaping positive media coverage
and the president's legacy. Democrats had an almost exclusive hold on this resource. No Republican could realistically hope to win over these thinkers and no
smart Republican would waste time trying.

Bush, for example, knew he stood no chance of winning support among the
establishment intellectuals and subsequently did not try. Bush could afford to

ignore this constituency because he knew the futility of soliciting its support. Columnist Michael Kelly described the attitude of mainstream intellectuals toward Bush: "It is accepted among establishmentarians that, now and again, a Republican is going to get himself elected president, due to the horribly large number of Americans who do not know better than to vote for the wrong people, no matter how often and how patiently the experts explain things to them."[28]

Yet this natural edge did not necessarily make the Democrats' job easier. They were coping with a more diffuse community, and they faced a tougher time in securing the support of such a community on their own. A Democratic president could not go to the liberal equivalent of the Hoover Institution, as candidate Bush had, and cite that organization's support as a proxy for the support of the broader liberal establishment. A Democratic president could not rely on the steady support of the counterestablishment network of think tanks, a network that could provide campaigns and administrations with ready staffers having some level of intellectual imprimatur.

Given this diffuse and, in some ways, less Washington-focused community, Democrats often found themselves able to mobilize monolithic support most easily in times of crisis. Establishment intellectuals as a group were generally lackluster about Bill Clinton until the Lewinsky scandal threatened his presidency, when they rallied around the Clinton presidency, providing support like the petition signed by 412 historians. Similarly, Al Gore received relatively little aid from the intellectual community until the 2000 election results came into dispute, at which point a remarkably similar petition appeared in the *New York Times*.

That is not to say that Democrats cannot score successes with the intellectual community during times of noncrisis. Clinton, as noted previously, had many ardent supporters like Sean Wilentz among the intellectual establishment. Wilentz did himself and his academic reputation no favor by defending Clinton in anything and everything he did. But Clinton gained such perfervid supporters by focusing on individual intellectuals, recognizing that it was impossible to gain the support of the community as a whole. While candidate Clinton worked mainly with one think tank, the moderate Progressive Policy Institute, to send the message that he was a different kind of Democrat, President Clinton took a very different path. Clinton knew that a visit to Princeton would not secure the support of the whole Princeton faculty, so he focused—through Sid Blumenthal—on an individual, and politically active professor, in Sean Wilentz. Similarly, he reached out to other intellectuals at different schools, whether by reading their books conspicuously or inviting them to the White House for strategy seminars. In this way, when he needed their support, he found steadfast loyalty.

Clinton's approach provides a model for a successful Democrat strategy—reach out to individual intellectuals in selected schools to build a base of support among the diffuse intellectual establishment. To do this, it is not necessary to hire a full-time intellectual adviser or even to be closely associated with one individual or school of thought. In fact, the more focused approach is risky and could lead to discontent, among either excluded individuals or the alternative ideological approaches. In short, Democratic presidents should adopt a diffuse strategy for appealing to a diffuse but powerful community that is generally inclined to support them.

REPUBLICAN STRATEGY: THINK TANK CADRES

Republican candidates had the opposite advantage and the opposite disadvantage. The disadvantage of the emergent conservative counterestablishment was that they could not shake the conservative label. While magazines, papers, and think tanks like *Time*, *Newsweek*, the *New York Times*, the *Washington Post*, and the Brookings Institution, which generally took liberal positions on issues, successfully portrayed themselves as mainstream, conservative organizations—the *Wall Street Journal*, the *Weekly Standard*, and the American Enterprise Institute—were always just that, conservative organizations.

Yet this disadvantage could also serve as an advantage. Bush, for example, could afford to ignore mainstream intellectuals because he understood that he had his own base of support among conservative intellectuals. Since the intellectual organizations on the conservative side were explicitly conservative organizations, Republican presidents, if they so chose, could reach out to organizations like Heritage, Hoover, and AEI, which could potentially support them. This support, of course, is not guaranteed. George H. W. Bush and John McCain, for example, did not receive the support of the conservative intelligentsia.

McCain failed to secure the backing of the conservative movement as a whole, even as he won the intellectuals around the *Weekly Standard*, which underscores the approach that works for conservatives. The pick-and-choose strategy, which works for Democrats specifically, does not work for Republicans because conservative intellectuals see such an approach as a lack of consistency. In the larger liberal intellectual establishment, such consistency will inevitably lead to discontent somewhere. Among conservatives, there is a better chance, although certainly no guarantee, of bridging the gap among conservative think tanks and intellectuals. While such thinkers may disagree with one another, presidents have a wide enough purview to satisfy their various conservative intellectual constituents.

THE LARGER PICTURE

The story of intellectual interaction with the White House is interesting for the tensions that the larger story reveals regarding the presidency, among American intellectuals, and for the American political system in general. For presidents, the need to deal with intellectuals reflects many trends, most of them developing as a result of the growth of government and the attendant increases in the complexity of public policy. These trends include the rise of think tanks, the fragmentation of the intellectual community, the increasing size of presidential staff, and, most recently, the development of the twenty-four-hour news cycle. With this backdrop, as government has become more important in people's lives, the media have focused more attention on government's actions. This, in turn, has led to a presidential focus on the media's importance in shaping a presidency, both while it is in power and later in the history books.[29]

While a government is in power, the media shape the image of the president, helping determine if he will get reelected and how much political capital he will have in the form of public support for his administration. In the longer run, the members of the press write the first draft of history and thereby control perhaps the most crucial portion of the presidential legacy. Furthermore, the media have become much more than the morning paper or the evening news. Twenty-four-hour cable news networks are starved for content, and presidents, whatever they are doing, make great filler. In the case of scandals, the quest for information about presidents becomes even greater. Similarly, Internet magazines and news content providers are constantly updating their coverage, seeking to press their advantage over the dated-as-soon-as-it's-printed paper media. In this environment, if presidents fail to define themselves, the media will do the defining, and it will not be what the president or his advisers would choose.

As the media have become more pervasive, however, the analysis has become more superficial and less sober. In the 2000 campaign, more Americans got their news from the humor monologues of Jay Leno and David Letterman than from the network news programs. In this world, shorthand characteristics—the pack journalism mentality that Al Gore called the meta-narrative—was often the sum total of what most Americans knew about presidents and candidates. As Gore described this concept to his Columbia University journalism students, "the meta-narrative is that Gore is stiff, Bush mangles his words and Clinton eats cheeseburgers." The shallowness of the meta-narrative approach cries out for someone to provide definition for a candidate.[30]

As a result, intellectuals became one, but only one, of the forces shaping the all-important meta-narrative. Interest groups, research organizations, corporations, unions, and other politicians all try to advance their own agendas by shaping the media's definition of a national politician, to advance (or damage) that politician's career and to enhance their own media profile. In order to cope with all of these competing—and sometimes cooperating—forces, political staffs, and in particular White House staffs, have grown as presidents have sought to reach out to every demographic and interest group. As the meta-narrative has become more important, political gurus have developed more important roles than intellectuals—witness Pat Caddell's role in the Carter campaign and administration or Karl Rove in the Bush campaign. But as dozens of aides focus on image, reaching out to intellectuals must become a key part of that image shaping.

In this context, intellectuals help shape the media. In fact, intellectuals become even more likely to participate. According to Irving Kristol, professors enter administrations precisely because of "the importance of the media." As Kristol explains, "professors do tend to be much more articulate than businessmen or bankers since, after all, they are lecturing to students all the time." Intellectuals serve a crucial role in helping frame the all-important media image.[31]

With or without a positive media image, however, the American presidency remains the most powerful post in the Western world. Presidents preside over a $9 trillion-plus economy, a $2 trillion government, a $300 billion military, and a huge staff of aides focused on serving the president's every whim. The president has image makers, press experts, and policy makers, all devoted to the cause of making the president look good. Yet presidents, for all their power, do not control what goes in the history books, which is shaped by the almost equally uncontrollable media reports that appear with ever increasing rapidity. They do not even control their own approval ratings, which are of the most immediate concern to presidents, not to mention their opponents.

This situation makes presidents, for all their power, extremely vulnerable. As a result, they understandably seek some magic elixir that can help shape their image among the voting public, the scribbling classes, and the history books. To some degree, intellectuals appear to have that power. If they cannot confer a positive image on a president, they certainly can help sully a president's image. Lyndon Johnson, for example, was one of the most powerful presidents of modern times, both in his understanding of the power of the office and his willingness to use that power. Yet he stood powerless against the campaign waged against him by intellectuals, most of whom probably belonged to his own party. And Johnson recognized his impotence on this front. As *The Nation* put it at the time, Johnson "was not oblivious to the fact that widespread antagonism among thoughtful citizens can be unhealthy for any President." As Johnson and later Nixon learned, this unhealthiness can prove politically fatal.[32]

As a result of these pressures, presidents look to intellectuals to help define their presidency. Presidents do this by paying attention at some level to what intellectuals are doing and by addressing intellectuals and intellectual developments in some fashion. The approach they take can vary, especially between Democrats and Republicans, but they must address the issue. If presidents are the lions of American politics, intellectuals are the mice. While the lions can smite the mice, the mice have the potential to remove—or insert—the thorn in the lion's paw.

INTELLECTUAL ROUNDHEELS

Needless to say, intellectuals are far less powerful than the president. First, however they are counted, they are fewer in number than any interest group meriting regular presidential attention. In 1974 Charles Kadushin catalogued the American intellectual elite as one hundred individuals, the public intellectuals who write multiple articles in the most prestigious intellectual journals. By even the most expansive definition—say, all humanities professors and think tank scholars in the entire country—they do not number more than 150,000. In addition to their relatively low numbers, American intellectuals are not organized in any coherent way and cannot remotely agree among themselves on anything, let alone ideology. Yet intellectuals have a soft spot for presidential attention. Just as presidents approach intellectuals in part on the basis of ideological considerations, so also intellectuals assess presidents through an ideological prism.[33]

American intellectuals, as noted above, are fragmented, split into a well-organized conservative community and a larger, better known, but less organized liberal establishment. Each side has its strengths and weaknesses, but it is important to recognize how the state of intellectuals differs today from what it was forty years ago. In 1960 Kennedy could reach out to a small group of Cambridge intellectuals and thereby gain the proxy for nearly the entire intellectual community. The whole intellectual establishment at the time was almost more analogous to the smaller, better-focused conservative intellectual community of today. In that forty-year period, there have been great changes in the intellectual community. The expanding media outlets—print, television, and the Internet—have opened the floodgates for the creation of far vaster numbers of talking heads, not all of them intellectuals. Think tanks, almost unknown in 1960, have exploded, creating housing for intellectuals beyond university campuses and magazine mastheads. Furthermore, the consensus school has disappeared as intellectuals have fragmented into differing ideologies, with no one school of thought capable of attracting the community as a whole.

These developments have taken place with surprising rapidity. The 1960s began with most intellectuals belonging to the consensus school of liberal anti-communism. The intellectual community split in the 1960s, making it difficult for any one figure to appeal to intellectuals across ideological lines. As Joseph Epstein put it in *Commentary*, in the late 1950s and early 1960s "it did not seem possible to be an intellectual and not be of the Left." In the 1960s and 1970s, however, the intellectual community fragmented, with both left and right wings forming on the traditionally liberal body.[34]

Conservative idea generators became so prevalent that by the 1980s and 1990s, to paraphrase Epstein, it did not seem possible to be a neoconservative and not be an intellectual. Indeed, in an article on the never-ending Great Books controversy, Emily Eakin of the *New York Times* referred to "disaffected traditionalists," as "Columbia historian Jacques Barzun, the Harvard biologist E. O. Wilson, and the neoconservative Irving Kristol." Unlike "professor" at Harvard or Columbia, "neoconservative," it seemed, spoke for itself. To be a member was to be an intellectual.[35]

This fragmentation has served an important purpose. While it is true that the consensus school intellectuals were in general agreement, it does not mean that they were lacking in ideology. Perhaps the advent of differing camps has revealed the ideologies of the intellectuals. By boldly challenging liberal claims that they were engaged in independent scholarship, conservative intellectuals made themselves vulnerable to the charge that they were not independent either. Perhaps the lesson in all this is that independent scholarship may be as mythical a concept as Atlantis or Utopia.

INTELLECTUAL AMBITION

Despite their fractures and limitations, intellectuals today are far more numerous, better compensated, and more influential than they ever were in the past. But this is not enough for an ambitious group, at least as individuals. As intellectuals become more influential, they grow more ambitious as well. As Mitchell Ross explained in *The Literary Politicians*, ambitious professors "seek power by acquainting politicians with their knowledge . . . they hope to catch the eyes of committee chairmen, who may invite them to testify at hearings, and of presidential candidates, who may ask them for advice."[36]

Professors are not the only intellectuals who seek proximity to power. Norman Podhoretz's 1968 book *Making It* was a how-to manual for ambitious intellectuals. According to Podhoretz, President Kennedy opened the doors to ambition among intellectuals. As a result of Kennedy's actions, "intellectuals were recognized as an occupational grouping that mattered in American life: from having carried a faint aura of disreputability, the title 'intellectual' all at once became an honorific, and much began to be made in Washington as elsewhere of leading representatives of this particularistic class." Podhoretz took full advantage of this recognition, and he was far from the only one to do so.[37]

But this ambition among intellectuals has its dangers as well. As Ross put it, "No one who moves freely between the worlds of politics and letters can help contradicting himself." Yet Ross has only captured part of the problem. Self-contradiction is one thing, and it is amendable; the taint of compromised principles is much harder to shake.[38]

In addition to their ambitions, intellectuals have a fair share of insecurity as well, never believing they are taken seriously enough. James Freedman, former president of Dartmouth, expressed this sentiment while speaking at a conference entitled Challenges in a New Century: The Engaged Intellectual. Freedman's great contribution was the insight that "the role of the intellectual is seriously undervalued." According to Freedman, "We need to appreciate that intellectuals are gifted individuals with unconventional angles of vision, and are often endowed with an exceptional capacity to advance the common good." Although Freedman's comments take intellectual self-congratulation to a new level, they also reveal an unhealthy level of insecurity, which mixed with ambition makes for a dangerous combination. Because intellectuals are so ambitious and so insecure, and because their reputations are so important, the question of possible taint becomes potentially devastating.[39]

Insecurity and ambition, when combined, make intellectuals an easy mark for presidents. Clinton, for example, often recognized and exploited this combination, with great success. Clinton read as many as four books per week. But he did not change or even create policy as a result of his reading. According to a report by Todd Leopold, "In the early days of his term, [Clinton] reportedly immersed himself in presidential biographies, from David McCullough's 'Truman' to Edmund Morris' volume on Theodore Roosevelt. Yet, the historians say, they apparently had little effect on his style or Presidency." Clinton, it seems, read for effect at least as much as to effectuate change.[40]

But Clinton was quite clever in his choice of reading, often using books to gain the undying support of their authors. According to Fred Greenstein, Clinton once conspicuously placed behind his desk Richard Reeves's book *President Kennedy: Profile of Power*, which discussed the disorganization of the Kennedy White House. According to Greenstein, "When that book was published Clinton had invited its author to meet with him and never touched on the theme of White House organization, which is one of the weak points of Clinton's leadership."[41]

Although there is certainly nothing wrong with succumbing to a presidential charm offensive, it can lead to compromised analysis. Sidney Blumenthal, for example, fell under this suspicion while covering Clinton for the *New Yorker*. Although Blumenthal's overt partisanship and sycophancy for all things Clinton was an extreme case, the issue goes far beyond Blumenthal's advising and covering the White House at the same time.

All intellectuals are subject to fears about their objectivity, but this issue looms larger for Democrats than for Republicans. As the Blumenthal example shows, Democrats have more concerns about being compromised. Conservatives have less to worry about because they start out tainted as conservatives—the very fact that they can't shake the conservative label means that tagging them with it cannot cause additional harm.

But conservatives have concerns on this front as well. In recent years, the line between conservative intellectual and Republican operative has become so thin that it is almost invisible. In fact, the advent of a Republican administration presents a powerful challenge to the integrity of the conservative intellectual movement. As David Brooks, himself a conservative, put it, "There is no longer a bright line separating the pool of conservative intellectuals and journalists from the pool of Republican officeholders. Now there is something of an expectation that activists, commentators, and rank and file conservatives should behave like Republican organization workers." When intellectuals fail to meet that expectation, they can expect a torrent of criticism from their colleagues in think tanks and conservative magazines.[42]

This is a problem on both sides of the aisle. As Brooks noted, "A similar transformation has occurred on the left—as the Lewinsky scandal made clear, when liberal groups universally betrayed their feminist principles to stand by their party leader." The point is not whether one side is less independent; according to Brooks, "this means that both liberalism and conservatism are less intellectually dynamic. Pressure to conform to the party line leads to groupthink, and narrows the parameters of acceptable debate." The rise of ideology over independent analysis has led to the development of two cadres of intellectual roundheels, who can largely be counted on to adhere to their own party line on a given issue. Such a development is useful for the parties, but it is potentially worrisome for the cause of independent scholarship.[43]

Because of the threat of tainted reputations, all intellectuals, right and left, must be wary of a president's charm. The Clinton example is particularly instructive in this regard. Intellectuals swooned over the attention Clinton lavished on them, but he did not give them much from a policy perspective. With the Third Way giving Clinton room to weave in and out of specific policy patterns, both liberal intellectuals and moderate DLC think tankers had cause to wonder about Clinton's commitment to their favored causes. But the intellectual swoon over Clinton was not Clinton's fault. He had a job to do in terms of winning intellectual support, and he did it well. Future presidents would benefit by learning from his actions on this front.

A policy role took a distant backseat under this symbolic approach. In today's environment, an intellectual with a real interest in policy can best serve by taking a line policy position rather than a generalist intellectual role. Policy advisers like Henry Kissinger in foreign policy or the economist Lawrence Summers in the

Clinton Treasury Department have served successfully in their respective roles, but they did not purport to serve as intellectuals or as emissaries to the intellectuals at large. The closest an intellectual has come to serving as both a policy adviser and an intellectual was Pat Moynihan. His situation as an antileftist Democrat intellectual in a largely anti-intellectual Republican White House was, as we have seen, unique.

FACILE FACULTIES

Ideological fragmentation was only one development that changed the intellectual community. Epstein drew a distinction between traditional intellectuals of the middle part of the twentieth century and the public intellectuals of the latter part of the century. A traditional intellectual, he argued, was an "amateur of the mind . . . distinguished from other mind workers, or intelligentsia, by his want of specialization. He knew not one but many things." The public intellectual, in contrast, was "a figure who as likely as not retains all or most of the political attitudes of the 1960s, suitably adapted for the moment, and who has become adept at packaging them in fancy academic dressing." As Epstein put it, the public intellectual "qualifies not by any particular mental power but by going public with one's intelligibility and one's mere opinions." The traditional intellectual, "the real thing," who wrote for serious journals but in an intelligible way, who rejected the abstruseness of academic specialization, was, according to Epstein, "on his way out." These new public intellectuals fell into two categories—specialist academics and glib pundits, albeit with some overlap.[44]

A number of factors contributed to the redefinition of intellectuals. First, affluence continued to allow more students to go to college, more degree holders to go to graduate school, and more intellectuals to find work in academia, think tanks, or a related field. As David Brooks explained in his *Bobos in Paradise*, "with the rise of a mass educated class, it has become ever more difficult to draw the line between the world of the intelligentsia and the rest of America. The gap between intellectuals and everyone else is now a continuum." As these people found jobs and careers, they became something very different from intellectuals of the past. As Irving Howe explained it, "Whenever intellectuals become absorbed into the accredited institutions of society they not only lose their traditional rebelliousness but to one extent or another *they cease to function as intellectuals*." This parsing of the word "intellectual" is partly a form of guild protection. Irving Howe and his colleagues believed that people whose operation differed from theirs did not merit being called intellectuals. Of course, as Epstein points out, Howe did accept a post at Brandeis, part of what Epstein calls the siphoning away of American intellectual life by the universities.

His own situation aside, Howe had a point. As American society valued intellectuals more, in terms of both remuneration and respect, opportunities abounded that took intellectuals away from their traditional roles. In addition to political and financial temptations, intellectuals faced media temptations, with cable TV and the Internet vastly expanding the opportunities for punditry. As these new media searched desperately for content to fill their twenty-four-hour-a-day requirements, the definition of a pundit, too often mistaken for an intellectual, expanded exponentially. At the same time, genuine intellectuals, seduced by a similar power to the one that attracted many of them to the corridors of power in the first place, seemed only too happy to hawk their wares on TV.[45]

With intellectuals succumbing to various temptations, it became harder for them to fulfill their traditional roles—to educate society, to break new scholarly ground, and to sustain a cadre willing to engage in legitimate criticism of the regime. All of these roles give way when intellectuals become pundits, presidential aides, or party regulars. Yet the temptations of twenty-first-century society often draw intellectuals into the very roles that prevent them from serving their societal function. Of course, no one is forcing intellectuals into working in the White House or appearing on television talk shows. It is certainly difficult to imagine Thoreau appearing on *Crossfire* or seeking political clearance for a White House job. But the temptations available to intellectuals in modern society do provide a potentially corrupting influence, and the temptations obstruct intellectuals from accomplishing their mission.

The presidency is just one among this expanding array of temptations but may be the worst of all. An intellectual could appear on television and still provide a coherent critique of the regime or produce groundbreaking scholarship the rest of the time. But the political world inflicts deeper wounds. To take just a recent example, the Clinton charm offensive exposed intellectuals both in and out of the White House. Sid Blumenthal and Sean Wilentz will have trouble presenting themselves as serious scholars in the years to come. Wilentz, in particular, damaged his reputation with his preimpeachment performance before the House Judiciary Committee, which was criticized on both the right and the left. Wilentz's near hysteria, and his claim to some monopoly over historical interpretation, inflicted real damage on his scholarly abilities.

So the presidency's flirtation with intellectuals is partially responsible for imposing a corrupting influence on the scholarly world. But it is by no means the only influence, and it is by no means an overwhelming or irresistible pull. Intellectuals can resist the charm offensive, and they can work with presidents while retaining their respectability. Arthur Schlesinger pulled this off under Kennedy, although he may have hurt himself by joining the Wilentz camp under Clinton. Unfortunately, while such a balancing act is a possibility, the increased political polarization of the intellectual world makes this an exceedingly difficult feat.

Whether or not intellectuals retain their integrity, the broader point remains. The traditional intellectual has faded away, and the new intellectuals are hard to distinguish from journalists, professors, or pundits. While an ambassador to academia can help a president appeal to all of these groups, the categories are just too broad, and the ideologies now too diverse, for one emissary to relate across the whole continuum.

Presidents seeking good relations with intellectuals and the resulting benefits may not be able to rely on a single intellectual as ambassador, but they still need to address the issue. The fact remains that intellectuals, even if they are no longer the homogeneous group they once were, are still important in shaping a president's image and reputation. The fragmentation of the intellectual community has made things both easier and harder for presidents seeking good relations with America's intellectuals. With the development of conservative intellectuals to counter the regnant liberal intellectual establishment, any president or presidential hopeful could find some intellectuals to both bolster his case and recruit more support among the intellectual's colleagues. Richard Nixon, for example, selected Moynihan because of the dearth of conservative intellectuals who could fill such a position. Yet Moynihan, while a committed Democrat, was disliked by most liberals and mistrusted by Republicans.

Today's presidents are not so limited. They can find intellectuals of all stripes, a veritable smorgasbord of intellectuals and policy experts, wide-ranging enough that anyone could find some measure of support. Of course, this fragmentation also means that no one intellectual can appeal to the whole community, as Arthur Schlesinger once could, or even bridge all the differences among all intellectuals on one side of the intellectual spectrum, as Martin Anderson tried to do. Furthermore, as the experiences of intellectuals in the White House have shown, just having one ambassador to the intellectual community has not always been sufficient. What presidents need is some kind of intellectual momentum. Presidents use intellectuals to show something about the candidate. Clinton showed he was a New Democrat; Bush showed both acceptability among conservatives and compassionate conservatism. Yet, even if more intellectuals of different stripes are available, the task is not always easy.

Despite the growing influence of intellectuals, it is a safe bet that they do not see themselves as sufficiently influential. Intellectuals have few votes, and even when they serve in high offices, they have relatively little influence. Yet as the Bush example shows, intellectuals remain important for presidents and presidential candidates alike. As Reagan and Clinton demonstrated, having good relations with intellectuals can help create a positive perception in the media, among party activists, and ultimately with voters. In contrast, mismanaging or, worse, ignoring relations with American intellectuals can contribute to the perception of a president lacking in conviction or in vision. To counter this problem, presidents need to work with intellectuals. Presidents must mollify the intelligentsia in order to avoid the pitfalls encountered by Carter or Bush Sr. Presidents may not need to hire an intellectual to succeed in this task, but they ignore the intellectuals at their peril.

WHAT IT MEANS FOR AMERICA

Intellectuals in the White House can serve as a guide, helping presidents navigate the expanding waters of American intellectual life. Although there is a potentially worthy purpose for intellectuals, there has always been a cynical element in bringing intellectuals into the White House, dating back to Roosevelt. Over the last few decades, however, the cynicism has increased. Intellectuals in the White House increasingly serve the purpose of selling the White House to the intellectual community, which in turn controls the tone of media coverage and other public opinion–molding mechanisms, a function that became especially clear in the Clinton impeachment saga. This is especially the case in Democratic administrations, where good relations with intellectuals can help with the media far more than those relations can help during Republican presidencies.

The presidents who use intellectuals in this way are not the only cynics involved. In other words, intellectuals have frequently shown themselves susceptible to manipulation by flattery, especially in administrations in which their seemingly great influence proved to be illusory. In the Clinton administration, for example, liberal academics often groused about Clinton's policies yet leaped en masse to his defense during the impeachment saga.

These developments are not all encouraging ones for our polity. The situation may not be as grave as Columbia University professor Jacques Barzun felt when he observed, "Thus the greatest danger to a democratic state is probably the contamination of its politics by Intellect." On the other hand, we clearly have cause for concern, as this study raises important question that intellectuals and their chroniclers need to address. What is the proper role for intellectuals with respect to the president? What is the appropriate position for presidents to take vis-à-vis intellectuals? To these questions, there are no easy answers, as Eric Goldman learned when Theodore White asked him the question that forms the subtitle of this book. White asked if intellectuals in the White House served as "philosophers, jesters, or technicians." The history of these last few decades teaches us that for intellectuals in the White House, the answer is, a little bit of each.[46]

APPENDIX: GUIDEBOOK FOR PRESIDENTS

THE DOS AND DON'TS OF EMPLOYING INTELLECTUALS IN THE WHITE HOUSE

Don't ignore intellectuals. It can come back to haunt you.

Don't be an intellectual. The American people might like their politicians to consult intellectuals, but they won't vote for eggheads.

Don't use an intellectual who lacks a reputation as an intellectual. It's like sending a man to be the White House representative on women's issues.

Don't forget your friends. If you rely heavily on an academic adviser in the campaign, make sure he or she is taken care of in the administration. Carter and Clinton made this mistake to some degree. Clinton got away with it; Carter did not.

Don't make meetings with intellectuals public and don't reveal what was said in such meetings in any official way.

Don't underestimate the capacity for flattery among intellectuals.

Don't try to latch on to a cutting-edge concept developed by a prominent intellectual, especially if the concept is alarmist or disconcerting, such as malaise.

Don't feel obligated to give your aides the same loyalty you demand from them.

Don't confuse intellectual advisers with policy advisers, and vice versa.

Do use intellectuals to express your vision. Having a group of thinkers affiliated with an idea—New Democrats, compassionate conservatism, or even supply-siders—is preferable to flailing about searching for the "vision thing."

Do use the president's meal times liberally as a way to garner support from intellectuals. Even if you don't back their policies, few people refuse a free meal at the White House.

Do call intellectuals and tell them you have read their works.

Do work with prominent think tanks and seek their guidance on issues in the campaign and their personnel during transition. Do not, as president, publicly rely on think tank guidance.

Do leak the existence of meetings with intellectuals, including the guest lists, and any amusing anecdotes that reflect favorably on one or more of the attendees.

Do let it be known when the president is reading a popular work by a well-known scholar, as long as it is not a Swedish planning text, à la Michael Dukakis.

Do make sure that any intellectuals brought into the White House are loyal to the president above all else. Loyalty is the most important characteristic for an intellectual in the White House.

Do expect that any public intellectual in the White House will produce a book describing the experience. Do your best to ensure that this is a positive book, as it will help shape your legacy. As Forrest McDonald wrote, "By and large, works by former White House aides are good sources of information on the subject. Presidents, in their memoirs, are less helpful."[1]

Do seek out advice from intellectuals, but do not rely on that advice.

NOTES

NOTES TO CHAPTER ONE

1. Cf. Allen J. Matusow, *The Unravelling of America: History of Liberalism in the 1960s* (New York: Harper & Row, 1984); Michael Barone, *Our Country: The Shaping of America from Roosevelt to Reagan* (New York: Free Press, 1991), 383–95; cover, *New York Review of Books*, August 24, 1967.

2. Richard Hofstadter, *Anti-Intellectualism in American Life* (New York: Knopf, 1963), 405.

3. Hofstadter, *Anti-Intellectualism*, 408.

4. Robert Wiebe, *The Search for Order, 1877–1920* (New York: Hill & Wang, 1967), 2–3, 111–32; Burton Bledstein, *The Culture of Professionalism: The Middle Class and the Development of Higher Education in America* (New York: Norton, 1976), 34.

5. Cf. Wiebe, *Search for Order*.

6. *Oxford English Dictionary*, compact ed.; Christopher Lasch, *The New Radicalism in America (1889–1963): The Intellectual as a Social Type* (New York: Knopf, 1965), ix; Talcott Parsons, "'The Intellectual': A Social Role Category," in Philip Rieff, ed., *On Intellectuals: Theoretical Studies, Case Studies* (Garden City, N.Y.: Doubleday, 1969), 18.

7. Cf. John Morton Blum, *The Republican Roosevelt* (New York: Atheneum, 1971).

8. Forrest McDonald, *The American Presidency: An Intellectual History* (Lawrence: University Press of Kansas, 1994), 280; cf. Alfred Dick Sander, *A Staff for the President: The Executive Office, 1921–1952* (New York: Greenwood, 1989).

9. Cf. Gil Troy, *See How They Ran: The Changing Role of the Presidential Candidate* (New York: Free Press, 1991), 160–89; Patrick Anderson, *The Presidents' Men: White House Assistants of Franklin D. Roosevelt, Harry S. Truman, Dwight D. Eisenhower, John F. Kennedy, and Lyndon B. Johnson* (New York: Doubleday, 1968), 21. "Brains trust" and "brain trust" are interchangeable terms. For reasons of consistency, except when quoting a source directly, I have chosen to use "brain trust."

10. David Kennedy, *Freedom from Fear* (New York: Oxford University Press, 1999), 119; Arthur Schlesinger, *The Age of Roosevelt: The Crisis of the Old Order* (Boston: Houghton Mifflin, 1956), 416.

11. Kennedy, *Freedom from Fear*, 124.

12. Adolph Berle, memorandum to Franklin D. Roosevelt, August 17, 1932, President Roosevelt's 1932 Campaign: 1932–1933, General Correspondence, O–W, Subject File, Container 16, "Roosevelt, F.D. 1932–March 4, 1933."

13. Harry Elmer Barnes, "The Liberal Viewpoint," *New York World–Telegram*, February 27, 1933, 18; Harry Elmer Barnes, "The Liberal Viewpoint," *New York World–Telegram*, February 28, 1933, 16.

14. Arthur Schlesinger, *The Age of Roosevelt: The Coming of the New Deal* (Boston: Houghton Mifflin, 1958), 182; Schlesinger, *Age of Roosevelt: Crisis*, 415.

15. Rexford Tugwell, Letter to Raymond Moley, February 4, 1964, Tugwell Papers, Container 2, Br–Ce, "Brains Trust Correspondence," Franklin Delano Roosevelt Library.

16. Raymond Moley, Letter to Rexford Tugwell, February 11, 1964, Tugwell Papers, Container 2, Br–Ce, "Brains Trust Correspondence," Franklin Delano Roosevelt Library.

17. Louis Brownlow, *A Passion for Anonymity: The Autobiography of Louis Brownlow* (Chicago: University of Chicago Press, 1958), 2:313, 396–97; Alfred Dick Sander, *A Staff for the President: The Executive Office, 1921–1952* (New York: Greenwood, 1989), 30; President's Committee on Administrative Management, *Administrative Management in the Government of the United States* (Washington: Government Printing Office, 1937), 2.

18. Richard Polenberg, *Reorganizing Roosevelt's Government: The Controversy over Executive Reorganization, 1936–1939* (Cambridge: Harvard University Press, 1966), 49–50.

19. Brownlow, *Passion for Anonymity*, 386; Polenberg, *Reorganizing*, 180–87.

20. John Kenneth Galbraith, *A Life in Our Times: Memoirs* (Boston: Houghton Mifflin, 1981), 38.

21. Milovan Djilas, *The New Class: An Analysis of the Communist System* (New York: Praeger, 1957); Daniel Bell, "The New Class: A Muddled Concept," in B. Bruce–Briggs, ed., *The New Class* (New Brunswick, N.J.: Transaction, 1979), 169–90; U.S. Department of Commerce, Bureau of the Census, *Historical Statistics of the United States: Colonial Times to 1970*, pt. 1 (Washington: Government Printing Office, 1975), 382, 285.

22. Hofstadter, *Anti-Intellectualism*, 3; Eric Goldman, *The Crucial Decade—And After: America, 1945–1960* (New York: Vintage Books, 1960), 224–25; Eric Sevareid, Letter to Carl McGowan, October 2, 1952, Papers of Adlai Stevenson, Illinois State Historical Society, Springfield. Stevenson evidently captured Sevareid's imagination as well. The supposedly objective reporter made this observation in a letter to Carl McGowan, Stevenson's top political aide, in which Sevareid advised McGowan on how Stevenson could win.

23. Porter McKeever, *Adlai Stevenson: His Life and Legacy* (New York: William Morrow, 1989), 207.

24. McKeever, *Adlai Stevenson*, 315, 247.

25. Lionel Trilling, *The Liberal Imagination* (New York: Secker and Warburg, 1950); Trilling quoted in George Nash, *The Conservative Intellectual Movement since 1945* (New York: Basic, 1976), 58.

26. Hofstadter, *Anti-Intellectualism*, 5.

27. John Kenneth Galbraith, *The Affluent Society* (Boston: Houghton Mifflin, 1958); David Riesman, *The Lonely Crowd* (New Haven: Yale University Press, 1950); C. Wright Mills, *The Power Elite* (New York: Oxford, 1956).

28. Galbraith, *A Life*, 296–97.

29. Eric Goldman, *The Tragedy of Lyndon Johnson* (New York: Knopf, 1969), 432; cf. Russell Jacoby, *The Last Intellectuals* (New York: Basic, 1987). Other names for the new intellectuals included "independent intellectuals" (Steven Biel), "universal intellectuals" (Andrew Ross), "literary intellectuals" (Mitch Ross), "idea brokers" (James Smith), "New Mandarins" (Noam Chomsky), "action intellectuals" (Theodore White), and "public affairs intellectuals" (Irving Kristol).

30. For more on the New York intellectuals, see Alan M. Wald, *The New York Intellectuals: The Rise and Decline of the Anti-Stalinist Left from the 1930s to the 1980s* (Chapel Hill: University of North Carolina Press, 1987).

31. Ben Wattenberg and Richard Scammon, *This U.S.A.* (Garden City, N.Y.: Doubleday, 1965).

32. Allen J. Matusow, *The Unravelling of America: History of Liberalism in the 1960s* (New York: Harper & Row, 1984), 405.

33. Hofstadter, *Anti-Intellectualism*, 397.

NOTES TO CHAPTER TWO

1. Kennedy won the Pulitzer Prize for John F. Kennedy, *Profiles in Courage* (New York: Harper & Brothers, 1956); his honor's thesis became John F. Kennedy, *Why England Slept* (New York: W. Funk, 1940); Theodore Chaikin Sorensen, *Kennedy* (New York: Harper & Row, 1965), 256.

2. "Stevenson Group Backing Kennedy," *New York Times*, June 17, 1960; Clipping, John F. Kennedy Library, The Papers of Arthur Schlesinger Jr., Writings, Box W-8, "Kennedy, John F., Reactions to Endorsement Of, By Arthur M. Schlesinger, Newsclippings."

3. Edward T. Thompson, introduction to *Theodore White at Large: The Best of His Magazine Writing, 1939–1986* (New York: Pantheon, 1992), xvii; Thomas Winship, "Kennedy Building Own 'Braintrust' of University, Industrial Leaders," *Washington Post*, December 26, 1969, A2.

4. Sorensen, *Kennedy*, 11.

5. Sorensen, *Kennedy*, 33.

6. Sorensen, *Kennedy*, 23.

7. Sorensen, *Kennedy*, 14.

8. Sorensen, *Kennedy*, 66; Theodore White, "The Action Intellectuals," *Life*, June 9, 1967; reprinted in White, *Theodore White at Large: The Best of His Magazine Writing, 1939–1986* (New York: Pantheon, 1992), 393.

9. Sorensen, *Kennedy*, 85.

10. Sorensen, *Kennedy*, 4.

11. Theodore White, "Perspective 1960, no. 1," *Saturday Review*, March 26, 1960; reprinted in White, *Theodore White at Large*, 267; Sorensen, *Kennedy*, 117.

12. Winship, "Kennedy," A2.

13. John F. Kennedy, Letter to Archibald Cox, January 18, 1960, JFK Library, The Papers of Theodore C. Sorensen, Campaign Files, 1959–60, Box 21, "Academic Advisory Committee"; Winship, "Kennedy," A2.

14. Invoice, John F. Kennedy Library, The Papers of Deirdre Henderson, Box 1, "Deirdre Henderson"; various memoranda, John F. Kennedy Library, The Papers of Deirdre Henderson, Box 1, "Theodore Sorensen."

15. Richard Goodwin, letter to Archibald Cox, February 9, 1960, JFK Library, The Papers of Theodore Sorensen, Campaign Files, 1959–60, Box 21, "Academic Advisory Committee."

16. Sorensen, *Kennedy*, 118; Abram Chayes, Oral History, JFK Library, Oral History Collection. Quoted in Thomas C. Reeves, *A Question of Character: A Life of John F. Kennedy* (New York: Free Press, 1991). 152.

17. Sorensen, *Kennedy*, 118.

18. Arthur M. Schlesinger Jr., *A Thousand Days: John F. Kennedy in the White House* (New York: Houghton Mifflin, 1965), 21–22; Sorensen, *Kennedy*, 48–49. On the issue of Kennedy's illness during the McCarthy vote, see Reeves, *Question of Character*.

19. Arthur Schlesinger, Letter to John F. Kennedy, July 7, 1959, JFK Library, The Papers of Arthur Schlesinger, Campaign Files, 1959–60, Box 25, "Arthur Schlesinger."

20. John F. Kennedy, Letter to Arthur Schlesinger, July 13, 1959, JFK Library, The Papers of Arthur Schlesinger, Campaign Files, 1959–60, Box 25, "Arthur Schlesinger."

21. Hubert H. Humphrey, Letter to Arthur Schlesinger, December 17, 1959, JFK Library, The Papers of Arthur Schlesinger, Private Files, Box P–16, "Hubert Humphrey (1947–1960)."

22. Arthur Schlesinger, Letter to Joseph Rauh, February 18, 1960, JFK Library, Papers of Arthur Schlesinger, Private Files, Box P–16, "Hubert Humphrey (1947–1960)."

23. Draft letter, March 19, 1960, JFK Library, The Papers of Arthur Schlesinger, Private Files, Box P–16, "Hubert Humphrey (1947–1960)."

24. Arthur Schlesinger, Letter to John F. Kennedy, March 17, 1960, JFK Library, The Papers of Arthur Schlesinger, Campaign Files, 1959–60, Box 21, "Campaign Material, General" (Folder 1).

25. Hubert Humphrey, Letter to Arthur Schlesinger, April 18, 1960, JFK Library, The Papers of Arthur Schlesinger, Private Files, Box P–16, "Hubert Humphrey (1947–1960)."

26. Arthur Schlesinger, Letter to Hubert Humphrey, May 2, 1960, JFK Library, The Papers of Arthur Schlesinger, Private Files, Box P–16, "Hubert Humphrey (1947–1960)."

27. Arthur Schlesinger, Letter to John F. Kennedy, May 11, 1960, JFK Library, President's Office Files, Box 32, "Schlesinger, Arthur Jr., 4/26/60–1/23/63 and undated."

28. "An Important Message of Interest to All Liberals," Open Letter, June 17, 1960, JFK Library, The Papers of Arthur Schlesinger, Campaign Files, 1959–1960, Box 23, "Liberals"; "Stevenson Group Backing Kennedy," Unsigned article, *New York Times*,

June 17, 1960, JFK Library, The Papers of Arthur Schlesinger, Writings, Box 8, "Kennedy, John F., Reactions to Endorsement Of, By AMS, Newsclippings"; Reeves, *Question of Character*, 160.

29. Walter Lippmann, Oral History, JFK Library, Oral History Collection, 6.

30. "For the 1960 Candidate, a Camp of Eggheads Is a Must," *Business Week*, June 18, 1960, 172.

31. Arthur Schlesinger, Letter to John F. Kennedy, August 30, 1960, JFK Library, Presidential Files, President's Office Files, Box 32, "Schlesinger, Arthur Jr., 4/26/60–1/23/63 and undated."

32. "Faculty Poll Supports Kennedy by 284 Votes," *Harvard Crimson*, November 8, 1960; JFK Library, President's Office Files, Staff Memoranda, Box 65, "Schlesinger, Arthur M., 11/60–2/61."

33. Richard Neustadt, *Presidential Power: The Politics of Leadership* (New York: Wiley, 1960); Richard Neustadt, Memoranda to John F. Kennedy, JFK Library, Papers of President Kennedy, President's Office Files, Staff Memoranda, Box 64, "Richard Neustadt, 1960."

34. Deirdre Henderson, various memos, JFK library, The Papers of Deirdre Henderson, Box 1, "Appointment Memos"; Deirdre Henderson, Memo to John F. Kennedy, November 22, 1960, JFK Library, The Papers of Deirdre Henderson, Box 1, "Deirdre Henderson."

35. Galbraith was an economist but professed an interest in looking at economic development in India. John Kenneth Galbraith, *Ambassador's Journal: A Personal Account of the Kennedy Years* (Boston: Houghton Mifflin, 1969), 1. Of course, an oft retold, perhaps apocryphal, tale has Kennedy sending Galbraith to India to get rid of him. In any event, Galbraith called the position in India his "prime aspiration."

36. JFK Library, Biography of Arthur Schlesinger; Mitchell S. Ross, *The Literary Politicians* (New York: Doubleday, 1978), 92.

37. Schlesinger, *Thousand Days*, 155; Arthur Schlesinger, Letter to Joseph Alsop, January 24, 1961, The Library of Congress, The Papers of Joseph and Stewart Alsop, Box 17, "General Correspondence, Jan. 1961."

38. Arthur Schlesinger, Memorandum to John F. Kennedy, January 9, 1961, JFK Library, The Papers of Arthur Schlesinger, Writings, Box W-8, "Kennedy, John F., Interregnum Correspondence 12/60–1/61."

39. Sorensen, *Kennedy*, 264; Richard Goodwin, *Remembering America: A Voice from the Sixties* (New York: Harper & Row, 1988), 142.

40. Edwin O. Guthman and Jeffrey Shulman, eds., *Robert Kennedy in His Own Words: The Unpublished Recollections of the Kennedy Years* (New York: Bantam, 1988), 38–39.

41. Kenneth O'Donnell and David F. Powers with Joe McCarthy, *Johnny, We Hardly Knew Ye: Memories of John Fitzgerald Kennedy* (Boston: Little, Brown, 1970), 243; Guthman and Shulman, *Robert Kennedy*, 419.

42. Guthman and Shulman, *Robert Kennedy*, 419.

43. Goodwin, *Remembering America*, 140.

44. He also did some work on Latin American affairs, which is beyond the scope of this survey, except as it related to Schlesinger's status as an intellectual; Galbraith, *Ambassador's Journal*, 28.

45. Arthur Schlesinger Jr., Memorandum to John F. Kennedy, February 6, 1961, JFK Library, President's Office Files, Box 65, "Disposition of Presidential Papers, 11/60–2/61"; Sorensen, *Kennedy*, 5.

46. Schlesinger, Memorandum to John F. Kennedy, February 6, 1961, JFK Library, President's Office Files, Box 65, "Disposition of Presidential Papers, 11/60–2/61"; Schlesinger, *Thousand Days*, 271.

47. Schlesinger, *Thousand Days*, x.

48. Arthur Schlesinger, Memorandum to John F. Kennedy, October 29, 1962, JFK Library, President's Office Files, Box 65A, "Arthur Schlesinger, October, 1962."

49. Arthur Schlesinger, Memorandum to John F. Kennedy, February 20, 1963, President's Office Files, Box 66, "Memos on the History of the Kennedy Administration, 10/63." "Cuba" referred to the Cuban missile crisis. "Skybolt" referred to the decision to test the airborne ballistic missile launched from the B–52 bomber.

50. Arthur Schlesinger, Memorandum to John F. Kennedy, March 6, 1963, President's Office Files, Box 66, "Memos on the History of the Kennedy Administration, 10/63."

51. Arthur Schlesinger, Memorandum to John F. Kennedy, July 17, 1961, JFK Library, President's Office Files, Box 65, "Schlesinger, Arthur, 7/61–9/61."

52. Schlesinger, *Thousand Days*, 681–82; Alfred Kazin, "The President and Other Intellectuals," *American Scholar*, Fall 1961, 504.

53. Kazin, "President," 514, 516.

54. Schlesinger, *Thousand Days*, 682.

55. Arthur Schlesinger, Memorandum to John F. Kennedy, January 20, 1962, JFK Library, President's Office Files, Box 65A, "Schlesinger, Arthur M., 1/62–3/62."

56. Arthur Schlesinger, Memorandum to John F. Kennedy, March 14, 1963, JFK Library, President's Office Files, Box 65A, "Schlesinger, Arthur M., 3/63"; Jules Feiffer, undated, JFK Library, President's Office Files, Box 65A, "Schlesinger, Arthur M., 3/63."

57. Arthur Schlesinger, Memorandum to John F. Kennedy, February 6, 1961, John F. Kennedy Library, President's Office Files, Box 65A, "Schlesinger, Arthur M., 11/60–2/61."

58. Arthur Schlesinger, Memorandum to John F. Kennedy, February 6, 1961, John F. Kennedy Library, President's Office Files, Box 65A, "Schlesinger, Arthur M., 11/60–2/61."

59. Schlesinger, *Thousand Days*, 672.

60. Arthur Schlesinger, Memorandum to John F. Kennedy, November 22, 1961, JFK Library, The Papers of Arthur Schlesinger, White House Files, Box WH–16, "National Cultural Policy, General (10/5/61–1/8/64 + undated)"; Schlesinger, *Thousand Days*, 11.

61. Arthur Schlesinger, Memorandum to John F. Kennedy, November 22, 1961, JFK Library, The Papers of Arthur Schlesinger, White House Files, Box WH–16, "National Cultural Policy, General (10/5/61–1/8/64 + undated)."

62. August Heckscher, Memorandum, "Conversation with the President of August 6," August 7, 1962, JFK Library, The Papers of Arthur Schlesinger, Writings Files, Box W–3, "The Arts Memoranda."

63. Arthur Schlesinger, Memorandum to John F. Kennedy, October 29, 1963, JFK Library, President's Office Files, Box 66, "Schlesinger, Arthur M., 10/63"; "JFK's De-

fense of Poetry," editorial, *New York Post*, October 28, 1963, Clipping, JFK Library, President's Office Files, Box 66, "Schlesinger, Arthur M., 10/63."

64. Arthur Schlesinger, Memorandum to John F. Kennedy, August 13, 1962, JFK Library, Papers of Arthur Schlesinger, White House Files, Box WH–18, "Politicking"; Arthur Schlesinger, Memorandum to John F. Kennedy, August 26, 1962, JFK Library, Papers of Arthur Schlesinger, White House Files, Box WH–18, "Politicking."

65. Sorensen, *Kennedy*, 353.

66. Arthur Schlesinger, Memorandum to John F. Kennedy, April 4, 1961, JFK Library, President's Office Files, Box 65, "Schlesinger, Arthur M., 4/61"; Schlesinger, *Thousand Days*, 690.

67. Benjamin Bradlee, *Conversations with Kennedy* (New York: Norton, 1975), 127.

68. Walter Winchell, "Walter Winchell of New York," *New York Daily Mirror*, August 31, 1962, Clipping, JFK Library, Arthur Schlesinger Papers, Writing Files, Box W–7, "Economic Growth Newsclippings"; cf. Neal Gabler, *Winchell: Gossip, Power, and the Culture of Celebrity* (New York: Knopf, 1994).

69. Robert Hartmann, "The ADA Liberalism: Its Impact on the New Frontier," *Los Angeles Times*, September 3, 1961. The three White House aides in the ADA were Schlesinger, Sorensen, and Harris Wofford. The three cabinet members were Orville Freeman (Agriculture), Arthur Goldberg (Labor), and Abraham Ribicoff (Health, Education, and Welfare).

70. Arthur Schlesinger, Letter to Violet Gunther, JFK Library, The Papers of Arthur Schlesinger, White House Files, Box WH–3, "ADA, 5/15/61–10/2/61."

71. Arthur Schlesinger, Letter to Paul Seabury, November 8, 1961, JFK Library, Papers of Arthur Schlesinger, White House Files, Box WH–3, "ADA 10/3/61–12/20/61."

72. Arthur Schlesinger, Memorandum to John F. Kennedy, January 19, 1962, JFK Library, President's Office Files, Box 65A, "Schlesinger, Arthur M. 1/62–3/62."

73. This exchange leaves little doubt regarding Baldridge as social secretary. In the days before computers, Baldridge sent the letter as was, inserting the correct word, "consulting," in the margin above the expression "Mamma Mia!" Arthur Schlesinger, Memorandum to Letitia Baldridge, November 29, 1961, JFK Library, Papers of Arthur Schlesinger, White House Files, Box WH–24, "White House Library 11/3/61–4/25/62"; Letitia Baldridge, Letter to Arthur Schlesinger, February 1, 1962, JFK Library, Papers of Arthur Schlesinger, White House Files, Box WH–24, "White House Library 11/3/61–4/25/62."

74. Arthur Schlesinger Sr., Letter to Arthur Schlesinger Jr., April 24, 1962, JFK Library, Papers of Arthur Schlesinger, Box WH–24, "White House Library 11/3/61–4/25/62." Schlesinger recommended the following individuals: "[Bernard] Bailyn (the new editor of the John Harvard Library), [Denis] Brogan, [Henry Steele] Commager, [Merle] Curti, John Hope Franklin, [Allan] Nevins, Henry Nash Smith, and, of course, Paul Buck and Howard Jones."

75. Arthur Schlesinger, Letter to Paul Buck, May 1, 1962, JFK Library, Papers of Arthur Schlesinger, Box WH–24, "White House Library 5/1/62–5/31/62"; Jacqueline Kennedy, Letter to Arthur Schlesinger, January 4, 1963, JFK Library, Papers of Arthur Schlesinger, Box WH–24, "White House Library 1/8/63–2/29/64 + Undated."

76. Arthur Schlesinger, Letter to Jacqueline Kennedy, January 9, 1963, JFK Library, Papers of Arthur Schlesinger, Box WH–24, "White House Library 1/8/63–2/29/64 + Undated."

77. Arthur Schlesinger, Letter to James Babb, February 29, 1964, JFK Library, Papers of Arthur Schlesinger, Box WH–24, "White House Library 1/8/63–2/29/64 + Undated."

78. John F. Kennedy, Letter to Arthur Schlesinger Sr., January 22, 1962, JFK Library, President's Office Files, Box 32, "Arthur Schlesinger, Sr. 1/22/62."

79. Richard Neustadt, Letter to Douglass Cater, December 15, 1961, JFK Library, President's Office Files, Box 64, "Richard Neustadt, 1960."

80. "Must Reading," *Newsweek*, June 19, 1961, 95.

81. Norman Podhoretz, *Making It* (New York: Harper & Row, 1967), 313.

NOTES TO CHAPTER THREE

1. Lyndon B. Johnson, Letter to Arthur M. Schlesinger, February 2, 1953, John F. Kennedy Library, Papers of Arthur Schlesinger, Private Files, Box P–17, "LBJ"; Johnson, Letter to Schlesinger, February 1, 1957, John F. Kennedy Library, Papers of Arthur Schlesinger, Private Files, Box P–17, "LBJ."

2. Schlesinger, Letter to Johnson, February 14, 1957, John F. Kennedy Library, Papers of Arthur Schlesinger, Private Files, Box P–17, "LBJ."

3. Johnson, Letter to Schlesinger, April 8, 1957, John F. Kennedy Library, Papers of Arthur Schlesinger, Private Files, Box P–17, "LBJ."

4. Schlesinger, Letter to Johnson, March 4, 1958, John F. Kennedy Library, Papers of Arthur Schlesinger, Private Files, Box P–17, "LBJ."

5. Johnson, Letter to Schlesinger, March 6, 1958, John F. Kennedy Library, Papers of Arthur Schlesinger, Private Files, Box P–17, "LBJ."

6. Arthur Schlesinger, Oral History, November 4, 1971, John F. Kennedy Library, Oral History Collection, p. 1.

7. Joseph Rauh, Letter to Schlesinger, November 7, 1958, Library of Congress, Papers of Joseph L. Rauh, Box 41, "Schlesinger, Arthur M., 1956–67," Folder 2.

8. Lyndon Johnson, Conversation with Doris Kearns Goodwin, cited in Doris Kearns Goodwin, *The Fitzgeralds and the Kennedys* (New York: Simon & Schuster, 1987), 780.

9. Lewis Mumford, "John Fitzgerald Kennedy: 1917–1963" (speech to the Academy of Arts and Letters), undated clipping, John F. Kennedy Library, Papers of Arthur M. Schlesinger, Writing Files, Box W–3, "The Arts Magazine Articles."

10. Eric Goldman, *The Tragedy of Lyndon Johnson* (New York: Knopf, 1969), 20, 23.

11. Steven Hess, *Organizing the Presidency*, 2d ed. (Washington, D.C.: Brookings Institution, 1988).

12. Arthur Schlesinger, Oral History, November 4, 1971, John F. Kennedy Library, Oral History Collection, p. 13.

13. Lee White, Oral History, John F. Kennedy Library, Oral History Collection, p. 370.

14. Arthur Schlesinger, Letter to Lyndon Johnson, January 25, 1964, Library of Congress, Papers of Averell Harriman, Box 502, "Arthur Schlesinger, Jr."

15. Lyndon Johnson, Letter to Arthur Schlesinger, January 28, 1964, Library of Congress, Papers of Averell Harriman, Box 502, "Arthur Schlesinger, Jr."

16. Alan Reinert, introduction to Billy Lee Brammer, *The Gay Place* (Austin: Texas Monthly Press, 1978); Billy Lee Brammer, *The Gay Place* (New York: Houghton Mifflin, 1961), 510.

17. Goldman, *Tragedy*, 117.

18. Goldman, *Tragedy*, 526.

19. Goldman's initial list of eight thinkers consisted of Robert Charpie, Fedel Fauri, William Friday, Simon Kuznets, Edwin Land, Phillip Moseley, Charles Reich, and Arthur Moss. Of the eight, only two, Reich and Kuznets, have anything close to enduring reputations. Eric Goldman, Letter to White House Group, December 7, 1963, Library of Congress, The Papers of Eric F. Goldman, Box 61, Scrapbook, "December, 1963." Goldman, *Tragedy*, 10.

20. Nelson attended and summarized the meeting. Richard Nelson, Memo to Lyndon Johnson, December 12, 1963, Library of Congress, The Papers of Eric F. Goldman, Box 61, Scrapbook, "December, 1963." Goldman, *Tragedy*, 9.

21. Richard Nelson, Memo to Lyndon Johnson, December 12, 1963, Library of Congress, The Papers of Eric F. Goldman, Box 61, Scrapbook, "December, 1963."

22. Bill Moyers, Memo to Lyndon Johnson, cc to Jack Valenti, December 3, 1964, Lyndon B. Johnson Library, White House Special Files, FG–11–8–1, Box 84, "FG–11–8–1/Goldman, Eric."

23. Goldman, *Tragedy*, 34.

24. White House Press Release, February 3, 1964; Pierre Salinger, Press Conference Transcript, February 3, 1964, Lyndon B. Johnson Library, White House Special Files, FG–11–8–1, Box 84, "FG–11–8–1/Goldman, Eric"; Arthur Schlesinger, Oral History, November 4, 1971, John F. Kennedy Library, Oral History Collection, p. 17; Arthur Schlesinger, Letter to Eric Goldman, February 29, 1964, Library of Congress, Manuscript Division, Eric Goldman Papers, Box 48, "White House Files, Books, General, 1964–66."

25. Finding Guide, Eric Goldman Papers, Manuscript Division, Library of Congress. Goldman's books included *Historiography and Urbanization: Essays in American History in Honor of W. Stull Holt* (Baltimore: Johns Hopkins, 1941); *Charles J. Bonaparte, Patrician Reformer: His Early Career* (Baltimore: Johns Hopkins, 1943); *John Bach McMaster: American Historian* (Philadelphia: University of Pennsylvania, 1943); *Rendezvous with Destiny: A History of Modern American Reform* (New York: Knopf, 1952); and, in his first endeavor into popular history, *The Crucial Decade: America, 1945–55* (New York: Knopf, 1956).

26. Eric Goldman, Letter to Lyndon Johnson, April 22, 1964, Lyndon Johnson Library, White House Special Files, FG–11–8–1, Box 84, "FG–11–8–1/ Goldman, Eric early '64–4/30/64."

27. Goldman, *Tragedy*, 476.

28. Goldman, *Tragedy*, 136; Adam Clayton Powell, Letter to Eric Goldman, February 4, 1964; Eric Goldman, Letter to Adam Clayton Powell, February 18, 1964, Library of Congress, Manuscript Division, Eric Goldman Papers, Box 53, "Correspondence, Peyser–Purnell, 1964–66"; cf. Wil Haygood, *King of the Cats: The Life and Times of Adam Clayton Powell* (New York: Houghton Mifflin, 1993).

29. Goldman, *Tragedy*, 476.

30. Goldman, *Tragedy*, 176.

31. Lady Bird Johnson, Various Speeches, Library of Congress, Manuscript Division, Eric Goldman Papers, Box 59, "Johnson, Lady Bird, 1965."

32. Eric Goldman, Draft Speech for Lynda Johnson to Roswell, New Mexico, October 19, 1964; Eric Goldman, Draft Speech for Luci Johnson to UJA Night of Stars, November 7, 1964; Eric Goldman, Letter to Lynda Johnson, December 20, 1965; Eric Goldman, Draft Letter to David Herbert Donald, December 20, 1965, Library of Congress, Manuscript Division, Eric Goldman Papers, Box 59, "White House Files, Johnson, Luci and Lynda."

33. Lynda Bird Johnson was born on March 19, 1944; Luci was born on July 2, 1947.

34. Eric Goldman, Memo to Lyndon Johnson, December 16, 1964, Library of Congress, Manuscript Division, Eric Goldman Papers, Box 63, "Scrapbook, Nov–Dec, 64."

35. Eric Goldman, Letter to Eliska Hasek, July 6, 1964, Library of Congress, Manuscript Division, Eric Goldman Papers, Box 62, "Scrapbook, July 5–17, 1964."

36. Eric Goldman, Memo to Jack Valenti, July 13, 1964, Library of Congress, Manuscript Division, Eric Goldman Papers, Box 62, "Scrapbook, July 5–17, 1964."

37. Eric Goldman, Memo to Lyndon Johnson, September 8, 1964, Library of Congress, Manuscript Division, Eric Goldman Papers, Box 62, "Scrapbook, September, 1964."

38. Eric Goldman, Memo to Lyndon Johnson, July 29, 1964; Lyndon Johnson, Undated Memo to Eric Goldman, Library of Congress, Manuscript Division, Eric Goldman Papers, Box 62, "Scrapbook, August 64."

39. Eric Goldman, Memo to Richard Goodwin, October 2, 1964, Library of Congress, Manuscript Division, Eric Goldman Papers, Box 63, "Scrapbook, October 64."

40. Eric Goldman, Memo to Bill Moyers, October 28, 1964, Library of Congress, Manuscript Division, Eric Goldman Papers, Box 63, "Scrapbook, 10/9–31, 64."

41. Eric Goldman, Memo to Lyndon Johnson, December 22, 1964, Library of Congress, Manuscript Division, Eric Goldman Papers, Box 57, "White House Files, Freedom Medal."

42. Arthur Goldberg, Memo to Eric Goldman, December 23, 1964; Eric Goldman, Memo to Arthur Goldberg, December 31, 1964, Library of Congress, Manuscript Division, Eric Goldman Papers, Box 63, "Scrapbook, Nov–Dec, 64."

43. William Shirer, Letter to Eric Goldman, February 20, 1964; Eric Goldman, Letter to William Shirer, February 22, 1964, Library of Congress, Manuscript Division, Eric Goldman Papers, Box 54, "Correspondence, Sheehan to Smylie, 1964–66."

44. Eric Goldman, Memo to Lyndon Johnson, December 21, 1963, Library of Congress, Manuscript Division, Eric Goldman Papers, Box 56, "General (2)."

45. Eric Goldman, Memo to Lyndon Johnson, December 21, 1963, Library of Congress, Manuscript Division, Eric Goldman Papers, Box 56, "General (2)."

46. Eric Goldman, Memo to Walter Jenkins, March 17, 1964, Library of Congress, Manuscript Division, Eric Goldman Papers, Box 62, "Scrapbook, March 64."

47. John Kenneth Galbraith, Letter to Eric Goldman, March 11, 1964, Library of Congress, Manuscript Division, Eric Goldman Papers, Box 56, "John Kenneth Galbraith, 1964."

48. Lyndon Johnson, Letter to Eric Goldman, March 23, 1964, Lyndon Johnson Library, White House Special Files, FG–11–8–1, Box 84, "Eric Goldman/FG–11–8–1, March, 1964." Attendees included John Davis, CCNY; John Ehle, assistant to North Car-

olina Governor Terry Sanford; Robert Faris, University of Washington, Seattle; John Fischer, Montana State College; Joseph Fisher, Resources for the Future; Paul Freund, Harvard Law School; Eli Ginzberg, Columbia; Earl O. Heady, Iowa State; Earl Higbee, University of Rhode Island; Harry Johnson, University of Chicago; Edwin Land, president of Polaroid; Edward Levi, University of Chicago; Margaret Mead, American Museum of Natural History; Richard Musgrave, Princeton; Daniel Pollitt, University of North Carolina Law; Roger Revelle, Scripps Institute of Oceanography; David Riesman, Harvard; Clinton Rossiter, Cornell; Richard Sullivan, Reed; Homer Wadsworth, Kansas City Association of Trusts and Foundations; and Paul Yvisaker, Ford Foundation. No-shows included Galbraith, Hofstadter, Clark Kerr, Eugene Rostow, and Robert Wood.

49. Eric Goldman, Letter to Sargent Shriver, April 1, 1964, Library of Congress, Manuscript Division, Eric Goldman Papers, Box 56, "General (2)."

50. Eric Goldman, Memo to Lyndon Johnson, April 2, 1964, Library of Congress, Manuscript Division, Eric Goldman Papers, Box 56, "General (2)."

51. Eric Goldman, Unsent Letter to James Reston, September 14, 1964, Library of Congress, Eric Goldman Papers, Box 53, "Quinn to Revelle, Correspondence, 1964–66."

52. Eric Goldman, Memo to Lyndon Johnson, September 15, 1964, Library of Congress, Eric Goldman Papers, Box 62, "Scrapbook, September 1964." Proposed Commission on White House Fellows, September 22, 1964; Eric Goldman, Memo to Jack Valenti, September 30, 1964, Library of Congress, Manuscript Division, Eric Goldman Papers, Box 62, "Scrapbook, September 1964"; White House Press Release, October 4, 1964; Francis Keppel, Letter to Eric Goldman, October 7, 1964, Library of Congress, Manuscript Division, Eric Goldman Papers, Box 63, "Scrapbook, October, 1964."

53. Goldman, *Tragedy*, 418.

54. Goldman, *Tragedy*, 418–19.

55. Eric Goldman, Memo to Lyndon Johnson, February 25, 1965, Library of Congress, Manuscript Division, Eric Goldman Papers, Box 63, "Scrapbook, March 1965."

56. Goldman, *Tragedy*, 420.

57. Goldman, *Tragedy*, 420.

58. Goldman, *Tragedy*, 421–25.

59. Robert Lowell, Letter to Eric Goldman, May 30, 1965, Library of Congress, Manuscript Division, Eric Goldman Papers, Box 64, "Scrapbook, May, 1965."

60. Goldman, *Tragedy*, 427–28.

61. Richard F. Shepard, "Robert Lowell Rebuffs Johnson as Protest over Foreign Policy," *New York Times*, June 3, 1965, 1, 3.

62. Goldman, *Tragedy*, 430.

63. Goldman, *Tragedy*, 430.

64. Goldman, *Tragedy*, 433–39.

65. Goldman, *Tragedy*, 443–45; Richard F. Shepard, "20 Writers and Artists Endorse Poet's Rebuff of the President," *New York Times*, June 4, 1965, 2. The *NYRB* began when the *New York Times*, and hence the *Book Review*, were on hiatus because of a strike.

66. Goldman, *Tragedy*, 447.

67. Goldman, *Tragedy*, 448–51. The four artists who declined specifically because of the Vietnam War were Robert Brustein, Alexander Calder, Jack Levine, and Paul Strand.

68. Goldman, *Tragedy*, 453–55.

69. Goldman, *Tragedy*, 455–60.

70. Goldman, *Tragedy*, 461.

71. Dwight Macdonald, "A Day at the White House," *New York Review of Books*, July 15, 1965, 12; Goldman, *Tragedy*, 471–73; Macdonald's seven signers were Thomas Hess, Herbert Ferber, Isamu Noguchi, Peter Voulkos, Willem de Kooning, Sam Hunter, and Reed Whittmore.

72. Howard Taubman, "Arts at White House: President's Reserve Noted at Festival Despite Official Welcome and Salute," *New York Times*, June 16, 1965, 46; Goldman, *Tragedy*, 474.

73. Dwight Macdonald, "A Day at the White House," *New York Review of Books*, July 15, 1965, 10–15.

74. Lady Bird Johnson, *A White House Diary* (New York: Holt, Rinehart & Winston, 1970), 287.

75. Johnson, *White House Diary*, 287; Goldman, *Tragedy*, 475.

76. Goldman, *Tragedy*, 475.

77. Eric Goldman, Memo to Jack Valenti, June 17, 1965, Library of Congress, Manuscript Division, Eric Goldman Papers, Box 64, "Scrapbook, June, 1965."

78. Eric Goldman, Memo to Lyndon Johnson, December 22, 1965; Bill Moyers, Memo to Eric Goldman, January 10, 1966; Joseph Califano, Memo to Eric Goldman, April 9, 1966, Library of Congress, Manuscript Division, Eric Goldman Papers, Box 60, "Presidential Professorships."

79. Eric Goldman, Memo to Bill Moyers, May 6, 1966, Library of Congress, Manuscript Division, Eric Goldman Papers, Box 59, "Speech at Princeton University."

80. Ronald Sullivan, "President Urges Scholars to Back War in Vietnam," *New York Times*, May 12, 1966, 1, 14; Eric Goldman, Memo for the Diary, May 11, 1966, Library of Congress, Manuscript Division, Eric Goldman Papers, Box 59, "Princeton Speech." The *Times* reported three hundred protesters, while Goldman saw only two hundred.

81. Eric Goldman, Memo for the Diary, May 11, 1966, Library of Congress, Manuscript Division, Eric Goldman Papers, Box 59, "Princeton Speech"; Eric Goldman, Letter to Lyndon Johnson, May 11, 1966, Library of Congress, Manuscript Division, Eric Goldman Papers, Box 64, "Scrapbook, March–May, 1966."

82. Goldman, *Tragedy*, 476–77.

83. Eric Goldman, Letter to Lyndon Johnson, August 23, 1966, Library of Congress, Manuscript Division, Eric Goldman Papers, Box 61, "Resignation."

84. Lady Bird Johnson, Letter to Eric Goldman, August 30, 1966, Library of Congress, Manuscript Division, Eric Goldman Papers, Box 52, "Correspondence, Johnson to Jones." Although Mrs. Johnson's letter is dated one day after the president's, Goldman received her letter on the thirtieth and the president's letter the following day (Goldman, *Tragedy*, 503).

85. Arthur Schlesinger, Oral History, November 4, 1971, John F. Kennedy Library, Oral History Collection, p. 13; Lyndon Johnson, Letter to Eric Goldman, August 29, 1966, Lyndon Johnson Library, FG–11–8–1, Box 84, "FG–11–8–1/Goldman, Eric." for comparison, see Lyndon Johnson, Letter to Douglass Cater, October 2, 1968, Lyndon Johnson Library, FG–11–8–1/Cater, Box 77, "Resignation": "I know of few men who have contributed so much to the enactment of progressive legislation in the 1960s."

86. Goldman, *Tragedy*, vii.

87. Arthur Schlesinger, Oral History, November 4, 1971, John F. Kennedy Library, Oral History Collection, p. 18.

88. Goldman, *Tragedy*, 504.

89. Transcript, White House Press Conference, September 8, 1966, Library of Congress, Manuscript Division, Eric Goldman Papers, Box 61, "Resignation."

90. Transcript, White House Press Conference, September 8, 1966, Library of Congress, Manuscript Division, Eric Goldman Papers, Box 61, "Resignation."

91. Transcript, White House Press Conference, September 8, 1966, Library of Congress, Manuscript Division, Eric Goldman Papers, Box 61, "Resignation."

92. Peter Lisagor, "White House Loses Link with Intellectuals," *Philadelphia Inquirer*, September 12, 1966, clipping, Library of Congress, Manuscript Division, Eric Goldman Papers, Box 61, "Resignation."

93. "So Long, Eric," editorial, *Washington Evening Star*, September 21, 1966, Clipping, Library of Congress, Manuscript Division, Eric Goldman Papers, Box 61, "Resignation 9/14–12/12/66."

94. Theodore White, Letter to Eric Goldman, December 12, 1966, Library of Congress, Manuscript Division, Eric Goldman Papers, Box 61, Resignation 9/14–12/12/66"; Theodore White, *Theodore White at Large: The Best of His Magazine Writing, 1939–1986* (New York: Pantheon, 1992), 389.

NOTES TO CHAPTER FOUR

1. See chapter 2.

2. Stephen Ambrose, *Nixon*, vol. 2, *The Triumph of a Politician, 1962–1972* (New York: Simon & Schuster, 1989), 82; Jonathan Aitken, *Nixon: A Life* (Washington: Regnery, 1993), 336.

3. Harry McPherson, Memo to Bill Moyers, June 28, 1965, "Moynihan Name File," WHCF, LBJ Library; Daniel Patrick Moynihan, *A Dangerous Place* (Boston: Little, Brown, 1978), 5.

4. Nathan Glazer and Daniel Patrick Moynihan, *Beyond the Melting Pot: The Negroes, Puerto Ricans, Jews, Italians, and Irish of New York City* (Cambridge: MIT Press, 1963). Glazer had also cowritten the best-selling *The Lonely Crowd*, making him a kind of Steven Spielberg of the university press circuit.

5. Glazer and Moynihan, *Beyond the Melting Pot*, 50–53; the authors specifically stated who wrote each chapter. Glazer wrote the chapters on blacks, Puerto Ricans, Jews, and Italians. Moynihan wrote the chapter on the Irish and the conclusion.

6. Glazer and Moynihan, *Beyond the Melting Pot*, 22.

7. Harry McPherson, Memo to Lyndon Johnson, July 16, 1965, "Harry McPherson: Memoranda for the President (1965) [1 of 2]," Office Files of Harry McPherson, Box 52, LBJ Library; *The Negro Family: The Case for National Action*, Unsigned Report by the Office of Policy and Planning, U.S. Department of Labor (Washington: Government Printing Office, 1965).

8. Daniel Patrick Moynihan, "The President and the Negro: The Moment Lost," *Commentary*, February 1967, 36.

9. Rowland Evans and Robert Novak, "Inside Report: The Moynihan Report," *Washington Post*, August 18, 1965; *Negro Family*, 5, 8, 48.

10. Moynihan, "President and the Negro," 37.

11. Mary McGrory, "Moynihan Conspicuously Ignored: The 'Non-Person' at the Rights Parley," *Washington Star*; reprinted in Lee Rainwater and William Yancey, *The Moynihan Report and the Politics of Controversy* (Cambridge: MIT Press, 1967), 256, quoted in Rainwater and Yancey, *Moynihan Report*, 212; Moynihan, "President and the Negro," 40.

12. James Farmer, "The Controversial Moynihan Report," *Amsterdam News*, December 18, 1965, reprinted in Rainwater and Yancey, *Moynihan Report*, 409–11; William Ryan, "Savage Discovery: The Moynihan Report," *The Nation*, November 22, 1965, reprinted in Rainwater and Yancey, *Moynihan Report*, 457–66; Frank Riessman, "In Defense of the Negro Family," *Dissent*, March–April 1966; reprinted in Rainwater and Yancey, *Moynihan Report*, 475–78.

13. Daniel Patrick Moynihan, *Coping: Essays on the Practice of Government* (New York: Random House, 1973), 21; Moynihan, "President and the Negro," 43.

14. Moynihan, *Coping*, 20–21.

15. Daniel Patrick Moynihan, *Maximum Feasible Misunderstanding: Community Action in the War on Poverty* (New York: Free Press, 1969), 25.

16. Pat Moynihan, Letter to Harry McPherson, September 22, 1966, "Office Files of Harry McPherson: Civil Rights (1)," Files of Harry McPherson, Box 22, LBJ Library.

17. Ambrose, *Nixon*, 124; James Reichley, *Conservatives in an Era of Change: The Nixon and Ford Administrations* (Washington: Brookings Institution, 1981), 69.

18. Ambrose, *Nixon*, 236; Reichley, *Conservatives*, 69; Theodore White, *The Making of the President, 1972* (New York: Bantam, 1973), 362; "A Whig in the White House: Daniel P. Moynihan," *Time*, March 16, 1970, 26.

19. Daniel Patrick Moynihan, *The Politics of a Guaranteed Income: The Nixon Administration and the Family Assistance Plan* (New York: Random House, 1973), 70; Rumsfeld quoted in White, *Making of the President*, 63; "The White House's Idea Man for Urban Problems," *Business Week*, September 27, 1969, 72–76.

20. Reichley, *Conservatives*, 70; Bernard Asbell, "Pat Moynihan: 'Too Much!' and 'Too Little!'" *New York Times Magazine*, January 2, 1969, 57.

21. Mary McGrory, "Long Day, Small Promises," *Washington Star*, January 27, 1969; clipping, "Presidential News Summaries, February, 1970," Nixon Archives, President's Office Files, Box 31.

22. Pat Moynihan, Memo to Richard Nixon, January 27, 1969, Nixon Archives, White House Special Files, John D. Ehrlichman Files, Box 21, "Miscellaneous" (Memos, 1969–70).

23. Pat Moynihan, Memo to Richard Nixon, January 27, 1969, Nixon Archives, White House Special Files, John D. Ehrlichman Files, Box 21, "Miscellaneous" (Memos, 1969–70); cf. Moynihan, *Politics;* William Safire, *Before the Fall: An Inside View of the Pre-Watergate White House* (New York: Ballantine, 1974), 50.

24. H. R. Haldeman, "Moynihan and Nixon," in *The Haldeman Diaries: Inside the Nixon White House, The Complete Multimedia Edition* (New York: Berkley, 1994).

25. "White House's Idea Man," 72; Moynihan, *Politics*, 488.

26. Reichley, *Conservatives*, 131.

27. Aitken, *Nixon*, 375; Reichley, *Conservatives*, 72. According to Aitken, Moynihan's other nine recommendations were John Adams, *Autobiography*; Lord Charnwood, *Abraham Lincoln*; Henry Adams, *The Education of Henry Adams*; Duff Cooper, *Talleyrand*; Lord David Cecil, *Melbourne*; Alan Bullock, *Hitler: A Study in Tyranny*; John Morton Blum, *The Republican Roosevelt*; and John Womack Jr., *Zapata and the Mexican Revolution*.

28. Pat Moynihan, Memo to Richard Nixon, January 31, 1969; Robert Bartley, review of *Maximum Feasible Misunderstanding, Wall Street Journal*, January 31, 1969, Nixon Archives, Clipping, President's Office Files, Box 1, "President's Handwriting January, 1969."

29. John Robert Greene, *The Limits of Power: The Nixon and Ford Administrations* (Bloomington: Indiana University Press, 1992), 28.

30. Quoted in Greene, *Limits of Powerv*, 28.

31. Moynihan, *Politics*, 51.

32. Moynihan, quoted in White, *Making of the President*, 69–70.

33. Moynihan, quoted in "The Limits of Politics," editorial, *Wall Street Journal*, June 20, 1969, Nixon Archives, Clipping, POF Box 2, "President's Handwriting, June 1969."

34. Pat Moynihan, Memo to Richard Nixon, June 20, 1969; "The Limits of Politics," editorial, *Wall Street Journal*, June 20, 1969, Nixon Archives, Clipping, POF Box 2, "President's Handwriting, June 1969."

35. Pat Moynihan, Memo to Richard Nixon, June 20, 1969, Nixon Archives, POF Box 2, "President's Handwriting, June 1969."

36. Pat Buchanan, Summary of Stuart Loory article in *Los Angeles Times*, March 6, 1969, Nixon Archives, POF Box 30, "Undated Press Summaries."

37. Pat Moynihan, Memo to Richard Nixon, June 14, 1969, Nixon Archives, FG 6–12, Box 2, "EX FG 6–12, 5/6/69–6/12/69."

38. Egil Krogh, Memo to John Ehrlichman, June 25, 1969, Nixon Archives, Files of Egil Krogh, Box 1, "Memos, June, 1969."

39. Pat Moynihan, Memo to H. R. Haldeman and John Ehrlichman, July 24, 1970, Nixon Archives, WHSF, Staff Member and Office Files, John D. Ehrlichman, Box 21, "Moynihan Report, July 24, 1970."

40. Pat Moynihan, Memo to H. R. Haldeman and John Ehrlichman, July 24, 1970, Nixon Archives, WHSF, Staff Member and Office Files, John D. Ehrlichman, Box 21, "Moynihan Report, July 24, 1970."

41. Pat Moynihan, Memo to H. R. Haldeman and John Ehrlichman, July 24, 1970, Nixon Archives, WHSF, Staff Member and Office Files, John D. Ehrlichman, Box 21, "Moynihan Report, July 24, 1970."

42. Pat Moynihan, Memo to H. R. Haldeman and John Ehrlichman, July 24, 1970, Nixon Archives, WHSF, Staff Member and Office Files, John D. Ehrlichman, Box 21, "Moynihan Report, July 24, 1970."

43. Pat Moynihan, Memo to H. R. Haldeman and John Ehrlichman, July 24, 1970, Nixon Archives, WHSF, Staff Member and Office Files, John D. Ehrlichman, Box 21, "Moynihan Report, July 24, 1970."

44. Pat Moynihan, Memo to H. R. Haldeman and John Ehrlichman, July 24, 1970, Nixon Archives, WHSF, Staff Member and Office Files, John D. Ehrlichman, Box 21, "Moynihan Report, July 24, 1970."

45. Pat Moynihan, Memo to H. R. Haldeman and John Ehrlichman, July 24, 1970, Nixon Archives, WHSF, Staff Member and Office Files, John D. Ehrlichman, Box 21, "Moynihan Report, July 24, 1970."

46. Pat Moynihan, Memo to Richard Nixon, August 4, 1970, Nixon Archives, POF Box 7, "President's Handwriting, August 1–15, 1970."

47. Pat Moynihan, Memo to Richard Nixon, August 4, 1970, Nixon Archives, POF Box 7, "President's Handwriting, August 1–15, 1970."

48. Pat Moynihan, Memo to Richard Nixon, November 13, 1970, Nixon Archives, Papers of H. R. Haldeman, Box 163, "Intellectuals."

49. Pat Moynihan, Memo to Richard Nixon, November 13, 1970, Nixon Archives, Papers of H. R. Haldeman, Box 163, "Intellectuals." Moynihan also recommended Sidney Hook, Lionel Trilling, Paul Seabury, David Riesman, and William Phillips.

50. Moynihan, List of Intellectuals, Undated (attached to November 13, 1970 memo), Nixon Archives, Papers of H. R. Haldeman, Box 163, "Intellectuals." Kristol was not technically a political scientist, having never received—or sought—a Ph.D. Those receiving biographic blurbs included Edward Banfield, Jacques Barzun, William F. Buckley, Lewis Feuer, Nathan Glazer, Sidney Hook, Kristol, Edward Levi, Seymour Martin Lipset, Robert Nisbet, Paul Seabury, Trilling, and Aaron Wildavsky.

51. H. R. Haldeman, Note to Pat Moynihan, undated, Papers of H. R. Haldeman, Box 163, "Intellectuals," Nixon Archives; Haldeman, *Diaries* (CD–ROM), November 17, 1970. The list was passed around the White House, with different people offering their advice. One copy of the list had the name of sociologist Seymour Martin Lipset crossed out.

52. Bruce Kehrli, Memo to Larry Higby, December 22, 1970, Nixon Archives, Papers of H. R. Haldeman, Box 163, "Intellectuals."

53. H. R. Haldeman, Memo to Richard Nixon, December 30, 1970; H. R. Haldeman, Memo to Larry Higby, undated, following December 30 memo, Nixon Archives, Papers of H. R. Haldeman, Box 163, "Intellectuals."

54. Greene, *Limits of Power*, 28; Hess, quoted in Reichley, *Conservatives*, 132.

55. Moynihan, *Politics*, 181; Ehrlichman, quoted in Wicker, 408.

56. John Whitaker, Memo to H. R. Haldeman, February 19, 1969, Nixon Archives, Council of Urban Affairs, Box 1, "Start–2/23/69."

57. Arthur Burns, Memo to Richard Nixon, March 17, 1969, POF Box 1, "President's Handwriting, March 16–31 1969," Nixon Archives; Haldeman, *Diaries* (CD–ROM), March 17, 1969.

58. Pete Hamill, "The Revolt of the White Lower Middle Classes," *New York*, April 14, 1969.

59. Pat Moynihan, Memo to Richard Nixon, May 17, 1969, Nixon Archives, POF Box 2, "President's Handwriting, May 1969."

60. Pat Moynihan, Memo to Richard Nixon, May 17, 1969, Nixon Archives, POF Box 2, "President's Handwriting, May 1969."

61. Arthur Burns, Memo to Richard Nixon, May 26, 1969, Nixon Archives, POF Box 2, "President's Handwriting, May 1969."

62. Cf. Daniel Bell, *The End of Ideology* (New York: Basic, 1958).

63. Pat Buchanan, Memo to Richard Nixon, September 2, 1969, Nixon Archives, POF Box 3, "President's Handwriting, September 69."

64. Reichley, *Conservatives*, 139–40.

65. John Ehrlichman, Memo to John Mitchell, December 7, 1969, Nixon Archives, The Papers of Egil Krogh, Box 12, "Domestic Staff [1969–1970]." In the Eisenhower administration, Burns had been the only adviser to stand with Nixon and support progrowth policies that would have eased Nixon's election in 1960.

66. Pat Buchanan, Undated News Summary, "POF 30 News Summaries-November 1969."

67. Moynihan also did some work in education that is beyond the scope of this survey.

68. Lyndon Johnson, Memo to Doug Cater, September 29, 1966, LBJ Library, Files of S. Douglass Cater, Box 15, "Cater, Douglass: Memos to the President, September, 1966."

69. Daniel Patrick Moynihan, ed., *Toward a National Urban Policy* (New York: Basic, 1970), 24, 3.

70. Pat Moynihan, Memo to Richard Nixon, January 9, 1969, Nixon Archives, H. R. Haldeman Papers, Box 49, "Memos to James Keogh, January 1969."

71. H. R. Haldeman, Memo to Len Garment, Nixon Archives, H. R. Haldeman Papers, Box 49, "Memos to James Keogh, January 1969."

72. Greene, *Limits of Power*, 49.

73. "Agenda for Council for Urban Affairs Meeting, January 9, 1969," undated White House document, WHCF, Subject Files, FG 6–12, Council for Urban Affairs (CUA), Box 1, "EX FG 6–12, Council for Urban Affairs, Begin–2/23/69," Nixon Archives.

74. Pat Moynihan, Memo to John Ehrlichman, September 30, 1969; Peter Flanigan, Memo to Darrell Trent and Harry Flemming, October 2, 1969, Nixon Archives, CUA, Box 2, "EX FG 6–12 10/1/69–10/18/69."

75. John Price, Memo to the Staff Secretary, April 14, 1969, Nixon Archives, CUA, Box 1, "EX FG 6–12 3/19/69–1/14/69."

76. Moynihan, Memo to Richard Nixon.

77. John Price, Memo for the President's File, February 11, 1970, Nixon Archives, CUA, Box 3, "EX FG 6–12 12/10/69–2/28/70."

78. Aitken, *Nixon*, 375; Pat Moynihan, Memo to Richard Nixon, November 13, 1970, Nixon Archives, Haldeman Papers, Box 163, "Intellectuals."

79. Moynihan, *Politics*, 545, 547–48.

80. Moynihan, *Politics*, 49–50, 124.

81. Pat Moynihan, Letter to Harry McPherson, September 22, 1966; Meeting Note, September 29, 1966, LBJ Library, Files of Harry McPherson, Box 22, "Office Files of Harry McPherson: Civil Rights (1)."

82. Richard Nixon, Memo to John Mitchell, Bob Finch, Bryce Harlow, and Pat Moynihan, Nixon Archives, H. R. Haldeman Files, Box 49, "Memorandum January 1969."

83. Moynihan, *Politics*, 86; Alexander Butterfield, Memo to Pat Moynihan, February 3, 1969, Nixon Archives, Haldeman Files, Box 49, "Memos/ Moynihan (February, 1969)."

84. Moynihan, *Politics*, 113, 93; Pat Moynihan, Memo to Richard Nixon, March 13, 1969, Nixon Archives, UAC, Box 1, "EX FG 6–12 2/25/69–3/18/69."

85. Ambrose, *Nixon*, 269. FAP was originally called the Family Security System.

86. Pat Moynihan, Memo to Richard Nixon, April 11, 1969, Nixon Archives, POF, Box 1, "President's Handwriting April 1969."

87. Ambrose, *Nixon*, 294.

88. Ambrose, *Nixon*, 315, 366.

89. Pat Moynihan, Letter to Anthony Lewis, June 10, 1991, quoted in Aitken, *Nixon*, 376.

90. Moynihan, *Politics*, 315.

91. Pat Moynihan, Memo to Richard Nixon, May 18, 1970, Nixon Archives, POF Box 6, "President's Handwriting, May, 1970."

92. Daniel Patrick Moynihan, "A Memorandum to the President-Elect January 3, 1969," in Murray Friedman, ed., *Overcoming Middle Class Rage* (Philadelphia: Westminster, 1971), 186, 189, 190.

93. Cf. Irving Kristol, "The Negro Today Is Like the Immigrant of Yesterday," *New York Times Magazine*, September 11, 1966, 50, 124–42.

94. John Ehrlichman, *Witness to Power: The Nixon Years* (New York: Simon & Schuster, 1982), 229.

95. Pat Moynihan, Memo to Richard Nixon, February 1, 1969, Nixon Archives, POF Box 1, "President's Handwriting February 1969."

96. Ray Price, Notes for the President's File, 11th UAC meeting, May 13, 1969, Nixon Archives, POF Box 78, "Memoranda for the President: Beginning May 11, 1969"; Ralph David Abernathy, *And the Walls Came Tumbling Down: An Autobiography* (New York: Harper & Row, 1989), 554.

97. Ehrlichman, *Witness to Power*, 229; Haldeman, "Moynihan and Nixon," 69; Richard Nixon, *The Memoirs of Richard Nixon* (New York: Grosset & Dunlop, 1978), 436; Moynihan, trying to keep his promise not to write a memoir, glosses over the Abernathy incident in his *Politics of a Guaranteed Income*, focusing only on Abernathy's relation to the FAP.

98. Ray Price, Notes for the President's File, 11th UAC meeting, May 13, 1969, Nixon Archives, POF Box 78, "Memoranda for the President: Beginning May 11, 1969."

99. Abernathy, *Walls*, 554; Nixon, *Memoirs*, 436; Haldeman, "Moynihan and Nixon," 69.

100. Ehrlichman, *Witness to Power*, 229; Haldeman, "Moynihan and Nixon," 70; Nixon, *Memoir*, 436.

101. Pat Moynihan, Memo to Richard Nixon, January 16, 1970, Nixon Archives, POF Box 5, "January 16–31, 1970."

102. Pat Moynihan, Memo to Richard Nixon, January 16, 1970, Nixon Archives, POF Box 5, "January 16–31, 1970"; Tom Wolfe, *Radical Chic and Mau–Mauing the Flak-Catchers* (New York: Farrar, Straus & Giroux, 1987).

103. Pat Moynihan, Memo to Richard Nixon, January 16, 1970, Nixon Archives, POF Box 5, "January 16–31, 1970"; William Safire, *Safire's Political Dictionary* (New York: Ballantine, 1978), 650. Safire, who had been one of Nixon's speechwriters, claims that Nixon wrote the "Silent Majority" speech "with no help from his speechwriters."

104. Peter Kihss, "'Benign Neglect' on Race is Proposed by Moynihan," *New York Times*, March 1, 1970, 1, 69.

105. Haldeman, *Diaries* (CD–ROM), March 1, 1970; John Osborne, "A Faithful Servant," *New Republic*, March 14, 1970, 12; Moynihan suspected someone at the Department of Health, Education, and Welfare, the same agency he had accused of leaking the Moynihan Report five years earlier. According to the *New Republic*, former subcabinet official Leon Panetta was a prime suspect. Nixon had just forced Panetta's resignation as deputy secretary for civil rights in the Department of Health, Education, and Welfare because Panetta opposed the White House approach to desegregation. His resignation came in February, after Moynihan submitted his memo but before the *New York Times* received a copy.

106. Anthony Lewis, "Neglect: Benign or Hostile?" *New York Times*, March 2, 1970, 36; "Moynihan Explains His Memo Urging Neglect of Racial Issue," *New York Times*, March 3, 1970, 24; "Neglect, but Not 'Benign,'" editorial, *New York Times*, March 3, 1970, 40.

107. Linda Charlton, "21 Rights Leaders Rebut Moynihan: Assert Benign Neglect Idea Is 'Symptomatic of Effort to Wipe Out Gains,'" *New York Times*, March 6, 1970, 1.

108. "Memorandum to Moynihan," editorial, *The Nation*, March 16, 1970, 291; "A Whig in the White House," 27; Nixon, *Memoir*, 436.

109. Haldeman, *Diaries* (CD–ROM), March 31, 1970; Greene, *Limits of Power*, 51.

110. Greene, *Limits of Power*, 50.

111. Pat Moynihan, Memo for the President's File, November 17, 1970 (written December 18), Nixon Archives, POF 83, "November 1, 1970–January 17, 1971"; Haldeman, "Moynihan and Nixon," 254.

112. Pat Moynihan, "Dr. Moynihan's Remarks to a Cabinet Meeting Prior to His Return to Private Life," December 21, 1970, Nixon Archives, POF Box 83, "November 1, 1970–January 17, 1971."

113. Haldeman, "Moynihan and Nixon," 268; Herb Klein, Memo to the White House Staff, December 24, 1970, Nixon Archives, POF Box 83, "November 1, 1970–January 17, 1971"; H. R. Haldeman, Memo to "ALL COMMISSIONED PERSONNEL," December 23, 1971, Nixon Archives, Egil Krogh Files, Box 8, "Pat Moynihan–Christmas Charge [1970–1972]."

114. William Randolph Hearst, "The World's Toughest Job," *Seattle Post-Intelligencer*, January 3, 1971, 1, 9.

115. Haldeman, *Diaries* (CD–ROM), January 2, 1971.

116. Bruce Kehrli, Memo to H. R. Haldeman, January 29, 1971, Nixon Archives, Files of H. R. Haldeman, Box 261, "ACTION"; H. R. Haldeman, Memo to John Ehrlichman, May 26, 1971, Nixon Archives, Files of H. R. Haldeman, Box 79, "John Ehrlichman, May 1971."

117. Haldeman, *Diaries* (CD–ROM), 165.

118. Irving Kristol, "Pornography, Obscenity, and Censorship," *New York Times Magazine*, March 28, 1971; George T. Bell, Note to Richard Nixon, undated, Nixon Archives, President's Office Files, Box 10, "March 16–31, 1971."

119. Philip Nobile, *Intellectual Skywriting: Literary Politics and the New York Review of Books* (New York: Charterhouse, 1974), 5; Diana Trilling, *The Beginning of the Journey: The Marriage of Diana and Lionel Trilling* (New York: Harcourt, Brace, 1993), 404–5; Irving Kristol, *Reflections of a Neoconservative* (New York: Basic, 1983), 15.

120. Neil Pickett, *A History of the Hudson Institute* (Indianapolis: Hudson Institute, 1992), 7.

121. Tod Hullin, Memo to Ken Cole, January 4, 1973, Nixon Archives; Herman Kahn, Nixon Archives, Briefing Book, FG–15, Box 4, "EX FG–15 Domestic Council [19 of 27, January, 1973–February, 1973]."

NOTES TO CHAPTER FIVE

1. "The President's Professor," *Time*, March 3, 1975, 20–22.

2. "President's Professor," 21.

3. Robert Hartmann, *Palace Politics: An Insider's Account of the Ford Years* (New York: McGraw-Hill, 1980), 390; Gerald Ford, *A Time to Heal: The Autobiography of Gerald R. Ford* (New York: Harper & Row, 1979), 350; Ron Nessen, *It Sure Looks Different from the Inside* (Chicago: Playboy Press, 1978), 81. Richard Cheney was Ford's deputy chief of staff.

4. Press Release, December 9, 1974, Gerald Ford Library and Archives, WHSF FG–6–11–1, Box 35, "FG–6–11–1/Goldwin, Robert 8/9/74–4/30/75 Exec"; "Robert A. Goldwin: Bridge between Thinkers and Doers," *Science*, January 24, 1975, 239.

5. Memo, Robert Goldwin to Gerald Ford, November 15, 1974, Ford Library, Robert A. Goldwin Files, Box 3, "Kristol–1."

6. Memo, Robert Goldwin to Dick Cheney, December 6, 1974; Memo, Robert Goldwin to Donald Rumsfeld, December 5, 1974, Ford Library, Robert A. Goldwin Files, Box 2, "Seminar 12/19/74." Goldwin attached accepted works from the three men, including Wilson's article "Crime and the Criminologists" in *Commentary* (July 1974); "Self-Liquidating Ideals," chapter 9 of Boorstin's *Democracy and Its Discontents* (Random House, 1974); and Diamond's 1973 American Enterprise Institute lecture, "The Revolution of Sober Expectations."

7. Transcript of Press Briefing, Ford Library, Ron Nessen Files, Box 4, Press Secretary Briefings, "12/9/74"; cf. Nessen, *It Sure Looks Different*. Nessen's funniest story involves the visit of Mexican American beauty Vikki Carr to the White House. When Carr asked Ford what his favorite dish was, Ford replied, "You are." Apparently Betty Ford did not find this amusing. Nessen, *It Sure Looks Different*, p. 24.

8. Transcript of Press Briefing, Ford Library, Ron Nessen Files, Box 4, Press Secretary Briefings, "12/10/74."

9. Letter, James Q. Wilson to Robert Goldwin, December 20, 1974, Ford Library, Goldwin Files, Box 3, "Wilson"; Memo, Goldwin to Ron Nessen, January 3, 1975, Ford

Library; Ron Nessen Papers (White House Press Secretary's Office), Box 129, "Goldwin, Robert (1)–(3), RAG (1)."

10. "Robert A. Goldwin," 239.

11. Fred Barnes, "Ford Welcoming Scholars to Share Their Wisdom," *Washington Star-News*, December 23, 1974.

12. Memorandum of telephone conversation with Irving Kristol, Robert Goldwin, November 20, 1974; Letter, Irving Kristol to Robert Goldwin, January 27, 1975; and Letter, Irving Kristol to Robert Goldwin, February 19, 1975; Ford Library, Robert A Goldwin Files, Box 3, "Kristol." Individuals who received Kristol's seal of approval included *Los Angeles Times* president Franklin Murphy, Harvard historian Oscar Handlin, Columbia sociologist Robert Merton, American Federation of Teachers president Albert Shanker (which Goldwin spelled "Shenker"), *National Review* editor William F. Buckley, University of Toronto professor Walter Berns, and Berkeley professor Paul Seabury.

13. Letter, Irving Kristol to Robert Goldwin, February 19, 1975; Ford Library, Robert A. Goldwin Files, Box 3, "Kristol."

14. Memorandum, Robert Goldwin to Gerald Ford, January 11, 1975, Ford Library, Robert Goldwin Papers, Box 2, "Seminar 1/11/75." Other participants included Rumsfeld, longtime Ford aide Robert Hartmann, Alan Greenspan, Martin Feldstein, former Nixon adviser Bryce Harlow, Gabriel Hauge from Manufacturers Hanover, and speechwriter Milton Friedman; Memorandum, Richard Cheney to Robert Goldwin, January 25, 1975, Robert A. Goldwin Papers, Box 22, "Richard Cheney (1)."

15. Letter, Irving Kristol to Robert Goldwin, January 30, 1975, Ford Library, Robert A. Goldwin Papers, Box 22, "Richard Cheney (1)."

16. Letter, Herman Kahn to Robert Goldwin, December 12, 1974; Letter, Robert Goldwin to Herman Kahn, December 17, 1974; Ford Library, Goldwin Papers, Box 24, "Herman Kahn."

17. Letter, Robert Goldwin to Harry Jaffa, January 23, 1975, Ford Library, Goldwin Papers, Box 24, "Harry Jaffa"; Harry Jaffa, *Crisis of the House Divided: An Analysis of the Lincoln-Douglas Debates* (Garden City, N.Y.: Doubleday, 1959). The divide between the East Coast and West Coast Straussians is far too complex to be covered fully here, but the basic dispute questions whether Strauss believed American founding represented the Aristotelean political ideal; the West Coasters believe that it did.

18. Letter, Harry Jaffa to Robert Goldwin, January 23, 1975, Ford Library, Goldwin Papers, Box 24, "Harry Jaffa"; Lee Edwards, *Goldwater: The Man Who Made a Revolution* (Washington: Regnery, 1995), 267–68.

19. Memo, Robert Goldwin to Donald Rumsfeld, January 31, 1975, Ford Library, James E Connor Files, Box 13, "Kristol, Irving—The Public Interest."

20. Memo, Robert Goldwin to Donald Rumsfeld, January 31, 1975, Ford Library, James E. Connor Files, Box 13, "Kristol, Irving—The Public Interest."

21. Memo, Richard Cheney to Robert Goldwin, February 14, 1975, Ford Library, Robert A. Goldwin Files, Box 22, "Richard Cheney"; Letter, Robert Goldwin to Martin Diamond, February 19, 1975, Ford Library, Robert A. Goldwin Files, Box 22, "Martin Diamond (2)."

22. Letter, Irving Kristol to Robert Goldwin, March 10, 1975, Ford Library, Robert A, Goldwin Files, Box 3, "Kristol, Irving"; Letter, Robert Goldwin to Allan Bloom, March 13, 1975, Goldwin Files, Box 4, "Ber–Bn."

23. Norman Podhoretz, "My Negro Problem—And Ours," *Commentary*, February, 1963, 93–101; Irving Kristol, "The Negro Today Is Like the Immigrant of Yesterday," *New York Times Magazine*, September 11, 1966, 50, 124–42.

24. Goldwin, quoted in *The Ford White House: A Miller Center Conference Chaired by Herbert J. Storing* (New York: University Press of America, 1986), 72.

25. Memo, Goldwin to Ford (through Cheney), June 25, 1976, Ford Library, Goldwin Files, Box 2, "Jewish Organizations (2)."

26. Memo, Goldwin to Ford (through Cheney), June 25, 1976, Ford Library, Goldwin Files, Box 2, "Jewish Organizations (2)."

27. Memorandum of telephone conversation with Irving Kristol, Robert Goldwin, November 20, 1974, Ford Library, Robert A. Goldwin Files, Box 3, "Kristol."

28. Letter, Thomas Sowell to Bob Goldwin, August 9, 1975; Memo, Bob Goldwin to Richard Cheney, undated, Ford Library, Robert A. Goldwin Papers, Box 27, "Sowell"; Letter, Thomas Sowell to Robert A. Goldwin, May 24, 1976, Ford Library, Goldwin Papers, Box 27, "Sowell."

29. Robert A. Goldwin, letter to Nathan Glazer, December 30, 1975, Ford Library, Robert A. Goldwin Papers, Box 23, "Nathan Glazer"; cf. Nathan Glazer, *Are We All Multiculturalists Now?* (Cambridge: Harvard University Press, 1997).

30. Gerald R. Ford, "Inclusive America, under Attack," *New York Times*, August 8, 1999, sec. 4, p. 15.

31. Memo, Goldwin to Cheney and Rumsfeld, June 26, 1975, Ford Library, Robert A. Goldwin Papers, Box 22, "Richard Cheney (1)."

32. Ron Nessen, *It Sure Looks Different*, xi.

33. Robert Hartmann, *Palace Politics: An Insider's Account of the Ford Years* (New York: McGraw–Hill, 1980), 431–34.

34. Cheney and Scowcroft quoted in *Ford White House*, 78; Nessen, *It Sure Looks Different*, xi, 149.

35. James Reichley, *Conservatives in an Age of Change: The Nixon and Ford Administrations* (Washington: Brookings Institution, 1981), 294; Goldwin, quoted in *Ford White House*, 27.

36. Handwritten note, Goldwin to Michael Raoul-Duval, Memo, Michael Raoul-Duval to Goldwin, December 1, 1975, Ford Library, Goldwin Files, Box 12, "President-Speech Ideas"; Ben J. Wattenberg, "Confessions of an Optimist in Time of Crisis," *Washington Star*, March 30, 1975, E1; Memo, Goldwin to Nessen, April 8, 1975; Memo, Nessen to Goldwin, April 10, 1975, Ron Nessen Papers (WH Press Secretary's Office), Box 129, "Goldwin, Robert (2)." *Note*: Goldwin also sent the column to eight other White House aides, including Hartmann.

37. Nessen, *It Sure Looks Different*, 80–82, 151.

38. Memo, Goldwin to White House Senior staffer, undated, Ford Library, Goldwin Files, Box 1, "Bicentennial (1)." Goldwin's document is clearly a product of the East Coast Straussian school, which appreciates the founding and yet recognizes its limits.

39. Hartmann, *Palace Politics*, 48, 397. Kristol does not have a doctorate.

40. Hartmann, *Palace Politics*, 397.

41. Memo, Robert Goldwin to Robert Hartmann, June 17, 1976, Robert Goldwin Files, Box 1, Bicentennial Speeches, Gerald R. Ford Library.

42. Hartmann, *Palace Politics*, 398; Ford, *A Time to Heal*, 352.

43. Letter, Goldwin to Ford, September 16, 1975, WHSF, FG–6–11–1, Box 35, "ExecFG–6–11–1/Goldwin, Robert 9/1/75–1/20/77."

44. Letter, Ford to Goldwin, September 17, 1975, WHSF, FG–6–11–1, Box 35, "ExecFG–6–11–1/Goldwin, Robert 9/1/75–1/20/77."

45. Reichley, *Conservatives*, 306.

46. Memorandum, Robert Goldwin to file, April 30, 1975, Ford Library, Goldwin Papers, Box 14, "Pres–Speeches–YLS, 4/25/75 (4)."

47. John Robert Greene, *The Presidency of Gerald R. Ford* (Lawrence: University Press of Kansas, 1995), 85.

48. Richard Reeves, *A Ford, Not a Lincoln* (New York: Harcourt Brace Jovanovich, 1975), 191.

NOTES TO CHAPTER SIX

1. Gaddis Smith, "Carter's Political Rhetoric," in Kenneth W. Thompson, ed., *The Carter Presidency: Fourteen Intimate Perspectives of Jimmy Carter* (New York: University Press of America, 1990), 203.

2. Kenneth E. Morris, *Jimmy Carter: American Moralist* (Athens: University of Georgia Press, 1996), 4; Burton Kaufman, *The Presidency of James Earl Carter, Jr.* (Lawrence: University Press of Kansas, 1993), 5.

3. Hamilton Jordan, *Crisis: The Last Year of the Carter Presidency* (New York: Putnam, 1982), 23; James Fallows, "The Passionless Presidency," *Atlantic Monthly* 243, no. 5 (1979): 33–48.

4. Jimmy Carter, *Keeping Faith: Memoirs of a President* (New York: Bantam, 1982); Fallows, "Passionless Presidency."

5. Morris, *Jimmy Carter*, 230, 239.

6. Morris, *Jimmy Carter*, 8.

7. Morris, *Jimmy Carter*, 155; Clifton McCleskey and Pierce McCleskey, "Carter and the Democratic Party," in M. Glenn Abernathy, Dilys M. Hill, and Phil Williams, eds., *The Carter Years: The President and Policy Making* (New York: St. Martin's, 1984), 127.

8. Fallows, "Passionless Presidency."

9. Stuart Eizenstat, Eizenstat Oral History, Jimmy Carter Library, Exit Interviews Collection.

10. Robert C. Wood, *Whatever Possessed the President? Academic Experts and Presidential Policy, 1960–1988* (Amherst: University of Massachusetts Press, 1993), 118–19.

11. Klein, quoted in Wood, *Whatever Possessed*, 123.

12. Wood, *Whatever Possessed*, 125, 129; Dilys Hill, "Domestic Policy," in Abernathy, Hill, and Williams, *The Carter Years*, 13.

13. Joseph A. Califano, *Governing America: An Insider's Report for the White House and the Cabinet* (New York: Simon & Schuster, 1981), 25.

14. Quoted in Morris, *Jimmy Carter*, 244

15. Goldman, quoted in William Leuchtenberg, introduction to Gary M. Fink and Hugh Davis Graham, eds., *The Carter Presidency: Policy Choices in the Post–New Deal Era* (Lawrence: University Press of Kansas, 1998), 10.

16. Cf. Fallows, "Passionless Presidency"; Califano, *Governing America*, 426.

17. Fallows, "Passionless Presidency."

18. Fallows, "Passionless Presidency."

19. Memo, James Fallows to Jody Powell, December 2, 1977, Jimmy Carter Library, Jody Powell Papers, Box 42, "7/5/77–12/07/77."

20. Memo, James Fallows to Jody Powell, December 2, 1977, Jimmy Carter Library, Jody Powell Papers, Box 42, "7/5/77–12/07/77."

21. James Fallows, Fallows Oral History, November 14, 1978, Jimmy Carter Library.

22. Names and Faces, *Business Week*, "Carter's Outside Insiders," June 27, 1977, 94.

23. Carter, *Keeping Faith*, 114; Morris, *Jimmy Carter*, 4.

24. "The Odd Combination of Jerry and Pat," *National Journal*, May 28, 1977, 814; "Carter's Outside Insiders."

25. "Carter's Outside Insiders."

26. Tom Morganthau and James Doyle, "The Mood of a Nation," *Newsweek*, August 6, 1979, 26.

27. Christopher Lasch, *The Culture of Narcissism: American Life in an Age of Diminishing Expectations* (New York: Norton, 1979), 17–18.

28. Sidney Blumenthal, "Mr. Smith Goes to Washington: Pat Caddell's Adventures in the Wasteland," *New Republic*, February 6, 1984, 17; Eizenstat Exit Interview, Jimmy Carter Library.

29. Carter, *Keeping Faith*, 115.

30. Carter, *Keeping Faith*, 116–18. In addition to staff, thirty-five members of Congress, twenty governors (including Bill Clinton), and eight mayors, attendees at the sessions included Eleanor Holmes Norton, John Gutfreund, Lane Kirkland, Vernon Jordan, Jesse Jackson, Robert Bellah, Clark Clifford, Sol Linowitz, and John Gardner. The economists were Lawrence Klein, Al Sommers, John Kenneth Galbraith, Walter Heller, Marina Von N. Whitman, and Arthur Okun. For a complete list, see Carol Steinbach, "They Came to Camp David," *National Journal*, July 21, 1979, 1224.

31. Memo from Gerald Rafshoon to Jimmy Carter, July 10, 1979, Jimmy Carter Library, Speeches, Box 50, "Speechwriters Chronological Files" (see Carter Chronological, pp. 389, 445/264).

32. Gerald Rafshoon, Oral History, Jimmy Carter Library, Exit Interviews Collection.

33. Blumenthal, "Mr. Smith Goes to Washington"; Eizenstat, Eizenstat Oral History, Jimmy Carter Library, Exit Interviews Collection.

34. Califano, *Governing America*, 428; Morris, *Jimmy Carter*, 261.

35. Eizenstat, Eizenstat Oral History, Jimmy Carter Library, Exit Interviews Collection.

36. "Who Makes Policy?" editorial, *Business Week*, August 6, 1979.

37. Blumenthal, "Mr. Smith Goes to Washington"; Morganthau and Doyle, "Mood of a Nation."

38. Blumenthal, "Mr. Smith Goes to Washington."

39. Memo, Bernard Aronson to Hendrik Hertzberg, July 29, 1980, Jimmy Carter Library, Speeches Subject File, Box 3, "Presidential Themes, 4/1/77–7/31/80."

NOTES TO CHAPTER SEVEN

1. Dinesh D'Souza, *Ronald Reagan: How an Ordinary Man Became an Extraordinary Leader* (New York: Free Press, 1997), 244.

2. David Stockman, *The Triumph of Politics: The Inside Story of the Reagan Revolution* (New York: Avon, 1986), 54; Memo, Bernard Aronson to Jack Watson, July 24, 1980, Jimmy Carter Library, Speeches Subject File, Box 3, "Carter Administration—Presidential Themes, 4/1/77–7/31/80."

3. Peggy Noonan, *What I Saw at the Revolution: A Political Life in the Reagan Era* (New York: Ivy, 1990), 280.

4. Martin Anderson, *Revolution* (New York: Harcourt Brace Jovanovich, 1988), 6; Noonan, *What I Saw*, 108.

5. Gregg Easterbrook, "Ideas Move Nations: How Conservative Think Tanks Have Helped to Transform the Terms of Political Debate," *Atlantic Monthly*, January 1986, 66.

6. Anderson, *Revolution*, 6–7.

7. Richard Reeves, *The Reagan Detour* (New York: Simon & Schuster, 1985), 48, 25.

8. Reeves, *Reagan Detour*, 32, 40.

9. Lou Cannon, *President Reagan: The Role of a Lifetime* (New York: Simon & Schuster, 1991), 132; D'Souza, *Ronald Reagan*, 8; Rowland Evans and Robert Novak, *The Reagan Revolution* (New York: Dutton, 1981), 5.

10. Don Regan, *For the Record: From Wall Street to Washington* (New York: St. Martin's, 1988), 6; Deborah Hart Strober and Gerald S. Strober, *Reagan: The Man and His Presidency* (New York: Houghton Mifflin, 1998), 100.

11. Memo, Lyn Nofziger to James Baker and Michael Deaver, March 12, 1982, Ronald Reagan Library, PR016–01, Box 20.

12. Memo, David Gergen to Ronald Reagan, January 15, 1984, Ronald Reagan Library, 19892855, FG001, Box 2.

13. Jay Winik, *On the Brink* (New York: Simon & Schuster, 1996), 95.

14. Theodore White, *America in Search of Itself: The Making of the President 1956–1980* (New York: Warner, 1982), 232.

15. White, *America*, 232.

16. Anderson, *Revolution*, 166, 198, xii.

17. Anderson, *Revolution*, 165.

18. Anderson, *Revolution*, 167–68.

19. White, *America*, 162–63.

20. Anderson, *Revolution*, 330; Evans and Novak, *Reagan Revolution*, 71.

21. Anderson, *Revolution*, 4; Blumenthal, quoted in Anderson, *Revolution*, 4–5.

22. Sidney Blumenthal, "The Conservative Elite: Outside Foundation Recruited the Inside Troops," *Washington Post*, September 24, 1985, A1.

23. Blumenthal, "Conservative Elite"; Ed Meese, *With Reagan: The Inside Story* (Washington: Regnery Gateway, 1992), 59–60.

24. Sidney Blumenthal and Thomas Byrne, eds., *The Reagan Legacy* (New York: Pantheon, 1988), 140; Ed Feulner, foreword to *Mandate for Leadership* (Washington: Heritage Foundation, 1981), viii.

25. Everett Carll Ladd Jr., "Pursuing the New Class," in B. Bruce-Briggs, ed., *The New Class* (New Haven: Yale University Press, 1979), 120.

26. Reeves, *Reagan Detour*, 23; John B. Judis, "Conservatism and the Price of Success," in *The Reagan Legacy*, 137.

27. Feulner, foreword to *Mandate for Leadership*, vii.

28. Sidney Blumenthal, "Conservative Elite," *Washington Post*, September 24, 1985, A1; Judis, "Conservatism," 139.

29. Anderson, *Revolution*, 201.

30. Evans and Novak, *Reagan Revolution*, 242–43.

31. Francis X. Clines, "Two Right Hands for the President," *New York Times*, December 9, 1983, A32; Robert Pear, "The Domestic Policy Staff Is Different under Reagan," *New York Times*, October 4, 1981, sec. 4, p. 2.

32. Meese, *With Reagan* 76; Pear, "Domestic Policy Staff," 2.

33. Meese quoted in Lou Cannon, "Top Aide of Reagan Resigning: Martin Anderson to Leave Post as Policy Director," *Washington Post*, February 4, 1982, A1; Stockman, *Triumph of Politics*, 4.

34. Steven Weisman, "President Getting a New Chief of Policy as Adviser Resigns," *New York Times*, February 5, 1982, A18; Lois Romano, "Reagan's Ranking Couple: Martin and Annelise Anderson's 20-Year, Ideological Odyssey to the Inner Circle," *Washington Post*, November 29, 1981, H1.

35. Cannon, "Top Aide," A1; Strober and Strober, *Reagan*, 59.

36. Howell Raines, "Policy Office Is Short on Clout and Long on Critics," *New York Times*, January 11, 1982, B7; Anderson, *Revolution*, 275–77.

37. Ann Crittenden, "Exodus of the Supply Siders," *New York Times*, July 25, 1982, sec. 3, p. 6.

38. Evans and Novak, *Reagan Revolution*, 243; Crittenden, "Exodus of the Supply Siders," 6.

39. Stockman, *Triumph of Politics*, 83; Strober and Strober, *Reagan*, 97–98; Easterbrook, "Ideas," 72.

40. Noonan, *What I Saw*, 171; Evans and Novak, *Reagan Revolution*, xii.

41. Paul Gottfried, "The Conservative Crackup Continued," *Society*, January–February 1994, 23–29.

NOTES TO CHAPTER EIGHT

1. Dan Quayle, *Standing Firm: A Vice-Presidential Memoir* (New York: HarperPaperbacks, 1994), 269; cf. Charles Kolb, *White House Daze: The Unmaking of Domestic Policy in the Bush Years* (New York: Free Press, 1994).

2. Kolb, *White House Daze*, 8, 5.

3. Don Regan, *For the Record: From Wall Street to Washington* (New York: St. Martin's 1988), 307; Anderson, quoted in Kolb, *White House Daze*, 347; Michael Duffy and Dan Goodgame, *Marching in Place: The Status Quo Presidency of George Bush* (New York: Simon & Schuster, 1992), 42; David Brooks, "Bush Family Values," review of Bill Minutaglio, *First Son: George W. Bush and the Bush Family Dynasty* (New York: Times Books/Random House, 2000); and George Bush, *All the Best: George Bush: My Life in Letters and Other Writings* (New York: Scribner, 2000); *New York Times Book Review*, October 17, 1999, 4; Kolb, *White House Daze*, 3.

4. Duffy and Goodgame, *Marching in Place*, 39.

5. Kristol, quoted in Duffy and Goodgame, *Marching in Place*, 46.

6. Duffy and Goodgame, *Marching in Place*, 41; Colin Campbell and Bert A. Rockman, eds., *The Bush Presidency: First Appraisals* (Chatham, N.J.: Chatham House Publishers, 1991); Campbell and Rockman, introduction to *Bush Presidency*, 25, 31; Campbell and Rockman, conclusion to *Bush Presidency*, 293.

7. Mark Rozell, *The Press and the Bush Presidency* (Westport, Conn.: Praeger, 1996), 55; Kolb, *White House Daze*, 4, 3.

8. Rozell, *Press*, 3; John Podhoretz, *Hell of a Ride: Backstage at the White House Follies, 1989–1993* (New York: Simon & Schuster, 1993), 82.

9. Kenneth Thompson, ed., *The Bush Presidency: Ten Intimate Perspectives on George Bush* (Lanham, Md.: University Press of America, 1997), 10:11; 11:xv.

10. Lou Cannon, *President Reagan: The Role of a Lifetime* (New York: Simon & Schuster, 1991), 793; Duffy and Goodgame, *Marching in Place*, 18.

11. George Bush, inaugural address, January 20, 1989.

12. Duffy and Goodgame, *Marching in Place*, 33.

13. Thompson, *Bush Presidency*, 10:104.

14. Robert Ajemian, "Where Is the Real George Bush? The Vice President Must Now Step Out from Reagan's Shadow," *Time*, January 26, 1987, 20.

15. William Schneider, "Voters May Be Seeking More Than Competence," *National Journal*, October 10, 1987, 2557.

16. Rozell, *Press*, 12.

17. Barbara Hinckley, *The Symbolic Presidency: How Presidents Portray Themselves* (New York: Routledge, 1990), 142; Kenneth T. Walsh, "The Passive Mandate," *U.S. News and World Report*, October 31, 1988, 20; quoted in John Robert Greene, *The Presidency of George Bush* (Lawrence: University Press of Kansas, 2000), 60.

18. Will, Buchanan, Broder, Phillips, and Thomas quoted in "National Briefing-Bush Reviews Improve . . . A Little," *Hotline*, March 13, 1989.

19. Duffy and Goodgame, *Marching in Place*, 252; Kolb, *White House Daze*, 25.

20. Fred Barnes, "Paradigm Regained," *New Republic*, April 13, 1992, 8; Duffy and Goodgame, *Marching in Place*, 269; David Mervin, *George Bush and the Guardianship Presidency* (New York: St. Martin's, 1996), 214; Dilys Hill and Phil Williams, eds., *The Bush Presidency: Triumphs and Adversities* (New York: St. Martin's, 1994), 4.

21. James P. Pfiffner, *The Strategic Presidency: Hitting the Ground Running*, 2d ed. (Lawrence: University Press of Kansas, 1996), 138; quoted in Rozell, *Press*, 20, 140.

22. Marlin Fitzwater, *Call the Briefing: Bush and Reagan, Sam and Helen; A Decade with Presidents and the Press* (Holbrook: Adams Media Corporation, 1995), 179.

23. Weber, quoted in Mervin, *George Bush*, 70; Dilys M. Hill, "Domestic Policy," in Hill and Williams, *Bush Presidency*, 142; Podhoretz, *Hell of a Ride*, 57.

24. Podhoretz, *Hell of a Ride*, 76; Thompson, *Bush Presidency*, 11:119.

25. Podhoretz, *Hell of a Ride*, 78; Joel D. Aberbach, "The President and the Executive Branch," in Campbell and Rockman, *Bush Presidency*, 237.

26. "National Briefing—Education Summit Crib Notes," *Hotline*, September 27, 1989; "National Briefing—Education Summit Wrap-Up," *Hotline*, September 29, 1989; "Focus—Cavazos Canned, Tenure Panned, Succession Planned," *Hotline*, December 13, 1990.

27. "White House '92—Bush: Everything Old Is New Again," *Hotline*, April 15, 1992.

28. Kolb, *White House Daze*, xiii; Podhoretz, *Hell of a Ride*, 84; Fitzwater, *Call the Briefing*, 215.

29. Fitzwater, *Call the Briefing*, 348.

30. Thompson, *Bush Presidency*, 11:54, 56.

31. Mervin, *George Bush*, 63; Duffy and Goodgame, *Marching in Place*, 64.

32. Kevin Philips, *The Politics of Rich and Poor: Wealth and the American Electorate in the Reagan Aftermath* (New York: Random House, 1990), xxii.

33. "White House '92—Bush: When in Doubt, Say Law-and-Order," *Hotline*, May 6, 1992.

34. George Bush, address to the nation on the civil disturbances in Los Angeles, California, May 1, 1992.

35. Quayle, *Standing Firm*, 268, 352.

36. Rozell, *Press*, 28–29.

37. Rozell, *Press*, 42.

38. Rozell, *Press*, 55; Freedom Forum Poll, 1995.

39. Mervin, *George Bush*, 115.

40. Rozell, quoted in Thompson, *Bush Presidency*, 11:121.

41. Duffy and Goodgame, *Marching in Place*, 21.

42. George Bush, remarks to the American Enterprise Institute, December 4, 1991.

43. Barnes, "Paradigm Regained," 8.

44. Duffy and Goodgame, *Marching in Place*, 86; Fitzwater, *Call the Briefing*, 378.

NOTES TO CHAPTER NINE

1. Michael T. Kaufman, "The Dangers of Letting a President Read," *New York Times*, May 22, 1999, B11; Dick Morris, *Behind the Oval Office: Winning the Presidency in the Nineties* (New York: Random House, 1997), 99.

2. Kaufman, "Letting a President Read."

3. Kenneth S. Baer, *Reinventing Democrats: The Politics of Liberalism from Reagan to Clinton* (Lawrence: University of Kansas Press, 2000), 2.

4. Lloyd Grove, "Al From, the Life of the Party; The Head of the Democratic Leadership Council, Finding Victory in Moderation," *Washington Post*, July 24, 1992, D1; Jonathan Chait, "The Slippery Center: The Self-Contradictions of the Third Way," *New Republic*, November 16, 1998, 19.

5. Jeff Faux, "The Myth of the New Democrat," *American Prospect*, Fall 1993, 20; William A. Galston, "A Student of Strauss in the Clinton Administration," in Kenneth L. Deutsch and John A. Murley, eds., *Leo Strauss, the Straussians, and the American Regime* (Lanham, Md.: Rowman & Littlefield, 2000), 433.

6. Baer, *Reinventing Democrats*, 202.

7. Michael Duffy, "A Public Policy Entrepreneur; Domestic-Issues Coordinator Al From Yanked the Democrats Back to the Center," *Time*, December 14, 1992, 51; Grove, "Al From"; Baer, *Reinventing Democrats*, 211.

8. Grove, "Al From"; Duffy, "Public Policy Entrepreneur."

9. "REAX," *Hotline*, January 15, 1993.

10. Dan Balz and Ronald Brownstein, *Storming the Gates: Protest Politics and the Republican Revival* (Boston: Little, Brown, 1996), 83; "REAX," *Hotline*, January 15, 1993.

11. "The New Administration—Jobs, Jobs, Jobs: Bitterness at the DLC?" *Hotline*, January 28, 1993; John B. Judis, "The Old Democrat: Is Clinton Dukakis II?" *New Republic*, February 22, 1993, 18; Balz and Brownstein, *Storming the Gates*, 83.

12. Jay Winik, *On the Brink: The Dramatic, Behind-the-Scenes Saga of the Reagan Era and the Men and Women Who Won the Cold War* (New York: Simon & Schuster, 1996), 84.

13. George Stephanopoulos, *All Too Human: A Political Education* (New York: Little, Brown, 1999), 363; Michael Barone, "A Vote for Smaller Government," *U.S. News and World Report*, November 28, 1994, 66; Galston, "Student of Strauss," 433–35.

14. Michael Kramer, "Clinton's Troops Turn Away," *Time*, July 10, 1995, 31.

15. "National Briefing—Hotline Rolodex: Galston Leaving; Cooper Managing," *Hotline*, March 20, 1995; Morris, *Behind the Oval Office*, 220.

16. Kramer, "Clinton's Troops"; Eliza Newlin Carney, *National Journal*, April 6, 1996.

17. Senator Daniel Patrick Moynihan, quoted in the *Congressional Record*, March 18, 1993.

18. Peggy Noonan, *The Case against Hillary Clinton* (New York: Regan, 2000), 61–68; John B. Judis, "Online Magaziner: Ira's Impractical Plan for the Internet," *New Republic*, December 28, 1998. The administration had initially estimated that creating the plan would cost less than $100,000.

19. Jon Aloysius Farrell, "Reich Redux," *Boston Globe*, April 2, 1995, Sunday Magazine, 26.

20. Robert B. Reich, *Locked in the Cabinet* (New York: Knopf, 1997).

21. Editorial, *The Nation*, August 10, 1998, 7.

22. Reich, *Locked in the Cabinet*, 271, 275, 300; Stephanopoulos, *All Too Human*, 329–30.

23. Stephanopoulos, *All Too Human*, 329–30.

24. Quoted in Jeff Faux, "The Myth of the New Democrat," *American Prospect*, Fall 1993, 20.

25. John Maggs, "Gilded Age, Newly Minted," *National Journal*, January 28, 2000; Burt Solomon, "Thinking Small," *National Journal*, January 24, 1998, 157.

26. Sidney Blumenthal, *The Rise of the Counterestablishment: From Conservative Ideology to Political Power* (New York: Harper & Row, 1988).

27. Howard Kurtz, "The Clintons' Pen Pal," *Washington Post*, June 16, 1997, C1.

28. Kurtz, "Clintons' Pen Pal," C1.

29. Michael Lewis, "I Liked a Pol," *New York Times Magazine*, November 21, 1999, 80.

30. Sidney Blumenthal, Affidavit to Federal Court, March 16, 1998; *Report of Independent Counsel Kenneth Starr*, appendix; Dana Milbank, "White House Watch: Sid's Id," *New Republic*, October 12, 1998.

31. Dana Milbank, "White House Watch: Sid's Id," *New Republic*, October 12, 1998; Baer, *Reinventing Democrats*, 259.

32. Jeffrey Toobin, "The Secret War in Starr's Office," *New Yorker*, November 15, 1999, 76.

33. Michael Isikoff, *Uncovering Clinton: A Reporter's Story* (New York: Crown, 1999), 357, 389 n. 1.

34. Jonah Goldberg, "Reaganism vs. Clintonism," *IntellectualCapital.com*, September 30, 1999, www.intellectualcapital.com/issues/issue306/item6656.asp; Jonah Goldberg, "Sid, Sid: He's Our Man!" Goldberg Files, *National Review Online*, February 1, 1999, www.nationalreview.com/goldberg/goldberg020199.html.

35. William Neikirk and Roger Simon, "Clinton's Lawyers Outline a Defense; Some Democrats Implore President to Admit Wrongs," *Chicago Sun-Times*, December 8, 1998.

36. Sean Wilentz, testimony before the House Judiciary Committee, Hearing on Impeachment Inquiry Pursuant to H. Res. 581, December 8, 1998, www.house.gov/judiciary/101325.pdf; Jonah Goldberg, "The Weakness of Wilentz," Magazine Arguments, *National Review Online*, February 22, 2000, www.nationalreview.com/goldberg/goldberg022200.html.

37. Historians in Defense of the Constitution, advertisement, *New York Times*, October 30, 1998, A15.

38. Jonah Goldberg, "It's Academic," Goldberg Files, *National Review Online*, December 9, 1998, www.nationalreview.com/goldberg/goldberg120998.html; Richard Blow, "Sidney Strikes Again," *George*, January 1999, 26; "Partisan Historians," editorial, *Augusta (Ga.) Chronicle*, December 30, 1998, A4.

39. Goldberg, "It's Academic."

40. Sidney Blumenthal, "Presidents and Democracy: An American History" (Willard and Margaret Thorp Lecture in American Studies, Princeton University, November 9, 1999).

41. Sean Wilentz, "Yawn," *New Republic*, February 28, 2000; Wilentz, "Give It a Rest," *New Republic*, March 6, 2000.

42. Emma Soichet, "Blumenthal Praises Clinton for Rescuing Party, Economy," *Daily Princetonian*, November 10, 1999.

43. Soichet, "Blumenthal Praises Clinton."

44. Richard Posner, *An Affair of State: The Investigation, Impeachment, and Trial of President Clinton* (Cambridge: Harvard University Press, 1999), 12, 14.

NOTES TO CHAPTER TEN

1. James Carney, "Why Bush Doesn't Like Homework," *Time*, November 15, 1999, 46.

2. George Hager, "California Think Tank Helps Staff Bush Team," *Washington Post*, June 8, 1999, E12; Robert McGrew and Henry Towsner, *Stanford Review*, front page, December 3, 1999.

3. McGrew and Towsner, front page.

4. Bill Minutaglio, "The Godfathers of 'Compassionate Conservatism': Authors' Works Have Helped Shape Candidate Bush's Core Philosophy," *Dallas Morning News*, April 16, 2000; Myron Magnet, *The Dream and the Nightmare* (New York: Morrow, 1993).

5. Minutaglio, "Godfathers"; Marvin Olasky, *The Tragedy of American Compassion* (Wheaton, Ill.: Crossway, 1993).

6. George F. Will, "Ready for the Big Leagues?" *Washington Post*, October 24, 1999, B7.

7. Michael Kelly, "The GOP Pilgrims' Sad Tale," *Washington Post*, February 9, 2000; Carney, "Why Bush," 46.

8. Michael Holmes, "Bush Circle of Diverse Advisers," Associated Press wire story, August 18, 1999.

9. The *Washington Post* called Gore's grades "generally middling." David Maraniss and Ellen Nakashima, "Gore's Grades Belie Image of Studiousness," *Washington Post*, March 19, 2000, A1.

10. Howard Kurtz, "MSNBC's Scoop Really a Double Dip," *Washington Post*, April 7, 1997, D1.

11. Myron Magnet, "Naomi Cries Wolf Over 'Racism,'" *Wall Street Journal*, November 16, 1999.

12. Muriel Dobbin, "Feminists, Others Say Gore Showed Poor Judgment in Hiring Naomi Wolf," Nandotimes.com, November 3, 1999; Maureen Dowd, "The Alpha–Beta Macarena," *New York Times*, November 3, 1999; "The Politics of Imperfection," editorial, *New York Times*, November 2, 1999; Deborah Orin, "Gore Lets Wolf Back in Pack," *New York Post*, July 6, 2000.

13. Ceci Connolly and Glenn Kessler, "Gore's Policy Team Finds Help Nearby," *Washington Post*, May 4, 2000, A1.

14. Connolly and Kessler, "Gore's Policy Team," A1; Dan Balz and Terry M. Neal, "Bush as President: Questions, Clues, and Contradictions," *Washington Post*, October 22, 2000, A1.

15. Jonathan Cohn, "The Old New Thing: Why Gore Can't Be a New Democrat," *New Republic*, April 17, 2000, 24, 38–42.

16. John J. Miller and Ramesh Ponnuru, "The DLC's Other Candidate," *National Review*, Washington Bulletin, April 18, 2000.

17. Fred Barnes, "John McCain, Winging It: He's Loosey Goosey on Domestic Policy, But Reporters Are Going Easy . . . For Now," *Weekly Standard*, January 3–10, 2000, 12–14.

18. Melinda Henneberger, "Bradley's Most Influential Adviser? Bradley," *New York Times*, January 21, 2000, A1.

19. Jonathan Chait, "Race to the Bottom: Why, This Election Year, It's Smart to Be Dumb," *New Republic*, December 20, 1999.

20. Richard L. Berke, "Head Games: What a Mind! In Politics, That's Not What Matters," *New York Times*, Week in Review, June 25, 2000, sec. 4, p. 1.

21. McGrew and Towsner, front page.

22. Chait, "Race to the Bottom."

23. Christopher Marquis, "Job of Clarence Thomas's Wife Raises Conflict-of-Interest Questions," *New York Times*, December 12, 2000, A1.

24. Peggy Noonan, "Write-Wing Conspiracy," *Wall Street Journal*, March 16, 2001, www.opinionjournal.com/columnists/pnoonan/?id=85000714.

25. Richard Morin, "Onward Christian Soldier," *Washington Post*, February 26, 2001, C1; Lynette Clemetson, "The Gospel According to John DiIulio, *Newsweek*, February 12, http://stacks.msnbc.com/news/526117.asp; Claude R. Marx, "Bush Adviser John DiIulio: Joe Pesci with a Ph.D.," Associated Press wire story, January 30, 2001; Michael Schaffer, "Philly-Based Faith Fighter," *U.S. News and World Report*, Outlook, March 12, 2001.

26. John F. Harris, "Leading Actor Bush Avoids Center Stage," *Washington Post*, April 14, 2001, A1, A8.

27. Michael Kelly, "The Quiet Man," *Washington Post*, April 18, 2001, A21; Jane Mayer, "School Ties: Can Yale Bring Back Bush?" *New Yorker*, April 23, 30, 2001, 54.

28. Michael Kelly, "The Quiet Man," *Washington Post*, April 18, 2001, A21.

29. Cf. David M. Ricci, *The Transformation of American Politics: The New Washington and the Rise of Think Tanks* (New Haven: Yale University Press, 1994).

30. Lloyd Grove, "The Reliable Source," *Washington Post*, April 5, 2001, C3. Gore made his comments, appropriately enough, in front of David Letterman, who then asked the class, "Am I the only one here who has never heard of the word 'metanarrative'?"

31. Irving Kristol, quoted in *Professors, Politicians, and Public Policy: A Round Table Held on July 29, 1977.* AEI Forum no. 10 (Washington, D.C.: AEI Press), 38. Other participants included Pat Moynihan, Robert Bork, and S. I. Hayakawa.

32. "Message to the Intellectuals," editorial, *The Nation*, November 18, 1968, 505.

33. Charles Kadushin, *The American Intellectual Elite* (New York: Little, Brown, 1974); National Center for Education Statistics, Encyclopedia of Education Statistics, www.nces.ed.gov.

34. Joseph Epstein, "Intellectuals—Public and Otherwise," *Commentary*, May 2000, 48.

35. Emily Eakin, "More Ado (Yawn) about Great Books," *New York Times*, Education Life, April 8, 2001, sec. 4A, p. 24.

36. Mitchell S. Ross, *The Literary Politicians* (New York: Doubleday, 1978), 302.

37. Norman Podhoretz, *Making It* (New York: Random House, 1980), 312.

38. Mitchell S. Ross, *The Literary Politicians* (New York: Doubleday, 1978), 110.

39. Lillian Ross, "Department of Big Thoughts: The 1845th," *New Yorker*, April 9, 2001, 39.

40. Todd Leopold, "Learning from the Masters: What Presidential Biographies Can Teach Presidents—and the Rest of Us," December 28, 2000, cnn.com/2000/books/news/12/28/presidential.books.

41. Leopold, "Learning from the Masters."

42. David Brooks, "The China Lineup: You Can't Tell the Players without a Scorecard," *Weekly Standard*, April 30, 2001.

43. Brooks, "China Lineup."

44. Epstein, "Intellectuals," 51.

45. David Brooks, *Bobos in Paradise: The New Upper Class and How They Got There* (New York: Simon & Schuster, 2000), 148; Richard Hofstader, *Anti-Intellectualism in American Life* (New York: Knopf, 1963), 397.

46. Jacques Barzun, *House of Intellect* (Westport, Conn.: Greenwood, 1978), 145–46.

NOTE TO APPENDIX

1. Forrest McDonald, *The American Presidency: An Intellectual History* (Lawrence: University of Kansas Press, 1994), 464 n. 5.

INDEX

ABOUT THE AUTHOR

Tevi Troy is the deputy assistant secretary for policy at the Department of Labor. Previously, Troy served as the policy director for Senator John Ashcroft (R–Missouri). From 1996 to 1998, Troy was senior domestic policy adviser and later domestic policy director for the House Republican Policy Committee, chaired by Christopher Cox (R–California). He has also served as the Herman Kahn Fellow at the Hudson Institute in Indianapolis and as a researcher at the American Enterprise Institute in Washington, D.C.

Troy has a B.S. from Cornell University and an M.A. and Ph.D. from the University of Texas at Austin; he also studied at the London School of Economics. He has written for numerous publications, including the *New Republic*, *Wall Street Journal*, *Washington Times*, *Weekly Standard*, *Journal of Commerce*, *National Review*, and *Reason*. He lives in Washington, D.C.

American Intellectual Culture

Series Editors: Jean Bethke Elshtain, University of Chicago,
Ted V. McAllister, Pepperdine University,
Wilfred M. McClay, University of Tennessee at Chattanooga

The books in the American Intellectual Culture series examine the place, identity, and public role of intellectuals and cultural elites in the United States, past, present, and future. Written by prominent historians, philosophers, and political theorists, these books will examine the influence of intellectuals on American political, social, and cultural life, paying particular attention to the characteristic forms—and evolving possibilities—of democratic intellect. The books will place special, but not exclusive, emphasis on the relationship between intellectuals and American public life. Because the books are intended to shape and contribute to scholarly and public debates about their respective topics, they will be concise, accessible, and provocative.

HUMAN RIGHTS WATCH BOOKS

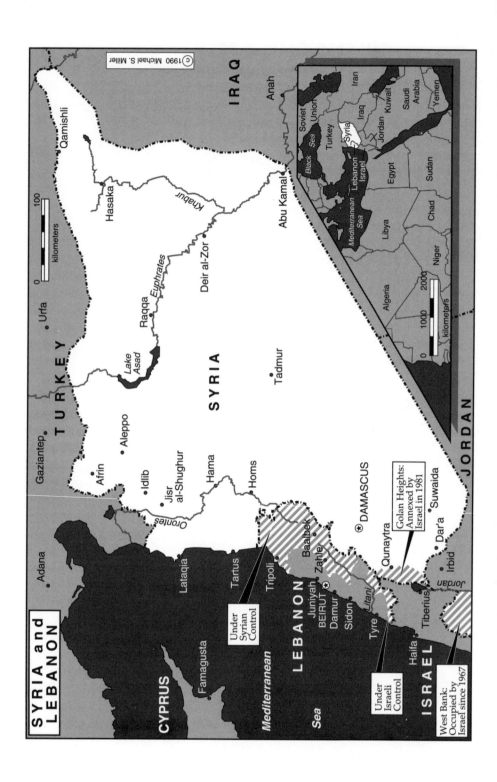

SYRIA and LEBANON

© 1990 Michael S. Miller

TURKEY

IRAQ

SYRIA

LEBANON

ISRAEL

JORDAN

CYPRUS

Gaziantep
Adana
Afrin
Aleppo
Idlib
Jisr al-Shughur
Hama
Homs
Orontes
Lat.aqia
Tartus
Tripoli
Famagusta
Juniyah
BEIRUT
Damur
Sidon
Tyre
Haifa
Litani
Tiberius
Jordan
Irbid
Dar'a
Suwaida
DAMASCUS
Qunaytra
Baalbek
Zahle
Tadmur
Homs

Mediterranean Sea

Urfa
Lake Asad
Raqqa
Euphrates
Deir al-Zor
Abu Kamal
Khabur
Hasaka
Qamishli

Under Syrian Control

Under Israeli Control

Golan Heights: Annexed by Israel in 1981

West Bank: Occupied by Israel since 1967

0   100
kilometers

Soviet Union
Black Sea
Turkey
Iran
Iraq
Kuwait
Jordan
Saudi Arabia
Yemen
Syria
Lebanon
Israel
Egypt
Sudan
Libya
Chad
Algeria
Niger

Mediterranean Sea

0   1000   2000
kilometers

MIDDLE EAST WATCH

Yale University Press   New Haven and London

Syria Unmasked was first published in slightly different form by
Human Rights Watch, copyright © September 1990.

Middle East Watch was established in 1989 to monitor and promote
observance of internationally recognized human rights in the Middle East
and North Africa. Human Rights Watch also includes Africa Watch,
Americas Watch, Asia Watch, Helsinki Watch, and the Fund for Free Expression.

Library of Congress Cataloging-in-Publication Data

Syria unmasked : the suppression of human rights by the Asad regime /
Middle East Watch.
p.   cm. — (Human Rights Watch books)
Includes bibliographical references and index.
ISBN 0–300–05115–8 (alk. paper)
1. Human rights—Syria.   2. Civil rights—Syria.
I. Middle East Watch (Organization)   II. Series.
JC599.S97S97   1991
323.4'9'095691—dc20   91–17065
CIP

Set in Times Roman type by The Composing Room of Michigan, Inc.
Printed in the United States of America by Vail-Ballou Press, Binghamton, New York.

The paper in this book meets the guidelines for permanence and
durability of the Committee on Production Guidelines for Book
Longevity of the Council on Library Resources.
10   9   8   7   6   5   4   3   2   1

CONTENTS

PREFACE

Since the summer and fall of 1989, when the research for *Syria Unmasked* was largely completed, two political earthquakes have sent tremors into Syria: the decline of Soviet might and the Persian Gulf war, precipitated by Iraq's invasion and occupation of Kuwait. Both have influenced human rights conditions with complex and mixed results.

The upheaval in Eastern Europe kindled hope among Syrian rights advocates that the government in Damascus might be the next to fall. Syria's government, long identified with the Soviet bloc, minimized the importance of European events. But fledgling movements for democracy in several Arab countries— and well-publicized elections in a number of neighboring countries, including Jordan—increased pressure for change. Even high Ba'th party officials are believed to have feared that Syria's aging president, Hafez Asad, might soon follow his East Bloc counterparts into oblivion. In November 1990, Asad completed two decades in power, with no successor in sight.

Beginning in 1989, rumors abounded that to strengthen his domestic base Asad would make major concessions: broaden the ruling National Progressive Front, release political prisoners, lift emergency laws, and allow new political parties to be formed. Initially, however, the government made only two small gestures. In April 1989, responding to a long-term campaign by the Arab Lawyers' Union, Asad released three lawyers who had been imprisoned since 1980. Then in June, Syrian officials met for the first time in eleven years with representatives of Amnesty International. Reformers waited hopefully for a major Ba'th party congress, scheduled for the fall, that was expected to signal a change in direction. The congress, however, was never convened.

Toward the end of 1989, latent domestic pressures on the regime emerged publicly for the first time since 1982. Mothers and wives of political prisoners and the "disappeared" demonstrated twice in front of the Presidential Palace. The gatherings were small, but they were significant—security forces showed unusual restraint, allowing them to proceed without incident. Then, on December 10, 1989, the Committee for the Defense of Democratic Freedoms and Human Rights in Syria was announced, becoming the first human rights organization inside the country in nearly a decade. Although it operated clandestinely within Syria, the group claimed to have members in several cities and made a strong statement from abroad regarding the need for fundamental change.

On February 19, 1990, as many as a hundred Syrian women held a third protest before the Presidential Palace, demanding the release of political prisoners. This time, the police intervened violently to disperse the demonstrators—but there were still no arrests.

Faced with such unusual public expressions of discontent, the Asad government made further gestures toward reform, though still with little substance. In January 1990, the Syrian cabinet restricted the scope of martial law, and in March it did the same for the state of emergency, which has suspended legal and constitutional protections since 1963. But these gestures left in place all measures "relating to state security"—the most objectionable and far-reaching provisions of martial law and the state of emergency.

On March 4, Asad announced the formation of special new courts to investigate abuses of authority by civil servants, a measure that meant little and had many empty precedents. Four days later, in a speech by Asad marking the anniversary of the Ba'th party's seizure of power in 1963, came a great letdown. Some observers had expected Asad to propose democratic initiatives; instead, he pointed to the threat inherent in having Israel as a neighbor as part of a lengthy justification for continuing the state of emergency. Such arguments have long been common in the regime's inflated rhetoric and in its rare public responses to charges of persistent human rights violations.

Syrian security forces continued to show little change in their rough tactics toward political dissenters. In early April, opponents of the regime painted unflattering slogans on walls in the little town of Yabrud, north of Damascus, comparing Asad with Nicolae Ceauşescu, the deposed dictator of Romania. Fifteen people were arrested almost immediately. One died a few days later, apparently from torture, and another was taken from prison to the hospital in critical condition.

Yet, a modest political opening took place in the spring of 1990. On May 22, Syria held national elections to replace the People's Assembly, whose term had expired. The government increased the number of openings from 195 to 250 "to provide more seats for independents" and issued a decree granting most Syrian citizens of voting age the right to present themselves as candidates.

Although an astonishing nine thousand candidates ran for office, the elections were highly controlled. Those outside the National Progressive Front—a body dominated by Asad's Arab Ba'th Socialist party, to give its full title— could run only as individuals, independent of party affiliation. Authorities forced at least forty-three candidates to withdraw and arrested at least one. Officials also prevented all mass meetings except those by the Front and insisted on prior censorship of electoral statements. Some independents dubbed it the "40 percent democracy," because Front candidates were, in practice, guaranteed at least 60 percent of the seats, in line with "predictions" announced well before the voting by Sulaiman Qaddah, a senior Ba'th party official.

Nonetheless, observers reported that the campaign was livelier than usual. Many candidates held meetings in their homes, where they criticized corruption, shortages, and inflation. Some even complained about the lack of democracy. But all conformed to the taboos of Syrian political life: none openly challenged the regime. Expressions of fidelity to President Asad were commonplace.

The overall results of the polling were no surprise. Front candidates took 166 seats—two-thirds of the assembly. Of those, the Ba'th party won 134 places, giving it a comfortable majority. The government did, however, apparently allow some "independent" seats to be filled on the basis of actual votes cast. As a result, some mavericks were elected, including sixteen Kurds openly active in Kurdish politics, the first such Syrian parliamentarians under Asad's rule.

As the position of the Soviet Union weakened in the region, the United States initiated an intensive "dialogue" with Syria, beginning in late 1989 and accelerating in early 1990. Many well-known political figures made visits to Damascus. The State Department conducted its own intense diplomacy toward Syria, led by U.S. Ambassador to Damascus Edward Djeridjian. In June 1990, Asad responded to this courtship, appointing his first ambassador to Washington in several years.

Syrian-U.S. relations warmed dramatically after the Iraqi invasion of Kuwait. Asad joined the U.S.-led coalition against his old foe, Iraqi president Saddam Hussein, eventually sending a division of Syrian troops to bolster coalition forces and increase Arab participation in the effort to dislodge Iraqi forces from Kuwait. For this he was well rewarded. According to reliable sources, Saudi Arabia offered at least a billion dollars, and other Gulf states made sizable contributions. Germany eventually offered another enormous aid package. The United States was said to have been an important broker in these transactions, and there was talk that after the war, the United States would lend its support to vital multilateral aid to Syria through such institutions as the World Bank.

Having bolstered Syria's previously weak economic situation, the United States appeared to accede to Syria's longstanding desire for a broader regional role. In mid-October 1990, less than a month after high-level talks between Asad and U.S. Secretary of State James Baker, Syrian forces went on the offensive in Lebanon, attacking army units under the command of rebel general Michel 'Aoun and his predominantly Maronite Christian supporters. Accompanied by forces of Lebanese president Elias Hrwawi, the Syrians routed 'Aoun and expanded their fifteen-year-long occupation to nearly two-thirds of the country.

Brutality marked the Syrian offensive. Widespread reports suggest that during and immediately after the push, Syrian forces executed at least a hundred prisoners, including civilians, in the area of 'Aoun's headquarters in Ba'bda and in the nearby towns of Dahr al-Wahash, Bsous, Houmal, and Beit Meri. Eyewitness reports say that many victims were shot in the head at close range, hands tied behind their backs. Thirteen high-ranking military officers were taken into custody by Syrian forces and transported to prison in Damascus. They were released months later. As the Syrians have expanded their control over Lebanese territory, the notorious Syrian Military Intelligence has tightened its grip by, among other measures, running private prisons.

One positive development has improved the otherwise grim Syrian rights record in recent months: in mid-March 1991, Syrian authorities released as many as two thousand Palestinian and Lebanese political prisoners. But these releases probably represent a facet of Asad's latest regional strategy rather than an improved human rights policy; at least a thousand Palestinians remain in custody.

Overall, in recent months, rights conditions in Syria have changed little from those described in the body of this book. Security forces operate with impunity, censors insist on conformity, minorities face continued persecution and discrimination, torture is a standard feature of interrogation, and thousands languish as political prisoners. With the rapprochement between Damascus and Washington that has developed since the summer of 1989, the United States has gained important leverage not at its disposal during the long years of political estrangement between the two countries. By focusing only on President Asad's complicity in terrorism, rather than on the legitimate human rights concerns of the Syrian people and that portion of the Lebanese populace subject to Syrian army rule, Washington is missing an opportunity to advance civil and political liberties in the Levant. It should not let this chance slip away.

ACKNOWLEDGMENTS

Human Rights Watch and Yale University Press express their appreciation to the J. M. Kaplan Fund for making this joint publishing program possible.

This book was written by James A. Paul, a consultant to Middle East Watch, based on extensive research he conducted in the Middle East, Europe, and the United States in 1989 and 1990.

Andrew Whitley, Executive Director of Middle East Watch, had overall editorial responsibility for the book. Susan F. Kinsley and Lisa M. Fleischman undertook additional research.

INTRODUCTION

Syria Unmasked looks at human rights in Syria during two decades of rule by President Hafez Asad. It also considers the human rights practices of Asad's predecessors, particularly the governments that emerged from the military coup d'état of March 8, 1963, under the banner of the Arab Ba'th Socialist party.

Syria, a country with a population of twelve million, has been a key player in contemporary Middle Eastern politics. In spite of limited oil revenues, the Asad regime has built a powerful army and security apparatus with the help of considerable foreign aid and a network of regional and international alliances. Such varied sources as the Soviet Union, Iran, and Saudi Arabia have provided more than a billion U.S. dollars a year in subsidies to Syria. European countries have recently begun to provide aid, and relations with the United States have been warming rapidly over the past two years, well before Iraq invaded Kuwait. That event, and the resulting shared hostility to the regime of Saddam Hussein, has produced the most amiable U.S. relations with Syria of the Asad years.

In the early 1980s, the Asad regime crushed its opposition with great violence, killing at least 10,000 citizens and jailing thousands more. Today, under a longstanding state of emergency, security forces routinely arrest citizens without charge, torture them during interrogation, and imprison them without trial for political reasons. At least 7,500 political prisoners languish in Syrian jails.

Syria is also a serious rights offender in Lebanon, where since 1976, its army has controlled more than half of the country. Using Lebanese proxy forces as well as its own army and security services, Syria has been responsible for widespread political imprisonment, torture, and massacres of hundreds of innocent civilians. The Syrian occupation, which effectively ended free expression in Lebanon, was an important factor in the demise of Beirut as the leading regional center of research, writing, and publishing. Much international commentary falsely treats Syria as a contributor to Lebanese peace and stability but overlooks the heavy price that has been paid by Arab society as a whole.

To secure its rule in Syria and Lebanon, the Asad regime relies on three institutions, in addition to the ordinary machinery of government. One is the Ba'th party—the "leading party" under the Syrian constitution—which has a virtual political monopoly in the country. It purveys the official ideology, censors opposing viewpoints, controls unions, professional associations, and mass organizations, and runs a large intelligence network.

The military is a second institution of rule. The Ba'thist regime came to power by military coup, and many of its leading figures, including Asad, are military officers. The military remains a major constituency and power base. Important military units are deployed near the capital, Damascus, to protect the regime from its domestic opposition.

The third institution of rule in Syria is the security apparatus. Today, fifteen different security and paramilitary forces watch one another and ensure the loyalty of the rest of the population. The security chiefs—almost all military officers from the 'Alawi sect—are among the president's inner core of advisers and, after Asad, are considered the most powerful people in Syria.

Syria's constitution affords many rights protections and its legal code, modeled in part on French jurisprudence, affirms many human rights principles. In practice, however, Syrian citizens enjoy few rights. The state of emergency overrides legal protections and authorizes sweeping powers of censorship, arrest for reasons of "state security," and unlimited detention without trial. The regime ignores the civil rights afforded by its own laws, and its practices regularly violate United Nations human rights conventions to which Syria is a party.

Yet critical thought survives in Syria. A strong human rights movement in the late 1970s was testimony to the widespread longing in Syria for the rule of law and democracy. And after many years of authoritarian rule, a movement for human rights and political freedoms may be building again.

SOURCES

Syria's human rights record has been difficult to document because of the lack of local rights monitors and the difficulty of gaining access to local sources. Syrian monitoring organizations sprang up in the late 1970s but they were short-lived. In 1980, the government dissolved them and threw their leaders in prison.

Throughout the 1980s, Syrian authorities refused to allow international human rights organizations to conduct any investigations in the country; nor did they answer inquiries from human rights organizations. For eleven years, 1978–1989, Amnesty International received no response from the Asad regime to dozens of communications, and its representatives were not allowed to enter Syria. The Arab Organization for Human Rights sent many unanswered communications to the Syrian government, and the International Committee of the Red Cross was refused access to provide humanitarian services to Syrian prisoners. During these years, the Syrian government did not even fulfill its basic reporting requirement to United Nations human rights committees.[1]

Middle East Watch wrote to President Asad on October 6, 1989, requesting permission to visit Syria. Copies of this letter were sent to Prime Minister Mahmud al-Zu'bi in Damascus, U.N. Ambassador Fathy al-Masri in New York, and Chargé d'Affaires Bushra Kanfani in Washington, D.C. Middle East Watch received no response to this request or to several follow-up efforts. On November 29, Middle East Watch spoke to a Mr. Kuttab, counselor in the Syrian embassy in Washington, who responded that further inquiry would not be useful. "Responsible officials in Damascus will deal with this and will do what is best," he said. "We are very busy and obviously cannot respond to every request of this kind that we receive."

Nevertheless, Middle East Watch was able to carry out extensive research on Syrian human rights for this book and even to make an unauthorized visit to Syria. The investigation also included interviews and documentary research in Egypt, Switzerland, France, the Netherlands, Great Britain, and the United States.

Many Syrian émigrés agreed to be interviewed for this report, in some cases at considerable risk, since Syrian security forces have been known to harass or even assassinate opponents of the regime living abroad. Several who testified to Middle East Watch were especially concerned about the safety of those who remain in Syria, who can be placed at risk by insensitive use of rights information. This book, therefore, depended on mutual trust as well as on mutual commitment to human rights. Thanks are due for this help and trust and for the support and encouragement so vital to the completion of the project.

This volume has also drawn on information and assistance from many non-Syrians: scholars, journalists, human rights experts, doctors, students, government officials, and others knowledgeable about Syria and Syrian-controlled Lebanon as well as technical issues. The Asad regime's great efforts to prevent negative information from getting out of the country have been only partially successful. Foreign press access has been limited (though some Western journalists have been granted freer access to Syria over the past two to three years), and officially sanctioned human rights research has been nonexistent; many foreign scholars, travelers, and officials have been able to visit the country and travel around with little restriction. Some émigrés also return to Syria for family visits, and many Syrians travel regularly to Europe. Middle East Watch was thus able to draw on many diverse and well-informed personal observations on current conditions in Syria. Middle East Watch is indebted to numerous people from many countries who generously gave of their time.

In addition to fieldwork and interviews, the book draws on documentary literature on Syria and Syrian rights in French, German, Arabic, and English.

Not least among these were documents, publications, and newspapers of the Syrian government. Many thanks to the libraries of Columbia University, New York University, and the University of California and especially the New York Public Library for their assistance.

Recognition is due to the French scholar Michel Seurat, whose courageous and pioneering criticism of the rights record of the Asad regime was cut short by his kidnapping and death in Lebanon in 1985. This book would not have been possible without the documentary record compiled by the United Nations Commission on Human Rights, the Committee for the Defense of Freedoms and Political Prisoners in Syria, and especially Amnesty International, whose fine work has been an invaluable foundation.

Finally, thanks are owed to a number of anonymous readers who carefully went over the text and provided many invaluable suggestions.

SCOPE OF RESEARCH

This book covers the traditional core of civil and political rights. Largely limited to the record of rights violations within Syria, it does not seek to analyze the causes of such violations, the social and economic context of Syria's internal conflicts, or the regional conflicts that may sharpen rights problems. Because of the need to concentrate on core issues and inevitable limits on time, resources, and access, this book looks most closely at rights abuses in major urban areas; it does not explore the rights abuses faced by peasants in rural villages, except in cases of massacres (such as the one in Sarmada, a village in northwestern Syria, in July 1980) or when broad patterns of abuse are evident, as with the forced relocation of Kurdish villagers in the northeast in the 1960s and 1970s.

Whether to cover human rights in those areas of Lebanon under Syrian military occupation posed a problem in planning and conducting the research. At first, we chose to concentrate solely on the rights situation within Syria, not only because Human Rights Watch reports usually concentrate on single countries but also because of the difficulty of obtaining information on civil war–torn Lebanon. However, charges of Syrian rights abuses in Lebanon were so abundant and the rights violations in the two countries so interrelated that it became necessary to integrate Lebanon into the text. For example, many political prisoners are arrested in Lebanon and interrogated there before being taken to Syria for long-term imprisonment. Many Lebanese disappear into Syrian prisons never to reappear. Syrian security forces feed on the smuggling, corruption, drug money, and violence in Lebanon. Only if one looks at rights abuses in Syrian-controlled Lebanon does the whole rights situation in Syria make sense.

Similar dilemmas arose with respect to the international operations of Syrian security agencies, as well as Syrian support for international terrorist organizations. These are clearly rights issues, since the Syrian government has almost certainly been responsible for killing, injuring, restricting free speech, and otherwise violating the rights of persons outside of territory it directly controls. Direct responsibility in these cases, however, is often difficult to determine. It was thus decided that in the limited time available it was best to concentrate on rights abuses within Syrian-controlled territory, where Syrian government responsibility can be clearly established.

Given the limited access to Syria and the regime's lack of cooperation in our research, some facts cannot be known with certainty. We do not know, for example, exactly how many political prisoners are currently held in Syria, how many have been tortured to death, and how many have "disappeared." By combining many sources and reports, however, it has been possible to make conservative estimates. The method and sources of these estimates are clearly stated throughout the book so that readers can reach their own conclusions. Even in more open societies, facts of this kind are often hard to establish; so any uncertainties should not inhibit our understanding the circumstances under which Syrian human rights violations occur.

SUMMARY OF CONCLUSIONS

Right to Life: The regime has massacred a large number of innocent civilians and carried out many summary executions. This was especially common in Syria in 1978–82; since then it has been a practice of Syrian forces in Lebanon. A disturbingly large number of persons have also died in custody, many from torture. Over the past twenty years, the regime has killed at least ten thousand citizens.

Right to Protection against Torture, Mistreatment, or Degrading Punishment: Torture and severe mistreatment are the security services' standard methods for interrogating political prisoners. Since 1984, an estimated one to two thousand persons—including those held by Syrian forces in Lebanon—have been tortured each year during interrogation.

Right to Decent Penal Conditions: Syria's prison conditions are appalling, especially for political prisoners. Cells are overcrowded and food rations inadequate. Many prisoners are not allowed visitors and face continual harassment and physical abuse. Long-term prisoners commonly develop such chronic health problems as heart conditions, paralysis, and loss of hearing and eyesight. Medical care in Syrian prisons is almost nonexistent.

Right to a Fair, Speedy, and Public Trial: Virtually no political prisoners are put on trial. They are never charged, are held incommunicado during interrogation, and never have access to a lawyer. Trials, when they do take place, are often in special courts that follow no established procedures or rules of evidence.

Freedom from Collective Punishment: The Asad regime has massacred neighborhoods, towns, and even cities as "collective punishment" for the acts of a few dissidents. Within Syria, the worst cases date from 1980 to 1982. Today, Syrian security forces employ collective punishment in Lebanon.

Right Not to Be Subject to Ex Post Facto Laws: In 1980, the Asad regime passed a retroactive law making membership in the country's largest political organization, the Muslim Brotherhood, a capital offense. A person can be punished for current or prior membership unless he or she confesses and asks for amnesty.

Freedom of Expression: The government owns and controls all mass media. It regularly censors broadcasting, publications, public lectures, and all other forms of expression. Those who violate official limits and taboos are often harassed, fired from their jobs and blackballed, and sometimes interrogated and imprisoned.

Freedom of Association: The regime does not permit any organization to exist that it cannot largely control. Opposition political parties are banned; those who belong to or cooperate with them may be arrested, interrogated, and imprisoned. Membership in the Muslim Brotherhood is punishable by death. When trade unions and professional associations called for democracy in 1980, the regime shut them down, imprisoned their leadership, and named new leaders.

Right to Democratic Participation in Government: The regime presents only one candidate in presidential elections: Hafez Asad. Most other elections— those for the People's Assembly, Muhafazat (local) councils, trade unions, and other bodies—offer just one slate of candidates that has been closely screened by the ruling Ba'th party. Syrian citizens fear their government—for good reason—and are almost completely excluded from participating in it.

A NOTE ON TRANSLITERATION

Common English usage has been used wherever possible. Where several different forms are in use in English, we have opted for the form that most closely represents the Arabic: thus Ba'th rather than Baath and Nasir rather than Nasser. Otherwise, transliteration has been simplified as much as possible, with only ayns signified by diacritics.

VITAL STATISTICS

Official Name: Syrian Arab Republic (Al Jumhuriyah al ʿArabiyah as Suriyah)

Area: 71,500 square miles, shares borders with Turkey, Iraq, Jordan, Israel, and Lebanon

Population: 12 million (1990 estimate)

Ethnic Groups: Syrians, 65 percent; ʿAlawis, 12 percent; Kurds, 8 percent; Christian Syrians, 6 percent; Druze, 3 percent; Palestinians, 3 percent; Armenians, 2 percent; Ismailis and Circassians, 1 percent

Religious Groups: Sunni Muslims, 76 percent; ʿAlawi Muslim, 12 percent; Christians (Greek Orthodox and Armenian), 8 percent; Druze, 3 percent; small minorities, including Jews, Ismailis, and Yazidis, 1 percent

Languages: Arabic (official); others include Kurdish, Armenian, French, and English

Government: President Hafez Asad, in office since February 22, 1971, is the head of state, chief of the armed forces, and president of the council of the magistrature. He may convene and dissolve the People's Assembly, approve all constitutional amendments, submit matters to referendum, and make laws when the Assembly is not sitting. President Asad is also secretary-general of the Baʿth party and chairman of the National Progressive Front.

The National Revolutionary Command Council

Baʿth Party Congress

People's Assembly, established in February 1971, 240 members

The Judicial System includes the Constitutional Court, Civil Courts, Military Courts, Exceptional Military Courts, State Security Courts and Military Field Tribunals. Islam is the basis of the legal system.

Administrative subdivisions: Damascus and 13 provinces.

Legal Political Parties: The National Progressive Front (includes the Baʿth Arab Socialist party, Syrian Communist party and three Nasirist parties: Arab Socialist Movement, Arab Socialist Union, and Socialist Unionist Movement—small opposition parties tolerated by the government)

Economy: GNP, $20.4 billion (1987); per capita income, $1,820 (1987); public debt, $3.6 billion (1987); foreign trade: imports, $7.1 billion (1987); exports, $3.8 billion (1987); tourism, $395 million (1986 re-

ceipts); industries include oil products, textiles, cement, tobacco, glass-
ware, sugar, and brassware; chief crops include cotton, grain, olives,
fruits, and vegetables

Natural Resources: crude oil reserves number 1.4 billion barrels; minerals
include phosphate and gypsum

Syria is party to the following international human rights treaties:

International Covenant on Economic, Social and Cultural Rights; accession
April 21, 1969. Reservations: does not recognize Israel.

International Covenant on Civil and Political Rights; accession April 21,
1969. Reservations: does not recognize Israel.

International Convention on the Elimination of All Forms of Racial Discrimination; accession April 21, 1969. Reservations: does not recognize Israel.

International Convention on the Suppression and Punishment of the Crime
of Apartheid; signed January 17, 1974, ratified June 18, 1976.

International Convention against Apartheid in Sports; signed May 16, 1986.

Convention on the Prevention and Punishment of the Crime of Genocide; accession June 25, 1955.

Syria is not a party to the Convention against Torture and Other Cruel, Inhuman or Degrading Treatment or Punishment.

SYRIA UNMASKED

1

BACKGROUND

LAND AND PEOPLE

Syria lies east of the Mediterranean, stretching south from the mountains of Turkey toward the deserts of the Arabian Peninsula. Its northwest coast faces the Mediterranean, in the center is a wide, uninhabited desert, and in the east the great Euphrates River descends from the mountains of Turkey to the plains of Iraq. Syria's land area—71,500 square miles—is about the size of Norway or the combined states of New York and Pennsylvania.

More than a third of Syria's people live in two big cities: Aleppo in the northwest, a center of trade and industry famed for its vast old *suqs,* or markets; and Damascus in the southwest, center of government and one of the world's oldest cities, with numerous handsome mosques and public buildings.[1] Many Syrians also live in half a dozen or so mid-sized cities: the Mediterranean ports of Lataqia and Tartus, Homs and Hama in the agriculturally rich Orontes River valley, Dar'a and Suwaida in the south near the Jordanian border, and Deir al-Zor, Raqqa, and Hassaka in the Euphrates-Khabur River valley to the east.

Fewer than half of all Syrians now live in the countryside and that proportion is declining steadily. These rural folk are mostly poor peasants. Over half work their own land and many have benefited from land reforms. The rest till the land of others, including absentee landlords.[2] Although the government has brought roads, electricity, and schools to many rural villages, peasants have a hard life.

Beginning in the 1950s (and especially in the early Ba'thist years) the Syrian government nationalized banking, industry, and trade, and the state now controls much of the Syrian economy. It maintains low prices for bread and other basic commodities, rations key food items, and provides many social services.

Syria is not plagued with the crushing urban poverty found in many Middle Eastern countries; there are virtually no shantytowns around its cities and malnutrition is rare. But its society is far from egalitarian. Many top government officials and private merchants own valuable enterprises, such as hotels, factories, farms, and construction companies; they live in elegant mansions and drive foreign luxury cars. The rest of the population, including most members of the middle class, lives very simply.

Further, the economic underpinnings of Syrian society have been eroding steadily over the past decade. In the early 1980s, Syria received as much as two billion dollars annually in foreign aid. It now gets one billion or less and the sum may continue to fall. The Soviets have other priorities, Iran is giving less, and the Saudis have cut their support as well.

Although foreign companies have recently made promising new oil finds, oil revenues will probably never be large enough to sustain Syria's economy. Oil export revenues peaked at one billion dollars in the early 1980s when prices reached new highs.

A large government bureaucracy, widespread corruption, and a costly military and security establishment burden the economy. Currency shortages and controls have starved many factories of essential raw materials, and productivity in state companies is notoriously low. Agriculture has recently suffered from two years of drought. Rampant smuggling and a flourishing black market are further signs of trouble, as are regular electricity and water cuts. Few Syrians can survive on government salaries and many are forced to work two jobs: teachers drive taxis at night, civil servants run deliveries, security agents dabble in the black market.

Economic and social reform, especially in the 1960s, sharpened opposition to the Ba'thist government. Merchants and landowners hated the nationalizations, land reform measures, and government controls. Pious shopkeepers and teachers disliked the government's secularism. Students, professionals, and intellectuals opposed military rule and wanted a return to democracy. By the late 1970s, these opposition forces were strong enough to seriously challenge Ba'thist rule. The Asad regime, however, could count on support from prosperous merchants, state employees, the security apparatus, and the army. With this backing, the regime was able to retain power, but only with extensive use of violence against the opposition.

Conflict in Syria also reflects religious and ethnic rivalries. Sunni Muslims make up about 70 percent of the population, and during the Ottoman era their leading families were the great landlords and administrators. Since then, such minorities as 'Alawis, Kurds, Christians, and Druze have struggled to improve their condition. The Asad regime draws its key personnel from one of these minorities—members of the 'Alawi sect, a heterodox branch of Islam. Until the 1960s, most 'Alawis were poor peasants in the mountains along Syria's Mediterranean coast. Today, although many 'Alawis remain poor and some have joined the opposition, thousands staff key political and military institutions. Some in the inner circles of power have profited handsomely and married into the old Sunni upper classes.

'Alawi solidarity is an important element of loyalty within the government, army, and security forces. But by recruiting so heavily from one minority, the regime has opened itself to charges of ethnic and religious favoritism. For a time in the late 1970s, the Muslim Brotherhood systematically assassinated a number of leading 'Alawis connected to the regime. Indeed, the dogged determination of Asad and his colleagues to maintain power is fueled by the fear of reprisals should they fall. Their use of violence against even the democratic opposition suggests anxiety and isolation at the pinnacle of power.

HISTORY

France and Great Britain carved today's Syria out of the collapsed Ottoman Empire after World War I, assigning it boundaries that had little to do with political economy, language, or history and endowing it with a political system that did not reflect the aspirations of the population.[3] A Franco-British agreement of 1920 assigned Syria to French control as a Mandate under the League of Nations. That year, nearly two years after Faisal ibn Husain had declared an independent state with its capital in Damascus, the French army marched in and imposed the Mandate by force.[4] This invasion and the subsequent division of geographical Syria left a strong sentiment among Syrians that the colonial boundaries were illegitimate and that Syria should be part of a much larger entity, such as Greater Syria or a unified Arab nation.[5]

The French occupiers confronted an organized and increasingly powerful nationalist movement in Syria, and their fight against it was a tragic dress rehearsal for present-day rights abuses. The Mandate regime imposed heavy censorship, confiscated presses, closed theaters, and set up the Service des renseignements, a large intelligence apparatus.

Worse still was the French reaction when organized resistance took to the streets. In October 1925, the French military bombed and shelled the commercial district of Hama to quell a revolt. They destroyed two markets and killed over three hundred people, including many women and children. After Hama, Damascus came under fire. The French besieged Damascus on three occasions—October 1925 and February and May 1926—subjecting it to aerial bombardment, shelling, and tank fire as well as looting and arson by troops. Several neighborhoods of the city were reduced to rubble, including the great Suq al-Hamidiya and the densely populated Maydan quarter. An estimated three thousand people were killed. The French also destroyed the Druze city of Suwaida and razed many rural villages in search-and-destroy missions. These events caused an international outcry but did not prevent the French military from again shelling Damascus for two days at the end of the Mandate in 1945.[6]

In 1928, in response to heavy nationalist pressure, French officials agreed to set up a constitutional assembly. The assembly was duly elected, but when it drew up a constitution that displeased Paris, the French high commissioner dissolved it and imposed a constitution of his own.[7] Rights guaranteed to citizens in France, claimed Mandate authorities, had no place in a colony. French clashes with the nationalists continued until Syria won its independence in 1946.

Independence for Syria brought a great improvement in human rights conditions: an end to censorship and the colonial intelligence agency, and elections free from the presence of colonial military forces.

But the new government was unstable. Run by the old merchant and landlord classes, it garnered little support from the bulk of the population, which sought social reform and a more vigorous nationalism. The Arab-Israeli War of 1948 further upset the political equilibrium. Syrians saw Arab defeat in that war and the founding of the state of Israel as Western aggression and were angry that their country was too weak to defend its interests. Nationalist sentiment, directed in part against the Syrian government, was again inflamed.

Foreign efforts to influence Syrian politics also destabilized the government. Foreign states—including France, Britain, Egypt, and Iraq—subsidized many Syrian newspapers and political parties, and foreign intelligence services intervened actively in Syrian politics, sometimes seeking to overthrow the government.[8]

After less than three years of weak democratic rule, a series of military coups shook Syria. The first coup, staged in 1949 by army chief of staff Husni al-Za'im, was backed by the U.S. Central Intelligence Agency.[9] Two others followed within nine months. The new military rulers built up the security forces and did not honor the rule of law. Human rights inevitably suffered.

After several years of unpopular military rule, civilian government re-emerged in 1954, but it lacked real authority and the military maintained an active role behind the scenes.[10] Further covert actions by the United States and Britain again undermined the fledgling Syrian democracy when Syria's government refused to join a planned regional alliance system known as the Baghdad Pact.[11]

The 1956 Suez War—when Britain, France, and Israel attacked Egypt—again aroused fierce national sentiment in Syria. The aftershocks led to the 1958 unification with 'Abd al-Nasir's Egypt, forming the United Arab Republic. Human rights, already poorly observed, suffered further as a consequence of the merger.

The Egyptian authorities imposed censorship, banned political parties, and arrested many political activists. Though popular at first, the union of Arab states lasted only two and a half years, falling apart amid recriminations over

Egypt's dominance. Parliamentary democracy followed for a stormy two years. Then, on March 10, 1963, another coup brought to power the military committee of the Arab Ba'th Socialist party.[12]

THE EARLY YEARS OF THE BA'THIST REGIME

The new military regime, inspired by radical nationalism, was similar to many that emerged in the Third World in the early 1960s. Led by a secretive National Revolutionary Command Council (NRCC), the regime proclaimed a commitment to nationalism and revolution but lacked a developed social and economic program, as well as an organized popular following. The civilian arm of the Ba'th party, moreover, was too small to hold its own against the military leadership. The NRCC soon declared a state of emergency and began to crack down on its internal enemies.[13]

Purges of the army officer corps began almost immediately as the Ba'thist leadership cashiered right-wingers as well as many Nasirists and Communists. Salah Jadid—a key member of the military committee along with Hafez Asad—took control of officer assignments and promoted several hundred loyal 'Alawi Ba'thists. Ethnic alliances joined ideological conflicts and personal aspirations in the struggle for power.[14]

Discontent and rivalries led to one coup attempt after another and a further series of purges. Three months after seizing power, the military committee dismissed Gen. Ziad al-Hariri, minister of defense and chief of staff, along with two dozen of his key supporters. The NRCC then went after the Nasirists, forcing over a thousand people in government ministries to resign, closing down the main Nasirist party—the Arab Nationalist Movement—and imprisoning a number of its leaders.

Sunnis and conservatives were the main losers in these battles, but they did not always accept defeat easily. In April 1964, opposition mobilized by the Muslim Brotherhood flared in the streets of Hama. On orders from Damascus, armored military units assaulted the city. Artillery and tanks blasted into dense residential neighborhoods, almost destroying the great Sultan Mosque where some of the rebels had gathered. The fighting left more than a hundred dead and large numbers wounded or homeless. Summary military courts tried and executed dozens more.

On February 23, 1966, Salah Jadid and Hafez Asad consolidated their power in an internal coup that moved the regime leftward and increased its 'Alawi complexion. Further purges of the army followed. Asad became minister of defense, while Jadid left his military command to take control of the Ba'th party.[15] The new leaders—embracing popular revolutionary rhetoric—

introduced many socialist measures and formed armed militias of workers and peasants. They set up mass-based "popular organizations": a Women's Union, Peasant Union, Writer's Union, and many more; and they purged the trade unions of those considered unsympathetic. More than ever, they relied on the strength of the state security apparatus to stay in power.

In June 1967, Israel, Syria, and Egypt fought a brief but devastating war, overwhelmingly won by Israel. During the war, Syria's military capability was weakened by Minister of Defense Hafez Asad's decision to hold some of his best military units in the rear, near Damascus, to protect the regime from its domestic enemies in case they should take advantage of the conflict and seize power.

The outcome for the Arab states was that Syria lost the Golan and the heights of Mount Hermon; Egypt lost Gaza and the Sinai; and Jordan lost the West Bank and East Jerusalem. Although this setback was a terrible blow to national pride, the regime was able to rally support by calling for a "people's war" to liberate Arab lands. Furthermore, it was increasingly able to exploit the threat of war to stamp out dissent.

In February 1969, Hafez Asad moved against his former ally and seized control of the major organs of the media. In succeeding months he tightened his hold over other institutions, all the while promising the public a less radical, more pragmatic approach to political life. Finally, in November 1970, he seized power in a bloodless coup, locking up Jadid and a score of his closest collaborators in al-Mezze Prison, Damascus. Casting himself as a political liberal, Asad sponsored elections, a parliament, and a new constitution. Under the National Progressive Front, other parties joined with the Ba'th. Economic liberalization measures, such as the easing of tight restrictions on private investment and trade, began to replace the socialist programs of Jadid.[16]

But Asad also set up new security services, tightened control over the mass media, and increased pressure for conformity in the schools and universities. The formal democratic institutions appeared promising at first but proved lacking in real influence. More than ever, power was concentrated in the hands of one man.

In October 1973, Syria and Egypt launched a war against Israel to regain territories lost in the 1967 war and settle the increasingly troublesome Palestinian question. Again, Syria and Egypt suffered defeat, but the Arab armies won the opening battles. Asad proclaimed "victory," and thereafter celebrated his patriotic accomplishments in the month of Tishreen (October). Once more, war led to tightened internal security as the government mobilized support in the name of national defense.

The war brought Asad financial benefits as well. The OPEC (Organization of Petroleum Exporting Countries) embargo had greatly boosted the price of oil, leading cash-rich Persian Gulf states to promise to underwrite Syria's postwar reconstruction and part of its military budget. Syria's own small oil exports soared in value, and many of its workers, after finding employment in the booming Gulf states, sent home large sums of money. A period of growth and prosperity ensued.

Internal strife, however, was not far from the surface. Protests flared up in Damascus in early 1972, in Hama and again in Damascus in March 1973, and again in Hama as well as Aleppo in June 1975; all were put down harshly. Throughout these years, Asad steadily reinforced the security apparatus and the paramilitary forces. In just one year, an opposition movement of unprecedented scale would confront his rule.

2

THE GREAT REPRESSION,
1976 TO 1982

Opposition exploded in the late 1970s, touched off by Asad's military intervention in Lebanon in 1976. Public discontent fed on many grievances: rampant
inflation, a housing crisis deepened by refugees from Lebanon, official corruption, security forces from which no one felt safe, and the domination of the
'Alawis. Over four years unrest spread to every sector of Syrian society, and by
the beginning of 1980 it seemed possible the regime would be overthrown.

The most powerful opposition came from the Islamists, a cluster of groups
usually known as the Muslim Brothers (al-Ikhwan al-Muslimin). This conservative, religious-based movement had fought the regime in the 1960s. Now it
drew ever wider support. Although its various factions adopted different
tactics—many believed in nonviolent opposition, but some organized into
secret, armed, and tightly organized guerrilla groups—all hoped to destroy the
regime to found a system based on Sunni orthodoxy.[1]

Meanwhile, the secular opposition, including well-organized underground
political parties of the left, professional associations, trade union locals, and
groups of teachers, writers, filmmakers, and other intellectuals, was growing
stronger. Though largely nonviolent and mostly confined to the middle class,
these groups seriously challenged the regime by weakening its ideological grip
and undermining its organizational strongholds.[2]

The first serious challenge to Asad came from within the armed forces.
Starting in the spring of 1976, many officers and troops rebelled against orders
to intervene in Lebanon in support of right-wing Maronite militias against the
Palestinians and the Lebanese left. In April security forces arrested some sixty
senior officers, but in May unrest spread to several air bases. Through the end
of 1976, military intelligence arrested dozens of officers and hundreds of
mutinous troops, but soldiers continued to organize opposition throughout the
armed forces.

On the heels of the military unrest, left-wing, Lebanese, and Islamist guerrilla groups began to attack public buildings and leading figures in the regime. In August 1976, the Damascus officers' club and a police station were bombed, and on December 1 of that year Foreign Minister 'Abd al-Halim Khaddam narrowly escaped an assassination attempt. Damascus University rector Muhammad Fadel, a leading 'Alawi, was shot down on February 22, 1977, and five months later, on July 4, a booby-trapped car exploded near Air Force Command in central Damascus, killing six soldiers and wounding four more.

At the same time, the democratic nonviolent opposition, protesting the Lebanon intervention, stepped up its calls for greater democracy and respect for the rule of law. After two lawyers—Tariq Haidari and 'Adil Kayali—died in detention, members of the Syrian bar founded a committee for human rights. They reported on this case and other abuses at a meeting of the Arab Lawyers' Union in Tunis in November 1976. Intellectuals joined in the criticism. In the summer of 1976, eighty-three leading authors, filmmakers, and other artists signed a petition protesting the war in Lebanon and the Syrian-backed massacre at the Palestinian camp of Tal al-Za'tar. Insisting on democracy, these respected figures found a wide audience in schools, universities, and the middle classes in general. Film club meetings turned into secular opposition gatherings, while university students began to organize political groups and issue publications.

As signs of opposition grew, the regime made gestures of reform. In the summer of 1977, Asad announced with great fanfare a "committee for the investigation of illegal profits."[3] But his real response was to reinforce the security apparatus; he built up the Presidential Guard and greatly expanded the Defense Brigades which his brother Rif'at commanded. These forces, however, were unable to stem either the rising tide of assassinations of 'Alawi officials and regime supporters or violent attacks on Ba'th party and government offices.

The more the regime felt under siege, the less the security forces, or mukhabarat, practiced restraint. On March 14, 1978, the People's Assembly passed an antiterrorist law that gave security agencies wider powers. Four days later, assassins gunned down Dr. Ibrahim Nu'ame, an 'Alawi member of the Regional Command and a relative of Asad. The mukhabarat threw up roadblocks and searched neighborhoods. Mobilizing all their forces to find the culprits, they detained an estimated fifteen thousand suspects and arrested some two hundred in connection with the crime.[4] Many suspects lost their jobs.

During the subsequent crackdown, many military personnel also lost their jobs. By the end of 1978, Asad had transferred in three waves 460 army officers out of sensitive posts, replacing all but three of Syria's most senior officers. He also ordered a house-cleaning within the Ba'th. On May 10, security forces arrested some four hundred leftists and opposition Ba'thists. Over the summer, the Ministry of Education fired a number of school teachers; at about the same time, many other state employees believed to be close to the parties of the opposition were either fired or arrested. On June 19, the director of the newspaper *al-Ba'th* was dismissed and a number of prominent journalists blacklisted. In December, another wave of arrests struck the secular opposition.[5]

Asad tried to win over the opposition as it gained strength by speaking about the need for greater respect for the rule of law.[6] Although lawless official behavior constantly belied the president's statements, many leaders of the secular opposition capitalized on the presidential rhetoric by running for office in the trade unions and professional associations in 1978 and 1979. Hundreds won, soundly defeating official candidates.[7] For the first time since the 1960s, many organizations escaped Ba'thist control.

The professionals, especially the bar associations, assumed leadership of the democratic movement. On June 22, 1978, the Damascus Bar Association passed resolutions demanding an end to the state of emergency and threatening lawyers with professional discipline if they collaborated with the government in illegal acts. Then, on August 17, the president of the Syrian Bar Association demanded that the government respect the rule of law and release all those detained without trial. The government ignored these demands, but the lawyers continued their campaign.

On December 1, the Syrian Bar Association held an extraordinary congress that made further demands, including independence for the judiciary and an end to censorship, torture, and executions. Just a few days after the congress, agents of Rif'at's Defense Brigades assaulted a lawyer and his wife on the streets of Damascus. The Damascus bar called a one-day strike and other bars joined in.[8]

Tensions within the regime appeared in the army and even in the security services. In March, Asad had fired Naji Jamil, Syria's most important security boss. Later in the year, rumors circulated of high-level retirements and command transfers. According to one reliable source, no fewer than forty generals were affected.

In the absence of any means for democratic change, the initiative passed to the violent opposition. On June 16, 1979, eighty-three young officer candidates at the Aleppo Artillery School—all 'Alawis—were murdered; the Sunni captain in charge of the cadets' political education masterminded the deed and carried it out with several accomplices.[9] The regime responded vengefully. Within a few days, security forces had detained an estimated six thousand people.[10] A televised trial charged fifteen most already serving prison terms, with complicity in the killing and membership in the Muslim Brothers; all were found guilty and swiftly executed. The official media spoke of "foreign plots." Four hundred more officers were cashiered from the armed forces in the next six months.[11]

Some high Ba'th party officials, such as Mahmud Ayubi and 'Abdalla al-

Ahmar, favored reform and concessions. On September 26, the Ba'th and its allies within the National Progressive Front published a thirty-seven-point communiqué criticizing conditions in the country, including the lack of democracy and basic freedoms and the misuse of existing laws. The communiqué called for the punishment of officials who broke the law.[12]

On October 9, a Ba'th party commission of inquiry invited a number of leading intellectuals to the amphitheater of Damascus University for what turned out to be an unprecedented seven-hour meeting. Many respected authors and intellectuals called for drastic changes. The long silence imposed through fear and censorship seemed to be lifting. Some of those present taped the proceedings and circulated copies throughout the country.

The regime also bowed to pressure from the working class. With many newly elected union officers no longer backing the regime, strikes, ordinarily not tolerated, began to break out. These included a major walkout in the critical oil field at Rumeila. Loath to confront workers head-on at such a delicate moment, the regime made concessions on pay and other demands.

The Ba'th party set up a special commission to study the crisis and make recommendations, and the Regional Command—the top policy-making body—began an inquiry on political prisoners. Party leaders promised renewed "dialogue" and a broadening of the National Progressive Front. In consequence, late in 1979 and again the following February, security services released dozens of political prisoners.

Within the regime doubts and defections took their toll. Most spectacular was the abrupt resignation on December 27 of Syria's ambassador to the United Nations Hammud al-Shufi, who announced at a press conference that he wanted to show his opposition "to the anti-democratic and repressive methods and corruption of the Asad regime."[13]

As the challenge to the regime continued to mount, Rif'at pushed for a hard-line approach. At the Seventh Congress of the Ba'th party (December 22, 1979, to January 7, 1980), he called for a "national purge" and for "labor and reeducation camps in the desert," insisting that no sacrifice would be too great to "defend the revolution." The congress, carefully prepared in advance, approved the hard-line approach, though not without a heated debate. Among other things, they agreed to "charge the comrade Minister of Education to eliminate all trace of adverse thought in his sector and modify the educational programs to coincide with the interests of the party and the revolution."[14]

The regime began to prepare its offensive. The first step was to secure its base. On January 20, the government doubled military pay and boosted civil service salaries as much as 75 percent. Next, it distributed arms to special militias set up by the party and by loyal branches of "popular organizations" like the Peasant Union and the Trade Union Federation. These militia were often as tough as the security forces and had little inclination to respect the law.

Encouraged by the president to defend the revolution at all costs, they searched homes, frisked pedestrians, detained people arbitrarily, and assaulted those they believed to be "enemies" of the regime. They even set up their own informal courts.

Meanwhile, the popular revolt continued to build. On February 28, the Syrian Engineers Association National Congress passed a strong resolution calling for an end to the state of emergency, the release of all political prisoners, and freedom of expression and association. On March 2, 1980, the Aleppo Bar Association struck for two hours to call again for democratic measures. Then, on March 8—the seventeenth anniversary of the Ba'th party's coming to power—strikes and demonstrations shook the whole country except Damascus. Merchants closed their shops, trade unions went on strike, public transport slowed, opposition posters and slogans covered the walls, and thousands of demonstrators marched in the streets calling for an end to the regime.

The medical association as well as the teachers' union now joined the lawyers in support of the democracy movement. On March 9, the professional associations of Homs made a joint declaration, joined two days later by those in Hama. The Hama professionals called for the army to get out of the streets of the cities and insisted on an end to the arming of "certain factions" (that is, the militias). Their resolution also called for an end to religious "confessionalism," a reference to both the 'Alawi regime and its Islamist opponents.[15] But the army, the party, and the security services remained loyal to the regime throughout these events.

A March 9 editorial in *Tishrin,* the mouthpiece for the Asad regime, vowed that the government would use "armed revolutionary violence to defeat the reactionary violence" and insisted that "those who used violence first" would bear responsibility for whatever happened.[16] Strikes again shook Aleppo and Hama on March 12 and 16, but by then the campaign of repression was already underway.

JISR AL-SHUGHUR, MA'ARRA, AND IDLIB
(MARCH 9–10, 1980)

In Jisr al-Shughur, a small town in the mountains between Aleppo and Lataqia, the regime struck its first blow of "revolutionary violence." On Sunday, March 9, townspeople demonstrated against the government and the party by marching on Ba'th headquarters and setting the building on fire. Some demonstrators broke into a nearby army barracks and seized arms and ammunition. Local police, completely unable to restore order, fled the scene.

Security officials immediately ordered Special Forces units helicoptered in from Aleppo. Arriving in the late afternoon, the commandos pounded the town with mortars and rockets. They regained control, but only after destroying twenty houses and fifty stores and killing or wounding dozens of citizens, including many innocent bystanders. Combing the town in house-to-house searches late into the night, the commandos executed some people on the spot and took at least two hundred others into custody.

The next day, authorities convened a military field tribunal, presided over by Tawfiq Salha, a member of the Ba'th Regional Command, who had flown in from Damascus. Although details of the court proceedings remain obscure, they were known to result in commandos executing more than a hundred detainees. Altogether, security forces killed an estimated 150–200 people in the town.[17]

People also protested on March 9 in the streets of Ma'arra and Idlib, both a few miles northeast of Jisr al-Shughur on the road to Aleppo. Security forces fired on the crowds, killing thirty people in Ma'arra and sixteen in Idlib. They arrested many more. Similar events occurred in other towns.[18] Although the official press said nothing, news of the crackdown quickly spread throughout the country.

REPRESSION AGAINST PROFESSIONALS (APRIL 1980)

Reacting to the arrests of some of its leading members and worsening abuses of law by the regime, the Syrian Bar Association set March 31 as the date for a nationwide strike. The Medical Association, pharmacists, and Association of Engineers took similar action. Many others, including merchants, followed their lead, turning March 31 into another major countrywide confrontation.

The Council of Ministers responded on April 9 by issuing a decree dissolving the professional associations, their national leadership, local leadership, and general assemblies. All association offices and research bureaus were immediately closed by the security services, and the next day, the regime set up new professional associations and named their governing boards.[19] Security agents rounded up nearly all the professional association leaders, and by mid-April the regime had imprisoned more than a hundred doctors and health professionals, a hundred engineers, and about fifty lawyers.[20] Among the lawyers arrested was Muwaffaq al-Din al-Kozbari, president of the Prisoners' Care Association and first secretary of the Syrian League for the Defense of Human Rights. These organizations were dissolved.

Many professionals were tortured; some were summarily executed. The victims included Dr. 'Umar al-Shishakli, a highly respected figure in the medical profession, president of the Syrian Ophthalmological Society, and officer of the Hama Medical Association. His badly mutilated body was recovered later. Security forces killed at least two other Hama doctors.[21] There were victims in Aleppo and Lataqia as well, including Burhan al-Din al-Tur, president of the Lataqia Bar Association.[22]

DISAPPEARANCES IN DEIR AL-ZOR (APRIL 15, 1980)

In the eastern city of Deir al-Zor, police and security forces clashed on April 15 with teenage demonstrators who assaulted and torched the local Ba'th party headquarters. A few hours later, security forces arrested thirty-eight youths. Some may have participated in the demonstration; others were probably arrested at random. They took the youths to a nearby detention facility. Three months later, still not having charged them with any crime, security forces moved them elsewhere. Parents and friends never found out what happened to them. Inquiries, including a letter to Asad, were to no avail.[23]

OCCUPATION OF ALEPPO (APRIL 1980–FEBRUARY 1981)

Aleppo, Syria's second city, was a center of both the democratic opposition and the Islamist campaign. In autumn 1979, its streets reverberated with clashes between the security forces and their opponents. Soldiers and security agents fired on peaceful student protesters and other demonstrators, inflicting many casualties. Armed cells of the Islamist movement attacked party offices and police patrols. Security troops retaliated against opposition centers and meeting places. In spite of the presence of five thousand commandos of the Defense Brigades and thousands of other security and police forces, Aleppo slipped steadily out of the government's control.[24]

In November, security troops arrested Shaykh Zain al-Din Khairalla, the leader of Friday prayers in the Great Mosque and a leading voice of the Islamists. From then on, the city became a battleground, with daily demonstrations, boycotts, and attacks on Ba'th party premises. The Islamist forces, armed and tightly organized, posed the most serious threat to the regime. But the nonviolent, secular opposition also challenged the system, commanding wide support especially among the middle classes, whose important Christian and minority components had no enthusiasm for the Islamists.

Once the Asad regime decided on a policy of force, Aleppo was the logical target. In mid-March, units of the Third Army Division under Gen. Shafiq Fayadh left their barracks in Damascus and posts in Lebanon and moved toward the city. Units of the Special Forces and additional commandos of the Defense

Brigades arrived outside the city as well. In all, more than thirty thousand crack troops, from units considered the most loyal to the regime, surrounded and sealed off Aleppo.

The Special Forces entered Aleppo on April 1. Five days later the Third Division entered in full strength, with hundreds of tanks and other armored vehicles. Troops fired rocket-propelled grenades and tank cannons right into residential buildings. They sealed off neighborhoods, searching every building for suspects and weapons. On the fourth day of the operation, General Fayadh reportedly stood on his tank turret and announced to the population that he was "prepared to kill a thousand people a day to rid the city of the Muslim Brother vermin."[25] By mid-April, civilian casualties numbered in the hundreds and prisoners jammed every possible detention site, including a Special Forces prison camp set up within the Citadel in the center of old Aleppo.

By May the city had settled down to a tense occupation. But that summer the regime began new reprisals. On July 1, in retaliation for an attack on a patrol, Special Forces troops rounded up people in the Suq al-Ahad quarter at random. Not pausing to check identification, they took all males age fifteen and over. When they had assembled more than two hundred men in an open space, they opened fire with automatic weapons, killing forty-two and wounding at least one hundred and fifty others.[26]

Again, on August 11, apparently in retaliation for an attack on a patrol, commandos of the Special Forces entered the al-Masharga quarter, forced male residents at random out of their homes and marched them to a nearby cemetery. Near the tomb of Ibrahim Hanano, the troops opened fire, killing eighty-three and injuring several hundred more. Every male resident of the neighborhood over age fifteen was equally at risk; a few of those killed were identified as loyal Ba'thists, government workers, and supporters of the regime.[27]

In the year the city was occupied, army and security forces are reliably estimated to have killed one to two thousand people—some in hot pursuit, some at random, many in summary executions. At least eight thousand more were arrested.[28]

TADMUR PRISON (JUNE 27, 1980)

On June 26, members of the Presidential Guard nearly succeeded in assassinating Hafez Asad, who escaped only slightly injured by a hand grenade. Holding the Muslim Brothers responsible for the deed, Rif'at immediately organized a reprisal against inmates of Tadmur Military Prison, where many Islamists were being held.[29]

At three o'clock on the morning, June 27, commandos from the Defense

Brigades were roused from their barracks in Damascus, briefed by Rif'at's son-in-law Mu'in Nassif, and sent to al-Mezze Military Airport. There they joined commandos from 'Ali Dib's 138th Security Brigade. Some two hundred troops then flew 150 miles by helicopter to a landing zone near Tadmur Prison, in the middle of the desert. Of these, about eighty men, heavily armed, were ordered into the prison. One of the soldiers, an 'Alawi from Lataqia, later described what happened:

> A Dodge truck came to take us to the prison. There they divided us into six or seven squads. In my squad there were about eleven, with Lt. Munir Darwish in command. . . . They opened the door of a communal cell for us. Six or seven of us went in and we killed everyone inside—that is, about sixty or seventy people. . . . Personally, I must have machine-gunned fifteen or so. Altogether, we must have killed about five hundred and fifty of those nasty Muslim Brothers; the Defense Brigades had one dead and two wounded. We left again. Lieutenant Ra'if 'Abullah went off to wash his hands and feet, which were covered with blood. . . . The operation lasted about half an hour. During it, there was a terrible tumult, with exploding grenades and cries of "Allah Akbar!" Finally, we got back in the helicopters. . . . At Mezze, Major Nassif welcomed us and thanked us for our effort. [30]

In fact, later evidence suggests that more than a thousand prisoners died that day. [31]

On July 1, an editorial in *Tishrin* signed by Rif'at al-Asad declared: "If necessary . . . we are ready to engage in a hundred battles, destroy a thousand citadels, and sacrifice a million martyrs to bring back peace and love, the glory of the country and the honor of the citizen." [32] And on July 7, the National Assembly passed Law 49, making membership in the Muslim Brothers—already outlawed—punishable by death. Members were given just thirty days (later extended to fifty days) to turn themselves in and avoid the full force of the law.

SARMADA (JULY 25, 1980)

On July 24, security forces struck Sarmada, a village near the northern border with Turkey. They may have been in hot pursuit of Islamic guerrillas or searching for arms traffickers. Whatever the reason, troops suddenly surrounded the village, and, ordering the inhabitants to remain indoors, stormed their houses and killed several people in a brief exchange of fire. The security forces then arrested about two hundred villagers and took them to the grounds of a school, where they interrogated and beat them. Some were summarily executed. Altogether, about forty persons were killed or disappeared. Before departing, the security forces razed part of the village.[33]

MUSLIM BROTHERS' ATTACKS, GOVERNMENT REPRISALS, AND CRACKDOWN

The Muslim Brothers now concentrated their efforts on terrorist actions in Damascus, stepping up bombings and attacks on 'Alawi officials. On August 17, a car bomb exploded outside the Council of Ministers building, inflicting at least a dozen casualties. On September 3, a car bomb that exploded outside air force headquarters killed about seventy people. Yet another car bomb killed an estimated two hundred people at Azbakia in the heart of the city on November 29.

The regime retaliated with sweeps, mass arrests, and summary executions. The mood in the capital was very tense, with security forces everywhere, many streets closed to traffic, major government buildings surrounded by concrete barriers, and heavy detachments of guards deployed.

In the summer and fall, though its main target remained the Muslim Brothers, the mukhabarat began to round up activists of left-wing parties: Nasirists, Communists, Ba'thists, and others. It struck most heavily at the Communist party Political Bureau, arresting its leaders and many dozens of top cadres, some of whom had been released from prison only a few months earlier. Many others, warned of the arrests, fled into exile. Security forces also jailed dozens of intellectuals, writers, artists, and teachers. Writer Michel Kilo, one of those who had been most outspoken at the Damascus University meeting, was taken off to jail on October 5.[34] Altogether, tens of thousands went into exile before the year's end.

HAMA 1981 (APRIL 23–26, 1981)

Hama, one of the centers of the opposition, took the brunt of reprisals the following spring. According to some reports, on Tuesday, April 21, armed *mujahidin* (Islamic guerrillas) ambushed a security checkpoint near an 'Alawi village on the outskirts of Hama. The revenge came two days later. Units of the Special Forces and the 47th Brigade moved into the city and began house-to-house searches. Street fighting erupted sporadically as soldiers sealed off neighborhoods and continued their probing. More troops then entered the city and a curfew was imposed.

That Friday morning, April 24, security forces dragged men out of their homes and shot them in the street without even an identity check. Between Thursday and Sunday, they killed at least 350 people and injured 600 more. Hama Hospital alone recorded 255 deaths.[35] One Hama citizen told of his experience:

> It must have been 1:30 in the morning on Friday, April 24. I wasn't sleeping. I saw two helicopters land in the neighboring cemetery. Soldiers came out and sealed off the neighborhood. Toward 2:00 shooting began. They assaulted the houses. They broke down the doors and rounded up all the men. When they gathered fifteen or twenty, they took them into an alley or into the entrance of a house and executed them, then went on to others.
>
> Toward 5:00, it was the turn of our house. They took two men from our neighbor's apartment. There are four apartments on the landing, but they must not have seen the third and fourth doors because there was no light in the corridor. By accident, they didn't come into our place. I had gotten dressed and prepared to go out, thinking that like last year it was just a matter of a short stint of four or five days [in prison] and after that we would be released.
>
> That's the way they did it last year: shooting in the air in every direction to terrorize the population. . . . This time, we didn't understand right away what was going on. That's why there wasn't any resistance, at least not in our neighborhood. The shots lasted until 9:00 or 9:30 in the morning. All this time, I heard from my apartment the wails of women . . . and the cries of men also, who must have been beaten before they were killed.
>
> Toward 11 A.M., I recognized the voice of my brother in the street. He does not live at our house, as he is married. I heard him cry: "They didn't leave a man or a boy in the neighborhood!" I went downstairs and took just a few steps before coming onto a pile of corpses, then another. . . . I looked at them a long time without being able to believe my eyes. In each pile there were fifteen, twenty, thirty bodies. . . . They were every age from fourteen on up, in pajamas or galabiya, in sandals or barefoot.[36]

HAMA UPRISING AND REPRESSION
(FEBRUARY 2–MARCH 5, 1982)

The opposition movement, terribly battered, receded further after the Hama massacre of April 1981. The regime had ousted over a hundred university professors and at least a thousand primary and secondary teachers. Three hundred medical professionals, lawyers, and engineers were behind bars.

Many trade union leaders who had challenged the Ba'thist candidates had also been arrested. Purges swept through the officer corps and the civil service. Writers, filmmakers, and political figures fled into exile. Many had disappeared. As many as twelve thousand people—more than half of them Islamists—were crammed into the jails and detention centers.[37]

Hama had suffered more deeply than any other city except perhaps Aleppo, yet political activity continued. The fourth-largest city in Syria, with a population of over 200,000, Hama had always been an opposition stronghold. During the Mandate, it was a bastion of the movement against the French and the site of some of Syria's first workers' strikes. In the early Ba'thist period, Hama was also a tough opponent of the government. Twice the city had endured harsh military attacks as punishment for its independence.

Hama is a deeply religious Sunni city, with over eighty mosques, but it also has a Christian population with several prominent churches. Wealthy Sunnis from old landlord families, fierce enemies of the regime, were the city's social leaders. The peasants who worked the landlords' fields in the surrounding countryside—some of the most exploited peasants in Syria—had also made Hama a center of the radical secular peasant-based socialist movement of Akram Hawrani. A Palestinian camp formed yet another opposition base. Islamists and Freemasons, landlords, shopkeepers, workers, and peasants, conservatives and revolutionaries, Syrians and Palestinians—nearly all opposed the regime. Among them, the Islamists were by far the most powerful and best organized, with a leadership committed to armed rebellion.

Hama was Syria's most beautiful city. Some say it was the most lovely city in the Middle East. Built on the gardened banks of the Orontes River, it was famed for its Great Mosque, giant wooden *norias,* or water wheels, and ancient neighborhoods with handsome homes and markets interwoven with narrow, bustling streets.

Sometime in late January 1982, the regime decided to end Hama's intransigent opposition. On February 2, a brigade of commandos from the Defense Brigades and units of the Special Forces entered the city to confiscate arms and round up the opposition. The city had remained unrepentant after the regime's previous two attacks. This time, there were to be no halfway measures.

The Islamists, understanding that it would be a critical test of strength, decided to resist. As security troops entered the narrow alleys of the old city, they fell into an ambush near a Muslim Brotherhood base in the al-Hader quarter. Other Islamist units went on the offensive. Then, from the minarets of the mosques, came the call to general insurrection: the people were told that they were not alone and that the time had come to drive the regime out of the city and right out of power. Rebels seized guns and ammunition from police armories, killed about a hundred government and party representatives, and barricaded large areas of the old city. The Islamist fighters, who originally numbered about four hundred, were joined by about two thousand citizens.

For two days fighting raged as security troops could not penetrate the old city. Then, on the third day, government forces gained the initiative as some of the toughest and most reliable military units—Defense Brigades, Special Forces, units of Shafiq Fayadh's 3d Armored Division, as well as the 47th Armored Brigade—joined the battle. Commandos seasoned by the battlefields of Lebanon blasted the city with helicopter-launched bombs and rockets, artillery, and tank fire. Entire neighborhoods were flattened. In some quarters, fighting raged from house to house. By February 5, the army occupied strategic positions in the city, but resistance continued in a few quarters, especially in al-Hader. By then fewer than a thousand rebels held out against more than thirty thousand troops.

Hama now endured a fierce collective punishment. For three days, security forces killed hundreds of people in a series of mass executions near the municipal stadium and at other sites. Troops pillaged stores and homes and fired weapons indiscriminately, treating all citizens as responsible for the insurrection. Army sappers blew up many of the buildings that still stood, sometimes with tens of people inside. Some reports say that security forces used cyanide gas to kill people inside structures. Tens of thousands fled the city, homeless and traumatized. Thousands of others, attempting to flee, were caught in the security ring and arrested.

Even though active resistance ceased in ten days, security forces continued to blow up buildings, including an important church. North of the Orontes, the dense, ancient neighborhoods had been reduced to rubble. Old quarters south of the river lay in ruins. Army bulldozers arrived to flatten the smoking shells of buildings.

Estimates of the number killed vary widely, but the most credible analysts put the number at between five and ten thousand people. Many, many thousands more were injured. With a third or more of the city's housing completely destroyed, between sixty and seventy thousand were left homeless. Even those whose homes remained intact deserted the city in panic. One credible report states that eighty-eight mosques and five churches were destroyed, along with twenty-one markets, seven graveyards, seven public bath houses, and thirteen residential neighborhoods.[38]

In 1989, Middle East Watch visited Hama. In spite of considerable rebuilding, the effects of 1982 were plainly visible. Of the Great Mosque, said to have been one of the most beautiful in the Middle East, nothing remained but rubble-filled foundations. On the north side of the Orontes, the city remains almost completely flattened. Amid this wasteland, construction workers labored on the skeleton of a new Meridien tourist hotel. Someday its pools, tennis courts, and terraced gardens will cover the ruins of the old city, now still so agonizingly raw. On the south, a few old buildings along the river have been rebuilt, including the ʿAzm Palace, which serves as the municipal museum. Even so, virtually every facade is pockmarked with shell holes, and people live in the broken remains of their houses. The people of Hama will not soon forget what happened to their beautiful city.

3

THE GOVERNMENT, POLITICAL
PARTIES, AND LEGAL SYSTEM

THE CONSTITUTION

The new Syrian constitution promulgated by Hafez Asad on March 14, 1973, declares the separation of legislative, executive, and judicial powers and enshrines many basic rights, including freedom of assembly (Article 39), freedom of speech (Article 38), and freedom of religion (Article 35).[1] It states that "sovereignty of law is a fundamental principle in society and state" (Article 25-2). It also declares that "every citizen is presumed innocent until convicted by a final legal decision," that "no one may be searched or arrested except in accordance with the law," and that "no one may be subjected to physical or mental torture or be treated in a degrading manner" (Article 28-1,2,3). The preamble of the constitution affirms that "[f]reedom is a sacred right and popular democracy is the ideal formula which ensures citizens the exercise of their freedom. This makes them dignified human beings, capable of giving and building, defending the homeland in which they live and making sacrifices for the sake of the nation to which they belong."[2]

The constitution provides for a president of the Republic, elected for a seven-year term of office, and a People's Assembly, elected for four-year terms, as well as one or more vice presidents, a prime minister, and a Cabinet or Council of Ministers. Two bodies—a State Council and a Constitutional Court—provide judicial review of administrative actions and legislation. Many provisions of the constitution are concerned with the organization and the independence of the judiciary (Articles 131–148).

Government leaders periodically assert the principles of the constitution in speeches and public forums. In a 1980 speech before the Regional Congress of the Ba'th party, President Asad spoke of the need to "affirm respect for the freedom of the individual, thus guaranteeing his security and safeguarding his dignity," and he called for "no laxity in the application of the principle of sovereignty of law."[3] More recently—on March 8, 1990, the Revolution Day celebrations—he asserted that "we, as Syrian Arabs and Ba'thists cannot but be freedom advocates and freedom seekers and fighters for the sake of freedom."[4] Annual declarations on Human Rights Day, published prominently in the press and broadcast on radio and television, make the same commitments.

Much in the constitution is unexceptionable. Intermingled with its fine, resounding phrases, however, are a number of potentially contradictory elements. The constitution establishes the "leadership" of the Ba'th party (Preamble) and speaks of it as the "vanguard party in society and state" (Article 8), enshrining in law Syria's particular form of one-party rule. Most dangerous are the broad powers given the president. They create an executive with virtually no effective constitutional, legislative, or judicial restraints or other forms of checks and balances.

Neither this constitution nor its predecessors, however, have ever been more than a legal shadow. Throughout Ba'thist rule a state of emergency has voided almost all constitutional protections of rights and liberties.

THE STATE OF EMERGENCY

The state of emergency (Hala al-Tawari') is the central legal mechanism and justification for the Syrian repressive system. The current state of emergency, declared as Military Order 2, of March 8, 1963, by the National Revolutionary Command Council, was one of the Ba'thist officers' first acts after seizing power. It was based on Syrian law, particularly on Legislative Decree 51, of December 22, 1962, declared by the previous regime, and on relevant passages in the Syrian constitution.

Syrian jurists pointed out to Middle East Watch that the state of emergency has never been legal, as it did not conform to provisions of either Legislative Decree 51 or the constitution. It was never approved by the Council of Ministers as chaired by the president of the Republic, nor was it submitted to the Syrian parliament, the People's Assembly. Both measures are required by Article 2a of Decree 51. Some jurists also argue that according to French legal precedent, influential because of the French origins of Syria's legal code, the state of emergency should be submitted to the People's Assembly for ratification with each new parliamentary session. This of course, has also never been done.[5]

The state of emergency is probably illegal in another way. According to Article 4, section 1, of the International Covenant on Civil and Political Rights, which Syria has ratified, a state of emergency is an allowable derogation from obligations for the protection of citizens' rights, as long as it is proclaimed in a genuine national emergency and lasts for a limited time. Such measures should be of "an exceptional and temporary nature," as the United Nations Committee on Human Rights has stated. The Syrian state of emergency, having been in force for over twenty-eight years, conforms to neither requirement. It is evidently unacceptable as a legal basis for the behavior of the regime toward its citizens.

Even the original Syrian legislation (Legislative Decree 51) asserts that the state of emergency is limited—namely, for "[a] situation of war or one in which war threatens to break out [or when] public security and order in the territory of the Republic or part of it is exposed to danger through the occurrence of international disturbances or general catastrophe" (Article 1b). These conditions do not hold at present—another reason the state of emergency should be considered invalid under Syrian law.

The Syrian regime has argued that it maintains a state of emergency because of its ongoing conflict with Israel.[6] As recently as March 8, 1990, Hafez Asad said that "[t]he state of war is the state in which we in Syria have been living since the Zionist movement occupied part of our Arab territory. We are in a state of war that was imposed on us and it continues to impose on us the enforcement of the emergency law for scores of years."[7] After twenty-eight uninterrupted years of a state of emergency, however, there is now an overwhelming presumption that the "emergency" is simply an excuse for the regime to suppress legitimate domestic opposition.

The state of emergency gives sweeping powers to the martial law governor[8] (the prime minister) and his deputy (the minister of the interior) to restrict freedom of assembly and movement; to censor mail, other communications, broadcasts, and publications; to confiscate, suspend, and close organs of the media; and to requisition or confiscate property. The state of emergency also includes a long list of offenses "Against State Security" and those which "Constitute a General Danger" (Article 6).

Given the vague definition of criminal activity and the sweeping powers contained in the state of emergency, one might imagine that the authorities could function within this legal framework. Yet the Syrian regime has broken even these laws in a number of important respects.

First, the procedure for arrest orders, which under the state of emergency must be signed by the martial law governor or his deputy (Article 4), is routinely ignored. According to widespread testimony, arrest orders are either signed blank and given to the security services or signed after an arrest is made. Second, and even more disturbing, the security services now ignore the courts altogether and do not bother even with the most perfunctory official charge and trial. Virtually all political prisoners in Syria are being held in preventive detention, some for years.

One of the most serious consequences of the state of emergency is that citizens lack any right to appeal the decisions of the martial law governor, including decisions to imprison persons for an unspecified period. There is no right of habeas corpus, no pressure to bring a person to trial, and no limitation on detention. This situation has continued to degenerate since 1963. Today the regime often fails to acknowledge whether particular people are prisoners or where they are being held—not only when they are first taken into custody but sometimes for months or years after their arrest.

By vastly broadening the limits of political crimes, by allowing unlimited detention without trial, and by legalizing methods of summary judgment (see below), the state of emergency has opened the way for an array of human rights abuses in Syria.

SPECIAL COURTS

Article 4 of the Emergency Law states that those violating the orders of the martial law governor shall be brought before a military court (al-Mahakam al-'Askaria). This has permitted the regime to bring its enemies before courts whose decisions it controls and whose standards and procedures protect the rights of the accused much less than those of the regular judiciary.

Legislation enacted since 1963 has further eroded the Syrian court system. Decree Law 6, of July 1, 1965, established exceptional military courts (al-Mahakam al-'Askariya al-Istithnaiya), courts separate from the ordinary military justice system and used especially for trying political cases. These courts have fewer procedural controls than the military courts mentioned in the original law.

Decree Law 6 also introduced vague, catch-all categories of political crimes:

SECTION A: "actions considered incompatible with the implementation of the socialist order, whether they are deeds, utterances or writing, or are done by any means of communication or publication"; SECTION C: "offenses against the security of the state"; SECTION E: "opposing the unification of the Arab states or any of the aims of the revolution or hindering their achievement."9

Almost any act of opposition could now be defined as illegal.

The abusive potential of these new arrangements were soon put to the test. In April 1964, after the new Ba'thist regime moved to crush protests in Hama, exceptional military courts judged and executed scores of citizens. Mustafa Tlas, a close collaborator of Hafez Asad and the present minister of defense, supervised this summary justice.

The regime went still further in March 1968 by promulgating Decree Law

47. This decree replaced the exceptional military courts with state security courts (Mahakam al-Amn al-Dawla), whose rules of procedure were specifically defined as not being "confined to the usual measures" prescribed in law for civil courts. In particular, evidence could be introduced that had no ordinary standing in law, such as hearsay or even the opinion of the prosecutor. Since the courts had no rules of procedure, there could never be an appeal on procedural grounds.

Decree Law 109 of August 17, 1968, set up yet another type of emergency court, the military field tribunal (sometimes referred to as the front-line military tribunal [Mahakam al-'Askariya al-Midaniya]), which could be set up anywhere during wartime or other military operations "in armed confrontation with an enemy." Although the law appears to refer to warfare with a foreign enemy, the regime soon applied the courts to confrontation with domestic enemies as well.

In both new types of courts, proceedings are closed and decisions unappealable.[10] At best, legal counsel appointed by the court only goes through the motions of representing the accused. After a verdict is reached, the president is required to confirm the decision, but this step can usually be taken for granted.

The president—or the minister of defense in the case of the field tribunals—appoints the judges, who are not required to have any legal training and in practice usually do not. Most are drawn from the ranks of military officers, Ba'th party officials, and the like. The courts are therefore completely outside the ordinary judicial system. Decisions usually appear to be reached in advance by the security agencies that make the arrest. With these courts in place, summary judgment has become the order of the day. Local bar associations began a fierce campaign against these abusive courts in the late 1970s. The Damascus Bar, in a famous resolution of June 22, 1978, stated that "all legal judgments issued by the special courts should be considered as contrary to the law and to the principles of Justice." The Damascus lawyers went further, demanding "that all lawyers not plead before the special courts and consider that if they do they are guilty [of a breach of discipline]. We must avoid having the prestige of the legal profession give credibility to these disastrous courts."[11] A few days later, the Syrian Bar Association followed suit. Over the next two and a half years, the fight to abolish these courts—and to abolish the state of emergency—was central to the democratic struggle led by the lawyers and to the democratic movement as a whole.

So widespread was public opposition to these courts and the dubious legal procedures they represented that the ruling National Progressive Front, in an effort to win over public opinion, felt compelled to criticize them. In a major public statement of September 27, 1979, it called on the regime to:

· Firmly apply the principle of sovereignty of law.
· Strengthen the [independent] authority of the judiciary.
· Respect and implement legal verdicts.
· Restrict the jurisdiction of the state security courts to crimes against the security of the state.[12]

Speaking in early 1980 at the Ba'th Congress, Asad himself called for: "The establishment of ordinary courts' dominance over the special courts as soon as possible. Instructions have been issued to the State Security Court to avoid looking into any case that does not deal with security [applause]."[13] Such pronouncements proved worthless. Far from improving the legal system, the regime took further steps in the opposite direction. It greatly increased its use of emergency and summary proceedings—including wide use of the military field tribunals—in Jisr al-Shughur, Aleppo, Hama, and the prisons.

It was just a short step from the summary justice of these special courts to the present-day arrangements, which date from the early 1980s. In political cases nowadays, court procedures are ignored altogether. Thus, through a series of steps begun under the initial State of Emergency law and continued through decrees and administrative action, the regime moved from a modicum of legality to a total disregard for legality; from courts, to summary courts, to no courts.

THE PRESIDENT

The enormous new presidential palace located on a hill overlooking Damascus makes other buildings in the city look Lilliputian by comparison. The building is a metaphor for the power of the president in the Syrian system. Under the constitution, the president[14] is not only head of state and government, he is also chief of the armed forces and president of the council of the magistrature. He may declare war and promulgate laws, and he "establishes the general policy of the state." He convenes and dissolves the People's Assembly, approves all constitutional amendments, submits matters to a referendum, and makes laws when the assembly is not sitting. He can even legislate over the wishes of the People's Assembly "in case of absolute need." He also, of course, has the constitutionally established right to "take emergency measures."[15]

The constitutionally specified checks and balances to presidential power—including the People's Assembly, the judiciary, and the Constitutional Court—are weak. The judges of the Constitutional Court, for example, are reappointed by the president every four years and are thus hardly able to exercise independence. Nor can the People's Assembly challenge the executive. All laws emanate from Asad's office and they are almost never blocked, or even amended, by the assembly.[16]

In practice, the president's power is almost unlimited, extending from direct control of the mass media to life and death over political prisoners. Asad names all the ministers and changes them at will. He appoints judges and can name anyone to preside over the special security courts. He nominates the prime minister, who is the martial law governor and whose powers of censorship and arrest are, in turn, very broad. Asad is said also to control all appointments to sensitive military and security posts.

Apart from his formal powers, Asad holds a number of other important posts, notably secretary general of the Ba'th party and chairman of the National Progressive Front. His appointees select all candidates for party office. The president controls the election of delegates to party congresses in a similar fashion. Even at the height of the opposition movement, when Asad's critics took over many Syrian institutions, the Ba'th stayed firmly under his control. By 1985, the party had become so supine that delegates to the Eighth Regional Congress asked Asad to directly appoint all ninety members of the party's Central Committee. At the previous congress, these members had been elected.[17]

An American political scientist described the scene:

> The standing ovation which greeted [Asad's] entrance was immediately broadcast to the most remote corners of Syria by a platoon of television cameras. These cameras carefully framed the president against a backdrop of gigantic wall-banners, which proclaimed him "leader of the struggle, champion of steadfastness and confrontation." . . . The congress opened with a long address by President Asad devoted mainly to foreign affairs. He spelled out Syria's policies toward Palestinian autonomy, Arab unity and socialist solidarity with a precision that left little room for debate. In the following days, when the Central Committee presented a detailed report on this subject, there was no dissent and little serious discussion. Instead, the regime's stance was simply rubber-stamped according to the traditional ritual: one delegate after the other took the podium to glory in Syria's "eternal mission" and to praise the achievements of "the champion leader."[18]

Not only is Asad's hold over the party and state firm, it is also very personal. Key field commanders in the army report directly to the president rather than through a chain of command to the chief of staff and the defense minister. The same is true in the security services. Communications, censorship, economic affairs, and foreign relations are all said to work in identical manner. Such personal governance has sapped the rule of law and made Asad's despotism possible. Loyalty has become more important than legality.

When Asad delegates authority, it is often to family members. His brother Rif'at, a leading figure in the Ba'th Regional Command and chief of the Defense Brigades, was the second most powerful person in Syria for many years. Though now living in exile in Paris and Marbella, Spain, Rif'at still holds the post of vice president for defense and security affairs.

Other family members in sensitive political posts include an in-law, 'Adnan Makhluf, head of the Presidential Guard, and a son, Basil Asad, a security officer who is being groomed to succeed his father. Another of Asad's brothers, Jamil, has been political boss of the port city of Lataqia and chief organizer of the 'Alawi community. Jamil's son Fawwaz serves as an intelligence official in Lataqia. A number of top people—including security chiefs 'Ali Duba, Shafiq Fayad, 'Ali Haydar, Ghazi Kana'an, and Mu'in Nassif—are cousins or have joined their children in marriage to the Asad family.

In recent years, this legal and personal dominance has been augmented by a carefully developed personality cult. Asad's image appears everywhere: on the walls of public buildings, on trucks, trains, and busses, in offices, shops, and schools—even in private homes. In some images he wears military commando gear, in others civilian dress; sometimes he is stern, at other times smiling avuncularly. Much is made of his name, which means "lion" in Arabic and connotes strength and dignity. The symbol is of especial significance in Syria, where icons of lions in ancient art symbolized rulers and their power. In Hama, two large lion statues watch over the main street just opposite the Ba'th party headquarters—a not-so-subtle reminder of who is in charge.

Almost every major meeting and congress, including international meetings held in Syria, is held "under the patronage" of Asad.[19] Public statements refer to him with such slogans as "leader of our people's and struggling party's march." Official newspaper editorials hope "that we may better apply the directives of Leader Comrade President Hafez Asad, party secretary-general and president of the Republic."

Ambitious officials and journalists quote Asad frequently, while Ministry of Information officials suggest to visiting journalists that he is a modern-day Saladin. His name appears on plaques dedicating hundreds of public buildings and public squares. There is Lake Asad and the Asad Library. And in recent years statues of Asad have taken prominent positions in the public squares of every city.

Today, though his likenesses are everywhere, Asad is rarely seen in public. Some say his poor health keeps him isolated, but parades and mass rallies have never been his style because he is not a charismatic figure. When he does make a public appearance, the delirious masses such as those that used to greet Egyptian president ʿAbd al-Nasir are not present. Even the casual visitor to Syria can tell that Asad is not the object of universal adulation. Why else would the imposing statue of the Hero-Comrade-President located in a square near the center of Aleppo need to be surrounded by barbed wire?[20]

Attempts to develop this personality cult are not sophisticated. Public comments critical of Asad—or any comment or representation that does not present him as a strong and wise father figure—are not permitted. Each week in primary school, a specially trained teacher leads students in songs praising Asad, and students are taught to applaud when his name is spoken.[21] A teacher from Darʿa reported that when any instructor enters the classroom in a primary school, the students stand and chant: "Our Chief Forever: Hafez Asad."[22]

A Syrian cartoonist has reported that no cartoon of Asad, no matter how flattering, has ever appeared in the Syrian press.[23] The media may not even hint that he might be responsible for any problems; foolish ministers, corrupt civil servants, or a lax and ungrateful public cause all errors, according to the Syrian press. Progress, as *Tishrin* is wont to assert, "requires that every one of us fully grasp President Asad's directives, which are the basis of our future action."[24] Not surprisingly, Asad's own guard sometimes refer to him as *al-muqaddas*— the sanctified.

THE BAʿTH PARTY

Both in law and in practice, the Baʿth party is an important force in the Syrian political scene.[25] As noted above, the constitution gives the party a "leadership" role and refers to it as a "vanguard party in society and state." The constitution also provides for the party's highest body, the Regional Command, to nominate the president of the Republic.

The Arab Baʿth Socialist party was founded in 1943 by three Syrian intellectuals and merged with the Arab Socialist party to form the Baʿth Socialist party in 1953. Its ideology combines support for pan-Arab unity, renaissance (*baʿth* means rebirth or resurrection), and socialism. The party's slogan, "Freedom, Unity, Socialism," sums it up. A map of the Arab world displayed in the party logo signifies the quest for Arab unity, a drive with strong historical roots in Syria.[26]

Before gaining power, the party was one of several on the secular left, where it competed with Communists and Nasirists. It faced far larger parties of the center-right, dominated by landlords and merchants, and, of course, the right-wing Muslim Brotherhood.

The Baʿth founders hoped the party would spread throughout the region and unify an Arab world humiliated and divided by colonialism. For years, the party had both a "national" (that is, Arab-wide) and "regional" (that is, Syrian) command structure. Where the ideological commitment to Arab unity has been strong, however, the practical results have been meager. As the union with Egypt failed, so did efforts to unite with the Iraqi regime, the only other Ba'thists in power. The two countries might have been an Arab powerhouse but for the fact that the Syrian and Iraqi parties have often protected and financed each other's opposition.

As for socialism, it became an important aspect of the party's outlook, though at a level more of sentiment than of a clearly defined program. Once in power, the Ba'thist governments nationalized industry, banking, trade, and some land. And in the late 1960s, the regime's socialist rhetoric, and even practice, took on a more serious air. Since Hafez Asad's Corrective Movement, however, both the party and the government have downplayed socialism. Although the public sector still dominates the economy, private enterprise has been quietly encouraged.

The Syrian Ba'th attracted a following among teachers and students (including military cadets) in the 1940s and 1950s, but its membership remained small and its electoral successes meager. Its rise to power owed everything to the small circle of Ba'thist military officers, including Hafez Asad, who seized power in 1963. From then until the coup of Salah Jadid in 1966, the civilian wing of the party may have held important posts, but real power remained in the hands of the military officers. Since then, the military wing has continued to gain dominance, even though many of the party's leading figures and most government ministers are civilians.

Only about 1,000–2,000 people belonged to the Ba'th party when it came to power; membership now numbers around 250,000, or about one in every twenty Syrian adults.[27] Those who want to get ahead in Syria are under pressure to join the party and may be threatened, denied jobs or promotions, or reassigned to undesirable posts if they refuse. Teachers, doctors, professors, and journalists all told Middle East Watch of such pressures.[28] Application forms for many jobs, including most positions in the state sector, ask for party affiliation.[29]

Although the party is the democratic face of the regime, it does not function democratically. Rather than being a vehicle for control of the government, orders come down from the top and the party mobilizes and controls the population. During Asad's rule, for all his emphasis on elections, democracy has actually decreased within the party. Whereas the lower ranks of the leadership had been elected before 1971, they have since been appointed from above. As one expert describes it, the party leadership "wields extensive powers to dissolve lower-level leadership organs and call for new elections, to discipline and purge members for 'deviation' from party goals or bad conduct and in 'emergencies' to suspend the rules and review all membership."[30]

Asad and his close advisers within the party and security apparatus carefully stage-manage party congresses and determine their conclusions in advance. At most, they allow delegates to vent complaints about corruption and incompetence. Asad ritually obliges by setting up investigations and punishing officials whose cases are particularly egregious. But such are the limits of popular control in the Ba'thist system.

The regime also uses the party in another way—as an instrument to gather information about more serious dissent. Every party member is expected to participate in the network by passing along information to party superiors. This system, larger than the most powerful security agencies, allows the party to monitor hundreds of organizations and thousands of small towns and villages. The intelligence center of the party, the Bureau of National Security, orchestrates this system.[31] The intelligence role of the party should not be exaggerated; the overwhelming majority of members join because of opportunism or pressure, so they are not strongly committed either to the party or to the regime. Yet the party remains one of the regime's most important listening posts.

The Ba'th party also plays an important role in censorship. The Bureau for the Training of Cadres, now headed by Ahmad Dargham, censors publications in all sensitive areas: politics, religion, and ideology.[32] Books in particular must pass through here for inspection, but Dargham has defined his portfolio broadly and intervenes in many other areas of intellectual life as well.[33] The regime also uses the party to control practically all institutions in the country, including trade unions, sports clubs, women's associations, peasants' unions, and associations of artists and writers.[34]

The party is especially active in training youth and students. As Asad asserted in a recent speech: "Our youth have been brought up to believe in the principles of the Arab Ba'th Socialist party."[35] If they don't believe, it's not for lack of effort by the Ba'thists. The party sponsors a large organization—the Revolutionary Youth Federation (Ittihad al-Shabiba al-Thawra)—to recruit and indoctrinate young people aged twelve to eighteen. Regular meetings, special summer training camps, and other activities prepare youth for party membership and set their sights on an eventual place in the regime or its security organs.

The party also sponsors the compulsory Ba'th Vanguard Organization (Munathama Talai'a al-Ba'th) for youngsters six to eleven years old. Twice a week, special teachers give children in this age group ideological instruction in the schools. They must memorize and recite party slogans, including homages to Hafez Asad. The head student in any class wears a red arm band marked with white letters with the word *muraqib* (observer), and is expected to report on all the other students. Observations might include unacceptable political behavior such as the failure to repeat party slogans with sufficient enthusiasm.

THE NATIONAL PROGRESSIVE FRONT

When Hafez Asad came to power, he promised to broaden the political base of the regime by bringing several opposition parties into a governing coalition with the Ba'th. After negotiations with other parties, the National Progressive Front—a grouping of five parties—was announced on March 7, 1982. Asad is its chairman and the Ba'th, with a majority of the seats on its Central Command, is its leading force.

The Front brought together the principal parties of the secular left: the Communist party, which dates back to the 1930s, and three more recent Nasirist parties. But soon a majority in these parties deserted to rejoin the opposition. This gravely weakened the Front's lesser parties and left them only marginally able to help "broaden" the base of the regime. By opting for legality and participation in the government, the Front parties gave up much of their independence; including their ability to criticize the Ba'th. As Communist party leader Yusuf Faisal recently told Kuwait's al-Watan: "We are allied with the ruling Arab Socialist Ba'th party not only on foreign policy but on all social issues. As long as there are social, peasant and worker organizations affiliated with the Ba'th party, the interests of the broad masses are unlikely to be overlooked. We only criticize negative points—and they are legion—but not from a posture of 'antagonism.'"[36]

Communist leader Khalid Bakdash told the same reporter that his party and all the others in the National Progressive Front are "nationalist parties and not against the regime."[37] Such a tame posture has been hard for the party leadership to sell to the rank-and-file, and all the parties in the Front continue to lose membership.[38]

Belonging to a party in the ruling "coalition" holds none of the perks of Ba'th party membership and brings many serious liabilities. Several rank-and-file members of Front parties told Middle East Watch that their parties feel compelled to praise Hafez Asad even louder and more slavishly than the Ba'th itself. Their parties cannot hold public meetings or events. Their newspapers cannot be sold on newsstands. They cannot establish youth federations, women's groups, or any party-related organization that might compete with the Ba'th-controlled "mass organizations." And party members are discriminated against in employment if they openly declare their affiliation.[39] Ironically, the parties of the Front lack a formal legal existence. Unlike most officially sponsored organizations, they have never received official authorization.

Under these conditions, the Front is largely a sham. Its Central Command rarely meets. It has no role in forming policy, planning, or any other exercise of political power. In elections to the People's Assembly, the regime sees to it that a few leading people from the Front parties are elected as token representatives. In the 1985 legislative elections, for example, these parties claimed about 16 percent of the seats in the People's Assembly.[40] Asad has also named a few people from these parties to lesser government posts over the years,[41] but all are loyal Asad allies. They cannot be said to symbolize pluralism in Syria.

THE OPPOSITION

As of late 1989, at least twelve Syrian opposition parties operated outside the Front, including the Muslim Brothers and a variety of secular left and nationalist parties: Ba'thists, Nasirists, and Communists.[42] Ten of the twelve were outlawed. The two opposition parties tolerated by the government, the Arab Socialist Union (ASU), originally a member of the Front, and the Workers' Revolutionary party (WRP), are both very small, riddled with intelligence agents, and politically irrelevant.[43]

The eight other parties of the secular opposition make various claims about their strength and effectiveness. All have undergone splits and have built alliances to reduce their vulnerability.[44] All share two things: opposition to Asad and reprisals from his regime. The government considers membership in an opposition party cause for imprisonment and torture, as discussed in chapter 5. Security forces have frequently arrested, interrogated, and imprisoned people merely for possessing the party literature or indicating sympathy for opposing positions.[45]

With the exception of the Muslim Brothers, these parties were tolerated to some degree during much of the 1960s and 1970s. There were relatively few political prisoners then, and the parties could function semi-legally and openly. During the Jadid period, a Communist was named minister of communications and veteran Communist party leader Khalid Bakdash returned to Syria after eight years of exile. Although the Communist party remained illegal, it was persecuted less than in the 1950s, during the military dictatorships and the union with Egypt.

The main exception to this tolerance was in Asad's treatment of opposition within the Ba'th party. When Asad came to power, he was especially harsh toward his Ba'thist predecessors, imprisoning hundreds first in a series of arrests and trials in the early 1970s, then in another wave in 1975. As the opposition movement gained momentum in the late 1970s, Asad cracked down on his opposition. In waves of arrests that hit all the main groups and caught many off guard, the regime imprisoned dozens of leaders and top cadres, especially in 1980. Continuing outbreaks of arrests decimated the parties. Some 1,00–2,000 party members have been arrested and badly treated each year since 1984 (the number was even larger before then). Today, an estimated 1,400 political prisoners sit in long-term confinement because of their affiliation with the secular opposition.[46]

The regime has treated the Muslim Brothers even more harshly. Given the violent methods of some Islamists, tough law enforcement was to be expected. However, the regime struck at the Muslim Brothers not only with fury but with a complete disregard for the rule of law. In the late 1970s, it began to identify the Muslim Brothers as a creature of foreign enemies.[47] A typical statement, issued by the National Progressive Front, called the Muslim Brothers "an armed gang, which has sold itself to the devil and is utilizing its resources to serve the nation's enemies." It also spoke of "onslaughts by the forces of darkness and malice and the agents of Israeli and U.S. intelligence."[48] In fact, some factions of the Muslim Brothers did receive outside support—mainly from Iraq, Jordan, and the Palestine Liberation Organization (PLO)—but the movement drew strength primarily from within Syria.

On July 7, 1980, the regime issued a law that not only banned the Muslim Brothers but made membership, even former membership, a capital offense. The law offered thirty days of amnesty—later lengthened by twenty days—for members to renounce their ties. This law aroused a great deal of criticism from both the Syrian opposition and international legal and human rights advocates. Retroactive laws are banned by the United Nations Covenant on Civil and Political Rights (Article 15-1), to which Syria is a party, and such laws are not acceptable under Syria's constitution (Article 30), legal codes, or traditions. But this made no difference to the Asad regime. According to official sources, about a thousand people took advantage of the amnesty. After that, the regime began to hunt down the Muslim Brothers with little regard for evidence and less for due process.

Even before the law had been passed, the regime had set up special courts to try Muslim Brothers. It also set up loyal militia to reinforce the police and security services. In August it published a new regulation requiring owners of buildings to identify their tenants—a requirement aimed specifically at hunting out Islamist followers.

According to eyewitness accounts given to Middle East Watch, security forces stopped people in the street and hauled them to prison on the mere suspicion of connection to the Muslim Brothers. Many were then summarily executed, either in detention facilities or in prisons. Apparently not all were executed, however, for the prisons filled with as many as five thousand prisoners suspected of some Islamist connection.

In January 1985, the Ministry of the Interior announced a special pardon for members of ʿAdnan ʿUqla's Fighting Vanguard Organization—the most militant of the armed Islamists—who had agreed to lay down their arms and reconcile themselves to the regime. A few returned from exile, but not many. Several hundred were released from prison. But 2,500 or more Islamists remained behind bars and arrests continued. The regime still treats the Muslim Brothers more ruthlessly than any other political group, with the result that it has effectively crushed their political power.

Every once in a while, when the regime feels a need to improve its democratic image at home and abroad, it circulates rumors that it plans to "broaden the Front" and release opposition political prisoners. Emissaries of the regime approach leaders in exile and invite them to come home and cooperate with Asad. Hope is kindled temporarily, but nothing ever changes and a harsh policy toward the opposition continues.

ELECTIONS

The Baʿthist regimes held no government elections at all from 1963 until 1970. When Hafez Asad took power, however, he promised that his Corrective Movement would install a new "popular democracy," with elections as one of its hallmarks. From then on, there has been no shortage of elections. First, there was a presidential election, ratifying Asad as head of state by a 99.2 percent majority on March 1, 1971. Following in rapid succession were a referendum on unification with Egypt, Libya, and Sudan that was never consummated (September 1, 1971); elections to local (*muhafaza*, or governorate) councils (March 3–4, 1972); a constitutional referendum (March 12, 1973), and legislative elections (May 25, 1973).

Like the presidential referendum, these exercises in popular democracy yielded predictable results. Although thousands had rioted against the proposed constitution, it was approved by 97.6 percent. The unification referendum likewise chalked up a victory of 96.4 percent.

The 1973 legislative elections may have been slightly freer of tampering than the three referenda. The non-Baʿth parties in the National Progressive Front still enjoyed residual independence, and Asad was interested in giving these first legislative elections an appearance of real choice. But after a moderately lively campaign, the results appeared fraudulent. Only 16 percent of the seats went to non-Baʿth Front candidates. Splits in the Front parties soon resulted. By the late 1970s, after further electoral disillusionment, few believed that Syrian elections offered a choice. As French expert Elisabeth Picard wrote at the time: "By effectively eliminating opponents and tightly controlling the voting process, the regime has assured itself in most cases a nearly absolute victory. But the level of voter participation—sometimes less than 10 percent and rarely more than 50 percent—shows the disaffection of the population toward electoral practices that fool no one."[49]

The regime now stages periodic elections: for the People's Assembly every four years, for the muhafaza councils every four years, and for the presidency every seven years. According to the Interior Ministry, in the 1985 presidential elections 99.97 percent of all votes cast were for Hafez Asad; in the whole country only 376 people cast a "no" ballot.[50]

There are many nongovernmental elections as well: for Ba'th party officers and Congress delegates, and for officers in the trade unions and other organizations, including the Writers' Union. These elections rarely offer voters a meaningful choice. The sole exception was the voting in the professional associations and mass organizations during the opposition movement in 1978 and 1979. With a real opposition slate, in some cases not a single Ba'th candidate won office. Of course, quite a few of those winning candidates are now in exile, in jail, or dead. Since then, organizational elections have returned to their predictable course.[51]

Parliamentary elections have never offered a surprise, but results from one election to another do shift, apparently reflecting the regime's changing strategy of co-option rather than changes in voting patterns. Far more independents won seats in the People's Assembly elections of 1986, for instance, than in 1982. The results of presidential referenda, by contrast, are monotonously regular. After his 99.2 percent victory in 1971, Asad won in 1978 by 99.6 percent, and then in 1985 by 99.9 percent.

Election campaigns are tame. Since there is no opposition press and no legal possibility for an unofficial election meeting, the only issues raised are such time-honored standbys as the need to fight corruption and the battle against inflation and food costs. Foreign policy comes up only when candidates want to arouse patriotism.

Not surprisingly, voter turnout for elections is small; so small that in recent years the regime has several times added an additional day for voting (this happens by law when turnout is less than 51 percent on regular election day). Officials admit a relatively low participation rate: 42 percent for the 1986 legislative elections, for instance, and much less in urban districts.[52] But independent observers have said that turnout is actually much lower, noting that many polling places are nearly empty on election days.[53]

Voter apathy reflects frustration and fear. A well-known Syrian writer told Middle East Watch that he crossed out all the top names on the electoral list in March 1986 as a protest. Shortly after leaving the polling place, an intelligence service summoned him for interrogation. It seems that an agent or informer had observed what he had done. He was told he would be forgiven if he cooperated. When he refused, he was imprisoned for over two years.[54]

4

THE SECURITY SERVICES,
OR MUKHABARAT

The Syrian political police or intelligence services—known in Arabic as *mukhabarat*[1]—have their roots in the French Mandate. The central government agency at the time was a security and propaganda department called the Special Services. Its powerful Intelligence Service (Service des Renseignements) formed the "cornerstone of the French administration."[2] Subject to little legal restraint, the service used detention without trial, torture, and summary execution, setting grim precedents for the postcolonial future.

After independence, political instability and foreign intervention set the stage for an expanded intelligence system. Shortly after Husni Za'im's CIA-backed coup in 1949, the new military leader centralized police and gendarmerie under the army, outlawed political parties, imposed press censorship, and enlarged the mukhabarat.[3] Za'im did not remain long in power, but his successors, especially Col. Adib Shishakli, continued the trend.

By the mid-1950s, although Syria had returned to civilian rule, Military Intelligence had become the paramount security agency. Led by Col. 'Abd al-Hamid Sarraj, Military Intelligence gained a reputation for ruthless efficiency and wielded considerable influence over the governments of the day. When Syria united with Egypt in 1958, President 'Abd al-Nasir named Sarraj minister of the interior for the Syrian "region," with responsibility for coordinating intelligence operations. Railing against "reactionaries," "provincialists," and other "opportunists," Sarraj gave the mukhabarat wide authority to stamp out the opposition—especially Communists—and to practice torture regularly for the first time since independence.[4]

After coming to power in 1963, the Ba'thist military regime relied on the mukhabarat to consolidate its rule. During the Jadid period of the late 1960s, Security Chief 'Abd al-Karim al-Jundi, head of the Ba'th party's Bureau of National Security, intimidated the country with abductions and torture. British author Patrick Seale, describing al-Jundi's "penchant for cruelty," told of the consequences of gossiping about the fearsome security chief: "When he heard that a group of lawyers and other professional men had gossiped about him at a private gathering, he moved to arrest them, forcing several to flee on foot to Lebanon where they remained out of harm's way until his downfall."[5]

Though al-Jundi's Security Bureau ruled supreme, Military Intelligence remained powerful. Political Security, another important agency, monitored opposition parties and movements. Hafez Asad controlled a fourth security service—Air Force Intelligence—while Col. 'Ali Haydar took charge of the newly created Special Forces, a military unit with intelligence missions.[6] Shielded by the state of emergency and the recently formed security courts, these agencies carried out their work with little restraint.

Following his coup of 1970, Hafez Asad enlarged the intelligence services and brought their chiefs into the inner councils of state. As a military man, he favored such military agencies as Military Intelligence and Air Force Intelligence. In 1971, he also set up a new paramilitary agency—the Defense Brigades—under his brother Rif'at. Originally intended to protect government buildings against military coups, the Defense Brigades soon won broad authority and built a powerful intelligence branch. By the late 1970s, they numbered more than ten thousand, mostly heavily armed commandos. Their bullying manner and reputation for violence and corruption made them the most hated and feared of the security forces.

In 1976, Asad set up a second praetorian guard under a relative by marriage named 'Adnan Makhluf. This agency, known as the Presidential Guard, was charged with maintaining Asad's direct personal security. It, too, rapidly grew to ten thousand or more, and included both paramilitary and intelligence branches.

Asad's security system was built on three pillars: the traditional mukhabarat, such as Political Security and Military Intelligence; the newer praetorian units, such as the Special Forces, Defense Brigades, and Presidential Guard, which mixed commando and intelligence functions; and special "political" military units, notably the Third Armored Division. These agencies and their powerful subdivisions are coordinated through the Presidential Security Council, formed by Asad in the mid-1970s. Syria's intervention in Lebanon, which began in 1975, accelerated the development of special commando forces and accustomed them to mass operations against civilian populations.

When popular support for the domestic Syrian opposition peaked in the late 1970s—and as the Islamists' use of violence intensified—these commandos and their intelligence counterparts acquired unprecedented power to hound and destroy the enemies of the regime through mass arrests, torture of prisoners, collective punishment, and summary executions.

With the opposition crushed, state violence has abated within Syria since

1982, though it continues at a high level in Lebanon. The Asad regime is no longer in immediate risk, but it has nevertheless maintained the extraordinary power and extensive apparatus of the security forces. Over the years, individual agencies have waxed and waned, chiefs have come and gone, and targets have varied. But the system has endured and remains central to Asad's rule.

THE SECURITY SERVICES TODAY

Some fifteen security agencies are currently at work in Syria. All are relatively independent, possessing separate administrative departments and chiefs who report directly to the president. All gather information and perform surveillance. To varying degrees, they also make arrests, interrogate prisoners, and supervise incarceration. Some have high-level "assets" in the mass media, the "popular organizations," the universities, and government ministries.

These agencies, not the regular police, deal with all political cases. And they handle every phase of such cases, from first investigation through imprisonment to surveillance after release. Ex-detainees who become informers usually report to the same agency that first arrested them.

Agencies overlap extensively, but they also specialize in different missions. Air Force Intelligence is known for its covert operations in foreign countries, Military Intelligence for its important role in Lebanon, Political Security for its close watch on the universities and the parties of the left, Palestine Branch for its control over Palestinians and Jews, and Special Forces for its role as shock troops in civil disturbances.

These agencies have virtually unlimited authority to carry out arrests, searches, interrogation, and detention. Since 1980, almost none of the thousands of persons they have imprisoned for political reasons has been tried in court.

The mukhabarat have arrested, jailed, and mistreated Syrians of all classes, religions, and political persuasions—without exception. Since the agencies frequently arrest military officers, government employees, and security personnel, it would appear that the regime fears threats from within as much as threats from without.

The security agencies are more than an arm of government. Their chiefs (virtually all 'Alawi military officers), belong to Asad's inner circle, along with heads of key army units stationed near the capital. This inner circle has held power longer—and is more powerful—than the Council of Ministers, where civilians and non-'Alawis are more in evidence.[7]

General Shafiq Fayadh, a cousin of the president who has commanded the army's Third Armored Division for nearly two decades, is an important member of this group. His unit was one of the first to go into Lebanon in 1976, it occupied Aleppo in 1980, and it helped to quell the Hama uprising in 1982. Stationed near Damascus, it guards Asad against potential coup-makers. Along with Fayadh, security chiefs who have been longtime members of the inner circle include 'Ali Haydar, head of the Special Forces from 1968 to 1988; 'Ali Duba, head of Military Intelligence; and Muhammad al-Khuly, head of Air Force Intelligence for more than twenty years and now head of the Presidential Security Council.[8]

Today, over fifty thousand persons work for the Syrian security services, including the military and paramilitary branches; some estimates run three times higher.[9] Even fifty thousand is a large number for Syria, representing 1 person in 240. Proportionately sized forces in the United States would employ over 1 million people.

Although the cost of operating such an extensive security apparatus is buried in the official budget, the mukhabarat weigh heavily on the Syrian treasury. By some estimates, as much as a third of the military budget is devoted to intelligence. That would come to about $750 million per year—or about 5 percent of Syria's gross national product (GNP).[10] The current economic crisis has forced the regime to reduce military spending, and it has been under pressure to trim security costs as well. The army had pared away two divisions by 1990, but most observers think that the security agencies will be last to undergo deep cuts.

REWARDS AND CORRUPTION

The high cost of the security forces comes not only from their tremendous size but also from the generous benefits the regime provides to ensure loyalty. Security personnel live well by Syrian standards. Their pay is higher than equivalently ranked civil servants and military personnel. They receive special loans and housing subsidies, travel allowances, priority access to public transportation, access to duty-free stores, and other privileges. Most officers have discretionary funds and can use low-level employees as personal servants.[11]

Security employees also make money selling favors. Many Syrians have testified to Middle East Watch about mukhabarat officers demanding money for prison visits, exit visas, permits, and authorizations of every kind. Impoverished Kurdish refugees have paid hundreds of dollars for passports, and desperate families in Lebanon have shelled out thousands of dollars for prison visits. Mukhabarat officials extort especially large sums when wealthy businesspeople need favors, such as import licenses.[12] Taking the practice further, Rif'at al-Asad is said to have made millions of dollars through a "protection" scheme in which he demanded a share of profits from large businesses.

Middle East Watch has also heard complaints that security officers have seized for personal use apartments and houses owned by Syrian political émigrés. Plunder by Syrian security personnel in Lebanon is especially common, with apartments, furniture, and automobiles reported as favorite booty. Lebanese sometimes refer to Rif'at as "King of the Oriental Carpets" because of his reputation for confiscating these prized objects, sometimes with the help of his personal Lebanese militia, the Fursan al-'Arab (Arab Knights), often known as the Pink Panthers.[13]

Syrian security chiefs have been deeply involved in the black market. Rif'at openly established a market in Damascus called the Soldiers' Suq that sold goods smuggled from Lebanon or stolen from the state.[14] Trucks of the Defense Brigades or the Third Division often travel the route from Beirut to Damascus loaded with contraband.

The Soldiers' Suq closed after Rif'at's exile, and smuggling by security forces is less flagrant today, but it continues to be big business. Rumors and occasional articles suggest that security chiefs have made fortunes selling arms, stolen automobiles, and Lebanese drugs.[15] Their substantial income above their official salaries is evident in the sumptuous houses, large landholdings, luxurious cars, and lavish family weddings they enjoy.

COMPETITION VERSUS CENTRALIZATION

Asad has built his security system with many overlapping services, thus preventing anyone from accumulating excessive power and assuring his access to many channels of information. He also orders agencies to watch one another. It is a costly exercise, but the mutual suspicion and "competition" gives Asad complete control.

Paramilitary agencies have counteracted one another in coup attempts. In March 1984, during the president's illness, Rif'at used his Defense Brigades in a bid for power. When his armor and commandos moved on Damascus, he was confronted by the Special Forces, the Third Division, and the Presidential Guard—all loyal to Hafez. Eventually, realizing that he could not win, Rif'at stood down in favor of his brother.[16]

Throughout the 1970s and early 1980s, the security agencies struggled with one another for influence and power. Sometimes one mukhabarat would search for a person already arrested by another or several agencies would search separately for the same person. Syrians told Middle East Watch of occasions when two teams arrived simultaneously from different agencies. While each heatedly disputed the other's right to make the arrest, their quarry managed to escape.[17]

Asad decided to impose greater central control, or at least better coordination, sometime in the mid-1980s by strengthening the Presidential Intelligence Committee (Lajna al-Mukhabarat al-Riasiya) and reducing the autonomy of other agencies. The anarchy that prevailed until the early 1980s is now past, so that multiple hunts for wanted persons, for instance, are no longer common. Interrogation is also more coordinated, with interrogation "committees" drawn from several agencies for important prisoners.

One sign of interagency cooperation was the massive wave of arrests that began in September 1987 and lasted until February 1988. Four security services—Political Security, Internal Security, Air Force Intelligence, and Military Intelligence—banded together, jailing as many as two thousand people from various left-wing parties. It was the first time in years that several agencies had carried out such a sweep.[18]

GUARDS AND GUARD DUTY

Within Syria, the security services are most visible guarding powerful people and important public buildings. During the years 1978 to 1982, when the Islamic opposition carried out a program of assassinations and car bombings, the Asad regime greatly increased the number of these guards. Damascus especially was swarming with them.

In 1982, French scholar Michel Seurat commented that a person's power in Syria could be measured by the number of his guards: the president had twelve thousand; heads of the security services enjoyed sixty each; the head of al-Ba'th, the party newspaper, twenty-eight; while just 4 were assigned to the dean of the dental school. Near a person's home, wrote Seurat: "Do the guards occupy a simple doorway, the sidewalk in front of a building, or is the entire street blocked off?"[19]

When the Iranian foreign minister came to Damascus to meet with several high-ranking Syrians, reported Seurat, "nine altogether sat down at the table, but since each had brought with him his personal bodyguard, no less than 300 people arrived in the neighborhood and tramped around near the restaurant."[20]

During that period, many lesser streets in Damascus were closed off entirely to protect the residences of important persons. Public buildings, depending on their significance, were often protected by two dozen or more guards. For the most important buildings, the mukhabarat built concrete barriers at the outer edge of the sidewalk to prevent the approach of any vehicle.

Today, far fewer streets are closed off. After Rif'at's exile in 1984, many streets in the capital were reopened, and people can go out at night without fear of encountering the tough commandos of the Defense Brigades. But many barriers remain. No one can walk along the sidewalk past the Central Bank, for example, or even approach the headquarters of Air Force Intelligence. Abu Zar Street, near the Central Bank, is closed to traffic. And near Amawyin Circle, where the Air Force General Staff and the Regional Command are located, the avenue narrows from two lanes to one to make room for heavy barriers on each side. The presidential palace is, of course, the most heavily guarded area, but one encounters forbidden streets, security patrols, and guards with submachine guns on almost any walk through Damascus.

For buildings of lesser importance, where the mukhabarat has never constructed barriers, guards stand watch to prevent an unauthorized approach or parking, waving away even pedestrians. At the entrances to the university, mukhabarat agents check student identification cards. And along the downtown sidewalks, patrols of security agents in commando fatigues stride in twos and threes. More than nine years after the regime crushed the opposition, security-conscious Damascus still has an edgy feel.

THE INFORMANT SYSTEM AND SURVEILLANCE

The Syrian mukhabarat's informers are ubiquitous. No one knows how many there are altogether, but knowledgeable Syrians guess in the tens of thousands. Some are paid, full-time employees, but many others are part-timers or paid occasionally. Some are simply expected to pass along information by virtue of their jobs, government posts, or party affiliation. And many become informers involuntarily after threats and torture. The net result is a society riddled with informers. Not surprisingly, Syrians are extremely conscious that anything they say or do may become known to the authorities.

According to knowledgeable Syrians who spoke to Middle East Watch, in order to drive a taxi in Damascus, one must agree to cooperate with the security agencies and pass along information. The same is true of many people in other occupations well-placed for observation: journalists, waiters, hotel personnel, bus station employees, street vendors, real estate brokers, and travel agents.[21] The mukhabarat also ensure that informers are present on university campuses, in youth groups, in factories—everywhere Syrians congregate. The following story is typical: "Five of us at the university got together one night for a discussion. We talked freely about the situation in the country and I was particularly outspoken in criticizing the regime. The very next day I was called in by the mukhabarat. They warned me I was going to get into trouble. Obviously, one of my comrades was an informer."[22] Such experiences are so common that Syrians are cautious in speaking about politics. In spite of their renowned hospitality, they are understandably careful about what they say to strangers.

Syrians generally discuss politics only among family and friends. Here, political discourse can be quite lively. But care is taken. It is understood that a gathering must remain small so that it will not be taken to be a meeting, in breach of security regulations. People may use euphemisms, lower their voices, or close the blind. It is not what is said but the context that can count the most. One Syrian reported on his understanding of the rules: "If I say to my wife I don't like Asad, there is no danger. If I say this in my home, to members of my family or two or three close friends, there is probably no problem either. If I say this to a dozen people in my home, I am beginning to run a real risk, even if they are friends. And if I propose to this group that we take action, my risk is very great indeed. Of course, if I make such a statement in public, I am certain to be arrested. These are the rules of the game."[23]

Syrians widely assume that telephone conversations are tapped and that foreign phone conversations are especially tightly monitored. These assumptions appear reasonable, at least in the case of high government employees, intellectuals, and persons with some history of political engagement. Many have been questioned or arrested for what they have said on the phone.

As a rule, foreigners are surveilled, though less obtrusively than in the past. Several years ago, a U.S. doctoral student was trailed for a year, eventually making the acquaintance of the person following him. Over the years, foreigners known to be critical of the regime, no matter how distinguished, have been considered personae non gratae. In one case in the mid-1980s, the regime forced a distinguished foreign historian to leave the country on twelve hours' notice because he had written articles considered unflattering to the state. Ordinary travelers, though, report no obvious signs of surveillance, and it is normal today to enter and leave Syria by air without a baggage search or personal questioning. For residents, the matter is very different. The security services tightly control citizens' foreign travel, requiring an exit visa in addition to a passport.[24] Many are refused travel—Jews and Palestinians in particular. Even well-known authors have been stopped at the airport and prevented from leaving.[25] No one can be certain of his or her travel plans.

In addition to physical surveillance of persons, houses, and offices, the security services also open and read every kind of mail. Even the most innocent items can be suspect, especially if they come from abroad. One Syrian was recently called in by a security service to explain why he was getting a book on modern art from a friend in Europe. He was allowed to take the book home only after a tense session in which he explained the book was a gift that he neither solicited nor anticipated receiving.[26]

Receiving mail with political content can have much more serious consequences. In one well-known case, Dr. Tawfiq Draq al-Saba'i, a neurologist and father of five, was arrested in Homs in May 1980 after security agents intercepted a letter from his relatives in Saudi Arabia expressing concern about the

Syrian political situation. Accused of endangering state security, he was tortured and imprisoned. As of mid-1990 he remained incarcerated in al-Mezze Prison.

It would be easy to exaggerate the success of informers, surveillance, and the other information-gathering efforts of the intelligence system. In fact, limits exist and the system is far from omniscient. A casual visitor to Damascus cannot fail to notice the confusion at airport immigration, the piles of untouched official forms, and the dusty, unused computer terminal. Local security offices convey the same disorderly impression with their yellowing stacks of forms piled on tables and officials chatting on the phone while supplicants wait anxiously to be heard. The atmosphere is one of chaos mixed with petty corruption and the exercise of bureaucratic power, not of a ruthlessly efficient police state.

The structure of Syrian society imposes other limits on the security services. The extended family, village, urban quarter, and religious sect all remain strong and provide counterintelligence networks. A Syrian from Damascus reported that his cousin's best friend is married to an officer in the mukhabarat; one day, the security man inadvertently revealed the identity of the neighborhood informer. Other Syrians tell similar stories, with different details.[27]

Many people claim to be able to spot mukhabarat agents. Often 'Alawis from the countryside, the agents' speech, dress, and questions give them away. According to one Syrian, even local agents are not terribly hard to spot; they often reveal themselves when closely questioned by canny people of the neighborhood.[28] Such limits have enabled outlawed parties to function, illegal literature to circulate, and political activists to remain safely underground for months or even years.

Syrians also use personal ties to protect themselves, their families, and friends from the security system. Some told Middle East Watch how they had used family, clan, and school ties with high officials. By pleading their cases, they sometimes managed to get a long-denied exit visa, eased censorship, or the release of a prisoner. But resorting to such methods can enmesh people in a system of clientage and dependency; by begging for favors, they concede their autonomy and dignity—one of the many ways the mukhabarat system takes its toll.

INTIMIDATION AND WARNINGS

The mukhabarat often summon people, question them, issue warnings and threats, and then let them go. Only rarely in such cases do they hold people overnight. Some Syrians told Middle East Watch of "polite and friendly" chats, with intimidation subtly veiled. Others reported harsher treatment: after they had waited for hours, an officer told them details of their personal life to show that they were being watched. Some spoke of interrogation and shouting, followed by pressure to provide information, support the regime, or explain some action considered suspicious or disrespectful of those in power. Still others say they were pushed around. Often a security officer delivers a blunt warning: unless the suspects change their ways, they will wind up in jail.

The mukhabarat issue thousands of such warnings each year. The process reminds Syrians that there is a line of behavior they cannot cross without running great personal risks.

ARRESTS

The mukhabarat make most of their arrests at night, between 10 P.M. and 5 A.M., to catch their prey at home, asleep, and off guard. Nighttime arrests also maximize the terror in the household and neighborhood. Here is one account of an unexpected arrest in a Damascus neighborhood:

> I was fast asleep. At about two in the morning, I heard knocks. I went to the door and asked who was there. A voice said: "Your neighbor, I want to talk." Without thinking, I opened the door and saw about ten people from the mukhabarat, some with automatic weapons. They pushed their way inside. Some searched every room of the house. They tore the place apart, looking for incriminating papers and documents. But they didn't find anything. Then they said: "You come with us. We want to talk to you." They let me get dressed, shoved me into one of the cars, put on a blindfold, and we drove away.[29]

Syrians are now wary of late-night knocks. Recently, a foreign visitor, passing the home of a Syrian friend late at night, innocently knocked at the door. Though not involved in any political activity, the shocked family became agitated. The sleepy foreigner at their doorstep was not what they expected to find.

The mukhabarat often make arrests singly, but most arrests occur in sweeps of dozens, perhaps hundreds, of people from the same political party, movement, or tendency. The Jadid Ba'thists have been rounded up seven times since 1970, the Communist Party-Political Bureau five times since 1980, and the Party for Communist Action ten times since 1977.[30] In September 1987, the mukhabarat launched their largest campaign since the early 1980s, as four agencies rounded up people suspected of left-wing connections. Mukhabarat agents simultaneously positioned themselves in a number of towns and cities, including Damascus, Aleppo, Homs, and Lataqia. They blocked access roads, sealed off neighborhoods, set up roadblocks, posted agents to watch bus and railroad stations, and then moved in to make arrests. They stopped cars, taxis, and buses. They raided cafes, restaurants, and movie theaters. Agents opened fire in crowded streets on those who fled, wounding innocent passersby as well as those pursued. In the end, two thousand people were arrested, some of them taken as hostages for others. Hundreds more were temporarily detained.

In a system without arrest warrants, formal charges, or any sort of legal procedures, prisoners' families, colleagues, friends, and neighbors can never be sure what lies in store for the person in custody. It is an agonizing time, when Syrians are acutely conscious of their powerlessness against state authority.

DIRECTORY OF AGENCIES

Of Syria's fifteen security services, five are military or paramilitary forces with security functions, like the Special Forces. Five are "ordinary" security agencies: two of these are nominally civilian, two are military, and one is attached to the Ba'th party. The remaining five agencies are technically subdivisions of the others, but they are so powerful that they virtually stand on their own, with independent headquarters, regional offices, and interrogation centers. Of these, three are branches of the most powerful agency—Military Intelligence. A description of each agency follows.

ORDINARY MUKHABARAT

"Civilian" Agencies

General Intelligence (Idarat al-Mukhabarat al-'Ama) is also known as State Security (Amn al-Dawla), its name until 1971. Brigadier General Majed Sa'id took over from Maj. Fuad Absi as the head of this agency late in 1988. Located on the Kafr Soussa traffic circle in southwestern Damascus, General Intelligence is thought to be Syria's second most important mukhabarat, after Military Intelligence. Although it is nominally a civilian agency and is formally under the jurisdiction of the Interior Ministry, it is in practice an autonomous entity, under military leadership and answerable only to the president.

General Intelligence is believed to have at least eight or nine major branches, the most important of which is Branch 251, the Internal Branch (Fara' al-Dakhili)—also sometimes known as General Intelligence Branch (Fara' al-Mukhabarat al-'Ama), State Security (Amn al-Dawla), and Internal Security (al-Amn al-Dakhili). Headquartered in the al-Sadat/al-Khatib area of Damascus, it is headed by Mu'n Nassif, a relative of Asad who is also deputy of General Intelligence. A key figure in his own right—and perhaps more powerful than the agency chief—Nassif is said to be very close to the president. His Internal Branch has independent quarters in Damascus and its own interrogation facilities. It is said to have special responsibility for Damascus and to be particularly active in the universities.

Other branches of General Intelligence, located primarily near the headquarters in Kafr Sussa, include the External Security Branch (Fara' al-Khariji), the Information Branch (Fara' al-Ma'lumat), the Administrative Branch (Fara' al-Idari), the Interrogation Branch (Fara' al-Tahqiq), the Prison Branch (Fara' al-Sijn), the Counter-Espionage Branch (Fara' Mukafahat al-Tajassus), and the Branch for Raids (Fara' al-Mudahama).[31] In addition to its central organization, the agency has many branches at the district and provincial levels.

Political Security (Idarat al-Amn al-Siyasi) is headed by Brig. Gen. 'Adnan Badr Hasan. This agency, one of Syria's oldest, has always made many political arrests, especially from the parties of the left and the Communists in particular. A special division, the Political Party Branch (Shu'bat al-Ahzab al-Siasiya), concentrates on such work. Other divisions are the Students and Student Activities Branch (Shu'bat al-Tulab wa al-Anshita al-Tulabiya), Surveillance and Pursuit Branch (Shua'bat al-Matlubin wal-Muraqabin wal-Mulahakin), and the City Branch (Shu'bat al-Madina), which oversees Damascus.

Although Political Security has always focused on controlling organized political forces, in recent years it has also taken on surveillance and control of the government. This task falls to the Branch for the Security of Governmental Institutions (Shu'bat Amn al-Muassasat al-Hukumiya).

As with Military Intelligence and General Intelligence, Political Security has a highly developed regional apparatus. For these reasons, many believe it to be the third most important agency.

A third agency, the Bureau of National Security of the Ba'th party (Maktab al-Amn al-Qawmi), is headed by Dr. 'Abd al-Rauf al-Kasm, a Sunni, who was prime minister until 1988. Al-Kasm appears to be the only civilian, non-'Alawi security chief. In theory, his agency, located in the al-Rawda area, controls all other security services. In practice, it has lost that role to the Presidential Security Council, and some dismiss the bureau as of only minor importance.

The bureau was once extremely powerful. Jadid loyalist 'Abd al-Karim al-Jundi, one of the original members of the Ba'th Military Committee, built up the bureau as the country's most powerful agency in the late 1960s. He held sway until March 1, 1969, when he committed suicide in anticipation of Asad's victory and his own fall from power. Since then, the bureau has been in eclipse.

It is no longer involved in arrests and interrogation, and it no longer has armed forces at its disposal. But it retains a significant intelligence-collecting role. By drawing on party members as well as operatives, the bureau's antennae reach into urban neighborhoods, small towns, and even remote rural areas—places the other mukhabarat cannot hope to cover effectively.

The bureau has expanded another important responsibility: screening proposed candidates for the People's Assembly, local councils, offices in trade unions, and "popular organizations." It also screens candidates for election to governing bodies of the professional associations. Even a delegate to the Arab Lawyers' Union Conference must gain approval here.

Military Agencies

Military Intelligence (Shu'ba al-Mukhabarat al-'Askariya), headed by Brig. Gen. 'Ali Duba, is located near Jamarik, a traffic circle in western Damascus. It is the largest and most powerful mukhabarat in Syria; it makes more arrests than any other agency and Duba is very close to the president. Military Intelligence is also the foremost agency in Lebanon, a major target of Syrian intelligence work in recent years.

Of Military Intelligence's numerous branches, some are prominent and relatively independent. These include the Palestine Branch (Fara' Falastin), headed by Col. Mazhar Faris. His agents have been known to arrest and interrogate many Syrians as well as Palestinians. This agency also closely monitors Jews and has been responsible for more deaths under torture than any other agency in recent years.[32] The interrogation center of the Palestine Branch is reputedly one of the country's most brutal.

The Commando Police (al-Dabita al-Fida'iya), led by Col. 'Abd al-Rahman 'Arafa, is formally a subunit of the Palestine Branch. In reality, however, it is autonomous, with its own central headquarters in the Mazra area of southeastern Damascus, a detention center on Baghdad Street in al-Qassa', and other branches at the Damascus Airport and at Yarmuk Camp. It, too, specializes in Palestinians.

Another branch of increasing importance is the Regional Branch (Fara' al-Mantiqa), headed by Col. Hisham Akhtiar. This department, which oversees the Damascus region, has made many arrests in the past few years. Like the powerful Internal Branch of the General Intelligence Agency, the Regional Branch may operative relatively autonomously from its parent.

The Military Interrogation Branch (Fara' al-Tahqiq al-'Askari) runs a large interrogation center by the same name that is sometimes ranked with that of the Palestine Branch as Syria's worst interrogation facility. Prominent opposition leader Riyad al-Turk has been held here since 1980 and reportedly has been tortured and abused almost continuously.

Another large and important division of the agency is the Syrian Military Intelligence in Lebanon (al-Istikhbarat al-'Askariya al-Suria fi Lubnan), whose extensive network has been responsible for many arrests and abductions there. General Ghazi Kana'an, chief of this branch, is believed to be the most important Syrian commander in Lebanon today.

Air Force Intelligence (Idarat Mukhabarat al-Quwwa al-Jawiya) was headed for a long time by Brig. Gen. Muhammad al-Khuly, who as chief of the agency helped Asad round up his enemies when Asad seized power in 1970. Located in the Abu Rumana area of north central Damascus, the agency is now run by al-Khuly's nephew, Col. Ibrahim Huwajy. Al-Khuly, chairman of the Presidential Intelligence Committee, is still considered highly influential in this agency; some even say that he remains effectively its chief.

Asad's air force background has meant especially close ties between the president and this agency. Air Force Intelligence has thus developed wide responsibilities that go far beyond military matters. It has long had a hand in arresting civilian opponents of the regime. It also has been very active in foreign covert operations. Al-Khuly is reported to have traveled often to Europe, especially to Switzerland and Germany, on intelligence missions. He was also named as the person behind the Hindawi affair, in which an El Al airliner narrowly escaped a midair bombing.

In addition to its headquarters building, Air Force Intelligence has five other centers in Damascus, as well as its own interrogation facility. It also has branches in three provinces: Aleppo, Homs, and Lataqia.

MILITARY COMMANDOS AND MILITARY POLICE SERVICES

Special Forces (al-Wahdat al-Khassa), with headquarters located in the Qabun area of Damascus, was founded in 1968. Brigadier General 'Ali Haydar headed the agency from its inception until September 1988. Asad finally replaced him with 'Ali Duba, nephew of 'Ali Duba, head of Military Intelligence.

As its name suggests, Special Forces is an elite military unit. With its own armor, helicopters, and weaponry, it is often described as the Asad regime's praetorian guard. Many of its ten to fifteen thousand specially trained commandos and paratroopers are 'Alawi. From 1978 to 1982, Asad used these troops to crush the opposition on several critical occasions. They were responsible for the Jisr al-Shughur massacre of March 1980, played an important role in the occupation of Aleppo in 1980 and were directly responsible for the massacres there. They also carried out the Hama massacre of 1981 and joined the forces crushing the uprising there the following year.

In addition to its military counterinsurgency mission, Special Forces acts as an intelligence and police agency, and over the years it has made many arrests.

Since 1985, its security police work has concentrated on Lebanon, where its bailiwicks are the northern districts—especially the city of Tripoli. There, it has imprisoned thousands of Lebanese and Palestinians and has been held responsible for many abductions and summary executions.

The Presidential Guard, sometimes known as the Republican Guard (al-Haras al-Jumhuri), was set up in 1976 after the Syrian invasion of Lebanon to protect the increasingly unpopular president of Syria. 'Adnan Makhluf, a nephew of Asad's wife, has always headed the agency, but some say the real chief now is a captain of the guard—the president's son, Basil—whom the media are starting to treat as heir to the throne. Officially, Basil heads Presidential Security (al-Amn al-Riasi), one of the guard's subunits on intelligence.

The guard, which long had an estimated strength of about ten thousand, has grown after the demise of the Defense Brigades (discussed below). Its responsibilities include not only the protection of the president but also general security in Damascus, a critical task it shares with other agencies.

The Third Army Division (al-Firqa' al-Thalitha), commanded by Gen. Shafiq Fayyad and headquartered in al-Qatania near Damascus, is an elite armored force of fifteen to twenty thousand men with hundreds of tanks and other armored vehicles. Its role in commando operations and internal security actions is unique among regular army units. It led the Syrian invasion of Lebanon, occupied Aleppo, and helped crush the Hama uprising. During the opposition period (1978–82), it also carried out search-and-destroy missions in the Syrian countryside, striking at villages believed to harbor opposition sympathizers or cadres. Because the Third Division plays such a prominent political role, it can be ranked with the Special Forces and defense companies. But its strictly intelligence role is limited, and it is rarely involved in arrests, interrogation, or similar activities.

The Defense Brigades (Saraya al-Difa' 'an al-Thawra, or Brigades for the Defense of the Revolution) are led by Rif'at al-Asad and headquartered in the al-Mezze area of Damascus. They were founded in 1971 at the beginning of the Asad presidency to protect government buildings from possible coups. Though more or less defunct today, the Defense Brigades grew during the late 1970s to as many as twenty thousand men—more than a full army division—at the height of their power in the early 1980s.[33] Composed of four elite brigades (three armored and one mechanized), they were even more heavily armed than the Special Forces. This military force was used to shield the regime against internal dissent and potential coup-makers, but when Rif'at turned it against his brother, the brigades were disbanded.

The Defense Brigades dressed in distinctive, light-reddish combat fatigues, which set them apart from other military and security forces. More than any other unit, they were led and manned by 'Alawis and—to a lesser extent—other minorities such as Christians, Druze, and Ismailis. The brigades had an active intelligence department, with branches for investigation, arrest, and interrogation, headed by Rif'at's son-in-law, Mu'in Nassif. They also ran several interrogation centers, including the Sha'lan Detention Center on the airport road outside Damascus.

When Rif'at was exiled after his abortive bid for power, Mu'in Nassif replaced him as commander and supervised a shrinkage of the forces. After two assassination attempts on high-placed enemies of Rif'at in 1985, Hafez decided to destroy his brother's power base and dismantle the brigades. Some intelligence personnel transferred to other security services, while the bulk of the forces were reorganized into a new armored division under the command of Gen. Hikmat Ibrahim. The much-feared brigades exist no more.

The Military Police (al-Shurta al-'Askariya), headed by Gen. Sari Rustum, theoretically falls under the jurisdiction of the Defense Ministry and the General Staff, but may operate semi-independently under the influence of Military Intelligence chief 'Ali Duba, whose headquarters is located nearby. Though it retains its role as a police force for the armed services, it has also assumed intelligence responsibilities in the civilian sector. In recent years, it has arrested dozens of civilian political activists.

Military Security (al-Amn al-'Askari) is a branch of the regular armed forces. Under the command of the General Staff, it is not controlled by 'Ali Duba's Military Intelligence. Though its primary focus is the armed forces, the agency has arrested many civilians over the years, especially in the period 1980 to 1982. Recently, it has been far less active in the civilian sector; no civilian arrests by this agency have been reported for the past two years. It remains as an active security service within the ranks of the armed forces.

5

PRISONS AND TORTURE

The journey of a Syrian prisoner is long and harrowing. Soon after arrest, the mukhabarat bring their captive to a place of temporary detention, usually an interrogation center. Here, they hold the prisoner incommunicado—cut off from all contact with family, friends, a lawyer, a doctor, or any other link with the outside world. The detainee confronts only inquisitors bent on wringing out a confession, information, and promises of future loyalty.

Judging from reports of those arrested, roughly half of all detainees are released soon after interrogation.[1] But the mukhabarat may also decide to hold the captive indefinitely. In this case, there will be no charge, no trial, and no sentence—just a decision made by nameless security officials. The prisoner may be held indefinitely at the interrogation center or, if lucky, transferred to a long-term prison facility.

On arrival at the prison, the prisoner is sometimes greeted with beatings, humiliation, and other abuse. He or she will then join tens of others in a foul, communal cell. There the prisoner will wait and suffer, with worsening health and deadened spirits, until he or she is released or dies. Scarcely a clan in all Syria has not had some of its members imprisoned, and so been taught the cost of opposing the Asad regime.

INTERROGATION AND TORTURE

Authorities routinely torture and severely mistreat Syrian prisoners, especially during interrogation. The mukhabarat use torture to extract confessions and secure information about others active in opposition organizations. They also use torture to punish, humiliate, and intimidate prisoners into renouncing their political affiliations and promising fidelity to President Asad.

In the basement of the Military Interrogation Branch, Damascus's largest interrogation center, is the Torture Courtyard (Saha al-Ta'dhib), which is surrounded by six or seven rooms where torture and interrogation are constantly taking place. Other facilities are similarly equipped with special rooms, staff, and apparatus for torture.

Interrogation sometimes begins immediately after arrest, but prisoners may be held in these centers for days—even weeks—before their interrogation commences. Severe mistreatment usually begins during this time to break the prisoners' spirit and will to resist. Guards may prevent captives from sleeping, force them to stand on one leg or to crawl on the floor, and pour boiling or freezing water on their naked bodies. Sounds of the torture of other prisoners echo through the halls.[2] Prisoners' fear builds and their physical strength ebbs as food is withheld and guards assault them with curses and threats.

Mistreatment includes psychological torture. In addition to hurling insults at the prisoners, guards tell them that their family members have been arrested and are being tortured, warn them of impending tortures, and threaten to kill them outright. Sometimes prisoners are told that a phony accidental death will be arranged: they will be thrown from a high place or killed in a car accident. Authorities sometimes even fake summary trials that invariably end in a death sentence.

Fierce beatings, however, are the most common form of torture. These can lead to permanent disability or death. Prisoners are kicked, whipped, and beaten all over their bodies—including their faces and genitals—with sticks, metal rods, leather straps, ropes, electric cables, rubber truncheons, and fists. Prisoners may face many methods of beating simultaneously.

But the period of interrogation makes this early abuse seem mild. Once questioning begins, those who do not or cannot answer confront special torture machines and methods designed to drive their bodies to the breaking point. Torture and interrogation can last for days or weeks, in rare cases months or years.

Prisoners under interrogation are often mistreated day and night. They are deprived of sleep. Guards beat, slap, and punch them continually—at mealtimes, when moving from cell to interrogation and back, or when using the toilet. Guards insult and threaten them, force them to stand naked for hours—sometimes in the freezing cold—and extinguish their cigarettes on sensitive parts of prisoners' bodies. Even when in their cells, prisoners live in fear of further sessions of interrogation. Here is the account of one prisoner who was tortured by Military Intelligence in Damascus:

> At first they put me in the *dullab* [tire] and beat me at least a hundred times on my feet. By the end, my feet were so swollen and bloody I couldn't walk, so they had to drag me along the floor to the interrogation.
>
> The interrogation committee asked me questions. "Who were you working with? Who were your contacts?" they shouted. A guard punched

me on my back and spine. Then they sent me back to the torture room, where an officer had an electric apparatus. Guards connected up wires to my body and they ran the current through me. As the officer turned up the voltage, I passed out several times and they had to throw water on me to revive me.

I was not given any food at all for four days. In one very bad torture I was tied upside down to a ladder and whipped and kicked. I was kicked in the face so that blood was pouring out of my nose and mouth. I could barely breathe.

They kept on for over a month and during that whole time I had very little to eat. I wore only underwear, which turned black with dirt and blood. It was hard to sleep because of the noise and the pain and I didn't even have a blanket to sleep on. By the end I was almost dead.[3]

Like this former prisoner, many others speak of the *dullab*—or automobile tire—as a common form of torture. The victim lies on his or her back, confined within the tire, with feet and buttocks through the bottom and knees and upper body through the top. Interrogators then beat the exposed soles of the feet and buttocks—perhaps a hundred times or more.

A related torture is called *al-farruj* (the chicken). Here the victim is tied to a bar resembling a roasting spit and is exposed to terrible beatings—on the back, buttocks, shoulders, head, and legs. Those who have been through these tortures say that people often pass out from the pain and cannot stand up for hours or even days afterward. Lying down to sleep is also virtually impossible because of the pain.

But other torture machines are even more horrible. There is *al-'abd al-aswad* (the black slave), to which the victim is strapped. It forces a heated metal skewer into the victim's anus. *Al-ghassala* (the washing machine), is a spinning drum into which victims must put their arms. As it rotates, the arms are caught, and arms, fingers or both are crushed and mangled. *Al-kursi al-Almani* (the German chair) has perhaps the worse reputation of all. It is a metal chair with hinges on the back. The victim is strapped in and part of the back is lowered backward, causing unbearable pain in the spine, neck, and legs. In a variation, knives are attached to the chair, cutting into the victim's flesh as the chair rotates. Victims often lose consciousness and some suffer permanent damage to their back and limbs.

The Syrian mukhabarat's torture methods are as varied as they are cruel: electric shock, sexual abuse, extraction of fingernails and toenails, breaking limbs, hanging the victim in the air, stretching the body to breaking point, burning, drowning, or cutting with razors. Amnesty International, which has monitored torture in Syria for many years, has recorded thirty-eight forms of torture in use today.[4]

Not even minors have been spared. Several teenagers—arrested as hostages, as political activists, or for some other "offense"—have been tortured. Haitham Kamel Mustafa, a political activist, was only fourteen when he was arrested in 1980. He was tortured and jailed six years before being released. In 1987, Military Intelligence arrested and tortured three fifteen- to sixteen-year-old Jewish youths in Damascus. All were released in 1988, but one remains partially paralyzed.

For people believed to be of any importance in the political opposition—even those seen as "uncooperative"—torture is especially long and intense. Authorities have occasionally continued to torture prisoners for years. The Military Interrogation Branch in Damascus is the scene of flagrant cases of this kind. Riyad al-Turk, general secretary of the Communist Party-Political Bureau, has reportedly been held and tortured and abused there for over nine years. His bones have been broken, his hearing and eyesight have been impaired, and his heart has been weakened. He has been so systematically tortured that he has been rushed to the hospital at least six times on the verge of death. His case is well known, but many others suffer in obscurity.[5]

Several persons abducted from Lebanon are among the long-term victims of the Military Interrogation Branch. Palestinian military officer Hassan Dib Khalil has been tortured in Damascus since his arrest in Tripoli in 1983, and Muhammad Daud, another Palestinian, has been tortured and held in solitary confinement since his arrest in Lebanon in 1985. Two other Palestinians from Lebanon, Diab Muhammad and Fayez ʿArafat, have been held and tortured for similar periods. An unidentified prisoner died under torture in this same place in fall 1989.

FAMILIES AND HOSTAGES

If the mukhabarat arrive at the home of a wanted person and that person has fled, they may take one or more family members as hostages. Hostage-taking was fairly common in the late 1970s; during the worst period, between 1979 and 1982, hundreds were taken. Many were women family members of Muslim Brothers. The mukhabarat routinely threatened them with sexual abuse and sometimes carried out those threats.

Security forces continue to take relatives of Muslim Brothers hostage, but do so less frequently for the secular opposition except in major round-ups or in cases considered especially important. When the mukhabarat take a woman hostage, especially an Islamist, the threat of what may happen to her exerts tremendous pressure on the fugitive and family.

Among the secular parties, women and whole families are sometimes involved in political activity, so it is not always clear who is a hostage and who is a suspect. Usama, Numair, and Mazin 'Asur al-'Askari are three brothers who were arrested in 1983 for their work with the Party for Communist Action while attending the University of Aleppo. In 1988, their sister Lina was held as hostage in lieu of another sister. In another striking case, on March 20, 1986, authorities arrested five family members and held them hostage for Palestinian journalist Samir al-Hassan.

If a fugitive does not surrender or is not captured, authorities may hold a hostage for several years. Grenda al-Jundi, a former science student from Aleppo, has apparently been held hostage for her father, Khalid al-Jundi, since the summer of 1984—six years so far. And her case is not unique.

The mukhabarat often holds onto the hostages even after the the fugitive is captured or surrenders. Mazin Rabi', a twenty-two-year-old Palestinian student, was arrested in early April 1986 with his sister Safa', both as hostages for their brother Jamal, an agricultural engineer and journalist. When Jamal was arrested later that month, Safa' was released. But Mazin remained in custody, under intense interrogation. According to reports from former prisoners, he has twice attempted suicide because of the brutality of his torture.

In a few cases, the mukhabarat even take hostages *after* the arrest to put pressure on the principal during interrogation. Hostages have reported being threatened with torture—and occasionally actually tortured—in front of the other family member.[6] Hostages have also been taken for escaped prisoners. In one documented case, no fewer than seven relatives were taken for Hamud Qabani in late 1984. Three were held for six years.

The mukhabarat may also put other kinds of intense pressure on family members. Prisoners' spouses may lose jobs, and families may be watched continually and isolated from their local communities. One woman reported what happened when her husband went into hiding:

> The principal of my school called me in and told me I could not work there anymore. I asked her why, and she said it was on orders from the mukhabarat. I protested and said that I was one of the best teachers at the school. She knew that, but there was nothing she could do. I could tell she was upset. I even went to the person who was in charge of education in the city. She knew me and was sympathetic, but she said that even if the prime minister and the minister of National Education approved my job, the mukhabarat could prevent it. Later, when I tried to get other jobs, the same thing happened, the Amn al-Siyassi blocked it. Our situation became very difficult.[7]

Another person reported: "People avoided us in the street. Even good friends would not come into our home. They knew we were being watched and felt that if they were seen near us that they, too, would be suspect. We felt very isolated, even though we knew that people secretly supported us. It was especially difficult in Syria, where all life is lived together in the local community."8

DEATHS IN CUSTODY, DISAPPEARANCES, AND SUMMARY EXECUTIONS

Deaths in custody usually result from torture or suicide. The two are closely connected. The authorities sometimes claim that prisoners have killed themselves when they have actually died under torture. And some prisoners do kill themselves—to escape the horrors of torture.

Human rights groups have documented about a dozen deaths in custody in Syria since the mid-1980s.9 Many more died during the fierce crackdown against the opposition from 1979 to 1982. Other cases probably go unreported because of families' fear of retribution. In Syrian-controlled Lebanon there are almost certainly more cases, but documentation there tends to be thinner.10 Recent reports from the United Nations Commission on Human Rights, Amnesty International, and the Arab Organization for Human Rights all express concern about death under torture.

The family is sometimes told that the prisoner died from natural causes or committed suicide; at other times, the mukhabarat disposes of the body and the family learns of the death much later, or never. In some cases the body is delivered in a sealed coffin which the family is told not to open. We have learned the fate of some prisoners from the testimony of other prisoners, from families who have dared to open such coffins and have noted the marks of torture, and from word leaked out through family networks.

Some of the recent documented cases follow:

'Abd al-Razaq 'Abazid, a member of the Communist Party-Political Bureau, died in custody in spring 1989. The mukhabarat arrested him in February 1988 in Dar'a and detained him without charge or trial. He was tortured at the Military Interrogation Branch in Damascus and his body was returned to his family on April 23. The family examined the body and reported that it bore the marks of torture.11

Ihsan 'Izzo died November 14, 1987, in Saydnaya Prison of heart failure following severe torture. Authorities apparently transferred his body to al-Mezze Prison Hospital to make it appear that he had received medical treatment before dying. The mukhabarat made the family bury the body immediately in Damascus rather than inter it in their home village.12

Muhammad al-'Arraj, a teacher from Lataqia who was a member of the Party for Communist Action, was arrested in late 1987. The mukhabarat transferred him to the Palestine Branch interrogation center in Damascus, where he died under torture in January 1988. His body was never returned to the family.[13]

Sulaiman Mustafa Ghaibur, a Syrian soldier from Hama, was tortured to death in 1986 while in the custody of Military Intelligence after he was found with prohibited literature. The mukhabarat returned his body to his family, telling them he had committed suicide in prison. The family disregarded instructions to bury the coffin immediately, examined the body, and discovered bruises and bullet wounds in the neck. He was apparently shot after dying under torture to make an explanation of suicide seem more plausible.

Amin Nassur, a university student, died in 1983 after three years in prison. Guards reportedly threw his body out a third-story window to make his death appear a suicide. Examining his body, his family found marks of torture, including burns induced by heavy electrical shocks.

An unidentified Palestinian died under torture in the Military Interrogation Branch in October 1989.

Disappearances also occur in Syria. In fact, all Syrian political prisoners "disappear" for a while. After someone is arrested, families are not told where the prisoner is, or even whether he or she is dead or alive. This disappearance may last for weeks or months. Eventually, the prisoner is released or the family discovers the captive's whereabouts from prison authorities, the mukhabarat, or a political organization.

Occasionally, however, the family is never informed. When questioned, the authorities may pretend never to have arrested or detained such a person. One especially long-standing case of this kind is that of Joseph Hammam, a Lebanese chauffeur abducted from Beirut in 1970 apparently because he witnessed an assassination in Beirut involving Syrian security forces. In spite of reports that he was seen in Syrian prisons, his family's inquiries have never been answered and his whereabouts are unknown.

In some cases, "disappeared" people believed dead are later discovered to be alive and in prison. Tawfiq Draq al-Siba'i, a medical doctor, disappeared after his arrest in May 1980 and was thought to have been killed in the Tadmur Prison massacre. Four years later, he was found to be alive in al-Mezze Prison. He is still being held.

Prisoners have also "disappeared" while in prison. Khalil Brayez, a writer and former Syrian military officer, was held in al-Hassakeh Prison for many years during his fifteen-year sentence. Two months after his sentence expired in October 1985 he was still in jail and has not been heard from since.

Within Syria, forces independent of the government are never responsible for disappearances. Although it may deny responsibility, the government controls all arrests and detentions, on whatever grounds. Nor is there recent evidence that groups other than the mukhabarat engage in abduction or political murder. Disappearances—other than short-term vanishings following arrest—are now relatively infrequent. But there are still many reports of disappearances at the hand of Syrian forces in Lebanon.

Summary executions began as a Ba'thist practice in the summer of 1963, just four months after the party seized power. Nasirist officers who had attempted a coup but surrendered were not pardoned or exiled, as had been previous Syrian practice. Instead, they were brought before a summary court and immediately shot. Later coup efforts were handled in the same way.

In 1979, the government tried a new kind of summary execution in response to the mass-based opposition movement and the assassinations of various figures in the regime. Security forces began to execute political prisoners, usually without even a summary trial, on presumption of guilt. Sometimes there were mass killings.

During the next three years, the army and mukhabarat summarily executed several thousand people in Hama, Aleppo, and elsewhere (see chapter 2). If the killings at Jisr al-Shughur and Sarmada in 1980, the Hama killings in 1981 and 1982, and other instances of summary executions in Damascus, Deir al-Zor, Homs, and elsewhere are added to this figure, it would appear that about fifteen hundred people were summarily executed in that period outside of prisons.[14]

The law of July 8, 1980, which made membership in the Muslim Brothers punishable by death, provided the justification for these killings. Because the law allowed direct execution on arrest, security agents sometimes killed suspects right in their apartments or on the street.

During these years security forces also executed hundreds in prisons, especially in Tadmur Military Prison, where many Islamists were held. Security forces killed over a thousand prisoners in the Tadmur massacre of June 27, 1980.[15] And, as many former prisoners have reported, hangings took place each week at Tadmur, al-Mezze, and other prisons. One former prisoner told Middle East Watch that at the height of the killings, a dozen or more prisoners were executed in al-Mezze every week. Another reliable source, someone who was held in Tadmur from 1981 until 1983, estimated there that were over six hundred executions in the prison during that time—an average of one a day. From the information available, we estimate that from 1979 to 1982 authorities summarily executed at least one thousand people inside Syrian prisons in addition to those killed in the Tadmur massacre.[16]

If the death toll outside and inside prisons are combined, we arrive at a total of 3,500 summary executions. At least 1,500 of those killed in the Hama uprising should probably also be included, since security forces executed at least that number both individually and in groups. This yields a minimum figure of 5,000 killings in four years, a rough estimate of the magnitude of summary executions at their height.

The situation has improved since the events in Hama in February 1982. Nevertheless, the Arab Organization for Human Rights (AOHR) reports cases of summary executions in Tadmur Prison in 1984 and in Sheikh Miskin Prison in June 1985.[17] In 1985, the AOHR sent a letter to President Asad that, among other things, inquired about one hundred people it claimed were summarily executed in Tadmur Prison, fifty-two of whom were named in an attached list.[18]

Since then, there have apparently been few summary executions, although the U.N. Commission on Human Rights reported in 1989 that it was investigating twenty-nine executions in Tadmur Prison "in recent years." According to the information of the U.N. special rapporteur, these prisoners were executed immediately after a summary trial in which they were given neither the right to legal defense nor the right to appeal.[19]

Syrian forces are reported more recently to have executed hundreds in Lebanon. In December 1986, Syrian commandos and security forces, acting with Lebanese groups under their control, killed over two hundred unarmed people in the Lebanese city of Tripoli. And in February 1987, Syrian forces entering Beirut are reliably reported to have executed twenty-five Hezbollah supporters in cold blood and to have hunted down Lebanese and Palestinian opponents of Syria in their apartments, killing many dozens outright and dumping their bodies in the streets. These cases did not involve combat and are clear examples of executions.

PRISON CONDITIONS

Physical conditions in Syrian prisons are poor. Buildings are in disrepair, cells are filthy, and food is minimal. Not surprisingly, perhaps, Syrian authorities have not permitted international monitors to enter these prisons.

Prisons in Syria vary, of course, but they have many features in common. Prisoners usually share large, communal cells with anywhere from 20 to 150 cellmates. Even cells that were built for a single person sometimes hold 5–10 inmates. Some are so crowded that prisoners cannot sleep lying down; they must either crouch on the floor or sleep in shifts while others stand.

Prisons rarely provide real bedding. At best, prisoners receive a plain cotton mattress a couple of inches thick; more commonly, inmates get one to four thin blankets, which must serve as both mattress and cover and provide little cushioning against the hard, damp floor.[20]

Sanitary conditions are usually very bad and toilet facilities are minimal. In

Tadmur and several other prisons, cells lack toilet altogether. Prisoners are allowed outside the cell to go to the bathroom only at fixed times—usually twice a day at most—which proves a source of great discomfort. Guards sometimes beat inmates en route.

The foulness of the cells can scarcely be imagined; lice, infected wounds, disease, and unwashed bodies are everywhere. But prisoner solidarity and mutual support help the inmates survive. One prisoner described the harsh conditions in a Damascus prison thus:

> There were about eighty of us living in just seventy square meters, with only one toilet in the cell. After being alone in the interrogation cells, it was good to be with others. Though we were very crowded, we could talk. The cellmates shared food, comforted those who were worried or depressed, and massaged those with bad pains. But it was very crowded. And the wait for the toilet in the morning was excruciating if you were toward the end of the line. Some eventually became incontinent, which worsened the hygiene problem.[21]

Hygiene is also lessened by the infrequency of opportunities to bathe. Many prisoners report getting only one cold shower every week or two. Light and ventilation are also inadequate. Some prisons have underground cells with no outside air or light except what comes through iron grates in the ceiling.

A number of prisons are unheated. Syria can be cold in the winter, and nights in spring and fall can be quite chilly in many parts of the country. The usual prison garb is not very warm, so prisoners are likely to get colds, bronchitis, and pneumonia. Insufficient food worsens their defenses so that over time they become weaker and weaker, increasing their susceptibility to diseases of all types.

Prisoners whom the authorities want to punish are sometimes held in the harrowing conditions of solitary confinement. There have been reports of inmates confined in tiny cells only one meter high and filled with excrement, with no human contact and almost no food for days and even weeks on end. Solitary confinement under marginally better conditions can last for months and even years.[22]

Exercise is also limited. Authorities usually allow inmates fifteen minutes of daily exercise in the prison yard, but some prisoners are given much less opportunity and some receive none at all (interrogation facilities almost never provide exercise). This exacerbates the effects of mistreatment. Sometimes "exercise" itself is a form of abuse. Prisoners report being whipped and beaten, kicked, stepped on, forced to crawl on the ground, and humiliated in other ways during exercise periods.

Food is poor or downright revolting, and prisoners may get either no food or just one meal a day as punishment. Even a full complement of meals provides little nutrition. Dinner might be watery soup and bread, perhaps with some cracked wheat or yogurt. At best, prisoners are fed meat only once or twice per week. Many inmates rely on food brought during family visits, but guards usually help themselves to this food, especially meat. Some prisoners also buy food from the outside, but prison guards charge exorbitant prices that many cannot afford.[23]

Laundry is another problem. Prison authorities often do not provide clean clothing or an opportunity for prisoners to wash their clothes. In some cases, inmates have to pay for laundry. Again, families often fill the gap, either by bringing fresh supplies or by bribing prison officials to allow an inmate to use the laundry. In one case, friends tried for months to persuade high officials to let them send a few clean shirts to an important political prisoner. Finally, an answer came: it had been decided "at the highest level" that no clean shirts were to be allowed.[24]

The terrible physical conditions appear to be part of the official effort to punish the prisoners and break their morale. But some of the bad conditions may be ascribed simply to corruption. Prison personnel are said to steal from the food budget and sell supplies. They also steal money sent to prisoners and charge inmates fees to improve their conditions—even for such basic privileges as exercising, washing, or using the toilet.

Some prisons are worse than others, and in general, military prisons are worse than civilian ones. Tadmur Prison is considered the worst of all. At the interrogation centers of Military Intelligence and Palestine Branch, discomfort, filth, and cruelty continue to test the limits of human endurance. By contrast, former leaders in the Salah Jadid group, who have been held since 1970 in al-Mezze Prison, enjoy minor comforts, including a radio in the cell, specially cooked food, access to books and newspapers, and broader-than-usual visiting rights. But this is rare.

Conditions also have varied over time. Between 1980 and 1982, when prisons were crowded with opposition activists, prison authorities were especially punitive. Frequent hangings in all facilities made prisoners extremely nervous. Today, conditions in most prisons, though still very bad, have improved: there is less crowding, no summary execution, and less brutality toward long-term inmates. Conditions at Syrian facilities in Lebanon, however, are said to be reminiscent of those earlier times.[25]

PRISONER PROTESTS AND STRIKES

Every once in a while, in spite of assured punishment for rebels, prisoners will protest their condition, either alone or en masse. Reports leak out each year of hunger strikes and other protests in nearly every Syrian prison.

Ghassan Najjar, an engineer imprisoned in the crackdown on professionals in 1980, has reportedly gone on two hunger strikes in recent years—once to protest his being held without charge and once, with others, to protest conditions in 'Adra Prison. According to reports from fellow inmates, prison guards beat him so badly when trying to force him to abandon his hunger strikes that he had to be taken to a hospital, where he was treated for spinal injuries and a heart condition. Recent reports say that he has again been hospitalized.

In the past two years, inmates at several facilities have staged hunger strikes. In Saydnaya Prison, they protested torture and mistreatment, while a strike in Tadmur Prison protested the extreme mistreatment of prisoner Munif Mulhim. In July 1989, Ahmad Swaidani, diplomat and former member of the Ba'th party Regional Command, is said to have gone on a hunger strike in al-Mezze Prison to protest the twentieth anniversary of his incarceration.

The authorities' retaliation is invariably harsh, and sometimes deadly. The AOHR has charged that striking prisoners in June 1985 were given an ultimatum to end the strike or die. When they did not capitulate, AOHR says, some were gunned down with automatic weapons.[26]

VISITS

Most prisoners are allowed periodic visits once they have been interrogated and placed in a regular prison. The main obstacle is that visitors often do not know where they are. Families must sometimes resort to connections, friends, family networks, bribes, and endless visits to those in authority to locate their loved ones. They may have to guess a location based on past patterns of arrests or wait until they receive news from a released cellmate.

Authorities in civilian prisons are generally more likely to allow visits than are those in military prisons. Regular visits are more widely reported in 'Adra Civil Prison or in the central prisons of Aleppo or Lataqia, for example. Tadmur Prison inmates are unlikely ever to see their families. Of course, some prisoners are held in facilities far from their families, making visits that much more difficult.

Visits are entirely at the discretion of the authorities, who often suspend visiting rights to put pressure on the prisoner or the family. They sometimes allow visitors to arrive at the regular time, keep them waiting outside all day long, and then send them away. This harassment can be repeated for days.[27]

Visiting is typically allowed twice a month. Family members are allowed into a special meeting area with bars on one side. The prisoner enters another barred area opposite. In between is a corridor, patrolled by one or more guards. Under such conditions, only the most perfunctory conversation is possible. All gifts are given to the guards, who take what they want before passing the prisoner what remains.

Sometimes, only bribery makes visits possible. The cost may be hundreds of dollars—a heavy burden for most Syrian families—and occasionally more; in Lebanon it is said to reach the equivalent of more than a thousand dollars. Still, many are willing to make great sacrifices to make sure that the prisoner is alive and well. Also, once aware of the place of incarceration, the family can begin efforts to secure the prisoner's release.

Ordinary visits are an opportunity to bring prisoners much-needed clean clothes, food, soap, medical prescriptions, and other necessities. These items are so important for the minimal well-being of inmates (including basic nutrition) that the interruption or cessation of visits can be devastating. Only rarely are visitors allowed to bring prisoners letters, photographs, books, newspapers, or other publications. Sometimes the authorities will forbid all gifts and restrict communication to a few words or gestures.[28]

MEDICAL TREATMENT

Political prisoners in Syria suffer a range of illnesses due to prison conditions and especially to torture. Prisoners often report kidney disease, which is probably the result of kicks and punches to the lower back, a common method of torture in Syria. Inmates also frequently suffer from spinal injuries and circulation problems, caused by torture aggravated by the cold and by sleeping on hard, damp floors.

Health problems described by prisoners in the past two years include: inflammation of the genito-urinary tract, stomach hemorrhage, paralysis of the hands and limbs, loss of sight, ulcers, inflammation of the kidneys, and various kinds of heart conditions. Then there are also the more common sores, wounds, broken limbs, burns, inflammations and infections, pneumonia, dysentery, and many other illnesses reported by former detainees. In prisons where sanitary conditions are the worst, prisoners have reported typhoid, cholera, and tuberculosis. With inmates living together in cramped unsanitary quarters, disease spreads rapidly.

Many prisoners suffer from mental disorders as a result of torture. Former inmates report that depression and other mental problems continue well after their release. Some prisoners break down altogether. One former prisoner told Middle East Watch that in his communal cell there were three inmates whose mental condition was so bad that they could no longer take care of themselves and had to be helped by fellow prisoners to eat and wash.

Prisoners suffering serious health emergencies may be simply neglected. One former inmate reported what happened in a Damascus prison in the 1980s:

At 3:00 or 4:00 in the morning, one of the prisoners in my cell began moaning with a severe pain in his chest. We decided it must be a heart attack. We pounded on the cell door and when the guard finally came we asked that a doctor come immediately, saying that the prisoner was in critical condition. The guard said it was not possible to get a doctor at that hour. Anyway, he said, the sick man would not be the first prisoner to die. At about 9:00 the next morning, the male nurse came and asked who was sick. By then, the man had died and his body was already cold. We carried him out and they later disposed of the body. The family was told only that the visits had been canceled. Finally, after a year, we managed to get word out to them.[29]

During the torture of Munif Mulhim in 1983, prison doctors at Tadmur told him he was in danger of dying. "Either you will be released and work with us, or you will die in prison," he was warned, according to former cellmates. Refusing to give in, he was tortured further. He has since developed problems of the urinary tract and cancer of the genitals but has been denied medical treatment. Some two years ago, prisoners at Tadmur went on a hunger strike on his behalf, but it is not known whether he has ever been hospitalized.

Those who enter the prison with existing health problems like diabetes, arthritis, or heart condition are especially at risk.[30] Almost all suffer permanent damage. Some prisoners die while in detention, others not long after. Muhammad Haitham Khoja, for example, died of kidney infection on June 1987, just three weeks after his release.

Most prisons are not staffed by full-time doctors, and many lack even a full-time nurse on call. Medical care for prisoners is grossly inadequate. When inmates ask to see outside doctors, prison authorities routinely turn them down. Occasionally, though, authorities take a prisoner to a hospital for special treatment, but usually only in critical cases when it has been decided that the prisoner should remain alive. Opposition leader Riyad al-Turk has reportedly been rushed several times to the hospital in the past nine years. In prison, he has been not only severely tortured but denied essential treatment for his diabetes. He is known, however, to have been taken to the hospital in critical condition in February 1981, January 1982, December 1983, December 1984, December 1987, and November 1988.

THE POPULATION OF POLITICAL PRISONERS

No one can say how many prisoners there are in Syria, since not even all the prisons and detention centers can be identified. Furthermore, since political prisoners and ordinary criminals are detained in the same institutions, there can be no straightforward count of each group, though they are generally segregated into different cells and often into different sections of the prisons.

It is possible nonetheless, to estimate the number of political prisoners held in Syrian prisons, using such sources as the testimony of former inmates, reports published by Syrian exile groups, by other Middle East human rights organizations, and by Amnesty International, and other published and unpublished accounts. This can be cross-checked with estimates of the size of prisons and detention centers: the number and size of cells and the number of their inmates. (Middle East Watch uses the term *political prisoner* to refer to those held for peaceful expression or association, or those held in apparent reprisal for politically motivated offenses for prolonged periods without charge or trial or after trials wholly lacking in due process. Like the other Watch Committees that make up Human Rights Watch, we do not use the term *political prisoner* for those convicted of crimes of violence in trials that provide a measure of fair process.)

From this information, it seems reasonable to say that the Syrian government holds at least 7,500 political prisoners in the country and in Syrian-controlled territory in Lebanon. This is a conservative estimate. As recently as 1987 Amnesty International reported that 5,000–6,000 political prisoners were being held in Tadmur Prison alone.[31] Our estimate thus appears especially conservative since it includes many Syrian-held political prisoners in Lebanon.

According to our estimate, Tadmur Prison holds 2,500 political prisoners (some think it still has 5,000 political inmates) and 'Anjar Detention Center in Lebanon contains 1,200; these two institutions together account for half of our estimate. The remaining prisoners are scattered over dozens of facilities, of which 'Adra, Saydnaya, al-Mezze, and Kafr Sussa are the most important.

As for the affiliation or nationality of the political prisoners, we can make some educated guesses. Here we are helped by published lists of prisoners—particularly those produced by the Syrian secular opposition—which appear to be highly accurate, though incomplete.[32] Palestinian groups have also published partial lists of their prisoners.[33] From these sources and prisoner testimony, it appears that Syrian prisons hold about 2,500 Islamist prisoners and a similar number of Palestinians.[34] There are also about 1,400 prisoners affiliated with the secular opposition, about 600 Lebanese and other foreign nationals, and 500 in all other categories, such as ex-officials and military officers and those accused of sympathies with Iraq (see tables 1 and 2). High estimates of political prisoners in Syria tend to run about twice those of Middle East Watch, or about 15,000.[35] Such estimates are plausible, but we are inclined to be cautious, recognizing that many of the numbers come from groups that may make exaggerated claims.

Table 1. Prison Population

Prisons	Estimates
Tadmur	2,500
'Anjar (Lebanon)	1,200
Saydnaya	400
'Adra	300
Al-Mezze	200
Kafr Sussa	200
Qatana and women's facilities	400
Local civil and military prisons	600
Interrogation centers and temporary facilities	900
Prisons and detention facilities in Lebanon	800
Total	7,500

Note: These numbers are informed estimates only.

LENGTH OF INCARCERATION AND CONDITIONS OF RELEASE

Few political prisoners in Syria today have been committed by courts to serve specific sentences. In the overwhelming majority of cases, as we have seen, prisoners are simply jailed without charge or trial for an indeterminate time. Some who were tried and sentenced years ago remain in prison though their jail

Table 2. Distribution by Types of Prisoners

Prisoners		Estimates
Islamists		2,500
Palestinians		2,500
Secular opposition group members:		1,400
Party of Communist Action	600	
Ba'th Party-Aflaq	400	
Communist Party-Political Branch	160	
Democratic Ba'th	100	
Nasirists	60	
Sha'biya	30	
Kurds and various groups	50	
Lebanese/other foreigners		600
All others (military, government officials, pro-Iraqis, unaffiliated		500
Total		7,500

Note: These numbers are informed estimates only.

terms have expired. Among them are people who were tried and committed in August 1971 for allegedly attempting to overthrow the regime while in league with Iraq. Among those handed fifteen-year sentences were: Jalal al-Din Mustafa Mirhij, Mustafa Tawfiq Fallah, Hussain Tahir Zaidan, and Mahmud Muhammad al-Fayyad. Four years after their sentences expired they remain in al-Mezze Prison. Another person sentenced about that time to fifteen years is the Syrian author and former military officer Khalil Brayez. He has not been released, and his whereabouts are unknown.

In all cases, prisoners are held for periods that suit the detaining authority. Some are released within weeks, most others within a few months to a year. In one wave of arrests from 1987 to 1988, for example, over two thousand people with alleged connections to left-wing parties, particularly the Party for Communist Action, were detained in all major cities. Roughly a year later, twelve hundred had been released and eight hundred remained in custody.

The mukhabarat are also known to hold political prisoners for very long periods. Mahmud Baidun, a Lebanese lawyer abducted from Lebanon by Syrian forces in 1971, is reportedly still in al-Mezze Prison, more than nineteen years later. His sole "crime" was to have been the publisher for a Lebanese newspaper that supported the regime of Salah Jadid and received Syrian subsidies. When Asad came to power, Baidun was asked to return all the money; he refused and suffered the consequences.

Several dozen—perhaps over a hundred—of those jailed during the early and mid-1970s have not yet been released. In addition to those jailed and tried in 1971 at the outset of the Asad regime, many others were arrested and held without trial later in the decade, quite a few of them Ba'thists with pro-Iraqi leanings.

A much larger number—probably a couple of thousand—have been held since the mass arrests from 1980 to 1982.[36] Sixty-eight engineers and ninety health professionals, for example, have been imprisoned since April 1980. A number of students and many Islamists who were arrested then are also still being held.

Until 1980, family and friends could often buy the release of a prisoner—especially one who was unimportant—for a sum equivalent to several thousand dollars. But prisoners rarely gain their freedom in this way today, and it is said that prisoner release orders can be signed only by Asad himself.[37] In Syrian-controlled prisons in Lebanon, though, the practice of buying one's way out remains common and has greatly enriched many mukhabarat officers. According to some reports, Syrian officials have charged up to fifty thousand dollars, or the local equivalent, for the freedom of a single prisoner.[38]

The reasons for releasing someone are ordinarily only partly related to the individual's case. The regime often frees dozens of prisoners at a time, in keeping with policy and security considerations. It released several hundred Islamic prisoners in 1985 and 1986, for example, as part of a general amnesty. In the early 1980s, when the government's policy on Syria's Kurdish minority shifted, it began to release Kurdish prisoners. And when strategy toward the PLO and other Palestinian groups has changed, these prisoners have also been released.

International campaigns to effect prison releases have had results, notably those aimed toward releasing imprisoned Jews and lawyers. Though the regime pretends to be impervious to international criticism and pressure, these campaigns have unquestionably produced results.

Most prisoners, however, report that the mukhabarat set conditions for their release. This is possible because a general release program toward a particular category of prisoner is simply an opportunity, not a guarantee of freedom. This became obvious in the case of the imprisoned lawyers. Although the regime was under considerable pressure to release all the lawyers arrested in 1980, it continued to hold a few who refused to agree to conditions imposed for their release.

The most common condition—said to have become almost a standard precondition for all political prisoners—is that the prisoner sign a statement promising to cease all political activity and thanking the president for his generosity in permitting the release. Some are also asked to renounce their former political affiliations and declare support for the regime. Another frequent demand is that the prisoner work with the security services as an informer. Refusing these conditions may add years to one's imprisonment. The former Ba'thist leaders imprisoned since 1970 are said to have been offered release in 1981 in return for pledges of support for the Asad government. Their refusals have already brought them nine more years in prison.[39]

Those who refuse may also be subjected to additional torture and mistreatment. One detained lawyer, Thuraya 'Abd al-Karim, was mistreated and held in prison for two additional years after refusing to sign a loyalty statement. Riyad al-Turk and four other prisoners from the leadership of the Communist Party-Political Bureau have also reportedly suffered worsened prison conditions by refusing to criticize their party and to announce their loyalty to Asad.[40]

WHAT THE SYRIAN GOVERNMENT SAYS

The Syrian government has rarely responded to charges of human rights violations, especially to allegations of false imprisonment, abuse, and torture. For ten years it refused to meet with Amnesty International and it has refused to receive a mission from Middle East Watch. It has, however, responded occasionally to allegations that the United Nations Commission on Human Rights has forwarded for comment or that have arisen in commission meetings.

On July 28 and November 9, 1988, the U.N. Commission on Human Rights wrote to the Syrian government alleging that it had killed prisoners through torture and summary executions. On December 21, the Syrian government replied, providing several lists of alleged acts of terrorism, sabotage, and assassination perpetrated by the persons who had been named. The Syrian government also stated that the information in the commission's allegations was "totally unfounded" and was "propagated by terrorist or extremist groups and social outcasts."[41]

Several aspects of this response are worthy of note. Even if the persons were guilty of crimes, they had not been charged or tried. Second, no crimes justify torture or summary execution. Finally, although the Syrian government questioned the validity of the information, it has not permitted international human rights organizations to investigate the charges.

Concerned foreigners have occasionally met with Syrian officials—even with President Asad—over the question of political prisoners. One foreigner reported that Asad become angry, saying: "There are no political prisoners in Syria, only traitors and criminals who want to destroy the country."[42] Asad and his officials have even told other supplicants that those persons whose release they seek have never been in Syrian jails. In one bizarre case, a person seeking information about a prisoner in al-Mezze was told: "We know nothing about such a prison. Give us the address and we will look into it."[43]

In official gatherings, the government constantly insists there are no political prisoners, only common criminals. Syrian representatives to U.N. human rights forums often refer to Syria's laws to "prove" that there can be no abusive treatment or torture in the country. Here is a typical statement made in 1983, one year after the events in Hama:

> As to the right of security of person and protection by the State against violence or bodily harm, whether inflicted by government officials or by any individual group or institution . . . we should like to remind the Committee that any person, victim of such violation, can resort to a competent Court of Justice, penal, civil or administrative, in view of suing a state organ, a civil servant, or any person or group of persons . . . to seek redress . . . and demand reparation for damages.[44]

In March 1986, the Syrian representative made an even more sweeping statement in a discussion of the question of torture:

> I would like to refer here to the constitutional and legal provisions in force in the Syrian Arab Republic. . . . The Syrian constitution stipulates that freedom is a sacred right; that the state shall guarantee citizens their

personal freedom and safeguard their dignity and safety; that the sovereignty of the law is a fundamental principle of the society and the state; that all citizens shall be deemed innocent until the final court judgment is rendered against him; that no person shall be investigated or detained except in accordance with the law; and that no one shall be tortured physically or morally, or be subjected to degrading treatment. The constitutional and legal provisions in force do not permit under any circumstances the subjugation of any citizen to torture or to cruel, inhuman or degrading punishment.[45]

Redress, legal protections, freedom from torture—many Syrian prisoners would find these notions highly fanciful.

DIRECTORY OF SYRIAN PRISONS

There are probably more than a hundred prisons, interrogation centers, and places of detention in Syria where political prisoners (including hostages) are held. One reliable source has published a partial list of twenty-two prisons in Damascus and Aleppo alone; our list names twenty-nine for those two cities.[46] These jails range from enormous centers with thousands of inmates to small local lockups. Some have reputations as places for terrible cruelty, while others are thought to be more benign.

The Syrian government has closed two or three of its oldest prisons and built several large new ones since 1985. Prison capacity has risen and prison populations have fallen, so there is considerably less crowding now than there was seven or eight years ago. In 1990, for instance, Tadmur Prison held only about half as many inmates as it did in 1982.

All prisons fall under civilian or military jurisdiction and are run by bureaus in the Ministry of Interior or the Ministry of Defense, respectively. But the distinction between "civilian" and "military" facilities is not clear-cut for political prisoners. Authorities move prisoners from military to "civilian" prisons and vice-versa without any obvious change in the prisoner's status.

Whatever the prison authority, political prisoners remain at all times under the control of a mukhabarat. Security officials may continue to interrogate and punish them throughout their incarceration. For this purpose, virtually all prisons contain special torture and interrogation facilities.

Central Prison Facilities

Tadmur Military Prison (sometimes known as Palmyra Prison), is the largest and most infamous of Syria's political prisons. Located near the Palmyra oasis, in the middle of the desert between Homs and Deir al-Zor, this institution holds the country's largest number of political prisoners. Harsh treatment, extremes of heat and cold in the desert and the absence of family visits make prison life here especially unbearable. The massacre of prisoners in 1980 has added to Tadmur's grim reputation, as have the many summary executions there—as many as ten hangings per week in the worst moments from 1980 to 1982.

Tadmur Prison has forty-one cells[47] for political prisoners in what is known as the *Jana al-Siyasiyin* (wing for politicals). A typical cell—measuring 5 meters × 20 meters and with no toilet—now holds about 60 to 70 prisoners. Former inmates have said that in 1982 there were 200 or more. Projecting from these numbers, it is possible to estimate that the prison now contains about 2,500 prisoners and that at one time it may have held as many as 8,000.[48] One cell is reserved for minors, including hostages, and another for females.

Tadmur is known as the Islamists' prison, for it is here that many of those suspected of membership in the Muslim Brothers and other Islamic groups have been held. This may explain why the number of inmates has dropped. The government has thinned the ranks of Islamic prisoners through amnesties and many individual releases since 1985. In contrast, a growing proportion of Tadmur inmates are now dissidents from the military and members of the secular opposition.

Al-Mezze Military Prison is located in the al-Mezze section of Western Damascus, within view of the new presidential palace and not far from the Sheraton Hotel. Because of this prominent location, the authorities have considered tearing it down. Apparently, they have transferred many political prisoners elsewhere in recent years, though quite a few remain. According to some recent reports, though, authorities have moved many additional political prisoners—mainly people who have been abducted in Lebanon—into the prison. Altogether, the political prisoner population of al-Mezze may now number two or three hundred.

Al-Mezze is a large prison, with a capacity of about one thousand. Its interrogation facility has sixty individual cells (1.5 meters × 2 meters) and rooms for torture and questioning. Long-term prisoners are held either in twelve communal cells (12 meters × 6 meters) or in twelve small cells (2 meters × 3 meters) for two to eight prisoners. Each communal cell has a single toilet for over fifty prisoners.

Many of Syria's most prominent officials languish in this prison, including former Ba'th party leader and military strongman Gen. Salah Jadid, former President Dr. Nur al-Din al-Atassi and former Interior Minister Muhammad Rabah al-Tawil. Marwan Hamawi, former director of the Syrian Arab News Agency, SANA, is also an inmate.

Some of Syria's longest-held prisoners are to be found in al-Mezze. Jadid, al-Atassi, al-Tawil, and fifteen others, for example, have been here since the Asad coup in November 1970—over two decades. Ahmad Swaidani, an army officer, diplomat, and Ba'th official, was imprisoned for alleged pro-Iraqi ties even before Asad came to power. He has been held in al-Mezze since July 11, 1969—over twenty-one years—without charge or trial.

Khalil Brayez, an author abducted from Lebanon in 1971, was also held here for many years. Other well-known figures have spent time in al-Mezze, including high army officers, cabinet ministers, lawyers, and journalists. Yasir 'Arafat was imprisoned here for a time in 1966; other major Palestinian figures, including George Habash and Salah Salah, have paid longer visits since.[49] In April 1962, Hafez Asad himself spent a few days here.

Al-Mezze is not only the prison for the most famous inmates, it has also been described as having Syria's most international community of prisoners. Here are found Lebanese, Palestinians, Iraqis, Jordanians—people from all over the Arab world and beyond. This is the Syrian prison whose name is best known in Lebanon. The phrase "They took him to al-Mezze" has now become a Lebanese colloquialism for people who disappear; it means "All hope is lost."

'Adra Civil Prison, located in the town of Duma not far from Damascus, is the third major location for political prisoners. This institution, with ninety-four communal cells,[50] holds some 3,000 inmates. Most are ordinary criminals. There is a separate section for political prisoners consisting of ten cells and a separate dining room. Each cell, measuring 10 meters × 5 meters, houses about 32 prisoners, so that there are probably about 320 political inmates altogether.

This prison contains many of the Communists, Nasirists, engineers, and others from the secular opposition. Among the well-known prisoners held here are 'Umar Qashash, former secretary-general of the Syrian Printers Union. He has been held since June 1978—more than twelve years. 'Abd al-Majid Manjouneh, a former minister and member of the council of the Aleppo Bar Association, was held here from April 1980 until his release in April 1989.

Al-Qala' Military Prison was decommissioned in 1984, but it should be mentioned as one of the most prominent landmarks of Damascus and one of Syria's best-known prisons. It is now being renovated as a tourist attraction.

A former fortress of Damascus's rulers, this citadel defends the northwest corner of the old city; the famous Suq al-Hamadiya runs along its southern flank. The large cells of al-Qala' each held about a hundred prisoners. Both common and political prisoners spent time here, including the leadership of the Syrian Kurdish Democratic Party. Conditions in al-Qala', in spite of its age, were considered better than in many other facilities in Damascus, and family visits were allowed. When it was closed, most of its inmates were reportedly transferred to 'Adra Civilian Prison, along with prisoners from Shaykh Hassan Prison, which also closed.

Saydnaya Civilian Prison, a large facility completed in 1987, is located in the

Christian village of Saydnaya, in the mountains north of Damascus. The building is four stories high and has three wings joined at the center like spokes on a wheel. Each wing contains twenty communal cells per floor, measuring 6 meters × 8 meters; on the first floor there are an estimated one hundred smaller cells. Each communal cell presently holds 20 or fewer persons. In 1989, the prison was said to hold about 2,400 inmates, with a regular capacity of up to 5,000, and a potential (with crowding) for up to 10,000.

The government supposedly built the prison for criminal offenders, but authorities have recently brought in an estimated 400 political prisoners. The prison is now equipped with full torture facilities, and at least one prisoner is known to have died there recently after severe torture.

Kafr Sussa Detention Center, built in the late 1970s, is located in the Kafr Sussa area of southwest Damascus, near the headquarters of its parent, the General Intelligence Agency. In addition to three interrogation rooms, the prison is said to contain six communal cells holding about sixty prisoners each, four smaller cells of 3.5 meters × 2 meters with five to eight prisoners, and six solitary cells. Altogether, the prison holds about four hundred detainees.

Although nominally used for temporary detention and interrogation, a number of prisoners report being transferred here *after* their interrogation was completed elsewhere. Kafr Sussa also holds many long-term prisoners. Haitham Kamel Mustafa, the political activist jailed at age fourteen and freed in mid-1986 after six years in custody, was one. Fatima al-Lazakani spent more than three years here before her release in 1984. Some think that about two hundred long-term prisoners are currently held here.

Qatana Civilian Prison, the main women's detention center, is located in the village of Qatana, a suburb southwest of Damascus. It houses ordinary criminals and political prisoners and reportedly mixes both types in the same cell. Women are also held in many other prisons, some of which under Syrian law are supposed to be for men only. These include the Aleppo Central Prison, the Lataqia Central Prison, and even the Tadmur Military Prison. There is said to be another women's prison, the Harasta Central Prison, in the town of Harasta near Damascus, which also mixes common criminals and political prisoners.

Local Civilian and Military Prisons
and Interrogation Centers

Each of Syria's eleven provincial capitals has a central prison (al-Sijn al-Markazi) or civilian prison (al-Sijn al-Madani). Some also have a military prison (al-Sijn al-ʿAskari). These prisons have special cells for political prisoners, though political prisoners may share cells with common criminals.

Almost all of these provincial capitals have interrogation centers—

ordinarily three—which are under the control of Military Intelligence, General Intelligence, and Political Security. Political prisoners have occasionally been detained for long periods in these centers, though they are usually transferred to the regular prisons or to Damascus for further interrogation.

The largest provincial prisons, where the most political prisoners are held, are those in Aleppo, Homs, Lataqia, and Deir al-Zor. Altogether, these provincial prisons hold several hundred such prisoners. In general, though, only those political prisoners considered to be less important are held permanently in the provinces.

Interrogation centers are to be found throughout the country, but by far the most notorious are located in Damascus. The best known and largest include the Kafr Sussa Center of General Intelligence and its Military Intelligence counterparts: Military Intelligence Interrogation Branch, located in the Jamarik area of Damascus, and the Palestine Branch, near ʿAdnan al-Malki Avenue. Military Intelligence also has at least two other centers in ʿAdawi and Qabun.

Interrogation centers are often located in the dark and airless basements of buildings that house the offices of the security service. There are two dozen or more of these centers in Damascus, including General Intelligence's center in al-Qasaʿ in northeast Damascus and Political Security's center in Abu Romana. Each mukhabarat runs at least one major facility, the largest of which are believed to hold more than a hundred detainees.[51] Together, such facilities hold over a thousand persons.

Temporary places of detention hold hundreds or even thousands of people during a large "sweep." The mukhabarat frequently use schools or sports clubs and sometimes, if the numbers are very large, sports stadiums or army camps.

Prisons and interrogation centers in Lebanon, under the control of Syrian security forces, are numerous. Among the most important are al-Mafraza in West Beirut and Madrasa al-Amrikan in Tripoli, both interrogation centers. Torture is common in here but is even more brutally practiced in the largest prison—ʿAnjar Detention Center. Located in a small Armenian town of the same name on the Damascus-Beirut road, just inside the Lebanese border, ʿAnjar holds at least twelve hundred inmates, almost all of whom are political prisoners.

6

ORGANIZATIONS, UNIONS, AND
PROFESSIONAL ASSOCIATIONS

The Asad regime seeks to dominate all organizational life in Syria, not just political parties but trade unions, sports clubs, women's associations, peasant unions, associations of artists and writers—almost any organization, whether it runs kindergartens, studies historical monuments, or shows films. The Ba'th party insists that its members become leaders of these organizations and that Ba'thist policy define their priorities.

Beginning in the mid-1960s, when Salah Jadid and the Ba'thist radicals were ascendant, the regime built a corporatist system of official organizations tied to the government and party apparatus. It constructed these "popular organizations" (al-Munazzamat al-Sha'biya) to mobilize the masses and build a new Ba'thist society. Syria was to become a "popular democracy" with institutions from base to summit uniting the people with the leadership. The regime aimed each organization at a key constituency and created each by passing a special law.

Some of these organizations—like the General Federation of Trade Unions or the National Union of Students—simply incorporated existing institutions. Some, like the Peasant Union, took over and developed smaller organizations, making them into large, national structures. And some, like the Revolutionary Youth Organization, broke new ground. In all, more than a dozen groups came into being between 1965 and 1970, including organizations for athletes, craft workers, teachers, writers, and journalists. Most were closely linked to a bureau in the Ba'th party's Regional Command: the party's Peasant Bureau supervised the Peasant Union while the Bureau of Higher Education supervised the National Union of Students.

These new organizations made positive contributions, especially in their early days. The Women's Federation brought thousands of women into public life and helped them achieve greater equality with men. The Peasant Union gave formerly powerless peasants a voice in local and national politics.

Because of this initial effectiveness, the organizations grew rapidly. According to one estimate, by the early 1970s the popular organizations encompassed as much as a third of the population. The Peasant Union, with 567 village branches, had organized in 15 percent of villages, giving the regime a rural base of support no previous Syrian ruler had ever enjoyed.[1]

The regime jealously guarded these organizations from the opposition's political influence. The charter of the National Progressive Front explicitly excluded the non-Ba'th parties from organizing among students, and Ba'thist leaders informally admonished Front parties not to organize among workers, women, and peasants either. Neither the Front parties nor the opposition, however, heeded these warnings. Among the teachers, the Muslim Brothers had a strong following, while in the trade unions Communists and Nasirists built a firm power base. Between 1978 and 1980, the high point of the opposition, some popular organizations slipped from the party's control—especially at the lower levels—while in others the party's domination was seriously eroded.

The party still had its strongholds, though—especially in the national leadership of the organizations—and it used them to defend the regime against the opposition challenge. In the early months of 1980, officials organized armed militia in most of the popular organizations and set them loose against the "enemies of the people."[2] In February and March of that year, Hafez Asad addressed special congresses of most of the organizations to urge them to take up the "revolutionary" challenge. The regime responded to the opposition with purges, rigged elections, and new organizational rules.

At the Seventh Party Congress, delegates recommended that the leadership "reinforce control over the popular organizations," and that is exactly what happened. During the crackdown of 1980, the opposition leaders disappeared into jails, slipped into exile, or retired to a silent anonymity. The organizations themselves, under a heavy-handed and undemocratic command, lost much of their earlier vigor. Their publications degenerated into didacticism and uncritical praise of the president. Their national congresses came to be little more than platforms for long-winded official speeches. The popular organizations are now virtually moribund, but they continue, marginally, to serve their constituents' interests. The Peasant Union, for example, has pressed the regime for further land reform and easier credit, while the Trade Union Federation recently lobbied to protect public enterprises and prevent privatization. This is a far cry from freedom of association, but it does show that the regime needs the support and cooperation of the popular organizations it helped create—and must concede to them a minimal influence in return.

In addition to the popular organizations, professional associations (al-Niqabat al-Mihni)—from agronomists and engineers to doctors and lawyers—

command an important position in Syrian society. Though organized by government laws, they have always been relatively independent; given Syria's decades-old brain drain, the government treads a little more gently when professionals and intellectuals are involved.[3] These associations were therefore the last to be tamed after the opposition movement of the late 1970s, in which they had played an active role. Ever since 1980—when the regime recaptured control by arresting the old leadership and imposing new leaders and laws— they have refused to collaborate as fully as Asad and his associates would like.

In the case of the lawyers, regional and international organizations such as the Arab Lawyers' Union—which promotes international standards of law and professional autonomy—have counterbalanced pressure from the regime. Doctors, engineers, and other professionals likewise look to international norms and frequently object to what they see as crude and stifling official interference in their affairs. Nevertheless, laws enacted in 1981 have imposed close Ba'th party oversight: the party must approve all candidates for association office and delegates to foreign conferences. Association meetings are illegal if a party representative is not present.

Members cannot simply abandon these organizations and start others. As with the popular organizations, by law there can only be one such body. Nor can individuals easily resign. Lawyers, doctors, and engineers are required to belong to their associations if they wish to practice their profession. Others— artists, teachers, and writers—are also under heavy pressure to participate, for the association provides housing subsidies, special cooperative stores, career advantages,[4] and a vehicle for getting such coveted official permits as travel visas.

Syria has thousands of organizations and associations in addition to the official popular and professional ones. Some rare groups, like the chambers of commerce, retain considerable autonomy and power. Others—such as the film clubs—have, at best, marginal room for maneuver. Most are firmly under the thumb of the party.

The Ba'th party employs both formal and informal means to supervise these groups; even small organizations and informal associations do not escape its net. In one case, the party insisted that its members join—and set the agenda for—an informal club in Aleppo organized to study the city's architecture. The original group disbanded in disgust.[5]

The party simply does not tolerate signs of independent association, however benign the purpose. As a general rule, no private organization can exist without an important, if not dominant, Ba'th presence. At a minimum, no group can hold elections for its governing board unless the Ba'th screens candidates or heavily influences their selection.

TRADE UNIONS

Trade unions emerged in Syria during the French Mandate from the labor conflicts of the 1920s and 1930s in the early days of Syria's modernization. Although workers set up a General Federation of Trade Unions after a general strike in 1938, they did not win the right to organize or strike until after independence. Law no. 279 of June 11, 1946, established these landmark freedoms; further reforms followed in 1948.[6]

In the late 1940s and 1950s, unions grew and fought hard for improved working conditions—often under left-wing leadership. (Some union leaders paid for their ties to leftist parties with stints in prison under the military dictatorships.) On April 5, 1959, two months after Syria's union with Egypt, the new government promulgated Law no. 59, imposing the Egyptian labor code on Syria. Although this code introduced some positive reforms, such as paid sick leave and mandatory notice for layoffs, it effectively shackled the trade union movement by banning strikes and mandating a single labor organization connected to the ruling party.[7]

Soon after the Ba'thist coup of 1963, the new regime began to assert control over the trade union movement, then dominated by Nasirists and Communists. In July, the regime forced out of office the leader of the General Federation of Labor, Nasirist Tal'at al-Thaghlabi, and replaced him with a Ba'thist, Khalid al-Hakim. Two months later, al-Hakim joined the party's highest body, the Regional Command. This joint directorate between the top leadership of the party and the unions continued for years.[8]

The new regime enacted a sweeping new trade union law giving workers several freedoms not allowed under the preceding Nasirist code on February 28, 1964. This new law, Decree 31, gave workers the right to freely elect representatives at all levels and ended bans on trade union political activity and on opposition to the government. Yet strikes and the formation of a competing national trade union, continued to be prohibited.

In spite of the formal ban on strikes, unauthorized labor stoppages were common in the first five years of the new regime. Many leading trade union figures called for workers' self-management and union autonomy from the state. They soon received their comeuppance. Even though Syria's provisional constitution of April 1964 had reaffirmed the principle of union independence from the government, the Ba'thist leadership quickly removed several union figures from their posts, beginning with Yasin al-Hafiz, secretary-general of the Federation.[9]

The purge reached a crescendo on August 21, 1964, when the minister of Labor replaced all members of the Federation's governing bureau with eleven persons chosen by the party—an action made legal by Article 60 of the new labor law passed earlier that year. In a transparent effort to break up the support base of the ousted leadership, the regime also proceeded to restructure the unions according to Decree 31, making industry rather than geographical region their new organizational base. The remaining leadership, assembled in Homs in October 1964, protested in vain.[10]

The government tested its newfound control during the December 1964 and January 1965 union elections. Although many workers spoke out against official meddling, the regime intervened openly, promoting fraud to aid its candidates. Not surprisingly, Ba'thist candidates won most seats. A few months later, at the Fourteenth Congress of the Federation, held April 15–23, 1965, the Ba'thists consolidated their control, naming Khalid al-Jundi president of the Federation.

During the rule of Jadid, the regime and the party further tightened the screws on the trade unions. The enlarged security apparatus, in coordination with the pro-Ba'th Federation leaders, carried out several waves of expulsions and arrests. Longtime trade unionists, even those who were party members, began to fear for their safety. In mid-September 1966, two members of the Federation leadership, including the former secretary-general Khalid al-Hakim, took refuge in Jordan and denounced the "anti-democratic practices" of the regime.

Under the direction of al-Jundi, the unions set up armed workers' militias (al-Kata'ib al-'Umaliya) in the summer of 1966 to defend the regime against its enemies. Jundi had been a close ally of Jadid, but he, too, soon fell victim to power struggles at the top. Accused in the press of corruption, he was forced to resign his post in July 1967. Five months later, he was charged with murder and imprisoned. After being released, he went into exile in Tunis, and Mahmoud Hadid, another Ba'thist, replaced him as president.

Al-Jundi was followed by Mansour Shadaida, who lasted barely a year. Jadid was unhappy with his stewardship of the union, and before new elections in spring 1968, Shadaida and most of his executive committee were warned not to stand for office. By the time the Sixteenth Federation Congress met in August 1968, Ba'th control over the unions was complete. On June 26, the government had promulgated Law 84, redefining the trade unions, not as independent organizations working for workers' welfare and rights, but as popular organizations, mobilizing people for national tasks.

The new legislation, followed and completed by other laws in 1969 and 1974, not only made it illegal for workers to establish unions other than those already sanctioned by the state[11] but gave the Ministry of Labor broad supervisory control over union finances: over gifts, donations, and legacies, over the financial records of union bodies at all levels, and over the unions' internal financial rules. Henceforth, unions were explicitly instruments of the "workers' state," no longer belonging to the workers themselves.[12]

There were, nonetheless, some gestures to union autonomy. In 1968, the regime enacted a law to set up "Workers' Production Councils." Allegedly a vehicle for self-management, these councils never helped workers exercise independent power, either at the work site, firm, or state level.[13] In public as well as private enterprises, the councils proved no more than political window dressing.

Before taking power in 1970, Hafez Asad had promised to open up the political system. Those promises were never fulfilled. In fact, the National Progressive Front, formed in 1972, worked to prevent any party other than the Ba'th from organizing within the workers' movement (though such organizing continued on a semiclandestine basis). And the Asad regime used its greatly enlarged security apparatus to make sure the trade union movement remained loyal.

At the 1974 Federation Congress, the regime introduced the idea of "political unionism"—the notion that workers should set aside "narrow demands" in favor of long-term efforts to achieve "liberation" and "the construction of Arab socialism."[14] One implication was unmistakable: strikes to win concessions on wages and working conditions were to be discarded for the greater good that the Ba'thist regime claimed to represent.

Although the regime did have its supporters among the working class—its nationalizations, welfare policies, and ideological slogans made it appear to be acting on workers' behalf—few bought the party line. And as political opposition to the regime gathered steam in the late 1970s, many union members joined in.

In spite of the regime's best efforts, the union elections of October 1978 were the most open in years. Opposition groups put forward their own lists, and a number of individual opposition candidates were able to run. Even the official lists, influenced by the political climate of the times, included a number of people who were relatively independent of the regime.

The Ba'th tried to maintain its position through the time-honored methods of fraud and heavy pressure. The authorities arrested potential candidates before the elections, rejected opposition lists for technical reasons, and intervened directly in many of the larger factories. At the Homs Oil Refinery, which employed 1,800 workers, for example, the governor came to the election—supposedly to prevent fraud but actually to try to prevent an opposition victory. The authorities intervened in the same way at the giant (6,000-worker) spinning and knitting mill in Damascus, the Hama steel mill, the country's big cement factories, and other industrial centers.[15]

In spite of these efforts, workers elected many opposition figures. In some unions, entire opposition slates were successful. For the Ba'th, the election was a disaster—and a practical reminder of the limits of its power. But at least the party and regime still controlled the top leadership.

During the late 1970s, strikes and other workplace showdowns also demonstrated the regime's loosening grip. Workers demanding better pay and improved work conditions walked off the job at the Rumeila oil fields in 1979. Unable to break the strike by force and unwilling to lose production, the regime was forced to make concessions. Similarly, the government offered large raises to state employees early in 1980 after pressure from key workers.

But, though conceding ground, officials simultaneously went on the offensive. In June 1978, security forces arrested the Communist leader 'Umar Qashash, secretary-general of the Syrian Printers' Union and the most powerful opposition figure in the union movement. In March and April 1980, the crackdown intensified, especially against unions and union leaders identified with the opposition parties.

In less than three years, the brief ferment of independent activity was over. By the summer of 1982, when union elections were again held, the Ba'th party had reimposed control. That year the Federation Congress again became little more than a platform for official speeches. Opposition since then has been minimal, though there were reports of wildcat strikes in the oil fields and construction sector in the mid-1980s.

In 1985, the regime once more promulgated legislation (Law no. 1) to curb union independence—this time governing the organization of civil service workers and others in the public sector. These workers do not bargain collectively for wages; they "discuss" minimum pay rates, and the responsible government ministry sets the scale. Their unions are especially closely tied to the regime and are under great pressure to conform. One labor activist told Middle East Watch that workers in the military industries sector have been reminded that any industrial action could be considered treason. One study shows how much the unions are now captives of the regime. According to Elisabeth Longuenesse, a French scholar at the University of Lyon who has analyzed Syria's union elections, workers rarely have a choice of candidates.[16] Workers told her that the official candidate list usually follows a set formula: one representative of each tendency within the Ba'th party, one person from a security agency, and one "neutral" or a member of one of the other Front parties. Sometimes this official list is not even voted on. At the Dibs Textile Factory in Damascus, where 2,000 workers are employed, for example, the list in 1982 was simply elected "by proclamation."[17]

This control over their leadership notwithstanding, unions continue to do more than just transmit discipline and ideology downward. They still function

.as an interest group, channeling information and pressure up to those in power. In an extensive study of trade union publications, Longuenesse found that they continued to speak quite freely of local conditions and worker problems at least until the mid-1980s. And in the past few years, union leaders have lobbied hard—and successfully—against the privatization of state-owned industries.

Asad tolerates union initiatives as long as they pose no threat to his leadership. But the limits of union independence are narrow, and if a union leader goes too far, the response is swift. In 1985, security forces imprisoned a Homs trade union leader when he publicly criticized the president's brother—even though Rif'at had already been exiled.

THE BAR ASSOCIATION

Under the Mandate, the French set up professional associations for doctors, pharmacists, lawyers, and engineers. Though state-sponsored, these institutions jealously guarded their autonomy and soon developed a lively independence. The Bar Association (Ittihad al-Muhamin) was especially active and has played the most prominent role in challenging the actions of successive governments. As early as 1924, it organized a two-week strike to protest a new French-imposed court system.[18] Lawyers remained in the thick of politics throughout the Mandate and during the postindependence years.

The bar clashed increasingly with the Asad regime, especially after the intervention in Lebanon in 1976, when many lawyers gathered petitions and organized protests. In response, the authorities detained two activist lawyers, Tariq Haydari and 'Adil Kayali. Both died in detention, apparently under torture. The Bar Association complained urgently to the government and reported on the cases at the Arab Lawyers' Union (ALU) meeting in Tunis in November 1976.[19]

About this time, Rashad Barmada and other concerned members of the Bar Association also set up a Committee for Human Rights to publish accounts of rights abuses and to persuade the government to accept reform. The group was not easily dismissed. Barmada, a leading Aleppo attorney and a pre-Ba'thist minister of Defense from the centrist People's party, was known as a liberal and not an enemy of the regime. Nonetheless, politically active lawyers like Ahmad Muhaffel were forced to seek exile in 1977 as repression mounted.[20]

By 1978, the bar had become a leading force in the secular democratic opposition. After the big government crackdown in May, 217 members of the Damascus Bar Association requested a special plenary congress to address the crisis. Meeting on June 22, they demanded an immediate end to the state of emergency, condemned the use of torture, and passed a motion warning lawyers that they would be subject to professional discipline if they collaborated with the government in illegal acts. On June 29, the Syrian Bar Association, meeting in plenary session, took similar steps. And on August 17, the president of the Syrian bar, Saba al-Rakabi, sent the government a plea that it respect the rule of law, abolish exceptional military courts, and release all those detained without trial.[21]

The leadership of the bar held discussions throughout the summer and fall with Ba'th party officials. When nothing materialized from those talks, the lawyers continued their campaign. On November 11, the General Congress of the Bar in Aleppo voted to support the June resolutions of the Damascus bar. And on December 1, the Syrian Bar Association, in an extraordinary congress, directed its leadership to meet with the president and demand that he end the state of emergency, disband the special courts, and assure the independence of the judiciary. The bar resolutions—adopted by overwhelming majorities— affirmed the unity of the legal profession behind the democratic movement.[22] Just a few days after the Congress, agents of the Defense Brigades assaulted a lawyer and his wife on the streets of Damascus. The Damascus bar responded by calling a one-day strike: all members were asked to refuse to appear before the courts. The bars of Hama, Homs, Aleppo, and Deir al-Zor passed resolutions of support. Again, the regime made no practical concessions, though Asad promised reform in a number of speeches.[23]

In late 1978 and throughout 1979, the opposition gathered force. It seemed the government would have to bend. Did not Asad need allies, some argued, against the violent sectarianism of the Muslim Brothers? Again taking the initiative, the Damascus bar passed a resolution at its congress on August 31, 1979, calling for an end to the state of emergency and respect for democratic rights. But the regime brushed aside the lawyers' campaign and redoubled its repression. Political cases flooded the courts, swamping lawyers with frightened defendants and unwinnable trials.

On March 1, 1980, the Aleppo bar met and decided on a two-hour strike the following day to highlight its call for democratization. In Homs, the engineering, medical, and bar associations again put out joint declarations on March 9. The same happened in Hama two days later.

The government reacted by rounding up several lawyers and throwing them in prison. In spite of the arrests, the Syrian Bar Association continued to fight back, calling a one-day strike for March 31. Associations for the engineers, health professionals, and many others joined the call. On the day of the strike, most magistrates suspended proceedings in solidarity with the striking lawyers.

Although the boycotts were peaceful, the government dealt with them harshly. Nearly fifty lawyers were arrested shortly afterward, including Sabah al-Rikabi, president of the Syrian Bar Association; As'ad Qa'dan, president of the Aleppo Bar Association; Muwaffaq al-Din al-Kozbari, president of the Prisoners' Care Association; Salim ʿAqil, former president of the Aleppo Bar Association; and Rashad Barmada of the Committee for Human Rights.

Continuing the crackdown, the Council of Ministers dissolved all professional associations on April 9, claiming that they had been "infiltrated by reactionary elements" and were dangerous to society. Officials closed down the national and local bars, their executive offices and research bureaus, the Human Rights Committee, and the Prisoners' Care Association. The next day, officials presented new bar associations, with newly appointed officers and executive councils. The legal community was aghast: even in the worst moments of the Mandate, nothing like this had ever happened.

The lawyers quickly mobilized international support for their cause. The Arab Lawyers' Union Executive Committee, meeting in Morocco in June, refused to recognize the newly appointed officers of the Syrian Bar Association. Soon afterward, the ALU Congress declared the government's actions null and void. Other international legal bodies joined the protest. Some even sent delegations to plead with Syrian officials, but the Asad regime refused to change course. Officials were well aware that opposition among lawyers ran deep and that the democratic majority might eventually recapture the new bar. As a precaution, Law no. 39 of August 21, 1981, ordered sweeping changes in the bar, turning it into a corporatist arm of the state and the ruling party.[24]

Article 3 of the new law required that the bar act "in conformity with the principles and resolutions of the Baʿth Arab Socialist Party." Article 4 stated that the bar must "work in coordination with the competent office of the [party's] Regional Command." According to Article 37, no Bar Association Congress could take place unless called and attended by a representative of the Baʿth party. Also under the new law, the Council of Ministers could at any time dissolve the regional or association councils as well as the Bar Association Congress.

Individual lawyers faced tight new regulations. No Syrian lawyer could join an international organization such as the ALU without the approval of the Syrian Bar Association—and hence of the regime. No lawyer could accept a case from a foreign person or entity without permission from the minister of Justice. Security forces were permitted to arrest lawyers and search their premises if they took on clients considered threats to "state security." Lawyers could even be disbarred for similarly vague reasons.[25]

Having muzzled the bar, the regime proceeded to break its spirit and corrupt its ranks. According to information gathered by Middle East Watch, officials systematically undermined the professional practices of lawyers deemed to be unfriendly. For example, officials might post security agents at the entrance of legal offices to scare away clients or pressure magistrates to rule consistently against such attorneys' cases. Increasingly, success in the law has depended on two factors: an attorney's close connections with those in power, and his or her skills at bribing judges and public officials.[26]

As time passed, the regime did release many of the imprisoned lawyers. But in 1985, five years after the original arrests, thirteen remained in custody. None had ever been charged or tried. In May 1986, when the ALU Executive Committee met in Damascus, Asad promised to free the prisoners, and ten were released early in December. But three remained in custody another three years—until April 1989—apparently because they refused to sign a statement thanking Asad for their release and promising to refrain from future political activity.

Throughout the 1980s, the regime kept a very firm hand on the bar, insisting on quiescence and conformity. The party closely scrutinized every candidate for office and packed the ranks of the bar with Ba'th officials, including many not trained as lawyers.

The regime let it be known that it expected lawyers going to foreign conferences to be its apologists and defenders. But in this goal at least it did not succeed. As ALU congresses repeatedly passed resolutions criticizing Syria—in Morocco in 1980, in Tunisia in 1984, and in Kuwait in 1987—Syrian delegates gave silent assent or cautiously left the chamber. In 1987, when a resolution asking the regime to free imprisoned Syrian lawyers again passed without effective opposition from the Syrian delegation, Asad held the bar leadership accountable. Two months later, he forced all members of the executive board out of office in the middle of their terms and installed a more reliable slate. Failing to find a suitable new president among practicing lawyers, the government was forced to pick Hassan Hamdan, not a lawyer at all but a retired security official and former director of Intelligence of the Damascus governorate.

7

MINORITIES

Feelings based on religious, ethnic, or national identity run deep in Syria. Urban neighborhoods often "belong" to one of the many such communities in the country—Christians, Kurds, Armenians, Druze, Jews, or Sunnis. For many Syrians, such identity is a primary fact of life, and the Asad regime—like many past Syrian rulers—has manipulated ethnic and religious feelings to strengthen its hold on power.

Arab Sunni Muslims are the largest group in Syria, making up about 66 percent of the population. After that, the most numerous are the 'Alawi Muslims (about 12 percent), and the Kurds (about 8 percent), who are Sunni but have a separate language and national identity. Christians, another significant minority (about 8 percent), are splintered into a dozen sects, the largest of which are Greek Orthodox and Armenians. There are also Druze (3 percent), Palestinians (2.5 percent), and a number of other small minorities, including Jews and such splinter Muslim sects as Ismailis and Yazidis (see table 3).

A HISTORY OF COMMUNITY CONFLICT: THE LEGACY OF THE MANDATE

The French Mandate in Syria nominally established a modern secular state with, in theory, equality of citizenship; in fact, it relied on what historian Philip Khoury calls the "exploitation of minority differences" as a principal strategy of control.[1] Lacking the money to maintain a large military and administrative presence in Syria, the French sought to keep segments of the population at odds with one another to weaken national solidarity and the anticolonial movement. (They also ranked the Syrian minorities in terms of their supposed intelligence and other "civilized" qualities, placing Westernized Christians at the top and Sunni Arabs, hated for their nationalist opposition to French rule, at the bottom.)[2]

Table 3. Syrian Population by Religious and Ethnic Group

Religion Ethnic/National Identity	Number	Percentage
Sunnis	9,080,000	76
Syrians	7,840,000	65
Kurds	960,000	8
Palestinians	280,000	3
'Alawis	1,500,000	12
Christians	940,000	8
Syrians	740,000	6
Armenians	180,000	2
Palestinians	20,000	—
Druze	380,000	3
Other Muslim	100,000	1
Ismailis	40,000	—
Circassians	30,000	—
Jews	3,800	—
Christian Sects		
Greek Orthodox	320,000	
Armenians	200,000	
Greek Catholics	160,000	
Syrian Orthodox/Jacobites	140,000	
Syrian Catholics	45,000	
Maronites	30,000	
Assyrians/Nestorians	15,000	
Chaldeans	10,000	
Roman Catholics	10,000	
Protestants	10,000	

Sources: Syrian census; Raymond, *La Syrie d'aujourd'hui*, pp. 87–107; Library of Congress, *Syria: A Country Study* (Washington, D.C.: USGPO, 1988); Elisabeth Picard, "Y a-t-il un problème communautaire en Syrie?" *Maghreb Machrek* 87 (January–March 1980), pp. 9–11; *Al-Nashra*, no. 115–16; Interviews, 1989.

Note: These figures are a rough approximation; the Syrian census omits most data of this kind. Total population in 1990 is estimated at 12 million.

One divide-and-conquer technique was to recruit minorities into ethnically homogeneous units of the colonial army and police force. The Troupes Spéciales du Levant included units of Armenians, Circassians, and Kurds, considered to be among the most reliable minorities. The French command used these units as shock troops during rebellions by the largely Sunni Arab populations of the cities. The terrible violence they let loose greatly deepened inter-community antagonisms.[3]

To further weaken their Arab nationalist foes, the French partitioned Syria by cutting away minority-dominated regions. They created Lebanon in 1920 as a separate state dominated by the Christian Maronites. They gave away the province and port of Alexandretta (with its large Turkish minority) to Turkey in 1937. They created ministates within Syria for the Druze in the south and the 'Alawis in the northwest. And they promulgated a constitution that assigned certain seats in the Syrian legislature on the basis of religious and ethnic affiliation.

This added to the bitterness Syrian nationalists already felt over the colonial break-up of their united Arab nation in 1920. What made Syrian nationalists, especially those from the Sunni majority, particularly cynical about minority claims was that the French had justified their policies as being "in defense of minority interests."

But nationalism was by no means a uniquely Sunni enterprise. In the era before independence, the nationalist movement was determinedly secular, a position summed up by the popular slogan "Religion for God, the Nation for All" (Al-Din lillah, al-watan lil-jami'). Syrian Christians were among the founders and leading ideologues of Syrian nationalism. Faris Khoury, a Christian lawyer, became one of the most important nationalist leaders of the late Mandate period, and Michel Aflaq, a Christian schoolteacher, founded the Ba'th party and was its most important thinker. For many Christian intellectuals—and those of other minorities—secular nationalism offered a means of escaping the religious domination of the past. French efforts to "protect" minorities, which simply inflamed differences, did not attract them.

Foreign manipulation of ethnic and religious communities continued after Syrian independence. The United States and Britain, for example, covertly armed bedouin tribesmen and members of the Druze minority in the 1950s.[4] Iraq and Jordan later lent secret support to the Islamic campaign of terror against the 'Alawis.

The extent of intercommunal rivalry and tension in Syria today is difficult to assess. Some warn that Syria could easily fall apart in sectarian strife. But to a recent visitor Syria appeared a relatively tolerant society, with minority communities coexisting fairly successfully.[5] Christians live without persecution in the city of Hama, known in the West for its "Muslim fanaticism." Jewish shops are popular in Damascus. Armenians and other Christians, notably Greek Catholics, are prominent in Aleppo's business, professional, and intellectual community. But to point out such tolerance is not to deny that serious group conflicts exist or to underestimate the regime's responsibility for perpetuating the French legacy of community rivalry as a ruling strategy.

THE INDEPENDENT STATE AND THE MINORITIES

In the early years of independence, the Syrian government's efforts to eliminate sectarianism and forge a single nation were energetic—and harsh. It violently crushed revolts in ʿAlawi- and Druze-populated mountain districts, largely destroying the principal Druze city of Suwaida in 1948 to assert its unchallenged authority over the territory. The government also insisted on a new geographical nomenclature to symbolize the Arab unity of the state: Jabal Druze (the Druze Mountain) became Jabal al-ʿArab (the Arab Mountain).

The Baʿth party constitution of 1947 expresses the fierce desire for unification, which continues to be a feature of official ideology: "The national bond is the sole bond of the Arab State. It guarantees harmony between citizens, puts them in the melting pot of one, unified nation and protects against religious, tribal, racial and particularist fanaticism."[6] In the party's thinking, the fire of nationalist unity would purify all sectarianist impulses, and the government of the day acted firmly to stamp out what it saw as unacceptable expressions of "particularism."

The Press Code of 1948, for example, provided penalties for "inciting to strife among the various sects or elements of the nation." Later, the Law of Associations and Private Organizations of 1958 provided for the "immediate dissolution of an association if it carries out activities of a sectarian nature affecting state security." A statute of 1954 makes it a punishable offense merely to refer to sectarian identity. These and other laws remain on the books and have been used for censorship; almost any independent voice or any claim to discrimination may be interpreted as leading to community "strife."

The Asad regime frequently declares itself to be nondiscriminatory. Not long ago, its representative proclaimed before a United Nations body: "Neither in law, nor in practice, does the Syrian Arab Republic make any distinction, exclusion, restriction or preference based on race, color, descent or national or ethnic origins. In view of the foregoing, the citizens of the Syrian Arab Republic cannot be divided along racial, ethnic or other compact or distinct groups."[7] In fact, the regime makes many such distinctions among its citizens. These categories are powerful dimensions of social consciousness in Syria, not least within the regime, and have led to a number of serious human rights violations.

Ironically, some believe the Asad regime to be the best defender Syrian minorities can hope for. Without a tough ruler like Asad, they argue, Sunni fundamentalists would threaten all non-Sunnis even more than they do now. As the recent reemergence of ethnic tensions in the Soviet Union and Eastern Europe shows, though, the only way to protect minority rights is to resolve community tensions through public discourse and political bargaining.

'ALAWIS

Hafez Asad and many of his associates are 'Alawis, Syria's largest minority community. The 'Alawis, who number about 1.4 million, have their origins in peasant villages in the Jabal al-Ansariya mountain chain near Syria's Mediterranean coast. There they lived in relative isolation until fairly recently, preserving their heterodox beliefs. Extremely poor, many farmed the land of absentee Sunni landlords from Lataqia or Hama (though there were also some 'Alawi landlords). The Sunni-'Alawi tension in Syria has its roots, in part, in this class distinction.[8]

In the 1940s, many ambitious 'Alawi youth entered the army or the Homs Military Academy—admission after 1945 was no longer based on social background—as a way of moving up in the world. And many did rise swiftly in the late 1940s and 1950s as military coups decimated the upper ranks of the officer corps. The Ba'th party also attracted some of these young 'Alawis, including Hafez Asad. By the early 1960s, many noncommissioned and junior officers were 'Alawis. Some of these young officers eventually led the party to power in 1963.

Unable to rely on mass support, the Ba'thist officers turned to reliable co-religionists to secure control over the military. An 'Alawi officer named Salah Jadid assumed control over military assignments and promotions. In 1963, he purged some seven hundred officers, replacing more than half with 'Alawis.

With Jadid's coup in 1966, an 'Alawi network emerged at the heart of the regime. Hafez Asad's coup in 1970 brought even more 'Alawis into top posts in the Ba'th party, security services, and key army units.[9] Since then, the security services and commands of the key military units at the division and brigade levels have been securely in 'Alawi hands. Some two-thirds of Military Academy students and over half of the top ranks of the officer corps are also 'Alawis. The Ba'th party, too, has been strikingly 'Alawi, though less so than the military-security nexus. Both the Regional Command and the Central Committee have had a markedly 'Alawi membership—between a quarter and a half of the total. The is also true of other key party organs.

At the very top, personal connections are narrower than 'Alawi status alone, and include relations to the Asad family, membership in Asad's "clan," or ties to his natal village of Qardaha. Many of the top security chiefs, such as 'Ali Duba and Muhammad al-Kuly, belong to these more intimate circles.

'Alawis have increasingly made large fortunes, usually through their connection to the state apparatus. They are to be found disproportionately among the country's foremost real estate magnates, construction millionaires, and wealthy black marketeers. Muhammad Haydar, for example, amassed a large fortune as the regime's economic chief in the 1970s; his kickbacks earned him the sobriquet "Mister Five Per Cent." Rif'at al-Asad became the richest of them all. With profits from smuggling and protection rackets, he built up an international portfolio of investments, including a casino in Malta, a hotel in Marseilles, a cement factory in East Beirut, a publishing company in Paris, and even a sizable bloc of shares in the Anglo-French Chunnel.

In addition to making money, many 'Alawis have risen through the university and joined the professions and intelligentsia. Although influence and favoritism may have helped some, a number are very gifted and have taken their place among Syria's foremost filmmakers and authors.

The regime has tried to organize the entire 'Alawi community as a base of support with partial success. Jamil al-Asad, another of the president's brothers, founded the 'Alawi-based Imam 'Ali Murtada Committee to galvanize 'Alawis behind the regime in the late 1970s, when it was most threatened. But such a blatantly sectarian group became an embarrassment and Asad disbanded it in 1983. There remain many poor 'Alawis who receive few benefits from the fact that they are so well represented at the top. Many 'Alawi intellectuals are sharply critical of the regime. And many 'Alawis are active in the secular opposition parties, especially in the Party for Communist Action, which is heavily 'Alawi both in its leadership and in its rank and file.[10]

At the same time, Sunnis, together with a handful of Druze and Kurds, have occupied many top posts, even if they may have been excluded from the innermost circles of power. Among the top Sunni officeholders are Vice President 'Abd al-Halim Khaddam, Defense Minister Mustafa Tlas, Ba'th Assistant Secretary-General 'Abdallah al-Ahmar, and Army Chief-of-Staff Hikmat Shihabi. Many of these figures have profited as handsomely as their 'Alawi counterparts. Tlas, for example, has amassed a fortune over the years and owns a well-known publishing company as well as agricultural properties and manufacturing concerns.

Nor has 'Alawi domination of the regime necessarily kept many Sunni merchants and businesspeople from prospering. Among the more prominent are Othman al-'Aidi, owner of the Sham and Merinid hotel chains, and Badr al-Din Shallah, president of the Damascus Chamber of Commerce and a trader in agricultural produce. Christians, such as Armenian construction magnate Pyzant Ya'qubian, also have an important place among the business elite, as do those from other minorities, such as Shi'i tourism king Saib Nahhas.

'Alawi favoritism is far from absolute. Nor is it in any way incorporated in law. But it is reasonable to conclude that the domination of the commanding heights by an 'Alawi clique has soured group relations in the country and detracted from the development of a secular and integrated Syrian society.

OTHER COMMUNITIES: KURDS, JEWS, AND PALESTINIANS

Every community in Syria makes some claim to discrimination, if only as the obverse of 'Alawi favoritism. This book is not the place to examine all such claims, which are often subtle and difficult to test against reality. Instead, we focus on three minorities—Kurds, Jews, and Palestinians—that face obvious discrimination for which the government is largely responsible.

The Kurds

About 960,000 Kurds, 8 percent of the population, live in Syria.[11] Most are Sunni Muslims.[12] They speak their own distinct language[13] and, though curtailed, have maintained distinct customs, including the ancient Persian holiday of Nawruz held at the spring equinox. Although Syrian Kurds have not suffered the extreme persecution of their kinfolk in Turkey, Iraq, and Iran, where they form larger minorities, the Syrian government nonetheless discriminates against them systematically.

The regime forbids any public discussion of the Kurdish question, even banning books that mention the existence of a Kurdish minority. It severely restricts Kurdish cultural and political organizations, bans the use of Kurdish in schools and in the media, and controls the celebration of Nawruz. Many tens of thousands of Kurds, deprived of their Syrian citizenship in the early 1960s after failing to prove that they had lived there since 1935 and were not illegal immigrants, remain trapped in Syria as stateless residents who cannot even legally emigrate. Possibly the worst abuse, however, was a plan to forcibly resettle Kurds living in the border areas of Jezira. Though never fully implemented, more than thirty thousand Kurds were driven from their villages from 1965 to 1975.

Most Syrian Kurds are peasants and live in three areas in the north and east, near the Turkish and Iraqi borders and adjoining other Kurdish majority regions. About 200,000, however, now live in major cities. Both Aleppo and Damascus have sizable Kurdish neighborhoods. Most urban Kurds are blue-collar workers, but some are employed in the state administration and the army and a few are professionals. Kurdish representation in the army, once important, declined after the mid-1950s.

Most Kurdish families settled within Syria's borders centuries ago, but a large minority arrived as refugees over the past sixty years, fleeing persecution in Turkey and Iraq. Damascus has been a rear base for Iraqi Kurdish guerrilla groups for many years.

Kurds generally prospered during the Mandate. The French opened the doors to Kurdish immigrants and offered them social advancement, especially through the armed forces. Kurdish nationalism grew, led by intellectuals such as the poet Cegerxwin. The French cautiously encouraged the movement as a counterweight both to Arab nationalism and the Communist party, then the Kurds' main defender.

Beginning in the mid-1950s—after Syrian independence—successive regimes saw Kurds as a threat to the unity and identity of Arab Syria. The government seized and destroyed Kurdish publications. It built schools in Kurdish communities but banned any language of instruction other than Arabic. And, to varying degrees in different periods, it decided that Kurdish activists would be best kept in jail.

The Kurds reacted by founding the Kurdish Democratic party of Syria (KDP-S) in 1957, a body similar to those organized in Iran and Iraq. It called for the recognition of Kurdish rights, land reform, and democracy—but not Kurdish independence. In addition to the KDP-S, the influential Syrian Communist party often defended Kurdish ethnic rights. Not coincidentally, many of its members were Kurds, including longtime party secretary-general Khalid Bakdash. The government, in turn, stepped up its arrests. Late in 1959 and again in August 1960, Col. 'Abd al-Hamid Sarraj's security forces imprisoned a number of KDP-S leaders and as many as five thousand other suspects. The government also pressured other local organizations in Kurdistan to drop their nationalist leanings.

The parliamentary government that followed the union with Egypt went even farther than its predecessor in oppressing the Kurds. In August 1962, it promulgated Decree 93, which called for a special census in the main Kurdish area of Jezira in the northeast. The stated purpose of this census was to discover how many people had illegally crossed the border from Turkish Kurdistan. Kurds had to prove that they had lived in Syria since at least 1935 or lose any claim to Syrian citizenship. Since many Kurds lacked written records, the census results stripped 120,000 people—over a fifth of the Kurdish population—of Syrian citizenship. Deprived of their passports, they faced difficulties of all sorts, from getting jobs to obtaining state services. They were not expelled, but many thousands eventually went into exile. Ironically, since they lacked a passport, it was especially difficult for these "noncitizens" to leave. Another irony: those young Kurdish men who remained had to serve, like citizens, in the Syrian armed forces.

The government also announced plans to create an "Arab Belt" 15 kilometers (about 9 miles) deep for a distance of 280 kilometers (174 miles) along the Turkish border. It planned to evacuate Kurds from 332 villages to create this zone, which was to be repopulated by "pure, nationalist Arabs."[14] In this draconian proposal, Syria foreshadowed an identical action adopted against

Iraqi Kurds first during the mid-1970s and again more ruthlessly in the late 1980s by its fellow Ba'th party in Baghdad.

The new Ba'thist government continued the crusade. Still friendly with Baghdad, it sent Syrian armed forces into Iraqi Kurdistan during 1963 to help quell the Kurdish autonomy movement there. Such cooperation between the two governments has not been repeated since.

In November 1963, eight months after taking power, the Ba'th party published a study on the Kurds by Jezira district security chief Muhammad Talib Hilal, who recommended stepping up the persecution. Making a claim echoed at different times throughout the region, he argued that Kurds have no real history or language and that they are by nature violent and destructive.[15]

The study made a number of policy recommendations for the Jezira region, among them systematically depriving Kurds of education and resources, forcibly transferring them to other regions, and then colonizing the area with Arabs. Another recommendation was to "unleash a vast anti-Kurd campaign among the Arabs, first of all to condition them against the Kurds, then to undermine the situation of the latter and sow in their midst the seeds of distress and insecurity."[16]

Since 1963, various Ba'thist governments have attempted to implement these ideas, especially in the years up to 1975. In 1967, school geography texts dropped all mention of a Kurdish minority in Syria. Government registry officials pressured Kurds not to give their children Kurdish surnames. The resettlement plan moved ahead under a new terminological cover. For "Arab Belt," for example, the government substituted "Plan to establish model state farms in the Jezira Province." "Agrarian reform" and "collectivization" provided a socialist excuse for the population transfer. At different times, the government built "model villages" and populated them with Arabs. The regime denied the benefits of the agrarian reform laws to the Kurdish villages and refused to give them electricity, roads, schools, and other resources.[17]

By 1972, Kurdish sources estimate that about 30,000 Kurds had left Jezira, about half because of government displacement efforts.[18] Arab colonization continued as the government moved in Arab peasants whose land was being submerged by the new Euphrates dam. In 1975, the government completed forty villages and installed some 7,000 Arab families; it may have moved as many as 25,000 families into Jezira in this way through 1976.[19]

The government also renamed Kurdish regions and villages to give them an "Arab identity," many through an administrative ordinance of 1977. The region of Kurd-Dagh (Mountain of the Kurds, in Kurdish), Syria's second-largest Kurdish area, was renamed Jabal al-'Uruba (Mountain of Arabism, in Arabic). Similarly, the important Kurdish town of 'Ifrin was renamed Madina al-'Uruba (City of Arabism), and the mountainous region of Jabal Hubkan was renamed

Jabal al-Thawra (Mountain of the Revolution).[20] In the summer of 1973, security forces arrested twelve Kurds, including KDP-S chairman Daham Miro and other party leaders, shortly after they had addressed a memorandum to President Asad protesting the resettlement plans and the condition of Kurds deprived of citizenship. Most remained in jail for the remainder of the decade.[21]

In 1976, as the opposition movement grew among Syrian Arabs, Asad sought to placate the Kurds, announcing an end to forced transfers from Jezira. As conditions improved, many Kurds enlisted in the security services and the army, in some units becoming second in importance only to ʿAlawis.

While easing up on its own Kurds, the Asad regime became a champion of Kurdish rights in Iraq, to put pressure on its enemy, Iraqi leader Saddam Hussein. Some Iraqi Kurdish groups, notably the left-wing Patriotic Union of Kurdistan of Jalal Talabani, have maintained offices in Damascus for over a decade and enjoy covert financial and military assistance. A Committee for the Defense of Human Rights in Iraq, based in Damascus, publishes a newsletter and lobbies foreign governments for the protection of Iraqi Kurds.

The regime has also supported groups of Turkish Kurds, such as the Marxist-Leninist PKK, or Kurdish Workers' party, which operates out of bases in the Syrian-controlled Biqʿa valley in Lebanon and infiltrates with fighters into Turkey through Syrian territory. According to one source, these foreign Kurdish groups celebrate Nawruz in fancy Damascus hotels accompanied by music and dancing—with high Syrian government and party officials usually in attendance.

Since 1980, the Syrian government has eased up even more on its Kurdish minority. It released five long-term Kurdish political detainees that year and let the rest go within the next five years. During that decade it also provided many Kurdish villages with electricity and roads for the first time.

Kurds may now openly celebrate Nawruz in the countryside, where music, dancing, and ritual fires do not attract attention. Yet the government's tolerance has limits. In the cities, holiday fetes other than the official functions for foreign Kurds are strongly discouraged. During Nawruz in Damascus in 1986, according to one account, security forces fired on people celebrating in the Kurdish quarter, killing one and wounding several. On the same night in Afrin, security forces allegedly killed three more Kurds. When the body of the Kurd from Damascus was brought back to Jezira for burial several days later, many thousands turned out in mourning and security forces arrested some eighty people.[22]

In a grudging sign of greater tolerance, the government now permits Kurds to play and sing their native songs in public. Tapes of Kurdish music, once banned, have reappeared for sale. In the cities, Kurds say that they no longer feel they must hide their Kurdishness, and many are again giving their children Kurdish names.[23] They can speak Kurdish in the streets as well as in their homes, where the use of Kurdish was never banned. But Kurds who lost their citizenship have not regained it, and their more deeply rooted difficulties continue. Not only are they denied passports and the possibility of work in the public sector, but they face problems getting hospital care, food coupons, and many other state benefits—including marriage licenses. International campaigns on their behalf have not been successful. As one Kurd reported:

> When I finished school I became a teacher. But in 1977, after three years of teaching, the authorities decided not to allow those in my situation to continue to work. So I left Jezira for Damascus, where I studied for the law. But when I graduated I learned I could not practice law and could not get any work in the administration or the public sector companies either. I tried to leave, but even that was denied me and I was questioned for a long time by the mukhabarat. Finally, in desperation, I got a false passport and escaped into exile.[24]

There are still no Kurdish-language broadcasts or publications in Syria, and Kurdish continues to be a forbidden language in the schools. All publications or public discussions about the Syrian Kurdish question, even in Arabic, also remain illegal. And periodic crackdowns on Kurdish cultural expression— such as the celebration of Nawruz—leave most Syrian Kurds feeling uneasy about the future.

The government does not permit any independent Kurdish political organization. It has threatened KDP-S leaders and played on party differences, prompting many organizational splits. Today, some splinters of the party are visible and tolerated, but, led by people considered to be pro-Asad, their discussions of the Kurdish question are muted. These shadowy parties are impotent, for they are unable to publish, hold meetings, or present candidates for elections. Independent Syrian Kurdish organizations exist only in exile.

A few Kurds sit in the People's Assembly and hold positions of local authority. Some, like former Prime Minister Mahmud Ayubi and Gen. Mahmud al-Kordi, former director-general of the Military Construction Enterprise and later minister of agriculture, have even been able to reach high-ranking positions.[25] Most observers agree, though, that these men would not have achieved these positions if they had shown any special Kurdish consciousness. None can be expected to speak for their community of origin, even in the conclaves of the party or regime.

The Jews

About 3,800 Jews live in Syria today, most in the Jewish quarter of the Old City of Damascus.[26] There synagogues, Jewish schools, and charities function openly. Although many Jews have prosperous businesses and professional practices,[27] the government seriously restricts the human rights of the Jewish community: political activity is impossible, surveillance intense, and emigration tightly restricted.

The community numbered fifty thousand in 1900, when many began to depart, lured by brighter prospects in the United States, Europe, and Latin America. Those who remained enjoyed good relations with Arab neighbors.[28] By 1945, however, the community had diminished to about fifteen thousand.[29]

Syrian Jews faced terrible changes in the late 1940s. On December 1, 1947—as soon as news broke about the United Nations partition of Palestine—Arabs attacked and badly damaged several synagogues, stores, and homes in Aleppo, at the time an old and flourishing Jewish community of six to seven thousand people. Police intervened only belatedly to restore order. Although no Jew suffered serious physical harm, the rampage was a heavy blow to community confidence. Many Jews left Aleppo then and emigrated to Lebanon or Turkey; some journeyed on to Israel, but most eventually went to the United States.[30]

In 1948 and 1949—during the Arab-Israeli War and its aftermath—attacks on the Jewish community continued. A bomb in a Damascus synagogue killed twelve worshipers, and vandals damaged Jewish stores and homes. In Aleppo, arsonists set fire to the major Jewish school.[31] The authorities gave Jews inadequate police protection and did little to prosecute those who destroyed Jewish property. Security forces, meanwhile, arrested a number of Jews on dubious charges. The frightened Jewish community pledged its loyalty to the government and became a pawn in Arab-Israeli rivalry. About seven thousand Jews nationwide emigrated during this period.

In the late 1940s, the government began to keep a keen watch on the Jewish community, using a special section of the security services. As part of the surveillance system—still in force—the mukhabarat keep dossiers on every Jew and closely follow their movements, money, and foreign communication.

Israel's mistreatment of the Palestinians in 1948 and 1949—especially the confiscation of Palestinian property—gave the Syrian government an excuse for even greater discrimination.[32] The regime restricted Jews' travel abroad and made legal emigration almost impossible, prohibited the sale of Jewish property, and confiscated the homes and businesses of those who left. Jews could not get responsible government jobs or serve in the army. *Musawi* (an Islamic term for Jew) was stamped in large red letters on Jewish identity papers.[33] Restrictions on money and travel made it difficult for Jews to continue in the export-import business.

Jews continued to enjoy freedom of religious practice. Although synagogues remained open, however, the mukhabarat sometimes sent agents to observe services—an ominous reminder that the community was being closely watched. Private Jewish elementary schools continued to function with little interference, as did other Jewish charitable institutions, though they, too, were carefully scrutinized.

Over the years, government policy has often changed suddenly and arbitrarily. Under Hashem al-Atassi in 1954, Jews who wanted to leave Syria were allowed to do so if they renounced claim to the property they left behind. But just a few months later, the government again imposed severe travel and emigration restrictions. Soon after the union with Egypt in 1958, President 'Abd al-Nasir greatly eased restrictions on emigration, only to ban it again a year later.

Conditions worsened after the Ba'th seized power. In March 1964, the regime restricted internal travel for Jews, insisting that they get prior permission for travel more than five kilometers (three miles) from their residence. For several years, the government also virtually forbade foreign travel. Under these suffocating conditions, a number of Jews tried to emigrate by secretly crossing the border. Those caught by the mukhabarat were imprisoned for weeks or months. Many were mistreated, and some were tortured.[34]

Asad's assumption of power in 1970 did not change these policies. During the 1973 Arab-Israeli war, though neither Jews nor their property were harmed, security forces imposed a strict curfew on the community for many weeks. As during previous wars, it was a time of great tension. Jewish businesses and professionals lost clients, and chauvinistic feelings ran high among the general Syrian population. A turning point came in March 1974, when four teenage girls were murdered while clandestinely trying to cross the border. The smugglers guiding them were apparently responsible for the crime. Several hundred people—Jews and Arabs—held a protest march in Damascus, and their campaign drew international support.

Beginning in 1976, the Asad regime relaxed restrictions on Jews.[35] Over the next two years, the government made internal and foreign travel as well as property sales and transfers easier. Emigration remained blocked (though in June 1977, in response to an American initiative, Asad permitted fourteen young, unmarried Jewish women to emigrate). Officials also replaced the large, red-lettered *Musawi* on identity cards with the word in smaller black type.[36] But, three years later, in March 1979, the government changed tack toward its Jewish minority once again. The return to a harder line coincided with the detention of several Jews who had tried to emigrate.[37]

A special section of Military Intelligence's Palestine Branch, under the direction of Col. 'Isa al-As'ad, continues to monitor Jews closely. Headquartered in Damascus's Rawda district, the section has a large local station in the Jewish quarter, not far from Suq Madhat Pasha, where twenty or more agents are said to work.

Jews told Middle East Watch that they must constantly inform the mukhabarat of their activities, whether business, a trip, or a bar mitzvah. If they fail to report meeting foreigners, for example, they can be called in for questioning. Every contact with the security police is difficult. As one recent émigré, a former Damascus shopkeeper, reported on his contacts with the mukhabarat: "When they came into my store, I never knew what was going to happen. Were they looking for a bribe? Were they checking my family? Had someone told them something about me that would get me into trouble? I felt powerless because whatever happened there was no recourse."[38] No other community in Syria faces such heavy surveillance and none is made to feel so completely powerless in the face of the authorities.

In December 1983, a pregnant Jewish woman, Lillian Abadi, and her two young children were murdered in Aleppo. The police did not apprehend the murderer but did step up patrols in the Jewish neighborhood. Although fear in the Jewish community lingered, daily life gradually returned to normal.

The government continues to impose onerous restrictions on Jewish travel and emigration, always the litmus test of its treatment of the community. Before making a foreign trip, Jews must appoint one or more persons to guarantee their return and must make a forfeitable deposit before they leave—recently S£25,000 (the equivalent of about $3,000 in 1989 purchasing power, a large sum by Syrian standards).[39] Other Syrians need no guarantors when they travel, and if they are asked for a deposit, the sum is considerably less.

Damascene Jews apply for travel permission to the head of the security station in the Jewish quarter. The application is then forwarded to headquarters, where agents scrutinize personal dossiers. The mukhabarat often refuse a request if other family members are already abroad or planning to go.[40] Those with property, including a house, continue to face special barriers to emigration. Regulations forbid Jews from liquidating their assets and they must report sales of assets to the mukhabarat. Like all Syrians, they are forbidden to transfer assets abroad.

A number of Jews do manage to leave Syria each year. Some cross the border clandestinely, some bribe their way out, and some receive permission to leave,[41] but most simply leave on approved travel and do not return. Total emigration may be about 150 people per year, most going to the United States—particularly Brooklyn.[42] In addition, government reprisals can never be ruled out.

In December 1985, security forces arrested Shehade Basso and his two sons

Salim and Jacques, apparently because a family member did not return from a foreign trip. Basso was seventy years old at the time and his health deteriorated during his incarceration. All three were held for ten months.

Security forces arrested ten Jews between September 1987 and July 1988 for violating emigration and travel restrictions and held all without charge or trial for over a year. Among those arrested were three clothing store owners (Jacques Lalo, another clothing store owner, was said to have been caught while trying to escape), thirty-two-year-old Zaki Mamroud, forty-eight-year-old Albert Laham, and Laham's eighteen-year-old son, Victor; and two pharmacists, Eli and Salim Swed. Zaki's brother, Faraj, was also detained, and three students were arrested.

The first four, accused of emigration-related offenses, were not formally sentenced until late in 1989. Three were released shortly afterward, and the fourth, Jacques Lalo, was released in the summer of 1990. As for the other two arrested during that period—pharmacists Eli and Salim Swed—the government said in December 1989 (two years after their arrest) that it planned to try them for "making contact with the enemy," which means that they traveled to Israel, a crime for any Syrian. But a martial proceeding on their case did not begin until autumn 1990, and as of March 1991 it was not clear when it would end.[43]

The three other arrests are also believed to be cases relating to emigration, possibly attempts at clandestine departure. All were minors—aged sixteen and seventeen—and all reported being tortured. They were released in 1988 after about six months' incarceration.

In October 1989, Vice President 'Abd al-Halim Khaddam offered to meet with Jewish leaders during his visit to the United Nations in New York.[44] It is not clear whether such a meeting took place, but shortly afterward, the U.S. State Department announced that the Syrian government had promised to take "a more flexible approach" to its Jewish population. This was to include a trial for two Jewish prisoners and a relaxation of emigration rules for unmarried Jewish women and those seeking family reunions.[45]

Almost a year and a half later, the Syrian government has made few moves, and nothing has changed on family reunions. At least four more Syrian Jews, including a pregnant woman, were arrested trying to leave the country in September 1990. (The woman was released after giving birth, but her husband and another of the four were still in detention in Aleppo six months later.) It remains to be seen whether the announcement was merely a Syrian public relations gesture, a temporary thaw, or a more lasting improvement.[46] In any event, the Asad regime has a long way to go before it can claim with any justification to be treating its Jewish citizens on the same basis as non-Jews.

The Palestinians

About 300,000 Palestinians live in Syria, most of them refugees from families who left Palestine in 1948.[47] Though well-integrated into Syrian society, few Palestinians are citizens,[48] and the government tends to harass them when its policies clash with those of the PLO. Since 1983, when Syrian-PLO relations deteriorated sharply, human rights abuses have increased significantly. The regime has interfered with Palestinian educational, cultural, and community organizations. It has also stepped up its surveillance and security presence in Palestinian neighborhoods. Security forces have opened fire on peaceful Palestinian demonstrators several times, and they have arrested and tortured a large number of Palestinian residents.

About three-quarters of all Palestinians in Syria live in and around Damascus, mostly in Yarmuk Camp, a large neighborhood south of the city with three- and four-story buildings and an air of modest prosperity.[49] Some Palestinians also live in poorer conditions in such rural camps as Qabr al-Sitt and Jarmana, while others live in such cities as Dar'a, Aleppo, and Hama. Many work in construction, quite a few have professional and technical jobs, and some are government workers, shopkeepers, or merchants. A few wealthy businessmen can be found, and one Palestinian has even become a general in the Syrian army.

Palestinian refugees were well received at first. When they arrived in Syria, the government set up the Palestine Arab Refugee Institution to take care of them. Starting in 1949, the government passed a series of laws giving Palestinians many rights. Law 260 of 1956 enabled them to be considered as Syrians in almost all things covered by law except the right to vote.[50]

Although Palestinians never received Syrian passports, authorities did issue them identity cards. Later, in 1960, it provided them with *laissez-passer* travel documents. Few jobs were closed to Palestinians except those in the Foreign Ministry, the intelligence services, and high levels of the political bureaucracy. A Palestinian could even become a mayor (ra'is al-baladiya).[51]

Beginning in the 1950s, some Palestinians joined various Syrian political parties—the Ba'th, the Communists, the Muslim Brothers, and the Nasirists—in the course of which activities they sometimes ran afoul of the authorities, exactly as Syrians themselves did. In the early 1960s, they also started to organize a national movement in exile.

The Ba'thist government allowed Palestinians a certain degree of freedom for self-organization—more so than Syrians had—because support for the Palestinian cause was, and remains, an important element of official ideology and propaganda. Palestinians were able to have their own institutions, including political organizations, clubs, cultural centers, and women's groups. They were able to speak out publicly on Palestinian political matters, but the mukhabarat always kept a close watch and the authorities expected Palestinian organizations to be on good terms with the regime—and to maintain close relations with the Ba'th party.[52]

The regime also created its own Palestinian organizations. Late in 1965, it set up the General Union of Palestinian Workers. In September 1966, it formed a Palestinian military force called Saiqa as a wing of the Ba'th party. Saiqa became, in effect, a branch of the Syrian army, led by Syrian officers and with many Syrians in its ranks.[53] Salah Jadid tried to use this force in his struggle with Asad. Once in power, Asad purged Saiqa of its pro-Jadid leaders and made the unit an instrument of Syrian policy in Lebanon.

To control its often restless Palestinian population, the Syrian regime built two powerful security forces within the Military Intelligence Agency: the Palestine Branch and the Commando Police. These have become among the largest and most feared security services, with a formidable capacity for surveillance, arrest, and interrogation. The Palestine Branch set up an especially notorious interrogation center: Fara' Falastin.[54]

The Syrian government has come down hard on Palestinians who protest Asad's policies affecting Palestinians in other countries. Police have frequently attacked and arrested peaceful Palestinian demonstrators. One of the first such clashes took place in September 1970.[55] The Syrian intervention in Lebanon in 1976 produced an even sharper conflict.[56]

But the aftermath of the Lebanon War, especially the Syrian-sponsored split in the PLO and the "war of the camps," led to the most serious official reprisals.[57] On May 23 and 24, 1983, when thousands of Palestinians marched through the streets of Yarmuk Camp, Commando Police opened fire on unarmed demonstrators, killing twelve and wounding many more. They arrested several hundred in the course of the two days.[58]

More arrests followed in July. On the twelfth, security forces seized Muhammad al-Amari, head of the al-Fatah office, and held him incommunicado for five years, most of the time in solitary confinement. The mukhabarat tortured al-Amari more than once and rebuffed efforts by Palestinian leaders to send him food and fresh clothing.

The regime also moved against all Palestinian organizations not directly under its control. On October 10, 1983, with the backing of security forces, Syrian-supported Palestinians seized PLO offices in the capital. These offices had focused primarily on education, culture, research, health, and other local community activities; thereafter their work was much reduced. Other organizations, notably the General Union of Palestinian Women, were compelled to end key community programs such as kindergartens.

Syrian attacks on Palestinian camps in Tripoli, Lebanon, in November ignited protests in Yarmuk and other Palestinian camps once more. Security forces intervened, again with many casualties and over a hundred arrests. By the end of 1983, according to reliable sources, Syrian security had arrested between one and two thousand Palestinians and had detained many hundreds more. Some prisoners later testified to mistreatment and torture. To gain their release, they had to promise to support Palestinian groups backed by Syria.

Since 1983, the regime has severely restricted travel for Palestinians, requiring not only an exit visa but also special permission from the Palestine Branch ten days before departure. Palestinian leaders who do not go along with Asad or are considered undependable often cannot get permission to attend international meetings. Palestinians never know, even when they go to the airport, whether they will be allowed to leave. "Not until the plane is actually in the air," said one, "do I know that I will reach foreign soil and not a Syrian interrogation cell."[59]

The relative freedom of Palestinians to organize public gatherings ended abruptly in 1983. Since then, the mukhabarat has kept a tight rein on all Palestinian meetings, requiring that all be approved in advance. The regime has not only blocked virtually all expressions of community solidarity but has even restricted such strictly cultural events as concerts.

According to some reports, the regime has also imposed economic sanctions on the community. It no longer allows Palestinians to buy more than one piece of property, and before any large purchase, Palestinians must show where the money has come from.

Security forces have released a few Palestinian prisoners each year, but they continue to make more arrests. Syrian forces have also rounded up many Palestinians in Lebanon, some of whom are brought to Syria for interrogation and detention. The extremely bad treatment of these prisoners is of serious concern to Syria's Palestinian community.

In June 1985, after reports of Syrian-supported killings in Palestinian camps in Lebanon, the Palestinian community again poured into the streets to protest. Thousands demonstrated in Yarmuk, and there were protests in other camps. Many Syrians reportedly joined in, making these protests the most important political event since 1982. In Yarmuk, security forces again opened fire on the crowds, killing several Palestinians and wounding dozens more. Police arrested an estimated seven hundred people this time. In reprisal, they also arrested Palestinians throughout the country, particularly in Aleppo and Homs.[60]

In succeeding years, security forces have continued to arrest many Palestinians, especially during protests against the "war of the camps" in December 1985 and May 1986 and during demonstrations on Palestinian Land Day, March 30, 1986. Among those arrested, beginning late in 1985, were scores of

Palestinians who had originally supported the pro-Syrian groups but now opposed the killing in the Lebanon camps.

The round-ups seem to have worked. Since mid-1985, public protests have been rare, but the level of intimidation required has been significant. As the regime has intensified efforts to silence the Palestinian community, reports have multiplied of prisoners tortured, even killed. Ahmad al-Kabra, a restaurant owner from Yarmuk arrested in January 1985, is one of those believed to have died under torture in the Military Interrogation Branch. His body was dumped in front of his family's house that summer, and they were told to bury it at night, without a funeral. Commando Police arrested Misbah 'Abd al-Haq, a sixty-year-old al-Fatah activist, about the same time. Friends discovered his body by accident in the morgue of Damascus's al-Mujtahid Hospital in April 1986. The condition of the body gave observers every reason to believe that his death was the result of torture.[61]

Mustafa Mahmud Hussain al-Khouri, a fifty-year-old Yarmuk resident arrested in July 1985, and Yahya Ahmad 'Abd al-Hafidh a thirty-five-year-old from Dera' arrested the next January, are also believed to have been tortured to death not long after their detention began. Altogether, at least ten Palestinians have been tortured to death since 1983. Of all the people from all groups tortured to death in Syria during this period, at least half have been Palestinians.

Torture has left many other Palestinians with permanent physical disabilities. A report of 1977 by the Committee for the Defense of Palestinian Prisoners in Syria tells of three inmates who suffered backbone damage and partial paralysis, five who suffered from heart disease and ulcers, and nine whose health was seriously endangered in other ways. In all these cases, it is reasonable to attribute the damage to torture.[62]

The human cost to the Palestinian community has been high. "When my friend Muhammad was finally released," reported a Palestinian to Middle East Watch, "he was totally changed. He had been cheerful and robust. After two years inside, he was pale, shrunken, and humorless. They tortured the spark of his life away."[63]

Of those swept up in the waves of arrests, many were hostages—often women—who were not even the target of the police search. On March 30, 1986, for example, security forces looking for Palestinian journalist Samir al-Hassan took as hostage his mother, wife, three sisters, and sister-in-law. At least a hundred other Palestinians have been taken hostage since 1983 in the same way.

Events on March 30, 1988, led to another wave of arrests. When Yasir 'Arafat came to Damascus for the funeral of PLO leader Abu Jihad, tens of thousands turned out to greet him in Yarmuk, among them many Syrians. Security forces did not intervene, but in the weeks that followed, they arrested dozens of Palestinians, even the leaders of some groups nominally allied with the Asad regime.

'Issam 'Abd al-Latif, a major figure in the Democratic Front for the Liberation of Palestine, had already been arrested in February 1987. Now it was the turn of Salah Salah of the Popular Front for the Liberation of Palestine, who was taken prisoner shortly after the demonstrations, along with many lesser cadres. Friends did not know whether these prisoners were alive or dead until their release in 1989.

A Palestinian reported to Middle East Watch on the fate of a daughter then studying at Damascus University: "One day they came and arrested her and some of her friends. We were crazy with anxiety, knowing what they do to people who are in prison. I called many people, used every connection I had, but I couldn't even find out where she was being held. Finally, after six months, they released her. Her friends, though, are still in jail [a year later]."[64]

As of the summer of 1990, Syria held at least 2,500 Palestinians as political prisoners, including about 2,000 within Syrian territory.[65] That is about one out of every 150 Palestinians in the country and twenty times the proportion of Syrians under arrest—a clear indicator of how seriously the Palestinian population is at risk.

Several high-level Palestinian and other Arab delegations have tried to improve the situation. In October 1987, four PLO envoys spoke with Asad and Vice President Khaddam about the release of Palestinian prisoners. On December 3, the Syrian government announced that it was studying the release of seventeen hundred prisoners, but nothing came of it.[66] Further negotiations took place when 'Arafat visited Damascus in March 1988 and when Palestinian leader Umm Jihad, Abu Jihad's widow, came the next spring. Algerian envoys have also raised the issue, but practical results—the release of several dozen prisoners—have been slim.[67]

Some observers have thought that Asad's recent diplomatic opening to Egypt and the Arab political mainstream would improve the lot of Syria's Palestinians. So far, there has been no sign of this. The Asad regime has much to correct in its dismal human rights record toward Palestinians, whom it defends so loudly in official propaganda—and treats so badly in practice.

8

CENSORSHIP, CULTURE,
AND THE MEDIA

The Ba'th party constitution states among its fundamental principles that "[f]reedom of speech, of assembly, of religion and of art are sacred. No authority [legitimately] has the power to suppress them."[1] Since seizing control of the state in 1963, however, the Ba'thists have shown little concern for free expression. The military government immediately laid the groundwork for censorship with the sweeping provisions of the state of emergency. According to Article 4b of this law, the state has the right to control newspapers, books, broadcasting, advertising, and visual arts—in other words, all forms of expression and announcements before publication. It may also stop, confiscate, and destroy any work deemed to threaten state security, or close down offices and places of printing.[2]

At the center of the system for the control of ideas is the Ministry of Information, which runs the mass media, conducts much of the censoring, and controls the distribution of printed matter. Ahmad Iskandar Ahmad, minister of information from September 1974 until his death in December 1983 and one of Asad's closest collaborators, "modernized" and centralized this system.

The mukhabarat have a role in censorship, too. They sometimes detain intellectuals, threaten them, or make it difficult for them to find work. But imprisonment and torture are reserved mainly for intellectuals from underground political parties—even though they may simply advocate free speech and a peaceful transition to democracy.

The regime tries to keep independent intellectuals in line primarily through bullying, praise, threats, bribes, fines, promotion (or demotion), and social pressures. Exacting such influence is easy, since most Syrian intellectuals are government employees. Some dissidents have been driven to despair, others forced into exile. Although many have given up, some still pit their wits against official orthodoxy. As a result, Syrian culture retains pockets of vitality, though it has been badly battered overall during the Asad years.

Even if the Asad regime has muted the voice of internal critics, it cannot prevent other viewpoints from reaching the Syrian public. Syrians maintain many links to the world. They receive news, information, and culture from diverse sources beyond state control. Among these are foreign radio and television broadcasts (that are considerably more popular than the propaganda-ridden official media), smuggled books, cassettes and videotapes, informal personal networks, and travel.

The censorship system is not absolute: it has gaps and inconsistencies and is relatively unsophisticated. Statements of criticism mediated by fiction, metaphor, euphemisms, fables, analogies, and historical parallels are commonly tolerated. Works of this kind are often very well received by canny Syrian audiences.

THE HISTORICAL ROOTS OF SYRIAN CENSORSHIP

Syria has a rich literary, artistic, and scholarly heritage. Its first press began printing in Aleppo in 1712, its first medical school is now nearly a hundred years old, and its first film production dates back sixty years. It would be difficult for any state, no matter how ruthless, to subdue such well-developed institutions and traditions.

But the French Mandate set dangerous precedents. Authorities jailed or exiled many Syrian writers, artists, and journalists who opposed French rule. The French even exiled well-known poets, such as al-Zirikly, in 1920 (condemned to death in absentia), and Khalil Mardam, in 1925.[3] They shut down newspapers, theaters, and cinemas, tightly controlled the only radio station, and imposed their authority over schools and universities.

After independence, diverse cultural institutions flourished for a time. Freed from censorship, many newspapers emerged (more than a dozen in Damascus alone), cinema and theater prospered, and books circulated openly. But military regimes again tightened censorship, beginning with the al-Zaʿim coup of 1949. As military rulers consolidated the police and security services within the army, they placed new restrictions on the press and recruited thousands of informants who made sure that their rules were enforced. The leash on free expression shortened even more during the merger with Egypt from 1958 to 1961. The government then set up a powerful Ministry of Culture and Information, based on the Egyptian model, which included a censorship department as well as a unit to run newspapers and other mass media. Independent newspapers and other media were banned.

After Syria broke with Egypt in 1961, the new government briefly restored free expression. When the Baʿth military committee came to power in 1963, it imposed ever tighter controls. It also won over many intellectuals—at least for a time.

Cultured, urban Syrians, not surprisingly, looked down on the rural military men who dominated the Ba'th leadership, but the new regime eventually mobilized many intellectuals with its appeal for radical nationalism and its promise to build a stronger, more dynamic nation. The state also enlisted intellectuals with carrot-and-stick policies: supporters were awarded good jobs and a comfortable living; critics often could not find work or were harassed and threatened as "agents of imperialism."

The Ba'th regime's record on freedom of expression—and its perceived betrayal of its own principles—eventually disappointed and embittered many of its intellectual supporters. Corruption at the top, rewards for second-rate ideologues, exile for many of the most talented—this was the stuff of disillusionment. The Syrian intervention in Lebanon in June 1976 was the last straw. From then until early 1980, opposition from cultural and educational institutions intensified. Then came the great crackdown. Many intellectuals fled into exile and those who remained muted their voices.

Since 1980, the regime has kept censorship very tight. Every lecture, book, and magazine—even Friday sermons in the mosques—must be approved in advance. Television news and print journalism are tightly controlled—and uniformly dull. Reflecting the regime's view of the media as docile servants of power, the minister of information recently hailed "the effectiveness of the media in developing and contributing to strengthening the march of growth and steadfastness—the march of the people and their great Ba'th Party under the leadership of the struggler comrade Hafez al-Asad."[4]

Official censors are less heavy-handed when it comes to fiction, theater, poetry, and cinema, which are allowed some creativity as long as authors do not engage in direct criticism.

The texture of life varies from city to city. In Damascus—headquarters of the state, swarming with military and security people—intellectual life has suffered most. In Aleppo, where the military is barely visible, café life flourishes and public conversation is less constrained. Although it tries, the state cannot control every institution. The cultural centers and film clubs put on poetry readings, film festivals, and art exhibits that sometimes delicately probe political limits. The central bureaucrats in Damascus simply cannot keep track of it all.

Dissenting intellectuals occasionally confront the regime—usually with great subtlety, but sometimes more directly. On March 24, 1989, fifty noted novelists, filmmakers, playwrights, poets, professors, and intellectuals—both in Syria and in exile—published a defense of Salman Rushdie in the Beirut-based newspaper al-Safir.[5] In the name of a free, secular, intellectual life nominally supported by the Baʻth party, the statement attacked the narrow orthodoxy of Khomeini's censorship and death threats against the Indian-born novelist. Not only did the protest clearly castigate Syria's main regional ally, Iran, but it implicitly criticized censorship and repression within Syria. By a quirk of fate, Asad had criticized Rushdie in an interview that appeared in *Time* magazine just days earlier.

The mukhabarat were quick to act. They summoned the Syrian organizers of the protest to security headquarters and asked whether the authors had intended to contradict the president of the Republic. "No," came the reply, for the petition had been circulated weeks before. Though unhappy, the regime could do nothing with such well-known intellectuals without provoking a storm of international criticism.

THE PRESS

The regime imposes strict control over the press. After the Baʻthist coup, authorities closed down all independent newspapers and established a press monopoly. The party organ *al-Baʻth,* founded in 1946, was joined by a new government paper, *al-Thawra* (Revolution), in July 1963. In October 1974, Hafez Asad launched a third national newspaper as his personal mouthpiece. Called *Tishrin* (October), it symbolizes the growing centralization and one-man rule of the Syrian political system.

Of the three papers, *Tishrin* is somewhat more polished and *al-Baʻth* more harsh and clichéd. But little distinguishes one from another fundamentally. The Ministry of Information oversees two of the three papers, and the Syrian Arab News Agency (SANA), an organization also controlled and funded by the ministry, writes most of the news reports. A recent study showed that in *al-Baʻth,* 95 percent of the national news copy and 90 percent of the international news came from SANA.[6]

In addition to the three national dailies, there are four regional dailies in Aleppo, Homs, Lataqia, and Hama,[7] but none are published in their own city. So centralized is the Syrian media system that, though edited locally, all are published in Damascus by the government's al-Wahda publishing house, producer of *al-Thawra*. Yet another sign of the press's ties the seat of power is indicated by the fact that of the eleven hundred professional journalists registered with the Journalists' Union in the mid-1980s, one thousand worked in the capital.[8]

Total circulation of all Syrian newspapers is only about 150,000—an extremely small number for a population of 12 million.[9] It is also unclear how many of these are actually read, since copies are distributed free to government and party offices and many other establishments.

The government also publishes such magazines as the army's *Jaysh al-Sha'b* (People's Army). Some of the nominally independent "popular organizations" also put out publications, but the state subsidizes and closely monitors everything.[10] Several local bodies—such as union branches—print papers, magazines, or newsletters. These small publications are not as tightly controlled as long as they steer clear of national politics. Elisabeth Longuenesse has reviewed many local trade union publications and found that they cover such issues as "problems on the job," the effect of inflation on workers' living standards, productivity bonuses, the introduction of new machines, and the housing crisis. In referring to national politics, however, they revert to obligatory, stock phrases, such as calling Asad "leader and symbol of the workers' struggle."[11]

Asad's effort to control the news media dates back to his ascent to power. On February 25, 1969, at the height of his struggle with Jadid, Asad sent his tanks into Damascus, straight to the offices of *al-Ba'th* and *al-Thawra* as well as to the Damascus broadcasting station. He removed their top editors and installed his loyalists, including Ghassan Rifa'i, chief of the army paper, who became editor-in-chief at *al-Ba'th*.[12] Those known to be accommodating, such as *al-Ba'th* editor Mahmud Kamil, remained at their posts.[13]

Asad tolerated some slight independence among journalists until 1978, but the mass opposition movement provoked a house-cleaning of all but the absolutely loyal. In mid-March, 'Ali Suleiman, editor-in-chief of *al-Thawra*, was dismissed for having improperly described the Israeli invasion of South Lebanon,[14] and on June 19, 1978, authorities fired the editor-in-chief of *al-Ba'th*, 'Adnan Baghajati, accusing him of turning his paper into a platform for "communist ideology." Also in June, ten journalists deemed too sympathetic to the opposition were barred from further press work; henceforth, the rest of the press was barred from even mentioning their names.[15]

Later in the year, many of Syria's best-known writers sent a petition to the Ministry of Culture and the Writers' Union demanding an end to blacklisting and a lifting of book censorship. A Damascus security chief summoned the organizers of the petition and threatened them with dire consequences if they continued to speak out.[16] From then until 1982, many other journalists were driven out of the media or resigned in disgust. By 1990, even a polite challenge was out of the question. A Syrian journalist is simply not expected to have a personal opinion.[17]

To train journalists, the Ministry of Information set up a press institute in 1970. Attached to the ministry, it ran a two-year program for those aspiring to the profession and provided training for those already employed. A diploma-mill for propagandists, the institute did not produce good reporters, even by the standards of the editors, who often refused to hire its graduates. As a result, the

Education Ministry created the Department of Communication at the University of Damascus in 1985. The department was supposed to provide better training and to ensure the quality of graduates by screening candidates at admission and during the course of study. According to reliable sources, however, the media chiefs remain discontent and usually prefer to hire writers who have learned their craft in other ways.

With few exceptions, young journalists must be Ba'th party members. The rare exemptions are protégés of generals or high officials. Once fledgling journalists begin work, their editors scrutinize their writing for political errors, and the mukhabarat make sure they have no suspicious contacts. Pay and promotion depend on unwavering adherence to the official line. As one exiled Syrian journalist has concluded: "Anyone who shows a critical or complaining or satirical spirit, or who sees matters from a pessimistic viewpoint—or who refrains from writing about certain subjects such as the presidential speech and against the regime's internal and external opponents—is subject to financial and administrative penalties."[18]

A journalist who wants a safe career must closely follow the daily guidelines issued by the Ministry of Information, the Office of Information of Vice President Khaddam, and the Presidential Press Office. Those who prove their skill and loyalty over the years—like editor Muhammad Khair al-Wady[19] and top political commentator Mustapha al-Fakir—are well taken care of. By Syrian standards their pay is very good, with generous bonuses, housing allowances, and opportunities for foreign travel. Some top journalists also supplement their income by serving as mouthpieces for powerful officials. Those who err, however, may suffer serious consequences. The worst offense is to join a banned political party. Rida Haddad, a popular editorial writer with *Tishrin,* was arrested in 1980 and charged with membership in the Communist Party-Political Bureau. Journalists 'Ali al-Kurdi (arrested in 1982) and Samir al-Hassan (arrested in 1986) were jailed for membership in the Party for Communist Action. All three remain in prison. Although they were not punished for their writings, their fate has had a chilling effect on other journalists.

In recent years, the security services have not imprisoned anyone simply for their writing, but they sometimes detain and interrogate journalists. In one case, an editor was questioned for printing a picture that made Asad look short and pot-bellied—though the photo was handed out by the presidential press office. Another editor got in trouble for a typographical error that inverted letters in one word, making the president a "drum" (*tabal*)—meaning "windbag"—rather than a "hero" (*batal*). Accused of insulting the president, he was interrogated for a week by Air Force Intelligence.[20]

One former editor reports that when he made "errors" (failed to follow the official line closely enough) in the mid-1970s, he was removed from his editorial job and given a desk job at the Ministry of Information. There, he says, he either did "nothing," worked in the office of the censor, or "just stayed at home and cashed my salary."[21] Having finally found another editorial job in 1977, he wrote a piece critical of the shah of Iran that was taken to be a subtle criticism of Asad; after that he was told he could no longer write. He kept editing but then lost the job entirely for reprinting a nineteenth-century text that called on people to oppose despotism. The Ba'th party censorship office told him there was no place for writers like him in Syria, so he left the country.[22]

In 1975, the mukhabarat arrested Marwan Hamawi, then head of SANA. Accused of pro-Iraqi sympathies, he was jailed in al-Mezze Prison. Fifteen years later he is still there.

More recently, Asad fired *Tishrin* chief 'Amid al-Khuly for a small editorial lapse. The incident says a great deal about Syrian censorship, as most Syrians saw Al-Khuly, editor-in-chief of Syria's most important newspaper, as a thoroughly reliable apologist for the regime.[23] He was nonetheless held responsible for a "mistake" in one paragraph.

In November 1987, *Tishrin* ran a Reuters wire report on the Amman Arab Summit, quoting the final communiqué that supported Iraq in its conflict with Iran. Although Asad had signed the communiqué, he remained hostile to Iraq and an ally of Iran. By running the story, *Tishrin* revealed Asad's dilemma. Some say al-Khuly checked the story with Vice President Khaddam and got an ambiguous go-ahead. But Asad reportedly was furious. Accusing his chief journalist of disloyalty, he immediately relieved him of his responsibilities. Asad replaced al-Khuly as editor with Yusif Maqdisi, said to be a mukhabarat man with no real journalistic experience. According to some sources, the security services vie to place their own candidates in top editorial ranks. Not surprisingly, newspapers read like police reports: dull, bureaucratic, and predictable. Filled with clichés and photos of Hafez Asad talking with dignitaries, they give tedious details of meetings with foreign delegations or lavish empty praise on high officials. An example of typical style in *al-Thawra*: "The revolution, particularly after the Corrective Movement that was led by the militant president, Hafez al-Asad, has marked the beginning of a new era of effective and positive national unity in the march of Syria's struggle and pan-Arab progressive course."[24]

The papers are also prone to roar bombastically at foreign and domestic enemies, using empty phrases, especially in view of the regime's record. Five months before the invasion of Kuwait, for example, Iraqi leader Saddam Hussein was charged with perpetrating "the most savage Nazi crimes in contemporary history."[25] Most Syrians have tired of reading about the "struggle against Zionism and imperialism" and the "fascist Saddam clique" while real Syrian issues and important world events are ignored.[26] The only relief from this tedium is the cultural section, where readers can sometimes find quality short stories, poems, reviews, and essays. The foreign press review section also occasionally runs an interesting (if carefully selected) piece from *Pravda, Le Monde,* or *Die Zeit.*

From time to time, Syrian newspapers run critical news stories, but the criticisms are carefully orchestrated by the daily press guidelines. For instance, papers may be encouraged to write about the housing crisis, the lack of adequate street cleaning, or occasionally even such issues as failures of the state sector, official corruption, or the sins of the new bourgeoisie. After the regime allows discussion of such matters, it often then decides that things have gone far enough and again closes this small opening.

Obviously, there are things no editor may ever allow into print. Criticism of Hafez Asad, no matter how indirect, is never permitted. No Syrian paper has printed a cartoon of Asad, even a favorable one, since he came to power.[27] The editors also do not allow any mention of an 'Alawi role in the regime. Indeed, any reference to 'Alawis—or any minority, for that matter—is taboo. Critical references to the military are out of bounds and any discussion of security agencies strictly forbidden. Criticism of the Ba'th party is dangerous, too, though it can sometimes be done with an exonerating formula: that the party is not worthy of the leadership of Hafez Asad, for example.

While the official press censors itself, censorship officials attend to the publications of the parties allied to the Ba'th in the National Progressive Front. The two Communist parties of Khalid Bakdash and Yussif Faysal put out publications called *Nidal al-Sha'b* (People's Struggle), and the Arab Socialists of 'Abd al-Ghani Qannut have *al-Ishtiraki* (The Socialist), all appearing more or less monthly. Even though these parties are part of the Front and have ministers in the government, they have never been given formal authorization to publish. Existing only by the tolerance of the regime, they praise Hafez Asad more loudly than do his own press organs, couch criticisms of the regime in indirect language, and usually refrain from negative comments on the Ba'th party.

In spite of these suffocating restrictions, the press of the legal opposition is more interesting and outspoken than the official press. (*Tishrin,* however, is in no danger of losing any readers to *Nidal al-Sha'b,* since neither the Communist party nor any other opposition group may sell papers directly to the public and must restrict distribution to party members.) A few other publications are tolerated in Syria, including two theoretical journals of the Communists, *al-Nahj* (The Way) and *Dirasat Ishtirakiya* (Socialist Studies). More influential have been the Palestinian newspapers and magazines. Iraqi Kurds have a newspaper of their own. All these publications are very tightly censored.

Some publications—the underground press of the opposition parties—are beyond the censors' reach. But one can be imprisoned and tortured merely for possessing these publications, which are presumed to indicate party membership. Sulaiman Ghaibur, a soldier who is believed to have been tortured to death in March 1986, was originally arrested because Party for Communist Action literature was found in his possession. If the price for mere ownership can be so high, anyone having a hand in producing or distributing such publications obviously takes an enormous risk. Remarkably enough, half a dozen such papers appear, though only irregularly. The Communist Party-Political Bureau puts out *Nidal al-Sha'b* and the Party for Communist Action publishes *al-Raia al-Hamra* (Red Flag). The Muslim Brothers' news sheet *al-Nadhir* (The Warner) and magazine *al-Ra'id* (The Guide) now appear only abroad.

Syrian censors also inspect foreign newspapers and magazines sold in the country, especially those in Arabic. In 1989 they blocked all publications from Iraq, Egypt, and Jordan but permitted friendly publications from Lebanon, the Persian Gulf, and the Soviet Union.[28] Censors review each issue before distribution and may order objectionable articles cut out. The Syrian Office for the Distribution of Printed Matter, set up in 1983, controls all distribution and may ban issues or titles that offend current policy.[29]

BROADCAST MEDIA

Syrian broadcasters air a good deal of fictional, cultural, and other material that is not directly political, so they are less drab than the newspapers. They also face greater competition, since foreign broadcasts are readily available and very popular. Even so, journalists, producers, technicians, and other broadcast staff face a system of control even tighter than that over the print media. Authorities are more sensitive to political presentations on television, probably because the audience is much larger. There are an estimated 1.5 million television sets in Syria, a number nearly ten times the country's newspaper circulation.

The regime and its broadcasting arm are one and the same. The state owns all radio and television stations[30] and runs them out of the Ministry of Information, where 'Abd al-Nabi Hijazi heads the Syrian Radio and Television Authority. Ahmad Hariri, head of Public Relations at the Ministry of Information, also works as a top television news anchor.

To ensure tight control, apparently nothing is broadcast live, except for the speeches of Asad and a few of his most trusted compatriots. Current affairs, news, sports, and culture are all taped and checked before they go on the air.

One insider claims that broadcasters "would even tape a discussion of Aristotle" for fear that "a stray comment" might anger a high official and end the career of the show's producer or the station chief.[31]

Broadcasting staff, especially those in news and current affairs, are closely watched. Like print journalists, they may be demoted, fired, or called in for questioning because of the slightest political "error." But none are serving long-term jail sentences except those accused of joining or collaborating with underground parties, as have Imad Naddaf and Amwar Bader. Naddaf, a television reporter, was arrested in 1982 and has been tortured and held in Tadmur Prison; Bader, a radio and television reporter, was arrested in December 1986 and has been held ever since in the Military Interrogation Branch. Both were accused of membership in the Party for Communist Action.

Such a closed and inflexible ideological system cannot produce convincing programming on public affairs. Some say the shows are so bad that they have little public influence. Films, video music, and reruns of old Egyptian and Lebanese serials fill much of the broadcasting day. Current programming also includes sports and local news, as well as large doses of reports from the "popular organizations"—unions, youth, peasants, and women. News relentlessly echoes the official propaganda line. Advertisements—for toothpaste, soap, and vacation homes—appear from time to time.

Programs frequently celebrate President Asad and affirm the people's love for him. One such show, aired in the summer of 1989, showed Asad standing in an open army truck, passing soldiers who waved, clapped, and generally appeared ecstatic at the sight of the head of state. This scene, accompanied by martial music, lasted for over an hour.

Asad's television speeches receive special dramatic treatment. Cameras recently showed him making his way toward a lectern through a throng of young women dressed in flowing white robes. As he passed, they bowed before him, as if he were a divinity.

Efforts by Syrian broadcasting to promote Asad-worship and present ideologically pure programming face serious obstacles. The two channels of Jordanian Television (JTV) come in clearly in Damascus and are said to be more popular than any Syrian broadcast. Syrians like JTV for its Western serials, cartoons, and soap operas, as well as for its polished style. Jordan also controls its television news, but merely by presenting another viewpoint JTV gains credibility from a jaded Syrian public. JTV's second channel includes public affairs programming and documentaries from the BBC, French, and West German television. Popular Western soap operas are a JTV drawing card. To compete, Syrian TV occasionally airs a European or American movie.

Outside the capital, Lebanese and Israeli stations reach southern parts of Syria, while Turkish television is available in Aleppo and along the northern border. Similarly, Iraqi television can be seen in Deir al-Zor and other areas along the Iraqi frontier.

Syrians are enthusiastic consumers of audio tapes and videocassettes, widely sold in all cities and towns. The Ministry of Culture, responsible for censorship in this domain, cannot control and censor these sales because most tapes enter the country on the black market. Syrians who can afford a video recorder (or who have a friend who can) today have access to virtually any film or other video or audio material, even if banned or considered subversive.

The government cannot control radio reception either. Syrians who are serious about following the news can easily listen to Radio Monte Carlo, Voice of America, Radio Cairo, the BBC Arabic Service, and other European state radios, many of which have Arabic-language programming and are available on medium wave. These radio stations punch a large hole in the government's attempts to monopolize all sources of information about current events.

CONTROLLING FOREIGN MEDIA AND JOURNALISTS

The Asad regime is not content to manage the news within Syria. It also controls the press in those areas of Lebanon occupied by its forces and tries to influence international news about Syria—with more success than might be imagined. In doing so, it has committed some serious human rights violations, including the physical destruction of presses and media offices and the torture and assassination of journalists solely because their ideas are not to the liking of the regime.

Almost as soon as Syrian armed forces appeared in Beirut—in early 1976—the Lebanese press became a target. On January 31, Syrian-controlled Saiqa[32] troops attacked two newspapers critical of Syria: *al-Muharrir* (pro-Palestinian) and *Beirut* (pro-Iraqi). After hitting the newspaper offices with rocket fire, Saiqa troops set them ablaze with gasoline, killing seven people and wounding many others, including the well-known Egyptian author and journalist Ibrahim 'Amr. At the same time, Asad demanded that President Elias Sarkis of Lebanon impose strict censorship on the Lebanese press. Under intense Syrian pressure, Sarkis agreed in principle to such censorship, although he did not implement it.

When the Syrian army entered Lebanon in force in the summer of 1976, pressure for press censorship increased. Late that year, the Syrian army occupied and closed down seven newspapers and one magazine in West Beirut, including Lebanon's most famous newspaper *al-Nahar,* as well as *L'Orient-Le-Jour, al-Safir,* and *al-Muharrir.* Only three pro-Syrian newspapers remained. The occupying forces are said to have removed files and equipment, including *al-Nahar*'s modern printing presses.[33]

Syrian forces also arrested several journalists, including *al-Safir* editors Muhammad Mashmushi and Tawfiq Sardawi, both critics of Syrian intervention. They were subsequently imprisoned in Damascus. After a major protest campaign, the Syrians withdrew from the occupied publications, and two months later they released Mashmushi and Sardawi. But *al-Safir* and other newspapers got the message; only rarely since then have they printed items that would seriously displease the Syrian regime.[34]

During the next three years many Arab publications left West Beirut. *Al-Hawadith* and *al-Dustur,* two of the most prominent, relocated to London. Only those prepared to be friendly to Syria remained.

In 1980, the Syrian regime began to threaten Beirut-based Western journalists who were filing stories about the Syrian opposition movement or whose coverage of the region otherwise irked Damascus. Bernd Debusman, the chief Reuters correspondent, was an early target. He began to get warnings, including threatening phone calls from staff at SANA. "They made it known they would take harsh measures," he recalls. In June 1980, Debusman was shot and seriously wounded in the street, moments after leaving a birthday party for BBC correspondent Tim Llewellyn. Most of the foreign press corps were there. "All the other correspondents knew about the warnings," he reports. "The shooting was carried out right under their noses. It was obviously meant as a general warning. After that, people became much more careful."[35]

Debusman left Beirut and began to cover the region from Cyprus. Several other correspondents—including Llewellyn and his colleague Jim Muir of the BBC—soon followed. Both had received death threats, reportedly delivered through informal channels and then confirmed by diplomats.[36] In July, the *New York Times* ran a story on these cases after the State Department expressed concern.[37] The BBC and Reuters seemed to be carefully chosen targets, commented the *Times*: the BBC because of its large number of listeners in the region, Reuters because it is the Western news service most widely used by the regional media.

Le Figaro soon moved its offices to Cyprus as well. From mid-1980 to mid-1982, dozens of other newspapers and electronic media gave up their permanent bureaus in Damascus.[38] Another incident accelerated the process: in May 1981, Syrian-backed forces detained four prominent American journalists in South Lebanon.[39]

Those who remained, or worked out of Cyprus, said far less about Syria. One dramatic example was the coverage of the April 1981 Hama massacre, which was late and sketchy. *Le Monde* did not break the news until May 13, three weeks after the event. The *Washington Post,* the only U.S. publication to cover the story, did not run its piece until late June. To excuse the delay, the *Post* dispatch described the situation journalists were facing:

The massacre reports, in trustworthy and untrustworthy variations, have been discussed in Damascus and Beirut in the last two months. In an atmosphere created by the wounding last June of Reuters correspondent Bernd Debusman, shot in the back by a gunman firing a silencer-equipped pistol, and threats against British Broadcasting Corp. correspondent Tim Llewellyn—both after stories considered by Damascus as unfriendly to Syria—the Hama reports have not been widely published from the area.[40]

It seems, in fact, that Western correspondents waited until stories broke in the Arab press before filing their own (news of Hama first appeared in Baghdad). By that time, the stories were "old news" and likely to be forgotten or buried on inside pages.

The Asad government also used more conventional means to suppress coverage: denying foreign journalists visas or making them wait for very long periods for them. Mary Curtius, a Jerusalem-based reporter for the *Christian Science Monitor*, spent two years trying to obtain a journalist's visa to go to Syria. When it became obvious that it would not come through, she finally traveled to the country on a tourist visa. After filing the story based on this trip, she was blackballed and could not return to Syria under any pretext. Many others have had the same experience.

In some cases, security forces have unceremoniously expelled journalists who attract official disfavor. In January 1986, mukhabarat agents came to get *New York Times* reporter Elaine Sciolino at the Damascus Sheraton a few hours before she was to interview Foreign Minister Farouq Shar'a. With no explanation, she was hustled to the airport and out of the country.[41]

The Syrian regime has dealt even more harshly with critical Arab journalists—especially in the early 1980s—whether they worked in Beirut, the Gulf, or Europe. Some, like exiled Syrian journalist Muhy al-Din Lazakani, who was then working in Abu Dhabi, say that publications were pressured to fire them.[42] Others say they were harassed or threatened.

Worse yet were the assassinations. In March 1980, at the height of the Syrian opposition movement, journalist Salim al-Lawzi was tortured and killed in Beirut. Editor of the Lebanese magazine *al-Hawadith,* he had recently moved his publication to London from Beirut to escape Syrian censorship. In London, he ran a number of articles critical of the Asad regime and its role in Lebanon. Having returned to Beirut for his mother's funeral, al-Lawzi was abducted on his way back to the airport, reportedly near a Syrian checkpoint. His disfigured body was later found in a Beirut suburb, with a right hand that was badly mutilated. This, it is said, was his writing hand—to warn others against angering Hafez Asad.

Two months later, 'Ali al-Jundi was shot. A Syrian journalist working in

Beirut who had published critical articles, he also is considered a victim of Syrian reprisals.[43] Then, on July 23, assailants shot and killed Riyad Taha in Beirut. A leading Lebanese journalist, newspaper publisher, and president of the Lebanese Press Union, Taha had been the key negotiator in the freeing of *al-Safir* reporters Mashmushi and Sardawi. Some say he was killed because he was a leading proponent of a free press in Lebanon, unafraid of standing up to Syria or traveling to Iraq. Many familiar with the case believe that Syria was behind the assassination. Salah al-Din al-Bitar, former Ba'th leader and editor of *al-Ihya al-'Arabi,* was gunned down in Paris just two days earlier—on July 21—in what is almost universally believed to be the work of the Syrian mukhabarat.[44]

Coverage of the great Hama uprising shows how much the Asad regime was able to manage the international press by 1982. Even though Syria's fourth largest city was under siege, the press did not break the story for more than a week. In addition to engineering the general climate of fear, the Syrian government kept journalists from visiting the site or sending dispatches.[45] It warned Syrians working for foreign agencies or media not to break the news prematurely. By the time the news came out—on February 11, nine days after the first incidents—the regime had imposed its will over the city.[46]

The Syrian mukhabarat did not let up the pressure. In April 1982, a bomb exploded outside the offices of *al-Watan al-'Arabi,* an Arabic weekly, in Paris's rue Marbeuf, killing one passerby and injuring forty others. The French government deported the Syrian military attaché shortly afterward, informing the press that it considered Syria responsible for the blast.

In September 1985, Michel al-Nimri, editor of the political bimonthly *al-Nashra,* was gunned down in Athens, where his magazine had just published several of his articles on the lack of democracy in Syria. On the day before he was shot, he wrote in his diary: "Calls from the lion's [Asad's] office that delivered a threat."[47]

The regime's insistence on managing foreign news sometimes leads to ludicrous situations. A former Reuters correspondent recalls one such incident. Late in December 1983, he filed a story about the death of Ahmad Iskandar Ahmad, the Syrian information minister. Seeing the Reuters story, the government issued a denial, even though funeral plans were already underway. One day later, the government announced the minister's sudden death. "Nothing happens unless they say it," commented the correspondent a few years later.[48]

Nothing can excuse or justify the Syrian regime's crude attempts to coerce the press. One ray of light for better international coverage of events within Syria comes, however, from the government's decision in 1988 to permit foreign journalists greater access. Western journalists covering the region from Jerusalem, previously banned simply on the strength of their home base, suddenly found that visas were available.

BOOKS AND WRITERS

The regime heavily censors books, plays, poems, occasional papers, lectures—any public expression of ideas—but censorship is heaviest on analysis of politics, ideology, religion, society, and economics, and especially on discussions of Syria or the Middle East. Nonfiction books must more or less reflect the official point of view, whereas fictional works are given far more latitude. As a result, while social sciences are in deep decline, fiction, theater, and poetry are surviving reasonably well.

Some of the biggest Syrian publishing houses, like the Ministry of Culture or the Ministry of Information, are state entities. Others are semiofficial, like the Arab Writers' Union, which is controlled by the Ba'th party and receives generous state subsidies.

There are also many privately owned firms. Their number has grown because of Asad's move to liberalize the economy and because of declining book imports from Beirut and Cairo.[49] Though ostensibly private, these publishing houses are closely related to the state. The largest private press in Syria, Dar Tlas, is owned by longtime minister of defense Mustafa Tlas, one of Asad's closest associates. That connection has contributed to Tlas's financial success. Among other things, he is able to take his pick of scarce paper imports to keep his presses rolling.[50] Tlas runs his publishing empire out of the Ministry of Defense, a building with prison cells in its basement. When authors speak to him, they rightly wonder whether they are speaking to a publisher or to a principal figure in the state apparatus of repression.[51]

Syrian publishers, all friendly to the regime, are unlikely to publish controversial books.[52] Nevertheless, censors check all books, both before and after publication. Before a manuscript is printed, the censor must stamp his or her approval on every page. After printing, the censor checks the book against the approved text.

The Ministry of Culture and the Writers' Union, two major official publishers, censor their publications. Some Syrians think that the minister of culture, Najah al-'Attar, has attempted to soften the censorship system within her domain, but she faces broad constraints.[53] The Writers' Union also censors most literary works. Other books are reviewed first by the Censorship Office (al-Raqiba) at the Ministry of Information. The most important censor of all is the Bureau for the Training of Cadres in the Ba'th party Regional Command, headed by Ahmad Dargham, former dean of the Faculty of Letters. All works that are directly political, ideological, or religious—that is, all the most sensitive and controversial materials—end up here.

More than one censor works on each book. The first censor reads the book and writes a report, which is sent on to a superior. Depending on the importance of the author, the sensitivity of the subject matter, and other factors, the superior may also read the book and write another report. So it goes, up the chain of command, through several offices. Eventually, the most sensitive matters reach the desk of the minister or of Dargham, one of whom makes the final decision. Obviously, each review up the line is also a check on the censor or censors below.

According to those close to the process, the censors work mostly with "understandings," as written guidelines are few. Censors must follow the latest policy developments, in case a sudden change makes new criteria necessary. Ten years ago, a book about Egypt would have had to be very critical, but today, as relations warm, Egypt can be spoken of in a new way. The worst fear among censors is that high officials will object to a work already approved for publication. So censors tend to err on the side of caution and block works that high-ranking watchdogs might let pass.

Authors can sometimes get their books approved through personal connections with people in high places, but only if the book is a borderline case, not an obvious violation of censorship norms. One author, facing the censors' displeasure, called a powerful minister who was a family friend. Unable to persuade the minister at first, the author called again many times, finally embarrassing the official into letting the book go through.

Even after publication, a book may not reach the bookstores. Any book or play is reviewed a final time before it is released. An important scholarly study was recently printed, bound, and ready for distribution when a final check revealed a problem. No one told the author what this problem was; he learned only that distribution was postponed indefinitely. Today this study of international interest is gathering dust in a Damascus warehouse.

Once a work is approved for distribution (or a play for performance), its future is still not guaranteed. High officials may decide that the censors have erred. The regime may then ban the work and even punish the censors. Not long ago, a censor gave final approval for production of a foreign play. In the play, characters referred to the Arab "invasion" of Egypt at the time of the prophet. When high officials saw the play, they decided that "invasion" was not acceptable and that the entry of Arab armies should have been referred to as "liberation." They banned the play and docked the censor's pay.[54]

"Errors" have also been spotted in university professors' textbooks well after they are in use. Opportunistic colleagues, keen to ingratiate themselves with the party, typically point out "ideological flaws" in the text. Sometimes the matter goes to the party's censors but more often it is handled within the university. The author, anxious to avoid more serious consequences, usually "corrects" the text and it is then reprinted. Threats to textbooks hit home with professors. Since sales are a vital supplement to their income, professors are usually extremely cautious in their writing.

Many writers have learned to work around the censors by using analogies. During the 1980s, a writer who wanted to talk about problems in Syria might have written about problems in Egypt. Since Egypt was out of favor, such a subject would have been not only acceptable but welcome. The reading public, long used to the censorship game, knows how to decipher the meaning. In this way, an adept author can manage to say a lot.

Like journalists, virtually all writers are state employees. They commonly work as translators, editors, teachers, or professors. Some work as censors. Because their income is tied to the state, writers are usually cautious about their political associations and publications. In 1980, when the bar and other professional associations made strong public demands for democracy, the Arab Writers' Union took no official stand, though its executive committee did meet privately with the president. To their concerns about censorship and lack of democracy, Asad is reported to have replied heatedly: "You are a living example of the freedoms here. After all your complaints, you are even received cordially by the president of the Republic!"[55] End of discussion.

The Arab Writers' Union—with its publishing arm, its journals and magazines, and its censorship role—is tightly controlled by the regime. All candidates for the twenty-five-member executive committee must be approved by the party, and most are handpicked. Only four or five seats are left "open." The candidates are screened, of course, but the final choice is made by election. Such are the limits of democracy for Syria's writers.

In fiction writing, where political issues are less overt, a number of excellent writers are at work today in Syria. Some are even handsomely supported by the government. Poets and playwrights 'Ali Kana'an and Mamduh 'Udwan, poet 'Ali Sa'id (Adonis), novelist and short-story writer Haydar Haydar, playwright Sa'dallah Wannus, and poet Shawqi Baghdadi have all won wide public recognition for their talent. Writers from other Arab countries, such as Saudi 'Abd al-Rahman Munif, have come to Syria because they find it more open than their own societies.

Talented favorites have leeway that others lack. Sa'dallah Wannus, who has won many prizes, has never joined the party. During the 1980s, he even gave an interview to an Egyptian newspaper, though most writers would not have dared commit such an offense.

Yet even star authors are not exempt from censorship. 'Udwan, one of the talented 'Alawis, ran into trouble with his play *Lail al-'Abid* (Night of the Slaves). His allegorical treatment of Islam's transition into a state religion apparently struck the censors as too obvious a reference to the Ba'th and they banned the play after one performance.

In 1988, authorities stopped 'Ali 'Akla 'Ursan, president of the (Syrian) Arab Writers' Union, from attending a meeting in Baghdad of the (Pan-Arab) Arab

Writers' Union, of which he was vice president. 'Ursan was detained at the airport at the last minute—a humiliating blow to a leading writer considered a friend to the regime.[56]

Shawqi Baghdadi also ran into trouble in his travels. A well-known Syrian poet, he was allowed to attend a meeting of the General Union of Palestinian Writers and Journalists in Tunis in November 1988. There, he read a poem that had been banned in Syria. When he arrived home, the mukhabarat immediately called him in, questioned him for three days, and warned him not to take such liberties again.

Over the years, some authors have been hit hard. The poet Muhy al-Din Lazakani reports that he was jailed for reading one of his works while a student in Aleppo in 1971. He was later suspended from the university and denied working papers. Al-Din eventually decided to emigrate.[57]

Khalil Brayez, a Syrian military officer in exile, wrote a critical book about the 1967 Arab-Israeli war called *Sukut al-Jolan* (Fall of the Golan) that greatly displeased the Syrian leadership. In 1970, the mukhabarat abducted him from Lebanon. After a cursory trial, he was sentenced to fifteen years in prison. Although his sentence expired in 1985, the authorities still had not released him as of March 1991, some six years later.[58]

The regime does not now imprison writers for their writing alone. Most writers imprisoned in recent years have been connected to underground political parties. Among them are poet Jamal Sa'id, who has been held since 1981 in Tadmur Prison, short-story writer Wa'il al-Sawah, who has also been held since 1981, and writer Mustafa Hussein, who has been held since 1987. All three are members of the Party for Communist Action. Haitham al-Koja, a short-story writer whose book *al-Qaht* (Drought) was published in Beirut, was imprisoned from 1980 to 1987 and is believed to have died as a result of torture. He belonged to the Communist Party-Political Bureau, as did Wadi' Ismandar, a novelist and short-story writer who was held from 1980 until 1986.

Some better-known Syrian writers avoid the censors by having foreign publishers produce their works. Such books may then be imported into Syria, since censors scrutinize imports less strictly than Syrian-published texts. Even if the book is never imported into Syria, though, authors living there must keep in mind the limits of official toleration. Notes one Syrian intellectual: "If you want to publish something that will make them mad, you can't stay in Syria. I avoid hitting them directly, otherwise I would have to pay a high price."[59]

The censors may be more lenient with imported books, but they nevertheless subject them to regular review. They ban books of authors who are considered "enemies" or who are personally out of favor, like Michel Aflaq, a founder of the Ba'th. His two books,[60] written in the late 1950s, say nothing about Asad or his regime (Asad was then just a young pilot). But since Aflaq sought refuge in

Iraq and later spoke out against Asad, the censors utterly forbid these writings, even though they are key texts in the history of Ba'thism. They also ban many books about politics and contemporary history of Syria and the Middle East. A seven-volume collection of early Ba'th documents, published in Beirut under the title *Nidal al-Ba'th* (Struggle of the Ba'th), is forbidden because it contradicts the current official history of the party. The censors ban any book that refers to 'Alawis or to sectarian differences, excluding for this reason virtually all Western studies of contemporary Syria. Patrick Seale's 1989 biography *Asad* is among those on the censors' list. Although Asad granted Seale many hours of interviews over the years, entertained him when he visited Damascus, and received him warmly after the book was published, he has decided that the book discusses too many controversial issues and has refused to allow its distribution in Syria.

Censors generally do not block imported works of literature, culture, and the arts. As one Syrian intellectual noted: "Banning *Macbeth* or *Richard III* because they deal with tyranny is too sophisticated for the Syrian censors. They are not concerned with things at that level."[61] But works on religious topics are considered sensitive. Islamic works of such authors as Sayid Qutb are banned, as are secular discussions and critiques of religion, including the well-known works of Damascus University professor Sadiq al-Azm.

Syrian censors may even target imported literary works if the author is identified with causes in official disfavor. The works of Naguib Mahfouz, Nobel Prize-winning Egyptian novelist, were apparently forbidden for this reason, although they were required reading in literature at Damascus University. Mahfouz had been a friend of Sadat and supported the Camp David Treaty, two of Asad's bêtes noires. The books, written primarily in the 1940s and 1950s, do not discuss contemporary politics, so the author himself was clearly the censors' target. Until recently, Syrian university students had to buy smuggled Mahfouz books in order to complete their literature course. The regime grudgingly tolerated this bizarre arrangement.

Once a year, the regime makes an exception to its book-banning—hosting the Damascus Book Fair on the grounds of the Asad Library. Publishers from the Arab world and beyond are relatively free to display and sell any book (as long as it does not criticize Asad, praise Iraq, discuss Israel favorably, or violate other major taboos). The fair is an enormously popular event, but the question remains: Why does a regime so systematically hostile to ideas and books host such a large book fair?

Because Western Europe is nearby, many Syrians travel there in the course of a year. To get around the censors, they often buy European books and bring them home. Smugglers also bring many banned books into Syria from Lebanon. Ironically, the mukhabarat are major smugglers, so occasionally what they ban with one hand they smuggle into the country with the other. Thanks to these sources, Syrian intellectuals and officials obtained Seale's banned biography of Asad shortly after its Arabic translation appeared in London in the early summer of 1989. In fact, there is almost no book that Syrian intellectuals cannot get.[62] Sometimes it seems that the aim of the regime is not to prevent people from reading certain texts but to impose fear and caution among all those who work in the realm of ideas.[63] At another level, though, the barriers do keep controversial ideas in a narrow circuit, preventing wider dissemination of critical texts and blocking alternative ideas among the literate public.

CINEMA

In spite of heavy censorship, Syrian filmmakers have made many excellent films. The censors have ruled out most realist films and documentaries, but they approve much social criticism that uses fictional forms. The regime might have dealt more harshly with the independent intellectuals who are the country's most successful filmmakers, but it has chosen not to do so. Rather than replace them with second-rate party hacks, it has supported their work while keeping up a constant pressure for conformity.

Syrian film production dates back to the 1920s. In the late 1940s, spurred by Lebanese financing and distribution, Syria began turning out several films a year, mostly light comedies and musicals. A new Syrian army studio also produced some serious films, and during the union with Egypt the government set up a short-lived state film studio within the new Ministry of Culture.[64]

In 1966, the Jadid regime established the National Film Center (al-Mu'assasa al-'Ama li-Sinama), a production unit planned as a propaganda arm of the state. Surprisingly, it soon began to release outstanding films, thanks to five or six talented young filmmakers on the staff. The center's director, Hamid Merei, encouraged their penchant for social criticism, hoping to justify the new regime by criticizing pre-Ba'thist society.

The filmmakers saw things differently. Young, committed, and idealistic, they wanted above all to examine the present without illusions. They set to work on a series of politically engaged documentary shorts and feature productions, their confidence strengthened by an international prize at the Carthage Film Festival in 1970.[65] But of twenty shorts produced, the censors banned five. In 1974, Asad dismissed Merei as head of the center and appointed a more conservative director who ruled out documentaries and decided that only fiction would be allowed. The center went on to produce over ten fiction features in the period up to 1980.

Best-known among the filmmakers of that period is 'Omar Amirallay, who finished his first full-length documentary film, *al-Hayat al-Yumia fi Qaria Suria* (Daily Life in a Syrian Village), in 1974. The film portrayed the failure of the Ba'thist agrarian reform program, which displeased party people who attended the preview. They tried to pressure Amirallay into adding a new, more upbeat ending. When he refused, they seized the negatives and banned the film, destroying two years' work of one of Syria's most promising filmmakers.[66]

In spite of the pressures, other filmmakers managed to produce and show engaging features and shorts. Nabil al-Malih did the humorous *Sayid al-Taqaddumi* (Mister Progressive), Burhan 'Alawiya *Kafr Qasim* (Qasim Village), and Muhi al-din Mu'adhdhin *Khan al-Armanazi* (The Armanazi Caravanserai). None of these serious films challenged the regime and they passed the censors. Amirallay was then asked to do a feature for television, which resulted in *al-Dajaj* (The Chickens), also about a rural village. This time, he steered away from economic problems and treated politics much more indirectly. The film, which gained a great underground reputation, was too much for the censors—apparently because of Amirallay's caustic symbolism and his treatment of religion in a Christian village. It never appeared on television and officials seized the negatives.

In the 1970s, the *nawadi al-sinama* (film clubs) located in every city became important gathering places. There, intellectuals of the secular opposition showed foreign films and organized lectures and conferences. Centers of opposition activity and safe meeting sites, they were the mosques of the secular intelligentsia.

The government crackdown in spring 1980 changed the equation dramatically, forcing the film clubs to curtail their programming. All the top filmmakers at the center went into exile, despairing of the future of Syrian cinema. Amirallay left for France in 1981, where he pursued a successful career in French television; the rest scattered to Germany, Greece, Libya, Kuwait, and the United States.

Remarkably, a talented new group of Syrian filmmakers emerged in the 1980s, also under the auspices of the National Film Center. Of this group, Muhammad Malas won acclaim in 1985 with his first feature film, *Ahlam al-Medina* (Dreams of the City), which earned first prize at the festivals of Valencia and Carthage. Malas deliberately chose a topic that predated the Ba'th era to get the film past the censors. The National Film Center continued to produce a feature-length film every year or so, and in the late 1980s two other widely praised films appeared: *Liali 'Ibn Awa* (Nights of the Jackal), by 'Abd al-Latif and 'Abd al-Hamid, and *Nujum al-Nahar* (Stars of the Day) by Usama Muhammad.[67] Although 'Abd al-Hamid's film won the censor's approval, his colleague's did not.

Muhammad completed *Stars of the Day* in 1988. Before it was released in

Syria, he sent the film abroad, where it won first prize at the Festival of Valencia and the International Festival of Rabat. A much-commended entry at Cannes, it gained commercial distribution in Spain, Germany, Switzerland, and France. Finally, in May 1989, Muhammad screened the film in Damascus at a special preview attended by high officials and military officers. Many did not like what they saw. Muhammad, an ʿAlawi, had depicted the moral crisis of a rural ʿAlawi family whose members move to the city and become involved in urban life and corrupt officialdom. The plot was a metaphor for the regime. After the preview, months passed. The censors did not ban the film, but neither did they approve it for distribution. Although the National Film Center funded and produced *Stars of the Day,* the film may never be shown in Syria.

In spite of such frustrations, the new generation of filmmakers has not given up. In early 1990, Malas began work on the first Syrian-French coproduction. Syria is now such an inexpensive production site for European-financed films that quality Syrian filmmaking may be able to survive in this way and escape the pressure of the censors.

Low production costs carry a danger for Syrian cinema, however. Many Arab companies, with money from Lebanon, Jordan, and the Persian Gulf, are increasingly making cheap TV serials in Syria, drawing away technical talent from serious projects. As one filmmaker complained, these serials, subject to the narrow requirements and censorship of the Gulf market, are more stiflingly censored by their producers than by the worst Syrian censors.[68]

Films for theatrical showing have also been made with Arab money. Among the most popular are the slapstick comedies of Duraid Laham, a former Syrian television actor. *Al-Taqrir* (The Report), a big hit in 1986, pokes fun at those in power without breaking rules of censorship. Although the plot tells of a vast scheme of corruption, it is not identifiably set in Syria, and the president of the fictional country never learns of the malfeasance.

The Syrian government controls film distribution through a state monopoly established in 1969. Censors examine every imported film and disapprove of some, but most commercial films encounter no problem. Syrian theaters show many foreign films, and audiences appreciate Egyptian and Indian melodramas as well as Hollywood action features like *Terminator,* which was popular in Damascus in the summer of 1989.

For political and intellectual film fare, Syrians sometimes circumvent censorship by attending film festivals at the cultural centers of foreign embassies. The film clubs, though not as freewheeling as they were in the late 1970s, also continue to screen interesting, politically controversial films. In spring 1989, with Soviet political reforms in official Syrian disfavor, the film clubs put on a weeklong festival of new Soviet cinema—another form of indirect commentary on Syria.

THE UNIVERSITIES

The battle over ideas in Syria has been most organized and intense in the universities—four large institutions that today enroll over 130,000 students and employ several thousand faculty members.[69] The regime uses a dense network of security agents and informants to keep track of campus activities. The Student Branch of the Political Security Agency is the mukhabarat with primary responsibility in this domain.

Faculty are under heavy pressure to conform. Failure to do so can easily cost them their jobs. Students are reminded constantly that independent thought is dangerous and cooperation the best route to jobs and economic success. Yet resistance to the regime is always just below the surface on campus. The well-mannered, prayerful young men and scarved women are a visible reminder of the Islamic opposition current. Other oppositions are also present, as hotly contested student elections in 1986 demonstrated.[70]

From its earliest days, the Ba'thist regime has sought to impose ideological control over the universities. One former faculty member recalled being summoned in 1963 by Dean (now Ba'thist security chief) 'Abd al-Ra'uf al-Kasm and questioned about the student movement. "In those days, you could still get away with refusing," he said. "Today, they do not forgive you so easily if you do not agree to collaborate."[71]

When Asad came to power, the campuses seethed with independent political activity—the worldwide student protests of May 1968 were then only two years behind. A half-dozen or more underground student publications circulated,[72] and a dozen or more underground groups worked side by side with rebellious Ba'thists and legal Communists. Students at Damascus University were the first group to protest Asad's ascent to power, organizing a demonstration in 1970 with the slogans "Down with the dictatorships! Down with the military regimes!"[73]

To eliminate this opposition, Asad brought in his brother Rif'at. In April 1975, the Sixth Regional Congress of the party named Rif'at head of the Regional Command Bureau of Higher Education, a post with authority over all universities. At the same time, of course, Rif'at was commander of the Defense Brigades and Syria's top security chief. He immediately enlarged the mukhabarat presence on campus, recruiting hundreds of informants to identify members of the student opposition. Many students were expelled, with no possibility of appeal.

Rif'at also stepped up classes in party doctrine and increased pressure on professors to join the party ranks. As one former faculty member reported: "I would run into Rif'at from time to time, and he would always ask me when I was going to take out party membership. More and more, he treated my refusal as insubordination. I began to fear what would happened to me if I held out much longer."[74]

Rif'at used the carrot as well as the stick. To friendly professors, he offered travel opportunities, security, and money. To high school students who enrolled in his special parachute training courses, he gave bonus points on their university admission tests, which helped them win places in the most sought-after programs.

His henchmen joined the faculty. Salim Barakat, an 'Alawi chief at the Bureau of Higher Education, appointed himself lecturer in Damascus University's Philosophy and Sociology Department, awarded himself a doctorate, and promoted himself to full professor. Meanwhile, Rif'at arranged a Ph.D. in economics from Moscow University for himself in 1974. His dissertation, widely known as a ghostwritten fraud, was even published in book form in Damascus.[75]

Though Rif'at strengthened the security apparatus on campus, he could not contain the opposition movement of the late 1970s. Students and faculty were among the most active supporters of the Islamist, liberal democrat, and leftist opposition movements. The regime finally struck. When Aleppo University students marched in fall 1979 to mukhabarat headquarters in al-Sabil, security forces opened fire, killing three, wounding many, and arresting over a hundred.

In the months that followed, student protests multiplied, culminating in the nationwide strikes of March 1980. The regime responded even more sternly. The army occupied Aleppo University, arresting hundreds of students. In Damascus and Lataqia, security forces arrested hundreds more. Ten years later, more than a hundred students had still not been released. Some may have been killed in detention.[76]

Professors felt the heat as well, especially beginning in autumn 1979. At the University of Damascus, officials dismissed four leftist professors and arrested nine others suspected of belonging to the Muslim Brothers. Also arrested were engineering professors Rif'at Siufi and Asif Shahin, two well-known critics of the regime. Two other professors fled for fear of their lives. In less than a year, from late 1979 through mid-1980, authorities dismissed or transferred to ministry jobs more than a hundred professors. The mukhabarat arrested or detained dozens more. The teaching program at the Faculty of Medicine was disrupted for over two years: no anatomy professors remained, though there was certainly no shortage of cadavers.

After the 1980 Regional Congress, Rif'at left his post at the Bureau of Higher Education, and Ahmad Diab, head of the party's National Security Bureau, replaced him. For the second consecutive time, the senior higher education post in the country went to a security chief.[77]

In the decade since, Syrian universities have been relatively quiet. Reminders of state security are everywhere. Mukhabarat agents check student identifications and other agents operate openly on campus. In the summer of 1989, at the al-Mezze arts campus of Damascus University, armed security agents guarded the campus entrance and four armored cars stood under tarpaulin covers outside a lecture hall.

Students must participate in weekly military training and are subject to military discipline. Political ideology courses are required, offered by instructors from the Ba'th party institute. In 1984, the government prescribed standard clothing on campus. Walls are adorned with banners and posters of Hafez Asad; his likeness is even spray-painted on campus buildings.

Admission to the universities is no longer as heavily influenced by political factors as it was at the apogee of Rif'at's influence. But military, security, and party chiefs continue to intervene in both admissions and grading. According to one professor, when high officials call him up "they do not issue an order, just a request for a favor which is hard to turn down!"[78] Intervention can be far from subtle. According to Patrick Seale, "The daughter of one security chief turned up for her examination with a posse of bodyguards and insisted that the professor help her write her paper."[79]

The Ba'th party awards many travel grants and scholarships for study abroad, especially to the Soviet Union and Eastern Europe. Political criteria are primary factors in getting a scholarship. Students can still win scholarships based solely on merit, but it takes a great deal of hard work and many prefer to take the easier route.

All faculty appointments are said to be screened by the mukhabarat and the party.[80] Professors who exhibit even the slightest independence are under intense pressure. Mukhabarat informers listen to their lectures. Party zealots comb their textbooks for ideological errors. If they are not yet party members, they are harassed to join. If they want to give public lectures, even on nuclear physics, they must ask permission of the mukhabarat.[81] If their intellectual work takes them along unusual avenues of thought, they may be called in to explain themselves. At any time the regime wishes, it can dispense with their services.

Hani Rahib, a professor of English at Damascus University and a well-known writer, is a case in point. Teaching for a time at the University of Sana' in Yemen, he returned to Damascus in the summer of 1985 to give a speech at an Arab Writers' Union meeting. His address criticized executive committee candidates as government informers and called for freedom of the press. He also remarked that freedoms were greater in Egypt than in Syria. Soon afterward, Ba'th official Ahmad Dargham called him in and accused him of "supporting

Camp David." A week later, security agents arrested him as he and his family were about to board a plane for Yemen. Although he was soon released, his passport was withheld. Five days later, the Education Ministry stripped him of his post at Damascus University. He could not leave the country for more than two years and now has a job at the University of Kuwait.[82]

9

FOREIGN RELATIONS AND THE HUMAN RIGHTS CONNECTION

In its annual report on human rights, the United States government regularly expresses concern for human rights violations in Syria. When it comes to action, however, the American record has been abysmal. The State Department takes the position that it cannot effectively raise human rights issues with the Asad government through public diplomacy, only in private conversations. But there is little evidence that the matter comes up in private, either. Judging from the many ways U.S. administrations could—but have not—subtly put the heat on Syria (through press leaks, for example, or by working through the U.N. Commission on Human Rights), it seems clear that human rights have received little consideration, even in the most stormy periods of U.S.-Syrian relations.

The United States is not alone in this approach to Syria. The Soviet Union, West Germany, France, and other major Western countries have a similar record. In Paris, an official at the Foreign Ministry explained to Middle East Watch: "We are concerned, but there is not much that we can do."[1] Indeed, far from encouraging Syria to protect human rights, the United States, France, the Soviet Union, Saudi Arabia, and other states have sometimes done the opposite. This record, unfortunately, stretches back over more than four decades.

THE ERA OF COUPS

Beginning not long after Syria gained independence from France, foreign governments supported a number of coups and covert actions that helped bring the country military rule and its strong security services. The coups undercut democratic forces and weakened chances for a constitutional political system— one that would protect fundamental human rights—to take root. British, French, Egyptian, Iraqi, and Soviet intelligence personnel were all active in the clandestine operations of that era,[2] but the United States was the most active of all. Recently uncovered classified documents have shed light on what happened.[3]

In the late 1940s, U.S. policymakers became alarmed when the Syrian government, bowing to public pressure, refused to let an American oil company build a pipeline through its territory. Washington also found the strong anti-Western sentiment and the large Communist party in Syria ominous. Concerned that Syria was "drifting leftward," the Central Intelligence Agency laid plans to overthrow Syria's three-year-old civilian government.

Early in 1949, CIA operatives Miles Copeland and Stephen Meade met in Damascus with a group of right-wing military officers—including the Kurdish chief of staff Husni Za'im—to discuss the possibility of installing a "military-supported dictatorship."[4] In one of his reports, Meade described the Syrian chief of staff as a "Banana Republic dictator type."[5] Meade and Copeland helped Za'im lay detailed plans for overthrowing the government. On the morning of March 30, 1949, army units took control of the capital and Za'im seized power. As the first military coup in the postcolonial Middle East, the putsch set a deadly precedent. Only weeks afterward, Meade enthusiastically reported to Washington that "over 400 Commies [in] all parts of Syria have been arrested."[6]

The pro-American regime did not last long. Za'im was overthrown after only a few months in power in a coup sponsored by British intelligence. Shortly thereafter, yet another coup brought to power Col. Adib Shishakli. At first, Shishakli shared power with civilians. But U.S. policymakers—again concerned about radical currents in Syrian politics—labeled Syria a "particularly sensitive danger spot."[7]

During several discussions, Copeland and U.S. embassy officials promised Colonel Shishakli arms and economic support in exchange for Syrian participation in a regional Western military pact. But the Syrian public resolutely opposed such an alliance. Eventually, Shishakli dissolved parliament at the end of November 1951 and set up a military dictatorship. Washington welcomed the move and soon offered economic aid.[8]

The following April, Shishakli suspended all opposition parties and banned the opposition press. Later, Assistant Secretary of State Henry Byroade commented to John Foster Dulles that "Shishakli represents the best available Syrian regime from our standpoint."[9] But the United States again grew concerned when prodemocracy military officers toppled Shishakli in February 1954 and restored elections and parliamentary politics. In May 1955, the CIA sent agent Wilbur Eveland to Damascus to encourage military officers to "save their country."[10] When Eveland failed to produce results, Washington joined with British intelligence to map out Operation Straggle—a complex effort to destabilize the government in Damascus. The plan involved fomenting border incidents, sabotage, and tribal uprisings. An army coup was to follow.[11]

American policymakers—encouraged by the success of the U.S.- and British-engineered overthrow of Iran's Prime Minister Mohammed Mossadegh two years earlier, which had restored Muhammad Reza Shah to his throne—saw the action as a similar blow against communism. President Eisenhower and Secretary of State John Foster Dulles publicly warned that Syria, under communist influence, might soon attack its neighbors. Though U.S. intelligence officials knew well that this assessment did not reflect Syria's military weakness,[12] Eisenhower believed that Syria was ripe for communism because it lacked a strongman like Egypt's ʿAbd al-Nasir.[13]

The operation got underway early in 1956, when the United States and Britain delivered arms to Druze and bedouin tribes. But Syrian counterintelligence, under Col. ʿAbd al-Hamid Sarraj, caught wind of the scheme and CIA officials aborted it.

That, however, was not the end of American involvement. Washington, concerned about Syria's weapons deal with the Soviets, set in motion another covert action known as Operation Wappen early in August 1957. When this failed, policymakers tried a second version of Operation Straggle: they moved the Sixth Fleet into the Eastern Mediterranean, sent American jets to a forward base in Turkey, persuaded Turkey to mass large military forces on the Syrian border, and sent State Department official Loy Henderson on a well-publicized emergency tour through the region to mobilize allies against Syria.[14]

The operation backfired dramatically; its main effect was to promote precisely the kind of Soviet influence it was meant to deflect. The Syrian government now turned to the USSR for long-term support against Western pressures to join the Baghdad Pact defense agreement.

But it was pressure from another, less predictable quarter that finally forced the United States to back down. In September 1947, King Saʿud of Saudi Arabia—a conservative American ally—arrived in Damascus to make several speeches affirming Syria's right to independence from foreign interference. Such strong Arab backing, especially coming from a friend of the United States, had a powerful effect in Syria. This Saudi-Syrian relationship would develop further in coming years.

THE SOVIET CONNECTION

When Communist party candidate Khalid Bakdash was elected to the Syrian parliament in 1954, the country was hardly poised on the brink of a workers' revolution. Indeed, Bakdash was the first (and only) Communist deputy in the Arab world. For reasons far removed from ideology, however, Damascus was poised to embark on a long-term strategic relationship with Moscow.

Both had a strong anti-Western interest in the link. The Soviets sought to counter the Western-established Baghdad Pact and recruit local allies in the widening cold war. The Syrian government needed arms and economic aid— which the West had refused to provide—and wanted to avoid joining a pact with the former colonial powers. In autumn 1955, the two countries signed their first arms deal.[15]

After the Suez War in 1956, the Soviet-Syrian relationship blossomed. (Britain had stopped supplying the Syrian air force, and neither France nor the United States would consider deals for arms or aid.)[16] During a trip to Moscow in the summer of 1957, Syrian defense minister Khalid al-'Azm concluded a $579 million economic cooperation agreement. In exchange for wheat, the Syrians received Soviet arms as well as economic support for the development of port facilities, dams, and factories.[17]

This relationship with the Soviets even survived Syria's union with Egypt, in spite of the country's imprisonment of many Syrian communists. As elsewhere in the world, the Soviet communist leadership found it convenient to ignore the plight of a local party when larger Soviet geopolitical interests were at stake. The ties also weathered several subsequent changes of government. After the coup of 1963, the new Ba'thist government continued to welcome Soviet overtures, even though most Ba'thists were harsh enemies of local communists. Salah Jadid's coup in 1966 brought the Marxist wing of the Ba'th to the fore, and relations with Moscow warmed correspondingly. Indeed, the Ba'th now even modeled itself after the Soviet Communist party. Syrian Communist leader Khalid Bakdash returned to Damascus from his exile in Moscow, while new agreements forged closer links between the two countries.

During the Jadid period, Hafez Asad was known for his opposition to Damascus's growing reliance on the Soviet Union.[18] An anticommunist responsible for purging many party members from the armed forces, he was expected to distance his regime from the Soviets when he came to power in 1970. Instead, Asad continued friendly relations with Moscow while developing a broader constellation of international allies, especially among the oil-rich states of the Arabian Peninsula. On his second trip to Moscow, July 5–8, 1972, Asad came away with a $700 million arms deal. During the October 1973 war with Israel, Moscow provided essential diplomatic and military backing; it resupplied Syria with arms and even threatened direct intervention if the Israelis advanced on Damascus.

Moscow's ardor cooled after Asad began to intervene in Lebanon early in 1976, though the Soviet Union continued to supply Damascus with arms and economic aid. But, in his hour of need, as internal opposition to the Syrian regime mounted in the late 1970s, the Soviets once more provided strong support to Asad. Since the Camp David accords between Egypt and Israel (Syria and the Soviet Union had been among the biggest losers as a result) Asad had become their most important regional ally.

The Soviet leadership thus welcomed the Syrian president to Moscow in June 1979 and agreed to a $500 million debt write-off, generous economic and technical agreements, and the largest arms deal the two countries had ever struck, including provisions for fourteen hundred tanks and two thousand armored vehicles. Some of those armaments were later used against the Syrian population in the harsh crackdown against internal dissent.

The Soviet connection also provided ideological fuel for the campaign against the Syrian opposition. In a long speech to the Seventh Regional Congress late in 1979, Rifa't al-Asad consciously drew on Soviet precedent to justify the crackdown, telling the Ba'thist delegates: "Stalin, comrades, liquidated ten million men for the benefit of the communist revolution, taking into account only unconditional adherence to the party and its positions."[19]

The Soviets demonstrated their backing for the beleaguered regime in a number of other ways. Moscow helped organize an international trade union meeting in Damascus in May 1980. On October 8, the two countries signed a long-term treaty of friendship and cooperation. Throughout the Syrian domestic crisis, Soviet arms supplies and advisers arrived in growing numbers.

Soviet-Syrian relations remained warm even after Asad's crisis ended. In the 1980s, the Soviets helped Asad toward his goal of "strategic parity" with Israel by providing generous credits and such sophisticated new weapons as advanced surface-to-surface missiles and latest-model Mig aircraft. Frequent meetings in Moscow and Damascus—accompanied by expressions of lasting friendship and close "strategic" relations—linked the two countries in an embrace of public diplomacy. In October 1982, the two countries signed a protocol of cooperation between the Ba'th party and the Soviet Communist party. The number of Soviet advisers in Syria—mostly military personnel—had grown to over three thousand by the mid-1980s.[20] And in April 1986, with Arab subsidies to Syria in decline, the Soviets baled Asad out by agreeing to a major rescheduling of Syria's $15 billion military debt to the USSR.

After Mikhail Gorbachev took over at the Kremlin, however, Soviet policy toward the Middle East underwent far-reaching change, in the course of which Syria's place in the firmament began to fade. By late 1986, Soviet supplies of military hardware had declined perceptibly, while Soviet journals began to criticize the Syrian idea of "strategic parity" with Israel.[21] If Asad still harbored any doubts about the way Moscow was heading, the message was drummed home by Gorbachev during a long toast to the visiting Syrian leader in April

1987. Relations nonetheless remained cordial, and in the summer of 1988 the two countries signed important new economic and military accords.

Serious strains in Soviet-Syrian relations began to appear only later that year, in part because of Soviet overtures to Israel and in part because of Soviet cutbacks in military sales. Then, on April 11, 1989, Syrian helicopters fired rockets at two Soviet naval ships cruising thirty-nine miles off the Syrian coast.[22] Although Syria apologized and called the incident an "error," Soviet advisers began to pull out. By early 1990, their number was down below five hundred. In November 1989, Soviet ambassador to Damascus Alexander Zotov told a *Washington Post* interviewer that Syria should stop trying to achieve strategic parity with Israel and that future Soviet weapons supplies would be available only as a "function of the Syrian capacity to pay."[23] Rumors circulated that the Soviets were pressuring Syria to begin repaying its arms debt.

With communism in serious disarray in Moscow, the Soviets no longer offered the Asad regime the ideological support they had in the past. As a result, Syrian censors increasingly found fault with Soviet magazines, which began to disappear from local newsstands. And in the summer of 1989, Syria cut back orders from the Soviet film export company.[24]

In spite of all this, the two governments maintained close ties and Soviet arms shipments continued, albeit on a much smaller scale than in the past. And at no time in the long history of their relations has Moscow expressed public concern about Syrian human rights, not even when its own closest supporters in local Communist parties were being purged, imprisoned, and tortured. By contrast, the Soviet Union is known to have intervened on several occasions with Iraq to try to protect Iraqi Communists.

THE SAUDIS AND OTHER REGIONAL ALLIES

Another decade passed after King Sa'ud's dramatic appearance in Damascus in 1957 before the Saudis widened ties with Syria—by cautiously offering financial relief in the wake of the Arab-Israeli war of 1967. But when Asad took power and began to search for wider international support, Saudi aid burgeoned. Radical Syria was observed to have a "very cordial foreign policy towards the conservative Arab states, particularly Saudi Arabia."[25] After the 1973 war, the Saudis led in reconstruction assistance and military aid to Syria. During a state visit to Damascus in January 1975, King Faisal promised $350 million for that year alone.[26]

Saudi generosity increased further the next year. It now included a subsidy to Syria's "Arab deterrent force" in Lebanon, pushing total Arab aid to nearly

$500 million for the year. Two years later, at a November 1978 summit in Baghdad, Arab oil producers agreed to a ten-year aid package, including $1.8 billion annually to support Syria's "confrontation" with Israel.[27] The consortium lived up to the promise for three years, with the Saudis alone providing nearly $1 billion a year. The cash flow began to dry up, however, after oil prices dropped and Syria backed Iran in the Iran-Iraq War, commencing in 1980. By 1987, annual support from the Arab states had fallen to $800 million. Yet the Saudis remained generous—apparently in an effort to prevent Iraq from dominating the Persian Gulf. In addition to money, they gave Syria free, or concessionally priced, oil, along with grain to help it through its drought crises. Support from the conservative desert kingdom totaled nearly a billion dollars in 1989—a substantial proportion of Syria's annual military and security expenses.

In 1990—although the Baghdad aid package had run its ten-year course—the Saudis were still financing Syria, though their assistance was reportedly in decline before Iraq's invasion of Kuwait on August 2. Asad has no doubt calculated that throwing in his lot with Saudi Arabia, the other Gulf states, and the West will repay him a financial dividend.[28]

THE UNITED STATES

Even after the United States gave up trying to arrange coups against the government in office and help install more U.S.-attuned rulers in Damascus, relations with Syria remained limited for over a decade. The Jadid government formally severed diplomatic relations when the United States backed Israel in the 1967 war. But when Hafez Asad came to power three years later, he sought to improve Syria's ties with the West and soon developed an active—if complex, and often sub rosa—relationship with Washington. This association, commonly described by officials as a "dialogue," has brought the two parties together on many issues, even while conflict between them formally persists. Relations improved dramatically in the wake of the 1973 Arab-Israeli war. Secretary of State Henry Kissinger visited Damascus many times to negotiate a cease-fire and disengagement accord between Syria and Israel, and Washington and Damascus restored diplomatic ties soon thereafter.[29] In 1974, the World Bank approved a $100 million loan to Syria, and the next year, U.S. economic aid began to flow into Syria at an annual rate of $60 to $100 million.[30] Private American and other Western investments followed, helping fuel Syria's postwar economic boom.[31]

By the end of 1975—a year and a half after the Golan disengagement agreement—the link was strong enough for Kissinger and Asad to strike an entirely different deal. The understanding would permit Syrian intervention in the Lebanese civil war on behalf of the Maronite Christian Phalange and against the left-wing forces and their Palestinian allies, who seemed about to prevail in the conflict.[32]

It began on October 16, 1975, when U.S. Ambassador Richard Murphy proposed that Asad promote "a balanced solution" in Lebanon and promised American support for the venture. Murphy said that Israel could be convinced to go along with the idea if Syria respected certain limits.[33] Israel gave that consent by late March 1976, with the understanding that Syria not deploy units in Lebanon south of a "red line" or maintain forces that would threaten Israel's defenses.[34] The State Department began to talk openly of a "constructive" role for Syria in Lebanon. Syria did not wait to take advantage of the opportunity. While Special Envoy Dean Brown was concluding final negotiations in Damascus and Jerusalem, the Syrian navy blockaded the Lebanese coast. On April 9, Syrian commando and Special Forces units quietly entered the country. At the end of May, regular Syrian units rolled across the border, and by July an estimated thirteen thousand Syrian troops with four hundred tanks were in control of large areas of Lebanon.[35] A few months later—with various Arab states providing financial support and token troops—the enterprise was rebaptized the "Arab Deterrent Force."

The United States government continued its "dialogue" with Syria after Kissinger's departure from the State Department in January 1977. Even though fierce differences later arose between Washington and Damascus over the Camp David Accords of 1978, the United States continued to support a Syrian role in Lebanon throughout the 1970s. Syria's abysmal human rights record notwithstanding, between 1977 and 1979 the Carter administration signed a new air transport agreement with Syria and gave funds and assistance for food and agricultural development, highways, and rural roads.

The level of assistance was not much different under President Jimmy Carter than it had been during the Kissinger era. Although Carter claimed to have made human rights central to his foreign policy, they appeared to have played no real role in his administration's relations with Syria. In fact, many of the worst rights abuses took place in Syria during Carter's term: the occupation of Aleppo and mass executions there; the Tadmur Prison massacre; mass executions at Jisr al-Shughur and Sarmada, and more. These abuses never came up in Washington's public dealings with the Asad government. In private, the Carter administration raised only one issue: the emigration of Syrian Jews.

United States policy toward Syria changed course only after the Reagan administration took office in 1981. Emphasizing the cold war dimension of international politics, Washington policymakers now publicly identified Syria as a Soviet surrogate and supporter of terrorism. Relations cooled dramatically, and aid stopped. Curiously, however, the new administration did not bring up Syrian human rights violations—even though it did so vociferously regarding other countries seen as cold war enemies. The administration even was restrained in its comments on the Hama massacre in 1982. In fact, on March 3 of that year, while the Syrian military was laying waste to the city and its inhabitants, Washington quietly eased earlier export restrictions.

The dialogue continued, often at the highest level, between Asad or Foreign Minister 'Abd al-Halim Khaddam and U.S. diplomats in Damascus, including special presidential envoy Philip Habib.[36] This, even though the Israeli invasion of Lebanon in mid-1982 further strained relations. While denouncing U.S. backing for Israel, Asad quietly sent his envoys to Washington: Rif'at al-Asad in August–September 1982[37] and Khaddam, who reportedly made several trips to the U.S. capital late that year.

Serious tensions developed over the role of American and Israeli forces in Lebanon after the Israeli invasion. United States Navy fighter planes struck at Syrian SAMs (Surface to Air Missiles) in Lebanon in 1983, and Syria shot down two F-14 reconnaissance fighters on November 10, 1983. Asad even mobilized 100,000 army reserves as a gesture of resolve during the crisis.

But by early 1984, the confrontation with Syria over Lebanon was proving increasingly unproductive, and Washington again began to seek more talks and cooperation with Damascus. In Senate Foreign Relations Committee hearings January 11, those testifying on military and intelligence questions overwhelmingly favored a warmer policy toward Syria.[38] Richard Murphy—former ambassador to Damascus and now assistant secretary of state for Near Eastern and South Asian Affairs—announced to the House Subcommittee on Europe and the Middle East on January 26: "We have informed the government of Syria that we are prepared to improve our relations and to cooperate to achieve concrete solutions to practical problems."[39]

Over the next six years, Murphy worked actively to broaden discussions with Damascus on such issues as Lebanon, the Western hostages being held there, and possible approaches to a wider Arab-Israeli peace settlement. Other U.S. envoys and intelligence chiefs were also involved, including CIA Director William Casey, who met with Asad in Damascus on July 29, 1986.[40] Not everyone in Washington, however, sought to thaw relations. In 1986, Vice President George Bush canceled a planned visit to Damascus because of congressional pressure. "U.S. policy towards Syria has been deeply ambivalent," complained Business Week in autumn 1986: "Administration officials have alternately described Pres. Hafez Asad as a stabilizing force in the Middle East and as a dangerous, Soviet-backed sponsor of terrorism." The article concluded that getting tough with Syria "conflicts with other foreign policy goals."[41]

The anti-Damascus faction in Washington again won out late in 1986, when a British court implicated Syria in the Hindawi Affair—the attempted bombing in London of an El Al airliner. On November 14, the Reagan administration withdrew Ambassador William Eagleton, reduced the embassy staff in Damascus, and banned all "high level" discussions with the Asad regime. The United States also imposed a variety of sanctions, including new export controls and a suspension of Export-Import Bank loans, subsidized wheat sales, and air service agreements. It also "recommended" that U.S. oil companies stop doing business in Syria, advice the companies, experienced in dealing with the shifting winds of international boycotts, quietly circumvented by moving their growing Syrian prospecting to European subsidiaries.[42]

In spite of the censure, the State Department seemed almost at pains at times to maintain good relations with Syria—even if it meant obscuring human rights issues. In January 1987, for example, when Voice of America correspondent Muhammad Gunaim was imprisoned for ten days in Damascus, the *Washington Post* reported that the State Department had tried to keep the incident quiet.[43] That month, the ban on high-level talks crumbled as well. State Department Syria specialist April Glaspie arrived in Damascus for talks and Murphy soon followed.

By the summer, the United States had dropped all pretense of wanting to end its Syrian ties. Late in June, President Reagan sent Asad a letter offering better relations.[44] On July 5, 1987, only eight months after the freeze was instituted, United Nations Ambassador and troubleshooter extraordinaire Vernon Walters arrived in Damascus for eleven days of talks, including lengthy private discussions with Asad. Walters later described his meetings as "very useful, very fruitful and very cordial."[45] By the end of August, Reagan was publicly thanking Asad for helping arrange the release of a hostage in Beirut, and Ambassador Eagleton returned to Damascus on September 6. The freeze was over.

The United States tried to broaden this dialogue by drawing Damascus into supporting Washington's Arab-Israeli peace plan. By 1988, the diplomatic activity had become so intense that it was being called the era of the "Glaspie-Murphy initiative."[46] Even though Asad remained cool to these proposals, active cooperation between the two governments over Lebanon increased.

On September 16–17, 1988, Murphy held intense negotiations with Asad over a joint U.S.-Syrian initiative centered on finding a mutually acceptable candidate for the Lebanese presidency. Though their bid failed, subsequent office holders are said to have been screened by Syria and the United States. Some analysts saw Murphy's move from the State Department to a post at the Council on Foreign Relations early in 1989 as a setback for the U.S.-Syrian dialogue. In fact, relations have continued to improve steadily under the Bush administration.

Signs of the growing cordiality have multiplied: in 1989, the United States Information Services arranged for twelve top Syrian journalists to visit the

United States. It was an unprecedented move, coming after years of anti-American hostility in the official Syrian media.[47] Early that July, the Syrian information minister told a *New York Times* reporter: "We are quite optimistic in our understandings with the Bush Administration and its policy towards the Middle East. . . . The dialogue is proceeding at the highest level between the U.S. and Syria."[48] In September, Secretary of State James Baker met with Foreign Minister Farouq Shar'a of Syria at the United Nations General Assembly. And on October 10, U.S. Ambassador Edward Djeridjian told the press in Damascus that the United States supported Syria's role in the Lebanese crisis.[49] Accompanied by former Secretary of State Cyrus Vance, Murphy, who remains a consultant to the State Department, led a delegation to Damascus in December 1989.

In addition to diplomatic exchanges, high-level security discussions between Syria and the United States were reported. For instance, a high officer of Syrian Military Intelligence in Lebanon is said to have visited Washington for talks with U.S. intelligence officials in September 1989.[50] United States officials would not confirm this story, but they told Middle East Watch that such a visit would be in keeping with the current dialogue.

That interchange had gathered so much momentum by spring 1990 that the Bush administration began to consider ending the sanctions. In late May, veteran journalist Patrick Seale said the talks between Washington and Damascus were of "unprecedented intimacy."[51] When Iraq invaded Kuwait, the Bush administration turned to Syria as an important regional counterweight. If the past forty years are anything to go by, little can be expected from Washington in the event of any future human rights outrage by the Asad regime, and perhaps less than ever following the warming of relations produced by shared hostility to Saddam Hussein.

PROSPECTS FOR THE FUTURE

As Western ties to Syria gradually expand, the cold war ends, and the aftermath of the Allied defeat of Iraq is resolved, it remains to be seen how these developments will affect conditions in Syria. Many of the constants of the Asad era are now in flux, but important continuities remain. On the international level, Syria is embroiled in two conflicts—those in Lebanon and with Israel—which tend to block any impetus to dismantle its strong military-security system. Syria's involvement in the anti-Iraq alliance and postwar Arab peacekeeping talks makes the Asad regime more vulnerable to U.S. pressure. The Bush Administration, however, is unlikely to press human rights issues that could undermine its new standing in the region.

10

CONCLUSIONS AND RECOMMENDATIONS

The Asad regime has been a gross violator of human rights throughout the more than two decades it has controlled Syria. Today, in spite of gestures toward liberalization, its practices remain repugnant. Having killed at least ten thousand of its citizens in the past twenty years, the Asad regime continues to kill through summary executions and violent treatment in prison. It routinely tortures prisoners and arrests and holds thousands without charge or trial. It persecutes some of its minorities.

The regime denies freedom of expression and association to its citizens and refuses them their right to democratic participation in government. It has imposed harsh conditions in its occupation of Lebanon, where it acts with even more violence than in Syria. Although conditions may have ameliorated somewhat at home, Syrian-inspired abuses in Lebanon today are as bad as any practiced in the past.

The time has come for this to stop.

The recommendations by Middle East Watch fall into three categories.

THE SYRIAN GOVERNMENT

Abolish the state of emergency, remaining aspects of martial law, and all exceptional legislation.

Abolish all special courts, including the exceptional military courts, the state security courts, and the military field tribunals.

Immediately release all prisoners held for their peaceful expression or association, as well as all family members detained in lieu of persons sought by the authorities or detained in retaliation for their flight.

Promptly bring to trial all others held by the security forces.

Guarantee to all those arrested, for whatever reason, immediate access to family, lawyers, and medical care.

Allow international organizations and private human rights groups access to Syrian territory to investigate charges of human rights violations and to verify human rights conditions.

Abolish all censorship, including control of the publication and circulation of newspapers, books, and periodicals, control of the cinema, control over universities and schools, and all other controls, de jure and de facto, over the expression of ideas.

Allow public meetings to be held without prior control.

Allow full freedom of association, including the formation of private organizations, professional associations, trade unions, and political parties without state interference.

Institute equality of rights and status for all political parties.

Treat all citizens equally, irrespective of religion, language, or nationality, and especially:

—take all necessary steps to assure citizens that no one community in Syria is the recipient of acts of favoritism;

—permit Kurds full freedom of language, celebration of holidays, and other expressions of identity, and review the claims of those deprived of citizenship in 1962;

—allow Jews full freedom of travel and of emigration, equally with all other Syrians, abolish special mention of their religious or ethnic affiliation on identity documents, and end all other discriminatory treatment;

—allow Palestinians freedom of expression, of travel, and of organization, equally with all Syrians, and cease all extraordinary security measures directed at this community.

THE UNITED STATES GOVERNMENT AND CONGRESS

Keep in place existing sanctions. Broaden their significance, making them contingent on improvements in Syria's human rights.

Publicly condemn the Syrian government for its human rights violations as documented in the State Department's annual report on human rights.

Work in the United Nations and U.N. Commission on Human Rights for resolutions condemning Syria for its gross rights violations.

Seek to engage the Syrian government in a dialogue on these human rights concerns.

Distance itself from relations with Syria, either directly or through its allies, which tend to give Syria political, economic, or strategic support—until such time as it proves that it has curbed its gross rights abuses.

Conduct public hearings in Congress on human rights violations in Syria.

THE INTERNATIONAL COMMUNITY

Bring pressure to bear on the Syrian government by political and other means to persuade it to cease its serious rights violations, including public statements of concern, support for multilateral sanctions, support for U.N. resolutions, and the like.

Through the United Nations and its various agencies, do everything possible to focus attention on Syrian rights violations and to call attention to Syria's commitments under the U.N.-sponsored international rights covenants.

APPENDIX A

TYPES OF TORTURE IN SYRIA
THE AMNESTY INTERNATIONAL LIST

"The following are details of allegations of torture and ill-treatment which have been made to Amnesty International over several years by former detainees. It should be noted that not all of the methods listed below are widely used in Syria. Some are said to be exclusive to certain prisons or detention and interrogation centers. They are said to include:

1. Beatings on all parts of the body, involving punching, slapping and/or kicking, administered with fists, feet, leather, belts, sticks, whips, hammers, braided steel cables or cables inside plastic hoses with the ends frayed;
2. *Dullab* (tyre): hanging the victim from a suspended tyre and beating him/her with sticks, clubs, cables or whips;
3. *Falaqa*: beating the soles of the feet;
4. *Bisat al-Rih* (Flying Carpet): strapping the victim to a piece of wood shaped like a human body and either beating him or her or applying electric shocks all over the body;
5. *As-Shabah* (the Phantom): tying the victim's arms behind the back and suspending him or her by them or by the feet. In both cases the victim may also be beaten or given electric shocks;
6. *Al-'Abd al-Aswad* (the Black Slave): strapping the victim onto a device which, when switched on, inserts a heated metal skewer into the anus;
7. *Al-Kursi al-Almani* (the German Chair): a metal chair with moving parts to which the victim is tied by the hands and feet. The backrest of the chair bends backwards, causing acute hyperextension of the spine and severe pressure on the victim's neck and limbs. This is said to result in difficulty in breathing almost to the point of asphyxiation, loss of consciousness, and, in some cases, the fracturing of the vertebrae. A variation of this device is known as *al-Kursi al-Suri*

or Syrian Chair. In this metal blades are fixed onto the front legs of the chair at the point where the victim's feet are tied, causing profuse bleeding from the ankles when pressure is applied. Both variations may be used in conjunction with beating or whipping.

8. *Al-Ghassala* (Washing Machine): a hollow spinning drum similar to that of a domestic washing machine into which the victim is forced to insert his or her arms, resulting in the arms and/or fingers being crushed;

9. Using domestic appliances to burn parts of the body such as the chest, back, genitals, buttocks, and feet. The appliances include electric boilers (hot water tanks) against which the victim's body is pressed; paraffin stoves covered with a metal sheet on which the victim is forced to sit; electric irons; electric welding machines;

10. Placing a piece of cotton wool soaked in petrol on various parts of the body and setting it alight; pouring petrol on the victim's feet and setting them alight;

11. Piercing the victim's back or chest with a pointed heated metal rod;

12. Extinguishing cigarettes on sensitive parts of the body; using gas lighters to burn the victim's beard, moustache or other body hair;

13. Applying electricity to sensitive parts of the body including the ears, nose, tongue, neck, hands, genitals, anus, and feet;

14. Applying salts and caustic substances (acidic and alkaline solutions) to the victim's wounds or burns;

15. Slashing the victim's face—lips, ears, nose—with shaving knives and razor blades;

16. Forcing the victim to stand in bare feet against a wall with the hands tied together above the head. The top of the victim's foot and toes are then crushed with the heel of a boot in a grinding motion;

17. Administering blows to the same areas of the victim's body (including the head) for prolonged periods with a long thin rod tipped with a metal ball;

18. Suspending the victim by the hands and feet to bedposts or by the feet from a ladder, and beating or whipping him or her;

19. *Al-Farruj* (the Chicken): strapping the victim to a revolving wooden bar resembling a roasting spit and subjecting him or her to beating with sticks;

20. Hanging the victim for prolonged periods by the neck in such a way that the neck is not broken;

21. Suspending victims from a rotating fan in the ceiling and beating them as they rotate;

22. Forcing the victim to lie fully clothed in a bathtub filled with water

for prolonged periods (sometimes overnight). Water may also be poured onto the victim at the same time.

23. Showering or pouring boiling hot or cold water alternately over the victim;
24. Plucking hair or skin with pincers or pliers;
25. Extracting finger and toe nails;
26. Sexual abuse or assault;
27. Forcing the victim to sit on bottle necks or inserting bottles or sticks in the rectum;
28. Forcing the victim to stand for long periods on one leg or to run carrying heavy weights;
29. Complete isolation in a small dark cell without any human contact at all for several days;
30. Switching on the light while the victim is asleep or keeping a bright light on for long or short periods day or night, possibly for several days;
31. Using loudspeakers to transmit noise, such as loud music and screams of people undergoing torture;
32. Subjecting the victim to mock execution, by holding his or her head below water almost to the point of suffocation;
33. *Al-Miqsala* (Guillotine): forcing the victim to lie on his or her back, facing the blade. A device on the machine ensures that the blade stops just before it touches the victim's neck;
34. Threatening the victim that his or her relatives or friends are in danger of, for example, torture, sexual abuse, assault, kidnapping, amputation of limbs, and execution;
35. Torturing other detainees in front of the victim;
36. Torturing or sexually assaulting the victim's relatives in his or her presence;
37. Degrading the victim by using obscene language or insults or by forcing him or her to undress in front of guards of the opposite sex;
38. Depriving the victim of sleep, food, water, fresh air, toilet or washing facilities, visits by relatives or medical treatment."

Tortures reported subsequent to this report include kneeling for hours on small stones or gravel and hanging by the hands from the ceiling. There are also many small modifications of all these methods.

Source: Amnesty International, "Syria: Torture by the Security Forces," September 1984, pp. 18-21.

APPENDIX B

FOREIGN ASSASSINATIONS

There is considerable evidence that Syrian security agencies have assassinated persons in foreign countries. In some instances, these agencies appear to have carried out assassination campaigns as an instrument of Syrian foreign policy. Patrick Seale said this about the Syrian regime's "undeclared war" on King Hussein of Jordan, 1983–1985:

> In October 1983, the Jordanian ambassadors to India and Italy were wounded in gun attacks; in November a Jordanian official was killed and another seriously wounded in Athens, and three explosive devices [were] defused in Amman; in December a Jordanian consular official was killed and another wounded in Madrid. In March 1984 a bomb exploded outside Amman's Intercontinental hotel and in November the Jordanian chargé d'affaires in Athens narrowly escaped being shot when his attacker's gun jammed. In December the Jordanian counsellor in Bucharest was shot dead. In April 1985 there was an attack on the Jordanian embassy in Rome and on a Jordanian aircraft at Athens airport. In July the Madrid office of Alia, the Jordanian airline, was machine-gunned and the first secretary of the Jordanian embassy in Ankara was shot dead. In August a Palestinian was arrested in Athens on suspicion of planning a second attempt on the life of the Jordanian chargé. It must be assumed that at least some of these assaults on Jordanians were the work of Syria. (Seale, *Asad,* pp. 464-65)

A list of some of the cases of assassination about which the greatest consensus exists follows. It should be remembered that this list is of prominent persons only. Many more ordinary citizens have likely been assassinated abroad under similar circumstances, most of them in Lebanon.

Muhammad ʿUmran   March 14, 1972

Leader of the five original members of the Baʿth Military Committee, ʿUmran held various military and government posts, including minister of defense. He was on the losing side in the Salah Jadid coup of 1966, was held in al-Mezze

152

Prison, and then released. 'Umran went into exile in Tripoli, Lebanon, where he was apparently planning a political comeback. He was murdered in Tripoli.

Kamal Jumblat   March 16, 1977

The top Druze chieftain, Jumblat had been a sharp critic of Syrian intervention in Lebanon and was the leader of the Left-Palestinian alliance within the Lebanese National Movement, which the Syrians opposed. He was assassinated in his car while driving from his home to a town in the Shuf.

Salah al-Din al-Bitar   July 21, 1980

A founder of the Ba'th party and prime minister during the early Ba'th years, al-Bitar had been in exile since 1966, first in Beirut and later in Paris. Condemned to death in absentia in 1969 and pardoned by Asad in 1970, he remained a thorn in the side of the regime. He was independent of Iraq and something of a rallying figure for the Syrian opposition. In 1979, he set up his own periodical, *al-Ihya' al-'Arabi* (Arab Revival), calling for more democracy and warning of the problem of 'Alawi domination of the regime. He was shot outside his home in Paris.

Riyad Taha   July 23, 1980

A leading Lebanese journalist, newspaper publisher, and head of the Lebanese Press Union, Taha played a leading role in pressing Syria to release Lebanese journalists arrested by their forces to restrict free expression. He was killed in Beirut, some say after returning from a trip to Iraq.

Salim al-Lawzi   March 4, 1981

Editor of the Lebanese newspaper *al-Hawadith* (Events), al-Lawzi moved with his paper to London to find greater freedom of expression than was possible in Lebanon under Syrian occupation. After publishing a number of articles critical of the Asad regime, he was abducted when he traveled to Lebanon to attend his mother's funeral. He was apparently tortured and killed and his body mutilated before being dumped in a Beirut suburb—his right hand is said to have been burned by acid as a warning to others whose writing might displease the regime.

Bayan [Binar?] al-Tantawi   March 15, 1981

The wife of 'Issam al-'Attar, a leader of the Muslim Brotherhood who opposed violence against the regime, she was killed in Aachen, Germany, when she opened the front door of her home. Her murder was an assassination attempt against her husband, who was not home at the time.

Louis DeLaMar   September 4, 1981

French ambassador to Lebanon, DeLaMar was killed in Beirut, allegedly in retribution for trying to set up a meeting between Yasir ʿArafat and the French foreign minister without a Syrian representative present. The Foreign Ministry of France believes that Syrians assassinated DeLaMar.

Michel al-Nimri   September 18, 1985

Editor of the Arabic-language political magazine *al-Nashra* (The Review), based in Athens, al-Nimri was killed in Athens after writing several articles about the lack of democracy in Syria. On the day before he was shot, he wrote in his diary: "Calls from the lion's [Asad's] office that delivered a threat."

Michel Seurat   Died while held captive in late 1985

A French researcher and writer who had written many articles critical of the Asad regime, Seurat was abducted March 22, 1985, in Beirut and died in captivity in Lebanon some months later. Some say he died of cancer, though he was not suffering from this disease at the time of his capture. Many with knowledge of the case consider the Syrians responsible.

Shaykh Subhi al-Salah   May 16, 1989

Vice president of the Higher Muslim Council of Lebanon, al-Salah was killed allegedly because he was working for Lebanese reunification outside of Syrian control.

CASES OF ATTEMPTED ASSASSINATION

Mudar Badran   September 1980

Prime minister and former security chief of Jordan, Badran was considered responsible for Jordanian support of violence committed by the Muslim Brotherhood in Syria. The Syrian security agents from Saraya al-Difaʿ who were assigned to carry out the assassination were arrested by Jordanian authorities as they attempted to cross the border into Jordan, and they later confessed on television.

'Issam al-'Attar   March 15, 1981

This assassination attempt killed his wife, Bayan [Binar?] al-Tantawi (see above). A leader of the Muslim Brotherhood, he is the brother of the longtime Syrian minister of culture. Ironically, he is the former leader of the faction of the Muslim Brotherhood that has opposed the use of violence.

Bernd Debusman   June 1980

A Reuters correspondent in Beirut, Debusman wrote a number of stories that displeased the Asad regime. He was shot and wounded after receiving threats from Syrian sources (see chapter 7).

APPENDIX C

SYRIAN POLITICAL PARTIES
AND PARTY ALLIANCES

National Progressive Front (al-Jubha al-Qawmia al-Taqadumia). Formed
March 23, 1972.
   Arab Ba'th Socialist party (Hizb al-'Arab al-Ba'th al-Ishtiraki)
   Syrian Communist party (Hizb al-Shuyu'i al-Suri). There are now two dif-
      ferent formations within the front by this name, headed by Khalid Bak-
      dash and Yusuf Faisal, respectively.
   Arab Socialist Union (al-Ittihad al-Ishtiraki al-'Arabi) (Nasirists). Headed
      by Fawzi Kayyali.
   Arab Socialist party (Hizb al-Ishtiraki al-'Arabi; or, al-Ishtirakiun
      al-'Arab). Headed by 'Abd al-Ghani Qanut.
   Socialist Unionists (al-Wahdawioun al-Ishtiraki al-'Arab). Headed by Faiz
      Ismail.

National Democratic Alliance (al-Tajammu' al-Watani al-Dimuqrati). Left-
      wing Opposition, formed January 1980.
   Ba'th Arab Socialist Democratic party (Hizb al-'Arab al-Ba'th al-Ishtiraki
      al-Dimuqrati). Movement of February 23; headed by Brahim
      Makhouss, Shamseddin al-Atassi, Michel Satouf, and 'Akab Yahid.
   Arab Socialist Union (Ittihad al-Ishtiraki al-'Arabi). Headed by Dr. Jamal
      al-Atassi.
   Communist Party–Political Bureau (al-Hizb al-Shuyu'i al-Suri-al-Maktab
      al-Siyassi). Headed by Riyad al-Turk.
   Workers' Revolutionary party (Hizb al-'Ummal al-Thawri). Headed by
      Tariq Abou al-Hassan.
   Arab Socialists (Ishtirakiun al-'Arab)

National Alliance for the Liberation of Syria (al-Tahlouf al-Watani li-Tahrir
      Suria). Founded March 11, 1982. Headed by Basil Yusuf.

Muslim Brotherhood (al-Ikhwan al-Muslimin). There are two factions—a majority faction, headed by 'Abd al-Fatah Abu Ghoddeh, and a minority faction, headed by 'Adnan Sa'deddin.

Ba'th Arab Socialist party (Hizb al-Ba'th). Michel Aflaq's pro-Iraqi faction, founded March 8, 1982.

Socialist Union (Ittihad al-Ishtiraki). Headed by Muhammad Derrah.

Salah Bitar group (not a party, but a splinter of the Ba'th). Headed by Nisim Safar Jalani, Khaled al-Hakim (trade unionist in Cairo), and Hamoud al-Shoufi.

Independent Groupings

Party for Communist Action (Hizb al-'Amal al-Shuyu'i). Founded first as the Movement for Communist Action in August 1976.

Arab Socialists (Ishtirakiun al-'Arab). Headed by Akram Hourani and followers.

Arab Socialist Union (Ittihad al-Ishtiraki al-'Arabi). Headed by Muhammad al-Jarah and Jasim al-'Ulwan.

Popular Nasirist Organization (Tanzim al-Nasiri al-Sha'bi). Headed by Hamad Khalifa.

Union of Communist Struggle (Ittihad al-Nidal al-Shuyu'i)

Popular Committees (al-Lijan al-Sha'biya)

There are also the following:

Committee for the Defense of Freedom and Political Prisoners in Syria (Lajna al-Difa' al-Hurriya wa-al-Mu'ataqlin al-Siyasiyin fi Suriya)

Committees for the Defense of Democratic Freedoms and Human Rights in Syria (Lijan al-Difa' 'an al-Hurriyat al-Dimuqratiya wa Huquq al-Insan fi Suriya)

APPENDIX D

IMPRISONED PROFESSIONALS

In April 1980, the Syrian government arrested more than 250 lawyers, engineers, and medical professionals who were officers of their professional associations or otherwise active in the protests for democracy (see chapters 2 and 6). None was charged with a crime or tried. All lawyers have now been released, except those like Riyad al-Turk held because of their connection to the political opposition, but many engineers, physicians, veterinarians, and pharmacists remain unaccounted for and are believed to be in custody.

After international protests, the government released a number of the imprisoned lawyers in the early 1980s, but thirteen remained in custody in 1985. The Arab Lawyers' Union (ALU) continued a campaign for their release, and in May 1986, President Asad promised delegates of the ALU who were holding an executive committee meeting in Damascus that the lawyers would be freed. Eventually, ten of the thirteen were freed on November 30. They were: Dibo Abboud, 'Adnan 'Arabi, Michel Arbash, George Atiyeh, 'Abd al-Karim Jurud, Muhammad Hamdi al-Khorasami, Haitham Malih, Bahjat al-Missouti, Sa'id Nino, and Assad 'Ulabi.

The ALU continued to pressure Asad to release the final three amid reports of their continued mistreatment. In 1989, the ALU finally managed to gain their release in April as part of arrangements for holding the ALU General Congress in Damascus in June. They were: Salim 'Aqil, Thuraya 'Abd al-Karim, and 'Abd al-Majid Manjuneh.

Among the medical professionals, ninety had not been released as of June 1990. They include: Farhan al-Azhari, veterinary surgeon from Homs; Muhammad Nizar al-Daqr, professor of dermatology, Faculty of Medicine, Damascus University; Ibrahim Faris, pediatrician from Lataqia; Usama al-Hashimi, dentist from Aleppo; Mahmud al-Jaziri, professor of surgery, Faculty of Medicine, Damascus University; Qasim Musa, ear, nose, and throat specialist from Lataqia; Muhammad Mukhlis Qannut, surgeon from Hama; Muhammad Nasir al-Siba'i, anesthetist from Homs; Fadil Sirajiyya, ophthalmologist from Aleppo; and Qaddur 'Ubaidan, general practitioner from Idlib.

Other medical professionals not yet released are: Zahi ʿAbbadi, Muwaffaq ʿAbd al-Dayim, Khulud al-ʿAbdallah, Tahsin al-ʿAbdallah, Hisham Zain al-ʿAbidin, Muhammad ʿUthman al-Abrash, Muhammad ʿAfissa, ʿAbd al-Bari al-Akhras, Mustafa ʿAraqil, Hisham ʿArnaʿut, Dr. Assaf, ʿAbd al-Qahir al-Atasi, ʿAbd al-Aziz ʿAttura, Yasir ʿAwni ʿAwna, Muwaffaq ʿAyyash, Muhammad Baradʿi, Nimr Barazi, Muhammad Asad Bisata, Muhammad Faiz Bismar, ʿAbd al-ʿAziz Bin ʿAbd al-Qadir Bitar, Ahmad al-Bushi, Ahmad Dalati, Kamal Kaba Dar, ʿAbd al-Majid Ghazal, Muhammad ʿAli Ghazal, Ghassan Mustafa al-Haj, Muhammad Halima, Ahmad Hazifa, Rfiq Ibrahim Ibrahim, Marwan al-Idlibi, Radwan ʿIqrin, Jalal Jalaghi, Darwish Janu, Husain Jarrah, Nadim Jawda, Mahmud Kassab, Salih al-Khoja, Adib Kirdawi, ʿAbd al-Rahman Kittanji, Walid Maʿmar, Hassan al-Mufti, Naji Muhabek, Hassan Najjar, Munib Zahri al-Najjar, Muhammad Nino, Ahmad Qaraquz, ʿAyuisha Qutaish, ʿArfan Ràshdiqi, Muhammad Mansur al-Rifaʿi, Hassan Saʿid, Badr al-Din al-Safadi, Bashir Saifu, ʿAbd al-ʿAziz al-Salih, Taisir Samsam, Muhammad Zakariyya Saqqal, ʿAbd al-ʿAziz ʿAbd al-Qadir Sawwan, Saʿid Shakir, ʿAbd al-Qadir Shallat, Fawwaz Ahmad Sharbak, Jamal Shuman, Khadr al-Sutari, Muhammad Dib Tahmaz, Fawwaz Taqi al-Din, ʿAbd al-Rahman Tutu, ʿAbd al-Rauf ʿUbaid, Usama ʿUrfali, ʿAbd al-Salam ʿUthman, Husam ʿUthman, Mustafa ʿUthman, ʿAdil ʿUthmani, Majid ʿUthmani, ʿAbd al-Fattah al-Wadi, ʿAbd al-Latif Yunusu, and Saʿid Zaidan.

Seventy engineers also have not yet been released. They include: Riad al-Bastati, secretary general of the Damascus branch of the Syrian Engineers Association; Salah Bin ʿAli al-Ibrahim, electrical engineer from Idlib; Hasan Jamal al-Din, civil engineer from Homs; Jalal Khanji, member of the Central Committee of the Syrian Engineers Association and lecturer at the University of Aleppo; Ghassan Najjar, member of the Central Committee of the Syrian Engineers' Association, from Aleppo; Maʿmun Sawwah, from Damascus; Talal Sufi, agricultural engineer from Lataqia; and Suhair Zuhri, military engineer from Idlib.

Other engineers not yet released are: ʿAdnawi al-ʿAdawi, Muhammad ʿAli Ajjaj, ʿAbd al-Hadi Akhras, Ibrahim Akhras, Muhammad Hassan ʿAlwani, Khalid Antar, Diham Atassi, ʿAwneh ʿAwneh, Badr ʿAwni, ʿAdnan ʿAyrut, ʿAbd al-Karim Barakat, ʿAdil Bitar, Radwan Dahhan, Ahmad Shafiq Dali, Jamal Dali, Riad Dali, Nihad ʿAbd al-Shaikh Dib, Ahmad Faris, Khalid Faris, ʿAli Ghabsheh, ʿUbaid Mustafa al-Hani, Yusuf Muhammad Saʿid Jabr, ʿAbdallah Ahmad Jadʿa, ʿAdnan al-Jassim, ʿAdideh Kaʿdan, ʿAbd al-Ghani Kharrat, Haithan al-Khatib, Muhammad al-Khatib, ʿAbd al-Qadir Koujou, Fadil Maʿakadeh, ʿAbd al-Karim Mahshiyyah, Talal Mahshiyyah, Bassam Mali, Jihad Missouti, ʿAbd al-Halim ʿAbd al-Muʿim, ʿUmar Musa, Fatih Najjar, Nadir Qarqanawi, Adib Qartawi, ʿAbd al-Majid Qattani, Talal Rai, Muhammad

Sayyid Rassas, Usama Sa'dun, Bassam Safur, Mustapha Sahyuni, Qassim al-Sa'id, Farid Bin 'Adnan Abu Salid, Rasul Sarraj, Muhammad 'Ali Satif, Shakir Bin 'Umr Sarwani, Ahmad Shaban, Bassam Najm al-Din Siba'i, Muhammad Zahi Sufi, 'Abd al-Latif Talib, 'Issam al-Tarabulsi, Usama al-Tarabulsi, Bashshar Tarazi, Hamid Hamid al-'Umr, Sami Walid, and Hassan Zeitun.

There is reason to believe that some of these persons are no longer living and may have been summarily executed or died under torture or otherwise died in captivity. Some may have been victims of the Tadmur Prison massacre. Many, however, are known to remain in custody.

APPENDIX E

PRISONS AND DETENTION CENTERS HOLDING POLITICAL PRISONERS IN DAMASCUS AND ALEPPO

Prison	Location	Intelligence Service
Damascus and Vicinity*		
1. Al-Mezze	al-Mezze (W)	Military Prison
2. ʿAdra	Duma	Civil Prison
3. Saydnaya	Saydnaya (N)	Civil Prison
4. Qatana (women)	Qatana (SW)	Civil Prison
5. Harasta (women)	Harasta (S)	Civil Prison
6. Military Interrogation Branch	Jamarik (W)	Military Intelligence
7. Palestine Branch	Malki (N)	Military Intelligence
8. Commando Police Interrogation	n/a†	Military Intelligence
9. Al-ʿAdawi Interrogation Center	al-ʿAdawi	Military Intelligence
10. Halbuni Prison	Near Hijaz Station	Military Intelligence
11. Qabun Detention Center	Qabun	Military Intelligence
12. Al-Qasa' Interrogation Center	al-Qasa' (NE) near Shifa' Hospital	General Intelligence
13. Kafr Sussa	Kafr Sussa (SW)	General Intelligence
14. Abu Rumana Interrogation Center	Abu Rumana (N)	Political Security
15. Sha'lan Detention Center	Airport Road (SE)	(Formerly Defense)
16. Rawda Detention Center	Rawda (SE)	n/a
17. Air Force Intelligence Prison	n/a	Air Force Intelligence
18. Special Forces Detention Center	n/a	Special Forces
19. Italian Prison	n/a	n/a

Prison	Location	Intelligence Service
Damascus and Vicinity*		
20. Abbasin Detention Center	n/a	n/a
21. Nabek Detention Center	n/a	n/a
22. Zabadani Prison	n/a	n/a
Aleppo		
1. State Security—Civil Prison	Muhafaza District	General Intelligence
2. State Security—Military Prison	Near Customs	General Intelligence
3. Central Prison	Muslimiya Road	Civil Prison
4. Military Interrogation Branch	Near Baghdad Station	Military Intelligence
5. Hanano Prison	Bab al-Hadid	Military Police
6. Political Security Prison	Jamiliya District	Political Security
7. Jina'i Detention Center	ʿAziziya District	n/a
8. Artillery School Prison	Ramussa District	n/a

*This is a partial list.
†Not available.

APPENDIX F

DRUG CULTIVATION AND TRAFFIC IN LEBANON

Considerable evidence has accumulated to suggest that high-ranking Syrian officials—especially military and security officials—are involved in narcotics trafficking. This traffic originates in areas of Lebanon controlled by Syria and in particular the Biqʿa valley, an area where cannabis was widely grown before Syria's intervention in 1976 and which is now increasingly devoted to opium cultivation.

Reports have often mentioned Rifʿat al-Asad, vice president and brother of the president, as a major figure in this traffic. An article in the French periodical *L'Express* (May 1987, pp. 34–41) provided evidence of Syrian links to Lebanese drugs and of Rifʿat's ties to international narcotics networks. In May 1985, having seized several heroin shipments, Spanish police held an inquiry that resulted in the expulsion of two high-ranking Syrian diplomats—the consul general and the chief of security at the embassy. The Syrian ambassador was cited by the Spanish media as a top figure in the Syrian drug connection, with close ties to Rifʿat.

The traffic in narcotics apparently puts huge sums of money in the hands of Syrian security chiefs, increasing their personal power and autonomy. In its article of May 1987, *L'Express,* citing the U.S. Drug Enforcement Administration (DEA), estimated that traffic in opium alone yielded Syrians about $1 billion in 1986 (p. 36; *L'Express,* also citing the DEA, stated that the hashish trade—after processing from raw cannabis—was worth $6 billion, though only a portion of that was thought to pass into Syrian hands.) Traffic in opium has grown fivefold since then.

Information on Lebanese production and related issues has been collected by the DEA and is available from the *International Narcotics Control Strategy Report (INCSR),* published annually by the Bureau of International Narcotics Matters of the U.S. Department of State. According to the 1989 edition of this report, opium production increased sharply in Lebanon in 1988 and it became a "major producer," though not one of the world's largest. In 1988, Lebanon produced 48,600 metric tons of cannabis, 700 metric tons of (processed) hashish, and 30 metric tons of raw opium. Opium production was up sharply from 6 metric tons the year before. Approximately 5 metric tons of heroin were produced from local opium crops during 1988. Since 1986, Lebanon has also become a major point for the transshipment of cocaine.

Some reports have suggested an even greater production of opium in Lebanon. An article in the French newspaper *Le Figaro* of June 11, 1988, estimated Lebanese production at 60 tons of raw opium annually. This article also reported on secret processing laboratories, the movement of drugs, and hundreds of millions of dollars of sales, shared among growers, processors, traffickers, and military forces.

The 1990 *INCSR* estimates that between 1988 and 1989 the land area in Lebanon under opium cultivation more than doubled—from 2,000 to 4,500 hectares (4,940–11,115 acres). In the same period, production is estimated to have increased from 30 to 45 metric tons. The report estimates that virtually all of this opium is converted into heroin in laboratories in Lebanon and Syria.

Lebanese drug production takes place in areas under the control of various forces, but the main area of cultivation is the Biqʻa valley, which is almost entirely under Syrian military control. According to the *INCSR,* Syrian forces protect growing areas and must approve shipments through Syrian military checkpoints. Some reports suggest that Syrian military vehicles are used in the shipment process (the *L'Express* article claims that drugs are also shipped in Syrian military helicopters).

Lebanese opium is converted into heroin in laboratories in the Biqʻa valley. Since 1987, laboratories have been set up in Syria. Aleppo is most often mentioned as a location, but other laboratories are said to exist in Damascus, Homs, and Hama. Given the tight security throughout Syria, it is inconceivable that these laboratories exist without the collusion of the Syrian government. In fact, it is inconceivable that the entire drug operation, in both Syria and Lebanon, goes on without the participation of the Syrian government. According to the 1990 *INCSR,* Lebanese drugs are shipped across various borders, some going out through Syria and some through Israel, but the bulk through Lebanon's Mediterranean ports—including ports controlled by Christian forces and those controlled by Syria, including Tripoli. Egypt has historically been the major destination for the hashish production. Other production goes out over Lebanese trading networks and Turkish and Syrian networks. The *INCSR* estimates that 40 percent of this heroin and 20 percent of the hashish reaches the United States.

The 1988 *INCSR* alludes to the involvement of the Syrian government and to individuals connected to the Syrian government, but bureau officials claim that they are not in a position to go further and that they lack information to substantiate such charges. The U.S. government may, however, have more information at its disposal than it admits, according to a former drug enforcement investigator who spoke with Middle East Watch. He said that he had worked on the Lebanese case and that a major DEA study has established many of the drug connections.

The 1990 *INCSR* goes slightly further than the 1989 report in establishing Syrian responsibility for this traffic. It states: "U.S. officials believe that individual Syrian soldiers and other officials stationed in Lebanon's Beka' Valley, as well as some higher level military officials, are involved in the drug trade . . . rumors persist of high-level Syrian military involvement in drug smuggling" (p. 367). The report also cautiously implicates the Syrian government: "Other than the Israeli security zone in the South and the Christian enclave of Lebanon, sixty-five percent of the country is controlled by Syria, including the prime drug producing area of the Beka' Valley. We believe that Syria tolerates and profits from the drug production and trafficking in the areas over which it exercises control" (p. 362).

Recent reports in the press have made disturbing allegations concerning French and U.S. collusion in this drug traffic, supposedly as part of deals for the release of hostages, but possibly motivated by other government interests. On November 19, 1989, an article in the *Toronto Star* referred to a confidential report written for Pan American Airlines by a former Israeli security figure. The report allegedly claimed that in 1988 the French government lent two top chemists to drug dealers in Syrian-controlled Lebanon to help set up heroin refineries there under the control of Syrian businessman Monzer al-Kassar, a European-based figure said to have close connections to Rif'at Asad. The same report was said to contain information about a CIA deal with al-Kassar in which the CIA was alleged to have helped Kassar get drugs into the United States in exchange for his "help." Kassar's brother is married to the daughter of 'Ali Duba, chief of Syrian Military Intelligence.

Other sources have identified al-Kassar as a figure involved in the Iran-Contra deals. It has been said that he worked on arms shipments to Iran and to the Contras. On September 26, 1989, *Middle East Insider* reported that "at the same time al-Kassar was wanted by the DEA, in 1985 he was organizing the shipment of 360 tons of East Bloc AK-47's to the Contras on behalf of the National Security Council" (p. 4).

Year	Cannabis	Hashish	Opium
1985	50,000	720	6
1986	50,000	720	6
1987	48,600	700	6
1988	48,600	700	30
1989	n/a*	905	45

Source: U.S. State Department, *International Narcotics Control Strategy Report* (Washington, D.C.: USGPO, 1989, 1990), p. 367.
*Not available.

APPENDIX G

LONG-TERM POLITICAL PRISONERS AND CASES OF ABDUCTION

LONG-TERM PRISONERS

The following are well-known cases of long-term political prisoners. There are probably at least 80 more persons arrested before 1978 who are still being held. The number of cases increased dramatically with those arrested in 1978 and especially from 1979 to 1982. At least several hundred remain incarcerated from that period. For 160 of those cases, limited just to medical professionals and engineers, see appendix D.

PRE-ASAD

Ahmad Swaidani: military officer, diplomat, and former member of the Ba'th Party Regional Command; arrested July 11, 1969, and accused of links to the Iraqi Ba'th

Jadid group: Ba'th party November 23 Movement; all arrested November–December 1970, except where otherwise noted; all held in al-Mezze Prison

Nur al-Din al-Atassi: medical doctor, former president and prime minister
Salah Jadid: army officer, member of the original Military Committee, army chief of staff and assistant secretary-general of the Regional Command of the Ba'th party, strongman of the country, 1966–70
Muhammad 'Id 'Ashawi: lawyer, governor of Dar'a and Hama, minister of the interior, and minister of foreign affairs
Muhammad Rabah al-Tawil: army officer, member of the Military Committee, minister of labor, member of the Regional Command, commander-in-chief of the Popular Army, and minister of the interior

Marwan Habbash: minister of industry

Kamal Hussain: diplomat, member of Regional command, and ambassador to France

Fawzi Rida: pharmacist and member of National Command

Hakim al-Faiz: Jordanian and member of National Command

'Abd al-Hamid Miqdad: member of National Command

Dafi Jam'ani: Jordanian, member of National Command

Haditha Murada: commandant of the Popular Army and member of the Regional Command

Yusuf al-Burji: Palestinian, teacher, and member of Palestine National Council

Mustafa Rustum: head of Ba'th Military Office and member of Regional Command

Muhammad Sa'id Talib: minister of agriculture and president of the Syrian-Soviet Friendship Society (early 1971)

Salman 'Abdallah: Iraqi and member of National Command (April–July 1971); abducted from Beirut

Hassan al-Khatib: Palestinian, member of Regional Command of Ba'th party in Jordan, and member of National Command (June 1971)

Mijali Nasrawin: lawyer, public prosecutor, and member of National Command (June 1971)

'Adel Na'issa: teacher and member of National Command (1972)

OTHER PRISONERS HELD SINCE BEFORE 1978
(HELD 12–20 YEARS)

1970

Khalil Brayez: Syrian army intelligence officer and author, abducted from Beirut, sentenced to fifteen years, not released on expiration of sentence in October 1985

Mustafa Fallah (*see* Zaidan)

Mahmud al-Fayyad (*see* Zaidan)

Joseph Hammam: Lebanese chauffeur, allegedly abducted from Beirut by Syrian security people for having witnessed the killing of his employer

Jalal al-Din Mirhij (*see* Zaidan)

Ahmad 'Abd al-Ra'uf Rummo: Ba'thist of the Aflaq tendency

Husain Zaidan: Syrian army officer, one of 350 brought to trial in August 1971 and charged with plotting to restore the pre-1966 Ba'thist government; sentenced to fifteen years' detention; not released when term expired in May 1985, moved to a different prison, and not heard from since mid-1985

1971

Mahmud Baidun: Lebanese lawyer, abducted from Tripoli for his involvement with an anti-Asad newspaper

1975

Marwan Hamawi: journalist, former head of SANA, imprisoned for his alleged pro-Iraqi sympathies

ABDUCTIONS (FOLLOWED BY LONG-TERM IMPRISONMENT)

1970

Khalil Brayez: Syrian military officer who left the country in 1968–69, wrote the book *Sukut al-Julan* (Fall of the Golan), which was embarrassing to the regime, and was abducted from Lebanon in 1970; tried and sentenced to fifteen years in prison but not released when sentence expired in May 1985

Joseph Hammam: Lebanese chauffeur with no involvement in politics, said to have witnessed the assassination of his employer by Syrian security; abducted in 1970 because he was prepared to testify as to what he had seen; disappeared, though he was reported several years ago to be in a Syrian prison

1971

Mahmud Baidun: Lebanese lawyer responsible for a newspaper that supported the Jadid regime, kidnapped in Tripoli in 1971; reported to have been held for some time in al-Mezze Prison, but lately there is no word of him

1977

George Atiya: lawyer who left Aleppo out of concern for his safety, was taken prisoner in Lebanon by Military Intelligence, disappeared for a period, and was reported to be held in a prison first in Damascus, then in Aleppo; there has been no news of his whereabouts in five years

Muhammad Daud Bashir: Syrian army officer from Lataqia who left the country in 1968, was arrested by Syrian intelligence in his apartment in Beirut, and was jailed in al-Mezze Prison

Muhammad Nijar Nahhas: Syrian army officer from Hama who left Syria in 1968, was kidnapped in Lebanon in 1977, and was subsequently held in al-Mezze Prison; his recent whereabouts are unknown

'Akl Qarban: lawyer from Damascus who left the country for political reasons in 1968 and was kidnapped in Lebanon; recent whereabouts are unknown

1982

Duraid Baridy: student from Deir al-Zor who was studying in France kidnapped by Syrian intelligence

Na'man Kawaf: lawyer from Lataqia who left Syria and was kidnapped in Cyprus in February 1982

APPENDIX H

ELECTIONS AND PARTY CONGRESSES

Elections

March 1, 1971	Presidential referendum
April 1971	Ba'th party elections for Regional Congress
September 1, 1971	Referendum on Union of Arab Republics
March 3–4, 1972	Local (Muhafaza) elections
March 12, 1973	Constitutional referendum
May 25, 1973	People's Assembly elections
March 1975	Ba'th party elections for Regional Congress
August 1–2, 1977	People's Assembly elections
February 8, 1978	Presidential referendum
November 1979	Ba'th party elections for Regional Congress
November 9, 1981	People's Assembly elections
February 20–21, 1983	Local (Muhafaza) elections
December 1984	Ba'th party elections for Regional Congress
February 10, 1985	Presidential referendum
February 10–11, 1986	People's Assembly elections
February 21, 1987	Local (Muhafaza) elections
May 22, 1990	People's Assembly elections

Ba'th Party Congresses (Asad era)

May 8–14, 1971	Fifth Regional Congress
April 5–14, 1975	Sixth Regional Congress
December 22, 1979–January 7, 1980	Seventh Regional Congress
January 5–20, 1985	Eight Regional Congress

People's Assembly Election Results

1973 (186 seats)

Progressive National Front	124 seats (66.6%)
Ba'th party	104
Communist party	6
Arab Socialist Movement	6
Arab Socialist Union	4
Socialist Unionist Movement	4
Independents	62

1977 (195 seats; 5 women)

Progressive National Front	159 seats (81.5%)
Ba'th party	125
Communist party	6
Arab Socialist Movement	6
Arab Socialist Union	8
Socialist Unionist Movement	12
Independents	36

1981 (195 seats)

Progressive National Front	195 seats (100%)
Ba'th party	60+%
Communist party	—
Arab Socialist Movement	—
Arab Socialist Union	—
Socialist Unionist Movement	—
Independents	—

1986 (195 seats)

Progressive National Front	154 seats (79%)
Ba'th party	123
Communist party	9
Arab Socialist Movement	5
Arab Socialist Union	9
Socialist Unionist Movement	8
Independents	41

1990 (250 seats)

Progressive National Front	166 seats (66%)
Ba'th party	134
Independents	84

NOTES

INTRODUCTION

1. A major report has been overdue since August 1984 and various other reports have been overdue since 1983, 1986, and 1987, according to United Nations sources in Geneva.

CHAPTER 1: BACKGROUND

1. In 1990, Damascus had a population of about 2.5 million, Aleppo a population of about 2.2 million.

2. In a conversation of spring 1990, Raymond Hinnebusch, citing the 1970 agricultural census, reported that about 60 percent of Syrian peasants own their land, approximately 20 percent are tenants, and about 20 percent are agricultural workers. He believes that since 1970 there may have been a shift away from landowners and toward workers as peasants have left the land for the cities.

3. The King-Crane Commission, sent by President Woodrow Wilson, investigated this issue and discovered that most of those they interviewed opposed the Mandates and favored an independent Arab state.

4. The state was conceived as ruling at least geographical Syria, what is today Syria, Lebanon, Jordan, Israel, and the Occupied Territories. The best history of the Mandate and the nationalist movement is Philip S. Khoury, *Syria and the French Mandate* (Princeton, N.J.: Princeton University Press, 1987). For a briefer rendition of the history and an excellent overview on Syria, see André Raymond, ed., *La Syrie d'aujourd'hui* (Paris: Editions du Centre national de la recherche scientifique, 1980).

5. An article in the abortive 1938 constitution, for example, stated that Syria was one and indivisible, including Lebanon, Transjordan, and Palestine. This factor is an important part of Syrian history, but it would be an error to see territorial expansion as a dominant feature of contemporary Syrian politics.

6. Khoury, *Syria and the French Mandate*, pp. 171–73, 174–80, 191–92, 195, 196–97, 616–17.

7. Ibid., p. 342.

8. Patrick Seale, *The Struggle for Syria* (New Haven and London: Yale University Press, 1987).

9. For a more complete account of this and other U.S. covert actions in Syria based on recently released classified sources, see Douglas Little, "Cold War and Covert Action: The United States and Syria, 1945–1958," *Middle East Journal* 44 (Winter 1990), pp. 51–76. These events are discussed at greater length in chapter 9.

10. For the history of this period see Seale, *Struggle for Syria,* and Tabitha Petran, *Syria* (New York: Praeger, 1972).

11. Destabilization and coup attempts prompted the Syrian government to strengthen the role of the security services, especially Military Intelligence, the main counterintelligence agency. Its chief, ʿAbd al-Hamid Sarraj, became one of the most powerful people in the country. For further discussion of these incidents see chapter 9.

12. The Military Committee had a core of six members, all of whom were from minorities. Among the members were Salah Jadid and Hafez Asad. Three were ʿAlawis, two were Druze, and one was Ismaili.

13. For the history of the early Baʿthist period, see Patrick Seale, *Asad: The Struggle for the Middle East* (Berkeley: University of California Press, 1989); Raymond, *La Syrie d'aujourd'hui;* and John Devlin, *The Baʿth Party: A History from Its Origins to 1966* (Stanford, Calif.: Hoover Institution Press, 1976). The classic short study by Nikolaos van Dam, *The Struggle for Power in Syria: Sectarianism, Regionalism, and Tribalism in Politics, 1961–1978* (New York: St. Martin's Press, 1979), is useful on the role of the ʿAlawis.

14. The relative weight of ethnic and ideological elements has been much discussed. The classic study on the ʿAlawi factor in the politics of this period is van Dam, *Struggle for Power in Syria.* Van Dam has consistently rejected crude interpretations of Syrian politics that reduce all analysis to the ʿAlawi factor alone.

15. Jadid remained Syria's strongman for nearly four years, but his official title—assistant secretary general of the Baʿth party—was modest. The three nominal leaders were radical doctors: Nur al-Din al-Atassi (president), Yusif Zaʿayyan (prime minister), and Ibrahim Makhus (deputy prime minister and foreign minister).

16. In 1972, Asad named a conservative, American-educated economist, Muhammad Imadi, as minister of economy. Imadi held this post until 1979 and emerged later as a powerful government figure.

CHAPTER 2: THE GREAT REPRESSION, 1976 TO 1982

1. On the Islamists see Hanna Batatu, "Syria's Muslim Brethren," *MERIP Reports* 110 (November–December 1982), pp. 12–20; Umar F. Abd-Allah, *The Islamic Struggle in Syria* (Berkeley: Mizan Press, 1982); and Haytham Manna, "Histoire des frères musulmans en Syrie," *Souʾal* 5 (1985), pp. 67–82.

2. For an overview of this period, two sources are especially helpful: Seale, *Asad,* chap. 19, and Michel Seurat and Olivier Carré, *Les frères musulmans, 1928–1982* (Paris: Gallimard, 1983), pp. 125–92.

3. Speech by Hafez Asad, broadcast on Radio Damascus, August 18, 1977. The committee, announced Asad, was to "investigate crimes of bribery, imposition of influence, embezzlement, exploitation of office, and illegal profits."

4. According to one account, these 200 all signed confessions of responsibility for the crime after long interrogation.

5. For these events, see Arab World File, I-S89, pp. 3–4, and *Le Monde,* June 11–12, December 27, 1978.

6. See, e.g., his speech on "Revolution Day," March 8, 1978.

7. For an analysis of the elections in the trade unions, which took place in October 1978, see Elisabeth Longuenesse, "Etat et syndicalisme en Syrie: discours et pratiques," *Souʾal* 8 (1988), pp. 104–5. Her evidence of the movement of opposition in the ranks of the factory workers belies the standard analysis, favored by the regime, that the opposi-

tion was restricted to Islamist fanatics and prosperous shopkeepers, merchants, and professionals.

8. On these events and other details of the campaign of the professionals, we have drawn on the recollections of a number of participants as well as on the excellent publication by the Comité de défense des libertés et des détenus politiques en Syrie: "Memorandum sur la dissolution des Barreaux d'avocats et des syndicats de médecins et d'ingénieurs par les autorités syriennes," no. 11 (April 28, 1980).

9. Michel Seurat, L'Etat de barbarie (Paris: Editions du Seuil, 1989), p. 66, and Seurat and Carré, Les frères musulmans, p. 135. Seurat reports that 282 out of 300 cadets at that time were ʿAlawis. He also states that this assassination had no connection to the Islamists, though others believe that it did.

10. Arab World File, I-S89, p. 3.

11. Seurat, L'Etat de barbarie, p. 68.

12. For a complete text see Foreign Broadcast Information Service (hereafter FBIS), September 29, 1979.

13. As quoted in Seurat, L'Etat de barbarie, p. 81.

14. Seurat and Carré, Les frères musulmans, p. 141.

15. Comité de défense, "Memorandum," pp. 34–37.

16. Seurat and Carré, Les frères musulmans, p. 145; also Seale, Asad, p. 328.

17. Among the more accessible published accounts are Seale, Asad, p. 327; Report from Amnesty International to the Government of the Syrian Arab Republic (London: Amnesty International, 1983), p. 34; and Seurat and Carré, Les frères musulmans, p. 145. Both Seale and Seurat and Carré speak of 200 dead, a figure our sources tended to confirm. Amnesty refrained from an estimate but said it had the names of 24 victims.

18. Arab World File, I-S100, p. 4, refers to these incidents. Reports of massacres in other towns at this time include, for example, Kannedeferat, where allegedly "nearly fifty" were killed, according to the Tribune (al-Minbar) 13 (December 1985), p. 26.

19. New laws governing these associations were finally decreed in the summer of 1981, which drastically reduced the freedom of association formerly enjoyed. For more on the professional associations, see chapter 6.

20. For lists of those still detained, and information about the campaign for release of the lawyers, see appendix G.

21. Suria al-Hurra (January 1989), p. 2. In Les frères musulmans, Seurat and Carré state that eleven doctors altogether were killed or disappeared in Hama, and this in addition to several other professionals. It seems that at this time in Hama security forces killed twenty or more people and detained hundreds. It was the first of three increasingly severe blows to the city over the course of three years. The following are the names of eight medical doctors of Hama in addition to ʿUmar al-Shishakli who are said to have been killed at this time: Alaal Barazi, Mulhim Barudi, Taher Haddad, Walid al-Hafiz, ʿAbd al-Kader Kondaqji, Ahmed Qassab, Kodr al-Shishakli, and Kamal al-Souad.

22. Seurat and Carré, Les frères musulmans.

23. For a list of these youths, see Report from Amnesty International, 1983, p. 32.

24. Published sources that refer to the events in Aleppo in this period include Report from Amnesty International, 1983, pp. 35–36; Seale, Asad, pp. 328–29; and Seurat and Carré, Les frères musulmans, pp. 145–46.

25. Seurat and Carré, Les frères musulmans, p. 145; Seale, Asad, p. 328.

26. See account in Suria al-Hurra (April 1988), p. 1.

27. This incident was widely reported. For one version, see Report from Amnesty International, 1983, pp. 35–36.

28. Seale estimates a death toll of 2,000 among the "Muslim opponents" of the regime. In a city with a large Christian minority, non-Muslim casualties were also significant. Our information suggests that a toll of 2,000 can reasonably be used to represent all deaths, irrespective of religion (Seale, *Asad*, p. 325). Seurat and Carré estimate 8,000 arrests, a number that others agree is soundly based (*Les frères musulmans*, p. 145).

29. The prison is sometimes referred to as the Palmyra Prison. The Arabic name of the town is Tadmur, but the English name is Palmyra (the name of the ancient Roman city on the site).

30. Seurat and Carré, *Les frères musulmans*, pp. 147–48. The soldier, 'Isa Ibrahim Fayadh, was a member of a team sent to Jordan to assassinate the prime minister. Arrested at the border before carrying out the operation, he told the Tadmur story as part of his confession. It was transmitted on Jordanian television in February and seen in Damascus. When news of the massacre eventually came out, the regime is said to have claimed that the prisoners had been condemned by a special field tribunal. These events are also discussed in Report from Amnesty International, 1983, p. 35; Seale, *Asad*, p. 329; *Suria al-Hurra* (August–September 1988), p. 6; and many other sources.

31. The commonly accepted number of those killed in the Tadmur massacre is 600. We are inclined to take seriously the report of Michel Seurat that an analysis by one of the security services put the number at 1,181 victims. Seurat, *L'Etat de barbarie*, p. 91.

32. As quoted in Seurat, *L'Etat de barbarie*, p. 62.

33. This incident has also been widely reported. One account is given in Report from Amnesty International, 1983, p. 35. The practice of punishing an entire village for harboring enemies is found in other pacification efforts, including those of Soviet forces in Afghanistan and U.S. forces in Vietnam.

34. He was not released until January 1983, when he went into exile.

35. For Hama Hospital deaths see *Suria al-Hurra* (April 1988), p. 2. For a version of the events and overall casualties see Report from Amnesty International, 1983, p. 36, and *Le Monde*, May 13, 1981. For a discussion of the delay in Western reporting of this incident, see chapter 8.

36. Seurat and Carré, *Les frères musulmans*, pp. 149–50. Extracts were published in the *Washington Post*, June 25, 1981.

37. For a detailed discussion of the number of political prisoners, see chapter 5.

38. Our account has drawn on interviews as well as extensive published literature. The Hama events are discussed and documented in many sources, including Seale, *Asad*, pp. 332–34; Report from Amnesty International, 1983, pp. 36–38; and Thomas L. Friedman, *From Beirut to Jerusalem* (New York: Farrar, Straus and Giroux, 1989), pp. 76–105. See also "Lettre de Hama," *Sou'al* 2 (1982), pp. 93–94. The extensive Arabic sources include: al-Dimokratiun al-Suriun, *Majzara Hama* (The Massacre of Hama) (Cairo?: al-Tahaluf al-Watani li-Tahrir Suria [Muslim Brothers], c. 1984); *Hama: Ma'sa al-'Asir* (The Tragedy of the Century) (Cairo?: al-Tahaluf al-Watani li-Tahrir Suria, c. 1983), and *Sawar min Medina Hama al-Shahid* (Pictures of the Martyr City of Hama) (Cairo?: c. 1983–84, containing a number of before-and-after photos that illustrate the city's destruction). For an accounting of the damage, complete with the names of the neighborhoods destroyed, see *Suria al-Hurra* (April 1988), p. 1. The number killed has been variously estimated from 1,000 to as high as 40,000. The range of 5,000–10,000 is a consensus, adopted by Seurat, Batatu, Drysdale, Seale, Amnesty International, and many other expert sources.

CHAPTER 3: THE GOVERNMENT, POLITICAL PARTIES,
AND LEGAL SYSTEM

1. A Constitutional Committee drawn from the presidentially appointed provisional People's Assembly drew up the constitution, which was adopted by the assembly on January 31, 1973, and adopted by popular referendum on March 12. The constitution was controversial mainly in one aspect: it removed the article in the previous constitution that made Islam the state religion. A provision that the president be a Muslim was not in the original draft and was added to placate popular pressure. For translated text and analysis, see Peter B. Heller, "The Permanent Syrian Constitution of March 13, 1973," *Middle East Journal* 28 (Winter 1974), pp. 53–66.

2. Constitution, Preamble, Basic Premises no. 4.

3. Closing speech to the Seventh Regional Congress, January 6, 1980. There are many other such statements, but we cite this one because of the irony of the repression that immediately followed.

4. FBIS, March 9, 1990, p. 30.

5. Interviews taken in fall 1989. For a longer discussion of the legal deficiencies of the state of emergency see the *Tribune,* various issues.

6. See, e.g., the comments of the Syrian delegate to the U.N. Human Rights Committee, Meeting 160, August 8, 1979.

7. Speech at the opening of the Fifth Congress of the Revolutionary Youth Federation as covered live by Damascus television. FBIS, March 9, 1990, p. 29.

8. Martial Law (al-Ahkam al-'Urfiya) is the body of laws, established by the Martial Law governor, that regulate the state of emergency and either restrict its scope or broaden it beyond the existing Emergency Law. The Syrian courts have disputed the legality of these laws, arguing that they have been extended beyond anything that could reasonably be justified as a threat to state security.

9. This law also included certain economic crimes, including monopolizing food products, "exorbitant price rises," and export of capital in breach of regulations.

10. The laws are very specific about the lack of a right to appeal. See Article 5 of Decree Law 47 and Article 8a of Decree Law 109.

11. Comité de défense, "Memorandum," pp. 21, 22.

12. FBIS, September 29, 1979.

13. Speech before the Seventh Regional Congress, January 7, 1980. FBIS, January 8, 1980.

14. There are two recent biographies of Hafez Asad: Seale, *Asad,* and Moshe Ma'oz, *Asad: The Sphinx of Damascus* (New York: Grove Weidenfeld, 1988).

15. The sections of the constitution relating to presidential powers are Articles 93–114. Article 111(2), for example, allows the president to promulgate legislation "in case of absolute need."

16. See comments on this by Al-Munthama al-'Arabiya li-Huquq al-Insan, *Huquq al-Insan fi al-Watan al-'Arabi* (Cairo: [Arab Organization for Human Rights annual reports; hereafter cited as AOHR], 1988), p. 84.

17. Yahya Sadowski, "Cadres, Guns, and Money," *MERIP Reports* 134 (July–August 1985), p. 3.

18. Ibid.

19. Even an organization like the Arab Lawyers' Union, which has criticized the Asad regime's imprisonment of lawyers, held its congress in Damascus under Asad's

"patronage" in June 1989, and the posters announcing the event gave far more space to the president's photo and the announcement of his patronage than to the event itself.

20. Observed in the summer of 1989.

21. Interview, fall 1989.

22. The army is also said to have similar slogans that are shouted out by troops as part of their politico-military training.

23. Interview, summer 1989.

24. *Tishrin*, September 22, 1979.

25. There is a considerable amount of literature on the Syrian Ba'th, including David Roberts, *The Ba'th and the Creation of Modern Syria* (London: Croom Helm, 1987), and Devlin, *Ba'th Party,* but no definitive source for the party in the recent period.

26. The Ba'th party, founded in 1943, merged in 1953 with the Arab Socialist party to form the present Arab Ba'th Socialist party.

27. Estimates of party size vary considerably, some being as low as 100,000. A plausible recent estimate, based on party records, puts membership in 1987 at 50,000 full members and 200,000 candidate members.

28. Interviews, summer and fall 1989.

29. Syrian politics are quirky and Ba'th party membership is not an absolute requirement for success. The occasional minister or successful author may get away with not joining the party, especially if they know Asad. But many others, lacking protection on high, find party membership a necessity.

30. Raymond A. Hinnebusch, "Political Recruitment and Socialization in Syria: The Case of the Revolutionary Youth Federation," *International Journal of Middle East Studies* 11, no. 2 (1980), pp. 143–74.

31. See chapter 4.

32. For more on censorship and the party's role in it, see chapter 8.

33. See chapter 8 for a number of examples, including a case involving a speech by a professor at the Arab Writers' Union.

34. For further discussion of the party's control over organizations, see chapter 6.

35. FBIS, March 8, 1990.

36. *Al-Watan,* February 11, 1990, p. 20, as reported in FBIS, February 14, 1990, p. 40.

37. *Al-Watan,* February 9, 1990, p. 21; FBIS, February 14, 1990.

38. The Communist party, for example, has split into three formations. One, led by Khalid Bakdash (party general secretary for over fifty years), is a member of the National Progressive Front. Another party, split from Bakdash's, is also a member of the Front and is led by Yusuf Faisal. Finally, there is the Communist Party-Political Bureau, led by Riyad al-Turk, which is outlawed and heavily repressed. This confusing situation is compounded by the fact that the parties all produce publications with the same name.

39. Interviews, summer and fall 1989. It seems that some Front parties have affiliates for women, peasants, peace, and the like but that these are even more illegal than the parties themselves and hence are underground.

40. For results of all parliamentary elections to 1990, see appendix H. In 1986 the results for the 195 seats were: Ba'th, 123 (66 percent); Communist party, 9; Arab Socialist Union, 9; Socialist Union, 8; Arab Socialist party, 5; and Independent, 41. The "independents" are not oppositionists and are certainly not independent of the regime, though they do not represent a party.

41. Nine of thirty-seven ministers in the government of 'Abd al-Ra'uf al-Kasm were from these parties, for example, including two from the Communist party.

42. The opposition Ba'thists belong to two main factions: the Michel Aflaq faction, with close ties to Iraq; and the Salah Jadid faction, more inclined to socialism. These reflect, of course, the two regimes that preceded Asad's.

43. The ASU, a Nasirist party, is headed by Dr. Jamal al-Atassi, a psychiatrist practicing in Damascus. The WRP is headed by Tariq Abu al-Hassan, who is said to work in a government ministry.

44. The parties and their alliances are listed in appendix C.

45. See discussions in chapters 5 and 8.

46. See chapter 5 for an estimate of how many prisoners there are from each party.

47. In fact, there is some evidence of foreign support for the Muslim Brothers—from Jordan in particular as well as from Iraq. But there is no doubt whatsoever that the movement was indigenous and drew its moral strength and most of its finances from within Syria.

48. Radio Damascus, FBIS, October 7, 1979.

49. Elisabeth Picard, "La Syrie de 1946 à 1979," in Raymond, ed., *La Syrie d'aujourd'hui,* p. 176.

50. A Syrian joke makes fun of these absurd results and the repression that lies behind them: After the election, an official congratulates Asad. "More than 99 percent, Mr. President, what more could you want?" To which Asad replies, "A list of the other 1 percent."

51. For a discussion of elections in unions and professional associations, see chapter 6.

52. An official source is said to have admitted that the turnout in the 1977 elections in urban areas was only 16 percent.

53. Interviews, summer and fall 1989. Michel Seurat wrote that overall turnout in the legislative elections of 1977 and 1981 was just 4 percent. This seems low, but it suggests the order of magnitude. Seurat, *L'Etat de barbarie,* p. 21.

54. Interview, fall 1989.

CHAPTER 4: THE SECURITY SERVICES, OR MUKHABARAT

1. The word *mukhabarat* is often translated as "security service" or "political police," but its more strict Arabic meaning is "intelligence service," since the root verb is *khabara,* to have knowledge of or to know. The use of the word *intelligence* in this context is as abusive in Arabic as is the similar usage in English.

2. Khoury, *Syria and the French Mandate,* p. 78.

3. See the description in Seale, *Struggle for Syria,* pp. 58–59.

4. For details as well as general context of this period, see Seale, *Struggle for Syria,* and Petran, *Syria.*

5. Seale, *Asad,* pp. 150–51.

6. A Palestinian military force called Saiqa, led by Syrian officers and affiliated with the Ba'th party, was also set up at this time, but it had no intelligence role.

7. For a discussion of this structure, see Hanna Batatu, "Syria's Muslim Brethren," *MERIP Reports* 110 (November–December 1982), p. 20. Patrick Seale, Michel Seurat, and many others have written about the military-security inner circle of 'Alawi officers.

8. For a discussion and identification of the members of the inner circle, see Seale, *Asad,* pp. 428–29, and Batatu, "Syria's Muslim Brethren," p. 20.

9. Partly at issue are what forces should be defined as "security forces" for this purpose. A reliable Syrian source estimated for Middle East Watch that the security services numbered in 1989 "somewhere between 100,000 and 200,000." This should be taken as potentially accurate, but we have opted for a far more conservative figure, since a security apparatus such as Syria's has a tendency to appear larger-than-life. The fact that the Defense Brigades, at the height of their power in 1982, may alone have numbered 25,000, however, suggests the magnitude of these forces.

10. Estimates here based on interviews, summer and fall 1989. For a baseline of Syria's government and military expenditures, see Patrick Clawson, *Unaffordable Ambitions: Syria's Military Buildup and Economic Crisis* (Washington, D.C.: Washington Institute for Near East Policy, 1989).

11. Interviews, summer and fall 1989.

12. Interviews, summer and fall 1989. Amnesty International, *Syria: Torture by the Security Forces* (London: Amnesty International, 1987), refers to extortion of sums for prison visits and releases in Lebanon in the mid-1980s—$6,400 to $12,700 for visits and up to $51,000 for releases. Security officers pocketing such sums would soon be rich by Syrian standards.

13. Interviews, fall 1989.

14. Yahya Sadowski, "Patronage and the Ba'th: Corruption and Control in Contemporary Syria," *Arab Studies Quarterly* 9, no. 4 (1987), p. 450. For other accounts of Rif'at's smuggling and related misdeeds, see Thomas Koszinowski, "Rif'at al-Asad," *Orient* 4 (1984), pp. 465–70, and Alasdair Drysdale, "The Succession Question in Syria," *Middle East Journal* 39 (Spring 1985), pp. 246–62.

15. For a brief discussion of the drug trade and the role of high Syrian officials, see appendix F. An article that discusses Rif'at al-Asad's connections to drug trafficking, smuggling, and the sale of stolen luxury automobiles is in *L'Express* (Paris), May 1987, pp. 34–41.

16. See the lengthy discussion in Seale, *Asad,* pp. 421–40.

17. Interviews, fall 1989.

18. *Suria: al-Sijl al-Aswad,* p. 33. Of course, in Aleppo in 1980 and in Hama in 1982, several agencies' paramilitary units joined forces, but that is a precedent of a different sort.

19. Gérard Michaud [Michel Seurat], "The Importance of Bodyguards," *MERIP Reports* 110 (November–December 1982), p. 29.

20. Ibid.

21. Interviews, summer and fall 1989.

22. Interview, summer 1989.

23. Ibid.

24. See chapter 7 for a discussion of cases in the context of Syria's minorities.

25. See chapter 8 for a recent case, as well as other examples of harassment of intellectuals.

26. Interview, summer 1989.

27. Interviews, summer 1989.

28. Interview, fall 1989.

29. Ibid.

30. *Suria: al-Sijl al-Aswad,* pp. 15–17, 22–24.

31. There is also Branch 279, which is in charge of questioning politically suspect Syrians living abroad when they return to the country. Without a clearance from Branch 279, such a person may be prevented from leaving the country and subject to arrest.

32. For more on this issue, see chapter 7.

33. An article in the *New York Times,* January 11, 1980, p. 2, a time when the Brigades were expanding, estimated their size at 18,000. Some sources believe that by 1982 they may have numbered 25,000 or more.

CHAPTER 5: PRISONS AND TORTURE

1. Consider, for example, the mass arrests in 1987–88, which hit the Party for Communist Action especially hard. With some 2,000 persons initially arrested, 800 were still reportedly in jail by mid-1989.

2. Syrian interrogators have been reported to play tapes of men and women screaming under torture to heighten the anxiety of the prisoners.

3. Interview, fall 1989.

4. For a list of types of torture, see appendix A.

5. For details on al-Turk's case, see below.

6. Interviews, fall 1989.

7. Interview, fall 1989.

8. Interview, fall 1989. Phone calls to prisoners' families have also been reported. The wife of a former prisoner had this to say about what happened to her family in the early 1980s in Damascus: "When [name] was in prison, we got calls at all hours of the night. Sometimes they shouted insults at me, sometimes they threatened me, and sometimes they even threatened the children. They told of terrible things that had happened to [name]—that they had cut off his tongue, that his body would soon be dumped in a field outside the city, and so on. This never stopped until he was finally released. Life became unbearable." Families of political suspects outside prison can also be harassed in various ways. If such a person travels abroad, family members may be prevented from traveling and held in Syria as hostages to guarantee the suspect's return.

9. Amnesty International devotes a section of its 1987 report to death under torture and provides seven cases of detainees who it believes died in this way between 1983 and 1986. Report from Amnesty International, 1983, pp. 16–18.

10. Amnesty International has reported four to six alleged deaths in custody per year during this period. These are only the cases of which it becomes aware and can document. Based on its discussions with former prisoners, Middle East Watch believes that many more cases go unreported, especially those among Islamist prisoners and former government or military personnel. Information is sparsest on Lebanon, where prisoners are routinely treated extremely harshly. An estimate of fifteen or more cases per year seems relatively conservative in this context.

11. This case has been taken up by both the United Nations and Amnesty International. See United Nations Commission on Extra-judicial Inquiry, Executions, Question of the Violation of Human Rights and Fundamental Freedoms in Any Part of the World . . . , February 6, 1989, p. 52.

12. This case has been taken up by both the United Nations and Amnesty International. See ibid.

13. This case has been taken up by both the United Nations and Amnesty International. See ibid. Recently mentioned by the United Nations is the case of Ahmad Mahdi: "Mahdi, arrested in March 1980, died at the end of April 1984, allegedly as a result of force-feeding and electric shock treatment." United Nations Commission on Human Rights, Economic and Social Council (hereafter COHR), Question of the Human Rights

of All Persons Subjected to Any Form of Detention or Imprisonment: Torture . . . (January 23, 1989), p. 20.

14. We arrive at this count as follows: Aleppo, 600; Jisr al-Shughur, 100; Hama (1981), 200; Sarmada, 30; Damascus and all others, 570. These figures would be for summary executions only, not total casualties.

15. See chapter 2.

16. We arrive at this total as follows: Tadmur, 600; al-Mezze, 200; all other prisons, 200. This is a very conservative figure, but we lack the information from other prisons that would confidently permit a higher estimate.

17. AOHR (1987), p. 58.

18. The names are listed in the *Tribune* 13 (December 1985), pp. 42–44. The unnamed victims are identified on the list simply as "12 inhabitants of the Village of Dana" and "35 officers of Idlib and Aleppo." These cases may date back to previous years, so it should not be concluded that they are definitely from 1985.

19. COHR, 45th sess., Question of the Violation of Human Rights . . . : Summary and Arbitrary Executions (February 6, 1989).

20. Interviews, fall 1989.

21. Interview, fall 1989.

22. Interviews, summer and fall 1989.

23. Interview, summer 1989.

24. Ibid.

25. Interviews, summer and fall 1989.

26. AOHR (1987), p. 58.

27. Interviews, summer and fall 1989.

28. Interview, fall 1989.

29. Interview, fall 1989.

30. Four cases of well-known prisoners who have been denied medicines for diabetes or other chronic illnesses, including Muwaffaq al-Din al-Kozbari, the general secretary of the Syrian Human Rights Organization, are cited in AOHR (1987), p. 61.

31. Amnesty International, *Syria: Torture*, p. 35.

32. See, e.g., the recent lists published in *Suria: al-Sijl al-Aswad,* which show the following totals: Democratic Ba'th (130), Communist Party-Political Bureau (122), Popular Nasirites (30), Popular Committees (35), Party for Communist Action (679), others (23).

33. See, e.g., "Nida 'Ajil" (Urgent Call), Committee of Palestinian Political Prisoners, March 1987, which provides about 200 names of those in bad condition, distributed among such categories as "partial paralysis, backbones destroyed, heart disease, [and] stomach bleeding."

34. See note on Palestinian prisoners in chapter 7. The Syrian government admitted to holding nearly 2,000 Palestinians in late 1988. In March 1990 the Palestinian Committee for Human Rights, based in Tunis, published a list of over 5,000 Palestinian prisoners. We consider the figure 2,500 to be conservative in this context.

35. Such a total might be broken down as follows: Palestinians, 4,000–5,000; Islamists, 4,000–5,000; Secular opposition, 2,000; Lebanese and other foreigners, 1,500; others, 1,500. Some people estimate that Tadmur Prison holds 5,000–6,000 and that all other prisons and detention centers have proportionately more inmates. 'Ali al-Bayanouni, head of the Syrian Muslim Brothers in Jordan, told correspondent Milton Viorst in the summer of 1989, for example, that "currently, there are between seven

thousand and ten thousand members of the Brotherhood in prison" (*New Yorker*, January 8, 1990, p. 56). Such orders of magnitude are not simply the claims of Syrian oppositionists. Michel Seurat estimated a Syrian political prisoner population of 12,000 in 1983. A knowledgeable expert told Middle East Watch in 1989 that he thought there were 13,000 political prisoners in Syria, but he hastened to add, "I can't prove it." The newly formed Committee for the Defense of Democratic Freedoms and Human Rights in Syria estimated 14,000 political prisoners in its first "Communiqué," December 12, 1989.

36. For details on the professionals held from this period, see appendix D.

37. Most knowledgeable sources agree that prisoners being held for long periods are kept on Asad's direct orders, not on the action of some unaccountable lower authority. See, e.g., AOHR (1988), p. 84.

38. See Amnesty International, *Syria: Torture,* p. 27.

39. See Amnesty International statement of October 23, 1985.

40. The four others are: 'Umar Qashash, Faiz al-Fawwaz, Faisal Tahhan, and Mufid Mi'mati. See AOHR (1987), p. 59.

41. COHR, Commission on Extra-judicial Inquiry, Executions, 45th sess., Question of the Violation of Human Rights . . . (February 6, 1989), pp. 52–53.

42. Interview, fall 1989.

43. Ibid.

44. COHR, Commission on the Elimination of All Forms of Discrimination, 29th sess., Consideration of Reports Submitted by State Parties . . . (July 21, 1983), p. 7.

45. COHR, 42d sess., March 11, 1986. Statement by Fahd Salim of Syria.

46. Report from Amnesty International, 1983, p. 7, gives a list of prisons. For Middle East Watch's list, see appendix E.

47. Some say that there are 55 cells, but 41 is the most commonly given figure.

48. Some former prisoners have estimated that as many as 12,000 were detained here in 1982. This would have meant on average three hundred prisoners in each 100-square-meter (about 900-square-foot) cell, which seems unlikely at first consideration. Such a density approaches that of a New York subway car at rush hour. As recently as 1987, Amnesty International estimated the prisoner population of Tadmur at 5,000–6,000, which shows how crowded the prison is believed to be (*Syria: Torture,* p. 35). Prison expert Herman Schwartz of the American University College of Law has told Middle East Watch that in his prison investigations, 1 square meter is close to the limit he has observed for long-term incarceration and 1.5 square meters is typical of "unpleasant" conditions in Third World prisons. One square meter, for example, does not permit all prisoners to lie down at once. But AOHR has reported extremes of crowding at Qasr al-Nihaya prison in Iraq, in which 4 persons are believed to be held in 0.75 square meters, and at prisons in Algeria where 100 are held in 60 square meters, AOHR (1987), p. 6. An Israeli detention cell in Ramallah Military Court was also observed with 60 persons held in 12.5 square meters (Yizhar Be'er, "The Punishment Machine in the Territories," *Ha'aretz,* December 1, 1989). By contrast, Alcatraz Prison in San Francisco had private cells that were 4.5 square meters! We can conclude from the sorry precedents in the region that if a "normal" range for Tadmur cells might be 70–100 prisoners, 200 per cell is not impossible. There may also be as many as 55 cells, and some cells may be larger.

49. Habbash was imprisoned for nine months in 1978–79, Salah Salah for nearly a year in 1987–88.

50. Some reports say that there are 120 cells, but we consider 94 to be a more reliable figure.

51. Political Security's facility, for instance, is said to contain "many" communal cells and six solitary cells, as well as two interrogation rooms. Internal Security's facility is said to contain two interrogation rooms, two communal cells, and thirteen solitary cells. Air Force Intelligence has three such facilities, including a headquarters unit said to contain one communal cell, one medium-sized cell, and seven solitary cells; interrogation and torture are said to be carried out not in a separate room but in the hallway. Military Interrogation, the largest, is said to have "many" communal and medium-sized cells, as well as forty-eight solitary cells. Palestine Branch is said to have "many" communal cells, as well as ten solitary cells. Other such facilities are those of the Farʿ al-Mantiqa and the Farʿ al-Khariji. The Faraʿ al-Madina of the Political Security is also said to have its own interrogation center with one large communal cell and sixteen solitary cells. Adding these interrogation facilities together, it becomes clear that in Damascus alone well over a thousand people are being held for interrogation at any time.

CHAPTER 6: ORGANIZATIONS, UNIONS, AND PROFESSIONAL ASSOCIATIONS

1. Raymond Hinnebusch, *Peasant and Bureaucracy in Ba'thist Syria* (Boulder, Colo.: Westview Press, 1989), p. 21.

2. For a discussion of these militias, see chapter 3.

3. Malcolm Kerr, citing Agence France presse, noted that a Syrian commission reported in 1973 that between 1956 and 1969 some 57 percent of Syrian professionals, mainly doctors and engineers, emigrated (Kerr, "Hafiz Assad and the Changing Patterns of Syrian Politics," *International Journal* 23 [1973], p. 689).

4. The Artists' Union organizes exhibitions; the Writers' Union publishes books and magazines.

5. Interview, fall 1989.

6. On the history of the trade union movement in Syria, see Elisabeth Longuenesse, "The Syrian Labor Movement," *MERIP Reports* 110 (November–December 1982), pp. 32–33, and Abdulla Hanna, *Al-Haraka al-ʿUmaliya fi Suria wa Lubnan, 1900–1945* (The Labor Movement in Syria and Lebanon, 1900–1945) (Damascus: n.p., 1973). Agricultural labor was excluded from most of the trade union laws.

7. Petran, *Syria,* pp. 86–87.

8. This section owes much to the excellent studies by Elisabeth Picard, "Une crise syrienne en 1965: les syndicats ouvriers face au nouveau régime ba'thiste," *Sou'al* 8 (1988), pp. 81–95; Elisabeth Longuenesse, "The Syrian Working Class Today," *MERIP Reports* 134 (July–August 1985), pp. 17–24; and "Etat et syndicalisme en Syrie: discours et pratiques," *Sou'al* 8 (1988), pp. 97–130.

9. Picard, "Une crise syrienne en 1965," pp. 85–86.

10. Ibid., p. 86.

11. Laws 250 of 1969 and 21 of 1974.

12. On a number of recent occasions the International Labour Organization (ILO) Committee of Experts has expressed concern about these laws and has stated that they are contrary to the ILO convention of which Syria is a signatory. International Labour Organization, International Labour Conference, 75th sess., 1988, Report 3: *Report of*

the Committee of Experts on the Applications of Conventions and Recommendations (Geneva, 1989), pp. 177, 223–24.

13. Jean Hennoyer and Michel Seurat, *Etat et secteur publique industriel en Syrie* (Beirut: CERMOC, 1979), p. 53.

14. Longuenesse, "Etat et syndicalisme in Syrie," p. 108.

15. *Le Monde,* December 27, 1978, p. 3.

16. Longuenesse, "Etat et syndicalisme en Syrie," pp. 97–130, esp. 102–9.

17. Ibid., pp. 104–5.

18. Khoury, *Syria and the French Mandate,* p. 141.

19. A memorandum entitled "Political Detentions in Syria" was presented to the ALU.

20. Interviews, summer and fall 1989.

21. Comité de défense, "Memorandum," pp. 17–27.

22. Ibid., pp. 28–33.

23. See chapter 2 and the section of chapter 3 on special courts for a discussion of this period.

24. For a commentary on Law 39 and the other new laws of the professional associations, see the *Tribune* 6 (March 1982), pp. 11–32.

25. The relevant sections of the law are: membership in foreign organizations (Article 79); foreign cases (Article 73); arrest (Article 78); and disbarment (Article 85).

26. Interviews, summer and fall 1989.

CHAPTER 7: MINORITIES

1. Khoury, *Syria and the French Mandate,* p. 58.

2. Personal communication from Philip Khoury. The Christians were very strongly favored. Though only 12 percent of the population in 1938, they represented over 30 percent of those attending school and their proportion in the university was even higher. Their role as merchants, factory-owners and professionals was similarly important. See also Raymond, *La Syrie d'aujourd'hui,* p. 83.

3. See, e.g., Khoury's description of the use of Armenian and Circassian troops to put down the revolt in Damascus in early March 1926 in *Syria and the French Mandate,* pp. 191–92.

4. For more discussion of these operations, see chapter 1.

5. New York, London, and Paris seem, at first glance, much more torn by intercommunity strife than does Damascus.

6. Section III, Article 2. For the text, see Raymond, *La Syrie d'aujourd'hui,* p. 210.

7. Statement to the 29th sess., United Nations Committee on the Elimination of Racial Discrimination, October 19, 1983.

8. Hanna Batatu emphasizes the convergence of sect and class factors in "Some Observations on the Social Roots of Syria's Ruling Military Group and the Causes for Its Dominance," *Middle East Journal* 35 (Summer 1981), pp. 331–34. Haytham Manna has pointed out some shortcomings of this view in "Syria: Accumulation of Errors?" *Middle Eastern Studies* 23, no. 2 (1987), pp. 211–14.

9. See van Dam, *Struggle for Power in Syria.*

10. The Party for Communist Action is one of the largest secular-left parties and, like others of similar beliefs, has always had a large minority representation, especially

'Alawi. In 1976, when the party was first founded, its leadership elections produced a five-person Political Bureau with two 'Alawis, one Ismaili, one Sunni Circassian, and one Sunni Arab. The eleven-person Central Committee had five 'Alawi members. Personal communication from one of the members, winter 1990.

11. The number of Syria's Kurds is variously estimated from under 500,000 to well over a million. Kurdish sources usually place the number at about 10 percent of the Syrian population, or about 1.2 million. Expert opinion varies but seems to tilt toward a count in the range of 900,000.

12. A small minority, estimated at less than 10 percent, are Yazidis, a Muslim sect.

13. It is estimated that over half of Kurdish families can speak no language other than Kurdish.

14. Gérard Chaliand, ed., *Les kurdes et le Kurdistan* (Paris: Maspéro, 1978), p. 316.

15. Ismet Cherif Vanly discusses this document at length in *The Syrian "Mein Kampf" against the Kurds* (n.p., n.d. [c. 1969]).

16. Hilal as quoted in ibid., p. 28.

17. Chaliand, *Les kurdes et le Kurdistan,* p. 319.

18. Ibid. In 1985, the Minority Rights Group estimated that some 60,000 Kurds from Jezira had left for other cities, Lebanon, and other foreign countries. Again, part of this migration would have been due to causes that cannot be attributed to government policies, since all rural regions were losing population.

19. Ibid. The government naturally did not allow any Kurdish refugees into Syria, though many were fleeing worse persecution in Turkey and Iraq. Only a few political leaders were admitted, in an effort to get leverage over these neighboring states who were usually considered unfriendly.

20. Some place name changes were later dropped or at least not insisted on. The city of 'Ifrin, for example, appears with its Kurdish name on recently printed government maps. Obviously, the inhabitants never stopped using the old name.

21. Besides Miro, this group included Kan'an Agid, 'Abdullah Mulla 'Ali, Muhammad Mulla Fakhri, Khalid Meshavikh, and Nazir Shams al-Din Mustafa. All were held without charge or trial.

22. Ismet Cherif Vanly, *Kurdistan und die Kurden,* vol. 3 (Göttingen: Gesellschaft für bedrohte Völker, 1988), p. 20.

23. Interview, summer 1989.

24. Interview, fall 1989.

25. Ahmad Kiftaro, the Syrian grand mufti, is also a Kurd.

26. The quarter is bounded by al-Amin Street, Suq Midhat Pasha, and the wall of the Old City. There is a Jewish community of about 500 in Aleppo and about 200 in Qamishle; the balance of 3,100 live in Damascus.

27. Well-informed sources told Middle East Watch that the most common Jewish occupation is that of shopkeeper. There are also some wholesale merchants and a few owners of small factories, as well as jewelers, tailors, office workers, teachers, and doctors. In the late 1980s, Jewish shops appeared to be thriving and drew many Arab customers, while Jewish doctors had numerous Arab patients. There were about thirty Jewish doctors in Damascus and about ten pharmacists, as well as several Jewish doctors in Aleppo, three of whom were women.

28. There are many such testimonies to be found in Joseph A. D. Sutton, *Aleppo Chronicles* (New York: Thayer-Jacoby, 1988), pp. 125–239.

29. *Encyclopedia Judaica* (New York: Macmillan, 1972), p. 646.

30. The events of 1947 in Aleppo are discussed by a number of respondents in Sutton, *Aleppo Chronicles.*

31. According to Seale, *Struggle for Syria,* p. 98, some of the attacks on the Jewish community in Damascus were carried out by an obscure group known as the Phalanges de la rédemption arabe, which was finally brought to justice when it sought to assassinate military strongman Adib Shishakli in October 1950. It is not clear what the goal of this group was or who backed it.

32. Ironically, the Syrian government loudly protested Israel's actions while adopting similar behavior.

33. When students at the University of Damascus protested about this to a visiting government minister in the early 1970s, he told them that this special form of identity for Jews would remain in force as long as Arabs in Israel were also separately identified on Israeli documents. The students were reported to be unhappy with this explanation. Interview, fall 1989.

34. Interviews, fall and winter 1989–90.

35. This may have been the result of diplomatic pressure from the United States and conversations between Asad and President Jimmy Carter—one of the rare cases where the United States introduced human rights issues into its diplomacy with Syria.

36. Though less prominent, the identity remained objectionable, since Jews were the only community in Syria so identified.

37. For the situation in the late 1970s, see House of Representatives, Committee on Foreign Affairs, Subcommittee on Europe and the Middle East, 96th Cong., 1st sess., "Impressions of the Situation of the Syrian Jewish Community," April 2, 1979 (Washington, D.C.: USGPO, 1979).

38. Interview, fall 1989.

39. This deposit must be given to the Office of Passport and Immigration Status (Idarat al-Hijra wal-Jawazat al-Jansiya).

40. Yet those Jews with special medical problems usually get speedy permission for foreign treatment.

41. According to the State Department, a recent arrangement allows unmarried Jewish women to gain exit visas for emigration. This same source said that four to six women per month got such visas in 1989.

42. A State Department source told Middle East Watch that 500 Syrian Jews a year travel to the United States, most for a short visit.

43. Letter of Syrian chargé d'affaires Bushra Kanafani to David Friedman, December 11, 1989; telephone interviews with Amnesty International, London, and the Council for the Rescue of Soviet Jews, New York, March 11 and 12, 1991.

44. *Jerusalem Post,* November 1, 1989, p. 1.

45. U.S. Department of State, press statement, November 8, 1989. The State Department had apparently received such assurances from the Syrian government, but given the record, one may wonder why the department did not wait to see concrete results before issuing such a statement.

46. Telephone interviews with Amnesty International, London, and the Council for the Rescue of Soviet Jews, New York, March 11 and 12, 1991. Diplomatic efforts to defend the Syrian Jewish community have included pressure from several European governments and political personalities. There have also been a number of visits to Damascus in the past two years by prominent American Jews.

47. An estimated 90,000–100,000 arrived as refugees at that time. In addition to the

natural increase of this population, Palestinians came from Jordan in 1970 and from Lebanon after 1983.

48. The fact that Palestinian refugees were not offered citizenship is not seen by either Palestinians or Syrians as an anomaly and still less as a human rights abuse. It was always expected that Palestinians would eventually return to Palestine.

49. Yarmuk is known as—and remains legally—a "camp." But the city has grown out and around it and with so many large multistory structures, it now resembles many other urban neighborhoods, though few of its streets are paved.

50. Laurie Brand, "Palestinians in Syria: The Politics of Integration," *Middle East Journal* 42 (Autumn 1988), pp. 624–26.

51. This office relates to the neighborhood of a large city, not to the city as a whole. Several Palestinians have been mayor of Yarmuk.

52. Brand, "Palestinians in Syria."

53. By the mid-1970s, when Saiqa intervened in Lebanon, an estimated three-quarters of its troops were believed to be Syrians.

54. In addition to Fara' Falastin, the two forces run some six other interrogation facilities. Military Interrogation Branch also interrogates Palestinians, especially those who have been brought from Lebanon.

55. Palestinians protested the events of "black September" in Jordan, including the Syrian military withdrawal from an intervention on the Palestinian side.

56. When Syria intervened in Lebanon, it took the side of the Maronite right against the Palestinians and their left-wing allies, supporting the destruction of Palestinian neighborhoods and camps, notably the camp of Tal al-Za'atar in Beirut.

57. Asad backed a PLO dissident, Abu Musa, who rebelled against 'Arafat and initially attracted popular sympathy among Palestinians. When it became clear that Musa was a captive of Syria, his movement lost support and significance. The "war of the camps" involved attacks on Palestinian refugee camps in Lebanon by Lebanese militias and army units backed by Syria. These frequent attacks resulted in the death or wounding of many innocent camp residents and the destruction of large areas of the camps.

58. *Maghreb Machrek* 10 (July–September 1983), p. 56.

59. Interview, summer 1989.

60. Interviews, fall 1989.

61. "Nida 'Ajil" lists many of these cases. For the mid-1980s see also Amnesty International, *Syria: Torture*, p. 17.

62. "Nida 'Ajil."

63. Interview, summer 1989.

64. Interview, summer 1989.

65. Palestinian sources have estimated the number of their political prisoners in Syria variously at 3,000–5,000. In March 1990, the Palestinian Committee for Human Rights, based in Tunis, published a list of over 5,000 names of Palestinian political prisoners in Syrian jails. In the summer of 1989, a knowledgeable journalist consulted by Middle East Watch estimated the number of Palestinian political prisoners at 2,500. The Syrian government, as noted below, indicated in late 1988 that it held 1,700 Palestinian prisoners. An estimate of 2,500 therefore appears conservative, especially if Palestinian prisoners in Lebanon are included.

66. *Maghreb Machrek* 119 (January–March 1988), p. 91.

67. In the summer of 1989, many publications reported that 185 Palestinian prisoners

had been released and that further releases were expected soon. Well-informed sources have told Middle East Watch that only about a dozen prisoners were actually freed at that time and only a few more since.

CHAPTER 8: CENSORSHIP, CULTURE, AND THE MEDIA

1. For French text, see Raymond, *La Syrie d'aujourd'hui*, p. 207.

2. See discussion in AOHR (1988), p. 83.

3. Others from different classes were also jailed and exiled, including the popular poet Badawi al-Jabal and the writer and patron of culture Fakhri Barudi.

4. Damascus Radio, February 14, 1990, in FBIS, February 15, 1990, p. 37.

5. *Al-Safir* is a Lebanese newspaper under the influence of Syrian forces in Beirut (for more on this, see below). Because a statement like the one on Rushdie would never have been printed by a Syrian paper and because *al-Safir* usually circulates in Syria as well as more widely in the Arab world, it was the chosen venue.

6. Yanka Ben Jemina, "Information Structures and Organizations in the Syrian Arab Republic," *Orient* 25, no. 4 (1984), p. 569.

7. There is also a small, English-language paper called the *Syria Times,* which is published by *Tishrin*.

8. Ben Jemina, *Orient,* p. 568. There appear to be fewer than 1,100 working journalists. Ben Jemina estimates that no more than 200 work for the three major dailies and about 400 work for all other organs; including SANA, radio and television, and magazines. The others on the union's roll probably work in government or party offices.

9. For circulation data, including estimates for each paper, see Ben Jemina, *Orient,* p. 570, and William A. Rugh, *The Arab Press,* 2d ed. (Syracuse, N.Y.: Syracuse University Press, 1987), pp. 3, 32.

10. These publications cover sports, women, trade unions, agriculture, and other subjects. One of the most important is *Kifah al-'Ummal al-Ishtiraki* (Socialist Workers' Struggle), the weekly magazine of the Trade Union Federation. There are two sports magazines, *al-Itihad* and *al-Mawqif al-Riyadhi,* a magazine on economics called *al-Iqtisad,* and the Writers' Union alone has four magazines.

11. Longuenesse, *Sou'al,* pp. 111–24.

12. In 1989, Rifa'i was head of SANA in Paris and was generally believed to be an intelligence operative.

13. Al-Kamil, one of the great journalistic survivors, is still an editor at *al-Ba'th.*

14. He is said to have described it as "the fifth Arab-Israeli war," which embarrassed Asad since Syria did not engage its forces. *Le Monde,* June 11–12, 1978, p. 5.

15. There were apparently many journalists, novelists, and poets whose names could not be mentioned.

16. *Le Monde,* December 27, 1978, p. 3. According to this account, the signers included authors Zakaria Tamer and Sa'dallah Wannus. The petition asked why censorship continued when the president said he was opposed to it and it asked why the Arab Writers' Union did nothing about the situation. Parties of the Front reportedly pressured writers not to sign or to withdraw their signatures.

17. See Adib Sadiq [pseud.], "The Road to Damascus Is Plagued with Censors," *Index on Censorship,* February 1990.

18. Ibid., p. 21.

19. Editor of *al-Thawra* who was promoted to the editorship of *Tishrin* in 1989.

20. Sadiq, *Index on Censorship*, p. 21; additional information from interview, fall 1989.

21. "Journalists in Syria Are an Extinct Species," *Index on Censorship* (June 1987), p. 42.

22. Ibid.

23. Amid al-Khuly, a Maronite, is no relation to Gen. Muhammad al-Khuly, the 'Alawite security chief.

24. *Al-Thawra,* March 2, 1990, p. 1.

25. *Al-Ba'th,* February 22, 1990.

26. Syrian newspapers give a very limited idea of what is happening outside Syria. In fall 1989, they gave scant attention to the crisis in Eastern Europe, which understandably makes the Asad regime nervous. When thousands marched in the streets and toppled one East European government after another, the Syrian press noted the crisis in only a few lines, referring in short news items to the "dangerous situation" or to the resignation of the government. Ironically, the papers carried several glowing stories about Nicolae Ceauçescu and his regime, complete with large photos of the Romanian leader, just before his fall.

27. Though they cannot poke fun at Asad, Syrian cartoons can be very good and quite effective as political criticism. For some reason, the government allows cartoons to go further than the written word and some cartoonists are therefore very popular.

28. Some foreign publications on sale in the summer of 1989 included *al-Safir* (Lebanese), *Sharq* (Syria's paper in Lebanon), *al-'Arabi* (Kuwaiti), *al-Hurria* (Palestinian), *Le Monde diplomatique* and *Scientific American* (Arabic versions), and the following Soviet publications: *Anba Musku, al-Ittihad al-Sufiyyati,* and *al-Marrat al-Sufiyyatia.* A Lebanese newspaper cost S£10, far more than a Syrian paper and too expensive for most people to buy. Publications in foreign languages, especially in English and French, are available at a few bookstores and newsstands, mainly in the five-star hotels. The censors appear to be less concerned about these, since they are too expensive for most Syrians to buy and are read almost exclusively by foreign travelers.

29. Ben Jemina, *Orient,* p. 565, says that in the mid-1980s the office reported imports of 195 "foreign" (i.e., non-Arab) publications and 146 publications from Arab countries.

30. Radio in Syria was founded in 1933 as a private business. The government established a public radio station just after independence in 1946. Television began in 1960, during the union with Egypt, as a government agency.

31. Interview, fall 1989.

32. Saiqa is a branch of the Syrian army that poses as a Palestinian military force. For more on Saiqa, see chapter 7.

33. Tabitha Petran, *The Struggle over Lebanon* (New York: Monthly Review Press, 1987), pp. 220–21.

34. Syria eventually forced the Lebanese government to impose a strict press censorship law, but this law was never effectively enforced. Direct pressure from the Syrian armed presence in West Beirut remained the major form of censorship.

35. Interview, winter 1990.

36. It seems that diplomats found out through their intelligence sources that the journalists were, in fact, on a Syrian hit list.

37. *New York Times,* July 3, 1980, p. 10.

38. Robert I. Friedman, "Journalists under the Gun in Beirut," *Nation*, December 15, 1984, p. 644, estimates that the number of foreign correspondents based in Beirut fell from about 400 in 1975 to about 200 in 1984.

39. This group included John Kifner and William Farrell of the *New York Times*, Jonathan Randal of the *Washington Post*, Julian Nundy of *Newsweek* as well as an Associated Press photographer. They were detained for sixteen hours at a checkpoint near Damour (Friedman, "Journalists under the Gun," p. 642).

40. *Washington Post*, June 25, 1981, p. 12.

41. Scott MacLeod, "How Asad Has Won," *New York Review of Books*, May 8, 1986, p. 26.

42. Lazakani, who was working for the newspaper *al-Wahda* in Abu Dhabi, tells his story in "Afraid of the Word," *Index on Censorship* (May 1986), pp. 16–18.

43. Both the al-Lawzi and the al-Jundi stories, apparently from State Department sources, are mentioned in the *New York Times*, July 3, 1980. Al-Lawzi's story is especially well known and widely reported, see Seale, *Asad*, p. 329.

44. Both the Taha and Bitar assassinations are widely attributed to Syria. See Seale, *Asad*, p. 329.

45. Michael Kennedy of the *Los Angeles Times* wrote that journalists were cautioned to stay away from Hama if they valued their lives. Foreign reporters apparently couldn't visit Hama until late April—ten weeks after the beginning of the uprising. Friedman, *From Beirut to Jerusalem*, p. 642.

46. See *New York Times*, February 11, 1982, p. 1.

47. Barbara Koeppel, *The Press in the Middle East: Constraint, Consensus, Censorship* (Washington, D.C.: MERIP, 1988), p. 9.

48. As quoted by Koeppel in *The Press in the Middle East*, p. 2. Since 1982, Western news agencies, television networks, and newspapers have had a hard time gathering independent news in Syria. Those correspondents with the best access have tended to reflect the point of view of the regime, like *Observer* correspondent Patrick Seale or Radio Monte Carlo reporter Louis Faris.

49. Beirut has been almost destroyed as a publishing center because of the civil war and the Syrian occupation. Cairo was out of favor with Asad for so long that book imports were cut off. Shortages of foreign currency have also restricted such imports.

50. Tlas is one of the most curious figures of the regime. A Sunni Asad loyalist, he is said to have relatively little responsibility as defense minister, since Asad retains personal control of military units. Tlas is the nominal author of many ghost-written books—from horticulture to poetry. His publishing house has done well with pirated editions of Mohammad Heikal's *Autumn of the Fury*, and he has even published a few banned books. Many say that Tlas has made a fortune through smuggling and arms dealing. He also owns some legitimate enterprises, including agricultural operations.

51. A foreign scholar confronted this problem not long ago shortly after arriving in Damascus, when a military officer arrived at his hotel and summoned him to the Defense Ministry. Fearing for his safety, the scholar was surprised to be ushered deferentially into the office of Minister Tlas, who welcomed him, offered him coffee, and began to converse about his field of specialty.

52. On the outer limit of the system is a publisher such as Dar Dimasq (Damascus House), which publishes Marxist works as well as Arabic translations of Marx and Lenin. The Soviets are said to have subsidized this house by buying some of its output. The mukhabarat is said to be especially concerned about the distribution of Marxist

books in the Syrian market but has been tolerant in this case because of friendly relations with the Soviets. No one in the army is permitted to read such literature, however, and bookstores with Marxist titles, especially outside Damascus and Aleppo, are reputedly scrutinized.

53. Syria's only female cabinet member, with a Ph.D. from Edinburgh University, Najah al-'Attar, belongs to a wealthy Damascene Sunni family. Her brother, 'Issam al-'Attar (in exile in West Germany), was the head of the Muslim Brothers. Said to be a close friend of Asad, she is not a Ba'th party member. Her inclination toward liberalism is well known at a personal level, but its practical effect has unfortunately been limited by the wider pressures of the censorship system.

54. Koeppel, *Press in the Middle East,* p. 12.

55. As reported in an interview, fall 1989.

56. The authorities knew of this trip long before 'Ursan reached the airport; that they arrested him there was a calculated act of humiliation.

57. See "Afraid of the Word."

58. Telephone interviews with Amnesty International, London, and the Council for the Rescue of Soviet Jews, New York, March 11 and 12, 1991.

59. Interview, fall 1989.

60. *Ma'rakat al-Masir al-Wahid* (Battle for the One Destiny) (1958) and *Fi Sabil al-Ba'th* (In the Cause of the Ba'th) (1959).

61. Interview, fall 1989.

62. Most such literature is not risky to own. A discovery by the mukhabarat of books and periodicals that suggest connections to the organized Syrian opposition put their owner at risk.

63. Vice president Rif'at Asad has also attempted to carry Syrian censorship into France by seeking to block distribution of Patrick Seale's biography of Hafez Asad there. Although some say that he is defending his own wounded pride (the book is very unflattering of him), others claim that he is simply carrying out his brother's wishes. In any case, it has been reported that he has hired more than twenty lawyers to bring suits against French bookshops that carry the book. There are also stories that Rif'at's henchmen have threatened bookstore owners with reprisals if they continue to carry the book. As a result, *Asad* is hard to obtain in Paris.

64. For a brief history and critical comments on Syrian films up through the late 1970s, see the article by Charles Vial in Raymond, *La Syrie d'aujourd'hui,* pp. 425–28.

65. The prize-winning film was *al-Rijal taht al-Shams* (Men under the Sun), a film with three sections, based on Ghassan Kanafani's short stories. The sections were directed separately by Nabil Malih, Muhammad Shahin, and Muhi al-din Mu'adhdhin.

66. Interview, fall 1989. See also "Entretien avec Omar Amiralay," *Cahiers du cinema* 290–91 (July–August 1978), pp. 79–89.

67. Both are by 'Alawi directors about 'Alawi subjects. The 'Abd al-Hamid film is about a junior officer in an 'Alawi village who tries to control his children but fails in the end. Some see it as a metaphor for Asad. The Muhammad film is an even stronger message and is thought to be another fable referring to the Asad clan (see below).

68. Improving relations with Egypt are also apparently encouraging a number of trashy commercial Egyptian-Syrian coproductions.

69. The four universities are: the Universities of Damascus and Aleppo, Tishrin University in Lataqia, and al-Ba'th University in Homs. Damascus University's oldest department, medicine, was founded in 1903 as the Institution Medicale Turc; the univer-

sity was founded in 1923, and by 1958 it encompassed thirteen departments, including law, engineering, and arts. The University of Aleppo was founded in 1958, Tishrin in 1974, and al-Ba'th in 1979.

70. It was reported that few official Ba'thist candidates were reelected and that radical students from the Bakdash wing of the Communist party took a leadership role. Security forces reportedly came into campus and arrested dozens of students.

71. Interview, fall 1989.

72. The publications included *al-Nashra, al-Jolan,* and *al-Thawriun.*

73. Fifty students were reportedly arrested.

74. Interview, fall 1989.

75. The dissertation was entitled "The Economic, Social, and Political Development of Syria."

76. A 1989 publication of a student opposition group lists names of those presumed still held. Selecting only the names of those arrested in 1980 turns up 34 from Damascus University, 31 from Aleppo University, and over 200 others from universities and institutions of higher education in Syria and Lebanon ("Save Syrian Students" [n.p., 1989]). AOHR (1989), p. 83, reports that 93 people from Aleppo, "mostly students," are still held from the years 1979–81.

77. At the same time, three Damascus University professors were elected to the party's twenty-one-seat Regional Command: Wahib Tannus, 'Abd al-Qader Qaddura, and Elias Ellati.

78. Interview, fall 1989.

79. Seale, *Asad,* p. 344.

80. Ibid., p. 459.

81. Syrian intellectuals are occasionally able to deliver a public lecture that indirectly criticizes the regime. As with the printed word, such lectures must use veiled analogies, historical references, and other such devices to make their point.

82. A longer version of this story (which Middle East Watch learned from its own sources) is found in Charles Glass, *Tribes with Flags* (New York: Atlantic Monthly Press, 1990), pp. 202–3. The Glass book contains numerous interesting anecdotes on censorship and intellectual life in contemporary Syria.

CHAPTER 9: FOREIGN RELATIONS AND THE HUMAN RIGHTS CONNECTION

1. Interview, fall 1989.

2. Although Syria's first coup was instigated by Americans, the second was apparently fomented by the British. Sami Hinnawi, who overthrew Husni Za'im, had the support of British intelligence.

3. Douglas Little has done the basic research, and the discussion that follows draws heavily on his recent article, "Cold War and Covert Action." Other major sources are the biographies of two important agents—Copeland and Eveland—as well as the groundwork done by Patrick Seale in *Struggle for Syria.*

4. Miles Copeland, *The Game of Nations* (New York: Simon and Schuster, 1980), pp. 50–55, and Little, "Cold War and Covert Action," pp. 55–57.

5. Little, "Cold War and Covert Action," p. 55.

6. Ibid., p. 57.

7. "Regional Policy Statement: Near East," December 28, 1950, as quoted in Little, "Cold War and Covert Action," p. 59.

8. Ibid., pp. 59–61.

9. Ibid., pp. 61–62.

10. Wilbur C. Eveland, *Ropes of Sand* (New York: W. W. Norton, 1980), pp. 119–24.

11. CIA chief Allen Dulles and his Middle East expert Kermit Roosevelt represented the U.S. side in these discussions. Another important figure in Middle East covert activities at this time was Archie Roosevelt, Kermit's cousin, who was often based in Beirut. The story on this operation, based on Arab sources, was first described in detail by Seale, *Struggle for Syria*, pp. 265–82. See also Copeland, *Game of Nations*, pp. 222–23, and Little, "Cold War and Covert Action," pp. 65–66.

12. Copeland, *Game of Nations*, p. 221.

13. Dwight D. Eisenhower, *Waging Peace*, p. 197, as quoted in Little, "Cold War and Covert Action," p. 70.

14. Seale, *Struggle for Syria*, pp. 297–302; Little, "Cold War and Covert Action," pp. 72–73. Seale notes that this was the fourth time in two years that Turkish forces had been mobilized at U.S. behest to pressure Syria.

15. This section draws especially on Efraim Karsh, *The Soviet Union and Syria: The Asad Years* (London: Royal Institute of International Affairs, 1988).

16. By January 1957, U.S. intelligence reports claimed Syria had acquired 24 MIG-15 fighter jets and 130 T-34 medium tanks. There were also said to be about a hundred Soviet technicians in the country. Little, "Cold War and Covert Action," p. 69.

17. Karsh, *Soviet Union and Syria*, p. 4.

18. Ibid.

19. As quoted in Seurat and Carré, *Les frères musulmans*, p. 140.

20. Much of the advanced arms deliveries to Syria approved by former Soviet president Yuri Andropov came as a reaction to the regional perception that the USSR had blanched at confronting the Israeli invasion of Lebanon in June 1982.

21. Karsh, *Soviet Union and Syria*, pp. 91–92.

22. *Maghreb Machrek* 214 (July–September 1989), p. 109.

23. *Washington Post*, November 20, 1989.

24. Interview, fall 1989.

25. Adeed Dawisha, *Syria and the Lebanese Crisis* (New York: St. Martin's Press, 1980), p. 56.

26. Aid from all Arab oil producers was $300 million in 1983.

27. Aid to Jordan, the PLO, the occupied territories, and Lebanon were also voted at this summit, which sought to block the American-sponsored peace treaty between Israel and Egypt.

28. We should also note Iranian support for Asad because of Syrian support for Iran in the Iran-Iraq War. Since the Saudis were financing Iran's enemy Iraq as well as Syria, this arrangement may seem odd, but it had a definite political and geostrategic logic. Beginning in 1983, Iran provided Syria with a million tons of crude petroleum free of charge, a subsidy worth $150–200 million. Iran also gave Syria additional oil at concession rates, with payment taking the form of loans. Iran and Syria worked together in Lebanon, and Syria apparently had a hand in funneling arms to Iran.

29. On the negotiations with Kissinger, see Seale, *Asad*, pp. 224–49. Many analysts note Asad's interest in developing better relations with the United States at this time, in

spite of disappointing results on the Golan negotiations. Dawisha, for example, refers to Asad's "quest for better understanding in Syrian-American relations," in *Syria and the Lebanese Crisis*, p. 56.

30. On February 27, 1975, agreements were signed for U.S. aid to Syria in education, agricultural production, and economic development. On June 30, a further agreement on finance for the Damascus Water System was signed. In 1976 there were agreements on aid for food aid, for the Euphrates Basin irrigation system, and for a road from Damascus to Dera'.

31. President Richard M. Nixon's visit to Damascus in June 1974 signaled warming relations. In 1976, Western loans reached $540 million.

32. One of the best studies of the relationship is Yair Evron, "Washington, Damascus and the Lebanon Crisis," in Moshe Ma'oz and Avner Yaniv, eds., *Syria under Asad: Domestic Constraints and Regional Risks* (London: Croom Helm, 1986), pp. 209–23. For the conflict in Lebanon and the relations of Syria, the United States, and Israel, see also Itamar Rabinovich, *The War for Lebanon, 1970–1985* (Ithaca, N.Y.: Cornell University Press, 1985); Naomi Joy Weinberger, *Syrian Intervention in Lebanon* (New York: Oxford University Press, 1986); Yair Evron, *War and Intervention in Lebanon: The Israeli-Syrian Deterrence Dialogue* (London: Croom Helm, 1987); and Dawisha, *Syria and the Lebanese Crisis*. The reasons why Syria intervened against its traditional allies in Lebanon and why the United States favored this initiative have been widely discussed. Israeli specialist Rabinovich concluded that the Lebanon intervention enabled Syria "while keeping a close relationship with the Soviet Union, to develop advantageous relations with the United States and the rich oil-producing Arab countries."

33. The proposal was said to be a letter from the U.S. government; see Eric Rouleau, "La Syrie dans le bourbier libanais," *Le Monde*, June 1, 1976, p. 1. Former ambassador Talcott W. Seelye, referring to the close Syrian-American ties that developed around Lebanon, discusses the shared goals, including "to keep leftist elements from coming to power," in "U.S.-Syrian Relations: The Thread of Mu'awiyah," *U.S.-Arab Affairs* 4 (Spring 1983), p. 40.

34. This accord, discussed over the preceding months, was made concrete in a letter from Israeli foreign minister Yigal Allon on March 24, 1990.

35. Evron, *War and Intervention*, p. 14.

36. Ibid., p. 216.

37. The nature of Rif'at's mission is not known, and the State Department felt obliged to deny any official contact. *New York Times*, September 3, 1982, p. 9.

38. House of Representatives, 101st Cong., 1st sess., "The Situation in Lebanon," July 1989 (Washington, D.C.: USGPO, 1989). Among those testifying were former CIA Director William Colby, former Secretary of Defense James Schlesinger, and former State Department official Joseph Sisco. The opinions of U.S. military commanders were transmitted to the committee by Sen. Christopher Dodd (D-Conn.).

39. House of Representatives, Committee on Foreign Affairs, Subcommittee on Europe and the Middle East, 98th Cong., 2d sess., "U.S. Interests in Lebanon," January 26, 1984 (Washington, D.C.: USGPO, 1984), p. 2.

40. *Washington Post*, July 29, 1986, p. 1.

41. "Why Reagan Won't Do More Than Slap Syria's Wrist," *Business Week*, October 10, 1986, p. 57.

42. Britain imposed the heaviest sanctions at the time and broke diplomatic relations.

Its European Economic Community partners also voted to impose sanctions, but voted again to lift them just six months later.

43. *Washington Post,* January 27, 1987.

44. Ibid., June 26, 1987, p. 14.

45. *Middle East Contemporary Survey,* 1987, p. 653.

46. See *Washington Post,* March 8, 1988, p. 27.

47. The Syrians included Yusif Maqdisi, editor-in-chief of *Tishrin*; Ahmad Hariri and Muhammad Jana'an of the Ministry of Information; and Muhammad al-Wady, chief editor of *Tishrin*.

48. *New York Times,* July 16, 1989, sec. 1, p. 9.

49. *Maghreb Machrek* 127 (January–March 1990), p. 180.

50. *Intelligence Newsletter,* September 27, 1989, p. 7. The official reportedly was Brig. Gen. 'Adnan Ballul.

51. Patrick Seale, "The Challenge to American Policy," *Mideast Mirror,* May 24, 1990, quoting a story from *al-Qabas*.

BIBLIOGRAPHY

Abd-Allah, Umar F. *The Islamic Struggle in Syria*. Berkeley: Mizan Press, 1982.

"Afraid of the Word." *Index on Censorship* (May 1986), pp. 16–18.

Allomi, Abdel Aziz. "The Labor Movement in Syria." *Middle East Journal* 13 (Winter 1959), pp. 64–76.

Amnesty International. *Annual Report*. London: Amnesty, various years.

———. *Report from Amnesty International to the Government of the Syrian Arab Republic*. London: Amnesty, 1983.

———. *Syria*. London: Amnesty, 1979.

———. *Syria*. London: Amnesty, 1983.

———. *Syria: Torture by the Security Forces*. London: Amnesty, 1987.

———. Various documents, including: *Amnesty International Newsletter, Amnesty Action,* and documents on prisoner cases, some entitled Urgent Action.

Arab World File/Fiches du monde arabe. Beirut: 1976–.

Association suisse pour la défense des libertés et des prisonniers politiques en Syrie. *Droits et libertés en Syrie*. Geneva, 1985.

Batatu, Hanna. "Syria's Muslim Brethren." *MERIP Reports* 110 (November–December 1982), pp. 12–20, 34.

———. "Some Observations on the Social Roots of Syria's Ruling Military Group and the Causes for Its Dominance." *Middle East Journal* 35 (Summer 1981), pp. 331–44.

Be'er, Yizhar. "The Punishment Machine in the Territories." *Ha'aretz,* December 1, 1989.

Ben Jemina, Yanka. "Information Structures and Organizations in the Syrian Arab Republic." *Orient* 25, no. 4 (1984), pp. 561–81.

Betts, Robert Brenton. *The Druze*. New Haven and London: Yale University Press, 1988.

———. *Christians in the Arab World*. Atlanta, Ga.: John Knox, 1978.

Boyd, D. A. *Broadcasting in the Arab World*. Philadelphia: Temple University Press, 1982.

Brand, Laurie. "Palestinians in Syria: The Politics of Integration." *Middle East Journal* 42 (Autumn 1988), pp. 621–38.

Chaliand, Gérard, ed. *Les kurdes et le Kurdistan*. Paris: Maspéro, 1978 [available in English as *People Without a Country*, London: Zed Press, 1982].

Clawson, Patrick. *Unaffordable Ambitions: Syria's Military Buildup and Economic Crisis*. Washington, D.C.: Washington Institute for Near East Policy, 1989.

Cohen, Hayim J. *The Jews of the Middle East, 1860–1972*. New York: John Wiley, 1973.

Comité de défense des libertés et des détenus politiques en Syrie. "Memorandum sur la dissolution des Barreaux d'avocats et des syndicats de médecins et d'ingénieurs par les autorités syriennes." No. 11. Paris, April 28, 1980.

Conférence internationale pour la délivrance des juifs au Moyen-Orient. Les juifs de Syrie: communauté en péril. Paris, 1974.

Copeland, Miles. *The Game of Nations*. New York: Simon and Schuster, 1980.

Cowell, Alan. "Trouble in Damascus." *New York Times Magazine,* April 1, 1990, pp. 28–33, 78.

Dawisha, Adeed. *Syria and the Lebanese Crisis*. New York: St. Martin's Press, 1980.

————. "Syria under Asad, 1970–78: The Centers of Power." *Government and Opposition* 13, no. 3 (1978), pp. 341–54.

Devlin, John. *The Ba'th Party: A History from Its Origins to 1966*. Stanford, Calif.: Hoover Institution Press, 1976.

————. *Syria: Modern State in an Ancient Land*. Boulder, Colo.: Westview Press, 1983.

Al-Dimokratiun al-Suriun. *Majzara Hama* (The Massacre of Hama). Cairo?: Al-Tahaluf al-Watani li-Tahrir Suria (Muslim Brothers) [c. 1984].

Documents du travail des congrès régionaux du Parti Baas arab socialiste, 1963–1980. Damascus: Office arabe de presse et documentation, 1981.

Drysdale, Alasdair. "The Asad Regime and Its Troubles." *MERIP Reports* 110 (November–December 1982), pp. 3–11.

————. "Ethnicity in the Syrian Officer Corps." *Civilisations* 29 (1979), pp. 359–74.

————. "The Regional Equalization of Health Care and Education in Syria since the Ba'thi Revolution." *International Journal of Middle East Studies* 13 (1981), pp. 93–111.

————. "The Succession Question in Syria." *Middle East Journal* 39 (Spring 1985), pp. 246–62.

————. "The Syrian Political Elite, 1966–1976: A Spatial and Social Analysis." *Middle East Studies* 17 (January 1981), pp. 3–30.

Encyclopedia Judaica. 16 vols. New York: Macmillan, 1972.

Eveland, Wilbur C. *Ropes of Sand*. New York: W. W. Norton, 1980.

Evron, Yair. *War and Intervention in Lebanon: The Israeli-Syrian Deterrence Dialogue*. London: Croom Helm, 1987.

Foreign Broadcast Information Service (FBIS). Middle East and North Africa. Daily Summary. Various years.

Friedman, Robert I. "Journalists under the Gun in Beirut." *Nation,* December 15, 1984, pp. 641–43.

Friedman, Saul S. *Without Future: The Plight of Syrian Jewry*. New York: Praeger, 1989.

Friedman, Thomas L. *From Beirut to Jerusalem*. New York: Farrar, Straus and Giroux, 1989.

Ghaliun, Burhan. *Etat et lutte de classes en Syrie, 1945–1970*. Paris: Bibliothèque des langues et de civilisation orientales, 1970.

Glass, Charles. *Tribes with Flags*. New York: Atlantic Monthly Press, 1990.

Gubser, Peter. "Minorities in Power: The Alawites of Syria." In R. D. McLaurin, ed., *The Political Role of Minority Groups in the Middle East*. New York: Praeger, 1979.

Haddad, Robert M. *Syrian Christians in Muslim Society*. Princeton, N.J.: Princeton University Press, 1970.

Hama: Ma'sa al-'Asir (Hama: The Tragedy of the Century). Cairo?: al-Tahaluf al-Watani li-Tahrir Suria (Muslim Brothers) [c. 1983].

Hanna, Abdulla. *Al-Haraka al-'Umaliya fi Suria wa Lubnan, 1900–1945* (The Labor Movement in Syria and Lebanon, 1900–1945). Damascus: n.p., 1973.

Harris, William. "Syria in Lebanon." *MERIP Reports* 134 (July–August 1985), pp. 9–16.

Hassan, Ibrahim. "La Syrie de la guerre civile." *Peuples méditerranéens* 12 (July–September 1980), pp. 91–107.

Heller, Peter B. "The Permanent Syrian Constitution of March 13, 1973." *Middle East Journal* 28 (Winter 1974), pp. 53–66.

Hennoyer, Jean, and Seurat, Michel. *Etat et secteur publique industriel en Syrie* (Beirut: CERMOC, 1979), p. 53.

Hilan, Riskallah. *Culture et développement en Syrie*. Paris: Anthropos, 1969.

Hinnebusch, Raymond. *Authoritarian Power and State Formation in Ba'thist Syria*. Boulder, Colo.: Westview Press, 1990.

———. *Peasant and Bureaucracy in Ba'thist Syria*. Boulder, Colo.: Westview Press, 1989.

———. "Political Recruitment and Socialization in Syria: The Case of the Revolutionary Youth Federation." *International Journal of Middle East Studies* 11, no. 2 (1980), pp. 143–74.

———. "Syrian Policy in Lebanon and the Palestinians." *Arab Studies Quarterly* 8 (Winter 1986), pp. 1–20.

Hizb al-Amal al-Shuyu'i fi Suria. *Suria: al-Sijl al-Aswad*. Paris, 1989.

Hopwood, Derek. *Syria, 1945–1986*. London: Unwin Hyman, 1988.

Index on Censorship. London: various issues.

International Commission for the Defense of Human Rights in Syria. *Bulletin*. Various numbers.

"Journalists in Syria Are an Extinct Species." *Index on Censorship* (June 1987).

Kaminsky, Catherine. *La Syrie: politiques et stratégies de 1966 à nos jours*. Paris: Presses universitaires de France, 1987.

Karsh, Efraim. *The Soviet Union and Syria: The Asad Years*. London: Royal Institute of International Affairs, 1988.

Kerr, Malcolm. "Hafiz Assad and the Changing Patterns of Syrian Politics." *International Journal* 23 (1973), pp. 689–706.

Khoury, Philip S. *Syria and the French Mandate*. Princeton, N.J.: Princeton University Press, 1987.

Kissinger, Henry A. *White House Years*. Boston: Little, Brown, 1979.

———. *Years of Upheaval*. Boston: Little, Brown, 1982.

Koeppel, Barbara. *The Press in the Middle East: Constraint, Consensus, Censorship*. Washington, D.C.: Middle East Research and Information Project, 1988.

Koszinowski, Thomas. "Die Krise der Ba'th-Herrschaft und die Rolle Asads bei der Sicherung der Macht." *Orient* 26 (1985), pp. 549–71.

———. "Rif'at al-Asad." *Orient* 4 (1984), pp. 465–70.

"Lettre de Hama," *Sou'al* 2 (1982), pp. 93–94.

Library of Congress. *Syria: A Country Study*. Washington, D.C.: USGPO, 1988.

Little, Douglas. "Cold War and Covert Action: The United States and Syria, 1945–1958." *Middle East Journal* 44 (Winter 1990), pp. 51–76.

Longuenesse, Elisabeth. "The Class Nature of the State in Syria: Contribution to an Analysis." *MERIP Reports* 77 (May 1979), pp. 3–15.

———. "Etat et syndicalisme en Syrie: discours et pratiques." *Sou'al* 8 (February 1988), pp. 97–130.

———. "The Syrian Labor Movement." *MERIP Reports* 110 (November–December, 1982), pp. 32–33.

———. "The Syrian Working Class Today." *MERIP Reports* 134 (July–August, 1985), pp. 17–24

Ma'oz, Moshe. "Alawi Officers in Syrian Politics." In H. Z. Schiffrin, ed., *The Military and the State in Modern Asia*. New Brunswick, N.J.: Transaction Books, 1976, pp. 277–97.

———. *Asad: The Sphinx of Damascus*. New York: Grove Weidenfeld, 1988.

Ma'oz, Moshe, and Avner Yaniv, eds. *Syria under Asad: Domestic Constraints and Regional Risks*. London: Croom Helm, 1986.

Manna, Haytham. "Histoire des frères musulmans en Syrie." *Sou'al* 5 (1985), pp. 67–82.

———. "Syria: Accumulation of Errors?" *Middle Eastern Studies* 23 (April 1987), pp. 211–214.

Middle East Contemporary Survey. New York: Holmes and Meier, 1976–77ff. Various years.

Middle East International. "Syria: Solvency from Oil?" March 31, 1989, pp. 18–20.

Al-Minbar [also *La Tribune* and the *Tribune*]. Publication of the Committee for the Defense of Freedoms and Political Prisoners in Syria. Nos. 1–14 (1980–June 1986).

Moniquet, Claude. "Armes, drogues, voitures: le trafic syrien." *Express,* May 3, 1987, pp. 34–41.

Munson, Henry, Jr. *Islam and Revolution in the Middle East*. New Haven and London: Yale University Press, 1988.

Al-Munthama al-'Arabiya li-Huquq al-Insan. *Huquq al-Insan fi al-Watan al-'Arabi*. Cairo [Arab Organization for Human Rights annual reports] 1987–1989.

Murphy, Richard W. "Lebanon at the Crossroads." Speech to alumni of American University of Beirut, October 29, 1988. Washington, D.C.: U.S. Department of State, 1989.

National Union of Syrian Students and Youth. "Save Syrian Students." N.p., 1989.

"Nida 'Ajil" (Urgent call). Committee of Palestinian Political Prisoners. March 1987.

Palazzoli, Claude. *La Syrie: la rêve et la rupture*. Paris: Sycomore, 1977.

Petran, Tabitha. *Syria*. New York: Praeger, 1972.

———. *The Struggle over Lebanon*. New York: Monthly Review Press, 1987.

Picard, Elisabeth. "Une crise syrienne en 1965: les syndicats ouvriers face au nouveau régime ba'thiste." *Sou'al* 8 (February 1988), pp. 81–95.

———. "La politique de la Syrie au Liban." *Maghreb Machrek* 116 (April–June 1987).

———. "Syria Returns to Democracy: The May 1973 Legislative Elections." In Guy Hermet et al., eds., *Elections without Choice*. London: Macmillan, 1978, pp. 129–44.

———. "Y a-t-il un problème communautaire en Syrie?" *Maghreb Machrek* 87 (January–March 1980), pp. 7–21.

Rabinovich, Itamar. "The Compact Minorities and the Syrian State, 1918–45." *Journal of Contemporary History* 14 (1989), pp. 693–712.

———. *Syria under the Bath, 1963–66: The Army-Party Symbiosis*. Jerusalem: Israel Universities Press, 1972.

———. *The War for Lebanon, 1970–1985*. Ithaca, N.Y.: Cornell University Press, 1985.

Raymond, André, ed. *La Syrie d'aujourd'hui*. Paris: Editions du Centre national de la recherche scientifique, 1980.

Roberts, David. *The Ba'th and the Creation of Modern Syria*. London: Croom Helm, 1987.

Rouleau, Eric. "L'énigme syrienne, qu'est-ce que le Baas?" *Le Monde diplomatique*, September 1967.

———. "La Syrie bassiste ou la fuite à gauche." *Le Monde*, October 13–19, 1966.

———. "La Syrie dans le bourbier libanais." *Le Monde*, June 1–4, 1976.

Rugh, William A. *The Arab Press*. 2d ed. Syracuse, N.Y.: Syracuse University Press, 1987.

Sadiq, Adib [pseud.]. "The Road to Damascus Is Plagued with Censors." *Index on Censorship* (February 1990).

Sadowski, Yahya M. "Cadres, Guns and Money: The Eighth Regional Congress of the Syrian Ba'th." *MERIP Reports* 134 (July–August 1985), pp. 3–8.

———. "Patronage and the Ba'th: Corruption and Control in Contemporary Syria." *Arab Studies Quarterly* 9, no. 4 (1987), pp. 442–61.

Saint-Prot, Charles. *Les mystères syriens*. Paris: Albin Michel, 1985.

Sawar min Medina Hama al-Shahid (Pictures of the Martyr City of Hama). [Cairo?: c. 1983–84.]

Schiff, Ze'ev. "Dealing with Syria." *Foreign Policy* 55 (1984).

Seale, Patrick. *Asad: The Struggle for the Middle East*. Berkeley: University of California Press, 1989.

———. "The Challenge to American Policy." *Mideast Mirror*, May 24, 1990.

———. *The Struggle for Syria*. New Haven and London: Yale University Press, 1987.

Seelye, Talcott W. "U.S.-Syrian Relations: The Thread of Mu'awiyah." *U.S.-Arab Affairs* 4 (Spring 1983), pp. 40–45.

Seccombe, Ian J. *Syria*. Santa Barbara, Calif.: Clio Press, 1987.

Seurat, Michel. *L'Etat de barbarie*. Paris: Editions du Seuil, 1989.

——— [pseud. Gérard Michaud]. "The Importance of Bodyguards." *MERIP Reports* 110 (November–December 1982), pp. 29–31.

Seurat, Michel [pseud. Gérard Michaud], and Olivier Carré. *Les frères musulmans, 1928–1982*. Paris: Gallimard, 1983.

Sutton, Joseph A. D. *Aleppo Chronicles*. New York: Thayer-Jacoby, 1988.

Suria al-Hurra. Washington, D.C.: National Alliance for the Liberation of Syria, U.S. Committee, 1988ff.

Tribune. See *al-Minbar*.

United Nations Commission on Human Rights, Economic and Social Council. Question of the Human Rights of All Persons Subjected to Any Form of Detention or Imprisonment: Torture and Other Cruel, Inhuman or Degrading Treatment or Punishment. (January 23, 1989, and previous annual reports in this series.)

———. Question of the Human Rights . . . : Question of Enforced or Involuntary Disappearances. (January 18, 1989, and previous annual reports in this series.)

———. Commission on the Elimination of All Forms of Discrimination, 29th sess. Consideration of Reports Submitted by State Parties under Article 9 of the Convention. Seventh Periodic Report of States Parties due in 1982, addendum, Syrian Arab Republic, July 21, 1983.

———. Commission on Extra-judicial Inquiry, Executions, 45th sess. Question of the Violation of Human Rights and Fundamental Freedoms in Any Part of the World, with Particular Reference to Colonial and Other Dependent Countries and Territories: Summary and Arbitrary Executions. (February 6, 1989, and previous annual reports in this series.)

United States Congress. House of Representatives. Committee on Foreign Affairs. Subcommittee on Europe and the Middle East. 96th Cong., 1st sess. "Impressions of the Situation of the Syrian Jewish Community." April 2, 1979. Washington, D.C.: USGPO, 1979.

———. 101st Cong., 1st sess. "The Situation in Lebanon." July 1989. Washington, D.C.: USGPO, 1989.

———. 98th Cong., 2d sess. "U.S. Interests in Lebanon." January 26, 1984. Washington, D.C.: USGPO, 1984.

———. Subcommittee on Human Rights and International Organizations. 101st Cong., 1st sess. "Human Rights in Lebanon." June 1, 1989. Washington, D.C.: USGPO, 1989.

———. Senate Committee on Foreign Relations. Subcommittee on Europe and the Middle East. "Policy Options in Lebanon." January 11, 1984. Washington, D.C.: USGPO, 1984.

United States Department of Commerce. "International Trade Administration; Foreign Economic Trends and Their Implications for the United States: Syria." Washington, D.C.: USGPO, 1988.

United States Department of State. Bureau of International Narcotics Matters. *International Narcotics Control Strategy Report.* Annual report. Washington, D.C.: USGPO, March 1989.

———. Bureau of Public Affairs. "Background Notes: Syria." Washington, D.C.: USGPO, June 1986.

———. Bureau of Human Rights. *Country Reports on Human Rights Practices: 1989.* Annual report. Washington, D.C.: USGPO, 1990.

Van Dam, Nikolaos. "Middle East Political Clichés." *Orient* 21 (January 1980), pp. 42–57.

———. *The Struggle for Power in Syria: Sectarianism, Regionalism, and Tribalism in Politics, 1961–1978.* New York: St. Martin's Press, 1979.

Vanly, Ismet Cherif. *Kurdistan und die Kurden.* Vol. 3. Göttingen: Gesellschaft für bedrohte Völker, 1988.

———. *The Syrian "Mein Kampf" against the Kurds.* N.p., n.d. [c. 1969].

Viorst, Milton. "The Shadow of Saladin." *New Yorker,* January 8, 1990, pp. 40–65.

Weinberger, Naomi Joy. *Syrian Intervention in Lebanon.* New York: Oxford University Press, 1986.

INDEX

ABOUT HUMAN RIGHTS WATCH

Human Rights Watch conducts systematic investigations of human rights abuses in some sixty countries around the world. It addresses the human rights practices of governments of all political stripes, geopolitical alignments, and ethnic and religious persuasions. In internal wars—such as those in Afghanistan, Angola, Cambodia, and El Salvador—it documents abuses by governments and rebel groups. Human Rights Watch defends freedom of thought and expression, due process of law, and equal protection of the law; it denounces murders, disappearances, torture, arbitrary imprisonment, exile, censorship, and other abuses of internationally recognized human rights.

With a staff that includes over thirty country specialists, Human Rights Watch annually carries out more than one hundred investigative missions to gather current human rights information. In country after country, this ongoing effort makes a difference—saving lives, stopping torture, freeing prisoners, and helping to create the space for citizens to exercise their civil and political rights. Human Rights Watch reports are unique, up-to-date, firsthand sources of human rights information worldwide.

Human Rights Watch began in 1978 with the founding of Helsinki Watch by a group of publishers, lawyers, and other activists and now maintains offices in New York, Washington, D.C., Los Angeles, London, San Salvador, and Hong Kong. Today it includes Africa Watch, Americas Watch, Asia Watch, Helsinki Watch, Middle East Watch, and the Fund for Free Expression. Human Rights Watch is an independent, nongovernmental organization supported by contributions from private individuals and foundations. It accepts no government funds, directly or indirectly.